1,000,000 Books

are available to read at

www.ForgottenBooks.com

Read online
Download PDF
Purchase in print

ISBN 978-1-334-05976-6
PIBN 10639014

This book is a reproduction of an important historical work. Forgotten Books uses state-of-the-art technology to digitally reconstruct the work, preserving the original format whilst repairing imperfections present in the aged copy. In rare cases, an imperfection in the original, such as a blemish or missing page, may be replicated in our edition. We do, however, repair the vast majority of imperfections successfully; any imperfections that remain are intentionally left to preserve the state of such historical works.

Forgotten Books is a registered trademark of FB &c Ltd.
Copyright © 2018 FB &c Ltd.
FB &c Ltd, Dalton House, 60 Windsor Avenue, London, SW19 2RR.
Company number 08720141. Registered in England and Wales.

For support please visit www.forgottenbooks.com

1 MONTH OF FREE READING

at

www.ForgottenBooks.com

By purchasing this book you are eligible for one month membership to ForgottenBooks.com, giving you unlimited access to our entire collection of over 1,000,000 titles via our web site and mobile apps.

To claim your free month visit: www.forgottenbooks.com/free639014

* Offer is valid for 45 days from date of purchase. Terms and conditions apply.

English
Français
Deutsche
Italiano
Español
Português

www.forgottenbooks.com

Mythology Photography **Fiction** Fishing Christianity **Art** Cooking Essays Buddhism Freemasonry Medicine **Biology** Music **Ancient Egypt** Evolution Carpentry Physics Dance Geology **Mathematics** Fitness Shakespeare **Folklore** Yoga Marketing **Confidence** Immortality Biographies Poetry **Psychology** Witchcraft Electronics Chemistry History **Law** Accounting **Philosophy** Anthropology Alchemy Drama Quantum Mechanics Atheism Sexual Health **Ancient History Entrepreneurship** Languages Sport Paleontology Needlework Islam **Metaphysics** Investment Archaeology Parenting Statistics Criminology **Motivational**

(THE

PUBLICATIONS

OF THE)

SURTEES SOCIETY

ESTABLISHED IN THE YEAR
M.DCCC.XXXIV.

VOL. CXXV.

FOR THE YEAR M.CM.XIV.

PRINTED BY
BEN JOHNSON AND CO., LTD.,
YORK.

YORK MEMORANDUM BOOK

PART II. (1388–1493).

LETTERED $\frac{A}{Y}$ IN THE GUILDHALL MUNIMENT ROOM.

Published for the Society
BY ANDREWS & CO., SADLER STREET, DURHAM, AND
BERNARD QUARITCH, 15, PICCADILLY, LONDON.
1915.

At a Council Meeting of the Surtees Society, held in Durham Castle, on Tuesday, March 1st, 1910, the Dean of Durham in the Chair,

IT WAS RESOLVED,

That the volume to be issued for the year 1914 be MS.$\frac{A}{Y}$ belonging to the Corporation of York, under the editorship of Miss Maud Sellers, Litt. D.

PREFACE.

My thanks are again due to Miss M. T. Martin, who undertook the task of transcribing the MS.

Mr. William Brown has given me invaluable help especially in seeing the book through the press. If, however, any mistakes still remain undetected, they are entirely due to me.

In a MS. where especially in the Anglo-French documents textual corruptions and scribal errors frequently occur, it seems preferable to leave them as they stand rather than correct silently, or burden the text with innumerable footnotes.

It is difficult for me to express adequately my gratitude to Miss Elinor Lucas and the Rev. W. Hudson, F.S.A. Their criticisms and suggestions have enabled me to correct, modify or re-state several points in the introduction.

M. S.

37, St. Mary's, York,
    August 27th, 1915.

CONTENTS.

INTRODUCTION:

    THE GOVERNMENT OF THE CITY ....

    FOREIGN TRADE xix

    MISTERIES xxix

    MISTERY PLAYS xli

    THE CHURCH AND THE CITY lxiii

TEXT 1–299

GLOSSARY 299–306

INDEXES:

    NAMES AND PLACES 307–322

    SUBJECTS 322–330

CORRIGENDA.

Page 5, line 24, for Mariemberg, read Mariemburg.
,,   6, line 12, for Mariemberg, read Mariemburg.
,,   6, passim, for Lynelandes, read Lyvelandes.
,,   8, line 2, for dicti, read dicte.
,,   10, line 11, for (1395), read 1398.
,,   13, line 3, for recuparent, read recuperarent.
,,   15, line 4, for precencia, read presencia.
,,   19, line 12, for linquit, read linquet.
,,   25, line 9, for secunda, read secundo.
,,   29, line 16, for serventiem, read servientem.
,,   32, line 21, for spectanti, read spectantis; line 30, for Yotton, read Yolton; line 31, for Birkton, read Bukton.
,,   33, line 22, for Grover, read Glover.
,,   42, line 1, for decollacio, read decollacionis.
,,   51, line 24, for senis, read senioris.
,,   54, line 1, from foot, for Nicholus, read Nicholaus.
,,   55, line 8, from foot, for canoniciis, read canonicis.
,,   63, line 6, for (1389-9), read (1398-9).
,,   64, line 3, for libarent, read liberarent.
,,   68, line 21, for suscipimus specialiter, read suscipimus, specialiter
,,   74, line 17, for Johannes Bedale; de xij., read Johannes Bedale, de xij.
,,   87, line 3, for ducius, read diucius.
,,   95, line 15, for Baurnburg, read Baumburg.
,,   103, head line, for undated, read (1421-22).
,,   146, line 34, for sort, read soit.
,,   148, line 31, for commisse, read connusse.
,,   150, line 10, for convencionis, read capcionis (?), word in MS. not clear.
,,   165, headline, for (1416-1428), read (1429-30).
,,   173, line 5, from foot, for Bobeon, read Bolron.
,,   195, 197, headline, for 1472, read 1473.
,,   218, line 20, for Fayefax, read Farefax.
,,   223, headline, for bequest, read gift; for Friar, read Friars.
,,   224, line 26, for misericordeam, read misericordiam.
,,   226, line 6, indulgenc(ie) the Breviary has indulgentiarum; line 9, Quamvis, a textual corruption, the Breviary has quae sumus.
,,   227, line 19, for successorebus, read successoribus.
,,   294, line 13, for Dauson, read Danson.

INTRODUCTION.

The division of the MS., labelled $\frac{A}{Y}$ in the Gild Hall Catalogue, into two volumes is entirely arbitrary; the MS. itself forms one uninterrupted whole of three hundred and eighty-one folios.[1] Paper folios numbered one to thirty-six are bound in the same volume; these are not printed, as it is exceedingly doubtful whether at any time they formed part of the original MS. They include a great deal of treasonable matter; possibly the wary York Council watched the swing of the pendulum between the claims of the Yorkist Richard III. and the Tudor heir of the house of Lancaster, and thought it wiser to omit them from the permanent register, when victory fell to Henry VII.

Broadly speaking this volume covers a century from 1388 to 1488. It is difficult to know why for so long historians looked askance at a period vitalized by Shakspere, immortalized by Agincourt, marked by extraordinary civic development and interesting constitutional experiments. Many investigators have found the evidence conflicting and have made little effort to reconcile seeming contradictions; they have given pictures either of unmitigated gloom or exhilarating prosperity—both equally misleading. It was essentially an age of transition,[2] with all the weaknesses and strength inherent in such a period. Constitutional progress had outrun the growth of adminstrative capacity; the machine had not a sufficient number of highly skilled men to guide it. But the chaos that resulted from this breakdown, disastrous as it was to men of the fifteenth century, ought to be stimulating and instructive to their descendants. The times were peculiarly rich in men of consummate ability but insatiable ambition. Still it is a century of startling contrasts; the pathetic failure of Richard II., the meteoric brilliancy

---

1. A Catalogue of the Charters, House Books, etc., of the Corporation of York, compiled by William Giles, Deputy Town Clerk, p. 7. All scholars interested in municipal history owe a debt of gratitude to Mr. Giles for this exceedingly valuable catalogue. To my predecessors in research among the York Archives, Drake, Davies, Scaife, and Dr. Collins, editor of the Freemen of York, it is impossible for me adequately to express my obligations.
.p 2. C. L. Kingsford, English Historical Literature in the Fifteenth Century,
. 2.

of Henry V., the tedious feebleness of Henry VI., the magnificent force of Richard III., offer dramatic possibilities of the highest order. With the exception of Henry VI., the kings, splendid failures as most of them are, failed through superabundance not through lack of initiative and enterprise. Too often crime cleared the way for the consummation of their activities, " God take King Edward to his mercy and leave the world for me to bustle in," is put by Shakspere into the mouth of Richard III., but the desire to be the foremost man of the age was common to the majority of the nobility; the large family of Edward III. had royalized too many of its members. The decimation of this class was the necessary prelude to the expansion of the real strength of the nation, the workers; the overweening ambition of the baronage facilitated their own destruction. From the evidence of the Memorandum Book, York, though strongly Yorkist in sympathy, stood aloof from these dynastic quarrels. The inhabitants were engaged in amassing wealth, the market place was more attractive to them than the battlefield. In spite of the terrible wastage of life, the black death had not affected cities so disastrously as country districts. The changes in centres of population, brought about by the great pestilence, were in favour of places connected with the woollen industry. Architectural activities[1] are a conclusive proof of progress, and York though it did not increase the number of its churches during the fifteenth century, beautified some, rebuilt or enlarged others; the common or gildhall belongs entirely to this period. This prosperity of York, at a time when so much indisputable evidence of decay and depopulation elsewhere exists, was due to its being the great centre of the northern textile trade.

In 1377 the population of York according to the poll-tax returns was 13,500, the total population of England being about two and a quarter millions. London had a population three times as great; Bristol was probably about the same size. Plymouth and Coventry[2] distinctly smaller; Norwich numbered

1. W. Cunningham, Growth of English Industry and Commerce, vol. I., p. 371.
2. The population of Coventry in 1520 was only 6,601 persons; see M. D. Harris, Coventry Leet Bk., Early English Text Society, 1907-1913, p. 675.

about 5,500 people,[1] Lincoln, Salisbury, Lynn, and Colchester had still fewer inhabitants. But although in population York was the second city in the kingdom, in wealth, according to the payments made to the loan demanded in 1397, it was only the sixth town in England. London paid £6,666 13s. 4d., Bristol £800, Norwich £333 6s. 8d., Lynn £266 13s. 4d., York £200 0s. 0d.[2] Compared with other towns in Yorkshire York paid twice as much as Hull, three times as much as Scarborough, more than four times as much as Pontefract, and ten times as much as Whitby.

Medieval statistics are not entirely trustworthy, but some idea of the number of people working in the textile industry can be gained from contemporary documents. In 1394 there were 800 weavers in or near the city.[3] There were 325[4] masters of different crafts either directly or indirectly connected with the trade ; if to these 1,125 workers apprentices and journeymen are added, a considerable proportion of the total population must have owed their subsistence to the woollen manufacture. The list of freemen bears out this contention. During the first half of the period, on an average, 105 people were added to the freemen each year, the highest total for a single year being 196, the lowest 31 ; in 1405, 136 men were enrolled, 41 trades were represented, of these 35 people are entered as having no trade. There are 8 mercers, 7 tailors, 6 weavers, 5 bowers, 5 clerks, 4 barkers, 3 millers, 3 barbers, and 3 mariners. Skinners, potters, dyers, masons, butchers, saggers, shearers, taverners, fishmongers, cordwainers, and spurriers, have each two representatives. One member of each of the remaining twenty-three trades, merchants, mercators, coopers, pinners, spicers, tilers, wrights, marshals, curriers, motlemakers, goldsmiths, shipwrights, lorimers, glasiers, tincklers, drapers, carvers, rapers, fletchers, cardmakers, joiners, locksmiths, chullours was enrolled, and 11 men claimed their freedom by patrimony. In 1408, 84 new freemen represented 35 different trades. Five years later 196 freemen were enrolled.

1. Records of the City of Norwich, vol. II., p. cxxii.
2. Quoted in Cunningham, *op. cit.*, p. 385.
3. Exch. K.R. Accts., 18 and 19, Ric. II., bdle. 345, No. 16, m. 1–20.
4. Mem. Bk., I., p. xxxiv.

They were engaged in 69 different industries.[1] It is with the doings of these men, the makers of industrial York, that the Memorandum Book is chiefly concerned. The leisured class were practically non-existent. They resided almost entirely in monasteries and nunneries, often as paying guests, and were, of course, outside civic jurisdiction. A few of the baronial class had residences in York, but they, as well as the heads of the great religious houses, were constantly absent.

The question of the percentage of inhabitants, who were not franchised, is difficult to answer. During the hundred years from 1388 to 1488, 84 women and 30 foreigners took their freedom. The liberties of the Castle, S. Mary's, S. Peter's, S. Leonard's and Davy Hall must have included many people who had trading and other privileges without being franchised or members of any mistery.[2] Doubtless they represent an element of freedom, for they must have acted as a drag on the wheel of the juggernaut of rigid gild organization.[3] The sanctuary dwellers, too, were not under civic control. The cappers recognized the undermining potentiality of these abnormal areas; in 1482 they passed an ordinance, which probably refers both to liberties and sanctuaries[4];
" No maistre of the said occupacion gyff no werk to wyrk to no maner of person dwellyng in Seynt Marygate, ne in Seint

---

1. Freemen of York, Surtees Soc., vol. 96, pp. 86–213. "The freedom of the city is to be obtained in three different ways. First, by servitude; that is, the applicant must have served his full time as an apprentice before his enrolment; secondly, by patrimony; that is, the children of a freeman can claim their freedom as their heritage; thirdly, by redemption; that is, by order of the Mayor and Court of Aldermen, which means that the recipient obtained it either by purchase or that it was given to him, without payment, as a reward for some more or less important services rendered to the city." p. xiii.

2. The phenomena of liberties has not so far had the attention to which its importance in civic development entitles it. They are a survival from the period when the city was under feudal government and represent the pre-constitutional phase of civic life. Probably the weavers' mistery in early gild history had some of the characteristics of the liberties. In York there was constant strife between the ecclesiastical liberties and the civic community in the thirteenth and fourteenth centuries, cf. Mem. Bk. I., pp. 13, 45, 216. F. Drake, Antiquities of York, pp. 326, 581. E. Gordon Duff, English Provincial Printers, pp. 56, 57, gives an example of a man moving from the liberty of S. Peter's to Blake Street, when he was obliged to become a freeman, though he had worked as a printer for several years.

3. G. Unwin, Gilds of London, p. 250.

4. Mem. Bk., p. 285. Rolls of Parliament, III., 504.

Leonardes, ne odyr placez ne santuaries¹ within this citie, where we have no power to correk tham and that no meistre of the said craft uttyr their werk." Evidently the number of workers who slipped through the fine sieve of mistery and franchise was sufficiently large to need restraint. As has already been seen, the average number of residents added to the franchise each year was 105, the population 13,500. Of this population probably about 120 men reached the age of twenty-one each year, and were eligible for freedom. According to this calculation there was an annual residium of 15 men who did not take up their freedom at all. Indefinite as the evidence is, it seems to justify the assertion that the bulk of the working population of York became freemen.² Of course there would be a certain number of casual immigrants within the walls; shipwrecked mariners and foreigners, criminals escaping from justice, and serfs hiding from their masters would add to the number of residents, though they would escape numeration. By one of the customs of the city no man could be taken from the city by any claim of villeinage before the matter had been investigated by law.³

The references in this volume to the government of the city by mayor and three bailiffs, that is before 1396, are few⁴; broadly speaking it is true that the city's constitution remained homogeneous throughout the whole period covered by the Memorandum Book. The communal period had closed before the register begins; the representative period, introduced by the Municipal Reform Act of 1835 was in the far future; the magisterial period was already inaugurated.⁵ The citizens of York, says Domesday Book, pay

1. Post, lxix.
2. I am under the deepest obligations to Mr. Archibald Harrower, F.F.A., who worked out the proportion for me. He based his calculations on the 1901 and 1911 census; as he says, the solution is only rough, but even an approximate suggestion seems to me of interest. In 1833 there were in York 2,400 resident freemen, 1,300 non-resident, out of a population of 35,362 only 2,400 residents voted. Population of Gt. Britain (Census Report), vol. II., 1833, p. 729.
3. Mem. Bk., p. 254.
4. Mem. Bk., pp. 11, 12, 15, 31.
5. Mem. Bk., vol. I., p. 163, xi. I am deeply indebted to Mr. Hudson for assistance in this section. The threefold division of civic government is his, not only have I, by constant reference to his Records of Norwich, cleared up many doubtful points in municipal development, but he gave me generous assistance by reading through the proofs of all the council meetings given in the Memorandum Book.

no relief. " But if you deprive a lord of these casualties," as Professor Maitland points out, " he is practically reduced to the position of a man with a rent charge."[1] So long as the King's representative was answerable for this rent and the rent was an uncertain quantity, obvious opportunities for peculation were presented : it was an important though undated step in the development of civic York, when it gained the right to pay a fixed annual rent farmed by the burgesses themselves, the firma burgi. The charter of Henry I. gave to York liberties, laws, and customs, and the right to have a merchant gild ; unfortunately this early charter is only known by an allusion to it in the charter of Henry II.,[2] who refers to his grandfather's charter. But that the merchants' gild was in existence in 1130 is proved by the pipe roll for that year, where it is stated that Thomas of York gave the King a coursing dog valued at 20s. that he might be alderman of the merchant gild.[3] The exact date when York substituted a mayor for a reeve or præpositus is unknown. London had a mayor in 1191, but certainly as late as 1206 possibly as late as 1211, there is a reference to Gerard, the bellfounder, præpositus of the city of York. In 1217 Hugh de Selby was mayor of York, so far he is the first mayor of York to whom authentic reference is made.[4]

The governing body consisted of the mayor, the twelve, three bailiffs, and the twenty-four. After the charter of Richard II. given on the 19th of May, 1396, when the city became a county by itself, and the sheriff of the county was excluded, the twelve became aldermen, two sheriffs took the place of the three bailiffs ; and after 1418, the twenty-four councillors consisted of ex-sheriffs.[5]

1. F. W. Maitland, Town and Borough, p. 71.
2. W. Stubbs, Constitutional History, p. 445. The municipality possesses this charter, but all traces of the earlier one are lost.
3. Pipe Roll 31, Henry I. (Record Commission), 1833, p. 34. T. Madox, History of the Exchequer, vol. I., p. 397.
4. Rot. Litt. Claus., vol. I. (Record Comm.), p. 341.
5. The twelve and twenty-four are sometimes classed together as probi homines, later as " counsaylours " ; the use of the word aldermen was slowly adopted, the twelve remained the usual expression during the greater part of the fifteenth century though the term aldermen is used in the custumal.

Two points emerge in which York differs apparently from the normal type of city governments, certainly from London and Norwich. One is the use of the terms " camera consilii," and " consilium camere," which does not seem to occur elsewhere. The meeting place on Ouse Bridge is called " the chamber of the council," and the body, which met there, is called " the council of the chamber." The assemblies had also two official meeting places, one in the chamber on Ousebridge, where the smaller meetings of the regular governing body were held, the other in the common hall, where the large popular meetings took place. Apparently other towns had only one hall of assembly.[1]

As, fortunately, the Memorandum Book includes a custumal[2] and an account of the mayor's court and the sheriff's court, it is possible from its own contents to compile a complete record of the machinery of the city's government, as well as to show the machinery at work. The custumal gives a succinct account of the mayor's court. " It is held before the mayor and aldermen either in the chamber in the ' Guyhall,' or in the ' Guyhall.' " In this court[3] all pleas and matters concerning apprentices and misteries were settled. All offences against the customs and ordinances of the city, breaches of the king's peace, and misconduct of the city's officials were punished in it. This court dealt, too, with all questions of debt, it administered the statute merchant and generally the statute staple. All wills, which dealt with land and houses, were brought " en pleine courte du mair " to be enrolled.[4] The will was proclaimed by the sergeant,

1. After the erection of the new common hall, the present gildhall, a room in it was called the council chamber, the first allusion to it in the Memorandum Book is on 21 September, 1416, " in cameram consilii infra aulam communem," p. 52. But the council chamber on Ousebridge was always used by the mayor and council in the fifteenth century.

2. The legalization of local customs was effected by royal ordinances ; the custumal is the city's own codification of a mass of customs which had grown out of local needs, but which were too numerous to be included in the king's charters ; naturally they differ considerably in different towns, probably all towns of importance had their custumal by the end of the thirteenth century. The account of the Sheriff's court is given in Mem. Bk., vol. I., pp. 137–139, lxxiii–lxxv.

3. Mem. Bk., pp. 251–253. A confirmation of the charter of the city by Henry III. mentions a court for holding pleas before the mayor and bailiffs. Municipal Com. Report, 1835, vol. xxv., p. 1737.

4. Mem. Bk., pp. 251–254, cf. Mem. Bk., vol. I., pp. xvii, lxiv., 13.

proved by two sworn witnesses, who were examined on oath as to the circumstances under which it was made, and the estate of the testator.

Unfortunately the custumal is undated, but it contains intrinsic evidence that it was copied into the Memorandum Book from another book, which had been compiled before 1396, for the three bailiffs, who were abolished in that year, are referred to in the custumal. Many of its provisoes were certainly in use in 1372, probably even at a much earlier date.

It also contains the oaths to be administered to the various municipal officials. These oaths are in London and in Norwich included in the Liber Albus.[1]

The oath of the mayor is brief. It contains no reference to his duty as the king's escheator; he simply swears that he will be faithful and loyal to our lord the king and preserve and guard the said city for our lord the king and his heirs; he undertakes to maintain the franchises, rights, laws, usages and customs of the same in every point, and to administer impartial justice as well to rich as poor; he concludes " and I will not neglect this for any reason, God helping me and the Saints." This oath shows him in the true light, he is supreme magistrate; his chief duty is to maintain law and order in the city. His fellow citizens approach him with almost servile respect, any insult is visited with severe penalties,[2] any effort to evade the office is regarded as a grave misdemeanour.[3] He was elected by the body of citizens from two or three of the aldermen nominated by the retiring mayor.[4] The recorder was the official civic lawyer; originally he was chosen each year, when the sheriffs were elected, " ils prendront un recordour que soit sachaunt de la ley et de bon fame a occupier

---

1. Lib. Alb. London, p. 306. Ibid. Norwich, fol. 182d, Records of the city of Norwich, p. 122. The Liber Albus of York seems to have disappeared, it is only referred to once in the Memorandum Book in 1392, this is earlier than the London Liber Albus, which was compiled in 1419.
2. Post p. xvi.
3. Post p. xv, p. 91.
4. This method of electing the mayor was altered twice by Edward IV. He placed the organization of the voting in the hands of the searchers of the various misteries who were to summons all the workers to the gildhall, they nominated two aldermen of the city, whose names were presented in writing to the mayor, aldermen and council, who selected one. 4 Edw. IV., pt. 2, m. 20, June 30th, 1464; 13 Edw. IV., pt. 2, m. 16 ; Dec. 23rd, 1473.

l'office de recordour par avys du meir et des bones gentz de la citee."¹ " He was the legal adviser of the mayor and aldermen especially when they acted in their magisterial capacity. He was appointed by the mayor, sheriffs, aldermen and twenty-four, the commons taking no part.

" For so myche as the ryght wurshipfull sir John Vavasour, late recorder of this wurshipfull cite, nowe beyng oon of the Kyngnes juges and the place of recordership void, it is by the said presence fully determyned and concluded, that the right wurshipfull sir William Fairefaxe, for certane considiracions, is most able and beneficiall fer that rowme. And so by the hole assent and consent of the seid presence, the said William Fairfaxe is elect and chosen to be recorder of this cite, and then and there sworne and admitted to the same office."² Miles Metcalfe seems to have held the office for nine years. On his resignation, the King, by " his mooste noble and severall letters " and the Earl of Northumberland " by mouthe," desired the position for Richard Green. The mayor, aldermen and sheriffs evasively replied, that if they had full proof of the circumspection and learning of the said Richard, " they may be rather inclined to call hyme to suche rowme, when any shal hapyn next to be voide." It is difficult to imagine their returning the same reply to the son of Henry VII. As Sir John Vavasour became recorder in 1486, the mayor's " rather inclined " seems to have been a polite form of refusal.³

Like Norwich, but unlike London, York had no special form of oath for the twelve, the aldermen. They were sworn in the same form and manner as the councillors. Their duties were probably similar. The custumal clearly defines what was expected from the councillors—they were " to counsel, assist, support and maintain the mayor in all his undertakings for the welbeing of the city."⁴ But the aldermen had a special power.

1. Mem. Bk., I., p. 40.
2. Mem. Bk., p. 293 [1489]. For list of recorders see F. Drake, *op. cit.*, p. 386.
3. Municipal Records, House Book, V., xv° die Februarii, anno regni regis Henrici vij, primo.
4. The custumal is not clear as to whether the thirty-six persons of the council to whom it refers consist of the twelve aldermen and the twenty-four councillors, or of a council of thirty-six, of whom twenty-four form a working committee. Mem. Bk., p. 256, ibid., p. 258.

They could arrest malefactors and commit them to the charge of the sheriffs. They were elected by the mayor and aldermen, " who assembled in the counsail chambre of Ousebrig, and ther and then of oon assent and consent elect and chuse the right honourable Thomas Scotton, merchant, to be of the number of the wershipful aldermen."[1] The sheriffs, however, rank above the twenty-four; sometime they take precedence of the aldermen. Their election was a public ceremony. On September 21st, the retiring sheriffs resigned their office in the presence of the mayor, aldermen, councillors and commons in the common hall. Then the election committee, " hii, ad quos elecio novorum vicecomitum civitatis pertenuit, ex ordinacione et consuetudine," apparently taken from the council, retired into an inner room and chose the new sheriffs. The mayor and commons remained in the large hall.[2] The sheriffs took over the duties of the bailiffs. They were accountable to the exchequer for the payment of the fee farm rent, and under the mayor had charge of the judicial administration in the city.[3]

The account of the sheriff's court, which is given in this volume of the Memorandum Book, is only a transcript of the regulations in force in the London sheriffs' court. A few of the clauses are missing, and there are various inaccuracies in the spelling due probably to the transcriber. Doubtless its presence in the city record is owing to the trade between London and York, as the dealings of merchants with each other form the subject of many of the regulations.[4]

An interesting case came into the sheriffs' court in July, 1416. A foreigner, Johannes Cuke from Bruges, had stolen money from Johannes Bell of Thirsk, and done him grievous bodily harm, so that he went in fear of his life. The jury found him guilty, but the court of chivalry interfered and took the case into their own

---

1. Mem. Bk., p. 292, 293. The position of the twenty-four is difficult to explain. Mr. Hudson suggests that they came into existence to help the bailiffs, in the same way that the twelve arose in an informal way to help the mayor.
2. Mem. Bk., pp. 75, 259, 260.
3. In the custumal the paragraph dealing with the duties of the sheriffs is headed vicountes on baillyffs." Mem. Bk., p. 259.
4. Mem. Bk., pp. 143–155. Munimenta Gildhallae Londoniensis, vol. I., pp. 202–221, cf. sheriffs' court. Mem. Bk., vol. I., pp. lxxiii–lxxvi, pp. 137–139.

hands, as the money stolen belonged to the king. This court instituted by Edward III. was presided over by the constable and marshal. Its chief work was to deal with matters pertaining to war within or without the kingdom, including trials by combat.[1] It invaded common law and Richard II. restricted its activities. There is no account of the election of the twenty-four, possibly it was less formal than other elections. In 1418 an ordinance was passed—probably it was only the re-enactment of a rule that had fallen into abeyance—that no one was qualified to become a member of the twenty-four, unless he had been a city sheriff. In case no ex-sheriff were available, then the choice was left to the discretion of the electors.[2] After the election of the mayor in the common hall, the aldermen and twenty-four returned to the council chamber on Ousebridge, and there chose the three chamberlains. They undertook the financial side of the city's affairs, and collected debts due to the commonalty; they also managed the common property except what was in charge of the bridgemasters.[3] The minor officials, the common clerk and the sergeants were chosen in the gildhall by the mayor, aldermen, and twenty-four.[4]

The government by council was in reality purely magisterial; theoretically, however, the whole scheme was based on the common will, on those large city assemblies, with their great though vaguely defined powers of moulding their city's history, which every citizen, not of course every resident, had a right to attend. Fundamentally the elaborate structure rested on the commons, " communis, tut la commonealte, tota communitas, multitudo copiosa," as they are called. They form the most interesting, at the same time the most elusive, part of the city's constitution. They possessed no adminstrative powers, those

---

1. 13 Ric. II., c. II., J. Selden, The Duello, p. 37.   Gregory's Chronicle, pp. 199–202, Camden Soc., 1876. Mr. Hudson has drawn my attention to the fact that this was the sheriffs' court of personal action, which still exists in Norwich, Records, I., cxxix, cxxx, cxlvi, 295–7. Mr. Spalding, town clerk of York, informs me that the sheriff's court of pleas, which is a court of record and served by the protonotary, is the successor of this court. Municipal Com. Reports, 1835, vol. 25, p. 1737.
2. Mem. Bk., p. 256, it is headed in the custumal " Le serment de trent six personns du counseil."
3. Mem. Bk., p. 256.
4. Ibid., pp. 257, 258.

were entirely in the hands of the council ; but when any important change, which involved the interests of the whole community, was contemplated, then the mayor summoned the whole body of freemen to the common hall. It is of course incredible that all the freemen attended, for about 100 freemen were added to the franchise each year.[1] Unfortunately on this subject the Memorandum Book gives little light. In 1379-80 the council is said to consist of the twelve, the twenty-four and the artificers,[2] but the times were revolutionary,[3] the councils of that period cannot be taken as typical. On July 4th, 1379, one of these large city assemblies was held, it is the only occasion on which a complete list of all the members by name is given. The twelve and twenty-four, qualified by having held important civic offices, occupy the first part of the list ; the forty-six names which follow[4] are those of craftsmen, none of whom had held office, the artificers of the previous entry.[5] The oath administered to the commons was identical with that taken by the twelve and twenty-four, but it was read to them by the common clerk, they then swore, by raising their hands, to support the mayor, " en tous poins a lour povoir."[6]

The Memorandum Book indulges in no tantalizing silences in its descriptions of the meetings of the citizens. It is rich both in accounts of the meetings in the council chamber and the assemblies in the common hall. No laboured account of the technique of medieval city government can give the vivid impression of its working that can be gained from these realistic pictures of the men themselves at their work of legislation, adminstration, consultation and arbitration. In 1417 a municipal undertaking, the re-erection of the public crane with its annexed buildings, had involved the city in great expense. The mayor, aldermen and " whole council of the chamber of the city " met, in the morning of the second of May, to discuss raising the

1. Ante, pp. iv, v.
2. Mem. Bk., I., pp. 39, v.
3. Mem. Bk., p. xlii.
4. A blank space for the insertion of two names is left in the MS.
5. Mem. Bk., I., pp. v–ix.
6. Mem. Bk., p. 256.

rent in order to reimburse themselves for the outlay.¹ They recognized that it was a matter about which the citizens had a right to be consulted. Later in the same day they therefore called a meeting of the commons in the common hall; the regulations they had drawn up were communicated to the commons, who sanctioned them, " coram communitate publicatum et per communitatem affirmatum." Although September 21st and February 3rd were favourite dates for proclaiming any new procedure, it seems doubtful whether, except for the elections, there were any fixed dates for the summoning of these general meetings.

On one occasion all the preliminary meetings are omitted, and ordinances of the utmost importance first appear in the Memorandum Book at a city assembly in the common hall on September 21st, 1419. The mayor, six aldermen, seventeen councillors, the whole of the community of citizens, " tocius communitatis civium," and the two sheriffs were present. The authorities were probably sure that they would carry their audience with them. The memory of " the Foul Raid," the consciousness that Scotsmen were only waiting a favourable opportunity to make another similar invasion, and that they were fighting with Frenchmen against Englishmen in France, had roused the feelings of the men of York to frenzy. This racial hatred had found an outlet in those stringent measures against the aliens, which the York council proposed, and the commons ratified with enthusiasm. No Scotsman nor any other alien, whatever his status, was " to occupy any position as searcher or constable or hold any official rank lofty or low; they were forbidden to enter the common hall or any other place in the city, where secret counsel or any city business could be overheard; they were not to hold meetings or to sit on assizes, or to be impanelled as jurymen for any cause whatsoever, but were to be excluded from every office for evermore."²

For the moment the Memorandum Book seems to have ceased to chronicle limited city affairs and to have plunged into a

1. Mem. Bk., p. 81.
2. Mem. Bk., p. 86.

whirlpool of international complications. The next proceeding, however, brings the assembly back to strictly civic matters. The same day new sheriffs had to be elected. Those, who had held office, had the previous year not conducted themselves with strict regard for the dignity of their own position or that of the " ful nobil city " which they represented. They had scandalized all right thinking citizens by appearing in the streets, no servant preceding or following them. Mayor, council and commons, in the presence of the two delinquents, solemnly and unanimously ordained that this should be prohibited, under a penalty of 100s.—unless some weighty, sudden accident should render such a disregard of decency inevitable. Probably the commons enjoyed sitting in judgment on their official superiors. But the day's work was not yet finished ; the same assembly had still to elect two members of parliament—Johannes Northeby and Thomas Gare, " cives et mercatores Ebor' fuerunt electi ad essendum pro civitate ista ad parliamentum tenendum apud Westmonasterium, xvj^{mo} die Octobris proximo extunc futuro."[1]

The list of the thirty officials, who were present on this occasion, shows how completely the government of the city had fallen into the hands of the cloth trade ; ten members were mercers, five mercators, three drapers, one was a dyer, and one a cloth dresser ; the trades of four are not given in the list of freemen, but, by family, they belonged to the merchant class ; two remain unidentified ; a butcher, a skinner and two potters are the only representatives of other industries. Possibly the reason of the animus against the retiring sheriffs was that one was a potter. It is suggestive that both the new sheriffs belonged to the popular official trade, and both members of parliament were mercators.[2]

A few months later another important meeting of mayor, twelve, twenty-four, sheriffs, and a great multitude of the searchers and other citizens, " unacum magna multitudine scrutatorum et

---

1. Mem. Bk., p. 87. As late as 1488 the parliamentary franchise was exercised by the assembly in Norwich. The Records of the City of Norwich, vol. I., pp. 107, 287.

2. Freemen of York, *op. cit. passim.*

aliorum civium," was held in the Common Hall.¹ Aldermen wishful to escape being chosen as mayor absented themselves from the city on the day of election. An ordinance was passed unanimously that the delinquent should pay dearly for his lack of civic spirit²; he was to be fined one hundred marks, sixty to go to the newly elected mayor to help to defray his expenses of office, forty to go to the sheriffs for the use of the city.

A resolution, that people should pay the taxes in the parish where they were living at the time when it was imposed, passed on this occasion, was later overruled. The mayor and commons rescinded the ordinance after a fortnight's interval; they substituted one, which ordained that the tax should be paid in the parish, where the people slept the night before the tax was collected. If, however, it could be proved that they had changed their domicile solely in order to pay at the lower rate, then they had to pay the tax in both parishes. Obviously the first resolution was passed with the object of preventing fraud. It is difficult to see the reason for the repeal; possibly a progressive party had rushed the measure through on a busy day, and a retrogressive party worked up opposition in the intervening fortnight.³

For three days during the month of September, 1436, a civic scandal caused great excitement in the city. Thomas Bracebridge, an alderman, had insulted the mayor; a discreet silence is maintained as to the form of insult. A city assembly was called in the gild hall, and " bi thadvise and thassent of the said maire,

---

1. Mem. Bk., pp. 90, 91. The presence of searchers as distinct from other citizens is unusual, especially as the interests of the various gilds are not involved.
2. The Patent Rolls give numerous examples of exemptions from holding civic offices granted by the King in return for service. " Exemption for life out of regard for last good Friday of William Selere of York, goldsmith, from being put on assizes, juries, inquisitions or other recognitions, and from being made mayor, sheriff, constable, bailiff, collector or assessor of tenths or fifteenths or other quota or subsidy, arrayer of men-at-arms, . . . or archers, or leaders of them, or other officer or minister of the King, against his will, 17 Ric. II., Pt. II., m. 3, May 2, 1394.
3. Some words in this passage are illegible but the sense seems clear. Was the absence of the council intentional? Did it arise from some disagreement between themselves and the mayor supported by the commons? " De concensu et unanimi voluntate maioris et *communitatis* in gildaula extitit ordinatum." The word communitas may include the whole council, twelve, twenty-four and the commons, but it would be an unusual description.

of all the said worshippful persones and of al the communalte of the said cite," he was " discharged of al offices within the cite and of al other occupacions and labours to the parliamentz." The next day this sentence was carried into effect in the council chamber on Ousebridge ; he was formally excluded in the presence of mayor, aldermen, and twenty-four, the commons were absent. The third day, however, the commons were once more summoned to the common hall to hear the repentant man's apology. His submission made, " the maire goodly with warme wordes and tendre admitted the said submission, and touk hym to favour and grace and restited and restored hym to his f[ranchise] and to the state of alderman in fourm as he stood afore."[1]

A servant of the mayor, who frequented a suspicious tavern by night, and said to one of the sheriffs " quod ipsam tabernam, dimittere nollet, eciam si maior vel Nicholaus Blakburn sibi inhibuerint " did not escape so lightly.[2]

An interesting case was brought into the council chamber on Ousebridge in 1397. Johannes Lyvelandes, son of Thoma Lyvelandes, was seized and claimed as a serf by Hanletheus Mauleverer. He was a member of the family of Mauleverer of Allerton Mauleverer ; the first of the family in England was Richard Leporarius, who gave the chapel of Allerton to the priory of Holy Trinity, York, " his gift being made with the consent of Robert de Brus, his lord and his heirs ; he at length returning from St. James [of Compostello] and being received at Marmontier, placed the said gift on St. Martin's altar, in the presence of Abbot Halgod."[3] In spite, however, of the good deeds of his ancestors, Hanletheus was forced to relinquish his claim. He did not confess that the claim was unjust, but declared that on account of the respect he bore the mayor, and the reverence he felt for the city of York, he gave Johannes his liberty.[4]

1. Mem. Bk., p. 143.
2. Mem. Bk., p. 55. For disrespect to an alderman see pp. 75, 76.
3. J. H. Round, Calendar of Documents, France (918–1206), p. 445.
4. The name Hanlath must come from some alliance with the Hanlathby family, now Halnaby in the parish of Croft. A potter of the name of Lyvelandey was made a freeman in 1379. Freemen of York, p. 77, cf. Mem. Bk. I., pp. 249, 250, lx, lxi.

The position of the serf was considerably modified by the black death, still his lot was far from enviable; on the death of his lord he was transferred to his successor with the rest of the live stock on the estate, the only court of justice to which he could appeal, was the manor court, where his lord presided; and he was unable to have his children educated unless he paid a fine.

When any question concerning the common lands or property came before the mayor, the commons seem always to have been consulted. A complaint was made that a little lane, between Bootham and *les leys*, although it was common property, had been closed. At once the mayor accompanied by the aldermen, the twenty-four, the commons, "communibus," and the searchers of the gilds of masons and carpenters went to examine the place. They found gates and posts had been erected at the entrance from Bootham; immediate orders were given for their removal. The willows growing near the meadow end of the narrow road were to be cut down; the bogs filled up with earth, so that men and beasts could pass safely.[1] This is only one example of the many delightful little pictures given in the Memorandum Book of the real life of the community, a true democratic spirit pervades it, all working together to put an immediate stop to a wrongful action. No costly litigation was entered upon; by the expert advice of those skilled in deciding these questions, surrounded by his thirty-six councillors, in the presence of many unofficial citizens, the mayor redressed the grievance. Still civic business was not always decided so expeditiously. On May 3rd, 1434, an indenture in the name of "nos maior et communitas civium civitatis Ebor'," was drawn up. It leased a newly built house in Hertergate[7] to Johannes Kyrkham, at an annual rent of twenty-six shillings and eightpence; the lease was only granted on condition that he supplied the city with all the plaster and lime they needed at a fixed price. The document was not attested by mayor, council and sheriffs until 20th December, 1436.[2]

1. Mem. Bk., pp. 109, 110.
2. Mem Bk., pp. 137–139. R. Davies, Walks through the City of York, pp. 76–78.

Johannes Bempton hoped to escape the vigilant eye of the city's guardians, when he built, out of his own head " ex capite suo proprio," a house on common land, behind his own garden and beyond the line of his neighbours' buildings. But the mayor, sheriffs, aldermen, and commons[1] went to the house in North Street, near the city moat; they scrutinized the evidence he laid before them, and then called in a mason and two carpenters, " secundum antiquam consuetudinem civitatis," to decide the matter. These three experts frustrated his plans; they declared that " from time to which the memory of man goes not back " the land had been held and enclosed in the same way, and that he must build his house within his garden walls and in no other manner.[2]

The city was not a rack renter, the grass land of the ditch called " le mote " within Mikelgarth bar on the south from " barra de Mikelgate " to the old Bailey was let for ten shillings a year. By the terms of the lease, the mayor and chamberlains had the right, if the rent were forty days in arrears, to reclaim the land without any opposition from the tenant, " in manus maioris et communitatis reseisire et rehabere."

But the meetings of the governing body in the hall on Ousebridge, in spite of the absence of the commons, were no dull assemblies for the transaction of unimportant routine business. It was a dramatic age, within a stone's throw of the place where the mistery plays were yearly enacted, scenes no less tragic though unrehearsed, took place. " On 27th February, 1390, Robertus de Ellerbek, mercer, with bare feet and uncovered head came into the chamber, and prostrated himself before Ranulphus del See in the presence of the mayor, bailiffs and council. With bitter tears, he addressed Ranulphus in all humility, saying, ' I beseech thee for the love of our Lord Jesus Christ, who redeemed the world by His precious blood shed on the cross, pardon and forgive me for the death of Ricardus[3] del See, thy father.' At these words, the mayor, bailiffs and

1. The expression used is " plures alii concives ejusdem civitatis," not the usual " communitas."
2. Mem. Bk., pp. 107, 108.
3. Mem. Bk., pp. 30, 31, cf. Drake, *op. cit.*, p. 199.

other worthies joined in petitioning Ranulphus 'that for the love of God the murder of the said Ricardus should be condoned.' Then the aforesaid Ranulphus, moved in spirit, turned to the weeping Robertus and said, ' For the love of God and for the salvation of the spirit of the said Ricardus, I pardon and absolve you of the death of the said Richard.' "

The Memorandum Book is peculiarly rich in references to foreign trade ; it is therefore fortunate, though entirely fortuitous, that the first document of this volume should be an agreement for the settlement of disputes between the English and the Prussians. This treaty was concluded (but never acted upon) between Richard II. and the Grand Master of the Teutonic Knights[1] in 1388. It is especially interesting to York for Thomas Gra, mayor of the city in 1373-4, was one of two ambassadors in whose charge it was sent to Marienburg :[2] his colleague was Walterus Sibelle, a London alderman, who represented the city in the parliament of 1377, and was suspected of having encouraged the peasants' rising of 1381.[3] Nicholaus Stoket accompanied them, apparently to give advice on questions of law. Momentous changes in national policy are passed over silently in the Memorandum Book, but it gives many apt illustrations of the fact that in the reversal of the policy of his grandfather Richard II. had the nation behind him. It is from this point of view that some account of the circumstances, which led to the treaty with Prussia, seems imperative. The encouragement of aliens had been the keynote of the policy of Edward III.[4] Richard II. introduced a new system ; he yielded to the pressure brought upon him by the towns, which argued with great plausibility that to treat foreigners in England as no English were treated in foreign lands

---

1. Originally a union of ship captains from Lübec for the succour of the sick and dying at Acre. The new order obtained vast possessions in Germany, and in 1228 drew their swords against the heathen Prussians, who since their massacre of St. Adalbert, had steadily resisted all attempts at conversion. From their head centre at Marienberg they slowly subdued the Pagans and laid the foundations of Modern Prussia. H. B. Workman, The Evolution of Monasticism, p. 267. Cf. A. Werminghoff, Der Deutsche Orden und die Stände in Preussen, pp. 1-9.

2. Close R. 11 Rich. II., m. 46. French R. 11 Rich. II., m. 3.

3. G. Unwin, *op. cit.*, pp. 137, 143, 147.

4. Stat. 11 Edw. III., cap. 5. W. Cunningham, Alien Immigrants, p. 107.

was an absurdity.¹ This pressure continued throughout the fifteenth century and brought the English policy more and more into line with the autonomous cities on the continent, which carried out a strongly protective policy with a high hand, though not always with entire success.² In 1382 the English government laid heavy taxes on the Hanse or German merchants³ in England ; the Grand Master of the Teutonic Knights retaliated by forbidding the English to trade in Danzic. He forced the English to retire to Elbing, and even there he imposed vexatious restrictions on them.⁴ After four years of armed neutrality in 1385 a small fleet of English ships attacked six Prussian vessels near Swin.⁵ The Grand Master at once ordered the seizure of all English goods in Prussia ; England replied by a similar order for all Prussian goods in England. These preliminaries led to the journey of Thomas Gra to Marienburg. The fact that York was the centre of considerable trade to the Baltic made the choice singularly judicious. The Teutonic Knights, long after their settlement in Danzic, continued to send out quasi crusades against the surrounding heathen lands, and many English knights, who in a previous century would have joined the crusades, fought under their banner in this European crusade. Henry Bolinbroke, afterwards Henry IV., was the best known of these military adventurers.⁶ The Percy family and the Yorkshire Scropes were represented too ; the trader followed in the steps of the soldier, and Danzic became the home of many merchants from York. Unlike the Hanse merchants in London, who were all congregated in one hall and led a separate existence, in Danzic, the English lived in the Prussian merchants' houses, and were apparently

1. W. Cunningham, Growth of English Industry and Commerce, vol. I., p. 377.
2. W. J. Ashley, English Economic History, vol. I., pt. II., p. 15. G. Des Marez, L'Organization du Travail a Bruxelles au xv. siècle, p. 495. G. Fagniez, Etudes sur l'Industrie à Paris au xiiie et au xive siècle, p. 128.
3. Dr. F. Schulz, Die Hanse und England, pp. 36, 37. Abhandlungen zur Verkehrs und Seegeschichte, v.
4. Hansisches Urkundenbuch, vierter Band, 1361-1392, No. 753, 759, 761, 786, 835.
5. Hanse Recesse 1256-1430, Band II., Nr. 309. Rymer Fœdera, VII., 581, 589, 601, 602, 647.
6. Dr. F. Schulz, op. cit., p. 15. T. Lindner, Die Deutsche Hanse, pp. 256-259.

allowed to trade even by retail. But as the rule of the Teutonic Knights, who were themselves not allowed to trade, weakened, the power of the burgher element strengthened; jealousy of the successful English trader grew.[1] The story of retaliations and reprisals is dreary reading. Henry Wyman, a German merchant living in York, was arrested in 1386, and only released at the request of the King. Probably he took part in the sending of the Embassy to Danzic for he must have held a prominent position in the city. In 1388 he was even exempted from the alien tax, and was mayor in 1407-1408.[2]

Many documents are preserved in the archives at Königsberg, which prove the extensive nature of the trade between York and the Baltic.[3] The complaints carried by Gra to Danzic are signed by numerous York merchants. The damages they claim throw light on the comparative position of York among other towns. Nine London merchants demand as compensation £386 3s. 4d.; thirty York men claim £1,636; nineteen merchants from Lynn demand £1,914 18s. 4d.; fourteen from Beverley £470; and fifteen from Norwich £937 13s. 4d. Although Lynn heads the list with its claim of almost £2,000,[4] the demand of York approaches it nearly, and is distributed among a greater number of traders. York had more than 3 times as many merchants trading to Danzic as London, $1\frac{1}{2}$ times as many as Lynn, more than twice as many as Beverley and exactly twice as many as Norwich.[5]

In 1404 a claim of £340 was advanced by Robertus Gaunt,[6] Henricus Hyndelay,[7] Ricardus Bantry,[8] Robertus Feriby and

1. P.R.O. Cl. R. 9 Rich. II., m. 46.
2. 11 Rich. II., pt. II., m. 8, 12 June, 1388. " Grant with the assent of the Council to Henry Wyman of Almaine, a citizen of York, who has long lived there with wife and house, and paid tenths, fifteenths and other taxes that he be exempt from the payment of 3d. in the pound, and other customs for his goods and merchandize paid by aliens, in addition to what the denizens pay, and license to him to acquire and sell lands, tenements within the realm, and to be held a denizen." Freemen of York, op cit., pp. 85, 110, 112. Cf. The Naturalization of Henry Market, Mem. Bk., pp. 185, 186.
3. Hanse Recesse, 2te Abteil, Band III., 1256–1430, passim.
4. Between £25,000 and £30,000 in modern money.
5. Hanse Recesse, op. cit., pp. 405, 406.
6. Freemen of York, op. cit., p. 97.
7. Ibid., p. 103.
8. Probably Bawtry ibid. p. 106.

xxii YORK MEMORANDUM BOOK

Rogerus Thornell,[1] who complain that 120 cloths, 25 pieces of worsted, 30 coverlets, 120 ells of frieze had been taken from them by the Prussians.[2] But the complaints of illtreatment of the people of Danzic by the men of York and Hull are equally numerous.[3]

Eighty years after the Marienburg treaty stories of the same kind are repeated. Evidence was taken at Nimeguen on September 15th, 1468,[4] Thomas Todde of York and the boatswain of the vessel give an account of their sufferings. "Thomas Todde of Yorke, merchant, in the shipp called the Valentyne, saith, that he sailed from Newecastell to Hulle and from thene to the Sounde and thider came on Wednesday at nyght in the moneth of Juyne last, and on the morrow about 7 or 8 of the clok came aborde a Karvell of Denmark, whereof was maister Nannyng Van Daryng [Duren], boren and havyng lyvelode in Campe, now dwellyng at Copemanhaven, and with hym shipper Tunes [Tymes] of Lubike and Vincent Stole in a blak shippe of Danske with certains yonkers of Danske, that is to seie Petre Van Plane, Hanze Servese [Servoese] and Hauze Knope and othir of Danske," . . . . "they entered upon theym and tok the rule of the saide shipp called the Valentyne and sente them to lande and putte them in prisone and toke from them all that they badde." The document in support of which this evidence is taken is headed complaint of John, Earl of Northumberland, and the merchants of York and Hull.[5] The Earl of Northumberland had not merely lent his name to strengthen the petition, he was the ship's owner, "*cujus navis predictus comes fuit proprietarius et possessor.*" The petitioners number thirty-one; twenty of them were York men.[6] An interesting side light on the concentration of civic power in the hands of the merchant class is afforded by this document, nine

---

1. Ibid., p. 100.
2. Hanse Recesse, Band V., No. 433, 434.
3. Hansisches Urkunden Buch, Band V., No. 153; Band VI., No. 288.
4. Ibid., Band IX., No. 519. Cf. Mem. Bk., pp. 86–89. Cf. J. H. Wylie, The Reign of Henry V., 328–332.
5. Ibid. No. 520, pp. 369, 370. Cf. Medieval Garner, Shipman's Law, p. 155. Life on a Hanse Ship, pp. 156–158.
6. Freemen of York, *op. cit. passim.*

of the twenty applicants had been mayors of the city. More details are supplied by other witnesses who say that the ship was attacked by 400 armed men from Danzic, Lübec, Rostock, Wismar and Stralsund. They seized both ship and cargo, captured the sailors and placed them in " vili carcere vocato le . . . . . profunde sub terra, ita quod nullus corum potuit videre alium." The evidence is long and confusing. One fact, however, emerges quite clearly that it was English disunion that was at the root of Hanse or German predominance in English trade. The death-blow to the Hanseatic power in England was delayed for nearly a century by the dynastic quarrels of the XV. century. But it would be difficult to gauge at its right value the strong feeling of animosity to the alien, which betrays itself in so much of the civic legislation, in so many of the gild regulations, unless the strong desire of mercantile England to concentrate English trade in English hands is recognized as an important factor in the matter.[1]

The next reference in the Memorandum Book to the Danzic trade is happily wholly pacific. It is an agreement[2] between Henricus de Hyndelay,[3] mercator, Rogerus de Thornhill,[4] mercator, Willelmus Denyas,[5] mercer, Johannes Somerby,[6] littester, Johannes de Raghton,[7] draper, and Johannes Eseby, burgher of Danzic, as to the division between them of the cargo

---

1. Prof. Dr. Dietrich Schäfer emphasized this view in his book *Die Hanse*, Leipzig, 1903. " Nothing could be more mistaken than the view that England merely by her geographical position had been predestined to commercial and maritime supremacy. . . . In the XVI. century, quite apart from the fact that England on account of her small area could never have been spoken of as a power besides Germany (if the latter had ever really been an Empire). economically and especially in commercial and industrial activity she was in no way superior to Germany and was considerably behind Holland. Her predominance under Queen Elizabeth was exclusively political. If the Hanse merchants could have been induced to maintain a continuous unity of purpose, the English merchant would have been obliged to curtail his aims. As it was he attained his object ; the nation united in a single state and represented by the strong will of an able woman triumphed over the isolated city states, the fragments of a league adapted to vanished conditions who were striving to defend the remains of their old magnificence."
2. Mem. Bk., p. 10.
3. Freemen of York, *op. cit.*, p. 103. Hanse Recesse, V., p. 332.
4. Ibid., p. 100. Ibid.
5. Ibid., p. 90. Denys here, Devys in Mem. Bk.
6. Ibid., p. 97.
7. Ibid., pp. 80, 92.

of a vessel called the "*Halygaste*," freighted from Danzic to Hull. Another entry, earlier in date but later in position, shows some of the difficulties of foreign trade. Johannes Topclyff came before the mayor to free himself from any responsibilities with regard to the trading ventures of Robertus Normanton, who had lately been his apprentice.[1] Robertus bound himself to pay one hundred marks, if his late master or his representative or his servants should be impleaded or proceeded against or have his goods and chatells arrested for any debt incurred by him, " tam citra mare quam ultra." Difficulties of this nature seem to have been common ; Johannes de Calthorn appeared before the mayor and other *probi homines*, and obliged his former apprentice, Perot de Casawas de Vasconia, to swear on the holy gospel of God that he had neither bought nor sold nor acted for Johannes de Calthorn, since his apprenticeship was finished.[2]

Twenty of the leading mercers and spicers had been holding an inquisition by order of the King on a case of cargo lost at sea. They gave their evidence on oath before the mayor, sheriffs and aldermen of the city, on the twentieth of March, 1415–16. The case furnishes another example of the precariousness of foreign trade.[3] Willelmus Warde, spicer, had made an agreement on the twelfth of December, 1415, with Willelmus Eseby.[4] By the terms of this agreement Eseby had to expend sixty-eight pounds in buying Flemish goods for Ward ; a special clause was inserted that this should be done at Warde's own risk. Eseby was to receive a commission of five per cent. The goods were bought and shipped from Selykey in Zealand, in a vessel called "*the Hulke*," to Hull. Between Yarmouth and Kyrkla, it was wrecked,' " in mari totaliter periclitata et perdita fuit." But Willelmus Eseby could get no payment from Willemus Warde, either for the capital he had expended, or for his labour. In 1419 Willelmus Eseby was again in the council chamber ; he brought a letter from the burghermaster, magistrates and

1. Mem. Bk., p. 14.
2. Mem. Bk., p. 29.
3. Mem. Bk., pp. 55, 56.
4. Can this be a relation of Johannes Eseby, burgher of Danzic ? p. 10. Willelmus Eseby appears as a freeman in 1392, no Johannis is in the roll. York Freemen, *op. cit.*, p. 92.

council of Bruges. They, at the suit of Jacques Weits, a burgher of Bruges, claimed twenty-three pounds, two shillings from Eseby, who was bound for that sum on behalf of Ricardus Heaton factor of Robertus Tup of Hull.[1]

In 1420 a curious bond was given by John Bukkiller, citizen and merchant of Danzic and John Dodyngton[2] of York for £100 to Robert Baumberg and John Dreng of Scarbrough, payable on November 11th, 1421. In case, however, John Bukkiller could prove that the vessel the two Scarborough men had seized, belonged to the merchants of Danzic, then the bond became null and void. Apparently John Bukkiller and John Dodington owed the Scarborough men money, who thinking the ship was John Bukkiller's personal property, seized it.[3] It belonged, however, to the merchants of Danzic, but Bukkiller and Dodington had to give a bond for £100 before it was allowed to sail. A letter was then obtained from Danzic, which proved the ship undoubtedly belonged to merchants in Danzic, then their bond was, as had been arranged, returned to them. The letters which passed between Danzic, Scarborough and York, are amusing examples of the epistolary style of the fifteenth century.

A testimonial letter under the seal of Danzic.

" In the presence of the honourable and most sagacious men, the mayor, sheriff and aldermen of the city of York in England,[4] our very sincere friends we, the proconsuls and consuls of the city of Danzic wishing for the increase of all good, ' cum tocius boni incremento,' publicly declare with protestation worthy of belief in these our letters, that a certain ship commonly called among us, the "*Marienkneche*," which Robertus Baumburg and Johannes Dreng of Scarborough took from Henricus Strunyng our fellow townsman, the governor and master of the said ship, on the Thursday before Pentecost last, by seizing her upon the

---

1. Mem. Bk., pp. 87–89.
2. Chamberlain in 1418, York Freemen, p. 127.
3. Mem. Bk., pp. 95, 98, 99. The man from Danzic appears in one set of documents as Bukkiller, in the other as Bokeler.
4. The words used are " dominis maiore, ballivo et consulibus," but obviously the sheriff and aldermen are meant.

sea with all the goods with which she was laden, for which afterward Johannes Bokeler, merchant of Danzic, and John Dodyngton, citizen of York, bound themselves to the aforesaid Robertus and Johannes Dreng, by a bond for £100, belongs entirely and lawfully[1] to certain inhabitants and townsmen of our city of Danzic and to no one else in any way."

In confirmation and fuller evidence of which we have caused these letters for which we desire to obtain firm and unhesitating belief to be confirmed by an impression from the reverse of our seal. *Written at Danzic, May 15th, 1421.*

The York officials at once wrote to Scarborough.

Richard Russell, mayor of the city of York, and the sheriffs and aldermen[2] of the same, men of a singular friendliness, to the bailiff and worthy men of the town of Scarborough.

" Greeting in Him who gives the gifts of eternal salvation. We, therefore, by reason of the profound affection which we bear towards you, counsel you and beseech you with warm and sincere goodwill that, on sight of the foregoing letters, testimonial, and these our present letters, you cause to be delivered the aforesaid bond to the aforesaid John and John, who are bound as is above stated, as is fitting, not only on account of our request and love, but still more observing with what constant affection and favour and peaceable disposition, the citizens of the aforesaid city of Danzic entreat our compatriots in their business relations every day."

Given at York, etc., 27th May, 1421.

The charming little port of Veere[3] near Middelburg still shows signs, in its grass grown quays, its beautiful harbour, its stately buildings, of the important position it held in the mercantile life

---

1. " Nomine " probably means enrolled in the city's register in their names.
2. Probi homines.
3. Cf. Hedon in Yorkshire, " A 12th century port with quays more than a mile and a quarter in extent must certainly have played a considerable part in the mercantile history of Holderness." Victoria History of Yorkshire, vol. II., p. 432.

of medieval Europe. A letter from the mayor, sheriffs, and aldermen of York " to the honorable, most potential, and ever dear Henricus de Borssalia, Lord of Campveer," proves that York was regarded as the principal city of northern England. A well-known sailor, Johannes Wacker from Veere, had been attacked and illtreated by some English sailors; the lord of Veere had written to demand redress from the mayor of York. But, as the mayor points out in his reply, the delinquents were men of Newcastle and Hull over whom he had no jurisdiction. Any attempt on his part to interfere might result in the abrogation of the privileges of York itself, " quod avertat bonus Jesus." Nevertheless he promises that, putting aside all slothfulness and procrastination, he will urge the mayors of Newcastle and Hull to bring the evildoers to justice.

There was considerable trade, too, with Dordrecht, a picturesque little Dutch town at the present time, but with a great wine trade, as its capacious cellars still testify, in the fifteenth century.[1]

There are a great many entries in the Memorandum Book of the naturalization of foreigners, Scotsmen especially,[2] but Henricus Market,[3] a Hanse merchant, who was enrolled as a freeman in 1411, was not naturalized until 1429-30, and then by act of parliament on the payment of £3 6s. 8d.

Petrus van Uppestall from Brabant,[4] who took up his freedom in 1402, paid twenty shillings for his naturalization in 1414. He brought the King's letter of naturalization to the mayor himself; it seems from the description to have been a gorgeous document, it was fastened with silken cords of red and green, and sealed with the great seal of green wax.

Another and less fortunate class of foreigners were often seen in York in the fifteenth century. Johannes Artays and Johannes Walter, born in Normandy and taken prisoners there, came into the council chamber and swore on the holy gospels of God on the

---

1. Mem. Bk., p. 82. Cf. B. Hagedown, Ostfrieslands Handel und Schiffahrt, vol. II., 140. From 1655 to 1751 Dordrecht was the mart for the Merchant Adventurers of England.
2. Eng. Misc., *op. cit. passim*, see index.
3. Mem. Bk., pp. 185, 186.
4. Mem. Bk., p. 50.

20th of May, 1419, that they would be good and faithful prisoners to Willelmus Barton, skinner, serve him faithfully, and not absent themselves from his service until their redemption money was fully paid.[1]

The disturbed condition of the country in 1459 led to increased stringency in the treatment of aliens in York. During and after the reign of Henry VI. all aliens in England paid double the amount of taxes paid by natives,[2] but York excluded them from all municipal offices,[3] and finally decided to follow London in its treatment of the Hanse merchants. On April 27th, the mayor, alderman, and councillors at a meeting in the council chamber[4] ordained that all foreigners " alienigine " coming to the city should dwell only in the hostel of the mayor and commonalty, " In hospicio maioris et communitatis," at the sign of the Bull in Coney Street, unless they obtained a special license from the mayor.[5] The penalty for disobedience was a fine of 40s. A few days later, this ordinance was recited by the mayor, read through by the common clerk, in the presence of many of the citizens in the gildhall, and was confirmed by their common assent and wish. This is the last entry in the Memorandum Book which is concerned with the treatment of the alien, except clauses which are common to all the gild regulations of the period.

The ordinances of forty-one misteries appear in the first half of the Memorandum Book, only twenty-six in the second. The predominance of the woollen industry in the period is uncontrovertible still, except the tapiters, no distinctly textile gilds are mentioned, though various trades subsidiary to the cloth trade, as cappers, listers, fullers, glovers figure largely. The architectural development of York in the fifteenth century led to great activity in the building trades, glasiers, carpenters, tilers and plasterers are constantly in the council chamber; sometimes as suppliants, oftener as arbiters in some dispute

1. Mem. Bk., p. 79.
2. Alien Merchants in England, trans. *Roy. Hist. Soc.* (new ser.), ix., 94.
3. Ante, p. xiii.
4. It is not stated whether it was the council chamber on Ousebridge or in the Gildhall.
5. Mem. Bk., p. 203.

about encroachments or rights of way. The growth of luxury had developed and differentiated the metalworking industries; cutlers, pinners, goldsmiths — occupy many pages of the Memorandum Book.

The mercers' is the first mystery to appear in this volume. One of their number had refused to hand over his weights for examination at the bidding of the searchers.[1] The custumal of the city expressly states that if any searcher finds any fault in workmanship or behaviour, he is to bring the offender before the mayor for the time being. The searcher was bound to do this by an oath sworn when he took office.[2] The preliminiary examination of the delinquent took place before the mayor and sheriffs; he pleaded not guilty. Twelve jurymen were then elected to try the case, and reported to the mayor and sheriffs that the charge was fully proved. It was decided by the same judges that he should be imprisoned, until he paid a fine. Finally the help of the aldermen was evoked to decide upon the amount of fine. The court thus augmented decided that for his disobedience, transgression, rebellion and contempt, the said Willelmus Hungate should forfeit ten pounds. He at once paid thirteen shillings and fourpence; the rest of the money he was allowed to retain, unless he transgressed again. These details are typical of all questions of gild discipline; the mayor and sheriffs dealt with them, often the aldermen joined, the twenty-four seldom, the commonalty never. When, however, any question arose affecting the pageant plays, then the citizens seem to have been summoned to all the deliberations. No ordinances of the mercers are found in the Memorandum Book. This omission is not surprising.[3] As mercers and merchants seem to have been interchangeable terms, and as the governing body of York were chiefly merchants, it would have been a work of supererogation to gain their consent to any change in their own enactments. The mayor and aldermen were the masters of the

1. Mem. Bk., pp. 8, 9.
2. Ibid., p. 260.
3. I have a copy of the earliest ordinances of the mercers made many years ago from a MS. which is now lost. It was in the possession of the late Canon Raine when heard of last. The Merchant Adventurers of York have made every effort to trace it, but failed.

mistery of mercers ; it was futile to bring ordinances, drawn up by themselves, into a council chamber over which they presided. But their royal charter, which emphasized their superiority to the smaller and less important misteries, is transcribed in its entirety.[1] It begins with the usual prologue, a contrast between the flourishing circumstances of the mercers in the past and their dire poverty in the present : " Whereas many men of the mistery of mercers of our city of York, abounding for a time and very rich as well in merchandize as in other worldly matters, afterwards by misfortune at sea and other mischances have come to misery and want so pitiful, that they have little or nothing whereof they may live or sustain themselves, except by the charity help and gratuities of faithful christians and religious people. Whereupon divers stable and capable people of substance and influence, belonging to the mistery of the same city, inflamed by zeal of charity, heeding its teaching, and not shutting up their bowels from the want and misery aforesaid, propose, as we have heard, to purchase with our license lands, tenements and rents . . . . to the honour of God and in aid and relief of the poor and indigent of the mistery aforesaid."[2] As the mistery had a large membership, it naturally included both the successful and unsuccessful trader, but this exaggerated picture of abject poverty is at variance with the account roll of the society for 1432, which tells a tale of prosperity and expansion. The York mercers, however, were always pedantically anxious to emphasize the difference between the gild or fraternity and the mistery. The head line of their account rolls is always " the account roll of A.B. master of the mistery of mercers and of the gild and fraternity of the Holy Trinity." Their gild was essentially a dual organization, each with its specialized functions ; the one mercantile and industrial, the other religious and social ; the one devoted to fostering the worldly advantage of its members, the other interested mainly in their spiritual welfare ; to the meeting of the one the members went accompanied by wives and sisters, to

1. Mem. Bk., pp. 135, 136, 137.
2. P.R.O., Pat. Rolls, 8 Henry VI., Pt. 2, m. 30, 12 July, 1430. Mem. Bk., pp. 135–137. Two contemporary copies of this charter are in the possession of the Merchant Adventurers of York.

the meetings of the other they went alone. But in the matter of the demand for a charter, they pursued a sound policy in allowing the fraternity to overshadow the mistery. The real state of affairs seems to have been that the mercers of York, a flourishing community of merchants carrying on both home and foreign trade, wished to consolidate their financial position. If they approached the government, who did not favour the concentration of wealth in the hands of an immortal trading community, with a simple statement of their wishes possible refusal loomed before them. But the amassing of wealth for charitable purposes was not regarded with so much suspicion; the mercers followed prescribed medieval etiquette in this verbose attempt to hide self-seeking under the cloak of charity.

Possibly they were actuated by another motive; taxation was capricious and the official world eager to pounce upon wealthy subjects; desirous as the mercers were to propitiate the government, they were even more anxious to avoid the appearance of wealth. The successful business man of the 20th century is the one, who creates an atmosphere of capital around him; the medieval trader's chief object was to create an atmosphere of poverty. However, the petition achieved its purpose; in return for £41 11s. the mistery was allowed to elect every year a governor and two wardens, who were empowered to purchase lands, rents and other possessions; to sue and be sued in any court, secular or ecclesiastical; and to have a common seal.[1] In addition, they were granted a license to acquire lands and rents in York to the value of £10, for the relief of the poor and the maintenance of a chaplain. As far as the direct evidence of the Memorandum Book goes, the weavers and the mercers are the only York misteries, which held charters directly from the King. Power to enforce the ordinances of the other misteries was granted by the mayor, aldermen and twenty-four. The Memorandum Book gives ample evidence of the " civic feudalism "[2] that prevailed in York; the merchants would certainly use all effort to prevent

---

1. This seal after having been lost for several centuries was restored to the York Company of Merchant Adventurers by the generosity of Mrs. Clayton, of Chesters, Hamshaugh, Northumberland.

2. G. Unwin, *op. cit.*, p. 157.

any other mistery obtaining the same advantage as themselves. Still probably the greater misteries in York, in desire though not in achievement, followed the lines of the London craftsmen.

Unimpeachable evidence exists of the steps by which a London mistery grew from a local institution, with ordinances legalized by the mayor, into a powerful company, with a charter granted by the king. As the desultory associations of men, whose only bond was a common craft, became more organic, they desired to become " a livery company," an association with the right to wear a distinctive dress, as a symbol of their trade. This stage of development continued for a considerable period. But as their wealth expanded their ambition grew ; they were no longer contented that their sole recognition as separate entities and their vague coercive rights should remain in the hands of the mayor. The next step, their desire to become a chartered company, with national and royal not merely local and municipal authorization, was not realized until the reign of Henry VI. He granted incorporation to nine London crafts ; the grocers in 1428, the fishmongers in 1433, the vintners in 1436, the brewers in 1437, the drapers in 1438, the cordwainers in 1439, the leather sellers in 1444, the haberdashers in 1447, and the armourers in 1452.[1]

The difference between London and York seems to be that in York the mercers had no rivals of sufficient standing seriously to challenge their supremacy. It has been already shown that the mercers, when they petitioned for a charter, emphasized the religious side of their organization ; apart, however, from their desire to obtain the charter, there were civic questions, which rendered this emphasis necessary. The mercers had secured political supremacy, but knowledge of the struggle for predominance among the London crafts must have brought home to them the importance of fortifying their position. The necessity for a strict regulation of industrial and commercial organization was never questioned by the practical medieval mind; but the merchants aimed at more than mercantile control, the retention of unquestioned political power in civic affairs was equally

---

1. G. Unwin, *op. cit.*, pp. 159, 160.

essential. On the surface, the mistery side of gild organization is the more important ; but subtle influences, social and religious, evanescent but vital, were bound up in the fraternity element ; the practical mayors and aldermen fully recognized the power of this weapon, the control of which was in their hands, not in the hands of the church.

Though the Memorandum Book gives no account of any fraternity in connexion with the mercers, it is quite clear from their account rolls that the gild or fraternity and the mistery were entirely interdependent. Members of the mercers' mistery were ipso facto members of the mercers' gild, and their religious, social and charitable undertakings were not merged in a separate organization ; the master of the mistery controlled both the mercantile and the religious policy. The marshals and smiths seem to have followed the same lines as the mercers, and drawn no distinct demarcation between the social and religious, that is the gild, and the mercantile, that is the mistery side of their society.[1]

The carpenters organized their fraternity and mistery differently. Although the two were probably for practical purposes as interdependent as in other crafts, still their ordinances emphasize the fact that if any carpenter belongs to the fraternity, he does so of his own free will ; whereas both mercers and marshals merge the two sides into a homogeneous whole. These ordinances of the carpenters' fraternity are of great interest and value. They contain a complete embodiment of the fraternity element ; the enforcement of these fraternity regulations by the municipality represents the first stage in the secularization of gilds, which was not completed until 1547. The mistery of carpenters requested the mayor, aldermen and twenty-four, " maiorem civitatis Ebor', et totum consilium camere," to consent to the addition of four

---

1. Mem. Bk., pp. 180–182. There is abundant proof of the development of the mistery of mercers from a religious fraternity or gild in the merchants' MSS. I have reserved for my volume on the Merchant Adventurers all discussion as to the origin of craft gilds. By the courtesy of Rev. J. P. Rushe, O.D.C., I have examined the transcript of the Goldsmiths of Avignon, which throw considerable light on the subject, but a more detailed examination, of the gild and mistery records of many towns, English and continental, is necessary before the question can be decided incontrovertibly. To generalize on insufficient data is a pitfall as alluring as it is fatal.

new ordinances in 1462 ; they dealt with three distinct subjects, the stranger, the unskilful and insubordinate worker, and the fraternity.¹ The stranger, who becomes a freeman of the city, can only set up as a master in the craft, if he pays iiij$d$. each year to the upkeep of the pageant and light on Corpus Christi day ; if he refuses, " than the maire fer the tyme beyng and the counseill of the chaumbre shal supporte the said craft to streyne the saide straungers as the lawe will."² In dealing with incompetency and disobedience the moral delinquent escapes the more lightly ; the sinner pays 3s. 4d., the bungler 6s. 8d. The clause dealing with the fraternity is the most interesting, " that every free man of this citee, that occupies as maister in the saide craft, not being of the fraternity of the same, shall pay yerely to the charges afore written³ as other wrights doo that be of the same fraternite."

Twenty years passed before the carpenters again appear in the council chamber. This time the fraternity ordinances are extraordinarily complete ; they afford such precious help in visualizing the social life of our medieval forefathers that a detailed analysis is necessary. The preamble shows how the civic spirit had grown in York until adjectives sufficiently strong to express it could hardly be found.⁴ The maior is called " the ryght honorabill," the carpenters belong " to this full nobill city," the council represent " the said full honourable cite." When trying to avoid taxation, when asking for a new charter, York brandishes her poverty and humble estate, but when no object is to be gamed, the loving pride of the citizens in their city knows no limit. Not only the virtues of the city but the antiquity and merits of the fraternity is recalled, " for as much as here afore thar hath beyn of old tym a brotherhode had and usyd emong the occupacion and craft above said, the which of long continuance have usid, and as yit yerely use is, to fynd of thar propir costes a lyght of dwyes torchis in the fest of Corpus

---

1. Professor Unwin informs me that municipal enforcement of fraternity regulations in London is not found much before 1460 ; the York marshals and smiths had their fraternity clauses acknowledged by the mayor in 1443. The whole of this section owes much to his Gilds of London, where the connexion between mistery and fraternity is thoroughly investigated.
2. Mem. Bk., pp. 193, 194.
3. *i.e.*, the pageant and lights.
4. Mem. Bk., pp. 277–283.

Christi day, or of the morn aftir, in the honour and worship of God and all saintes ; and to go in procession with the same torchis with the blessed sacrament from the Abbey[1] foundyd of the Holy Trenite in Mykylgate in the said city ; and also have done and usyd diwyrs odir right full good and honourabill deidis, as her aftir it shall more playnly apeir." With pathetic faith in the stability of things they ordain, " that the said fraternite and bredirhode shalbe hereafter for ewyr kept and continued, as it has beyn in tymis passid." Suddenly reverting to practical affairs, they declare that each brother has to pay sixpence for the sustentation of the fraternity—but a rider leaves to the option of the carpenters, whether they join the brotherhood or not, " provydyng allway that everyman of the said occupacion within the said cite shalnot be compellid ne boundyn to be of the said fraternite ni broderhod, ne noyn to be thar of bot soch as will of thar free will." In addition to the Corpus Christi festivities, there were two occasions on which there were public manifestations of the bond of brotherhood, " the said fraternite shalbe togiddir ij tymys in the yere, the Sunday after Saint Helen's day, and the Sunday after or before All Hallows." All the brethren then paid one penny to the brotherhood, and thirty successive daily masses were to be said in the priory of Austin Friars[2] for the souls of dead brethren and sisters. The absent brother was fined a pound of wax to be given to the fraternity, and sixpence " to the behove " of the chamber of the city. " Also it is ordeyned that yf ony of the said fraternite dy, the said bredirhode shal gyfe for a trentall of messis to be dooyn for hys sawll in the said Freir Austens, vs."[3] If the burial took place within the city precincts, the torches belonging to the fraternity were to be lent for the occasion ; they were to be carried by those in whose keeping they were and brought " home agane of the bredir cost,

1. J. Solloway, Alien Benedictines of York, pp. 19, 234, 247, 253, 258, 268, 298, 307.
2. In 1458-9, the meeting for the election of the new mayor was held in the refectory of the Austin Friars. Possibly this close connexion between citizens and friars was due to the fact that the mayor and citizens in 1382 had given them a piece of land in Ald Conyngstrete (Lendal), adjoining their house. Mem. Bk., p. 207. Cf. Mem. Bk. I., pp. 153, 205.
3. Mem. Bk., pp. 278, 279. Cf. R. R. Sharpe, Calendar of Letter-Books of the City of London, L., pp. 194, 265.

and not of the cost of the deid person." The brother, who had fully kept all the ordinances, was not left to die in poverty, " Yf ony of the said fraternite fall to povert, so that tha may not wyrk, or happyn to be blynd, or to leis thar gudes by unhapp of the world, then the forseid bredyrhode to gyffe them iiij$d$. every weke, as long as tha liff, by way of almusse." But every precaution is taken that charity is only given to the really destitute, " who was sworn apon a buke that he shall trewly lyffe apon hys allmous and his awn gude, without wast or gyffyng away of tham, and what so ewyr he levys at hys dying that longs to hymselff, his dettes payd and his beriall resonably done, shall remain to the said fraternitie as thar own propre gudes."[1] Such extensive schemes required a great deal of supervision; four keepers were appointed " the wich shall make thar reknyng every yer." An embryo labour exchange was also started in connexion with the fraternity; " Thar shalbe every yer a brodir chosyn and assigned of the said fraternite, to whom every brothir that is owt of wark shall make knawlege that he is owt of wark, so that he that would have a workman may have knawlege of hym that is owt of wark."[2] It may be impossible to make men moral by act of parliament, but the fraternity aimed at making men brotherly by ordinance, backed up by heavy fines; " it is ordeyned that if ony of the said bredir have nede to a warkman at ony tym, and a nodir of hys bredir is owt of wark, and has no wark to doo, than the said brodir, that has neid of a warkman, shall rather take in to wark hys brodir of the said fraternite, than ony odyr that is not brodyr, yf he will wyrk as he may deserif, upon payn of forfatour of xx$d$."[3]

In case of non-payment of any of the fraternity dues, the keepers and searchers, acting under the orders of the mayor and

---

1. Ibid., p. 280.
2. A somewhat similar arrangement was in vogue among the blacksmiths of London in 1434, Ashley, *op. cit.*, pt. II., p. 117. " ' From henceforth, when any stranger cometh to London to have a service, any of the servants (that) knoweth that he will have a service shall bring him to a master to serve, and to warn the warden that is their governor (*i.e.*, of the yeoman) that he may be at the covenant making '—a practice precisely similar to that in modern trades unions where a man seeking work sends up his membership card to one of the workmen, that he may inform the employer or his foreman."
3. Mem. Bk., p. 280.

with the assistance of his officers, could distrain for the payment of the dues owing to the fraternity, as well as for the dues to the city chamber. Not only the offender, but anyone who helped him to evade justice, was heavily fined.

These twelve strictly fraternity ordinances are followed by six of the ordinary mistery type; four of them deal with the apprenticeship and journeyman question, two with trades subsidiary to the carpenters. In none of these is the word fraternity used, but a seventh ordinance is added, which applies to both fraternity and mistery. "Also it is ordeyned by the actorite abovesaid, that yf ony of the said fraternite or eny of the said craftes discowyr or disclose the counsell or ony thyng that the said bredir or ony of said occupacions or eny of tham says at the day or days of thar assemblys, that tha meit for the weill of thys cite and of the said occupacions, that he or tha, that so disclosys the said counsell, shall forfate as oft tymys as tha ar thar in foundyn defective xl$d$." Two more ordinances concerning the duties of the searchers follow. The ordinances of the fraternity and mistery are inextricably mixed; it is only by intrinsic evidence that the one can be differentiated from the other. Still the compilers have left no possibility of error. The fourteen fraternity clauses have either the word fraternity or brotherhood or brother expressly used; in the remaining eight mistery ordinances these words are absent—occupation, master, apprentice, youngman take their place. The fraternity qua fraternity completely ignores the pageant plays. The carrying of torches (six according to an earlier and a later entry)[1] in the procession of Corpus Christi is obligatory, but the pageant duties are left to the mistery.

Although the gild of Corpus Christi was inaugurated in 1408, it was not incorporated until 1459,[2] possibly the entire severance of the pageant from the procession was not completed until the later date. Before Friar Melton's revival both pageant and procession were on the same day. Even as late as 1462, the carpenters' fraternity is said to pay to the charges of "thair

1. Mem. Bk., pp. 118, 295.
2. R. H. Skaife, Guild of Corpus Christi, Surtees Soc., vol. 57, passim.

pageant and lights on Corpus day Christi (sic)," as if there was some connexion between the plays and the procession. Although the carpenters in 1482 were not forced to belong to the fraternity, they had to pay for the " lyght the morn after Corpus Christi day." Unfortunately no list of pageant plays for a later date than 1415 has so far come to light ; in that schedule underneath the carpenters and opposite the play acted by them, " Jesus resurgens de Sepulcro," is added in a later hand joiners, cartwrights, carriers, sawyers, none of whom are assigned a separate play. By 1563 a union of the five crafts under the name of the carpenters had taken place,[1] but the phraseology of the ordinance in 1482, which deals with these different crafts, points to their being subsidiary rather than submerged in the carpenters.[2] As the early drama originated in ecclesiastical shows, it seems just possible that in the earlier stages of gild development, the fraternity, over which originally the church had much influence, undertook the production of the plays, but as ecclesiastical supervision waned they became entirely secularized, and the mistery took over what had originally been fraternity work. An indenture dated February 24th, 1486-7, which seems to merit quotation as it completes the picture of the carpenters' fraternity, gives a hint of some connexion between fraternity and pageant ; the pageant brought out by the carpenters was the Resurrection,[3] the name of the fraternity of the carpenters was " the holy fraternite of the Resurrection." The indenture is headed,

Freer Austynsyns of York.

" This present indentour maide at York, in the fest of Saint Mathie appostell, yere of the reign of King Henry the vij after the conquest of Englonde the second, betwixt freer William Bewyk, prior of the house of the order of freers Augustyns within the citie of York, and the convent of the same of the oon partie ; and Richerd Bischope, John Couper,

1. York Municipal Records, $\frac{B}{Y}$, fol. 234a.
2. Mem. Bk., pp. 281, 282.
3. L. Toulmin-Smith, York Mystery Plays, pp. 396-420. Printed from the Ashburnham MS. Cf. Towneley Play, Resurrectio Domini, Surtees Soc., vol. 3.

serchours of the occupacion of the carpenters within the said
citie,—James Wynsell, Michael Clerk, William Johnson, and
Thomas Hunt, Keepers of the holy fraternite of the Resur-
reccion of our Lord mayntened by the carpenters of the said
citie on that other part; witnesseth that the said prior and
covent, of ther holle assent and consent, for them and ther
successours for evermore grauntes tham to syng every yere
two trentalles of messes for the saules of all the brether and
systers of the said fraternite, and that the said prior and
covent of ther hole assent and consent graunts them to syng
a trentall of messes for every brother of the said fraternite,
that truly doeth his duyte, after his disceasse, uppon resonable
warnyng of his discease. And the forsaid kepers and
serchours of the hole assent and consent of them and ther
occupacion fastly byndes them and ther successours and
kepers of the said occupacion of carpenters for the tym
beyng, to pay to the said prior and convent and ther successours yerly for evermore xs. of lawfull money of Englonde
for syngyng of the forsaid two trentalles, as afore it is rehersed,
at two termes of the yere, that is to say at the fest of the
invencion of the holy cross (May 3) and of all halows by evyn
porcions, and for every trentall of messes for every brother
disceased as afore it is expressed, vs. of lawfull money of
England, and for contentacion and payment of vj$s$. viij$d$.
parcell of the said xs. yerely to be paid as affore is specified,
we the said serchours and kepers of the hole assent and
consent of us and all our said occupacion grauntes and by
thes presentes lettes to ferme to the forsaid prior and convent
two meases with ther appurtenances upon the corner of the
lendyng next saynt Leonerdes to the watter of Ouse adjoynyng
to the forsaid house of freers, and conteigneth in lenght
ixth yerdes and in breid viijth yerdes and di., to have and to
hold the said two meases with ther appurtenaunces to the
forsaid prior and convent and successours, from the forsaid
fest of Saint Mathie the yere abovesaid unto the ende
and terme of iiij^{xx} xixth yeres fully complet. And the
forsaid prior and convent and ther successours the forsaid
two meases with the appurtenaunces during the terme

afforsaid of ther aun propre costages and charges shall
reparell and uphold, provyded alway that if the forsaid
priour and convent and ther successours fall of syngyng of
the said two trentalles of messes as affore it is expressed,
that then it shalbe lefull to the said serchours and kepers
and ther successours to entre into all the forsaid ij meases
with the appurtenaunces in ther olde estate, and tham to
occupie thies presentes indentures notwithstandyng. In
witnes wherof to the oon partie of thies indentures to the
forsaid prior and convent remaynyng, the said serchours and
kepers haith sette ther seales. Yeven the day, yere and
place abovesaid."[1]

It is obvious from this document that the fraternity,
represented by the keepers, had no legal status apart from the
mistery, represented by the searchers; fraternity and mistery
were completely interdependent. The fact, too, that the fraternity
is called the fraternity of the Resurrection of our Lord, and the
pageant play, acted by the carpenters, had as its subject, the
Resurrection, seems to show that at some period the fraternity
played a more important part in the production of the pageant
than the silence of the carpenters' fraternity rules would seem to
indicate.

The gild of Corpus Christi was not fully organized until
1459, the allusions in the Memorandum Books to the lights
carried in the procession of Corpus Christi are few in number
in comparison with the constant references to the plays.
In 1443 the marshals and smiths obtained the mayor's
consent to several[2] new ordinances: "That al the lightes and
torches that langes to both the saide craftes, as wele in the
mynster as in other places, fro nowe furth be made at the costes
and expenses of both the said craftes, and spended to the use of
eithere of thaym, as wele in the procession upon Corpus Christi
day, as at beriall of every man and of thaire wifes that er or
shalbe of the said craftes."[3] But all the eight enactments have

1. Corporation Records, $\frac{B}{Y}$, fol. 201b.
2. These ordinances were apparently agreed to by the mayor, William Bowes, acting alone, neither aldermen nor sheriffs being present.
3. Mem. Bk., pp. 180, 181. Cf. Blacksmiths, *op. cit.*, p. 247.

a fraternity ring in them; possibly the marshals and smiths were not so numerous or so important as the carpenters (the official advisers of the city on all questions of property),[1] and had not such a highly organized fraternity. The shipmen have a similar ordinance passed in 1478 by mayor, aldermen and twenty-four. " Firste, that every man occupiyng eny shipping at the stahe (sic) of this worshupful cite and is fraunchest, whether he be denisen or forant dwellyng, be contributori to the said shipmen, that is to say, every man salyng as maister with a freman pay yerely ij$d$.; and he that salys as a felowe, pay jd., to the susteutacion and upholdyng as well of the pageant of Noe as of the bringing furth and beryng ef certan torches before the shryne of Corpus Christi yerely."[2] It seems probable that the shipmen, many of whom of necessity would be frequently absent, would have a small fraternity or possibly even join the fraternity of some other craft.

The Memorandum Book contains an extremely interesting and full account of the pageant plays, from 1376 to 1493. The first allusion occurs in the first volume, under the date 1376; but the entry proves conclusively that they were an ancient institution even at that early date.[3] In 1394 an order was issued that the pageants should be played in the places appointed of old times.[4] In 1397, Richard II. visited York and attended the performance of the plays.[5] The municipal authorities voted £11 13s. 1d., towards the expenses of the pageant on this occasion. Richard, duke of York, father of Edward IV., anxious

1. W. R. Lethaby, Westminster Abbey and the King's Craftsmen, pp. 362–364.
2. Mem. Bk., p. 215.
3. Mem. Bk., vol. I., p. 10. Mr. Robert Davies in 1843 published an invaluable account of the Corpus Christi festival in York, he had collected several extracts from the Memorandum Book, and requotes several given by Drake. Miss Toulmin Smith in her York Mystery Plays followed Davies closely, but does not appear to have paid much attention to the Memorandum Book. " Brit. Mus. Addl. MS. 35290, recently Ashburnham MS. 137. The MS. dates from about 1430–40, and appears to be a register or transcript made for the corporation of the 'origenalls,' in the hands of the craft. In 1554 the register was kept by the clerk at the gates of the dissolved Holy Trinity Priory." E. K. Chambers, The Mediæval Stage, vol. II., 409–10.
4. Mem. Bk., vol. I., p. 47.
5. " We learn this fact from a fragment which has been accidently discovered of the chamberlains' account for this year," R. Davies, Municipal Records, Appendix, p. 230.

for popularity, in 1454 came to York for the same purpose. "As to my Lorde Yorke, he abydyth aboute York tille Corpus Christi Feste be passyd, and wyth grete worship ys there resseyved."[1] But popular as the plays were with the audience, the study of the Memorandum Book reveals another phase of the question. The pageant plays appear for the first time in an atmosphere of discord, controversy and hostility, they disappear in an acrimonious dispute between bladesmith and blacksmiths, the mayor making a final effort "for appeasing of diverse matiers of variences."

The first entry in the second volume gives the keynote to all the other entries. In 1387, Johannes de Duffield, Johannes de Calton, and Robertus de Malton, representatives of the skinners, bakers and dyers attacked Robertus de Waghen, because he had failed to fulfil the contract that he had undertaken to keep in good repair the house in Toft Green, where the pageants, that is the movable stages on which the plays were acted, were lodged. This house was city property and paid a rent of two shillings a year.[2] Robertus Wagen was forced to find a surety, who, in case the house was allowed to fall into disrepair again, would make good the damage.

The following year cs., which Thomas de Bukton[3] had given to provide four torches for the procession on Corpus Christi day, were handed over to Stephanus de Yolton, who in return paid 6s. 8d. each year to the pageant authorities for the loan; the mayor himself was pledge for the return of the capital. The medieval world must have been ideal for lenders, unattractive for borrowers, if $6\frac{2}{3}$ per cent. had to be paid even when the surety was unimpeachable.[4]

The ordinances of the various crafts do not occupy so much space as in the previous volume; still the misteries continue to be the predominant influence in the industrial life of the people. But like all other institutions in all ages, it tried to distract attention from the decrease of its essential importance as a factor

1. Paston Letters, vol. I., p. 85.
2. Mem. Bk., vol. I., p. 10.
3. Mem. Bk., pp. 31, 32.
4. Ibid., p. 32.

in the city's development by the increase of its spectacular demonstrations. The references to the pageant plays augment in number and interest as the century progresses. One point emerges clearly; the men themselves found the upkeep of the plays an vexatious burden. The crowds that thronged the streets undoubtedly appreciated the show; those, too, deriving profit from the visitors, whom it attracted to the city, were equally appreciative; but time after time the sorely burdened craftsman appeared in the council chamber on Ousebridge to beg for exemption. The puritanic opposition to the drama, in the sixteenth century, had probably its roots in the inherited prejudice provoked by these enforced contributions to the medieval stage in the fifteenth. Another new feature forces attention in these later mistery regulations, the foreigner, not necessarily an alien, but always a man from another town or country, is more frequently provided for in the ordinances. The failure of total exclusion had forced the position; the foreigner filtered through; obviously it was safer to acknowledge his presence than to leave him uncontrolled. Though chronolical sequence is not strictly followed, the new gild legislation belongs chiefly to the fifteenth century. The number of entries about the pageant plays testifies to the important place they held in the life of the city. One investigator suggests that it would almost appear as if in Shrewsbury the gilds existed for the sake of the procession on Corpus Christi day.[1] The Coventry Leet Book contains endless allusions to the pageant plays in that town.[2] It is, however, important to remember that the pageant plays were by no means the spontaneous expression of the sheer joy of life of men actuated partly by religious zeal, partly by social exuberance; the grudging craftsmen rather regarded them as an intolerable and vexatious burden, from which they were unable to free themselves.[3] The first important entry concerning the plays does not occur until 1417. The notability of the occasion may be gauged by the fact that as the meeting was

1. F. A. Hibbert, Influence and Development of English Gilds, 63, quoted by Professor Ashley.
2. M. Dormer Harris, op. cit., pp. 195, 206, 312, 417, 556, 558, 716, ix.–xi.
3. Ibid., p. 115. "The smiths complain that they are forced to produce a pageant . . . the leet insists upon their continuing the practice."

held in the common hall, not in the chamber on Ousebridge, evidently a large attendance was expected. It is the most representative meeting of the community that the Memorandum Book has registered. The mayor, both sheriffs, nine aldermen, the recorder, thirteen of the twenty-four, both chamberlains, and a multitude of other citizens, " unacum multitudine aliorum civium," were present. The first business was the recapitulation of the ordinance passed in 1398-9, which had decided that the pageants should be played at the doors of the important civic officials as well as other places. The first act of the long day's work began at the gates of the priory of the Holy Trinity; the pageant then passed down Micklegate, where four performances were given; four more took place in Coney Street, one at the Castlegate end, another at the end of Jubbergate (Market Street),[1] the next at the house of Henry Wyman,[2] the last before the common hall. The play then moved up Stonegate, where the players stopped once, at the house of the late Adam del Bryg; the three final performances were given at the gates of the Minster, in Low Petergate, and upon the Pavement.[3] But apparently the populace had resented the amount of money made by those, before whose houses the plays were enacted. "The mayor, ' the probi homines,' and the whole community, therefore, by their unanimous consent and assent passed a [new] ordinance. Those, who receive money for the stands, which they erect before their doors in the aforesaid places upon ground belonging to the community from those, who sit upon them, shall pay every third penny of the money thus received to the treasurers of the city, to be applied for the use of the said community. If they refuse to pay the third penny in this way or to make some other equitable arrangement with the chamber, that then the play shall be transferred to other places at the discretion and wish of the mayor for the time being and of the council of the chamber of the city— no one opposing this ordinance with the exception of a few owners of stands in Micklegate."[4]

1. R. Davies, Antiquarian Walks through York, pp. 72-74.
2. Ante p. xxi.
3. Mem. Bk., pp. 62-65.
4. Ibid., p. 63.

And it was further ordained by common consent "that the banners of the play of Corpus Christi, painted with the arms of the city,[1] should be delivered yearly, on the eve of Corpus Christi, to be erected at the places where there is to be a play of the pageants on the following day; and that the banners themselves every year shall be brought back to the council chamber of the city without delay, on the day following the said feast of Corpus Christi."[2]

At a smaller meeting held a few days after in the council chamber, the mayor and council restated the case; " seeing that everyone according to his condition bears his burden in the maintenance of the said play, it was unanimously ordained that for the benefit of the community the places for the playing of the aforesaid play shall be altered, unless those, before whose houses it was formerly played, shall pay to the community some fixed sum in return for their own individual advantage, which they thus receive each year. And that in all subsequent years as long as that play shall happen to be played, it shall be played before the doors and houses of those who are willing to pay most richly and well to the chamber, and to do the most for the benefit of the whole community for the sake of having the play in the same place—not showing any favour to any person for any individual advantage, but only what is held to be the public welfare of the whole community of York."[3]

Johannes Morton, who was to be mayor the following year, had at the first meeting opposed the motion, as the owner of a house in Micklegate, before which the pageant was represented. At this second meeting, however, he completely withdrew all opposition, " and the aforesaid reverend man Johannes Moreton, in respect of his tenements submitted himself entirely to the discretion and ruling of the mayor and council with reference to

---

1. The scene in the York Pageant of 1909, where the mysteries appeared before Richard II. bearing banners with the arms of the mysteries inscribed, was as effective as it was historically incorrect. The arms shown on the banners were the arms of the London companies, mostly of the seventeenth century, not the arms of the York misteries of the fourteenth century. The arms of the London companies are all given on a few pages in Stow's Survey of the Cities of London and Westminster, bk. v., p. 262 et seq.
2. Ibid., p. 63.
3. Ibid., p. 64.

the aforesaid play, in respect of the play before the gate of his dwelling in the street of Micklegate, and in other tenements in the city."[1]

In a natural reaction from the misstatement of Mr. Toulmin Smith,[2] there is a tendency to forget that although the procession of Corpus Christi had no direct connexion with the pageant plays, still it was in existence long before the gild of Corpus Christi was inaugurated,[3] and that as it took place for several years on the same day as the pageant plays were acted, doubtless the craftsmen took a prominent part; in fact, the number of torches to be borne in the procession by each craft is twice given in the Memorandum Book,[4] and fines imposed by the misteries are sometimes appropriated to keep up processional lights and torches. Marshals, smiths and shipmen all had special ordinances dealing with the subject.[5] Unfortunately the festival was often connected in the minds of law-abiding citizens with tumults and disturbances. In 1419, the skinners came to complain to the mayor that as they bore their lighted torches in the procession "coram Corpore Christi ibidem presenti," several men of the crafts of carpenters and shoemakers attacked them with sticks and axes. Not only was this a serious breach of the peace, but it also impeded the procession. Two carpenters and a cordwaner were imprisoned and then brought before the mayor. They threw themselves on the mercy of the chamber; they were bound over to keep the peace by a bond of £100, and eight sureties undertook in writing to be answerable for them.[6] In 1421 the saucemakers, tilemakers, turners, hayresters, bollers and millers asked that their plays, " the Suspencio Jude, the Condemnacio Christi, the Flagellacio et Coronacio cum Spinis, and the Particio Vestimentorum Christi" should be combined into one play. The mayor and council agreed; but the amalgamation seems to

1. Ibid., p. 65.
2. Toulmin Smith, English Gilds, E.E.T.S., p. 141. Dr. Brentano's introduction, lxxxv.
3. Ibid., p. 32, R. H. Skaife, Register of the Gild of Corpus Christi, Surtees Soc., vol. 57.
4. Ibid., pp. 118, 295.
5. Ante, pp. xl, xli.
6. Ibid., p. 79.

have resulted in disputes as to payment. In the following year the craftsmen submitted to arbitration. The decision was that the production of the play should be entrusted to the saucemakers and tilemakers; the millers should pay them ten shillings a year, but two of them should accompany the pageant and share the refreshments " in cibo potuque solacia percipiant." The hayresters only paid five shillings, and only one of their craft went with the pageant. Apparently the men were attempting to use the pageants as a means of advertizement; this effort was sternly repressed. None of the trades should place any sign of their trade above the pageant—the arms of the city only were tolerated. Ten years later the saucemakers, too, retired and paid five shillings to the tilers in preference to acting themselves.[1]

In 1422 the painters, stainers, pinners and latoners suggested to the mayor and council that it would be a distinct gain to the audience if the two plays, for which they were answerable, were amalgamated and curtailed. The mayor, aldermen and council of the chamber benignantly accepted, and cordially commended the craftsmen for their laudable proposition. They decreed that from that time the painters and stainers should be exempt from bringing out a play, but should pay five shillings annually to the pinners and latoners,[2] who would undertake to bring out the two abbreviated plays in their new form.[3]

Three years later a new and vivifying force was brought to bear on these Corpus Christi festivals. It seemed as if a spiritual power was about to raise them from the atmosphere of tumults, quarrels and grudging performance into a

---

1. Ibid., pp. 171–173.
2. Ibid., pp. 102–104.
3. The pinners seem to have suffered much from foreign competition. In 1564 the council grappled with the evil. " Upon a bill of supplicacion exhibited by the pynnars, it is agreed for amendement of the sayd craft that the tynclars and makers of fyshehookes and other wares belongyng the pynnars craft shalbe contributory and paye yerely towards the chardge of pynnars pageant iiij*d*. a pece. Item, that all forynars pynnars from hensforth shall resort to Thursday market there to sell their pynnes and wares openly; and none of theym to be suffred to goe hawkyng about the cite or to mens bowses to sell their wares. And that it shalbe leeful to the serchars of pynnars of this citie to serche the sayd forynars wares, and also to take pageant money of them of every suche forynar usyng to sell pynnes or other their stuff aforesayd within the sayd citie, iiij*d*. a pece in the yere." Municipal Records, House Book, xxiii., fo. 163.

higher plane, where they should become a permanent means of recalling a sordid people annually to their religious duties. Willelmus Melton, a brother of the order of friars minors, learned in the scriptures, preached earnestly to the people that they should leave off the noisy drunken riots, which disgraced the celebration of the festival. He showed them that they imperilled their immortal souls, and lost all the indulgences granted by the blessed Pope Urban IV. His eloquence was so convincing that the mayor called a special council meeting to discuss the matter. Evidently they were anxious to avoid committing themselves to quite such a gloomy view of the effect of the festivals on the morals of York, as that held by the revivalist.[1] They met the predicament with circumspection. They prefaced their decision by the safe platitude that it could not be a crime nor could it offend God, if good were turned into better, " quod delictum non est, nec Deum offendit, si bonum in melius commutetur." But they refused to act until they had felt the popular pulse ; so they convened a large city assembly in the common hall. The more democratic assembly showed the greater religious zeal. It was solemnly proclaimed by common consent that procession and plays should be held on separate days ; the plays to be acted on the day before the feast, the procession on Corpus Christi day. Thus, citizens and visitors could perform all their religious duties, obtain the indulgences, and still not sacrifice their traditional love of the dramatic representations.[2] The influence of Willelmus soon passed,

1. G. G. Coulton, a Medieval Garner, pp. 570–575. From a MS. volume of English sermons, written at the end of the fourteenth century. The preacher is arguing against those who defend miracles plays. " But here— against they sayen, ... oftentimes by such miracle-playing men and women seeing the passion of Christ and of his saints be moved to compassion and devotion, weeping bitter tears. Then they be no scorning of God but worshipping." To this the preacher replies, " But the weeping that falleth to men and women by the sight of such miracle-playing as they be not principally for their own sins nor of their good faith within sorry, but more of their sight without [therefore their] sorrow is not allowable before God but more reprovable. For, sithen Christ Himself reproved the women that wepten upon Him in His passion, much more they be reprovable that weepen for the play of Christ's passion, leaving to weepen for the sins of themselves and their children, as Christ bade the women that wepten on Him." Cf. Behind the Scenes at a Miracle Play, ibid., 701–703.

2. Ibid., pp. 156–158.

the people obtained two holidays, but continued to perform their plays on Corpus Christi day and relegated the religious procession to the following day. In other directions, however, the friar was more directly successful, he induced the citizens to close their shops on Sundays; and anxious to destroy sin, being a lover of virtue, "volens peccatum destruere et amator honestatis," he persuaded the mayor to put an old ordinance in force, which obliged whores either to find sureties for good behaviour, or to relinquish their manner of life, or to leave the city.[1]

In 1431 the goldsmiths came into the council chamber with a piteous story of their overburdened condition. The recital of their woes loses much by translation, still the passage gives such a terse and vivid picture of the burdensome nature of the pageant policy that the whole seems to merit reproduction.

"In the name of God, Amen. It must not be overlooked but rather committed to memory that the goldsmiths of the city of York, during years gone by, have borne a grievous burden and enormous costs on account of their two pageants in the play of Corpus Christi. But now the world is changed for them, they have become poorer than they were wont to be, their wealth has decreased in the way mentioned before. They came in great numbers to appeal to the great men and the council of the chamber in order to get assistance in this matter for the relief of their burdens, which were too heavy to be borne. But if this is impossible, they ask that they might be relieved from one of their pageants with its attendant expenses, which increase continually, for [they said] that they could no longer bear the burden of both their pageants without enormous trouble to themselves. On the other hand the masons of this city grumbled among themselves about their pageant in the play of Corpus Christi in which Fergus[2] was scourged, because the subject matter of that

1. Ibid., pp. 158, 159.
2. Miss Toulmin Smith writes: "This play, founded on a well-known incident in the apocryphal legend of the death of Mary, is the only one, all trace of which is wanting in the Register." *op. cit.*, p. xxvii. But neither Drake, nor Davies, nor Miss Toulmin Smith have noticed this allusion to it.

pageant is not contained in holy scripture and gave rise to more laughter and noise than devotion. Sometimes quarrels, disputes and fights arose from it among the people ; and they could seldom or never produce and play their pageant by daylight like the earlier pageants. The masons, therefore, desired with a great desire to be freed from this pageant, and to be allowed another, which should be in accordance with holy scripture and could be produced and played by daylight. And for the fulfilment of these their desires both the parties aforesaid [the goldsmiths and the masons] made applications and prayers to the mayor and council to obtain their willing consent and good will in this matter. Whereupon Thomas Snaudon, mayor, and also the aldermen and council of the chamber, graciously forwarding the wishes and desires of the men of the aforesaid crafts, and deeming them in accordance with what was fitting, gave judgment that the aforesaid goldsmiths for the decrease of their grievous burdens should be relieved of one of their pageants—namely, that of Herod. And likewise that the masons should be relieved and quit of the pageant of Fergus. And that the said masons shall have for themselves and their craft the aforesaid pageant of Herod, which the goldsmiths previously had produced ; and produce it at their expense and play it in a more fitting manner, which is seemly for the honour of the city, as often as the aforesaid pageant shall happen to be played in the aforesaid city."[1]

In 1476 an effort was made to raise the standard of the performances. The mayor and council ordained " that yerely in the tyme of lentyn there shall be called afore the maire .... iiij of the moste conyng discrete and able players .... to serche here and examen all the plaiers and plaies and pagentes thrughoute all the artificers belonging to the Corpus Christi play."[2] Only those players " sufficiant in personne and conyng " were accepted, " insufficient personnes either in conyng, voice, or personne to discharge, ammove, and avoide." Two years later

1. Ibid., pp. 123, 124.
2. Corporation House Books, vol. I., fol. 14a. I am indebted to Mr. Giles for connoting this extract with the original.

a new station for the performance of the plays was instituted. The extract is interesting as it gives some idea of the amount of money those, who paid for the right to have the plays enacted before their houses, expected to get for the trouble and expense of erecting grand stands. Henricus Watson and Thomas Diconson, pikemongers, in Ousegate at the east end of Ousebridge, paid 11s. a year, for a twelve years' lease of this right.

The twenty-four misteries, which brought their ordinances into the council chamber to have alterations or innovations ratified by the mayor and council, cover almost a century—the first is dated 1409, the last 1493. Unfortunately there is a long period from 1431 to 1463, when there was either no new gild legislation, or it was not considered sufficiently important to be registered. Marshals and smiths, stringers, parchmentmakers, plasterers and tile makers, fullers and shearers, cooks, goldsmiths, tilers and wrights, curriers, walkers, glasiers, broggers, tapiters, patoners, botellers and bowgemakers, listers, sadlers, shipmen, tanners, pinners and wiredrawers, cutlers, carpenters, cappers, blacksmiths and bladesmiths, vintners and hatmakers all appealed to the civic government to settle their disputes, to legalize their new ordinances, or to approve of their pageant procedure.

Drake quotes a city ordinance of 1519, in which the mayor and his brethren claim that the punishment of craftsmen for breach of their ordinances was in their hands, not in the hands of the searchers of the mystery.[1] But the whole tenor of the Memorandum Book shows conclusively that this ordinance was only a reiteration not an innovation. One of the customs claimed by the city is that if the searchers discover any breach of the ordinances of the craft, they shall bring the matter before the mayor for the time being.[2] Naturally the hold of the council on the crafts would ebb and flow as the tide of the popularity and power of the mayor and his brethren fluctuated; but that during the whole of the period

1. F. Drake, *op. cit.*, p. 215. Cf. W. J. Ashley, *op. cit.*, pt. ii., p. 28. I am much indebted to the illuminating chapter on the crafts in Professor Ashley's economic history, where occasionally I have differed from him it has been owing to the fact that I have had materials unpublished when he wrote.
2. Mem. Bk., p. 260, ante p. xxix.

of the Memorandum Book their power over the crafts was undisputed is clear. It is, of course, possible that in any struggle between council and crafts, if victory fell to the crafts, the council did not register their own defeat; but judgment must be based on general impressions gained from the general tendency of the crafts as a whole, and even the most cursory survey reveals the servility with which the crafts approach the civic rulers. "Dominus maior"[1] is not sufficiently expressive of their lowly attitude—"reverendus dominus,"[2] "right worshipful sir maiour of this wirshipful city"[3] are terms used. In 1482, when new ordinances were brought into the council chamber by the cappers, they were endorsed by the mayor and "the hole counsell," to the clause dealing with the duties of the searchers a rider is added " providyng all way that the mair for the tym beyng have the examinacion and correccion herof."[4] The fact that the cloth industry was supreme in the council would strengthen its hold over the crafts subsidiary to that trade, as the cappers and fullers. The last named mistery were granted the search over foreign[5] fullers, in 1425. The council meeting was unusually large and strongly representative of the woollen interests; with one exception, a goldsmith, the twenty-seven members were mercers. Both the mayor of the city and the mayor of the staple were there; seven of the twelve aldermen and sixteen of the twenty-four were also present. But the right of search was accompanied by a strong exhortation to the searchers to deal fairly by these outsiders. "Ita quod non ostendant eis odium nec maliciam in scrutando."[6] The stringers' ordinances, too, show clearly how strong was the hold of the council on the crafts; any bowstrings that were found

---

1. Mem. Bk., p. 163. This is an unusual expression, dominus is here probably only a courtesy "Sir," used to parsons, not the word lord, as used before the mayors of certain cities in modern times. The first example given in the N.E.D. is c. 1554. But "false nets condemned to be burnt by my lord maire (1485) occurs in Letter-Book L, p. 229, with Dr. Sharpe's note · 'this is an earlier instance of the use of the title "Lord Mayor," than hitherto supposed.' Cf. "Cal. Letter-Book K," p. 243n.
2. Ibid., p. 167.
3. Ibid., p. 297.
4. Ibid., p. 284.
5. *i.e.*, fullers from the villages in the neighbourhood of York.
6. Mem. Bk., p. 159.

on search to be defective were to be brought to the council chamber and there remain until they were burnt.¹

In 1463-4 the lack of work among the walkers in the city seriously alarmed the governors of the city. " In tyme passed men of the said craft of walkers, inhabitauntes within the saide citee wer wont to full and wirke all manere of clothe made within this citee, and also grete parte of clothe made in the contree aboute the saide citee, at which tyme were many honest and thrifty men of the said craft inhabitaunt in the same citee, and nowe thay be fewer and porer for lak of wark, that goeth at thies dayes into the contree." They passed an ordinance at the request of the craft that no citizen should have his cloth fulled by walkers from the country. But a rider was added, which shows how completely the city controlled the crafts. "Forseyne alway that if it can be thoght to the maire, aldremen and counseill of the chaumbre and comons at eny tyme after this to be eny hurt, prejudice, or inconvenient in this ordenaunce or any parte ther of to the comon wele, worship, or profitte of this citee, that than it shalbe lefull to thayme to adnull, adde, correcte, refourme, and amende this ordenaunce, and every parte ther of, after thaire wisdomes and discrecions, to the honour of the citie and wele of the crafte."² This is the most autocratic statement of the absolute authority claimed by the mayor and his brethren that the Memorandum Book furnishes.

But the disagreements between the different crafts certainly strengthened the hands of the mayor and council, and enabled them to put their latent power into force without rousing general resentment. The history of the mistery of tanners brings out this point very clearly. In 1427 a great controversey raged between tanners and cordwainers, as to the search of tanned leather. Both disputants bound themselves to submit to the judgment of the mayor and council. The award begins with a counsel of perfection, all men of both crafts are to be good friends for ever, there was to be no renewal of discord. They were not, however, called upon to kiss each other, a ceremony often insisted

1. Ibid., p. 123.
2. Mem. Bk., pp. 206, 207.

upon by mayors of a freakish disposition.¹ But the feelings of the council were obviously against the tanners ; eight searchers of tanned leather were to be appointed, two from each of the crafts tanners, cordwainers, girdlers, and curriers. Cordwainers were to go to the house of the tanner, inform him of the kind and amount of leather required, and the price was to be settled ; then the tanner, at his own expense, was to send the leather to the common hall, where in a room appointed for the purpose, it was to be searched. If on search the leather was found to be satisfactory, it was sealed with the tanners' seal. If the searchers failed in their duty, they were to be judged at the discretion of the mayor and council. If, in spite of all these precautions, the cordwainer found his leather defective, his case was submitted to the mayor, and tried either at the king's or complainant's suit, according to the statute provided for such occasions.²

Evidently the tanners had not submitted to these humiliating terms without a struggle, in which they must have been deprived of their rights as freemen ; the year following, however, the franchise was restored to them. Ricardus Russell, the new mayor, seems to have had his sympathies enlisted on their side. The tanners came to him and the council with urgent requests and humble petitions, and submitted their ordinances " in alto et basso," to them. The civic governors, anxious as they said, to spare them the tedious and excessive inconvenience of the elaborate system of search instituted under the previous mayor, made new arrangements. But first and before all things, they gave back to them the liberty of the city, which had been taken from them on account of their transgressions. So long as the leather was tanned by themselves, their right of search was restored without let or hindrance of the men of other crafts. It had to be sealed with their ancient and customary seal, and then they had a free passage whithersoever they wished by land or water. The use of a trade mark was general among the crafts

1. Mem. Bk., pp. 15, 174.
2. Cf. W. Cunningham, *op. cit.*, p. 514, the whole question of the relation of tanners, curriers, cordwainers and girdlers was settled by statute by Henry VII. and Henry VIII.

at an early period.[1] But apparently it was not until later and only in the textile trades that the council assumed complete control over them.[2] The leather, however, bought from the country tanners had still to be taken to the common hall to be searched. Again the story illustrates the subordination of the crafts. One year the entire constitution of the mistery is changed, the searchers only exercise their right under the tutelage of other crafts, the masters are deprived of their civic position; the next year a wave of the civic wand and the mistery is restored to its former position.[3] But the tanners seem to have learnt caution by experience, nearly half a century elapses before they again evoke the civic help; then the changes they require are of minor importance. One, however, shews that entrance to the mistery is still jealously guarded; "first if there be any maner man that is not of the tanner craft and shall hapan to wedde and take to wife a widowe of the same craft, then that man shall paie er he occupie, and by his sersours of the saide craft admitted thereunto, xls., the oone half unto the chaumbre of the citie, and the other half to the supportacion of the pageaunt and charges of the saide craft."[4]

There is little in the Memorandum Book to support the theory that "the England of the fifteenth century possessed a definite system of technical training."[5] The ordinances of the lorimers of London in 1269 stipulated that no apprentice should be taken for less than ten years. But that some sort of training must have grown side by side with the specialization of industry

1. Mem. Bk., I., pp. xli., 136.
2. The tapiters have two stringent ordinances dealing with the subject; "that the sayd serchers shall come from tyme to tyme yerely to the chambre for seales of leade to pay in hand for every dowzen . . . . , to th'use of the chamber according as hayth bene used. Item, that every maister of the sayd craft from hensforth shall have and use a severall and proper marke to himselfe, whiche he shall sett and worke in every suche peace of stuff, as he shall make to be beamed from others, apon payne of xijd. for every suche peace wantyng his sayd marke, th' one half to the chambre and th'other to th' occupacion; and that the patirne of every theire sayd severall markes shalbe presented on Use-bryge and their entred in the chamorelaynes boke from tyme to tyme." Municipal Records, House Bk., xx., fo. 70, 14 Aug., 1551.
3. Mem. Bk., pp. 162–166.
4. Ibid., p. 167.
5. O. J. Dunlop and R. D. Denman, English Apprenticeship and Child Labour, p. 29. G. Unwin, op. cit., p. 85.

is of course obvious. Unfortunately the register of apprentices for York does not begin until the year 1461,[1] and the earliest indenture which has come to light is for the year 1371.[2] From that indenture the master, a bower, and the apprentice's sponsor, Thomas de Kyghlay, a chaplain, seem more concerned with the youth's moral and physical well being than the development of his technical skill. But the earliest dated set of ordinances of the York craftsmen yet discovered, those of the girdlers of 1307, had an apprenticeship clause : " Also that na maister take na apprentice in that craft for to lere hym, but alanely ane, and that apprentice sall abide with his master foure yere at the lest."[3] The idea that " Not many of the provincial towns or gilds made regulations until the fifteenth century, *e.g.*, rules were made in York in 1415, Northampton in 1430, Exeter in 1450,"[4] is entirely erroneous. In 1415 there were at least eighty-two different crafts in York ; the majority of these had certainly gilds with both a fraternity and a mistery side in the fourteenth century. Possibly many of them existed in the thirteenth century. It is true that during the fifteenth century many of those of a much earlier date brought their ordinances into the council chamber to have new clauses added, but this does not, of course, mean initiation, only alteration and innovation.

Fullers, bowers, saddlers, tailors, shearers and listers had their ordinances revised in the fourteenth century. Apprentices are legislated for in each case, nor is there a hint that the apprentice was a novelty.[5] So general had apprenticeship become by the fifteenth century that of the twenty-four misteries that brought their ordinances into the council chamber in the fifteenth century, only five marshals 1409,[6] parchment makers 1422,[7]

---

1. W. Giles, *op. cit.*, p. 53. " Register of apprentices ; commences temp. Edwd. IV. (1461), and with certain omissions, continues to 1502. This book is much decayed—many of the entries being illegible."
2. York Municipal Records, $\frac{B}{Y}$, fo. 3a, printed in Mem. Bk. I., pp. 84, 85.
3. Mem. Bk. I., p. 181, Cf. Mem. Bk. I., p. 134.
4. O. J. Dunlop and R. D. Denman, *op. cit.*, p. 32.
5. Mem. Bk., I., passim.
6. Mem. Bk., p. 178.
7. Ibid., p. 129.

plasterers and tilers 1422,[1] glasiers 1463,[2] hatmakers 1493[3] have definite seven year apprenticeship clauses; of the remaining seventeen fifteen regard the subject as settled, and pass it over in silence. The stringers' ordinances of 1420[4] lay down the rule that neither man nor woman could take an apprentice for less than four years; the curriers have a six years' apprenticeship.[5] But even had this definite evidence been non-existent, it is entirely incredible that York should only have inaugurated in 1415 a system that was practised in London in 1269, if not earlier. There was less difference between the York and London of the fourteenth than the twentieth century. That it should have been almost a century and a half later in development than London is contrary to all existing evidence of its economic condition.

But the same ordinances, that prescribe an apprenticeship, also provide a loophole by which those willing to pay can escape the tedium of training. A rule for the admission of non-apprentices is common to almost all the misteries of the fifteenth century; he had only to pay a higher fee, if he started as a master, than the man that had served his apprenticeship, and to satisfy the searchers as to his ability. Probably the desire to avoid paying the enhanced entrance fee rather than any desire for technical training was one reason why apprenticeship became so general. It was also a means of obtaining the freedom of the city without a fee for those, who could not claim it by inheritance.

The prevention of excessive competition was the keynote to much of the economic policy of medieval times; the masters achieved this by limitation of the number of apprentices each master could take, but evidence on this subject in the Memorandum Book is meagre. The glasiers had a regulation, "bott oon at once unto the tyme that iiij yere of the said vij yeres be fully complete";[6] the patoners only one at

1. Ibid., p. 127.
2. Ibid., p. 209.
3. Ibid., p. 286.
4. Ibid., p. 123.
5. Ibid., p. 167.
6. Ibid., p. 209.

once until the sixth year.¹ The parchment makers in 1422 could only have one apprentice at once, " hoc unum ad semel " ;² in 1474 this was repealed. Masters were then empowered " to take into thaire services iij, ij, er j apprentesses or apprentes tageders attones by indenture to be made betwyx theyme in that behalfe for such yeres and termes as the maisters or maister on that one partie and the same apprentes gan agre emonges theymsiffe, any acte, ordynaunce or constitucion made in the dayes and tyme of Thomas Esyngwald, standing maire of the forsaid cite of Yorke, to contrarie of this present ordynaunce not agaynstynge."³ The matter must have excited much attention for the meeting was unusually large, mayor, aldermen, sheriff and twenty-four all being present. As well as the ordinary apprentice, the finisher, a youth intermediate between the apprentice and the journeyman, was a recognized part of the carpenters' training system.

"Yf a yongman, that is not cunyng in wark of the said occupacion, cum in to thys cite to lern the said occupacion bettyr yf he be hyryd in the said occupacion for mete, drynk, and xx$s$. be yere or above, than hys said maister, that so hyrys hym, within a quarter of a yer than next aftir shall pay xx$d$. ; . . . . and yf he hyr hym ondyr the some of xx$s$., the said maister, that so hyrys hym, shall pay xl$d$. in the furm above said, to be devydid and paid."⁴ There seems to be here a faint hint of " das wanderjahr," that was such a powerful influence in the development of technical skill in Germany during the second half of the fifteenth century.⁵

Evidently apprentices were sometimes sent out to work without supervision, for the masters of the plasterers and tilers are fined, if they allow either apprentices or servants to work

1. Ibid., p. 140.
2. Ibid., p. 129. The cutlers at a very early date, if one can judge by language for the document is undated, enforced both a seven years' apprenticeship and limited the apprentices to one. " Item, ordeigne est que nul meistre de la dite artifice desormes preigne ascun apprentice pur meyndre terme fors quez pur septz ans, ... que nul maister de mesme lartifice tiendra ou overa plusours apprenticez ensemble, mes solement un apprentice apres autre." Mem. Bk., I., p. 134.
3. Ibid., p. 238.
4. Ibid., p. 281.
5. Gustav Schmoller, Strassburg zur Zeit der Zunftkämpfe im XV. Jahrhundert, p. 66.

"extra presenciam magistri sui," unless with the consent of the searchers.[1] The curriers have the most elaborate rules for their workers, "servientes," whether they worked by piece, "merces," or for a salary, were to pay iiij$d$. to the pageant fund yearly, if they had served apprenticeship within the city, and viij$d$.[2] if they had not. They were not to give work to men of evil reputation or dishonest life, "qui erit male fame aut vite inhoneste," nor to intice any workman from any master to whom he was bound. Agreements for work could only be made for a whole year; but if a servant wished to transfer his services to another master, after serving his first master for three months, he could on the payment of 6s. 8d. for his release, leave him.[3] Any stranger, coming to the city in search of work, could be hired by one master for a week, and by another master for another week, and so on, week by week, until all the masters wishing for his services had employed him; no license from the searchers was required unless the stranger wished at his coming to be hired for a whole year.[4] One of the ordinances of the vintners reads as if it belonged to a more modern and sanitary age; "that it be not leful to eny maner men, retaling wynez herafter within this said cite, to hold or have eny servant, man, childe, or woman to retail his wyne, which is corrupt and unclen nature, uppon the payn of forfatour of xx$s$."[5] The tapiters were forbidden to take any apprentice, who was not born under the allegiance of our lord the king.[6]

A cursory survey of these gild regulations leaves a general impression of a prevailing family likeness, but closer study reveals a bewildering differentiation. The marshals and smiths have the clearest rules as to the terms on which, after apprenticeship was over and the journeyman period passed through, a man could begin work as a master. There were four grades; the son of a freeman who had served an apprenticeship; the apprentice whose father was not free; the native who had not been

1. Ibid., p. 127.
2. Ibid., p. 168.
3. Ibid., p. 168.
4. Ibid., p. 169.
5. Ibid., p. 277.
6. Ibid., p. 190.

apprenticed in the city; and the unapprenticed alien. The fee was graduated the first grade paid nothing, the second a small fee, the third a higher, the fourth the largest. "That every man of the said craftes, that has been pryntes within this citee, shall pay at his first settyng upp as a maister in the said craftes xviij$d$., to the lightes of the said craftes, except thaym that er fraunchest men sonnes." "If eny man of the saide craftes com to this citee, that has not bene prentes within this citee, and will occupy as maistr, he shall pay at his first settyng upp ij$s$. to the lightes of the said craftes." "If eny aliene come to this citee and will occupy as maister, he shal at his first settyng up vj$s$. viij$d$., the one halve to the chaumbre and this other halve to the craftes."[1] The tapiter, who had been apprenticed, paid 6s. 8d., when he started business for himself; the fee was doubled for the unapprenticed tapiter. The fee for the tanner "of the contre that hath not be apprentice within this citie," was higher still, xiij$s$. iiij$d$.[3] The stringers' ordinances make no reference to any payment when beginning the trade, but all stringers must first " be received into the liberty of this city," and pass an examination as to their ability to do skilful work.[4] The cappers drew a distinction between, the man, "who cumys in by redempcion to the libertes of thys cite" and the one, who obtained his freedom by servitude. The first paid 6s. 8d. when he became a master, the last "shalbe admitit as a maister withowt ony thyng giffyng or payng for hys uppsett."[5]

In view of the important position taken by the women of France in the industrial life of their native country, the fact that in medieval times their position as members of misteries was more fully recognized than in England is interesting. In Paris not only were they accepted as members of the corps de métiers on the same terms as men, but they organized and controlled gilds of their own.[6] In Brussels, too, women workers

1. Ibid., pp. 180–182.
2. Ibid., p. 197.
3. Ibid., p. 166.
4. Ibid., p. 123.
5. Ibid., p. 284.
6. E. Boileau, Les Métiers et Corporations de la Ville de Paris, passim.

were recognized.[1] English legislation notices women but does not take them very seriously. A man has to choose his craft and stick to it; a woman could turn her hand to almost any craft that she liked.[2] Parliament recognized women brewers, bakers, weavers, spinners, but they were to receive lower wages.[3] In York, cappers, parchment makers, listers, freshwater fishers, ironmongers, barber surgeons, fishmongers, stringers, cooks and vintners have definite ordinances dealing with women. All misteries, however, seem to have accepted the widow of a master as his legitimate successor; though in the case of the tanners, if she took a second husband, a very high entrance fee was exacted, before he was admitted to the craft.[4] The tapiters were even more extortionate, they not only exacted the same fee, but the new master was only admitted on the condition that he should employ a skilled foreman, " habeat hominem sufficientem instructum et in arte predicta eruditum."[5] In fact the widow's second husband was really in a worse position than the alien, he paid the same money, but the alien was not hampered by the foreman.[6]

During the fifteenth century constant disputes arose beween the different crafts, because members took advantage of overlapping to work at more trades than one; but the quarrels generally focussed on the payment towards the upkeep of the pageant plays. Innumerable examples are furnished in the entries concerning the Corpus Christi procession and pageants.[7] Thomas Wyllardeby came into the council chamber and by his own wish relinquished his work as a coiner, " in arte monetarii et myntarii," and chose to join the mistery of pewterers. He was sworn into his new occupation in the presence of the mayor,

1. G. des Marez, L'Organisation du Travail à Bruxelles au xve siècle, pp. 107-115.
2. W. Cunningham, *op. cit.*, p. 353.
3. Rolls of Parliament, vols. II., fol. 278a, 281a, iv., fol. 112b. Cf. Mem. Bk., vol. I., p. xxix.
4. Mem. Bk., p. 166.
5. Ibid., pp. 191, 192.
6. Ibid., p. 190.
7. Ante, pp xlvi, xlviii.

four aldermen and the common clerk.¹ These endless petty restrictions must have been extremely galling to many of the more enterprising of the craftsmen, but there is little evidence to show that there was ever any real consistent strenuous opposition to them. Professor Ashley's opinion " that to create even such a business conscience as we now enjoy, the medieval system of supervision was a necessary stage, and that the law was our schoolmaster to bring us to liberty "² is verified by the Memorandum Book. Certainly any effort, such as was made in York in 1519, to introduce laissez-faire methods was abortive.

During the fourteenth and fifteenth centuries probably about one thousand people in York were leading a monastic life or ministering to those who followed it. Over this monastic element the mayor had little jurisdiction. It appears only fitfully in the Memorandum Book. When any dispute as to property arose ecclesiasticism had to seek civic help, and submit to the decision of searchers of the gilds connected with the building trade. But this volume contains none of those cases of disputed jurisdiction between abbot and mayor, which enliven the earlier pages of the Memorandum Book. Possession of corpses, rights of way, attempts at enclosure are relinquished without discussion; the mayor is undisputed ruler of the city. As the medieval merchant walked through York and saw the lordly buildings of the Benedictines, the Franciscans, the Dominicans, the Carmelites, the Augustinians, he might possibly think that sufficient wealth had already been diverted to monasticism. The influence of Richard Rolle, hermit, poet and mystic, might prevail to a certain extent inside the gates of St. Mary's Abbey, but it did not reach the city's governors in the neighbouring Gild Hall.³ A brief account of the efforts of Willelmus Melton, a brother of the Friars Minors,

1. Mem. Bk., p. 76. Cf. W. Cunningham, *op. cit.*, p. 353, *n*. W. J. Ashley, *op. cit.*, p. 93.
2. W. J. Ashley, *op. cit.*, p. 73.
3. M. Deanesly, The Incendium Amoris of Richard Rolle, p. 53. His teaching would not have been popular with the merchant class even had it been known. " In another place Rolle describes the men whom he considers most sure of future damnation—perpetratores . . . those who bought to sell for exorbitant profits, offending against the medieval doctrine of the just price," *ibid.*, p. 43.

" a famous preacher of the word of God,"[1] to stir religious enthusiasm in York, is given : he was not so successful as St. Bernardine in Siena.

In all ages the man of deeds has looked on the man of thought with suspicion ; in 1391[2] the mayor, two aldermen and their clerk were added to the commission to report on S. Leonard's hospital ; possibly the knowledge thus obtained of the inner life of the institution did not tend to increase their veneration. A few years later, Thomas Thurkyll, who figures in the Memorandum Book, an alderman of the city, acted as substitute for the Master of S. Leonard's for six months. During his brief tenure of office he worked a financial reformation ; had he only remained, a witness at a subsequent visitation declared, the hospital would soon have been freed of debt.[3] Lay experiences of this kind changed the earlier civic attitude of deference to ecclesiastical power first into criticism then into scorn.

The study of the Memorandum Book leaves the impression that the real link between municipality and church was the chantry priest ; in the chantries the mayor and his brethren had a personal, a vivid interest. The long document with a head line, a reminder that mortuaries should not be exacted from the priests in York, shows that the civic officials regarded the priests as being peculiarly in their charge.[4] On the death of a chantry or stipendiary priest, the rectors and vicars of the various churches in York claimed his second best gown with his hood as a mortuary. The defence of the exaction of a mortuary was a curious piece of reasoning. It was assumed that inadvertently even a devout churchman might have omitted to pay as much tithe as he could have done, therefor as such an omission was a mortal sin, in the interest of his immortal soul the dead parishioner's estate must pay what often amounted to 33 per cent. of his personal property. The custom had no foundation in law, and was different in amount in

---

1. Mem. Bk., pp. 156–159, ante p. xlvii.
2. Cal. P. R. Rich. II., vol. V. (1391–1396), p. 79.
3. Victoria History of Yorkshire, vol. III., p. 341. This article by Mr. Little throws a flood of light on monastic life in York.
4. Mem. Bk., pp. 17–24.

different districts, Wales escaped entirely, many parts of England paid little, some nothing.[1] Whatever feeling there was in York with regard to the exaction from laymen, this document leaves no shadow of doubt as to the civic attitude with regard to the priests. The claim was vehemently contested on behalf of the numerous poor clergy, by the mayor and citizens. Twelve of the leading official citizens lent their weight and authority to the decision of the mayor. He publicly declared "that all the chantries of this city have been and are founded by the citizens and notabilities of this city; therefore, both the priests of this city and suburbs having chantries, and the stipendiary priests not having chantries, are the special officials ' orators ' of the citizens, their patrons and masters."[2] Obviously it was the bounden duty of the citizens to defend their servants against any action that might be burdensome to them. In addition to the mayor's speech, a lawyer, Johannes de Waltham, declared the exaction contrary to all law on the plea that the clergy were exempt from anything of the kind. The result was that the rectors after deliberation among themselves declared unanimously that they withdrew their contention. The mayor ordered the decision to be inscribed in the city records.[3] This document is of considerable interest for York was peculiarly rich in chantries, and the mayor and council seem to have had an exceptionally strong position with regard to all the chantries in the city, not only, as might have been expected, those of which they were trustees by special appointment. The work of the chantry priest was of a three-fold nature. His primary business was to celebrate masses for the souls of the departed founders. The

---

1. G. G. Coulton, Priests and People before the Reformation, Medieval Studies, No. 8, pp. 3–5. Medieval Garner, p. 593. The reverend man John Snyffemore, rector of Silverton claims that, from time immemorial " if the wife of any parishioner of the aforesaid parish die, in what place or manner soever, forthwith the right of taking and having her husband's second best possession or beast, which the said husband had in his wife's lifetime, under the name of a mortuary and as a mortuary, belonged, belongeth and should belong even in future to the rector of the aforesaid parish church." He therefore demands one red ox valued at 18s., which John Laven, having lost his wife Matilda, had hitherto refused to render " to God and the aforesaid church."
2. Mem. Bk., p. 19.
3. Ibid., p. 24.

deed of foundation generally named various members of the founder's family for whom prayers were to be recited, and in whose gift the appointment of the priest's successor was vested. He was also expected to help the parish priest in his work, although he was entirely independent of any rectorial supervision; in fact he held his chantry as an independent benefice; he worked side by side with the rector but no idea of subordination existed, nor was the chantry priest available for parochial visiting. A Durham founder expressly stipulates that his two chaplains are to devote themselves entirely to reciting masses, saying prayers; he gives the quaint reason that "dum colitur Martha expellitur Maria," when Martha is mistress, Mary is shewn the door.[1] The chantry priest, however, found ample compensation in his scholastic work for any loss of influence through lack of social intercourse; York had three schools, the cathedral grammar school with its abbey boarding house, and two small schools attached to S. Leonards and Fossgate hospitals; none of these can be claimed as of chantry origin.[2] But in the immediate neighbourhood at Northallerton, Farburn, Ripon, Tickhill and Hemingborough the chantry priest was the schoolmaster.[3] Still his essential function was to say masses; the mysticism of some of the medieval writers, the spectacular splendour of some of the open-air shows, the pseudo-chivalry of the court tend to obscure the intrinsic practicality of the average citizen of the middle ages. Abstract discussions as to the soul's welfare had no attraction for them; they believed in the efficacy of masses to free the dead from torture; they had, however, an equally fervent belief in the necessity of increasing their worldly goods. The prosperous merchant carried his business habits into his spiritual life, specialization was in the air; while the layman pursued wealth, he paid the chantry priest to intercede for his health and prosperity in life, for his soul after death. The use of the word "magistri" in the claim of the mayor and citizens to

---

1. A. Hamilton Thompson, The Chantry Certificate Rolls for the counties of Nottingham and Northamptonshire. I am much indebted to Mr. Hamilton Thompson for help in elucidating this document.
2. A. F. Leach, *The Schools of Medieval England*, pp. 119, 244, 279, 329.
3. Ibid., pp. 197–199, 200, 211.

be " patroni et magistri " of the chantry and stipendiary priests is unusual. Possibly it has special reference to the stipendiary priest, who only received annual salaries and could be dismissed at will, the word patroni would hardly cover this second class.[1]

The names of the priests officiating at the chantries in S. Helen's, Stonegate, S. Sampson's, S. Mary the Elder, S. Mary at the gate of the Castle, S. Martin in Coney Street, S. Saviour's in Marisco, and the chapel on Ousebridge are given in the document as if they were a committee chosen to represent the forty city chaplains.[2] When the rector of the church was non-resident and his duties performed by the vicar, his resident deputy, the chantry priest who helped him, still held his altar, his stipend, his house as freehold. Although all chantry priests in York were nominally under the ægis of the city council, the chantry priest, who officiated in St. William's chapel on Ousebridge, was regarded as attached to the council by even closer ties. The allusions to him in the Memorandum Book are both numerous and interesting. In 1413 the mayor and citizens " communitas " gave a license to Johannes de Hamerton, chaplain of S. William's chapel, to build a certain room or dwelling suitable for himself, at his own expense, at the north side of the chapel. If the said John agreed to endow a suitable chaplain, who would say mass in the aforesaid chapel, then the mayor and commons, in case they were appointed trustees, offered that the newley erected dwelling should be a perpetual possession of the chaplain and his successors. The license was sealed with the seal of the city not of the mayor.[3] In May, 1416, Thomas Howran was presented by Willelmus Selby to the mayor for admission to a chantry founded in memory of Hugo Selby,[4] in S. William's chapel; the following January

1. Mr. Hamilton gives succinctly but comprehensively the distinction between chantry and stipendiary service. " The emoluments of the first were held by the chantry priests in mortmain ; the chantry was his benefice, to which institution was necessary. The revenues of the stipendiary service were the property of feoffees, who paid an annual sum to a priest or ' conduct ' for his services, but had the disposal of the money and could use it for other purposes, if necessary."
2. The sentence "communitas rectorum . . . pretendent fore consuevit " as in the text would gain by an emendation suggested by Mr. Hudson " pretendit fore consuetudinem." Mem. Bk., p. 18.
3. Mem. Bk., pp. 39, 40. Cf. W. Hudson, *op. cit.*, pp. 227, 261, 263.
4. Ibid., pp. 51, 52.

Willelmus Selby, the patron of this perpetual chantry, confirmed a chantry by which the chaplain granted a yearly rent of 13s. 4d. for twenty years to Thomas del Gare.[1] On July 13th, 1447, Cuthbertus Cotes, chaplain, resigned his chantry in the chapel of S. William, and by the third of August, his successor, Johannes Palyser, was presented by Willelmus Bulmer, knight, and admitted by the mayor; apparently the celerity of business habits permeated even the city chantries.[2]

The undated custumal of the city claims by ancient custom " that constables, sergeants and other people and officers of the city have the right to take to the Kidcote and imprison breakers of the peace going about the city by night and other men and women, chaplains, and men and women of religion found in suspicious places with any woman, and carry them before the ordinary, to be punished according to the law of holy church."[3] The ordinary means, of course, the ordinary judge, who in such cases was generally the Bishop, but might be someone else.[4]

When it is remembered that there were thirty-nine churches in York, about sixty abbeys, priories, monasteries, hospitals, maisons dieu, and chapels the rarity of the allusions to those who held office or dwelt in them is remarkable; it shows how essentially the Memorandum Book is a specialized history of civic York.

An interesting insight into the working of two characteristic medieval institutions, the one economic, the other ecclesiastical is given in a letter from the King addressed to the mayor and constables of the staple.[5] The great statute of the staple was planned on similar lines to the statute merchant.[6] The staple was originally the town, appointed by the government, to which all English merchants were obliged by law to take their wool or

---

1. Ibid., p. 53.
2. Mem. Bk., p. 273.
3. Mem. Bk., p. 254, vol. I., p. 203. Cf. G. G. Coulton, Priests and People before the Reformation, Medieval Studies, No. 8, p. 17. A. Hamilton Thompson, Visitations of Religious Houses (1420-1436), pp. xii, xiii.
4. E. Gibson, Codex Juris Eccl., 1, p. 436, 1 Henry VII., c. 4. " Priests and religious men being incontinent the ordinaries may commit them to prison, without charge of false imprisonment."
5. Mem. Bk., pp. 27, 28.
6. Mem. Bk., vol. I., pp. 12, 13, xvi., xvii

any other staple goods for sale. It was settled to facilitate the collection of custom duties, but became a useful weapon in the hands of diplomatists.[1] Calais, Bruges[2] and Antwerp were successively staple towns. In 1353, however, it was decided to try the plan of holding the staple in England, and Newcastle, York, Lincoln, Norwich, Westminster, Canterbury, Chichester, Winchester, Exeter and Bristol were appointed as staple towns.[3] Each staple town had a mayor of the staple, before whom debtors were required to execute a bond, which was signed in the presence of the mayor. In Bristol " the old mayor delivered unto the new mayor the king's sword, and his hat, and the casket with the seal of office, the seal of the statute of the staple, the seal of the statute merchant, with other authentic seals included in the same."[4] In Norwich the seal of the statute merchant and statute staple were the same.[5] In the December of 1391 the letter from the king arrived; it tells clearly and briefly that Johannes de Lyndesay had incurred a debt, according to staple law, of sixty-six pounds to Johannes Burdon and Willemus Sherman. Unable to discharge his obligations he had fled to the monastery precints " ad domum et ecclesiam " of the friars preachers :[6] an unfortunate man, Ricardus Kyng, who had been his surety, was seized and put in prison. The king, therefore, ordered the mayor and constables of the staple together with the mayor of the city and

1. W. Cunningham, *op. cit.*, pp. 315, 316, 415, 493. W. J. Ashley, Economic History, pt. II., pp. 21, 22. W. E. Lingelbach, The Merchant Adventurers of England, pp. xxv, xxvi. [Translations and Reprints from the original sources of European History.]

2. R. Häpke, Brügges Entwicklung zum Mittelalterlichen Weltmarkt, passim.

3. 27 Edw. III., m. II. (Ordinances of the Staple).

4. Ricart's Calendar, quoted by Professor Ashley. Sir Richard York was twice mayor of York and also mayor of the staple. The late perpendicular window in S. Helen's commemorates these facts. Possibly, too, the large light representing " Our Father in pity exhibiting His crucified Son," refers to his connexion with the merchants' company whose seal represents the same subject; G. Benson, Churches of York, pp. 117, 118. *British Association Hand Book.* Freeman of York, *op. cit.*, p. 188, 203.

5. W. Hudson, *op. cit.*, p. 269.

6. Ad domum et ecclesiam is really tautological, often in the middle ages " ecclesia " is used for monastery.

the keepers of the crown pleas[1] to go within the monastic precints,[2] seize him and force him to pay the debt, thus obtaining the liberation of his surety. This could be done by law and according to the form of the said statute. Twelve years before this occurrence debtors had abused sanctuary rights so frequently that parliament had been forced into action. The statute proclaimed that after five successive weekly summonses at the gates of the sanctuary, where the debtor was, if he failed to appear before the king's justices, his goods and lands were forfeited.[3] All churches and churchyards were sanctuaries for felony; the sanctuary knocker of All Saints, Pavement, is a modern myth. There are references to sixteen sanctuaries in York during the thirteenth century. According to the coroners' rolls of the city between 1349 and 1359 there were eleven fugitives, who took sanctuary at All Saints, Pavement, S. Crux, S. Lawrence, S. Martin Coney Street, S. Martin Micklegate, S. Saviour, Holy Trinity, S. William's chapel, and the church of the Carmelites.[4] But the fame of Beverley sanctuary overshadowed all others; the refuge extended a mile and a half in every direction; the privilege, however, intensified as the high altar and frith stool were approached. The register from 1478 to 1539 is still extant, 495 names are entered, the largest number 208 came for debt. These sanctuary men were allowed to be members of trades gilds in Beverley, though there is no trace of any regulation of the kind in York.[5]

A quarrel between a priest and the craft of tixtwriters, lumers, noters, turners and flurrisshers was submitted to arbitration by the command of " the right reverent fadre in God, the

---

1. The coroners, 4 Edw. L, "De Officio Coronatoris" does not give any explicit rules with regard to this part of a coroner's duty; the legal tracts of the reign, Bracton, Britton and Fleta, treat the subject fully. J. C. Cox, Sanctuary and Sanctuary Seekers, pp. 12, 13.

2. Evidently here as at Westminster, St. Martin's le Grand, Whitefriars, there were houses within the monastic precincts to which felons and (by abuse) debtors resorted. The Rolls of Parliament, III., 504, give a graphic picture of the lawlessness of the district of St. Martin's le Grand in 1379.

3. 2 Rich. II., st. ii., c. 3. Quoted by Dr. Cox.

4. Dr. Cox, *op. cit.*, 295.

5. MSS. Harl. 4292. Surtees Soc., Registers of the Sanctuaries of Durham and Beverley, vol. 5. I am indebted to the Rev. A. A. R. Gill for information on this point. Cf. A Réville, L'Abjuratio Regni, Revue Historique, vol. 50, p. 1.

archbishop of York." The award is not dated but from intrinsic evidence it must belong to the end of the fifteenth century. The arbiters are two merchants, a goldsmith and a grocer. The subject of dispute was as to whether the priests had the right to take apprentices and to sell books. The judgment is clear and uncompromising.

"Wee deme and award that the said Sir William and all other prestes within this citie, suburbes and fraunchiesse of the same frome hensforth take noon apprentice ne hiredman to set on wark in the said occupacion upon the payn of xl*s*., as oft tymes as thai or any of thaime ar founden defective whereof, the oon halff to be imploid to the common well of this citie and the other halve to thoccupacion of tixtwriters abovesaid, provided alway that the said Sir William Inceclyff and all other prestez that haith any wark or bukes in wrytyng at the tyme of makyng of this award have respect to finych all such bookes afore the feist of purification of our lady next ensewing after the date of this award. Also we awarde and deme that it be leffull to the said Sir William Inceclyff and all other preistes within this [citie], suburbes and fraunchiessez of the same to write and make bookes to there awn proper use or to giffe in almose and charitie at ther pleasour, so that the same bukes or any of thame by the same Sir William or any of the said preistes or any other in his or ther namez colerable be not put to any sale under the payn to forsaid."[1]

Over one section of the industrial life of York the church held undisputed sway. The men employed in building the minster seem to have been a class apart. In 1407, after the collapse of the belfrey, William Colchester, mason, had to be protected by a special mandate from the King, " for him and his deputies and the workmen and labourers and their goods."[2] An entry in the patent rolls of the following year prove the

1. York Municipal Records, $\frac{B}{Y}$ f. 39, *b*.
2. Pat. Rolls, 9 Hen. IV., pt. 1, m. 21, Dec. 14, 1407.

futility of the protection. A commission was appointed to inquire about "divers conspiracies among certain stone cutters and other evil doers of the county of York and elsewhere to hinder the work of the fabric of the church of S. Peter, York, and to maim William Colchestre, ' mason ' and the stone cutters and masons taken by him according to letters patent, and to do other evils."[1]

The longest entry in the book is the copy of the triple indenture in which the prior, John Multon, of the order of preaching friars in York, pledged his order in 1463 to perpetual gratitude for the benefactions of dame Eufemia Langton, widow of John Langton knight. This honourable and discreet lady, who had on previous occasions bestowed many gifts upon the order for the especial love she bore them, had recently discovered with much distress that the friars were in danger of forfeiting to their creditors sundry jewels, books, vestments and other ornameuts on the security of which they had incurred debts, which they were unable to meet. Whereupon dame Eufemia presented to them a sum of money sufficient to redeem their goods and ornaments which, without her timely aid, would have been lost to the convent for ever.

In the exuberance of their gratitude the prior and brethren unanimously, with the consent of the provincial of the order in England, their venerable father in Christ, brother John Kyng doctor of theology, pledged themselves and their successors in perpetuity to the following observances :—

(1). A mass of the Blessed Virgin Mary was to be said at the altar of the Holy Trinity in the conventual church for the welfare and prosperity of Eufemia and her six children, John, Robert, Henry, William, Thomas and Margaret and for the souls of John Langton knight and his parents, friends and ancestors and of Eufemia whenever she should depart this life and all her friends and relations and of any persons connected by any ties whatsoever with John and Eufemia. This mass was to be said every day except on the last three days in Holy Week, between the hours of eight and nine, with the special memorials for benefactors and for the faithful departed and with three strokes

---

1. Pat. Rolls, 9 Hen. IV., pt. II., m. 8 d, July 26, 1408.

on the small bell, and was to be called the Langton Mass. Three times in the year the friar, to whom this duty was entrusted, was to swear upon the Gospels to fulfil it faithfully, and he was to observe strictly the appointed hour, unless he had been informed that dame Eufemia or one of her children, heirs or executors was intending to be present, in which case he might wait for their arrival.

(2). The names of dame Eufemia and her children and of her late husband and all their friends and relations, living and dead, were to be inscribed in a list and placed upon the altar before the eyes of the friar celebrating the Langton Mass; they were also to be read aloud daily in chapter; and at Nones every day the psalm De Profundis was to be recited in the choir of the conventual church and on Good Friday the seven penitential psalms with a litany were to be said by all the brothers of the convent for the welfare of their souls whether living or dead.

(3). A memorial service was to be held annually for the soul of John Langton and all his departed friends and relations on the eve of St. Mathias' Day with a mass on the following day, at both of which services the big bell was to be rung thrice and the prayers *Deus indulgentiarum* and *Inclina Domine* were to be used.

And when dame Eufemia herself should die, a similar mass was to be instituted on the anniversary of her death with a memorial service on the eve with similar prayers and ceremonies.

(4). The children of dame Eufemia and all their lawful descendants were to be admitted as brothers and sisters in the chapter of the order and to participate in the masses, preachings, fasts, pilgrimages, abstinences, watchings, prayers and other good works and devotions of the order.

(5). On the demise of dame Eufemia or of any one of her children or of her children's children, their names were to be sent to every convent of the order throughout England, in order that *Placebo* and *Dirige* might be said on their behalf with the other prayers, which were used for a brother of the order.

(6). And in order that these observances should be duly remembered, this memorandum was to be read publicly twice a year in the presence of all the brothers on Maundy Thursday and the 15th day of September.

And to ensure the due observance of this agreement the prior and convent pledged themselves and all their goods, whether consecrated or otherwise, to Eufemia and her heirs and to the Mayor of York and his successors that every time they failed in performing the above devotions and observances, they would pay a penalty of 100 shillings of which 40 should be for the use of the chamber of the city and 60 should be distributed to the poor by the Mayor or by Eufemia's children on the day of her anniversary. And if the convent should fail in any of these observances, it should be lawful for Eufemia or her heirs or the Mayor or his successors to enter the church, buildings or lands of the convent and distrain upon their goods, consecrated or otherwise, without regard to any privileges or liberties conferred by the pope or the king, until such time as the fine with all the costs of the distraint should be duly paid. Nor should the order have the right to retaliate in any way for such action, either by a sentence of excommunication or by legal proceedings or in any other way.

This agreement was confirmed by the provincial of the order and sealed with his seal as well as with the prior's seal and the common seal of the convent.

And copies of the indenture were to be deposited in perpetuity with the prior and convent, the heirs and executors of dame Eufemia, and the Mayor and community of the city of York.[1]

Another lady, Maria Brathwayt, who figures in the Memorandum Book, was more practical in her gifts. In 1421 of her own free will she gave twenty marks to be spent in building a new stone cross in Thursday market; the money was given to Johannis Sturtevant, but the mayor was appointed to supervise the expenditure.[2] A tantalizing mystery hangs over Elizabeth Troghton, " a discrete woman of the city of York," who was the subject of a unfinished letter from the mayor, sheriff and aldermen of Newcastle.[3]

1. J. J. Jusserand, Piers Plowman, pp. 88-94. Mem. Bk., pp. 223-230.
2. Mem. Bk., p. 100.
3. Ibid., p. 272.

The book is often referred to as a register, but the name is inadequate. A register belongs to the dry-as-dust category, whereas this Memorandum Book pulsates with the vitality of a vital age. It is no colourless mechanical report of every proceeding of the civic council: selection is its charm. It contains what contemporary thinkers considered to be of significance to themselves as citizens of York. There is no allusion to the insurrection of Robin of Redesdale, who led a tumultuous crowd to the gates of York, Lancastrian in sympathy. The numerous occasions on which royalties came with glittering retinues to the city, or sent the heads of their enemies to rot over its bars, are passed over in silence.[1]

But it does afford an authentic revelation of the whole community from " the ryght honorabill mayor " in all his civic pomp, in the council chamber on Ousebridge,[2] to the widow with her scanty dole in the neighbouring almshous, " le meson du super pontem."[3] No aspect of the city's life is omitted. We see the people at work, at play, in health, in sickness, in war, in peace, at home, abroad, at church, and in the tavern. No circumstance is too trivial, none too momentous for the civic chronicler.

When first the curtain is drawn back, we see upon the stage so heterogeneous a crowd, whose grouping is so fortuitous that we fail to discover any dramatic unity. And yet closer scrutiny reveals an underlying purpose. It is as if some playwright had deliberately filled his stage with a motley throng in order to emphasize the fact that the city's true life is neither ecclesiastic nor military—or even industrial—but corporate and communal.

1. Sir. J. H. Ramsay, Lancaster and York. II., p. 339. C. L. Kingsford, *op. cit.*, pp. 17, 149, 172, 175, 178, 181, 183, 191.
2. Mem. Bk., p. 278.
3. Ibid., p. 33.

YORK MEMORANDUM BOOK.

Part II. (1388—1493).

Composicio terre Prusse.[1]

(*fo.* 150). In nomine summe et individue Trinitatis, Patris et Filii et Spiritus Sancti. Amen. Cum pacis auctor pacificos volens filios esse beatitudinis ac execrabilem pacis emulam a Christianorum finibus exulare : ea propter, ad perpetue rei memoriam, noverint universi tenorem presencium visuri et audituri, quod orta dudum inter serenissimum principem et regem, Ricardum Dei gracia regem Anglie et Francie, ac dominum Hibernie, ligeosque suos Anglie parte ex una, necnon venerabilem et religiosum dominum, dominum Conradum Czrolner de Rotenstein, magistrum generalem ordinis beate Marie domus Theotonice, terramque suam Prussie, et subditos ejusdem, parte ex altera, dissensionis seu discordie materia ; predictus dominus magister generalis, usus consilio, suos honorabiles nuncios ad supradictum serenissimum principem et regem versus Angliam destinaverit, ad proponendum et querelandum sibi violencias et injurias Prutentis ab Anglicis, ut dicitur, illatas ; propter que nonnulla bona ligeorum Anglie arestata fuerunt in terra Prussie. Quorum querelam dictus serenissimus princeps benevolenter et amicabiliter admisit, recepit, et acceptavit, ac, post multa verba in tractatu hujusmodi habita, eos ad propria benevolenter remisit, promittens literatorie dicto venerabili domino magistro generali, quod suos ambassiatores ad terram Prussie vellet destinare. Unde de anno Domini millesimo trecentesimo octogesimo octavo, honorabiles et reverendos viros magistrum Nicholaum Stoket, utriusque juris licenciatum, Thomam Gra, et Walterum Sibille, Londoniensis

---

[1]—For translation see R. Hakluyt. *The Principal Voyages of the English Nation.* Vol. I. pp. 122—128.

et Eboracensis cives civitatum, cum sufficienti potestate mandatoque pleno dictum negocium tractandi, discuciendi, et finaliter terminandi, necnon cum litera credenciali ad dictum venerabilem dominum magistrum generalem, destinavit. Quos quidem ambassiatores, una cum Johanne Bevys de London', informatore eorundem, ac literis predictis, et eorum ambassiata, idem venerabilis dominus magister generalis, in castro suo de Mariemburg, vicesimo octavo die Julii anni predicti reverenter et honorifice recepit et admisit, animoque arbitrabatur digno dictas causas tractandas et decidendas ; sicque ambassiatoribus predictis, tres de suo consilio, videlicet, honorabiles et religiosos dominos, Conradum de Walrode, magnum commendatorem, Sifridum Walpod de Bassenheim, summum hospitalarium et commendatorem in Elbyngo, et Ulricum Hichenberg, thesaurarium, ordinis sui predicti, pro parte sua adjunxit. Quibus sic tractantibus, post multos tractatus inter se habitos, in hunc modum et sub forma que sequitur, unanimiter et concorditer extitit condescensum et concordatum. Primo, videlicet, quod omnes arestaciones, represalie et inpingnoraciones quorumcumque bonorum et mercandisarum in Anglia et Prussia, ante datam presencium facte, sint de presenti quiete, (*fo.* 150, *b*) libere et solute, omni fictione et dissimulacione postpositis ; adeo quod dampna, sumptus, et dispendia hinc inde ratione hujusmodi arestatorum in futurum a quoque nullatenus repetantur ; sed inefficax sit et esse debet in hac parte cujuscumque repeticio, causeque hinc inde si, que occacione dictorum arestatorum intentate fuerint, mortue sint penitus et extincte.

Item, secundo, concordatum est, quod omnes et singuli Pruteni in portu de Swen ab Anglicis pretendentes se fuisse gravatos, vel etiam alibi ubicumque, quomodocumque, et quandocumque, ante datam presencium, acceptis literis dicti venerabilis domini magistri generalis, et civitatum suarum habitacionum, ire debent versus Angliam ad dictos honorabiles ambassiatores, qui ipsos juvare debent, ut querelam eorum dicto domino regi deferant et proponant. Qui quidem serenissimus princeps et rex operam ad hoc dare teneatur, ut dampnum passis fiat bonorum restitucio, vel saltem justicie complementum et judicium indilatum. Et, conformiter, singuli de Anglia per Prutenos, ubicumque, quandocumque, et quomodocumque, dicentes se gravatos, cum sui regis ac civitatum suarum habitacionum literis, ad sepedictum venerabilem dominum magistrum generalem ire tenentur, suas querelas et causas eidem proposituri. Qui et consimiliter, ut ablata seu dampna restituantur, vel saltem ut expeditum judicium et indilatum fiat eisdem, operam dare teneatur. Hoc premisso in quibuslibet clausulis, quod salvum et liberum sit cuilibet, agere et civiliter querelare volenti, hoc posse facere per se, vel procuratorem sive procuratores suos.

Item, tercio, concordatum est, quod si quis esset de Prussia qui in Anglia suas querelas criminales proponere vellet criminaliter, ut, puta, frater suus vel affinis interfectus, vulneratus vel mutilatus sit ab Anglicis, ille idem ad civitatem London' in Anglia, et ad dictos ambassiatores transire dignetur, literas deferens dicti venerabilis domini magistri generalis, ac civitatis sue habitacionis; qui liberam et plenam habere debent potestatem, juxta querelas hominum de Prussia, et secundum responsa Anglicorum, amicabilem reconciliacionem seu honestam emendam inter partes hujusmodi faciendi et cedandi; quam vero reconciliacionem partes sic concordate servare teneantur indubie et indilate. Si quis vero fuerit de Anglicis, qui dictorum ambassiatorum composicioni seu arbitrio temerarius contradictor extiterit vel eciam contemptor, ex tunc habent ambassiatores predicti dictos Prutenos conquerentes ad regie majestatis presenciam deducere, necnon supplicare quod hujusmodi conquerentibus fiat justicie complementum seu judicium indilatum, prout hec sunt placitata. Si quis vero de Anglia, contra quem aliquis de Prussia (*fo.* 151) suas acciones vellet intentare, se in termino absentaverit, dicti ambassiatores ad proximum terminum ex tunc sequentem eundem Anglicum evocare seu constituere debent, ne Pruteni conquerentes sine judicio seu juris suffragio secedere seu recedere videantur. Quod si evocatus contumax extiterit, dicti ambassiatores habent referre et requirere prout superius dictum est. Et conformiter per omnia fiet Anglicis in Prussia conqueri volentibus, videlicet, civitate de Danskz, ubi proconsules ejusdem civitatis et Elbingensis civitatis, coassumptis sibi duobus consulibus, uno de Danskz, altero vero de Elbyngo, qui quidem quatuor consimilem per omnia habeant potestatem omnes querelas criminales, criminaliter per Anglicos contra Prutenum seu Prutenos propositas, per amicabilem reconciliacionem seu honestam emendam si fieri poterit, decidendi, discuciendi, et terminandi ; quod si amicabiliter fieri non poterit, seu si aliquis Prutenus arbitrio seu composicioni hujusmodi non paruerit, ymmo contradictor seu contentor extiterit, extunc dicti iiii^{or} proconsules et consules dicto magistro generali terre predicte referre et debite requirere teneantur, quod dictis Anglicis conquerentibus fiat judicium indilatum et justicie complementum. Si vero contingat aliquem aut aliquos reos principales mori hinc inde aut esse jam defunctos, extunc liberum sit agenti prosequi jus suum in bona sive heredes jam defuncti. Ad premissa vero exequenda termini ponuntur infrascripti ; primus, videlicet, in Dominica qua Quasimodi geniti decantatur proxime futura, cum vii^{tem} diebus sequentibus ; secundus, in festo Sancte Trinitatis proxime eciam futuro, cum vii^{tem} diebus sequentibus ; tercius, in octava Sancti Johannis Baptiste extunc proxime, cum vii^{tem} diebus sequentibus ; quartus terminus ultimus et peremptorius erit in festo Sancti Michaelis extunc proxime futuro, cum vii^{tem} diebus sequentibus. Et extunc omnes cause, que tangunt mortem, vel membri mutulacionem cum accionibus civilibus ex eisdem descendentibus, sint perpetuo mortue penitus et extincte. Et si forte aliquis dictorum ambassiatorum interim moriatur, extunc duo potestatem habeant tercium eligendi. Et si post datam presencium aliqua causa insurgat vel emergat, parva seu magna, debet judicari in Anglia et Prussia sicud antiquitus et ab antiquo extitit usitatum.

(*fo.* 151, *b.*) Item, ultimo concordatum existit, quod ligii mercatores Anglie quicumque liberam habeant facultatem se applicandi cum navibus, bonis et mercandisis quibuscumque ad quemcumque portum terre Prussie, necnon hujusmodi bona et mercandisas ulterius ad quemcumque locum in dicta terra Prussie se transferendi, ibique cum quacumque persona libere contrahere et mercari, sicut antiquitus et ab antiquo extitit usitatum.

Quod quidem in omnibus et per omnia Prutenis concessum est in Anglia. Et si post datam presencium, inter dictum regnum Anglie et terram Prussie aliqua dissensio seu discordia de novo

emerserit, quod absit, extunc dictus serenissimus princeps rex
Anglie, et dictus venerabilis dominus magister generalis habeant
se mutuo literatorie et per nuncios certificare et intimare de
hujusmodi materia causam dissensionis seu discordie inducente,
que quidem intimacio, pro parte dicti serenissimi principis, fiet
in dicto castro de Marienburg; pro parte vero dicti venerabilis
domini magistri generalis, fiet hujusmodi intimacio in civitate
London', predictis consulibus civitatis ejusdem, ut extunc facta
hujusmodi denunciacione seu intimacione, libere et tute annum
possint et valeant ligei Anglie et subditi terre Prussie, cum bonis et
mercandisis suis ad propria redire et remeare, si interim saltem
hinc inde composicio seu amicabilis tractatus non intervenerit
quovismodo. Et ut premissa omnia solidius et sub fide hinc
inde debite demandentur execucioni pro pace et tranquillitate
firmiter et inviolabiliter observanda; necnon premissorum omnium corroboratione et consolidacione tres supradicti honorabiles
et religiosi domini, a dicto venerabili domino magistro generali
commissarii pro hujusmodi ordinacione seu composicione assignati,
sua sigilla presentibus appenderunt; dictamque ordinacionem
seu composicionem consimilis tenoris que literam de verbo ad
verbum, per omnia prout presentibus inseritur, a supradictis
tribus ambassiatoribus serenissimi regis Anglie suis sub sigillis
mutuo receperunt.

Dat. in castro de Mariemberg predicto anno Domini ut supra,
vicesima prima die mensis Augusti.

(*fo*. 152). Serenissimo principi et domino, domino Ricardo,
regi Anglie et Francie, ac domino Hibernie, frater Conradus
Crolner de Rotenstein, ordinis beate Marie domus Teutonice
Jerosolomitane magister generalis, specialem in Domino affectum
et amorem. Noscat vestra serenitas quod anno Domini millesimo
ccc^{mo} lxxxviii de mense Julii xxviii die, honorabiles viri ambassiatores, magister Nicholaus Stoket, licenciatus in utroque jure,
Thomas Gra, Walterus Sibile, Londoniensis et Eboracensis
civitatum cives, in castro nostro Marienberg, litera credenciali
ac mandato procuratorio a vestra illustri magnificencia in nostra
presencia comparuerunt, audita et accepta eorum ambassiata

consulte et mature agere volentes, adjunximus vestris honorabilibus ambassiatoribus seu nunciis de nostro concilio tres honorabiles et religiosos viros, dominos conpreceptores nostros, Conradum de Walrode, magnum commendatorem, Siffridum de Bassenheim, summum hospitalarium et commendatorem in Elbyngo, et Ulricum Hacenberger, ordinis nostri thezaurarium, qui juxta continenciam literarum sigillis eorum communitarum unanimiter convenerunt. Quorum composicionem seu ordinacionem firmiter et inviolabilite gratificamus, ratum et gratum habere volumus, omni postposita ficione. In cujus gratificacionis testimonium sigillum nostrum duximus presentibus apponendum. Dat. in castro nostro Mariemberg anno Domini millesimo ccc^{mo} lxxxviii xxi die mensis Augusti.

Cum Hanletheus Mauleverer et alii sibi associati ceperunt Johannem Lynelandes, filium Thome Lynelandes, quondam civis Ebor', extra stratam de Layrthorp, infra limites, bundas et procinctum libertatis civitatis Ebor', ac ipsum Johannem Lynelandes ut nativum ipsius Hanlethei exinde abduxerunt et detinuerunt. Super quo facto habito processu coram justiciariis domini regis de pace in civitate et suburbiis Ebor' assignatis versus transgressores predictos, et demum interventu tractatu cum consilio ex parte dicti Hanlethei ac aliorum transgressorum, venit enim idem Hanletheus cum aliis strenuis viris ac quibusdam aliis de predictis transgressoribus coram Willelmo Frost, tunc maiore dicte civitatis Ebor', Thoma Gra, Thoma de Howom, Thoma Thorkyll, Simone de Quixlay, Willelmo de Selby, et Johanne de Brathwayt, aldermannis, Thoma de Houeden, tunc vicecomite dicte civitatis, ac pluribus aliis venerabilibus personis dicte civitatis, Willelmo Gascoigne, Johanne Woderof, et (fo. 152, b) Ricardo de Gascoigne, tunc eciam ibidem presentibus, duodecimo die Aprilis 20 Ric. ii. (1397) in camera maioris super pontem Use in Ebor', et ibi submiserunt se gracie ad honorem dicti maioris et proborum, et ob reverenciam dicte civitatis promiserunt personaliter restituere prefatum Johannem de Lyneland, in predicta camera, coram dicto maiore et aliis probis hominibus dicte civitatis, die Mercurii proximo post festum Dominice in Ramis Palmarum (April 18). Quo die, prefatus Johannes de Lyneland restitutus fuit in forma predicta.

De guttera in tenemento communitatis in Fossegate.

Inquisicio capta coram maiore, vicecomitibus, et probis hominibus, viij° die Marcii, 21 Ric. ii. (1397-8), de cursu aque cujusdam guttere in tenemento communitatis juxta terram Ade del Brigg in Fossegate, per Willelmum Palmer de Fossebrigg, Laurencium de Leverton, Willelmum de Muston, Willelmum Lyons, Ricardum del Chaumbre, Thomam Catour, Abraham de Colton, Robertum Loksmyth de Fossegate, Johannem de Hillom', *smyth*, Johannem Couper de Fossegate, Johannem de Paston, et Thomam de Kylburn. Qui dicunt super sacramentum suum, quod cursus aque guttere predicte non habuit antiquitus, nec habet ulteriorem exitum, nisi usque ad murum lapideum, in cornerio dicti tenementi communitatis, et ibi descendit in terram in loco vocato a *synk*, et sic oportet tenentes ibidem evacuare aquam suam propriam.

(*fo.* 153). Excellentissimo domino Regi, in cancellaria sua, sui ligei humiles et subditi maior et communitas civium civitatis vestre Ebor' vestro regali imperio se subjugant, cum omni humilima servitute. Cum in carta vestra, nobis in hac parte concessa, contineatur quod nomina vicecomitum dicte civitatis vestre Ebor' statim super electionem eorundem, sub sigillo communi dicte civitatis, in cancellariam vestram mitterentur; virtute carte predicte electi sunt vicecomites secundum formam et effectum ejusdem A et B ad occupandum dictum officium vicecomitum dicte civitatis per unum annum integrum proxime sequentem datam presencium. In cujus rei testimonium huic certificatorio sigillum commune dicte civitatis fecimus apponi. Datum apud Ebor', in festo Sancti Mathei Apostoli anno regni vestri etc.

Venerabili et discreto viro, domino cancellario domini nostri regis, maior et communitas civium civitatis Ebor', omnimodam reverenciam et honorem. Cum in carta dicti domini nostri regis, nobis in hac parte concessa, contineatur quod quilibet maior civitatis predicte, qui pro tempore fuerit, eo ipso et quam citius in maiorem ibidem electus fuerit, sit eschaetor dicti domini regis et heredum suorum in predicta civitate Ebor', suburbiis, et procinctu eorundem, ita semper quod statim de nomine eschaetoris predicti singulis annis ad scaccarium dicti domini nostri regis et heredum suorum sub sigillo communi dicti civitatis Ebor' certificaretur ; virtute cujus carte A.B., maior electus civitatis predicte, eschaetor est dicti domini regis civitatis predicte Ebor', ad occupandum dictum officium eschaetoris secundum formam et effectum carte predicte, per unum annum integrum proxime sequentem datam presencium. In cujus rei testimonium huic certificatorio sigillum commune civitatis fecimus apponi. Datum apud Ebor' tercio die Februarii anno regni domini regis Henrici primo.

Venerabilibus et discretis viris, domino thesaurario et baronibus de scaccario domini regis, A et B, vicecomites civitatis Ebor', omnimodam reverenciam et honorem. Scire velit vestra laudabilis dominacio quod, virtute carte domini nostri regis in hac parte concesse, assignavimus et loco nostro posuimus dilectos nobis in Cristo A et B attornatos nostros conjunctim et alterum eorum per se divisim ad profra nostra coram vobis faciendum, necnon ad computandum, quando vobis placuerit, loco nostro de rebus unde computabiles sumus virtute officii nostri vicecomitatum, et ad omnia alia facienda que nos ipsi faceremus, si coram vobis personaliter interessemus secundum formam et effectum carte predicte,[1] necnon ad recipiendum nomine nostro omnimoda precepta per waranta domini Regis scaccarii predicti nobis . . . . juxta formam et effectum statuti nuper inde editi.[1] In cujus rei testimonium sigillum commune civitatis predicte presentibus est appensum. Datum etc. anno etc.

Waranta domini regis scaccarii predicti nobis.

Venerabili etc. A B, maior civitatis Ebor', eschaetor domini regis dicte civitatis Ebor', suburbiorum et procinctuum ejusdem civitatis, omnimodam reverenciam et honorem. Scire velit vestra laudabilis dominacio quod virtute carte domini nostri regis in hac parte concesse assignavi et loco meo posui dilectos michi in Cristo A et B attornatos meos conjunctim.

Repetition of last, but in the singular and without ([1]) . . . ([1]).

(fo. 153, b.) Presentatum est coram Thomas Gra, maiore civitatis Ebor', Willelmo de Sallay, et Johanne de Hewyk, vicecomitibus ejusdem civitatis, per Rogerum de Barton et Robertum de Jarum, scrutatores artificii mercerum civitatis Ebor', quod ubi ipsi per preceptum maioris predicti et aldermannorum ejusdem civitatis jurati fuerunt ad officium scrutatorum in artificio predicto fideliter faciendum et exequendum; dicunt quod ipsi, die Veneris in septimana Pentecostes ultimo preterita, venerunt ad shoppam Willelmi de Hugate, *mercer*, ad pondera sua prout onerati fuerunt probanda, et pecierunt pondera sua eis liberari, prout alii ejusdem artificii ante fecerunt; ibi dicunt quod Willelmus pondera sua eis liberari renuit et recusavit. Et cum dicti scrutatores pondera ibidem ceperint, ipse Willelmus ea ab eis violenter eripuit, et fecit eis rescussum in contemptum etc.; super quo, dictus Willelmus, ad certos diem et locum coram prefatis maiore et vicecomitibus de rescussu et transgressione predictis allocutus, dicit quod ipse de aliquo rescussu non est culpabilis. Ideo queritur etc.

Et postea, videlicet, die Jovis proxima post festum Nativatatis Sancti Johannis Baptiste, xij juratores coram prefatis maiore et vicecomitibus ad hoc electi, triati et jurati pro domino rege, videlicet, Willelmus de Brignall, Henricus de Preston, *mercer*, Johannes de Osebaldwyk, Robertus Hayne, *mercer*, Johannes de Newland, Johannes de Sharowe, Robertus de Popilton, Robertus Cooke, *junior*, Nicholaus de Westyby, Rogerus de Lyndesay, Willelmus de Hovyngham, *boucher*, et Johannes de Snayth. Qui dicunt super sacramentum suum quod dictus Willelmus culpabilis est de rescussu predicto, prout versus eum presentatum est etc.

Ideo consideratum est per prefatos maiorem et vicecomites quod dictus Willelmus eat prisone, quousque fecerit finem etc.; et quo ad finem consideratum est per prefatos maiorem, vicecomites et aldermannos, quod predictus Willelmus solvat ad opus communitatis civitatis predicte, pro rescussu et transgressione, rebellione et contemptu predictis, decem libras sterlingorum. De quibus solvit in manibus xiij *s*. iiij *d*., et ix *li*. vi *s*. viii *d*. remanent in respectu in manibus ipsius Willelmi, sub bono gestu suo in futurum custodiendi etc.

Appointment by Thomas de Leycestre of London, grocer, before William Frost, mayor of York, of Thomas de Fryseton and William Roundell, citizens of York, to gather his farms from his tenants, and if necessary to distrain and prosecute for the same.

York, 24 September, 5 Hen. iv. (1404).

(*fo.* 154¹). Wednesday after S. Peter ad vincula, 19 Ric. ii. (4 Aug. 1395) attornment " per unum denarium," by Joan, widow of Thomas Basy to Roger de Crane for a tenement in Skeldergate, which she held for life, after her husband's death, made before Thomas de Staynlay, then mayor of York, Nicholas de Warthill, Adam del Stok, Walter de Topcliff, William de Touthorp, John de Wheldale, William de Wirkeworth, and other servants of the community.

24 Jan., 22 Ric. ii. (1395-9). The following measures and weights were delivered to Robert de Ripon by order of the mayor and consent of the good (*proborum*) men, videlicet, unum busselum eris, dimidium bussellum et pek ligni, tercia pars lagene, lagena, potella et quarta ligni pro cervisia, una trona ad ponderandum, unum hopir cum scala, et unum strikill ligni, lagena, potella et quarta eris pro vino, sigillum pro mensuris vini, et aliud sigillum pro mensuris ligni, pro blado, braceo, cervisia et aliis rebus sigillandis, simul cum ponderibus, videlicet, dimidium centum, quarterium et dimidium quarterium plumbi in corio consuta.²

Hec est concordia facta apud Ebor', decimo nono die Aprilis, A.D. 1403, inter Johannem Eseby, burgensem de Danszik, ex una parte, et Henricum de Hyndelay, Rogerum de Thornhill, Willelmum Devyas, Johannem Somerby, et Johannem de Raghton, ac alios mercatores socios suos, qui habuerunt bona et mercandisas in nave Allardi Harmanson de Hardewyk, vocata Halygaste, freghta per prefatos Henricum et Rogerum usque Kyngston super Hull, in Anglia, ad opus predictorum mercatorum ex parte altera, videlicet, quod de bonis et mercandisis, que erant in nave predicta, per predictos Henricum et alios mercatores cum eo superius nominatos, et socios suos, seu per aliquem eorum recuperatis, prefatus Johannes Eseby habebit inde porcionem suam sibi pertinentem, faciendo et solvendo sumptus et expensas, prout pro porcione sua predicta de jure et bona fide requireretur, et eodem . . . . , dictus Johannes Eseby, ex

1—There is no fo. 155.
2—" Plus in folio sequente," is written in margin.

parte sua, de bonis et mercandisis predictis recuperaret, et eciam dicti Henricus et alii mercatores cum eo superius nominati, habebunt porciones suas, prout . . . . inde in . . . . faciend' et declarand' pro ratis porcionis sue . . . . de jure et bona fide requiret.

(*fo.* 154, *b.*) Placita curie Ebor', tenta ibidem coram maiore et ballivis civitatis Ebor', die Lune proximo ante festum Sancti Augustini (25 May, 6 Ric. ii., 1383).

Henricus de Bolton, *couper*, et Johannes de Bedale, *littester*, queruntur de Johanne del Wode, *marshall*, de placito assise frisceforcie de libero tenemento suo in civitate Ebor'; plegii de prosequendo, Johannes Bell et Willelmus Bell. Querela attachiatur infra quarentenam etc. Virtute cujus querele preceptum est subballivis curie predicte, quod summoneant per bonos summonitores xxiiij probos et legales cives de dicta civitate Ebor', quod sint hic coram maiore et ballivis civitatis predicte, die Lune proximo futuro, scilicet, primo die Junii, anno supradicto, ad faciendum recognicionem assise predicte, etc. Et quod interim habeant visum. etc. Et quod ponant per vadia et salvos plegios predictum Johannem del Wode vel ballivum suum etc., quod tunc ibi auditurus illam recognicionem etc. Et quod habeant ibi tunc nomina recognitorum et plegiorum etc.

Placita curie Ebor', tenta ibidem coram maiore et ballivis civitatis Ebor', die Lune, primo die Junii, anno supradicto. Ad quem diem assisa frisceforcie venit recognitura si Johannes del Wode, *marshal*, injuste, etc., disseisivit Henricum de Bolton, *couper*, et Johannem de Bedale, *littester*, de libero tenemento suo in civitate Ebor' post primam etc. Querela attachiata infra quarentenam etc. Et tam predicti Henricus et Johannes de Bedale quam predictus Johannes del Wode in propriis personis suis veniunt. Et unde predicti Henricus et Johannes de Bedale queruntur quod predictus Johannes del Wode disseisivit eos de duobus mesuagiis cum pertinenciis in predicta civitate Ebor' infra quarentenam etc. Et predictus Johannes del Wode respondet, ut tenens dictorum mesuagiorum in visu positorum, et dicit quod nullam eis inde fecit injuriam seu disseisinam, et de hoc ponit se super assisam etc.; et predicti Henricus et

Johannes de Bedale similiter. Ideo capiatur inde inter eos assisa etc. Et quia modo recognitores non veniunt etc., ideo assisa predicta ponitur in respectum hic usque diem Lune, scilicet, in festo Sancti Willelmi episcopi proximo futuro etc. Et preceptum est subballivis curie, quod habeant corpora recognitorum hic ad eundem diem, et quod apponant decem tales etc., quod habeant corpora eorum ad eundem diem. Et quod interim faciant visum etc., et idem dies datus est partibus predictis.

Placita curie Ebor' tenta coram prefatis maiore et ballivis, die Lune in festo Sancti Willelmi episcopi, anno supradicto. Ad quem diem veniunt partes predicte etc. Et quia modo recognitores non veniunt, ideo assisa predicta ponitur in respectum hic usque diem Lune, scilicet, proximum post festum Sancti Barnabe apostoli proximo futurum etc. Et preceptum est subballivis curie predicte, quod distringant recognitores predictos etc., ad eundem diem etc. Et quod interim faciant visum etc. Et idem dies datus est partibus predictis.

Placita curie Ebor' tenta ibidem coram prefatis maiore et ballivis, die Lune proximo post festum Sancti Barnabe apostoli anno supradicto.

(*fo.* 155). Ad quem diem veniunt partes predicte etc. Et predicta assisa ponitur in respectum hic usque diem Lune, scilicet, proximam ante festum nativitatis Beati Johannis Baptiste proxime futurum etc. pro defectu visus etc. ; et interim faciant visum etc. Et preceptum est subballivis curie predicte quod distringant recognitores etc., sicut prius contra eundem diem etc. Et idem dies datus est partibus predictis etc. Et modo, scilicet, ad prefatum diem etc. veniunt partes predicte etc. ; et similiter recognitores veniunt etc., scilicet, Robertus del Gare, Willelmus Giry, Ricardus de Alne, Willelmus de Dureme, Adam del Bank', Willelmus de Cawode, *bucher*, Johannes de Duffield, *skynner*, Robertus de Hoperton, Willelmus de Bedlyngton, Johannes Candeler, Willelmus del Freres, *skynner*, et Stephanus Littester, ad hoc electi, triati et jurati, ex assensu partium. Qui dicunt super sacramentum suum quod predicti Henricus et Johannes de Bedale fuerunt seisiti de mesuagiis predictis in visu positis in dominico suo ut de libero tenemento suo, quousque predictus Johannes del Wode eos injuste et sine judicio disseisivit, sed non vi et armis, ad dampnum predictorum Henrici et Johannis de Bedale, quadraginta solidorum. Ideo consideratum est quod predicti Henricus et Johannes de Bedale recuparent inde seisinam suam versus predictum Johannem del Wode per visum recognitorem seisine predicte et dampna sua predicta ad quadraginta solidos assissa. Et predictus Johannes del Wode in misericordia etc.

Memorandum quod duodecimo die Junii 16 Ric. ii. (1393), deliberata fuerunt Willelmo Tundu, ex precepto maioris et consensu proborum, mensura et pondera subscripta, videlicet, unum busselum eris, dimidium bussellum et pek ligni, tercia pars lagene, lagena, potella, et quarta ligni pro cervisia, una trona ad ponderandum, j hoper cum scala, et j strykel ligni, lagena, potella et quarta eris pro vino.

Receipt by Walter Randolf, servant of the late Hugh Rose, citizen and merchant of London, to John Middleton of York, mercer, for four bonds, one acquittance, two cloaks, a coverlet with a blanket, a mantle, five shillings in coin, and thirty-four pounds of onion seed, which the said John was charged before the official of the court of York to deliver to him. Seal of the mayor. York, 31 Jan., 17 Ric. ii. (1393-4).

Thursdaymarket.

(*fo.* 155, *b.*) Feoda custodum fori de Thoresdaymarket.

De quolibet equo veniente ad forum predictum cum victualibus venalibus	quad.
Et de quinque ovibus venalibus	ob.
Et de quatuor porcellis venalibus	ob.
Et de qualibet carecta carcata cum sale venali ...	j *d.*
Et eadem si ibidem remaneat per unam noctem et usque mane	ij *d.*
Et de quolibet summagio cirporum venalium	quad.
Et de quolibet summagio salis venalis	quad.
Et de quolibet extraneo veniente ad predictum forum cum speciebus venalibus	ob.
Et de quolibet extraneo veniente cum ciphis, discis, scaphis, perapcidibus et aliis hujusmodi rebus venalibus	ob.

15 June, 19 Ric. ii. (1396), grant in the presence of William Frost, mayor, Thomas Gra, Thomas de Howom, William de Selby, Simon de Quixlay, John de Howdon, Thomas Smyth, John de Brathwayt, Thomas de Staynlay, Robert de Talkan, Robert Warde, John de Bolton, Robert de Louthe, John de Askham, John de Ceszay, and other good men of the commonalty, to Sir Thomas de Barneby, chaplain, on account of the poorness of the chantry he was then occupying, of the next chantry in the presentation of the mayor and commonalty of greater value, which should be vacant.

Memorandum quod, 2 die Junii, 1 Henry iv. (1400) venerunt coram maiore civitatis Ebor', in camera consilii super pontem Use, in Ebor', Thomas de Staynlay, Thomas de Kelfeld, Stephanus de Parys, et Willelmus del Bothe, *clericus*, et recordati fuerunt quod quedam concordia finaliter facta fuit inter Johannem de Topclyff, civem et mercatorem Ebor', et Robertum de Normanton, nuper apprenticium ipsius Johannis, de omnibus accionibus, demandis et debatis, inter ipsos motis seu pendentibus seu aliqualiter exactis. Et super hoc quod dictus Robertus diu stetit in servicio ipsius Johannis, et plures empciones ac vendiciones rerum ac diversarum mercandizarum eo tempore fecerat, tam in partibus transmarinis quam citra ; ob hanc causam dubium esset an forcitan dictus Johannes, aut attornatus ejus, seu servientes sui, poterint implacitari, seu calumpniari, aut bona et catalla sua arestari, aut alio modo dampnum incurrere ideo ut ipse Johannes et sui sint in hac parte securi, prefatus Robertus se obligavit per scriptum suum obligatorium prefato Johanni in centum marcis sterlingorum, solvendis eidem Johanni, sub hac condicione, quod si dictus Johannes ammodo calumpnietur, implacitetur, seu occasionetur racione alicujus vendicionis, empcionis, recepcionis, seu liberacionis dicti Roberti, tam bonorum seu mercandizarum dicti Johannis, seu alterius cujuscumque, videlicet, pro tempore elapso quo idem Robertus exstiterat apprenticius seu attornatus dicti Johannis tam citra mare quam ultra etc.

(*fo.* 156). Hec indentura testatur, quod cum discencio et discordia exorte fuerint inter Johannem de Popilton, personam ecclesie de Patrikbrunton, et Nicholaum de Skelton de Ebor', super edificacione tenementi predicti Johannis et participacione terre inter eos in debato existentis et simul adjacentis in Walmegate in Ebor', super quibus quidem discencione et discordia inter eos motis ad instanciam et in precencia Roberti Sauvage, maioris, Rogeri de Roseton, Johannis Bouthe, et Thome de Horneby, baillivorum civitatis Ebor', magistri Johannis de Clifford, Johannis de Berden et aliorum ibidem existencium, predicti Johannes de Popilton et Nicholaus, juramentis suis astricti, posuerunt se in arbitracione et discrecione quatuor hominum, scilicet, Willelmi de Levesham et Stephani de Parys, ex parte dicti Johannis electorum, et Johannis de Quixlay et Simonis de Elvyngton, ex parte dicti Nicholai electorum, annexis sibi quatuor scrutatoribus carpentariorum artis, videlicet, Johanne de Ledes, Willelmo de Barneby, Johanne de Setryngton, et Roberto de Waghen, ad arbitrandum, discussiendum et finaliter determinandum omnia debata et defectus inter eos habita, de tenementis suis ibidem simul adjacentibus. Qui quidem arbitratores, simul cum avisamento et informacione predictorum scrutatorum ad premissa discussienda electi, monstratis coram eis gravaminibus utriusque partis predictorum Johannis et Nicholai, et visis defectubus, tam in edificacione quam in dimissione terre inter eos in debato existentis, invenerunt dictum Johannem de Popilton edificasse super solum dicti Nicholai, latitudine unius manus hominis ante versus regiam stratam, et similiter inferius in gardino super solum ejusdem Nicholai, ponendo unum postem ejusdem domus dicti Johannis, latitudine dimidii partis unius pedis hominis. Et similiter invenerunt dictum Nicholaum protravisse quandam particulam unius parietis lapidei et lapides inde asportando et vendicasse certam particulam terre soli dicti Johannis, extendentem ab exteriore domo dicti Nicholai usque ad aquam de Fosse retro. Omnibus hiis visis, examinatis et inspectis per informacionem predictorum scrutatorum, adjudicaverunt, primo quod predicti Johannes et Nicholaus essent amici ad invicem et quod simul osculentur; et quod ad edificacionem factam super solum dicti Nicholai ante, et ad posicionem postis inferius in gardino indebite positi, adjudicaverunt et consideraverunt, quod edificacio et posicio postis per dictum Johannem facte starent imperpetuum, absque impedimento seu calumpnia dicti Nicholai seu heredium suorum. Et predictam particulam terre sic existentem a domo dicti Nicholai usque ad aquam de Fosse, adjudicaverunt et consideraverunt dicto Nicholao, habendam sibi et heredibus suis imperpetuum, prout inter eos dividitur per pilos interpositos inter bundas dictorum Johannis et Nicholai.

Item, viso exitu aque descendentis et supervenientis in gardino dicti Nicholai, tam ex parte dicti Nicholai quam dicti Johannis, adjudicaverunt dictum Nicholaum ducere aquam illam sic venientem per gardinum dicti Nicholai usque ad quandam gutteram, in pariete dicti Nicholai existentem, et quod tunc aqua illa exeat per gutteram predictam in gardinum dicti Johannis, et sic exiet per gardinum dicti Johannis usque ad aquam de Fosse. Et sic concordati sunt. Ad quam quidem concordiam ex utraque parte tenendam, et imperpetuum duraturam, utraque pars alteri seisinam in propriis personis suis, ut predictum est, liberavit; et sigilla sua hiis indenturis alternatim apposuerunt.

Datum apud Ebor', die Lune proximo ante festum Sancti Thome apostoli, 16 Dec., 16 Ric. ii. (1392).

(*fo.* 156, *b.*) Concordia facta inter Willelmum Brisgreve et Johannem de Skypton de Ferybrigg.

Memorandum quod penultimo die Maii, 16 Ric. ii. (1393), hec concordia facta fuit inter Willelmum Brisegreve de Ebor', *cordewaner*, ex una parte, et Johannem de Skypton de Feribrigg, ex parte altera, de debatis et transgressionibus inter eosdem, per decretum Thome Gra, Johannis de Berden, Willelmi de Selby, et Thome Smyth, arbitratorum electorum ad concordandum partes predictas, cum consensu et supervisu Johannis de Brathwayt, tunc maioris electorum; videlicet, quod predictus Willelmus Brisegreve relaxaret dicto Johanni de Skypton quadraginta solidos sterlingorum, quos dictus Willelmus recuperavit versus ipsum Johannem in curia domini regis coram ballivis Ebor'; et eciam idem Willelmus solveret et satisfaceret dicte curie de expensis in placito inter ipsas partes in dicta curia prosecuto. Et quia videbatur dictis maiori et arbitratoribus, quod hii qui fuerunt in inquisicione inter partes predictas et injustum veredictum inter ipsas reddiderunt, prout coram dictis maiore et arbitratoribus quidam eorum publice recognoverunt, ideo ix^{em} eorum concesserunt dare prefato Johanni de Skypton pro expensis suis factis in castro Ebor', gentes de Curia in banco domini regis, tunc ibidem existente, xiij s. iiij d. Et super hoc utraque pars alteri fecerunt hinc inde acquietancias generales omnium actionum.

23 Jan., 17 Ric. ii. (1393-4). Venerunt in camera maioris super pontem Use in Ebor' coram Johanne de Brathwayt, tunc maiore, Alicia uxor Johannis de Cartmell de Ebor', *barbour*, Robertus Talke, tunc camerarius, Johannes de Kilvyngton, Hugo Gardyner, Johannes de Man, *tapiter*, et alii vicini ipsius Johannis de Cartmell, testificantes quod quia ipse Johannes nimis languidus fuerat de quadam infirmatate vocata le stane, peciit et requirebat quod Johannes Catlewe de Ebor', *barbour*, curam suam sibi imponere vellet ad afferendam petram ; et sive viveret seu moreretur, ipse Johannes Catlewe quietus fore deberet ab omni impeticione, calumpnia, et demanda per ipsum seu dictam Aliciam uxorem suam, aut quemcumque alium aliqualiter in hac parte facienda.

(*fo.* 157). Memoracio de exactione mortuariorum a presbiteris Ebor' non exigendorum.

Memorandum quod cum nuper inter communitatem rectorum et vicariorum ecclesiarum parochialium civitatis et suburbiorum Ebor', ex una parte, et communitatem presbiterorum tam cantarias in dicta civitate et suburbiis habencium quam eciam presbiterorum stipendiariorum hujusmodi cantarias non habencium, parte ex altera, occasione cujusdam pretense consuetudinis super exaccione mortuariorum presbiterorum hujusmodi infra dictas civitatem et suburbia decedencium, gravis suborta fuisset materia questionis, demum xx die Maii A.D. 1388, 2 Ric. ii., in quadam camera infra capellam Sancti Willelmi supra pontem Use dicte civitatis, camera maioris vulgariter nuncupata, coram venerabili viro, Willelmo de Seleby, tunc maiore dicte civitatis, Roberto Howom, Simone de Quixlay, R. Savage, Johanne de Berden, Roberto de Ampilford, Willelmo de Burton, Johanne de Rypon, Johanne de Styllyngton, Henrico de Yharom, Johanne de Cesay, Roberto Wrench, Thoma del Garth, civibus, et aliis quampluribus civibus honorabilibus civitatis predicte, presente me Willelmo de Chester, notario publico et clerico

communi civitatis predicte, ac magistro Willelmo Feriby de
Ebor', cur(ie) Ebor' advocato, testibusque subscriptis, comparuerunt venerabiles viri, magister Willelmus Broghton, Sancte
Trinitatis in Gothrumgate ; Johannes Suthewell, Sancti Wilfridi ;
Robertus Apylgarth, omnium Sanctorum in Northstrete ;
dominus Johannes Pykeryng, Sancte Marie super pontem castri,
ecclesiarum parochialium dicte civitatis rectores, nomine suo et
aliorum rectorum et vicariorum supradicte civitatis et suburbiorum
ad tunc ibidem absencium, necnon dominus Thomas de Garton,
capellanus cantarie Sancti Michaelis in ecclesia Sancte Elene in
Stayngate, Ebor' ; dominus Ricardus de Thornton, capellanus
cantarie Sancti Johannis Baptiste in dicta ecclesia Sancte Elene ;
Robertus de Fowton, capellanus cantarie Beate Marie in ecclesia
Sancti Sampsonis ; Johannes de Lutton, capellanus cantarie
Sancte Katerine in ecclesia beate Marie Veteris ; dominus
Johannes de Ascham, capellanus cantarie Sancti Johannis
Baptiste in ecclesia beate Marie ad portam castri ; dominus
Johannes de Molcroft, capellanus cantarie beate Marie in ecclesia
Sancti Martini in Conyngstrete ; dominus Robertus de Bylton,
capellanus cantarie beate Marie in ecclesia Sancti Salvatoris in
Marisco ; dominus Johannes Flemmyng, capellanus cantarie
Hugonis de Seleby in capella super pontem Use ; dominus
Willelmus de Coventre, dominus Thomas Waryn, dominus
Robertus Lacer, dominus Willelmus de Wyghton, dominus
Willelmus de Sonyngton, dominus Willelmus de Brayton, necnon
alii quamplures capellani civitatis et suburbiorum predictorum,
numero circiter xl. nomine et communitatis presbiterorum ante-
dictorum. Ac Willelmus de Seleby maior predictus dixit et
exposuit ibidem in presencia et audiencia omnium et infra-
scriptorum, quod nuper ad ipsius et aliorum civium dicte civitatis
pervenit noticiam quod communitas rectorum superius memorata
pretendent', fore consuevit in dictis communitate et suburbiis,
quod singuli rectores et vicarii superius memorati et eorum
successores habebunt a singulis presbiteris locorum predictorum
infra suas (*fo.* 157, *b*) parochias decedentibus meliorem vestem
suam cum capucio nomine mortuarii et pro mortuario, et sic
dicebat dicta communitas rectorum precessores et predecessores
suos habuisse et percepisse a presbiteris decedentibus ut prefertur

per tempus et per tempora cujus contrarii sive inicii memoria hominis non existit.

Pretextu cujus pretense consuetudinis quidam dominus Robertus Ede traxit in causam quemdam dominum Thomam Wirkesworth, executorem testamenti domini Thome de la Ryver, quondam capellanum (*sic*) cantarie Sancte Trinitatis in Fossegate dicte civitatis, et qui dominus Robertus Ede hujusmodi auctoritate cessit et renunciavit, ac mandatum alias per ipsum datum procuratori suo ad agendum in hac parte in presencia suorum parochianiorum revocavit, quia recognovit se non habere justiciam in prosecucione sua, prout per instrumenta publica super hujusmodi revocacione et recognicione confecta plene liquit. Super quam materiam, cum fuisset aliquamdiu altercatum ibidem inter maiorem cives et presbiteros ac rectores predictos, demum Willelmus maior predictus ibidem, de consensu omnium civium ibidem presencium, dixit et publice declaravit quod omnes cantarie istius civitatis et suburbiorum fuerunt et sunt fundate a civibus et nobilibus istius civitatis, et presbiteri istius civitatis et suburbiorum cantarias habentes, et alii stipendiarii cantarias hujusmodi non habentes, sunt speciales oratores civium, patronorum suorum et magistrorum suorum, a quibus habuerunt et habent hujusmodi cantarias et stipendia, unde vivunt; ideo pertinet civibus, qui nunc sunt heredes dictorum fundatorum, et aliis omnibus habentibus stipendiarios presbiteros, diligenter advertere, ne aliqua nova consuetudo introducatur contra dictos presbiteros que foret ipsis onerosa, et si aliqua questio in hac parte contra ipsos seu eorum aliquem moveatur, eisdem eorum defensioni assistere ut patroni et magistri superius memorati. Insuper dixit idem maior, quod an rectores predicti fundent peticionem suam in exaccione mortuariorum de jure communi ignoravit, sed bene sibi constabat ut dixit et . . . .[1] aliis civibus ibidem presentibus, ut singuli dixerunt, quod temporibus suis de quanto eis constabat nullus rector seu vicarius civitatis aut suburbiorum predictorum habuit mortuaria a presbiteris decedentibus infra suas parochias aut executoribus ipsorum, ut audivit dictus maior aut aliqui cives ibidem presentes, ut dixerunt, a senioribus suis, quod hujusmodi mortuaria per

1—A word has been erased here.

executores presbitorum rectoribus solvebantur, sed temporibus suis, ut eis constabat, et predecessorum suorum, ut ab eis audiverunt, fuerunt dicti presbiteri immunes a prestacione hujusmodi mortuariorum. Constabat insuper dicto maiori, ut dixit, quod temporibus suis quamplures presbiteri hujusmodi decesserunt, et eorum executores absque prestacione alicujus mortuarii libere bona hujusmodi defunctorum ministrabant, nec uncquam, ut dixit, audivit hujusmodi mortuaria peti ab aliquo presbitero, excepto quod quidam dominus Hugo de Saxton, vicarius ecclesie Sancti Martini in Conyngstrete, petebat mortuarium a quodam Thoma del Garth, executore testamenti domini Johannis de Thresk, presbiteri, qui in parochia Sancti Michaelis de Berefrido Ebor' diem suum (*fo.* 158) claudebat extremum. Super qua materia consultus magister Johannes de Waltham, quondam officialis curie Ebor', respondit quod hujusmodi peticio fuit omnino injusta, nec aliquo jure colorata, ymmo omni juri contraria, quia ab ipso dono, ut dixit, sunt clerici ab hujusmodi omnibus exempti. Unde finaliter dictus maior dixit, quod tempore quo ipsum contingeret esse in officio maioritatis non deberet aliqua hujusmodi nova consuetudo, que est verius abusio sive coruptela, de quanto impedire potuit, introduci. Et in sentenciam per maiorem ut prefertur dicti concordarunt singuli cives predicti, per ipsum maiorem seriatim requisiti, et maior et cives predicti dixerunt quod ea, que per ipsos ibidem dicta fuerunt, processerunt de unanimi consilio omnium civium civitatis predicte. Dixerunt insuper iidem maior et cives, quod presbiteros suos predictos in hac parte pro posse suo defenderent, et ipsis in sua defensione assisterent laboribus et expensis. Insuper requisivit ibidem dictus maior presbiteros ibidem presentes an constabat eis de aliquibus presbiteris temporibus suis mortuis, et quid actum fuerat ad exactionem mortuariorum hujusmodi presbiterorum decedencium, dicti vero presbiteri porrexerunt maiori quandam cedulam continentem nomina presbiterorum, qui suis temporibus decesserunt, que cedula inferius recitatur. Et jurarunt dicti presbiteri, quorum aliqui noverunt dictam civitatem per lx. annos, aliqui per amplius tempus, ut dixerunt, quod nuncquam audiverunt quod aliquis presbiterorum, in dicta cedula nominatorum, seu aliquis alius presbiter dicte civitatis, solvebat hujusmodi mortuarium, sed executores ipsorum presbiterorum mortuorum de visa et sciencia sua libere ministrabant in bonis ipsius sine exaccione, solucione, aut prestacione alicujus mortuarii, de quo superius memoratur. Tenor vero cedule continentis nomina presbiterorum defunctorum, de qua superius memoratur, talis est:—De ecclesia Sancti Nicholai in Mikylgate, dominus Robertus Cuke, dominus Willelmus de Ledys, dominus Robertus de Ascham. De ecclesia Sancti Gregorii, dominus Georgius. De ecclesia Sancti Martini in Mikylgate, dominus Johannes de Bergh, dominus Johannes de Kyrtlyngton. De ecclesia Sancte Marie la Alde, dominus Johannes de Horton, dominus Willelmus de Warthill. De ecclesia Omnium Sanctorum in Northstrete, dominus Gregorius de Neuton, dominus Johannes de Staflay, dominus Willelmus de Langtoft, dominus Johannes de Thorp. De ecclesia Sancti Johannis ad pontem Use, dominus Patricius, dominus Nicholaus de Ripon, dominus Thomas de Kyghlay, dominus Robertus Yhedyngham, dominus Willelmus Orre, dominus Johannes de Topclyff. De ecclesia Petri Parvi, dominus Alanus de Corbrygge, dominus Willelmus de Shirbrun, dominus Thomas de Nassington, dominus Johannes de Thirsk, dominus Johannes Gothland. De ecclesia Sancti Sampsonis, dominus Johannes Broune, dominus Johannes de Ottelay, dominus Adam de Norton, dominus Johannes de Ampilforth, dominus Willelmus de Screkyngton, dominus Johannes de Hovyngham, dominus Johannes de Tykyl, dominus Ricardus de Thornton, dominus Johannes de Gayteforde, dominus Johannes de Flasby, dominus Johannes Schirbron. (*fo.* 158, *b.*) De ecclesia Sancti Martini in Conyngstrete, tempore Hugonis de Saxton rectoris, dominus Willelmus de Driffeld, dominus Willelmus de Ottelay, capellanus parochialis, dominus Johannes de Rudscharth, dominus Willelmus de Gyllyng, tempore domini Roberti de Ottelay rectoris, dominus Thomas de Thorpe, in discordia pro mortuario ejusdem, dominus Adam de Munkegate. De ecclesia Sancte Crucis in Fossegate, dominus Johannes Moys, capellanus parochialis, dominus Willelmus de Appilby, dominus Walterus de Sutton, dominus Ricardus de Driffeld, dominus Symon de Barneby. In tempore Johannis de Pykeryng alias dicti Lang' rectoris, dominus Robertus de Merston, dominus Johannes de Queldryk. In tempore Thome de Escrik rectoris, dominus Stephanus de Driffeld, dominus Robertus de Grimston, dominus Willelmus de Thresk. In tempore domini Willelmi de Pikeryng rectoris, dominus Willelmus de Preston, dominus Thomas de Molendinis. Item in tempore Alani de Setrington, dominus Philippus de Cotum, dominus Laurencius de Merston, dominus Adam de Burbrigge. Item in tempore Willelmi de Hedon rectoris, dominus Johannes Baron, dominus Thomas de Hathelsay. Tempore Roberti Wyclyf rectoris, dominus Robertus de Craven, dominus Robertus de Lyland, dominus Robertus de Flaynburgh. In tempore Henrici rectoris ecclesie Sancte Trinitatis in curia regis, dominus Jordanus Gudeale, dominus Robertus de Thurverton, dominus Johannes de Buston, dominus Alexander de Cotyngwyth. In tempore Nicholai de Burton rectoris, dominus Willelmus de Salton, dominus Johannes Marschall, dominus Robertus de Carlton, dominus Johannes de Hutou, dominus Philippus de Heworth. Tempore domini Willelmi de Kyrkton, rectoris ecclesie Sancte Trinitatis in Gotherumgate, dominus Willelmus de Yhucflete, dominus Hugo Botoner. Tempore domini Johannis Lukes rectoris, dominus Robertus Yhedyngham, dominus Johannes Eryome. In tempore domini Johannis de Pykering, rectoris ecclesie Omnium Sanctorum in Usegate, dominus Willelmus de Burton, dominus Johannes de Salton, Thomas Gundall, dominus Robertus Colvell, dominus Walterus de Haxholme, dominus Johannes de Burton, dominus Ricardus de Midilton, dominus Robertus de Neuton, dominus Willelmus de Neuton.

De ecclesia Sancte Elene in Stayngate tempore Thome Langtoft rectoris, dominus Johannes de Sprotton, tempore Thome de Helysbech rectoris, dominus Robertus Dolfyne, tempore domini Ricardi de Eshwra rectoris, dominus Willelmus de Donyngton, dominus Willelmus de Croftes, dominus Willelmus de Thornton, dominus Johannes de Palasgarth, dominus Johannes capellanus, Johannes de Ledys. De ecclesia Sancti Dionisii, dominus Thomas de Midylton, dominus Johannes Broune, dominus Willelmus de Scarburgh. De ecclesia Sancti Olavi dominus Henricus de Hoton, dominus Ricardus de Clyfton. De ecclesia Beate Marie ad portam Castri, dominus Ricardus de Pomfrayt, dominus Thomas de Midilton, dominus Thomas Payne, dominus Willelmus Swaynland, dominus Thomas de Brumpton, dominus Willelmus de Clyff, dominus Symon de Neuwerk, dominus Willelmus de Munkton, dominus (*fo.* 159) Thomas Osgodby, dominus Thomas Graa, magister Johannes Pykeryng. De Berefrido, dominus Radulphus de Stanesby, dominus Johannes de Helperby, dominus Robertus de Farlyngton, dominus Ricardus Anderby, dominus Willelmus Disford. De ecclesia Sancti Wilfridi, dominus Johannes Ulrom, dominus Willelmus de Yhedyngham, dominus Thomas de Burbryg, magister Johannes de Crakynthorp, dominus Willelmus de Topclyff. De ecclesia Sancti Johannis de Pyke, magister Adam de Twyslyngton, dominus Johannes de Barton, dominus Willelmus de Massam. De ecclesia Sancti Andree, dominus Robertus de Cotom, dominus Robertus de Rypon, dominus Robertus de Carlton, dominus Philippus de Hellowe. De capella super pontem Use, dominus Robertus Verdnell, dominus Ricardus de Burton, dominus Willelmus de Bridsall, dominus Johannes Schale, dominus Robertus de Horneby, dominus Thomas de Driffeld, dominus Robertus de Flasby, dominus Stephanus de Gisburn. De ecclesia Sancti Michaelis tempore magistri Johannis de Heryse, dominus Johannes de Brerton, dominus Radulphus de Ledys, dominus Stephanus, dominus Johannes de Ricall, dominus Thomas de Kyghlay. De ecclesia Sancti Clementis, dominus Johannes de Swyne, dominus Ricardus de Boltby, dominus Johannes de Crayke, dominus Ricardus de Neuton, dominus Thomas de Haxby.

Demum maior et cives predicti petebant a prefatis rectoribus quod ipsi permitterent et dimitterent presbiteros predictos stare in pace quo ad premissa et gaudere ea libertate et immunitate quantum ad exaccionem et prestacionem hujusmodi mortuariorum, prout retroactis temporibus fuerant et eos ipsi rectores in adventu suo ad civitatem predictam invenerant, nec aliquam vanam consuetudinem seu exaccionem contra ipsos presbiteros introducere seu inchoare presumerent. Quibus peticionibus ipsi rectores, habita penes se deliberacione, responderunt unanimiter quod pro temporibus suis libenter consenserunt peticionibus predictis. Dixerunt tamen quod noluerunt renunciare alicui juri quod eis vel successoribus suis pretextu hujusmodi concessionis possit competere quovismodo. Et quia dicti presbiteri dixerunt quod quidam dominus Robertus de Ottelay, vicarius ecclesie Sancti Martini in Conyngstrete, quoddam mortuarium accepit, ymmo verius extorsit, a Willelmo de Scausby, executore testamenti domini Thome de Thorp, presbiteri dicte civitatis, ne hujusmodi percepcio seu extorsio esset ipsis presbiteris vel successoribus suis aut juri ipsorum in posterum prejudicialis, petebant deliberacionem et restituccionem ipsius mortuarii, qui dominus Robertus ibidem publice respondit et dixit quod, pretextu hujusmodi percepcioniis noluit nec intendebat futuris temporibus, si ipsum aliquam accionem in hac parte manere contingeret, reportare commodum vel pretendere se esse in possessione percipiendi hujusmodi mortuaria. Unde finaliter maior et concives, habita super premissis pene se deliberacione matura, dixerunt, Volumus et mandamus quod omnia hic coram nobis gesta, acta et recitata inserantur in archivis et libris nostris, ut sit heredibus, posteris et successoribus nostris in exemplum, quod sicut nos non permittimus aliquam consuetudinem vanam nostris temporibus contra presbiteros introduci, sic heredes, successores et posteri nostri sequentes nostra vestigia resistant temporibus suis, ne alique vane consuetudines vel abusiones aut coruptele suis temporibus inducantur, acta sunt hec.

(*fo.* 159, *b.*) Writ to Sheriffs and other ministers of the King not to execute any judgment delivered by John de Beaumont, admiral, against Thomas de Howome and Thomas de Hesill at the suit of Richard Gell ; in accordance with a writ of *supersedeas* of the same date.

Westminster, 5 February, 14 Richard ii. (1391).[1]

Memorandum quod Adam Miles venit in camera consilii xxiiij^{to} die Novembris 14, Ric. ii. (1390) et recognovit se fecisse statum Nicholao de Skelton in feodo contra voluntatem suam de duobus cotagiis cum curtilagiis in Munkgate in suburbio Ebor', ubi dictus Adam non habuit statum nisi ad terminum vite sue

---

1—This case is given in full on folios 130–134b, printed in Vol. I., pp. 224—235.

per curialitatem, etc., et ultra recognovit Willelmum, filium
Rogeri Archibald, esse verum heredem tenementi predicti,
presentibus Willelmo de Helmeslay, tunc maiore (*fo.* 160)
Johanne de Houeden, Thoma Smyth, Johanne de Brathwayt,
Johanne de Stillyngton, Willelmo de Wytton, Willelmo Palmer,
Willelmo de Scauceby, et Thoma de Robton, tunc camerariis et
multis aliis probis hominibus.

*De officio custodis de Thuresdaymarket concesso Johanni de
Dyghton de juramento ejusdem in secunda folio sequenti.*

Memorandum quod 12 Oct., 5 Henr. iv. (1403), concessum
est Johanni de Dyghton, *marsshall*, officium custodis fori de
Thoresdaymarket per maiorem et probos homines consilium
civitatis Ebor', ad instantem rogatum et peticionem dicti domini
regis per litteras suas, et juratus est ad custodiendum fideliter
dictum forum et officium suum debito modo ibidem excercendum,
ac forisfacturas presentandas in camera maioris ut tenetur etc.
Et invenit plegios, videlicet, Johannem Hatlessay seniorem,
Johannem Hatlessay juniorem, Johannem Bukler, et Johannem
Travers, *marsshall*, pro fidelitate sua in officio predicto gerenda
etc.

(*fo.* 160, *b.*) Privilegium Fratrum Minorum civitatis Ebor'.
Letters Patent. 28 July, 33 Edw. iii. (1359).[1]

*Concordia facta inter Johannem Catclogh, et Aliciam de Beleby,
quondam uxorem Johannis de Beleby, et Emmam filiam ejusdem
Alicie :—*

(*fo.* 161). Fait a remembrer que come debat nadgaires
estoit entre Johan Catclogh Deverwyk, *barbour*, dune parte, et
Alice que feust la femme Johan de Beleby Deverwyk, Emmot
sa feile, et Henri de Beverlay Deverwyk, *mercer*, dautre parte,
pur une maheyme que la dite Emmot ad en la destre partie de
son bouche, nepurquant al honour de Dieu et pur nurrir amour et
charite entre veisynes, les parties avauntditz se mistrent en
larbitracion de Johan de Bukland, William de Bolton, Johan de

---

1—Printed by Drake, p. **xlvij**.

Beverlay, et Johan de Halghton Deverwyk, *barbours*, et firent suretee a ester et loialment parfourner daumbe partie la garde et ordinance faitz par les arbitrours avauntditz. Les queux arbitrours, considerantz bone foy et equite dune parte et dautre, ount agardez que final acorde soit entre les parties avauntditz en la fourme qensuit. Ceste assavoir que le dit Johan Catclogh paiera en meyns a la dite Emmot pur amendes du trespas del maheyme avauntdit dys livers desterlinges, et puis apres que acquitances generales de toutz actions personels sount faitz et ensealez daumbe parte ; et outre sount obligez au dit Johan Catclogh les avauntditz Alice, Emmot et Henri, William de Beleby Deverwyk, *mercer*, Johan de Derfeld *marchaund*, et Thomas de Thwayt *goldbeter*, en C. livers, a paier au dit Johan Catclogh en certeine jour, come piert pleinement par une escript obligator ent fait, sur tiel condicion que si[1] le dit Johan Catclogh ne soit enpesche par les ditz Alice, Emmot, et Henri, ne par ascun deaux, ne par le baron de la dite Emmot, en cas qele soit marie en temps avenir, par cause du dit maheyme ou action de trespas, chalange, ou demaund, pur chose fait entre eaux en temps passe. Estre ceo les ditz Alice, Emmot, et Henri sount obligez en une escript obligator de C. livers. Et auxint le dit Johan Catclogh est oblige par soy en une autre escript obligatore de C. livers a les avauntditz arbitrours, sur tiel condicion que les ditz arbitrours ne soient chalangez ne enpeschez en temps avenir par cause de lour dit arbitracion, ne pour nul chose touchaunt lour tretee ou acorde entre les parties avauntditz. Et ensement les ditz Alice et Henri sount obligez a les avauntditz Johan de Derfeld et Thomas de Thwayt, et a chescun deaux singulerment, par trois obligacions chescun de C. livers en suretee pur les sauver et defendre lours heires et lours executours saunz perde et damage vers le avauntdit Johan Catclogh ses heires et ses executours, par cause del avauntdit obligacion de C. livers en quele les ditz William, Johan de Derfeld, et Thomas sount obligez al avauntdit Johan Catclogh. Et pur avoir tesmoigne et evidence de veritee de cest present acorde en temps avenir, les parties avauntditz ount requis et priez au meir de la citee Deverwyk que ceste remembrance soit entree en la chaumbre de counseil

1—Si obscures the sense, possibly the scribe's error.

sur le pount d'ouse en Everwyk, et a lour request ceste remembrance est escript en le blank liver pres de le fyn de le dit liver, le quart jour de Novembre (16 Ric. ii., 1392).

Memorandum quod Gilbertus Johannensson de Werk, ultimo die Februarii, 20 Ric. ii. (139$\frac{2}{7}$) juratus est [ad] essendum fidelis ligeus domini regis et quod diu antea fuit, et invenit Robertum del Hall et Thomam de Wheldall plegios quod ex nunc stabit et fidelis etc.

Memorandum quod Johannis Sym . . s . .[1] *smyth*, de Dunbarre juratus ad sacrosancta Dei evangelia, quarto die Julii . ., Henry iv., amodo esse fidelis ligeus dicti domini regis.

Breve quod debitores non debent recipi apud Fratres pro immunitate ecclesiastica ad excludendum creditorem de debito suo.

(*fo*. 161, *b*.) Ricardus, Dei gracia rex Anglic et Francie et dominus Hibernie, maiori et constabulariis stapule Ebor', salutem. Ex parte Ricardi Kyng de Ebor' nobis est supplicatum ut cum ipse, simul cum Johanne de Lyndesay de Ebor' et pro eodem Johanne, in sexaginta et sex libris Johanni Burdon et Willelmo Sherman ad certum terminum solvendis, juxta formam statuti ejusdem stapule obligatus fuisset; et quia predictus Johannes de Lyndesay terminum solucionis predicte non observavit, nec eisdem Johanni Burdon et Willelmo de debito predicto nondum satisfecit, et ad domum et ecclesiam Fratrum Predicatorum Ebor' se retraxit, et in feodo ecclesie ibidem se tenet, quominus ad solucionem ejusdem debiti compelli potest, predictus Ricardus tanquam plegius ejusdem Johannis de Lyndesay in hac parte captus et prisone nostre commissus est, ibidem quousque predictis Johanni Burdon et Willelmo de debito predicto satisfactum fuerit moraturus; et cum idem Ricardus ad solucionem ejusdem debiti non sufficiat ut accepimus, velimus manus nostras ad compellendum ipsum Johannem de Lyndesay pro solucione ejusdem debiti et deliberacione ipsius Ricardi in hac parte apponere adjutrices. Nos, supplicacioni predicte quatenus justum fuerit annuentes, vobis precipimus quod si ita sit, ut predictum est, tunc assumptis vobiscum maiore civitatis nostre

---

1—Symoneson? faded.

Ebor' ac custodibus placitorum Corone nostre accedatis ad locum, ubi predictus Johannes de Lyndesay se tenet in ecclesia, ipsumque Johannem de Lyndesay, nisi seipsum felonem et de facto de felonia culpabilem coram dictis custodibus cognoverit de recordo, pro qua immunitatem ecclesiasticam de jure habere debeat, ab eodem loco ecclesiastico extrahi, et ad solucionem dicti debiti in exoneracionem ipsius Ricardi in hac parte, quatenus de jure et secundum formam dicti statuti facere poteritis, compellatis et hoc non omittatis. Damus autem prefatis maiori et custodibus tenore presencium in mandatis, quod vobis in execucione premissorum intendentes sint, respondentes, et auxiliantes prout decet. Teste me ipso apud Westmonasterium quinto die Decembris, anno regni nostri quinto decimo (1391).

17 Feb., 15 Ric. ii. (1391-2). Oath of John Carum, weaver, elected keeper of the market in Thursday market.

7 Feb., 22 Ric. ii. (1398-9), also of John Farleham.

Memorandum quod Ricardus de Alne, Robertus de Hoperton, Johannes de Wighton, Johannes de Grandon, et Johannes Hogin, fratres hospitalis Sancti Thome Martiris extra le Mykellyth in suburbio Ebor', unacum Nicholao de Warthill ac aliis fratribus dicti hospitalis die Jovis proximo ante festum Sancti Michaelis Archangeli (26 September, 16 Ric. ii., 1392), protulerunt Margarete, que fuit uxor Thome de Nessefeld, in domo sua in Northstrete in Ebor', viginti libras auri et argenti bone et legalis monete, secundum formam convencionis inter ipsam et dictos fratres de hospitali predicto prelocute et in hac parte concordate, quam pecuniam dicta Margareta recipere recusavit. Et super hoc predictus Nicholaus cum fratribus predictis eodem die coram Roberto Sauvage, tunc maiore, Johanne de Craven et Johanne de Penreth, tunc ballivis, Johanne de Bernardcastell et Johanne de Crayk tunc camerariis, Thoma Gra, Johanne de Berden, Johanne de Ripon, Johanne de Doncastre, Johanne de Stillyngton, Willelmo de Sallay, et multis aliis probis hominibus ibidem presentibus visa et ostensa a . . . . ata . . . . predicto . . . . sufficienter quod dicti fratres parati sunt ad solvendum dictam pecuniam . . . . prefate partes . . . . concordate sunt et pecunia predicta soluta est.

(*fo.* 162). Memorandum quod Johannes de Calthorn, *armurer*, et Perot de Casawas de Vasconia venerunt in camera coram Roberto Sauvage, tunc maiore, et aliis probis hominibus, xiij die Decembris. Et dictus Perot juravit ad sancta Dei Evangelia, quod a tempore quo completum fuerat tempus apprenticiagii ipsius Perot, a medio quadragesime ultimo preterito, quod ipse Perot nichil extunc emebat, vendebat, seu ministrabat ad opus ipsius Johannis, nec in servicio suo stetit, aut extunc dictus Johannes aliquid pro ipso Perot aut pro factis suis in nullo respondere tenetur, sed cciam dictus Perot a servicio predicti Johannis exnunc ut extunc totaliter sit exoneratus. Anno xiiij (7 March, 139$\frac{0}{1}$).

Memorandum quod xx° die Marcii anno regni regis Ricardi secundi etc., Bertinus Longespy comparuit coram maiore in camera cum quadam domisella Katerina filia sua, et peciit eam sibi deliberari ut filiam et serventiem suam[1] unde ipsa examinata fatebatur, quod nemo haberet jus servitutis in eam, nec ea alicui servire tenetur, nec cum aliquo commorare tenetur nisi dicto patre suo, et cum eo gratis recessit. Queritur cujus etatis sit, et dictum fuit quod isto die 'est etatis xj annorum.

Demise of a house with a chamber towards the Tofts, in the holding of the late John de Essheton, to Richard Gardyner for a term of ten years from Whitsunday (2 June), 1392, at a rent of 6 *s.* a year.

Clausula testamenti Henrici le Scrop', militis.

In nomine Patris et Filii et Spiritus Sancti, Amen. Ego, Henricus le Scrop miles, in bona memoria existens condo testamentum meum in hunc modum. In primis lego animam meam suo Creatori etc., prout in dicto testamento continetur cum quadam clausula in dicto testamento contenta que sequitur inferius in hec verba. Item lego Johanni filio meo unum hospicium meum in Ebor', situatum infra cimiterium Sancti Martini Conyngstrete etc. Datum in manerio meo de Clyfton super Joram in vigilia Sancti Thome apostoli 15 Ric. ii. (20 Dec., 1391).

1—Filia et serviens in MS.

Receipt by Robert Wrenche of York, attorney of John de
Bolton, abbot of the monastery of S. Mary of Fourneys, and the
convent, for 10 *l*., from Robert de Eure paid by hand of Robert
Barry, son of Robert Barry, and Thomas de Neuton, clerk of the
said Robert de Eure ; being payment for Michaelmas term,
17 Richard ii. (1393), in part of 200 *l*., in which Robert de Eure
is bound to the said abbot and convent by statute merchant.

(*fo*. 162, *b*.) Memorandum quod Thomas del Syker, *tapiter*,
venit in camera maioris coram Willelmo de Selby, tunc maiore,
Thoma del Garth, Willelmo de Birkheued, et Johanne de Topcliff,
tunc camerariis, ac aliis probis hominibus, xviij die Januarii
12 Ric. ii. (1388-9), et recognovit se ad solvendum communitati
Ebor' xl *s*., si ipse amodo nominet unum verbum vocatum *Pissyng-
peny*, in obprobrium textorum Ebor', quod legitime probari
poterit.

Elyas de Ulskelf de Ebor', *wever*, venit in camera coram
Thoma Smyth, tunc maiore Ebor', et aliis probis hominibus ibidem
tunc presentibus, et recognovit se solvere xiij *s*. iiij *d*. videlicet
vj *s*. viij *d*. ad opus communitatis Ebor', et vj *s*. viij *d*. aldermanno
artificii textorum Ebor' ad opus firme domini Regis de dicto
artificio debite, si dictus Elyas erga dictum aldermannum et
artificium suum predictum in solucione et collectione firme
domini Regis, aut in aliis imposicionibus in dicto artificio racionabiliter imponendis seu levandis, ammodo rebellis inveniatur.

Memorandum quod penultimo die mensis Februarii, videlicet,
die tunc vicesimo septimo die ejusdem mensis, anno Domini
millesimo ccc^{mo} nonagesimo et regni Regis Ricardi secundi post
conquestum Anglie quarto decimo, congregatis in camera maioris
super pontem Use in Ebor' Roberto Sauvage, tunc maiore, Johanne
de Houeden, Johanne de Doncastr', tunc ballivis, Johanne de
Ripon, Roberto del Gare, Roberto Warde, Johanne de Bolton,
Willelmo de Rumlay, Hugone Straunge et multis aliis probis
hominibus, inter quos presens personaliter interfuit Ranulphus
del See, filius Ricardi del See de Ebor', unde ipsis vero tractantibus
et sequentibus, venit quidam Robertus de Ellerbek, *mercer*, nudis
pedibus et capite discooperto, in cameram predictam coram
dictis maiore, ballivis et aliis probis hominibus supradictis, et
coram dicto Ranulpho del See genuflectendo se prosternens, et

humiliter ac lacrimando prefatum Ranulphum exoravit in hec verba dicens, Precor te, Ranulphe, pro amore Domini nostri Jesus Christi, qui precioso sanguine suo in cruce humanum genus redemit, ut perdones et michi remittas mortem Ricardi del See patris tui. Ad quod v[erbum] prefati maior, ballivi et ceteri probi homines rogaverunt simul cum ipso Roberto de Ellerbek prefatum Ranulpum ut [pro] amore Dei remitteret ei mortem predicti Ricardi patris sui. Qui quidem Ranulphus anima motus se adversus Roberto flendo, dixit, ad reverenciam Dei et peticionem istorum reverendorum virorum et pro salute anime dicti Ricardi, remitto et relaxo tibi imperpetuum mortem predicti Ricardi del See, patris mei.

(*fo.* 163.) Trinity Sunday before Corpus Christi, 50 Edward iii., (8 June, 1376). Edward, prince of England and Wales, first born son of Edward iii. died at . . . .[1] and was buried at Canterbury.

Sunday before the feast of the Nativity of St. John the Baptist 51 Edward iii. (21 June, 1377), Edward iii. died at Shene near London. He reigned 50 years and 21 weeks. Buried at Westminster on Sunday before the feast of the translation of St. Thomas, archbishop of Canterbury and Martyr (5 July).[2]

Cristendome.

(*fo.* 163, *b.*) Memorandum quod tempore Johannis de Quixlay et sociorum suorum ballivorum anno vj^{to} in curia coram Simone de Quixlay, tunc maiore, et ballivis predictis capta fuerunt pro vadiis de Roberto de Cristendome pro taxacione sua de dupplici taxacione, videlicet, quinquaginta marcarum, videlicet, v *s.*, unum lotorium pendens et unum catabrum, appreciata ad v *s.* per Rogerum Cooke de Fossebrigg et Thomam Cook de Coppergate die Sabbati proximo ante Purificacionem anno predicto (31 Jan., 1382-3) in curia predicta.

Memorandum quod cum quedam discordia nuper mota fuerat inter Robertum de Waghen, *wright*, ex una parte, et Johannem de Duffeld, *pelter*, Johannem de Calton, pistorem, et

1—A space is left in the MS.
2—Printed in Letters from the Northern Registers, Rolls Series, p. 418.

Robertum de Malton, *littester*, ac homines de illis tribus artificiis suis, ex parte altera, de edificacione et reparacione cujusdam domus super les Toftes ad hospitandum paginas suas de Corpore Christi, tamen sub hac forma concordati sunt, videlicet, quod predictus Robertus de Waghen faciet edificare et reparare competenter dictam domum ad hospitandum tres paginas predictas infra eandem citra festum Pentecostes, 10 Ric. ii. (26 May, 1387) per visum maioris et proborum civitatis ad electionem dicti maioris, qui tunc temporis fuit. Et ad hoc bene et fideliter tenendum et perimplendum dictus Robertus de Waghen invenit Johannem de Ruddestan de Ebor', *barker*, plegium et manucaptorem, qui quidem Johannes obligavit se et executores suos ad faciendum domum predictam, si dictus Robertus in edificacione et reparacione domus predicte defecerit, quod absit.

Memorandum quod xxix° die Augusti xviij Ric. ii., Willelmo de Helmeslay tunc maiore, presentibus Thoma C . . . . ., Roberto de Howom, Johanne de Berden, Willelmo de Sallay, Johanne de Houeden, et multis aliis probis hominibus in camera congregatis, concessum est Thome de Barneby, capellano, ex consensu eorundem presentacionem cantarie primo vacature donacioni maioris spectanti.

(*fo.* 164). Memorandum quod Simon de Durem pelliparius venit gratis in camera coram Willelmo de Selby, tunc maiore Ebor', xiiij die Julii, 11 Ric. ii. (1387), [et] juravit, quod ammodo non habeat neque faciat aliquod opus de pellura nisi habeat secum unum hominem sufficientem ad operandum pelluram competenter, et omne opus pellure quod fecerit ostendet scrutatoribus.[1]

Memorandum quod Willelmus de Seleby, tunc maior Ebor', deliberavit Stephano de Yotton de Tollerton c *s.*, quos magister Thomas de Birkton dedit sub certa forma ad inveniendum iiij^{or} torcheas circa Corpus Christi, in eodem festo ardentes in processione viij° die Maii, 11 Ric. ii. (1388) et dictus Stephanus solvet ad opus luminis predicti vj *s.* viij *d.* usque Purificacionem proximam, et predictus Willelmus de Seleby plegius pro pecunia predicta.

[1]—This entry is crossed through and in the margin is written **vacat**.

Receipt by Nicholas Charwod, attorney of John att More, citizen of Norwich, executor of John Anable of Salle, for 40 s. from John Crayk of York, mercer, in full payment of 60 s. which he owed to the said John Anable. York, 14 November, 16 Ric. ii. (1392).

Plegii pro Roberto de Ledes, custode pontis de Fosse, Willelmus . . . . eg Ricardus . . . . et admissus est ad dictum officium die lune . . . . in crastino Sancte Katerine Virginis anno regni Regis Henrici quinto (26 November, 1417).

(fo. 164, b.) Demise of "fossatum cum gutta inter les Holmes et causeiam apud le Neutour," with the fishing to John de Gotteshalve, fisher, from Whitsunday, 1388, for a term of five years, at 6 s. 8 d. a year.

Friday, 9 Feb., 14 Ric. ii. (1390-1) admission of Simon Vasour as sergeant of the chamber. Sureties for good behaviour, William de Kepewyk and Gilbert de Twys.

Memorandum quod xiiij die Aprilis, xiiij Ric. ii. (1391) Willelmus de Willesthorp, unus adminstratorum bonorum que fuerunt Johannis de Gysburn de Ebor', venit in camera cum Simone de Quixlay et Willelmo de Palmour, executoribus testamenti Ricardi de Wardeby, quondam civis Ebor', coram Roberto Sauvage, tunc maiore Ebor', Willelmo de Clyveland et Edmundo Grover, tunc camerariis, et optulit ibi xx^{ti} marcas in auro, quas prefatus Johannes de Gysburn, unus executorum testamenti predicti Ricardi de Wardeby, habuit in custodia sua ad emendum quandam perpetuitatem ad opus pauperum in le Mesendu super pontem. Et ex consensu parcium predictarum dicte viginti marce liberate sunt dictis maiori et camerariis ad ponendum in usum predictum. Et super hoc et sub hac forma posite sunt in thesauro, et sub eadem condicione dicta pecunia deliberata est Ricardo de Caunton et Thome de Staynlay custodienda. Thomas de Staynlay solvit thesauro in partem xij marcas vj s. viij d. iiij die Junii, 5 Henry iv. (1404). Item v li. in plenam solucionem.

A touz ceaux etc. le Meir etc., saluz etc. Pur ceo que un Johan Gardyner de Scoce jadys chaumbirlayn au count de Douglas veynt devant nous, en notre chaumbre sur le pount de Ouse, en la dite citee Deverwyk, et plusours autres honestes persones ovesque lui, le vynt et tierce jour doctobre, 15 Ric. ii.

(1391) et illeoques humblement requist nous et prit, pur lamour de Dieu et en oeuvre de charitee, que nous voerasmes prendre sa serement pur estre loial lege homme a nostre tres redotee seignour le roi. Et nous considerantz la persone du dit Johan, et sa bone volente al honour de Dieu, et a la request des bones gentz, qi veyndrent ovesque le dit Johan, et a sa humble prier, nous le chargeasmes sur les seintz Evaungeles que desormes il serroit loial lege homme a nostre dit seignour le roi, et ceo il graunta, et a ceo loialement tenir pour touz jours, saunz fraude ou mal engyne, il jura sur les ditz seintz Evaungeles, et en oeuvre de charitee a recorder veritee nous en avons fait cestez noz presentz lettres patentz ensealez du seal del office de maiaraltee de la citee avauntdite. Escriptz a Everwyk le jour et lan susditz.

Sachent touz gentz qe nous avons pris serement de J. de H. quil serra loial lege homme a nostre seignour le Roy Henry et ses successoures, roys Dengleterre, et esterra a les loys et les gardera a son poair a terme de sa vie. Et a ceo bien et loialment faire J. et R. soient devenuz plegges etc.[1]

(*fo*. 165). Release by Thomas de Hemmyngbrough, chaplain, one of the executors of Gilbert, late vicar of Ilkelay, to William Barneby of York, merchant, of all personal actions. York, 23 Dec., 10 Henry iv. (1408).

Similar release to the same by Thomas de Hemyngburgh one of the executors (not here called chaplain). York 1 January, 10 Henry iv. (1408-9).

Grant by Thomas Horle of York, "*peuderer*," to Richard London and John Clerk, citizens and mercers of York, of all his goods. Witnesses, Henry Wyman, mayor, John Moreton, Robert Gaunt, sheriffs, Master John Levyngton, William del Both. York, the feast of S. Peter's chains, 10 Henry iv. (1 August, 1409).

Release by William Norton, citizen of York, to William de Bolton, sheriff of York, of all personal action. York, 24 January . . .[2] Henry iv.

(*fo*. 165, *b*.) Release by John de Kenlay the younger to Robert de Middelton, citizen and merchant of York, and Katharine

---

1—Two lines are illegible.
2—Faded.

his wife, in tail, with remainder to the right heirs of Hamo de
Hessay, of a tenement in Patrikpole in York, formerly of Hamo
de Hessay, late citizen of York, extending in breadth from the
highway of Patrikpole and from a tenement late of William de
Santon, to Fenkelstrete, and in length from the street of Benet
place before, to a tenement formerly of Adam Colyer behind.
Witnesses, John de Bolton, mayor, Robert Gare, John Northeby,
sheriffs, Henry Wyman, Robert Holme, William Bowys, John
Hewyk, Richard Soureby, Richard Russell, Thomas Brasebrigg,
John Threpeland. York, 12 May, 11 Henry iv. (1410).
Acknowledged before the mayor, Richard Soureby, Richard
Russell, John Threpland, Thomas Bracebrig, Thomas Roderham,
Robert Louth, Richard Neuland, William Neuland and Richard
Spencer, 24 May, 11 Henry iv. (1410).

Bond by the same to the same, for 100 *l*. to be paid upon
the feast of the Nativity of S. John the Baptist next. 11 May,
11 Henry iv. (1410). Seal. To be void unless the said John
alienate the lands, which he holds for term of life, or the lands
which he inherited after the death of Katharine Kenlay, his
mother, which late belonged to Hamo Hessay, except in urgent
necessity, if he be taken prisoner in war or if he kill a man.
Acknowledged as above.

(*fo.* 166). Hoc scriptum indentatum testatur quod cum
Henricus, filius Nicholai Appilby de Ebor', se senserit erga
Robertum Ottelay, clericum, gravatum, prout per quandam
cedulam per prefatum Henricum erga predictum Robertum
monstratam plenius apparet, cujus tenor sequitur in hec verba :
En primes la ou le dit Henry vendist a dit Robert un tenement
in Conyngstrete, 15 Ric. ii. (1391-2) en le temps que Robert
Sauvage[1] fuist meir pur c marcz et c *s* de annuel rent issaunt a dit
Henry a terme de sa vie, de quele somme le dit Henry ne fuist
unqes paie forsqes de xl marcz, nient obstant que ledit Robert
promitta par sa foy que ledit Henry serroit prestament paie de
les c marcz suisdites, des quelx xl marcz le dit Robert prist du
dit Henry pur certeyns munumentz, quelx Andrew Monymaker et
sa femme, soer au dit Henry, mistrent en gage a Johan Hoser
Deverwyk pur ij marcz. Auxint que iiij ans apres en le dit

temps, quaunt Thomas Stanlay[1] fuist meir, et le dit Henry demaunda son annuyte, le dit sire Robert ne lui vorroit graunter sa annuyte de c s. devaunt que le dit Henry soy oblige par son fait qil ne serroit james espense come le dit fait pleynement purport. Auxint le dit Henry mist en gage a dit Sire Robert xx s. par an de la annuyte de c s. pur ix *li*., quel annuyte de xx s. le dit sire Robert ad ew par xj ans. Auxint le dit Henry mist en gage a dit sire Robert un annuel rent de vj s. viij d. pur 1 s. le quel annuel rent il ad ew par ix ans. Auxint le dit sire Robert ad diverses neccessores du dit Henry, quelx sount en le tenement de Conyngstrete suisdite, a la valu de c s. Auxint le dit Robert fist par son consiel et mayntenaunce le dit Henry estre arestu al suyt de partie, a graund damage et vilany a lui et a touz ses bienvilantz.

Super quibus dictus Robertus et Henricus se posuerunt in arbitracione et ordinacione quatuor proborum et legalium hominum per partes predictas electorum, videlicet magistri Ricardi Arnald, commissarii officialis curie Ebor', magistri Willelmi Pelleson, receptoris archiepiscopi Ebor', Willelmi Selby et Thome Hesyll, civium Ebor'. Qui quidem arbitratores (*fo.* 166, *b*.) primo examinaverunt cedulam predictam ac omnia in eadem contenta minime vera et nullius reputacionis, tamen ad excitacionem et instantem rogatum predictorum arbitratorum, predictus Robertus ex sua mera voluntate concessit eidem Henrico quendam annuum redditum xx s., percipendum de omnibus terris et tenementis suis in Ebor', prout in quodam scripto indentato inde confecto plenius apparet. Et predictus Henricus, in presencia predictorum arbitratorum, non coartatus nec min tus,[2] sed spontanea voluntate sua concessit se, si gracia divina mediante se contigerit aliquam mulierem ducere in uxorem, infra quatuordecim dies tunc proximo sequentes post sponsalia solemnpnizata ac celebrata reliberare ac sursum reddere prefato Roberto scriptum predictum annui redditus, cum omnibus denariis medio tempore a data presencium inde receptis. Et ad hoc fideliter perimplendum se sub juramento super sancta Evangelia obligavit sub pena

---

1—Robert Savage was Mayor in 7, 14, and 15 Ric. II. and Thomas de Staynlay in 18 Ric. II.

2—Minatus with a omitted ?

xx *li*. solvendarum prefato Roberto, si defecerit in aliquo articulo prenotato. Et ulterius predicti arbitratores consideraverunt ac arbitraverunt, quod si dictus Henricus aliqua verba inhonesta seu contumeliosa, dolum aut dedecus de prefato Roberto loquatur per se aut per alium ex suo consensu, quod probari poterit, quod tunc idem Henricus solvet prefato Roberto xx libras sterlingorum. Ad que omnia et singula prescripta ex parte dicti Henrici perficienda, tenenda et perimplenda, ut supradictum est, predictus Henricus in presencia predictorum arbitratorum ac aliorum fidedignorum ad sacrosancta Dei Evangelia corporale prestitit juramentum. In cujus rei testimonium arbitratores predicti partibus hujus scripti indentati sigilla sua apposuerunt, quarum una pars remanet erga predictum Robertum, et altera erga predictum Henricum. Ac eciam idem scriptum irrotulatur tam in camera maioritatis civitatis Ebor' quam in scaccario domini archiepiscopi apud Ebor', in fidem et testimonium premissorum. Datum apud Ebor' quintodecimo die Decembris anno Domini millesimo cccc decimo.

Grant by John Helmeslay, son and heir of William Helmeslay, late citizen and merchant of York, by licence of the King,[1] for the souls of the said William and of Alice, his father and mother, to Sir George Helmeslay and his successors, chaplains at the altar of the Holy Trinity in the church of S. Sampson, York, of four messuages in the city and suburbs, viz.: a messuage in Patrikpole now in the tenure of John Brome, extending in width between land of William Horneby of York and land of William Alne, and in length from the high street of Patrikpole before to land of Robert de Middelton of York, mercer, behind; a messuage in Patrikpole now in the tenure of William Haryngton, between a tenement of the prior and convent of Newburgh and land of Robert del Gare; a messuage in Gotherumgate between land of the prior and convent of Malton and the King's gutter or ditch; and a messuage without le Mikellyth in the suburb of York between land of the grantor and land of . . . .[2] Askham; also a yearly rent of 14 *s*. from a tenement in Girdelergate, now

1—Licence in mortmain granted 28 May, 1405, Yorkshire Chantry Surveys, Surt. Soc. xcii, p. 559.
2—A space is left here.

inhabited by John Byrdesall, patoner. The grantor and his heirs shall present to the said chantry within a month of vacancy, and in their default, presentation shall remain successively to twelve parishioners, and to the mayor and commonalty. The chaplain shall celebrate and say *Placebo* and *Dirige* daily for the souls of William and Alice, except on the feasts of Christmas and Easter, and shall receive 8 *s.* by the year. The obits of William and Alice shall be celebrated by eight chaplains, each receiving 2 *d.* If there be not this number of chaplains celebrating constantly in the church, the chaplain shall procure others for the obits, and he shall pay to the clerk for ringing the bells 4 *d.*, to the under clerk 2 *d.*, and 4 *d.* to the town-crier (campanario civitatis Ebor') for ringing a bell through the city, as the manner is, to excite people to pray for the souls of William and Alice; and shall provide two wax candles, which shall burn on their tomb during mass of the dead.[1] Witnesses, Henry Wyman, mayor, Robert de Kirkeby, John Usburn, sheriffs, Nicholas Blakburn, John de Bolton, mercer, Robert de Louth, Robert Ledes, John Hewyk, Thomas Doncastre, William Wynkburn, Thomas Esyngwald, William Wortelay, William del Both, clerk, citizens of York. York, 12 September, 8 Henry iv. (1407).

(*fo.* 169). 12 February, 12 Henry iv. (1410–11). Writ of *supersedeas* to the sheriffs of the city of York upon a writ from the exchequer dated 3 June, 7 Henry iv. (1406), ordering them to levy 20 *li.* from the goods and chattels of the citizens and commonalty of that city within their bailiwick, which were due to Joan, queen of England, the King's consort, being part of a fine of 200 *li.* which she had made with him for all the liberties, franchises, etc., surrendered into his hand.

(*fo.* 169, *b.*) Release by William de Blenkowe, son and heir of Thomas de Blenkowe, to William de Stapilton of Edenale, of the manor of Jonby, co. Cumberland, and the hamlet of Kesclyff, co. Westmorland. Witnesses, Nicholas Blakburn, mayor, Peter Bukcy, Thomas Essyngwald, sheriffs, William de Selby, John de Brathwayt, John Blakburn, Thomas Bracebrigg. York, 10 April, 13 Henry iv. (1412).

1—Seal also common seal of the city and seal of the chaplains.

ASSIZE OF NOVEL DISSEISIN (1413/4)

Grant by Robert de Middelton of York, mercer, to William Laysyngby, John Bolton of York, merchant, master John de Carleton and John Bolton, forester, of all his goods. Witnesses, Nicholas Blackburn, mayor, Thomas Essyngwald, Peter Buksy, sheriffs, William Bowes, merchant, John Hewyk, Robert Jarum. York, 29 March, 13 Henry iv. (1412).

(*fo.* 170). Will of William Strykell son and heir of Roger Strykell, citizen of York. 12 September, 1 Henry v. (1413).

(*fo.* 170, *b.*) [1] . . . . ¯

(*fo.* 171.) Robertus Tirwhit et socii sui justiciarii domini regis ad quandam assisam nove disseisine quam Willelmus de Fulthorp, miles, Walterus Tailboys, miles, Alexander del Lound, miles, et Johannes de Leuesham, clericus, arrainiaverunt coram nobis versus Gerardum Salvayn, chivaler, et alios in brevi originali domini regis inde contentos, de tenementis in civitate Ebor' capiendam assignatis, vicecomitibus ejusdem civitatis, salutem. Ex parte domini regis vobis precipimus quod venire faciatis coram nobis apud quendam locum ubi Crux stat, in regia via, que ducit a civitate Ebor' versus villam de Overfulford, juxta pontem ligneum ex australi parte ejusdem pontis in confinio civitatis predicte et comitatus Ebor', die Martis in septimana Pasche proximo futuro assisam predictam,[2] in omnibus secundum vim, formam et effectum ejusdem cum summonicione et attachiamento et omnibus aliis adminiculis assisam illam tangentibus plenarie executam et arraiatam. Proviso semper quod attachiamentúm inde fiat per xv dies ante prefatum diem Martis. Et ita vos habeatis in premissis pro vestrum defectu assisa predicta a . . . . remaneat capienda. Et habeatis ibi tunc dictum breve originale assise predicte, et hoc mandatum in omnibus prout decet arraiatum. Datum apud Ebor' xv die Marcii 1 Henry v. (1413-4).

Copia carte Johannis Hamerton, clerici capelle Sancti Willelmi super pontem Use, de camera per eum edificanda in parte boriali ejusdem capelle.

1—A writ from Henry IV. almost illegible, the names of Tailboys, Alexander del Lound, Gerard Salvayn and John Halyden are quite clear.
2—Some omission here.

Omnibus Cristi fidelibus, ad quos presentes litere pervenerint, maior et communitas civitatis Ebor' salutem in Domino sempiternam. Noveritis nos unanimi assensu et consensu nostris concessisse et licenciam dedisse Johanni de Hamerton, clerico capelle Sancti Willelmi super pontem Use in Ebor', ad faciendum et sumptibus suis propriis de novo edificandum quandam cameram seu mansionem sibi decentem in parte boriali dicte capelle. Tenendam et habendam eandem mansionem eidem Johanni ad totam vitam suam, et post ejus decessum, uni honesto assignato suo ad totam vitam ipsius assignati cum libero introitu et exitu ad eandem absque impedimento aliquali. Et ulterius, si contingat prefatum Johannem aut assignatum suum in vita sua dare et assignare prefatis maiori et communitati terras, tenementa, redditus seu possessiones sufficiencia ad sustentacionem unius idonei capellani, in predicta capella divina celebraturi pro anima dicti Johannis et animabus benefactorum suorum atque omnium fidelium defunctorum, ad electionem maioris qui pro tempore fuerit, et secundum composicionem ejusdem Johannis aut assignati sui inde legitime faciendam, quod tunc predicta mansio cum pertinenciis suis sit et manet eidem capellano et successoribus suis capellanis pro mansione sua ibidem habenda imperpetuum. In cujus rei testimonium sigillum commune civitatis predicte nos presenti scripto nostro fecimus apponi. Datum apud Ebor' xx^{mo} die Januarii anno Domini millesimo cccc^{mo} terciodecimo et 1 Henr. v. R. BURTON.

(*fo.* 171, *b.*) Release by Thomas de Ledes of Westwyk, son of Robert de Ledes of York, to Thomas Emlay of York, tailor, of all actions real and personal, concerning lands which Nicholas Blakburn the elder, citizen and merchant of York, has by enfeoffment of William Nessefeld of Hewyk and Henry Doncaster of York, skinner, in the city and suburb of York, and in Langtoft super le Wald, which were late of Agnes de Wandesford of York, grandmother of the said Thomas de Ledes. York, 14 May, 3 Henry V. (1415).

Similar release by the same, to Beatrice de Remyngeton, prioress of Clementhorp by York. Same date.

(*fo*. 172). Similar release by the same, to Agnes de Ledes, formerly wife of the said Robert de Ledes, father of the grantor. Same date.

Letters of attorney by the same, appointing Nicholas Blakburn the elder, citizen and merchant of York, attorney in all actions concerning the said lands. Same date.

(*fo*. 172, *b*). Memorandum quod xiij die Junii, xiij Henry iv. (1412), insinuatum et conquestum fuit Nicholao Blakburn, maiori, et probis hominibus civitatis Ebor', quod portitores civitatis negligenter et nimis juste fecerunt, et (*sic*) opus suum in portacione sua, et noluerunt portare summagia sive pondera sua ad loca consueta pro stipendio et salario suis competentibus prout continetur in registro maioratus et communitatis dicte civitatis, etc. Ac eciam insinuatum et conquestum fuit dicto domino maiori et probis hominibus, quod nonnulli portitores ceperunt bona et mercandizas tam indigenorum quam[1] forinsecorum in aqua Use, et cum eisdem bonis sepissime fugam fecerunt, et alia enormia dicte communitati intulerunt ad grave dampnum etc. Et super hoc iidem dominus maior et probi homines cum consilio jurisperitorum constituerunt Willelmum Lekenfeld, porter, Johannem Lund, Johannem Chartres, porters, Robertum Proktour, Robertum Russell, et Thomam Stubbes, portours, quasi principales portitores et supervisores juratos, quod nullus portitor ministrabit nec amodo illo officio utetur nisi sufficiens inventus fuerit ad respondendum pro opere suo et actibus suis ad solvendum et restituendum recte et juste de bonis et denariatibus sibi traditis; et quod omnes portitores recipiant grana, carbones et omnia alia bona per sufficientem mensuram; et quod portent summagia sua ad loca constituta et ordinata prout intitulatur in dictis registris, secundum consuetudinem dicte civitatis. Et ad ista perimplenda etc. predicti portitores superius nominati super sancta Dei Evangelia corporaliter fidem suam attribuerunt. Testibus, etc.

1—In right hand margin, " portars," and " Constitucio de portoribus, et est alia in registro majore quasi in medio folio xxxij et alia in vjti folio hujus registri post principium," is written.

Chronica H. Scrope decollacio.[1]

12 February, 12 Henry IV. (1410-11) Licence in mortmain[2] to John de Munkgate, Nicholas de Holm, William de Strensall and Thomas Carnaby, clerks, to grant a messuage called le Tylehouse, in the suburbs of York, which they had had of the grant and feoffment of Joan, widow of Roger de Well, citizen of York, held of the King in burgage, as was all the city of York, and worth 6 s. 8 d. a year, as had been ascertained by an inquisition taken before John de Bolton, mayor of the city and king's escheator in the same, to the warden of the habitation of the vicars of the cathedral church of S. Peter called *le Bederne*, and to the same vicars, in part satisfaction of another licence in mortmain granted on 22 May, 19 Richard ii. (1396) authorizing them to acquire lands, tenements, and rents to the yearly value of 40 marks.

Libertates archiepiscopi Ebor' confirmate de falsis monetariis allocate per W. Alne, maiorem, W. Ormeshed, Ricardum Spencer, vicecomites civitatis et alios.

[3]Willelmus, archiepiscopus Ebor', summonitus fuit ad respondendum domino regi de placito quo waranto clamat habere duos cuneos monetales in civitate domini regis Ebor', sine licencia et voluntate domini regis etc. Et archiepiscopus per attornatum suum venit et dicit quod ipse clamat predictos cuneos tali waranto, quod ipse et omnes predecessores sui a tempore a quo non est memoria fuerunt in seisina habendi duos cuneos, et ad maiorem evidenciam dicit, quod tempore Henrici regis, filii conquestoris, quidam Odo, vicecomes Ebor', impedivit quendam Gerardum, tunc archiepiscopum Ebor', quominus habere potuit placita in curia sua de monetariis et judicia (*fo.* 174, *b.*) eorundem, per quod idem archiepiscopus, senciens se esse gravatum, accessit ad predictum dominum regem, et ostendit seisinam suam et jus ecclesie sue sancti Petri Eboracensis, per quod idem dominus rex mandavit predicto vicecomiti literam suam patentem in hec verba :—Henricus, Dei gracia rex Anglorum, vicecomiti et R. filio Gizonis salutem. Volo et precipio ut Gerardus, Eboracensis

(*fo.* 173). 1—Printed by Drake. App. xvi.
(*fo.* 174). 2—Pat. R. 19 Ric. II., pt. 2, m. 8.
3—Printed in *Placita de Quo Waranto*, p. 198.

archiepiscopus, in terris ecclesiarum suarum et in omnibus terris Eboracensis archiepiscopatus placita sua in curia sua habeat de monetariis suis et de latronibus et de omnibus aliis, et omnes leges et consuetudines suas et ecclesiarum suarum de omnibus habeat, sicut et Thomas archiepiscopus melius habuit tempore patris vel fratris mei ; et nova statuta mea de judiciis sive de placitis latronum et falsorum monetariorum exequatur et faciat per suam propriam instanciam in curia sua, nec ipse aliquid perdat vel ecclesia sua pro novis statutis meis, sed ea, ut dixi, in curia sua faciat per propriam suam instanciam secundum statuta mea. Teste R. Cestrensi episcopo apud Wyntoniam in Pascha.[1] Predicta clausula continetur et confirmatur inter alias libertates et franchesias, venerabili in Christo patri et domino, domino Henrico Bowet, Eboracensi archiepiscopo, per dominum Henricum quintum, Dei gracia regem Anglie et Francie et dominum Hibernic illustrem, concessas. Unde quidam Johannes Esyngwald dicti archiepiscopi in palacio suo Ebor' monetarius, et coram Willelmo Alne, maiore, Willelmo Ormersheued et Ricardo Spenser, vicecomitibus civitatis Ebor', accusatus super eo quod ferramenta sua ad cuneanda in ipsa civitate private fabricari fecit, visa carta confirmatoria libertatum dicti domini archiepiscopi, examini et judicio ejusdem archiepiscopi quo ad hunc articulum traditur, et ipse et manucaptores sui, quos dictis vicecomitibus in hoc casu invenit, liberantur indempnes.

(*fo.* 175). 12 July, 3 Henry v. (1415). Writ to the Mayor of York, the King's escheator there, Nicholas Blakeborn, senior, John Craven, Robert Holm, Thomas de Santon, and John de Bolton, citizens of York, to inquire whether John de Stokton, late citizen of York, who was said to have died without an heir, died seised of a messuage in Walmegate, in the parish of St. Denis, with three shops and solars built thereon in front, in breadth between land late of William de Dalton and Joan his wife, on the one side, and the land of William Bulmer and Katherine his wife, which had belonged to John de Neuton of York, cook, on the

1—R. de Limesey, bishop of Chester, 1086-1117, removed the see from Chester to Coventry, 18 April, 1102. If he changed his title at the same time the date of the charter is brought within narrow limits, between 1100 the date of the translation of Gerard from Hereford to York, and that of the removal of the see from Chester to Coventry.

other, and in length from the king's highway of Walmgate in front to the water of Fosse behind ; and of another messuage in Girdlergate, lying in breadth between the land lately belonging to John de Langton, and the land of John Gervas, and in length from the king's highway in front to the land lately belonging to John de Langton behind. Stokton was further said to have devised them to St. Denis's church without having obtained a licence in mortmain. Return to be made into the exchequer at Michaelmas. Witness, W. Lasynby, Westminster. "By a certain schedule delivered at the exchequer which is amongst the bills of Trinity Term, third year."

Answer to the said writ :—Inquisition taken at York on Wednesday after the Nativity of the B.V.M., 3 Henry v. (11 September, 1415), before William de Alne, mayor and eschaetor, Nicholas Blakebourne, senior, John Craven, Robert Holme, Thomas Santon, and John de Bolton, by the oath of Thomas Roderham, Richard Newland, William Lyons, *sadeler*, William Barton, *skynner*, Thomas Sharrowe, Thomas Holbek, William Brandesby, John Brydlyngton, Thomas Newton, Richard Lygeard, Robert Feriby, and John del See. John de Stokton, late citizen of York, was seised in his life (of the tenements in Walmegate and Girdlergate mentioned above). (*fo.* 175, *b.*) Katherine de Boynton is his nearest heir. He did not devise the said tenements to St. Denis's church.

19 October, 3 Henry v. (1415) John Symond of York, draper, delivered a bill before William Alne, the mayor, stating that William de Burton had made a false statement in the exchequer that John Stokton was seised in his demesne as of fee, and died so seised, of certain tenements in Girdlergate, of which Symond was seised and in which Stokton had only had an estate for 25 years, as appeared by evidence of record and deed sealed. And that on this false statement a commission was directed to the mayor and certain aldermen to make inquiry, and that the jurors, who neither saw nor were informed of these evidences and deeds, found that John Stokton died seised of these tenements and that Katherine Boynton, was his heir, which was contrary to fact. Symond prayed that, as the verdict had not been sealed, it might be amended. The mayor sent for the jurors and showed

them the indenture and defeasance given below. Stokton held the estate William de Fryston had had in the tenements in Girdlergate.

Lease by William de Friston of York, girdler, and Agnes his wife, to Thomas de Stokton of York, girdler, of a messuage in Gloverlane, extending in breadth between land late of John de Langton and land of John Gervas, and in length from the high street before to land late of the said John de Langton behind; to hold from Whitsunday 1375 for term of twenty-five years, for a sum of money paid beforehand. Seals. Witnesses, Thomas Gra, mayor, John de Houeden, William Savage, John de Braythwayt, bailiffs, Henry de Colton, John de Staynelay, William de Langlaythorp, John de Hewick, girdlers of York. York, 27 April, 1375, 49 Edward iii.

(*fo.* 176). Indenture of defeasance. Whereas William de Fryston of York, girdler, is bound by statute merchant to Thomas de Stokton of York, girdler, in 20 *l.* to be paid at York at Christmas next; and also whereas Agnes, wife of the said William, 9 May, 1375, before the commissary general of the official of the court of York[1] swore to pay 20 *l.* to the said Thomas at the marriage of John her son at Easter next, as appears in the register of the said court, the said bond and undertaking shall be void upon condition of the lease, made by William to Thomas, rent free (as above) seals. York, 18 May, 1375, 49 Edward iii.

(*fo.* 176, *b.*) By these indentures it was quite clear that Thomas Stokton did not die seised of the tenements in Girdlergate, and that John Simond occupied them as required by law, and that Katherine (Boynton) had no right in them.

7 September, 3 Henry v. (1415), general pardon at the request of the commonalty of the kingdom of England in the last parliament, to the mayor, sheriffs, aldermen and commonalty of the city of York, for offences committed before 8 December last, "contrafactores misterie monete, et cunagii multiplicatores, et lotores auri et argenti cum cunea nostra cunatorum, et tonsores monete nostre, probatores communes

---

1—Coram domini officialis curie Ebor' commissario generali in eadem curia pro tribunali sedente judicialiter.

et notorii latrones seu felones, qui abjuracionem fecerunt, non existentes." Witnesses, John, duke of Bedford, guardian of England. (*fo.* 177.) Westminster.

14 February 1415-6, 3 Henry v., Thomas Santon, Richard Russell, John Moreton, and William Lambert, arbitrators chosen to settle a dispute between Geoffry Forester and Alice, his wife, late wife of John Unkthorp, lyttester, on the one part, and William Rodes, lyttester, on the other, before John Northeby (*fo.* 177, *b.*) mayor, in the council chamber on Usebridge. They award that Rodes alone with his family and household shall inhabit the messuage, in which Geoffrey, Alice and William dwell in Northstrete, during the term Alice has in it for her life, paying Geoffrey and Alice six marks sterling a year. Geoffrey and Alice to do all repairs.

Grant by Thomas de Ledes of Westwik, son of Robert de Ledes of York, to William de Nessefeld of Hewik, and John de Whixley of Ripon, of the manor of Westwik; also of all his lands in the city of York, in Dalton and Neusom, in Broghtonlith within the liberty of Richmond, in Ripon, Knaresburgh, Kyllynghall, Weton, and Helithwayte. Seal. Witnesses, William de Ledes of Ripon, William Stowe, William de[1] Fencotes, John Pygot, William de Tanfeld. Westwik by Ripon, 5 September, 13 Henry iv. (1412).

(*fo.* 178). Release by John de Whixley of Ripon to William de Nessefeld of Hewyk, of the manor of Westwyk and lands (described as above) which the said John and William had by enfeoffment of Thomas de Ledes of Westwyk, son and heir of Thomas de Ledes of York. Seal. Witnesses as above. Westwyk 10 March, 3 Henry v. (1415-6).

Similar release by the said Thomas de Ledes to the said William de Nessefeld. Seal. Same witnesses. Westwyk, 14 March, 3 Henry v. (1415-6).

(*fo.* 178, *b.*) The three preceding deeds were acknowledged before John Northeby, mayor, John Blakburn, William Lamberd, Robert Gare, Robert Lokton, Nicholas Blakburn the younger, Master John Suthewell the younger, William Bothe, clerk, and

---

1—*de* is omitted in the next deed but not in the following one.

Roger de Burton, common clerk of the city of York, upon oath by the said Thomas Ledes that he had not made nor had knowledge of any other deeds or estate of the said lands. 26 March, 4 Henry v. (1416).

Grant by William Nessefeld of Hewyk by Ripon to William Witton of the reversion of lands in Hosyergate in York, between a tenement of William de Alne and a tenement of Roger de Selby, extending in length from the highway of Hosyergate before to a tenement of John Mergrave behind; now held for term of thirty-five years by Agnes, formerly wife of Robert de Ledes of York, mother of the said William Wilton, the reversion being held by the said William Nessefeld by enfeoffment of Thomas de Ledes of Westwyk, son of the said Robert. Seal. Witnesses, Nicholas Blakburn the elder, John Blakburn, John Mureton, John Beverlay, John Lofthous York, 24 March, 4 Henry v. (1415-6). Acknowledged before John Northeby, mayor, Thomas Davy, chamberlain, Roger de Burton, common clerk, John Stirtavaunt and John Kirkeby esquires, 27 March, 4 Henry v. (1416).

(*fo.* 179). Copia litere ballivorum ville Salopie de libertate ipsius ville allocanda, missa maiori Ebor' et aliis Christi fidelibus.

A touz yceux qe cestes lettres verront ou orront David Rathebon et Johan Shelton, baillifs de la ville de Salop', saluz en Dieu. Et pur ceo que nostre cher et bien ame veisyn et comburgeys David Fuyster du dit ville ad travaille, et ungore purpose de travailler, si bien a la citee d'Everwyk comme a autres villes et lieux deinz le roialme d'Engleterre, pur achater arkes et autres choses appurtenantz a sa dite art, et officers, sibien de la dite citee d'Everwyk come dez autres villes et lieux, luy demandont tol et autres custums pur ycellez, la ou il est et deust ent estre quit et fraunk, come pleinement appiert par noz chartres et liberteez, a nous par les progenitours nostre seignour le roy qor est grauntez, et par luy ratifiez et confirmez par tout le dit roialme. Sur quoy nous, lez avauntditz baillifs, emprions a touz les lieges nostre dit seignour le roy, sibien de la dite citee d'Everwyk come des autres villes et lieux, qils suffrent lavauntdit David Fuyster, nostre comburgeys, venir entre eux et fraunchement ove son chafer passer, et luy avoir et tenir quit et excuse de tol et touz aultres custumes, et a luy faire en tiel manere come ils voillont et desiront que nous ferrons a eux, et a lours veisyns, venantz a la dite ville de Salop' pur vendre ou achater illoeques ascun manere marchandise ou aultres choses, a cause de ceste nostre priere et recorde. A quelle nous avons mys le seal de nostre office de dite ville. Done a Salop' le septisme jour de Novembre lan du regne du roy Henry quint puis le conquest tierce (1415).

Recordum seisine Leverton.

Universis Christi fidelibus presentes literas inspecturis vel audituris, Johannes Northeby, maior civitatis Ebor', salutem in Domino. Noverit universitas vestra quod decimo die mensis Februarii, anno regni regis nunc tercio (1415-16), venerunt in camera consilii super pontem Use in civitate predicta, domini Robertus Dalby, Robertus Gammyll, Willelmus de Burton, capellani, necnon Rogerus de Burton, clericus communis dicte civitatis, Johannes Axiholme, Thomas Wardale, *glover*, Johannes Hebbe, *sadeller*, Ricardus Bradeshagh, Edmundus Heceham, Thomas Carleton, Johannes (*fo.* 179, *b.*) Clegg, Robertus Dunnyng, Thomas Barbour, Willelmus Brukeshagh, Thomas Greteham et Johannes Munckgate, cives Ebor', et expresse ibidem recognoverunt et dixerunt quod personaliter presentes, videntes et audientes fuerunt sextodecimo die mensis Januarii, anno regni regis predicto, unacum multis aliis quando Johannes Boydon de Ebor', *coureour*, et Katerina uxor sua, consanguinea et heres Johannis Stokton, quondam civis Ebor', in bona et sana memoria existentes, liberarunt et dederunt possessionem et seisinam Thome Lyverton et Ade Heceham, civibus Ebor', unius mesuagii cum tribus shoppis et solariis supra edificatis in fronte ejusdem mesuagii cum suis pertinenciis in Walmegate, in parochia Sancti Dionisii in Ebor',[1] prout jacet in latitudine inter terram nuper comitis Northumbr', ex parte una, et terram hospitalis Domini nostri Jhesu Christi et Beate Marie Virginis in Fossegate in Ebor', ex altera, et in longitudine a regia strata de Walmegate ante usque ad aquam de Fosse retro. Habendum et tenendum

---

1—St. Dennis, Walmgate, was, in reality, the parish church in York of the earls of Northumberland. Drake, *Eboracum*, p. 306.

predictum mesuagium cum tribus shoppis et solariis supra edificatis cum suis pertinenciis, prefatis Thome Lyverton et Ade, heredibus et assignatis suis, libere, quiete, integre, bene, et in pace de capitalibus dominis feodi illius per servicia inde debita et de jure consueta imperpetuum, reddendo inde annuatim eisdem Johanni Boydon et Katerine ad totam vitam ipsius Katerine duas marcas sterlingorum, ad terminos Pentecostes et Sancti Martini in hieme, per equales porciones, et infra annum proximum post decessum ejusdem Katerine, viginti libras sterlingorum custodibus fabrice predicte ecclesie Sancti Dionisii, in opere ipsius ecclesie expendendas ad voluntatem et disposicionem custodum fabrice antedicte. Et si predictus annuus redditus duarum marcarum a retro fuerit post aliquem terminum supradictum in parte vel in toto per quadraginta dies, tunc bene liceat predictis Johanni Boydon et Katerine et assignatis suis ad totam vitam dicte Katerine in omnibus predictis mesuagio, shoppis et solariis supraedificatis distringere, districciones inde fugare, ducere, asportare, et penes se retinere quousque predictis Johanni Boydon et Katerine, et assignatis suis, de dicto annuo redditu et ejus arreragiis, si que fuerint, plenarie fuerit satisfactum. In cujus recognicionis testimonium sigillum officii maioratus civitatis predicte presentibus est appensum. Datum apud Ebor' xiij die mensis Februarii, 5 Henr. v. (1415-16).   Burton.

Recordum brevis domini Regis.

xxviij° die mensis Aprilis anno Domini millesimo ccccxvj^{mo} 4 Henr. v., venit personaliter Petrus van Uppestall, *merchaunt* et civis Ebor', coram Johanne Northeby, tunc maiore civitatis Ebor', et in presencia sua, Ricardi Sourby, Thome Davy, et Willelmi Houyngham camerariorum, Roberti Gare, magistri Johannis Carleton, Willelmi Housom, *sergeant*, et aliorum, et quasdam literas patentes dicti domini nostri Regis, cum cordulis sericis colorum rubei et viridis, suo sigillo magno in cera viridi pendente sigillatas, ostendit, quas Rogerus de Burton, clericus communis, de mandato dicti maioris, et ad peticionem dicti Petri, hic irrotulavit, quarum verus tenor sequitur et est talis.

Henricus, Dei gracie Rex Anglie et Francie et dominus Hibernie, omnibus ad quos presentes litere pervenerint, salutem.

D

Sciatis quod de gracia nostra speciali, et pro viginti solidis nobis (*fo.* 180) solutis in hanaperio nostro, concessimus et licenciam dedimus pro nobis et heredibus nostris, quantum in nobis est, dilecto nobis Petro van Uppestall in Brabancia oriundo, quod ipse ex nunc pertractetur et in omnibus teneatur tanquam verus et fidelis ligeus noster, infra regnum nostrum Anglie oriundus, et quod idem Petrus adeo liber sit in omnibus aliis locis extra dictum regnum nostrum Anglie, ubi dominia nostra existant, sicut aliquis ligeus noster infra idem regnum nostrum Anglie oriundus ; et quod ipse terras, tenementa, redditus, et alias possessiones quecumque infra regnum et dominia nostra predicta adquirere possit, habenda et tenenda sibi heredibus et assignatis suis imperpetuum, quodque ipse omnimodas actiones, tam reales quam personales, in quibuscumque querelis habere, ac implacitari et responderi possit, modo et adeo libere et integre, sicut unus ligeus noster infra dictum regnum nostrum oriundus, absque perturbacione vel impedimento nostri aut heredum nostrorum seu ministrorum nostrorum vel heredum nostrorum quorumcumque. Proviso semper quod predictus Petrus homagium ligeum nobis faciat, ac lotto et scotto contributorius existat, necnon taxas, tallagia, custumas, subsidia, ac omnia alia onera et denaria nobis et heredibus nostris solvat, eodem modo quo alii ligei nostri infra dictum regnum nostrum oriundi faciunt et facient in futurum. In cujus rei testimonium has literas nostras fieri fecimus patentes. Teste me ipso apud Leycestr' vicesimo secundo die Maii anno regni nostri secundo (1414). Per ipsum Regem. (Clerk.)

[1]Grant by Edmund Barneburgh, citizen of York, kinsman and heir of Master Robert Sprottesburgh,[2] late rector of the church of S. Margaret in Briggestrete, London, to Thomas Butiller citizen and fishmonger of London, of lands in the parish of Neuton and in the vill of Walleworth, co. Surrey. Seal. Witnesses, Henry de Acclom, Thomas Roderham, Thomas Snowedon,

1—On fo. 181 there is a letter of attorney similar to the one above but dated a day earlier with a note in the margin that it should have been registered here.
2—Robert de Sprotborough was appointed to the rectory of St. Margaret, New Fish Street, on April 1, 1375, by the abbot and convent of Westminster. He died early in 1400. *Novum Repertorium Londiniense*, p. 275.

Richard Maresshall, William Newland, 10 April, 4 Henry v. (1416). Acknowledged before John Northeby mayor, Thomas Santon, William Alne, William Bowes, Henry Preston, Richard Sourby, Thomas Davy and Roger Burton, common clerk of the city of York, 30 April, 1416, 4 Henry v. (*fo.* 180, *b.*) Letter of attorney by the same appointing Robert Warcope and Richard Blenkensope to deliver seisin of the said lands. Seal. Same date. Acknowledged as above.

Inquisition held at York on Friday before the feast of the Apostles Simon and Jude, 3 Henry v. (25 Oct., 1415) before William de Alne, mayor and escheator, by virtue of his office; by oath of William Gatesheued, Richard Cleseby, John Stele, Thomas Emlay, John de Man, Robert Harpham, Thomas Holbek, Hugh Gardener, John Stafford, Roger Pountfreyt, William Skyres and John Candeler. Henry Lescrop, knight, who forfeited his property to the King, held, within the city of York, lands of the yearly value of 10 *l.* payable at Martinmas and Whitsuntide. Richard Wakefeld of York, merchant, at Martinmas, 14 Henry iv. (11 Nov., 1412) had in loan from the said Henry Lescrop, 100 *l.* of which he repaid before the forfeiture 97 *l.* 5 *s.* 6 *d.*, and thus 54 *s.* 6 *d.* remained in the hands of Richard and are received from him this day by the said mayor and escheator, who shall answer to the King therefor.

(*fo.* 181). Admissio domini Thome Howran, capellani, ad cantariam pro anima Hugonis Selby senis in capella Sancti Willelmi fundatam. Memorandum quod octavo die mensis Maii, anno Domini millesimo ccccxvj^{mo} et 4 Henr. v., Willelmus Selby, aldermannus et civis Ebor', presentavit Johanni Northeby, maiori Ebor', dominum Thomam Howran, capellanum, ad cantariam in capella Sancti Willelmi super pontem Use Ebor' pro animabus Hugonis Selby, senis, antecessorum suorum et omnium fidelium defunctorum antiquitus ordinatam, adtunc vacantem per mortem domini Johannis Algude, ultimi possessoris et capellani ejusdem, et ad presentacionem dicti Willelmi Selby spectantem. Quem sic presentatum et presentem idem Johannes Northeby, maior, xij° die dicti mensis Maii, anno Domini supradicto, in camera consilii super pontem predictum, in presencia Ricardi Sourby, Thome Davy, Willelmi Houyngham, Rogeri de Burton, notarii publici, clerici communis, et aliorum, virtute presentacionis predicte admisit ad dictam cantariam cum oneribus eidem cantarie ex forma ordinacionis ejusdem incumbentibus, et omnia terras, tenementa, et redditus dicte cantarie qualitercumque pertinencia eidem domino Thome assignavit suo perpetuo possidenda; ita semper quod idem dominus Thomas in dicta capella celebret et ministret in divinis in omnibus et per omnia sicut precessores et predecessores sui, capellani cantarie predicte, facere debuerunt et consueverunt, et secundum quod ordinacio sepedicte cantarie et usus antiquus dicte capelle exigunt et requirunt. Et de omnibus hiis per ipsum fideliter servandis idem dominus Thomas ad sacrosancta Dei evangelia per ipsum tacta suum corporale prestitit juramentum.   Burton.

(*fo.* 181, *b.*) De xij, Johannes Northeby, maior, Willelmus Selby, Johannes Braythwayt, Robertus Howom, Johannes Craven, Thomas Santon, Willelmus Bowes, Johannes Moreton, Ricardus Russell; vicecomites, Thomas Bracebryg, Robertus Burton; de xxiiij^{or}, Thomas Gare, Johannes Hewyk, Johannes Bouthe, Henricus Preston, Thomas Doncastre, Johannes Usburn, Thomas del More, Robertus Lokton, Willelmus Muston, Johannes Petyclerk, Petrus Buksy, Thomas Esyngwald, Willelmus Wynkburn, Galfridus Sauvage, Ricardus Spenser, istis omnibus congregatis in aula communi, necnon communitate hujus civitatis ibidem in magna multitudine astante, die Lune, videlicet, festo Sancti Mathei Apostoli, 21 Sept., 1416, 4 Henr. v., habito consilio maturo, consensum et ordinatum extitit per maiorem, probos homines, et totam communitatem, quod omnes fines, exitus forisfacti et amerciamenta racione justiciarie pacis ante hunc diem forisfacta et debita respectuentur, et quod fines exitus forisfiendi et amerciamenta racione justiciarie pacis proventura et debenda de cetero leventur et colligantur per vicecomites hujus civitatis, qui pro tempore fuerint, et eorum ministros, de quibus maiori et camerariis dicte civitatis, qui pro tempore erunt, statim integraliter respondeant in camera consilii civitatis. Et, hoc facto, electores quorum intererat secesserunt in cameram consilii infra aulam communem, et unanamiter elegerunt in vicecomites civitatis pro anno proximo futuro Johannem Waghen, *mercer*, et Thomam Snawdon, *pewderer*. Eodem die ordinatum erat per maiorem, vicecomites, aldermannos et communitatem in aula communi hujus civitatis, quod forum venale pro bobus, vaccis, ovibus, porcis, et animalibus omnibus mactandis ad sustentacionem hominum, ab hac die in antea vendantur super lez Toftes, infra civitatem Ebor', mercato ad hoc assignato, tociens quociens talia animalia ducta fuerint ad civitatem ut vendantur, et in nullo alio loco. Et eodem die similiter ordinatum est quod mercatum equorum venalium de cetero teneatur qualibet septimana die Veneris super lez Toftes predicta, et non alibi infra civitatem Ebor' suburbia vel procinctum ejusdem.

Lease by Robert Middilton, citizen and mercer of York, to Robert Lovell, son and heir of William Lovell of Hoton-on-Derwent, of a capital messuage called le South Appilgarth, a tenement with a garden, ten bovates of land, and all *le forland* in Hoton-on-Derwent, which the said Robert Middilton had by enfeoffment of the said Robert Lovell. To hold from Martinmas 1416 for term of three years at a yearly rent of five marks. Seals. York, the feast of S. Martin (11 Nov., 1416). Acknowledged, for enrolment before Roger Burton common clerk, 4 Oct., 1416, 4 Henry v.

(*fo.* 182). Confirmation by William Selby, citizen of York, patron of the perpetual chantry founded by Hugh de Selby formerly citizen of York, in the chapel of S. William by the bridge of Use in York, of the following charter.

Grant by Thomas Howeram, chaplain of the said chantry, to Thomas del Gare, citizen and merchant of York, of a yearly rent of 13 *s.* 4 *d.*, from Whitsuntide 1417, for term of twenty years, from lands of the said Thomas Howeram belonging to the said chantry, as they lie by the Ouse in York, between lands of the said Thomas del Gare and lands formerly of William Frost, and, on the third side, the bank of the Ouse and *le Fysshlendyng*. Seals. York, 13 Jan., 4 Henry v. (1416–17). Confirmation tested by John de Northeby mayor, John Waughan, Thomas Snawedon, sheriffs, John de Morton, William Bowes. York, 15 Jan., 4 Henry v. Enrolled by consent of the parties.

(*fo.* 183.) Tuesday before the Conversion of S. Paul, 4 Henry v. (19 Jan., 1416-17). Inquisition at York before John Northeby mayor, escheator, by virtue of his office, by the oath of William Pirler, William Barton, Roger del Hay, William Rowlay, William Gudale, Robert Stillyngton, William Coupland, *taillour*, William Barnet, *bower*, Thomas Garleker, John Shirwod, *boucher*, William Kendall, Robert Hobschort, John Spaldyng and William Warde of Bouthom, jurors. John Bryghenhall of York, buklermaker, hung for felony and treason, had on the day of his arrest by Thomas Bracebrygg and Robert Burton, lately sheriffs of the said city, certain goods and chattels; that is, half a thousand fagottes with astelwod, 14 *s*.; one brewled, three wortled, two cauldrons, 13 *s*. 4 *d*.; three brazen pots with three small dishes 6 *s*. 8 *d*. Two basons, with two vessels and four candlesticks, 4 *s*. Two worn out coverlets, 5 *s*. Three pair of sheets with three blankets, 3 *s*. 4 *d*. He had on the day of his arrest by William Wynkeburn, Geoffry Sauvage, lately sheriffs of the said city, a dublet 2 *s*. and a mailsaddle 12 *d*.

(*fo*. 183). Release by William de Strensall, son of Thomas de Strensall late of York, goldsmith, to Agnes de Croxton, late wife of John de Croxton late of York, chandler, of all actions of debt concerning the repair, occupation or waste of his tenements. Seal. York, 10 Feb., 4 Hen. v. (1416-17).

(*fo*. 183, *b*.) Writ to the mayor, sheriffs and aldermen of York, upon the complaint of William Eseby, merchant of York, to hold the inquisition which follows on fo. 185. Westminster, 12 Feb., 4 Hen. v. (1416-17).

(*fo*. 184). Grant by Margaret Keldsyk, late the wife of Thomas Morele of Tyndale, daughter of William de Keldsyk of Cokermouth, to Thomas de Keldsyk of Cokermouth, of all lands in the vill of Cokermouth and elsewhere in the county of Cumberland, which can descend to her in future. Seal. Witnesses, John Threpland, William Cowpland of York, William del Dykes, William del Sandes, Robert de Lathes of Cokermouth. 8 Feb., 4 Hen. v. (1416-17). Acknowledged before William Bowes, mayor, Roger Burton, John Somerby, chamberlains, and Roger de Burton, common clerk, 9 March, 1416, 4 Hen. v. Release by the same to the same of the same lands. Seal. Same witnesses and date. Acknowledged as above.

(*fo*. 184, *b*.) Johannes Moreton, maior, de xij Nicholus Blakburn, senior, Willelmus Alne, Johannes Northeby, Willelmus

Bowes, Ricardus Russell; vicecomites, Robertus Jarom, Johannes Loftehouse; de xxiiij^{or}, Johannes Hewyk, Johannes Peticlerk, Willelmus Ormesheued, Johannes Gascoigne, camerar(ius), N. Blakburn, junior, congregati fuerunt hic in camera xxviij die Junii anno Domini M°ccccxviij° (6 Hen. v.), consenserunt et pro meliori considerarunt quod Nicholaus Walker, serviens maioris et communitatis, non portet clavam suam, sed ipsam deponat, quousque maior et probi homines melius fuerint deliberati, pro eo quod idem Nicholaus tabernam Johanne Caldecotes frequentare presumpsit, et hoc in horis et locis suspectis de nocte contra prohibicionem maioris, pro eo eciam quod dixit Johanni Loftehouse, uni vicecomitum, quod ipsam tabernam dimittere nollet, eciam si maior vel Nicholaus Blakburn sibi inhibuerint.

(*fo.* 185.) In Magno Rotulo 4 Henr. v. in civitate Ebor'. *Civitas Ebor'*, Johannis Northeby, nuper maior et escaetor regis in civitate Ebor', suburbiis et procinctu ejusdem, reddit compotum de x *li.* iiij *s.* x *d.* de exitu escaetrie a tercio die Februarii, anno regni domini regis nunc tercio, usque tercium diem Februarii proximo sequentem ($141\frac{5}{6}$—$141\frac{6}{7}$), sicut continetur in compoto suo inde rotulo compotorum de escaetrie. In thesauro x *li.* iiij *s.* x *d.* in iij talliis per dictum nuper maiorem et escaetorem. Et quietus est. *Prioratus de Bridlyngton.* In rotulo domini regis in castro Ebor' continetur clausula subscripta de annuo redditu solvendo domino regi. De priore et canonicis de Bridlyngton pro diversis libertatibus, privilegiis, donacionibus et concessionibus per regem prefatis priori et successoribus suis xiij *s.* iiij *d.* Et de eodem priore et canoniciis pro finibus wapentagii de Dykryng ij *s.*

Marcand(isa). Flandrea. Inquisicio[1] capta apud Ebor' die Veneris in tercia septimana quadragesime, 4 Henr. v. (20 March, 1415-6), coram Willelmo Bowes, maiore civitatis Ebor', Johanne Waghen et Thoma Snawedon, vicecomitibus civitatis predicte ac aldermannis ejusdem civitatis, virtute commissionis domini Regis eisdem maiori, vicecomitibus et aldermannis directe, per sacramentum Thome del More, Petri Bukcy, Thome Bracebrygg,

---

1—The writ directing that this inquisition should be held, is given on fo. 183, *b.*

Johannis Louthe, Roberti Yarum, Thome Aton, Willelmi Fenwyk, Thome Neuton, *mercer*, Johannis Wakeman, Johannis Austenmore, Willelmi Bedale, Ricardi Fendard, *spicer*, Johannis Brounflete, Roberti Belton, *spicer*, Willelmi Aukebarowe, Henrici Rothewell, *merchant*, Johannis Aspey, *spicer*, Ricardi Soureby, Johannis Cutberd et Roberti Dodmor, juratorum, qui dicunt super sacramentum suum quod quedam convencio facta fuit apud Ebor', circa duodecimum diem Decembris anno regni Regis Henrici quinti supradicti tercio (1415) inter Willelmum Warde *spicer*, de Ebor, ex una parte, et Willelmus Eseby, ex altera parte, quod predictus Willelmus Eseby ad usum et proficuum predicti Willelmi Warde in Flandrea emeret pro eodem Willelmo Warde, super periculo ejusdem Willelmi Warde, diversa bona et marcandisas ad summam sexaginta et octo librarum secundum formam cujusdam bille de parcellis eorundem bonorum et marcandisarum sic emendorum, manu predicti Willelmi Warde scripte et eidem Willelmo Eseby deliberate, et quod perciperet de predicto Willelmo Warde pro labore suo ad quaslibet viginti libras in empcione eorundem viginti solidos, et quod bona et marcandise predicta ex aventura dicti Willelmi Warde devenirent. Et dicunt quod predictus Willelmus Eseby, virtute convencionis predicte bona et marcandisas predictas ad summam predictam attingencia in Flandrea emit, et ea cum aliis bonis et marcandisis diversorum mercatorum civitatis Ebor' in quadam navi, vocata le Hulke de Selykey, in Seland, recte apud Kyngeston super Hull velando skippavit et frettavit, et quod dicta navis, per infortunium et magnam maris tempestatem cum hominibus, bonis, et mercandisis in eadem navi existentibus, velando versus predictam villam de (*fo.* 185, *b.*) Kyngeston super Hull, inter Yermuth et Kyrkla super costeris Anglie, in mari totaliter periclitata et perdita fuit. Item dicunt quod predictus Willelmus Eseby sepius de predicto Willelmo Warde petiit satisfactionem et solucionem sibi fieri pro bonis et marcandisis predictis ad dictam summam se extendentibus, ac pro labore et expensis suis in hac parte factis, et quod predictus Willelmus Warde ea facere omnino recusat ad grave dampnum ipsius Willelmi Eseby. In cujus rei testimonium juratores predicti huic inquisicionim sigilla sua apposuerunt. Data die anno et loco supradictis.

Johan fitz et frer des rois, duc de Bedford, count de Richemond et de Kendale, et conestable Dangleterre, a noz chiers et bien amez, lez mair et viscontz Deverwic, saluz. Come en une cause ou busoigne moeve et pendante devaunt nous en nostre courte de chivalerie parentre Johan Belle del counte Deverwic, partie poursuiant, dun part, et Johan Lough et Robert Zarom, partie defendaunt, dautre parte, par cause ou occasion du spoliacion dun prisoner appelle Johan Cook de Brugges, monstre nous ad la dite partie defendaunt, que vous avez en voz gardes et archives diverses scriptures, processes, actes, ou munimentz la cause et especialment la defense du dicte partie defendant concernantz et touchantz, et a dite partie defendaunt necessaries et busoignables pur la dite defense, et lesquelles en mesme la defense la mesme partie defendant voet user comme il dist, sicomme la dite partie defendant judicielment ad fait son serement sur lez seintz evangelies en dhue fourme, en nostre dite courte, nous requerant diligentment noz lettres compulsories a lui graunter a vous directes celle partie. Si nous attendantz la dite request juste et consonant a reason, vous mandons et chargeons que vous enserchez ou facez enserchier le dis et neofisme jour du mois davril prochein venant (1417) vos archives, et touz scriptures, processes, actes, ou munimentz illoques trovez, ou en vostre garde esteantz, touchantz ou concernantz la dite cause, sanz riens adder ou amenuser, que chaunge la substance du fait, envoiez a nostre dite courte bien e secretement enseelez encloses desoubz voz seelx ove ycestes noz mandementz, le tierce jour de Maii prochein venant. Entendantz que la dite partie pleintif est dhuement garniz destre present legalement ove vous a dit jour du serche, si lui semble expedient pur veier le dite scrche estre fait, et outre ce faire que de ley appartient a faire celle partie. En tesmoignance de quelle chose a ycestez noz lettres nous avons fait mettre nostre seel de nostre office de constablerie. Donn le primer jour du mois du marche lan du regne mon tres redoute seignour le Roy Henry quint puis le conquest quart (1416-7). Sequitur certificacio ejusdem.

(*fo*. 186). A treshault et trespuissant prince et leur tresgraciouse seignour, Johan, fitz et frere des rois, duc de

Bedford, count de Richemond et de Kendale et conestable Dangleterre, William Bowes, meir, John de Waghen et Thomas Snauedon, viscontz de la citee Deverwic, honours et touz maners de reverence. Vostre honourable mandement a nous direct et a ycestes noz lettres fiche nadgairs nous avons reverentment receu, comme appartiegne de la liverance de Johan Lough et Robert Jarom en y celle vostre mandement nommez. Par vertue de quelle mandement, le dis et neofisme jour du mois daveril venaunt, lez ditz Johan et Robert et Johan Bell de count de Everwic faisasmes estre preconizez publicment pur estre legalment ove nous pur voier et oier par nous et devaunt nous estre procede et fait en touz pointz comme vostre dit mandement requerast ; et eulx nient comparantz mes touz absentz, nous veulliantz eschuer toutdis contempt de vous et de vostre honourable courte de chivalerie, en labsence de lez ditz Johan, Robert, et Johan, enserchasmes et faisasmes enserchier touz noz archives diligentment, et par ensercher fait trovasmes loialment contenu et escript en les rolles del courte nostre seignour le roi de la dite citee Deverwic que un Johan Bell, de Thresk, fist attacher un appelle Johan Cuke, Selander, esteant en la dite citee Deverwic, pur responder a lui en un plee de trespasse, et que ceo faite mesme le Johan Cuke, Selander, fist attacher Johan Bell, de Thresk, trove deinz la citee, pur responder a lui en un plee de trespasse. Lez quelx ambideux plees feurent terminez en la courte nostre seignour le roi de mesme la citee devaunt Thomas Bracebrig et Robert Burton, a celle temps viscontz illocques, sicomme pleinement appert en le recorde des mesmes lez plees, enseelez, enclosez, a ceste nostre certificate annexe. Et outre tout ceo nous avons trove auxi par diligent ensercher fait de lez archives de la dite citee que le Lundy prochein avaunt le fist de translacion de Seint Thomas, lan de regne nostre tressoverein seignour le roi qor est quatre (6 July, 1416), pendantz lez plees suisdites devaunt Johan Northeby a cele temps meir, et ses compaignons aldermen de la dite citee, justices del pease deinz la dite citee, suburbez, et procinctz de la mesme assignez par chartre nostre seignour le roi, seantz en execucion et esploit de leur office en la gildesale de la dite citee, vient un William Bell, clerc, soy disant filz de dit Johan Bell de Thresk, et illocques a eux en pleine courte monstrast et deliverast une bille en Englois endente, escripte en papire envers le dit Johan Cuke, le tenour de quelle bille del mote en mote pleinement appiert en une cedule enclose deinz le dit recorde; la quelle bille illocques receu, lye, et entendu, lez ditz meir et aldermen, et Thomas Bracebrig et Robert Burton, lez viscontz suisdites, fesoient estre fait une public proclamacion en la gyldesale devaunt la communaltee de la dite citee, et autres gentz assemblez illocques, que si le dit Johan Bell ou aucuns autres vouldrent aucun chose et matere dire, purposer ou monstrer pur nostre seignour le roi encountre le dit Johan Cuke, qils viendrent en le Samady prochein ensuiant en la courte nostre seignour le roi de la dite citee, et pleine droit averoient. Et sur ceo, Thomas Bracebryg et Robert Burton, lez viscontz suisdites, aresteront le dit Johan Cuke et lui garderont en baille tanque a le dit Samady. Et cele Samady venant, lez ditz meir et viscontz feurent bien certifiez par divers officers de bone credence de nostre seignour le roi que le dit Johan Cuke ne fuist endite de la matere contenu en la dite bille ne dautre queconque, et lez ditz Thomas et Robert, viscontz, ceo regardantz, en mesme le Samady en pleine courte de nostre seignour le roi de la dite citee (*fo.* 186, *b.*) derechief fesoient un public proclamacion que si aucuns a cele temps vouldrent aucune mater purposer pur nostre seignour le roi ou le dit Johan Bell, ou aucune autre encountre le dit Johan Cuke, qils viendrent illocques en la courte et serroient bien oiez et averoient pleine droit. Et en certein nulle matere fuist de novelle illocques monstre encountre le dit Johan Cuke. Et puis cele darrein proclamacion, le dit Johan Cuke alast deinz la dite citee a sa voluntee pesiblement par certeins jours sanz empeschement ou chalange de nullui. Et le verray tenour de tout le fait et processe des plees suisdites, le verray tenour auxi de la ville suisdite, envoions a vostre honourable courte de chivalerie bien et secretment enseeles, encloses desoubz les seel x de noz ditz offices ensemble ove vostre mandement, et ceste nostre certificate, selonc la fourme de celle mandement, ne addantz riens ne amenusantz que chaunge la substance dufait. Doun a Everwic le dis et neofisme jour du mois daveril suisdite, lan du regne nostre tressoverein seignour le roi Henry quint puis le conquest quint (1417).

Curia domini regis civitatis Ebor', tenta ibidem die Sabbati proximo post festum Sanctorum Apostolorum Petri et Pauli, coram Thoma Bracebrig et Roberto Burton, vicecomitibus predicte civitatis, iv. Henr. v. (4 July, 1416). Johannes Bell de Thresk queritur de Johanne Cuke, Selander, de placito transgressionis, plegius de prosequendo Johannes Asper, *spicer*; defend(ens) attach(iatur) per plegiagium Thome de Aton et Johannis Louth. Et unde idem querens in propria persona sua dicit quod dictus defendens die Dominica proxima post festum Sancti Barnabe Apostoli, 4 Henry v. (14 June, 1416) in Bouthom, in parrochia Sancti Olavi infra libertatem civitatis Ebor', vi et armis, videlicet, gladiis et aliis armis etc. venit, et in predictum querentem ibidem insultum fecit ipsumque falsum et infidelem appellavit, per quod bonam famam et credenciam suas valde amisit, et adhuc amittit injuste, etc., et sex libras sterlingorum in pecunia numerata ipsius querentis ibidem inventas cepit, et asportavit injuste et contra pacem domini regis etc. Et unde dictus querens dixit quod deterioratus est et dampna habet ad valenciam xx *li*. etc. Et inde producit sectam etc. Et predictus defendens per Johannem Alman, attornatum suum, venit et defendit vim etc. quicquid etc., quando etc., et dampna xx *li*. etc., et dicit quod dictus defendens in nullo predictorum est culpabilis prout dictus querens superius versus eum narravit etc., et de hoc ponit se super patriam etc. Et predictus querens dicit quod dictus defendens est culpabilis prout ipse querens superius versus eum declaravit etc., et de hoc ponit se similiter super patriam etc. Ideo veniat inde inter eos jurata etc. Et deinde processus continuatur de die in diem secundum cousuetudinem civitatis predicte pro defectu juratorum usque in diem Mercurii proximum ante festum assumpcionis beate Marie Virginis, anno supradicto (12 Aug., 1416), et tunc ibidem xij juratores ad hoc electi, triati et jurati secundum consuetudinem etc., dicunt super sacramentum suum quod dictus defendens in nullo predictorum est culpabilis prout superius versus eum dictus querens narravit etc. Ideo consideratum est per curiam quod dictus querens nichil capiat per placitum et pro injusta querela sua sit in misericordia etc. Et defendens eat inde sine die etc.

JOHN COOK AND JOHN BELL (1416)

(*fo.* 187). Curia domini regis civitatis Ebor', tenta ibidem die Sabbati proximo post festum Apostolorum Petri et Pauli coram Thoma Bracebrig et Roberto Burton, vicecomitibus predicte civitatis, 4 Henr. v. (4 July, 1416). Johannes Cuke, Selander, queritur de Johanne Bell de Thresk de placito transgressionis, plegius de prosequendo Thomas de Aton. Defend(ens) attach(iatur) per plegiagium Andree Ferur et Johannis Asper, *spicer*. Et unde idem querens per Johannem Alman, attornatum suum, dicit quod dictus defendens venit injuste hic in Ebor' infra libertatem die Lune proximo ante festum Corporis Christi 4 Henr. v. (15 June, 1416) et ibidem vi et armis, videlicet, daggariis et aliis armis, et in ipsum querentem insultum fecit, ipsumque falsum et infidelem appellavit, per quod bonam famam et credenciam suas valde amisit, et tantas minas dicto querenti ibidem fecit ad verberandum et insultandum, quod ipse querens fuit in desperacione vite sue, ac bona et catalla ipsius querentis ibidem inventa, unum equum cum sella et freno, precii 1 *s.*, unum gladium, unum daggarium, unum pautener, unum par de lynclathes, et j kerechief, precii omnium x *s.*, unam bursam de lathir, precii xij *d.*, simul cum xij *s.* et vj *d.* sterlingorum in pecunia numerata, cepit, abduxit et asportavit, ipsumque querentem a dicto die Lune usque ad diem Dominicam tunc proximo sequentem imprisonavit et in prisona detinuit, per quod dictus querens fuit in desperacione vite sue, et circa negocia et necessaria sua facienda ibidem nec alibi ire potuit, injuste et contra pacem domini regis etc.; et unde predictus querens dicit quod deterioratus est et dampna habet ad valenciam xx *li.* etc.; et inde producit sectam etc. Et predictus defendens per Robertum Orwell, attornatum suum, venit et defendit vim etc., quidquid etc., quando etc., et dampna xx *li.* etc., et dicit quod ipse defendens in nullo predictorum est culpabilis prout superius versus eum declaratur etc., et de hoc ponit se super patriam etc. Et predictus querens dicit quod dictus defendens est culpabilis prout ipse querens superius versus eum declaravit etc., et de hoc ponit se super patriam similiter etc. Ideo veniat inde inter eos jurata etc. Et deinde processus continuatur de die in diem secundum consuetudinem civitatis predicte pro defectu juratorum usque in diem Sabbati proximum post festum translacionis sancti Thome martiris anno supradicto

(11 July, 1416) et tunc ibidem xij juratores ad hoc electi, triati, et jurati secundum consuetudinem etc. dicunt super sacramentum suum quod dictus defendens culpabilis est de transgressionibus predictis, prout superius versus cum declaratur, insultu vi et armis tanto modo excepto etc., et assidant dampna dicto querenti pro transgressionibus predictis ad vj *li.* etc. Ideo consideratum est per curiam quod dictus querens recuperet dampna sua per inquisicionem assessa ad vj *li.* etc., et defendens in misericordia etc. Et ibidem dictus querens petit execucionem de dampnis suis predictis versus plegios dicti defendentis etc. Et concessum est per curiam etc.

Tenor vero cedule de qua superius memoratur sequitur et est talis :—We pray and require of the Kynges behalve of Inglond yow, mayre and sherefs and all the Kynges officers that here bene present, that ye make seure this John Cooke that her ys present and putte hym in safe warde, for he ys a felloun and has stollen vj *li.* of mone and more of the Kynges taxe of the towne of Thirske, oute of the house of John Bell, and also other gode and catell of the forsayd John, till a grete value in the forsayde towne of Thirske, and that the forsayde John Cuke in no wyse escape before the justys of deliverance sitte for to deliver the jayll, for we lat yow wytte that this same John Cooke ys indited of thys (*fo.* 187, *b.*) same thing, and therfor sen ye may noght termyn this felony within yow, for als mykyll als the felonye ys done oute of your franchise and jurisdiction, we pray for the King that ye be sure of the forsayd John Cooke, als ye wyll answer to the King befor the forsayd justice of deliverance at youre perill.

(*fo.* 187, *b.*) Willelmus Bowes, *maior*; Johannes Waghen, Thomas Snawdon, *vicecomites*; Willelmus Seleby, Johannes Brathwayt, Robertus Howom, Johannes Craven, Thomas Santon, Johannes Northeby, Johannes Moreton, Johannes Bedale, Johannes Blakburn, Willelmus Wandesford, *recordator*; Thomas Gare, Johannes Hewyk, Johannes Bouche, Henricus Preston, Thomas Doncaster, Johannes Usseburn, Thomas del More, Robertus Lokton, Thomas Esyngwald, Robertus Gare, Willelmus Ormeshed, Thomas Bracebrig, Ricardus Spenser, *de xxiiij*; Rogerus Burton, Johannes Somerby, *camerarii*; omnes isti congregati fuerunt in aula communi unacum multitudine aliorum civium vij^{mo} die mensis Junii, anno Domini millésimo ccccxvij^{mo}, regni autem regis Henrici quinti post conquestum Anglie anno quinto, et licet contineatur in quadam constitucione seu ordinacione antiqua facta tempore Roberti Talkan, dudum maioris Ebor', anno regni regis Ricardi secundi xxij^{do} (1389-9)[1] et ibidem perlecta de ludo in festo Corporis Christi in civitate Ebor' sustinendo, videlicet, quod ob commodum civium ejusdem civitatis et omnium extraneorum illuc veniencium in festo predicto, omnes pagine ludi, vocati, *Corpus Christi play*, sint sustentate et producte suo ordine per artifices dicte civitatis, ad honorem precipue et reverenciam Domini nostri Jesu Christi et comodum civium predictorum, et ludus singularum ipsarum paginarum esset primo, ad portas prioratus Sancte Trinitatis in Mikelgate ; secundo, ante ostium Roberti Harpham ; tercio, ante ostium quondam Johannis Gyseburn ; quarto, apud Skeldergatehend et Northstretehend, quinto, ad finem de Conyngstrete versus Castlegate ; sexto, ad finem de Jubritgate ; septimo, ante ostium quondam Heurici Wyman in Conyngstrete ; octavo, ante aulam communem in fine Conyngstrete ; nono, ad ostium quondam Ade del Bryg in Stayngate ; decimo, in fine de Stayngate ad portam monasterii beati Petri ; undecimo, ad finem de Girdelergate in Petergate ; duodecimo et ultimo, super Pavimentum, prout in constitucione et ordinacione ista antiqua in registro isto versus principium scripta plenius continetur ; nichilominus maior, probi homines et tota communitas predicta eorum unanimi consensu et assensu ordinarunt quod omnes illi qui pro skafaldis, quas ante eorum ostia super solum communitatis edificant in locis predictis, de supersedentibus monetam recipiunt, solvant tercium denarium monete sic recepte camerariis civitatis, ad usum communitatis ejusdem (*fo.* 188) applicandum ; et si hujusmodi tercium denarium solvere vel alias cum camera honeste concordare recusaverint, quod tunc ludus transferatur ad alia loca ad disposicionem et voluntatem maioris, qui pro tempore fuerit, et consilii camere civitatis, nemine ordinacioni hujusmodi contradicente, paucis possessoribus skaffaldorum in Mikelgate

1—See Drake *op. cit.*, App. xxxii. Miss Toulmin Smith *op. cit.*, xxxiii. Davies *op. cit.*, p. 241.

dumtaxat exceptis. Et ulterius ordinatum erat communi consensu quod vexilla ludi Corporis Christi, sub armis civitatis depicta, libarentur annuatim in vigilia Corporis Christi, ponenda in locis ubi erit ludus paginarum die sequente, et quod vexilla ipsa singulis annis reportentur ad cameram consilii civitatis sine mora, in crastino dicti festi Corporis Christi ad manus maioris et camerariorum civitatis, et ibidem custodiantur per totum annum proximo sequentem, sub pena vj $s.$ viij $d.$, ad opus communitatis applicandorum, per illum et illos, qui vexilla illa ultra crastinum illum detinuerint et ea non liberaverint modo qui prefertur. Et quia propter dicti festi Corporis Christi propinquitatem et temporis brevitatem dicta materia non potuit plene execucioni mandari, predicti, igitur, Willelmus Bowes, *maior*, Johannes Waghen, Thomas Snawdon, *vicecomites*; Willelmus Seleby, Johannes Brathwayt, Robertus Howom, Johannes Craven, Thomas Santon, Johannes Moreton, Johannes Bedale, Johannes Blakburn, Willelmus Wandesford, Thomas Gare, Johannes Hewyk, Johannes Bouche, Henricus Preston, Thomas Doncastr', Johannes Usburn, Thomas del More, Robertus Lokton, Thomas Esyngwald, Robertus Gare, Willelmus Ormeshed, Thomas Bracebrig, Ricardus Spenser, Rogerus Burton, Johannes Somerby, congregati in camera consilii, xij^{mo} die Junii annis Domini et regis supradictis (1417), considerantes quod indecens esset et contra comodum communitatis quod ludus predictus annuatim luderetur in eisdem certis locis et in nullo alio, cum unusquisque juxta statum suum onus suum portet pro ipso ludo sustinendo, unanimiter, igitur, ordinaverunt pro utilitate communitatis quod loca ad ludendum ludum predictum mutentur, nisi ipsi, ante quorum loca antea ludebatur, aliquod certum quid solverint communitati pro ipso comodo suo singulari sic annuatim habendo, et quod in omnibus annis sequentibus, dum ludus ille ludi contingerit, ludatur ante ostia et tenementa illorum, qui uberius et melius camere solvere et plus pro commodo tocius communitatis facere voluerint pro ludo ipso ibidem habendo, non impendendo favorem alicui persone pro aliquo commodo singulari, sed tantum quod consideretur utilitas publica tocius communitatis Ebor'. Et reverendus vir, Johannes Moreton supradictus, pro tenementis suis se submisit totaliter disposicioni et regimini maioris et consilii camere, quantum ad ludum supradictum pro ludo ante portam habitacionis sue in vico de Mikelgate et in aliis tenementis suis in civitate.

Et eodem die ordinatum erat quod omnes extranei mercatores, de quacumque parte venientes, extunc hospitentur omnimodas res et mercandisas suas qualescumque fuerint, quas ad istam civitatem vendendas adducent, in domibus crane communitatis apud Hyngbryg, et non in alio loco, et ibidem expectent quousque plenarie vendentur, reddendo inde firmam custodi crane predicte ad opus communitatis, sicut cum eo poterit racionabiliter concordare, majorem vel minorem, secundum quod hujusmodi res et mercandise ibidem jacuerint hospitate, sub pena gravis amerciamenti ab hujusmodi mercatoribus levandi, per maiorem et camerarios hujus civitatis pro tempore existentes, si ipsi mercatores istius ordinacionis contrarium fecerint in futurum. Et quod statera et alia pondera legalia in dicta crana omni tempore parata existant ad ponderandum res et mercandisas ibidem mercatorum predictorum, que per ponderacionem vendentur.

(*fo.* 188, *b.*) Memorandum quod viij die mensis Novembris anno regni regis Henrici quinti quinto (1417) Johannes Ithen, *shipman*, venit coram Willelmo Bowes, maiore, hic in camera et monstravit unam literam patentem Thome comitis Dorset', et duas literas patentes domini regis quas peciit ibidem irrotulari per Rogerum de Burton, notarium publicum, quarum tenores sequntur et sunt tales.

Thomas, Cont de Dorset, constable doste de mon seignour le Roy, admiral Dengleterre, Guienne, et Dirland, et capitain de Harefleu, a tous ceaux que ces noz lettres verront ou orront, salutz. Savoir faisons que nous considerantz la bon service que William Derby, meistre de la nief appelle Mary de York, ad fait a mon dit seignour le roy en icest son present viage et sa longe demourre en cestes parties, donnons a cellui William nostre bon licence et conge daler et conduier la dit vessell devers quelque part Dengleterre, que luy plerra ou aillours la ou busoigne luy serra. Donne soubz nostre seel a Hareflieu le vij jour Doctobre lan du reigne de mon seignour le roy Henry quint tierce (1415).

E

Henricus, Dei gracia rex Francie et Anglie et dominus Hibernie, omnibus ad quos presentes litere pervenerint salutem. Sciatis quod cum Willelmus Miller, magister craiere vocate Marie de York, qui ad deserviendum nobis cum craiera sua predicta in ultimo viagio nostro ad partes regni nostri Francie de nobis vadia percepit, nobis in eodem viagio cum craiera sua predicta, durante tempore vadiorum suorum predictorum bene et fideliter servierit, nos ea consideracione concessimus prefato Willelmo licenciam versus partes suas proprias vel alibi quo sibi placuerit transeundi et redeundi. Et hoc omnibus quorum interest innotescimus per presentes. In cujus rei testimonium has literas nostras fieri fecimus patentes. Teste me ipso apud abbatiam nostram Sancti Stephani juxta Caen in ducatu nostro Normannie, primo die Septembris anno regni nostri quinto (1417). Per ipsum regem. Sturgeon.

Similar licence to Robert Grice, for the same reason given on the same date.

(*fo.* 189). Writ to the mayor and escheator of York to hold the following inquisition. Westminster, 5 December, 5 Henry v. (1417).

Inquisition held at York on Friday after the feast of S. Lucy, virgin, 5 Henry v. (17 December, 1417) before Henry Bowes, mayor and escheator, by oath of John Elvyngton, William Scorburg, Thomas Holbek, John del Man, Peter Wright, Hugh de Gill, Robert Hobshort, Richard Walker, Robert de Lonsdale, Walter Marshall, Thomas Sutton and John Hobshort. William Sheffeld held a messuage and a garden adjoining upon Bishophill in the City of York, for term of life with reversion in tail male to John, son and heir of Miles de Stapilton, a ward of the King. The premises are of the clear yearly value of 40 *s*. and are held of the king in free burgage as is the whole city. William died on Wednesday before the feast of the Nativity of S. John the Baptist, 9 Henry iv. (20 June, 1408).

Immediately after his death, Brian de Stapilton, knight, now deceased, and Robert Conyers of York, yeoman, who still lives, entered into the premises, by what title the jurors know not, and received the profits until the death of Brian on

20 September last, and since then Robert has received them until this day. John Holme of Holdernesse is kinsman and heir of William, viz., son of Margaret his sister, and is aged forty years and more.

(*fo.* 189, *b.*) Release by Alice, late the wife of Adam Gower of Thornton, co. Lincoln, son of John Williamson of Whallesgrave by Scardeburgh, and William Whallesgrave of York, glover, son of the said Adam and Alice, to Robert Mauldson of Scardeburgh, of his lands in Whallesgrave. Seal. York, 12 February, 5 Henry v. (1417–18). Acknowledged on the feast (*fo.* 190) of S. Valentine, martyr, 5 Henry v. (14 February, 1417-18) in the time of John Moreton, mayor, and enrolled by Roger de Burton, common clerk. Release by the same to the same of land in Hatterbergh by Scarborough.

Writ to the mayor and escheator of York to deliver the messuage and garden adjoining upon Bishophill, held by William de Sheffeld deceased, to Richard Norton and Roger Crome, to whom the king has committed the custody of the same during the minority of the heir, at the yearly rent of 40 *s.* and 6 *s.* 8 *d.* increase. Westminster, 29 January, 5 Henry v. (1417–18). This writ was delivered to John Moreton, mayor and escheator, by Roger Crome, 10 March, 5 Henry v. (1417–18) and was executed by William Ryllyngton, sub-escheator.

Memorandum quod iiij^{to} die Julii, 6 Henry v. (1418). Willelmus Neuland, Thomas Bemeslay, Johannes Danby, et Johannes Hall, arbitratores electi ad concordandum Johannem Besyngby seniorem et Henricum Appilby de omnibus actionibus, litibus, et querelis, inter eos motis et habitis usque in hunc diem, venerunt hic in camera coram Johanne de Moreton, maiore, Roberto Hovyngham, [Johanne] Aldestanmor, Rogero de Burton, clerico communi, Johanne Stertavant, et aliis, et recordabantur quod concordarunt predictas partes de omnibus premissis; et quod inter alia corum erat arbitrium et judicium, quod si probari possit decetero quod predictus Henricus vocaverit predictum Johannem Besyngby, publice vel occulte, usurarium, seu quidquam aliud de eo dixerit, quod bonam famam ipsius Johannis ledet, vel in ejus obprobrium sonare poterit in futurum, quod tunc predictus Henricus amittet vj *s.* viij *d.* ad opus communitatis

Ebor', et vj *s.* viij *d.* ad opus pontis Fosse et fabrice capelle Sancte Anne ibidem ; et hoc audito predictus Henricus dixit quod ordinacioni, judicio et arbitrio predictis obediet bona voluntate. Burton.

(*fo.* 191). Release by William Thuresby, son of Richard Thuresby, late citizen and merchant of York, to John Aldestanmore, citizen and merchant of York, and Agnes his wife, for term of life of Agnes, of a capital messuage in Micklegate. Witnesses, William Bowes, mayor, John Waughen, Thomas Snawdon, sheriffs ; William del Both, Robert Mason, clerks. York, 27 March, 5 Henry v. (1416-17).

(*fo.* 191, *b.*) Honorius episcopus, servus servorum Dei, dilecto filio B., rectori capelle supra pontem fluminis Huse, salutem et apostolicam benedictionem. Cum a nobis petitur quod justum est et honestum, tam vigor equitatis quam ordo exigit racionis, ut id per solicitudinem officii nostri ad debitum perducatur effectum. Eapropter, dilecte in Domino fili, tuis justis postulacionibus grato concurrentes assensu, personam tuam cum omnibus bonis que impresenciam racionabiliter possides, aut in futurum justis modis prestante Domino poteris adipisci sub beati Petri et nostra protectione suscipimus specialiter, autem capellam supra pontem fluminis Use cum pertinenciis suis, sicut eam juste, canonice ac pacifice possides, auctoritate tibi apostolica confirmamus et presentis scripti patrocinio communimus. Nulli ergo omnino hominum liceat hanc paginam nostre protectionis et confirmacionis infringere vel ausu temerario contraire. Si quis autem hoc attemptare presumpserit indignacionem Omnipotentis Dei et beatorum Petri et Pauli apostolorum ejus se noverit incursurum. Datum Lateran' iij idus Maii pontificatus nostri anno septimo (13 May, 1223[1]).

xiiij^{mo} die Junii, 6 Henry v. (1418) Willelmus Sauvage de Ebor' venit hic in camera consilii hujus civitatis super pontem Use, coram Johanne de Moreton, maiore Ebor', et Roberto Yarom, Johanne Loftehouse, vicecomitibus ejusdem, Johanne Petyclerk, Johanne Lyllyng, Johanne Gascoigne, Johanne Dodyngton, Rogero de Burton, clerico communi, Johanne

1—(Honorius iij).

GRANT OF THE MANOR OF LETTEBY (1418)

Kyrkeby, armigero, et Johanne Wersworth, et aliis, rogavit Willelmum Alne, civem et mercatorem Ebor' ibidem presentem, ut solveret pro eo Thome Garton, clerico, viginti libras sterlingorum, quas idem Thomas Garton clamabat de Willelmo Sauvage predicto, per quandam obligacionem xx li inde factam. Et predictus Willelmus Alne ad instanciam et rogatum predicti Willelmi Sauvage promisit solvere predictas xx li predicto Thome Garton pro dicto Willelmo Sauvage. Et xv die Junii, anno predicto, Willelmus Alne predictus venit hic in camera et recognovit quod solvit predicto Thome Garton xx li pro dicto Willelmo Sauvage ad rogatum suum, et in fidem et testimonium solucionis predictarum xx li ostendit hic in camera objuracionem predicti Willelmi Sauvage factam per eum predicto Thome Garton de xx li predictis, cujus obligacionis verus tenor sequitur (*fo*. 192) et est talis :—Bond by William Sauvage of York to Thomas Garton, clerk, for repayment of a loan of 20 *l*. on the feast of the Purification next. Seal. The feast of S. Martin, bishop, 3 Henry v. (11 November, 1415), " Jhs in sigillo sculpt'."

Burton.

Grant by William Bempton of York, and William Norton, vicar of Esyngwald, to John Scharrowe, citizen of York, and Agnes his wife, of the vill, manor and lordship of Letteby, with the homage, rents, and services of Robert Bullyng, John Pogethorpe and Margaret Wymmer. Witnesses, Marmaduke Darrell, Thomas Malebys, Richard Grene, John Wath, Adam Bacoun, clerk. Letteby, 14 March, 4 Henry v. (1416–17). Acknowledged by the said William Bempton and Agnes Scharrowe, before John de Moreton, mayor, sir Adam Bacoun, Roger de Burton, common clerk, John Laxton, John Askham, citizens, 27 June, 1418, 6 Henry v.

Burton.

(*fo*. 193). Two entries concerning encroachments.

(*fo*. 193, *b*.) Memorandum quod 5 Ric. ii. (1381). xxiiij[to] die Novembris, fuerunt omnes carte conventus Fratrum Ordinis Predicatorum Ebor' confirmate per dictum regem et confirmaciones in regis rotulo rotulate. Et eodem anno fuerunt muri terrestres versus muros civitatis destructi et ad solum redacti, et magne porte tam versus Usam quam versus kynges toftes ablate per communes civitatis insurgentes die Lune proximo post festum

Corporis Christi, hoc est xvij° die mensis Junii anno Domini millesimo ccc^{mo} lxxx^{mo} primo. Et in sequente xl^{ma} fuit Simon de Quixlay, qui tunc fuit maior civitatis supradicte, compulsus per consilium regis in cancellaria ad reformandum et reparandum muros et portas superius memoratos in expensis civitatis. Ad quod faciendum ante festum nativitatis Johannis Baptiste proximo tunc futurum fuit obligatus per recognicionem in cancellaria regis sub pena quinque millium marcarum; et quod de cetero illi de civitate non inferrent violenciam loco fratrum supradictorum sub pena superius memorata. Hec omnia procurata et prosecuta fuerunt per reverendum virum fratrem Johannem Paris in expensis suis propriis. Et alia clausula carte predictorum fratrum scribitur infra, folio cc^{mo} primo.

(*fo.* 194). Letters Patent dated 3 August, 1428; it recapitulates the order, by which Richard II. forbade butchers to throw offal into the Ouse in the neighbourhood of the monastery of the Friars Minor.

Congregati fuerunt hic in camera super pontem in crastino Sancti Laurencii, anno regni Regis predicti sexto, et perlecto dicto brevi et intellecto, assenserunt quod ammodo fimi, feditates, exitus et (*fo.* 194, *b.*) intestina bestiarum et alia sordida quecumque, proveniencia tam de carnificio tam de aliis locis infra civitatem Ebor', ponantur et proiciantur et laventur ad tempus procul a gardino predictorum Fratrum Minorum, inter lez Holmes et aquam de Ouse, prope locum ubi naves emendari et de novo fieri solent, ex opposito Clementhorp, ubi homines de Fulford et aliis villis cum batellis suis et navibus suis, fimos, feditates, exitus, et intestina predicta possint abducere, pro cultura et compostacione terrarum suarum; quousque maior, probi homines et consilium civitatis istius, melius deliberentur de loco congruo, ubi fimi, fedetates, exitus, et intestina predicta poni, lavari et proici possint, sine nocumento predictorum fratrum. Et super hoc facta est premunicio scrutatoribus carnificum Ebor.'

Et cum quedam discordia mota erat inter fratres gilde Sancte Trinitatis, que per aliquot annos sustentata erat in ecclesia conventuali fratrum predicatorum Ebor', ubi in multo major et sanior pars ipsius gilde consensit quod fieret unio et annectio ipsius gilde fraternitati Sancti Antonii in Ebor', paucis numero quasi xxxvij fratribus ejusdem gilde dissencientibus et clamantibus torcheas et alia bona communia ipsius gilde ad se pertinere, ducentibusque juxta eorum sacramentum in recepcione sua ad dictam gildam factum in ecclesia conventuali predicta dictam gildam teneri et velle sustinere. Et durante discordia hujusmodi quidam de numero majori fratrum ipsius gilde die Martis crastino ad Vincula Sancti Petri dictam ecclesiam conventualem ingressi fuerunt, et quandam longam cistam dicte gilde ibi stantem, in qua securitatis causa torchee et alia bona communia dicte gilde ponebantur, ceperunt et extra conventum predictum removerunt ; qua de causa inter predictos priorem et conventum et predictos fratres dicte gilde pauciores et dissencientes, ut predictum est, ex una parte, et reliquos fratres ejusdem gilde in numero multo majores, ex altera parte, discordia pejor priori mota erat, ipsis priore et conventu clamantibus predictam cistam et omnia in ea inclusa ad se pertinere tanquam eis et loco suo oblata, et asportatores ipsius ciste in excommunicacionis majoris sentenciam incidisse, et ipsos eos occasione ipsa excommunicatos v. ll^e denunciare non cessantes quousque restitucio inde fuerit eis facta, et delinquentes in hoc casu absolucionis beneficium in forma juris meruerint obtinere, fratribus majoris numeri dicte gilde hoc fieri denegantibus. Tandem tamen personarum indifferencium mediante tractatu omnes partes predicte se submiserunt ordinacioni, judicio, et consideracioni maioris et consilii camere de et super discordia et bonis predictis. Unde die, mense et annis Domini et regis predictis, Johannes de Moreton et omnes alii probi homines predicti, habita communicacione matura et diligenti de premissis, invenerunt quod dicta gilda Sancte Trinitatis fundata et sustentata erat in loco predicto sine licencia domini nostri regis Anglie, qui nunc est, vel aliquorum antecessorum suorum regum Anglic, et contra ordinaciones et statuta regni Anglie, quod diucius tolerare noluerunt. Ideo, ordinarunt, judicarunt, et considerarunt quod dicta gilda Sancte Trinitatis cessaret et super (fo. 195) sederet, et hii qui fuerunt fratres ipsius gilde extunc non facerent nec haberent inter se aliquam congregacionem in loco predicto nec alibi, nec aliquam liberatam in capiciis vel aliis signis vel rebus darent, nec reciperent, nisi ad hoc faciendum graciam et licenciam habuerint a domino nostro rege, et quod imago Trinitatis, in cujus honore et sub cujus vocabulo dicta gilda fundata erat, remaneat dictis priori et conventui unacum quodam candelabro coram predicta imagine pendenti et candela supra ipsum candelabrum posita, pro eo quod imago, candelabrum, et candela ipsa fuerunt res spirituales et oblata predictis priori et fratribus remansura sine intencione et animo removendi; pro eo tamen quod videbatur eis quod predicte torchee et cista, in qua reponebantur, fuerunt bona et catalla temporalia predicte gilde in sepulturis fratrum et sororum dicte gilde ad disposicionem custodum ejusdem, extra dictum conventum remotiva sine requisicione vel assensu prioris et conventus predictorum, ideo consideratum erat quod ipsa cista reportaretur ad et in ecclesiam conventualem predictam racione capcionis et spoliacionis, quas dicti prior et fratres pretendebant, et facta reportacione ipsa quod tunc ipsa cista portaretur ad capellam Sancti Willelmi super pontem Use Ebor', et esset postea ad dispocionem maioris, et torchee que in ea erant deservirent dum durant et comburerentur in capella predicta in solempnizacione celebracionis divinorum, et quod pecunia, si qua fuerat in thesauraria de communitate fratrum dicte gilde Sancte Trinitatis, deliberarentur maiori, et expenderentur circa construccionem nove capelle Sancte Anne apud pontem Fosse in Ebor', quodque predicti prior et conventus extunc cessarent et supersederent de quarumcumque excommunicacionis et aliarum censurarum ecclesiasticarum sentenciis, et alio quocumque processu juris ecclesiastici et secularis. Cui quidem consideracioni partes predicte adquieverunt, et facta restitucione predicte ciste predictis priori et conventui, portata erat ab hinc ad et in capellam Sancti Willelmi predictam, et postea demandata et disposicioni maioris posita hic in camera, pro thesauro, rotulis et libris civitatis in posterum custodiendis.

Item eisdem die et annis Domini et regis, maior et probi homines predicti admiserunt ordinaciones factas de novo per piscarios de Ousegate, et assignaverunt extraneis piscariis, pro vendicione piscium suorum aque recentis veniencium ad hanc civitatem locum supra pontem Use, ubi venditores pomorum et aliorum fructuum stare solebant, et quod batelli extraneorum piscariorum, cum venerint ad civitatem, non stent de cetero cum batellis piscariorum hujus civitatis, sed per se procul ab eis in aqua Use ex opposito venelle de Thruslane, et super hoc proclamacio facta est.

Taxa de Bouthom.

Item quo ad xliiij *s.* quos collectores de Northridingo clamant colligere pro taxa domini regis de inhabitatoribus de Bouthom, quod est suburbium hujus civitatis, consensum est et concordatum quod statim post festum Michaelis proximo futurum consilium civitatis communicet cum consilio dictorum collectorum apud London'; et de consilio amborum eligant viam meliorem quam sciverint pro triacione in scaccario domini regis utrum inhabitatores de Bouthom solvere teneantur et debeant xliiij *s.* predictos cum patria Northridingi adjacente vel non. Et pro hujusmodi triacione facienda promiserunt maior et probi homines predicti, quod cives nostri Ebor' erunt contributorii pro expensis in hac materia faciendis. Burton.

(*fo.* 195, *b.*) Responsum Johannis de Moreton, maioris civitatis Ebor'.

Tenorem securitatis pacis de Willelmo de Preston coram me et sociis meis capte coram domino rege in cancellariam suam mitto secundum formam hujus brevis huic eidem brevi consuti. Memorandum quod die Lune proximo ante diem Dominicam in Ramis Palmarum anno regni Regis Henrici quinti sexto[1] apud Ebor', coram Johanne de Moreton, tunc maiore civitatis Ebor', et sociis suis, aldermannis ejusdem civitatis, tunc custodibus pacis et justiciariis domini Regis infra civitatem predictam et suburbia ac libertatem ejusdem civitatis, Johannes Dodyngton de Ebor', *marchaund,* Willelmus Aukebarowe de eadem, *marchaund,* Thomas Goddesbroke de eadem, *marchaund,* et Johannes Duffeld de eadem, *marchaund,* venerunt in propriis personis suis et manuceperunt pro Willelmo de Preston de Ebor', *irynmanger,* quod ipse dampnum vel malum aliquid Roberto de Feriby de Ebor' de corpore suo non faceret nec fieri procuraret quovismodo, et quod extunc predictus Thomas Salvayn' gereret

1—There was no Monday before Palm Sunday in 6 Henry V. This day was 14 March (1417–18), 5 Henry V., or 3 April, 1419, 6 Henry V.

pacem domini regis erga predictum Robertum et quemcumque de populo domini regis, sub pena cujuslibet manucaptorum predictorum viginti librarum, quas coram prefatis justiciariis tunc ibidem concesserunt fieri et levari de bonis et catallis, terris et tenementis suis et eorum cujuslibet, ad opus dicti domini regis, si predictus Willelmus de Preston contra pacem dicti domini regis modo quo premittitur limitatam in aliquo contravenerit in futurum; et predictus Willelmus de Preston, similiter in propria persona sua tunc ibidem existens, coram eisdem justiciariis concessit quadraginta libras de bonis et catallis, terris et tenementis suis, fieri et levari ad opus domini Regis, si ipse Thomas Salvayn contra pacem domini Regis prout superius annotatur, quidquid attemptare presumeret in futurum.

Certificate of searchers of Carpenters.[1]

(*fo.* 196, *b.*) Johannes de Moreton, maior; Robertus Howom, Nicholaus Blakburn, senior, Thomas Santon, Willelmus Alne, Willelmus Bowes, Ricardus Russell, Johannes Bedale; de xii, Johannes Hewyk, Johannes Bouche, Henricus Preston, Thomas Doncaster, Johannes Usseburn, Robertus Lokton, Johannes Petyclerk, Petrus Buksy, Thomas Esyngwald, Robertus Midelton, Willelmus Ormesheued, Galfridus Sauvage, Thomas Bracebryg, Ricardus Spenser, Johannes Waghen, Thomas Snawdon; de xxiiij, Robertus Yarum, Johannes Loftehouse, vicecomites, congregati fuerunt, primo hic in camera consilii, et deinde in aula communi hujus civitatis Ebor', die Mercurii, festo Sancti Mathei apostoli et evaungeliste, anno Domini millesimo ccccxviij, 6 Henry v. (21 September), et de eorum unanimi consensu et assensu necnon voluntate tocius communitatis in dicta aula presentis ordinatum erat et stabilitum quod [2]. . . . . [2]

Et hoc ordinato, statim surrexerunt Robertus Yarom et Johannes Loftehouse, vicecomites hujus civitatis Ebor', et ut moris est, sursum reddiderunt officia sua vicecomitum coram maiore, probis [hominibus], et communitate congregata. Et hii, ad quos electio novorum vicecomitum civitatis pertinuit, ex ordinacione

[1]—English Miscellany, Surtees Society, vol. 85, p. 12.
[2]—2—Six and a half lines have been erased here.

et consuetudine ejusdem accesserunt in interiorem cameram apud gildam aulam, maiore et communitate in aula remanentibus, et unanimiter elegerunt Robertum Midelton, mercerum, unum de xxiiij^{or}, nuper custumarium in portu de Kyngeston super Hull, et Johannem Baynbryg, *potter*, cives Ebor', in vicecomites, ad occupandum officium vicecomitum in hac civitate per annum proximo sequentem. Et jurati sunt ut mos est civitatis, et plegios invenerunt.

Subsequenter antepenultimo die Septembris anno regni Regis predicti ix°, tempore Ricardi Russell maioris, ordinatum erat quod nulli de cetero eligantur in numerum xxiiij, nisi prius fuissent vicecomites civitatis, si tot ex eis inventi fuerint habiles ad illum numerum implendum, et si tot ex eis non fuerint habiles ad illum numerum implendum, tunc eligantur alii habiles juxta discrecionem eligencium ad occupandum illum numerum etc.

Certificate of searchers of masons and wrights.[1]

Lease by Christopher Spenser of Langtofte to Philip Appylby of York, tailor, of a garden and nine selions of land without Walmgate bar, in the suburb of York, by the hospital of S. Nicholas. To hold from Whitsuntide 1489 for term of eighty years, at a yearly rent of 6 s. to Christopher, and 3 s. 4 d. to the monastery of S. Peter of York. Philip shall build a cottage and a barn upon the said garden within four years, under penalty of 20 s. Seals. Witnesses, John Moreton, mayor, Robert Yarom, and John Loftehous, sheriffs, Richard Haukeswell, Thomas Forster, Thomas Whetall. York, 26 February, 5 Henry v. (1417–18).

Certificate of searchers of masons and wrights.[2]

(*fo.* 197). Johannes de Moreton, maior; Nicholas Blakburn, Thomas Santon, Willelmus Bowes, Ricardus Russell, de xij; Johannes Hewyk, Thomas Doncaster, Robertus Lokton, Thomas Esyngwald, Willelmus Ormesheued, Thomas Bracebryg, Johannes Waghen, Thomas Snawdon, de xxiiij^{or}, congregati fuerunt hic in camera xviij° die mensis Novembris, 6 Henry v. (1418), et conquestum erat coram eis quod Johannes Charters, portour communis, noluit pondera carbonum et aliarum mercandisarum

1—Eng. Misc. *op. cit.*, p. 13.
2—Eng. Misc. *op. cit.*, p. 13.

in aqua Use veniencium portare, cum fuerat requisitus pro salario constituto in antiqua ordinacione civitatis, et quod idem Johannes verba obprobriosa publice in aperto dixit et intulit Willelmo Bowes, aldermanno, unde lectis constitucionibus de portitoribus editis et factis, predictus Johannes posuit se in misericordia et gracia maioris et proborum hominum predictorum, et peciit de Willelmo Bowes predicto.

Grant by Richard Richemond of Ripon, son of Richard Richemond of the same, with the assent of Robert Richemond and Richard Richemond his sons, to Robert Percy of Scotton, Thomas Percy, chaplain, John Scotton, vicar of the church of Farnham, and William Walthewe, chaplain, of a burgage in le Marketsted in Rypon, between a burgage of William Ingilby and a burgage of William Tanfeld, and extending in length from the high street before to the ditch of the archbishop of York called le Halgarthdyke behind. York, 21 December, 6 Henry v. (1418). Acknowledged before John de Moreton, mayor.

Ultimo die mensis Decembris anno Domini millesimo ccccxviij° et 6 Henry v., Thomas Wyllardeby venit hic in camera coram Johanne de Moreton, maiore Ebor', Willelmo Alne, Thoma Gare, Johanne Waghen, Thoma Snawdon, Rogero de Burton, clerico communi, et de sua propria voluntate recusavit de cetero operari in arte monetarii et myntarii, et elegit amodo tantum artem peudrariorum occupare, et ad hoc corporale prestitit sacramentum.

Appointment of Richard Hawkeswell, mercer, William Scoreburgh, merchant, John Man, tapiter, and Thomas Wetherby, osteler, all of York, as collectors in the city and suburbs of two tenths and fifteenths granted by the last parliament; of which, one shall be paid at the feast of the Purification next, and the other at the same feast then next following. Westminster, 18 December, 5 Henry v. (1417).

(*fo.* 198). [1]Jacobus, Dei gracia Rex Jerusalem et Cipri, serenissimo principi et domino, domino Ricardo, Dei gracia Anglie Regi, illustri fratri nostro carissimo. Serenissime et

---

1—Printed in Letters from the Northern Registers, Roll Series, p. 425.

illustrissime princeps, frater carissime, salutem et fraterne dilectionis continuum incrementum.

Literas vestre serenitatis amicabiles et graciosas cum gaudio recepimus, per quas nobis recommendatis nobilem consanguineum vestrum, Johannem, dominum de Roos etc. Frater carissime, non expedit vos aliquos vestros nobis recommendare, cum sint nobis multum cari omnes qui de regno vestro huc accedunt, et ita libenter eos videmus et habemus gratos, quando dignentur nos visitare, tanquam fratres et amicos benivolos, et tunc cognoscimus quod nos diligunt. Quapropter, carissime frater, si casus contingeret aliquem de regno vestro huc accedere dignum (*fo.* 198, *b.*) literis vestre celsitudinis nos visitare, et nobis notificare illos qui erunt de hospicio vestro, et eos multum suscipiemus gratos. Et quia vestros nostros, et nostros vestros, tenemus et reputamus, et si aliqua reperiuntur hic vestre celsitudini grata, que per nos possunt fieri, nobis dignemini confidenter intimare, quia toto cordis affectu totoque posse nostro ea curabimus adimplere. Et super hoc quod nobilis consanguineus vester, dominus Henricus Perci, retulit vobis nos sibi fecisse curialitatem et honorem, et de hoc nobis regraciamur, frater carissime, ipse dixit sua curialitate et nobilitate quid sibi placuit. Sed nos tenemus quod ipse nobis fecit maximum honorem nos visatasse et sibi multum regraciamur. Altissimus conservet vestram celsitudinem feliciter et votive. Datum Nicossie die xv Julii mcccxc tercio.

Inquisicio capta apud Ebor' die lune proximo ante festum conversionis Sancti Pauli, 6 Henry v. (23 January, 1418-9), coram Johanne de Moreton, maiore civitatis Ebor' ac escaetore ejusdem, per sacramentum Johannis Waghen, Ricardi Stryghtlay, *girdeler*, Willelmi Pirler, *bower*, Willelmi Rowlay, *capmaker*, Johannis Preston, *bokelmaker*, Rogeri del Hay, Johannis Symondson, Willelmi Barton, Johannis Gargrave, Johannis Sharrowe, Johannis Kyrspyn, Roberti de Neuton, Thome Whittik, et Johannis Marsshall juratorum. Qui dicunt super sacramentum suum quod Robertos Wenceley de Ebor', *bower*, utlagatus in comitatu Ebor' die Lune proximo post festum Epiphanie Domini anno supradicto (9 January, 1418-19) ad sectam Roberti de Waterton de placito debiti, et virtute cujusdam brevis domini regis eidem vicecomiti inde directi, coram justiciariis domini Regis de banco, apud Westmonasterium in octavis Purificacionis Beate Marie Virginis retornandi, habuit dicto die utlagarie sue diversa bona infra civitatem predictam, videlicet, unum dorsorium cum suis b . . k . . r, et sex cosshyns precii vj d., unam cathedram, vj stoles, j formam precii iiij d., unum lectum et unum coverlet, ij blankettes, ij lintheamina, j . . . . precii xij d., j brandreth et j spytt precii ij d., unam ollam et unam pelvem precii xij d., j waterkan precii iiij d., duas ollas pro cervisia precii iiij d., duas standes precii iiij d., unam cistam debilem precii iiij d., j qiver . . . precii iiij d., unam tondre et unam mensuram precii iij d., unam pelvem cum uno lavacro precii xij d. Et residium omnium bonorum aliorum appreciatur per dictos juratores ad iij d. Et habuit ibidem focale precii viij d. Et dicunt super sacramentum quod predictus Robertus Wenceley nulla habuit plura bona seu catalla dicto die utlagarie predicte infra civitatem predictam, nec sunt aliqua bona seu catalla alicujus alterius utlagati infra eandem civitatem prout aliquo modo eisdem juratoribus constare potest. In cujus rei testimonium predicti juratores huic inquisicioni sigilla sua apposuerunt. Datum die, loco et anno supradictis.

(fo. 199). Two certificates of searchers of masons and wrights.[1]

(fo. 199, b-200, b.) Placita apud Westmonasterium coram Ricardo Norton et sociis suis, justiciariis domini regis de banco de termino Sancti Hillarii 6 Henry v. (1417-18). Rotulo ccxj.

Marmaduke Darell of Sessay, knight, and Joan, his wife, are ordered to return to John Bouche and Mary, his wife, a house and outbuildings, situated in Bootham.

Johannes Artays et Johannes Walter, nati in Normannia, capti ibidem tempore guerre, venerunt hic in camera coram Johanne de Bedale, maiore, et jurarunt ad Sancta Dei evaungelia, xx^{mo} die mensis Maii, anno Domini millesimo ccccxix° 7 Henry v. quod erunt boni et fideles prisonarii Willelmi Barton de Ebor', *skynner*, et cum eo morabuntur, et sibi servient fideliter,

1—Eng. Misc. *op. cit.*, pp. 13, 14.

et non absentabunt se a servicio suo, quousque eorum redempciones et financie fuerint predicto Willelmo magistro suo plenarie persolute.

Certificate of searchers of daubers and carpenters.

(*fo.* 201). Johannes de Bedale, maior; Nicholaus Blakburn, Robertus Howom, Thomas Santon, Johannes Northeby, Johannes Moreton, Ricardus Russell, Johannes Blakburn, Thomas Gare, de xij; vicecomes Johannes Baynbryg; Thomas Hewyk, Johannes Penreth, Henricus Preston, Thomas Doncaster, Willelmus Lamberd, Thomas More, Johannes Peticlerk, Thomas Esyngwald, Robertus Gare, Willelmus Wynkburn, Willelmus Ormesheued, Thomas Bracebryg, Robertus Burton, Robertus Yarom, de xxiiij^{or}; congregati fuerunt in camera consilii super pontem Use hujus civitatis Ebor', die crastina festi Corporis Christi (16 June) in anno Domini millesimo ccccxix° regni vero regis Henrici quinti septimo contingente, ubi venerunt diversi artifices de *skynnercrafte* et gravem querelam fecerunt, quod diversi artifices carpentariorum et allutariorum civitatis predicte, in festo Corporis Christi annis predictis, ipsorum torcheas accensas, et ut portarentur in processione dicti festi coram Corpore Christi ibidem presenti, fregerunt et deorsum traxerunt cum fustibus suis et carlelaxaes, quos illuc portaverunt, et alia enormia fecerunt in gravem perturbacionem pacis domini regis et impedimentum ludi processionis Corporis Christi. Super qua quidem querela capti fuerunt et imprisonati Simon Calton et Benedictus Williamson, carpentarii, et Thomas Durem, *cordewaner*, et predicti Simon et Benedictus coram maiore et consilio civitatis, hic in camera venientes, objecta sibi transgressione predicta, recognoverunt se predicta fecisse, et posuerunt se in misericordia, gracia et ordinacione maioris et consilii camere civitatis, et ad hoc faciendum predicti Simon et Benedictus, necnon Johannes Mosse, Johannes Bolron, Willelmus Kyrkeby, Ricardus Ferrour, Willelmus Cunsby, Johannes Haxeby, Thomas Cunnysburgh, et Johannes Skathelok, *wryghts*, et cives Ebor' per scriptum suum obligatorium obligantur in centum libris sterlingorum ut in eodem plenius continetur.

Memorandum quod ubi Thomas Dene de Ebor', *mason*, clamavit de Roberto Barry quod faceret et edificaret quandam domum ipsius Roberti in Coliergate Ebor', in tenura Roberti . . . . *sadeler*. virtute cujusdam convencionis inter ipsos Thomam Dene et Robertum Barry inde facte, ut dicebat. Super quo xxvj^{to} die Maii, 9 Henry v. (1421), venerunt hic in camera consilii coram Ricardo Russell, maiore Ebor', Johannes Ampilford, Johannes Thorp, *masons*, Johannes Askham et Thomas Beste, carpentarii, scrutatores jurati cementariorum et carpentariorum hujus civitatis Ebor', et recordabantur quod de mandato Thome Gare, nuper maioris Ebor', examinacionem et diligens scrutinium fecerunt inter partes predictas de materia prenotata, sed tandem invenerunt quod predictus Robertus Barry nullam talem convencionem fecit cum Thoma Dene predicto alicujus virtutis, sed quod libere potuit facere predictam domum suam edificari per aliquem alium hominem, cum quo de edificacione illius domus voluerit et potuerit concordari, sine aliquo defectu, calumpnia, vel impedimento juris predicti Thome Dene. Burton.

(*fo.* 201, *b.*) Judicium scrutinii facti inter abbatem et conventum de Melsa, ex una parte, et priorem et conventum Fratrum Carmelitarum in civitate Ebor', ex altera.

Johannes Ampilford, Willelmus Cunsby, et Willelmus Warter, scrutatores jurati artificiorum de *lez masons* et *wryghtes* in civitate Ebor', suburbiis et procinctu ejusdem, assignati per Henricum Preston, maiorem predicte civitatis Ebor', ad separandum et limitandum quandam clausuram ligneam vel lapideam, ponendam inter solum predictorum abbatis et conventus et terram gardini predictorum fratrum, partibus premunitis, secundum consuetudinem civitatis considerant et judicant per sacramentum suum quod predicti prior et fratres ponant et erigant clausuram gardini sui eisdem modo et forma, sicut certi postes et palus ligneus predictorum prioris et fratrum ibidem pro presenti ponuntur, a cornerio exteriori domus molendini predictorum prioris et fratrum usque ad vivarium de Fosse. Et quia non potest evadi quin futuris temporibus postes predicti diuturnitate temporum corrumpentur, igitur prior et fratres per judicium scrutatorum predictorum in prima posicione postium et pali predictorum posuerunt deorsum in fundo sub pede cujuslibet postium predictorum magnum lapidem, ut exinde certitudinis memoria in premissis facilius et melius habeatur in futurum. Burton.

De crana. Memorandum quod cum crana hujus civitatis Ebor' sit jam de novo edificata et constructa loco consueto apud Hyngbryg, cum certis domibus eidem annexis de magnis sumptibus communitatis, ideo de consensu Willelmi Bowes, maioris, Johannis Waghen et Thome Snawdon, vicecomitum, necnon aldermannorum et tocius consilii camere ejusdem civitatis, volencium incrementum firme crane predicte et proficuum ac melioracionem reddituum ejusdem civitatis in futurum, ordinatum erat secundo die Maii, anno Domini millesimo ccccxvij^{mo} 5 Henry v., et eodem die in aula communi coram communitate publicatum et per communitatem affirmatum, quod omnimoda mercimonia, species, vina, wadda, madera, alumen et omnes alie mercandise, que sunt per pondus vendende, extraneorum mercatorum ad predictam civitatem ex quacumque parte per aquam veniencia, decetero hospitentur in crana predicta et domibus ejusdem et non alibi, de et cum supervisu custodis crane predicte pro tempore existentis, et ibidem morentur et expectent quousque plene vendantur in grossa et integra vendicione, et non per retalliam. Et quod species, madera, alumen, et omnes alie mercandise de averio de pondere mercatorum extraneorum, que venient per aquam in *bales* vel in barell', ponderentur apud cranam predictam cum stateris et ponderibus communitatis, et ibidem vendantur. Et quod omnia predicta mercandise, vina et mercimonia non vendantur alicui apud cranam predictam nisi civibus hujus civitatis, et non forinsecis. Et si probatum fuerit quod aliquis hujus civitatis cooperiat vel sustentet aliqua talia mercimonia, vina, res vel mercandisas de quibus prefertur, ut alibi hospitentur quam in crana predicta et domibus ejusdem, nisi fuerit de licencia speciali maioris hujus civitatis et sociorum suorum pro tempore existencium, quod quilibet talis perdet libertatem suam et reputabitur ut infidelis civitati amodo non confidendus. Et quod universi mercatores extranei, cum predictis rebus et mercandisis singulis temporibus quando per aquam venient, concordent racionabiliter cum custode crane predicte de precio ab eis solvendo pro hujusmodi mercandisis et rebus, ut prefertur, hospitandis;

et si crana predicta et domus ejusdem non sufficiant ad hospitandum res predictas, tunc maior, qui erit pro tempore, providebit mercatoribus ipsis extraneis de domibus aliis necessariis, quousque domus sufficientes edificentur apud cranam predictam. Et super hoc deliberata fuerunt [*sic*] quedam trabes magna, que quondam fuit stapula lanarum cum grossis scalis eidem pertinentibus Johanni Northeby, mercatori, custodi crane predicte, ad ponderandum omnimodas mercandisas per pondus vendendas, cujuscumque fuerint generis vel speciei. Burton, R.

(*fo.* 202). Bond by William Wadman, merchant, Adam Heseham, John Heseham, Robert Dunnyng and John Sutton, litsters, citizens of York, to Godfrey Rust of Duredraght, merchant, for a loan of 100 *l.*, of which 50 *l.* shall be repaid on the feast of S. Peter's Chains (1 August) next and 50 *l.* the following Martinmas. Seals. 15 April, 5 Henry v. (1417). Acknowledged before John de Bedale, mayor, 20 June, 1419, 7 Henry v. The bond shewn by Henry Enghebert, attorney of the said Godfrey.

Cum quedam controversia mota fuit inter Jacobum Toucotes, armigerum, ex parte una, et executores Willelmi del Lee, nuper civis et *bower* Ebor', ex altera parte, pro reparacione cujusdam tenementi predicti Jacobi in Stayngate in Ebor', quod nuper fuit in tenura predicti Willelmi dum vixit, et modo est in tenura Isabelle, que fuit uxor ejusdem Willelmi, igitur Johannes Ampilford, Johannes Thorp, scrutatores cementariorum Ebor', Willelmus Cunsby, Johannes Mosse, scrutatores carpentariorum, Robertus Kereby et Johannes Kyrkeham, plasterarii et tegularii, assignati et jurati coram Johanne de Bedale, maiore Ebor', et electi per partes predictas ad terminandum controversiam predictam, considerantes quod predictus Willelmus del Lee magnas fecit expensas in plasteratura et tegulatura in tenemento predicto, judicabant et considerabant quod executores predicti solvant Jacobo predicto viginti sex solidos, octo denarios, pro reparacione que est necessaria ad presens in tenemento predicto, in plasteratura et tegulatura, et pro clavis, ferro, meremio, et omnibus aliis expensis ad carpentariam et *grundyng* dicti tenementi pertinentibus et necessariis . . . . . bus xlij *s.* viij *d.* Et quod uxor predicti Willelmi del Lee et omnes alii executores ejusdem quieti sint versus predictum Jacobum pro quacumque reparacione predicti tenementi pro omnibus annis et terminis preteritis, et quod predictus Jacobus predictis executoribus inde quietus sit. Burton. Redditum fuit istud judicium in crastino nativitatis Johannis Baptiste, 7 Henry v. (25 June, 1419.) Burton.

(*fo.* 202, *b.*) [1]Audita gravi querela per scrutatores et alios artifices tannatorum hujus civitatis Ebor' frequenter facta quod usus est allut[1] [arius].

Certificate of searchers of masons and wrights.[2]

In magno Rotulo de anno vj^{to} Regis Henrici quinti in civitate Ebor'.

Johannes de Moreton, nuper maior et escaetor regis in civitate Ebor' ac suburbio et procinctu ejusdem, reddit compotum de xj *s.* vij *d.* de exitibus ejusdem escaetrie a tercio die Februarii anno v^{to} usque tercium diem Februarii anno vj^{to} ($14\frac{17}{18}$-$14\frac{18}{19}$), sicut continetur in compoto suo inde rotulo compotorum de escaetria. In thesauro xxvj *s.* viij *d.* in ij talliis. Et habet surplusagium videlicet x *s.* j *d.*

Billa Ducis Excestrie.

Be it knawen to all maner of men that if ther be any persone of what astate or condicion that he be, to whom the Duc of Excestre oweth any moneye, be it for vitayle, marchandise or other thyngs what ever it be, taken by hym or eny of hys officers or servants for hym and to hys use of any suche persone, and yit unpyed fore, or if thay canne complayne upon the sayd Duc or eny of hys sayd officers for eny extorsion done unto hem on the sayde Dukes behalf, that all suche persones comme unto I . . hie Caxton, receyvour generall of the forsayd Duc, and shewe suffisiantly, be yt be writyng or other trewe record, what ys dewe unto hem for eny suche vitaille or marchandise taken of hem or extorsion done unto hem, as it ys above sayde, and they shall be payde or agreed in suche wyse that thay shall hald hem content, yif God wyll. And if ther be any man in thys cite, or in thys cuntre, that will comme at Seint Bartilmeus day to Shalford in in [*sic*] Conyngstrete to William, the lewde frer of Munk grace, of

1—1—This entry is unfinished and is crossed through.
2—Eng. Misc. *op. cit.*, p. 15.

all finale payements he sall pay tham, and of all grete payment he sall gare them be sur. Proclamatum xvij die Augusti, 7 Henry v. (1419).

(*fo.* 203). Johannes Bedale, maior; Nicholaus Blakburn, Thoma Santon, Willelmus Bowes, Johannes de Moreton, Ricardus Russell, Robertus Howom, de xij; Robertus Gare, recordator; Robertus Midelton, vicecomes; Henricus Preston, Petrus Buksy, Thomas Esyngwald, Thomas Doncastr', Johannes Penreth, Johannes Petyclerk, Thomas Bracebryg, Willelmus Lambert, Robertus Lokton, Robertus Jarom, Galfridus Sauvage, Johannes Bouthe, Johannes Waghen, Robertus Middilton, Johannes Hewyk, Thoma Snawdon, Thoma Esyngwald, de xxiiij^{or}, xxvj^{to} die Augusti, 7 Henry v. (1419), congregati fuerunt in camera consilii super pontem Use, ubi maior declaravit quod dominus Henricus de Athedill, chivaler, ipsum oneravit ex parte domini regis, quod fortificaret honorabilem dominum Henricum Percy, comitem Northumbr', custodem de *lestmarche* versus Scociam, cum copia bonorum hominum defensabilium, ad resistendum malicie Scotarum, qui infra breve essent hostiliter invasuri regnum Anglie, in gravem destructionem ejusdem. Et quia maior et probi homines vocabunt in dubium an predictus dominus Henricus Percy de Athedill predicta dixit mocione et capite proprio vel de mandato predicti domini comitis, ideo consenserunt quod Johannes Stertavaunt et Johannes Kyrkeby, armigeri, mitterentur ad dictum dominum comitem ad sciendum certitudinem premissorum. Et predicti Johannes et Johannes, ad dictum comitem euntes et ab eodem redeuntes, retulerunt quod predicta fuerunt dicta sine sciencia predicti domini Henrici comitis. Nichilominus pro casu qui contingere poterit, maior et probi homines hoc scripto consenserunt et ordinaverunt quod decem homines armati ad lanceas, et viginti sagittarii bene arraiati, ordinarentur sumptibus parochiarum in omnibus sicut fiebat tempore Willelmi Bowes, maioris.

(*fo.* 203, *b.*) Writ to John de Bedale, mayor and escheator, to hold a second inquisition after the death of Miles de Stapilton, who held fourteen cottages in the city of York, upon Bishophill, and four cottages without Mykellyth in the suburb of York;

the first inquisition not having specified his estate therein. 9 July, 7 Henry v. (1419).

Answer of the Mayor.

Inquisition held at York on Monday before the feast of the Nativity of the Virgin, 7 Henry v. (4 September, 1419), before John de Bedale, mayor and escheator ; by oath of John Besyngby, John Brounflete, William Neuland, Roger Shalford, Richard Bryan, John Laxton, Robert Kettyll, Thomas Emlay, Thomas Whityk, Thomas Spencer, John Stafford and Thomas Horneby. The said Miles held the said eighteen cottages in tail male with remainder to the right heirs of Brian de Stapilton, knight, his father.

(*fo.* 204). Universis Christi fidelibus presentes literas inspecturis, Johannes de Bedale, maior civitatis Ebor', Robertus Middilton et Johannes Baynbryg, vicecomites ejusdem, salutem in Domino. Mandatum domini Regis in hec verba recepimus :—

(Writ of *certiorari* to send to the chancery, record of the following assise ; dated 1 July, 7 Henry (1419.)

. . . .

Nos igitur volentes informari super veritate premissorum cepimus inquisicionem virtute brevis predicti, die Jovis in vigilia nativitatis beate Marie Virginis, 7 Henry v. (7 September, 1419), in gilda aula dicte civitatis, per sacramentum Johannis Sharrowe, senioris, Ade Heseham, Willelmi Neuland, Henrici Dubber, Ricardi Neuland, Willelmi Semer, Willelmi Coupeland, *draper*, Johannis Waghen, *cutler*, Ricardi Broghton, Dionisii Westerdale, Johannis Huthwayt, Willelmi Coupeland, *taillour*, Roberti Ketyll, Johannis Coucher et Johannis Preston, *buklermaker*, qui dicunt super sacramentum suum quod Johannes de Ripon et Willelmus Tundue, in predicto brevi nominati, nuper arrainiaverunt coram Thoma Graa, nuper maiore Ebor', et Willelmo Sallaye et Johanne de Hewyk, nuper vicecomitibus ejusdem civitatis, quandam assisam frisce forcie sine brevi domini regis secundum consuetudinem dicte civitatis, versus Johannem Alkebarewe, Willelmum Wortelay, Roger Shalford, Thomam Emlaye et Willelmum de Braweby, in predicto brevi nominatos, de quodam tenemento cum pertinenciis in Stayngate in Ebor', modo in tenura Roberti Chaundeler, et per eandem querelam dictum tenementum recuperaverunt. In cujus inquisicionis testimonium, tam sigillum officii maioratus civitatis predicte quam sigilla dictorum juratorum presentibus sunt appensa. Datum apud Ebor', vij^{mo} die Septembris, (7 Henry v.)

(*fo.* 204, *b.*) Johannes de Bedale, maior; Nicholaus Blakburn, Thomas Santon, Willelmus Bowes, Johannes de Moreton, Johannes Blakburn, Thomas Gare, de xij; Johannes Hewyk, Johannes Bouthe, Johannes Penreth, Thomas Doncastr', Henricus Preston, Johannes Usburn, Robertus Lokton, Thomas More, Thomas Esyngwald, Galfridus Sauvage, Thomas Bracebrig, Robertus Gare, Willelmus Ormeshed, Thomas Snawdon, Robertus Jarom, Robertus Burton, Johannes Waghen, de xxiiij^{or}; Robertus Middilton, Johannes Baynbrig, vicecomites, congregati fuerunt in aula communi in festo Sancti Mathei apostoli anno Domini millesimo, ccccxix° 7 Henry v. (21 September), ubi et quando de consensu eorum et tocius communitatis civium ibidem congregata ordinatum erat quod nulli Scoti nec aliqui alii alienigene, habitantes et habituri infra libertatem civitatis hujus, cujuscumque artificii vel status fuerint, ab hac die in antea gerant vel occupent officia scrutatorum, constabulariorum aut aliqua alia officia civitatis, qualiacumque fuerint, majora vel minora, nec habebunt aliquem modum intromittendi vel regimen in civitate ista, nec intrabunt nec venient in aulam communem vel aliqua alia loca civitatis, sub pena imprisonamenti xl dierum, ad videndum vel audiendum secreta consilia vel negocia hujus civitatis, nec inter se congregaciones aliquas aut conventicula aliquo tempore facient, nec in assisis vel inquisicionibus aliquibus pro re vel causa aliqua impanellati vel jurati erunt, sed ab omnimodis officiis, occupacionibus et omnibus aliis premissis sint imperpetuum penitus exclusi. Et quod predicta officia occupaciones et alia premissa expediantur et perpetuis temporibus occupentur per cives et homines hujus civitatis, qui de bona noticia hominum nati sunt et erunt infra regnum Anglie et sub ligeancia domini nostri regis Anglie et heredum suorum regum Anglie.

Et quia Robertus Middilton et Johannes Baynbryg, dum erant vicecomites hujus civitatis Ebor', presumebant super se ire per vicos et placeas civitatis publice sine aliquo servientum suorum ad clavam eos precedente, vel aliqua honesta familia

eos a tergo sequente, ad gravem inhonestatem, scandalum et
verecundiam tocius hujus civitatis predicte, igitur maior et
probi homines et communitas, premissa nolentes ducius tolerare
sed remedium apponere, unanimiter consenserunt et ordinarunt
quod omnes vicecomites hujus civitatis, qui sunt et pro tempore
erunt, non eant decetero infra civitatem, suburbia et procinctum
ejusdem nisi habeant ante eos unum servientem ad clavam ad
minus precedentem, et ad minus unum honestum hominem eos
a tergo sequentem, sic quod pro vicecomitibus ab aliis hominibus
possint cognosci; et hoc nullo modo omittant nisi gravis, subita et
inevitabilis necessitas et casus emerserint, sub pena forisfacture
centum solidorum, usui communitatis sine pardonacione solvendorum a quolibet vicecomite pro vice qualibet quando istius
ordinacionis contrarium fecerit, et super hoc convictus fuerit
quoquomodo.

Et eodem die Johannes Bolton, *mercer*, et Thomas Davy
draper, electi fuerunt in vicecomites hujus civitatis Ebor' pro
anno extunc futuro.

Et eodem die Johannes Northeby et Thomas Gare, cives et
mercatores Ebor', fuerunt electi ad essendum pro civitate ista
ad parliamentum tenendum apud Westmonasterium, xvj^{mo} die
Octobris proximo extunc futuro.

(*fo.* 205). In festo Sancte Austraberte virginis, 7 Henry v.
(20 October, 1419), venit hic in camera coram Johanne de Bedale,
maiore Ebor', et aliis ibidem presentibus, Willelmus Eseby, civis
et mercator Ebor', et ostendit quoddam scriptum patens cum
alio scripto patenti eidem annexo, et ipsum irrotulari peciit hic
in camera, cujus tenor sequitur et est talis. De la demande que
Jaques Weyts, bourgois de Bruges, fist pardevant la plaine
chaumbre des Eschins de Bruges a Willime Esby, merchant
de Yorc, comme plesge et respondant pour Richard Eton, facteur
et attourne, sicome len dist, de Robert Tup de Hull, de la somme
de vint et trois livres, deux solz, de gros monnoie de Flandres,
disant le dit Jaques Weyts que japieca il vendi en la ville de
Bruges a Robert Hugon, comme facteur et attourne de Johan
Waen, certaine quantite doile dolive, de la quele le dit Robert
Hugon lui demoura debteur de la dite somme de vint et trois
livres, deux solz, gros, et le dit Richard Eton, comme facteur

dessusdit, en demoura plesge a le paier a certain terme japicea passe. Et pour ce que le dit Jaques Weits avoit, apres le terme du paiement escheu et non paie, fait prenre et arrester en la dite ville de Bruges le dit Richard Eton, comme plesge du dit Robert Hugon, et que le dit Richard Eton nestoit mie pour lors aisie, si quil disoit, de paier la dite somme de deniers, et que pour ce le dit Williame Esby demoura plesge pour le dit Richart de le paier avant que le dit Richart se partiroit de Bruges, et ce non obstant yceli Richart se soit parti de Bruges sans le dit Jaques Weyts contenter et paier de la dite somme de deniers. Requist yceli Jaques Weits le dit Willame Esbi, que comme plesge du dit Richart Eton il lui paiast la dite somme, le dit Willame Esby ad ce respondant en confessant loyaulment soy a la peticion et requeste du dit Richart Eton, facteur et attourne de Robert Tup dessusdit, estre demoure plesge pour le dit Richart envers le dit Jaques Weits de la dite somme de deniers, et quil estoit prest de faire son devoir par ainsi quil puist recouvrer sa indempnite sur le dit Richart Eton, ou sur Robert Tup son maistre, ou sur Robert Hugon et Jehan Waen son maistre. A este dit et jugie par lesdiz eschins que le dit Willame Esby, comme plesge de Richart Eton, estoit tenu de paier la dite somme de vint et trois livres, deux solz, groso au dessusdit Jaques Weyts; reserve a ycelui Willame son action de recouvrer ycelle somme de deniers sur le dit Richart Eton ou autres, ou il lui semblera bon, en temps et en lieu que droit et raison vouldront. Actum le xij^e jour de Mars lan mil quatrecens dix et sept. Ainsi est il signe en livre de la ville de Bruges folio ij. Duheu[1] abra(ges).

Et tenor scripti predicto scripto annexi cum sigillo scabinorum et burgensium de Bruges convexo sequitur et est talis. A toucz ceulz que ces presentes lettres verront ou orront, bouremaistre, eschins et conseil de la ville de Bruges, salut. Pour ce que droit veult et raison donne que len tesmoigne choses veritables, est il que nous nous certiffions et tesmoignons par ces presentes que de et sur la demande que Jaques Weits, bourgeois de Bruges, fist par devant la plaine chambre des eschins de Bruges a Willame Esby, merchant de Yorc, comme plesge et respondant pour

---

1—*Sic*; but *Du Mem.* on fo. 205b.

Richard Heton, factour et attourne, sicome len dist, de Robert
Tup de Hull, de la some de vint et trois livres, deux solz, de gros
monnoie de Flandres ; a par nous, eschins desusdiz, este dit et
jugie en la meisme fourme et maniere que la copie extracte de
noz registres, signe (fo. 205, b.) de la main de nostre clerc secretaire,
maistre Julien du Hein, parmi la quele ces noz presentes lettres
sont infixees, contient et declaire plus a plain. En tes-
moingnance de ceo avons nous ces presentes fait sceller du seel
aux causes de la dite ville de Bruges, qui furent faites et donnees
lan mil quatrecens dix et sept, le xiiij^e jour de Mars.

Johannes de Bedale, maior ; Thomas Santon, Willelmus
Bowes, Johannes Penreth, de xij ; Petrus Buksy, Johannes Waghen,
Thomas Bracebrig, de xxiiij., congregati fuerunt xxix° die Januarii,
7 Henry v. (1419-20), et consenserunt quod deliberacio fiat Johannis
Davy, pelliparii, die aliquo in prima septimana Quadragesime
proximo futura, super eo quod idem Johannes indictatus est de
furtiva capcione unius bovis cujusdam Simonis Grymston, civis
et *boucher* Ebor'.

Release by Robert de Thorneton of York, to Thomas Duffeld
and Margaret, his wife, Peter Thoresby of York and William
Grissop of Thouthorp, of the manor of Skelton by York. Seal.
30 January, 7 Henry v. (1419-20). Acknowledged before John
de Bedale, mayor, 31 January, 7 Henry v. Burton.

(fo. 206). Memorandum quod herbagium fossati vocati le
mote infra Mikelgarth barre ex parte australi, prout se extendit
in longitudine subtus muros civitatis a barra de Mikelgate usque
ad vetus ballium, dimittitur ad firmam Hugoni Gyll, *walker*,
habendum et tenendum eidem Hugoni a festo Sancti Martini
in yeme (11 November) in anno Domini millesimo ccccxix° usque
ad finem novem annorum, extunc proximo sequencium plenarie
completorum ; reddendo inde annuatim custodibus pontis Use,
qui erunt pro tempore, quinque solidos sterlingorum ad festa
Pentecostes et Sancti Martini in yeme per equales porciones.
Et, si predictus annuus redditus quinque solidorum a retro fuerit
non solutus in parte vel in toto, si petatur, per quadraginta dies
ad aliquem terminum in quo solvi debeat, tunc bene licebit
maiori et camerariis predicte civitatis, qui erunt pro tempore,
predictum herbagium fossati predicti in manus maioris et

communitatis reseisire et rehabere, sine contradictione vel impedimento predicti Hugonis, presenti dimissione in aliquo non obstante. Et predicti maior et communitas herbagium predictum Hugoni predicto ad terminum sexdecim annorum predictorum pro annuo redditu quinque solidorum predictorum warantizabunt et defendent. Salvis semper maiori . . . . tempore . . . . et exitu pro muris civitatis supervidendis et reparandis, quociens fuerit oportunum.

In Magno Rotulo de anno primo Regis Henrici sexti in comitatu civitatis Ebor'.

Henricus Preston, nuper maior et escaetor regis in civitate Ebor' ac suburbiis et procinctu ejusdem, debet xxiiij $s.$ x $d.$ de exitu ejusdem escaetrie in civitate, suburbio et procinctu predictis, a tercio die Februarii, 9 Henry v. (1421–22), usque tercium diem Februarii anno dicti domini Regis nunc primo (1422–23), sicut continetur in compoto inde Rotulo comptorum de escaetriis. In thesauro xiij $s.$ iiij $d.$ xxx^{mo} die Novembris anno primo. Et debet xviij $d.$

Deliberacio mensurarum Johanni Alman.

(*fo.* 206, *b.*) Memorandum quod die Mercurii post festum Sancti Mathei apostoli, 7 Henry v. (27 September, 1419), deliberata fuerunt Johanni Alman per Thomam Gare, maiorem, et Willelmum Louthe, Johannem Brounflete et Thomam Brereton, camerarios, mensure et pondera subscripta, videlicet, unum sigillum magnum de ferro ex empcione propria predicti Johannis Alman pro mettys et bussellis sigillandis, j sigillum camere de ferro pro mensuris cervisie sigillandis, j sigillum parvum camere de litera M. pro mensuris vini et pro ponderibus sigillandis; j hopir camere; j bussell' camere de ligno; j scala camere; j geauge camere de ferro pro latitudine et pro profunditate modiorum sigillandis. Et [1]postea omnia predicta deliberata fuerunt Ricardo Lucas, qui juratus est ad exercendum fideliter officium mensuratoris et presentandi forisfacturas.[1]

Johannes Bedale, maior; Nicholaus Blakburn, Thomas Santon, Johannes Northeby, Willelmus Bowes, Johannes

---

1—1—These words are added.

Moreton, Johannes Blakburn, Thomas Gare, Johannes Penreth, de xij; Johannes Hewyk, Johannes Bouthe, Willelmus Birkheued, Henricus Preston, Thomas Doncastr', Johannes Usseburn, Willelmus Lamberd, Thomas More, Robertus Lokwood, Petrus Buksy, Thomas Esyngwald, Willelmus Ormesheued, Galfridus Sauvage, Thomas Bracebryg, Johannes Waghen, Robertus Barton, Thomas Snawdon, Robertus Jarom, Johannes Loftehouse, de xxiv.; vicecomites, Johannes Bolton, Thomas Dany, congregati fuerunt in aula communi hujus civitatis Ebor', in festo Sancti Blasii, 7 Henry v. (3 February, 1419-20), una cum magna multitudine scrutatorum et aliorum civium hujus civitatis, et ibi, de voluntate et assensu maioris, proborum hominum et tocius communitatis ibidem congregate, plene ordinatum fuit et unanimiter consensum quod si quis aldermannorum hujus civitatis, qui pro tempore erit, quem verisimilem esset eligi in maiorem in electione proxima maioris, se absentaverit a civitate erga diem electionis maioris ne elegatur maior pro anno futuro, quod quilibet sic se absentans de cetero solvat centum marcas sterlingorum sine pardonacione aliqua, quarum centum marcarum quadraginta libre solventur maiori, qui erit in anno proximo, in subsidium expensarum suarum illius anni, et quadraginta marce solventur camerariis, qui pro tempore erunt, ad usum et proficuum communitatis hujus civitatis Ebor'. Et nichilominus erit maior si ipsum contingerit postea eligi in maiorem predicte civitatis. Et . . . maiorem et probos homines hujus civitatis . . . . et dent taxam suam domino regi de parochia illa, in qua habitantes fuerunt cum familia sua tempore concessionis taxe hujusmodi. Et voluerunt . . . . ista locum teneat et effectu hac . . . . melius avisamentum suscepit in hac parte. Sed quia apparebat multis quod constitutio ista non erat consona racioni, ideo xviij die Novembris, anno Domini Mccccxx (18 Henry v.), (fo. 207) de consensu et unanimi voluntate maioris et communitatis in gilda aula extitit ordinatum quod decetero universi homines predicte civitatis solvant taxam suam domino regi in parochia illa, in qua cubantes et levantes inventi fuerint cum uxore et familia sua tempore collectionis taxe, et non alibi infra civitatem nec suburbia nec procinctum ejusdem. Et si forte probatum fuerit quod aliquis de civitate diverterit moram suam per fraudem de una parochia in aliam tempore assessionis vel collectionis taxe, ea intencione ut minus solvat in una parochia quam in alia, ordinatum est per maiorem et communitatem in gilda aula quod talis, quiscumque fuerit, solvat taxam suam in utraque parochia sine spe venie alicujus.

Burton, R.

Certificate of searchers of masons and wrights.[1]

In Magno Rotulo de anno septimo Regis Henrici quinti in civitate Ebor'.

Johannes Bedale, nuper maior et escaetor in civitate Ebor' ac suburbiis et procinctu ejusdem, reddit compotum de xxxiij *s.* vij *d.* de exitu ejusdem escaetrie a tercio die Februarii, anno sexto regis nunc, usque tercium diem Februarii, anno vij, sicut continetur in dicto compoto suo inde Rotulo compotorum de escaetriis. In thesauro xxxiij *s.* vij *d.* in tribus talliis. Et quietus est.

(*fo.* 207, *b.*) Grant by John Dey, son of Thomas Dey of York, mariner, to Hugh Latham of Congleton, of one burgage with two acres of land in Congleton, which John inherited after the death of Maud, relict of the said Thomas, daughter of John Cady, grandfather of the said John Dey. The burgage lies in breadth between a burgage of Richard Brodok and a burgage of Roger de Moreton, and in length from the high street called Milnestrete before to a burgage of the said Roger behind; the land lies an acre and a half in le Overwestfeld and half an acre in le Nethirwestfeld. Seal. York, 27 March, 1420 (8 Henry v.)

Letter of attorney by the same, appointing Lawrence Hewester of Congleton and Robert Chircheleghes, chaplain, to deliver seisin of the said burgage and land. Same date. Seal.

(*fo.* 208). Clause from Close Rolls, dated 7 May, 1359, concerning Saint George's Chapel.

[2]Memorandum quod xvj^{to} die Maii, 8 Henry v. (1420), Thomas Gare, maior Ebor', concessit et ad firmam dimisit de visu et voluntate proborum hominum, Thome Wardale, *glover*, certam

---

1—Eng. Misc. *op. cit.*, p. 16.

2—2—The whole of this entry is crossed through and " Vacat quia **erat** in nocumentum morancium ex utraque parte porte," is written in the **left** margin.

quantitatem terre ex utraque parte porte magne ecclesie cathedralis beati Petri Eboracensis aperientis versus Stayngate, ita quod ibi ponere possit scabellum et stare cum rebus suis venalibus, longitudinis unius ulne et unius quarterii strictim et latitudinis dimidie ulne strictim ; reddendo inde per annum proximum duos solidos ad festa Pentecostes et Sancti Martini in yeme per equales porciones. Et si post finem anni placuerit maiori et predicto Thome, tunc idem Thomas recipiat licenciam standi in placca predicta sub forma premissa ad terminum decem annorum.

Certificate of searchers of masons and wrights ; crossed through.

(*fo.* 209). Cum quedam controversia mota fuisset inter abbatem et conventum monasterii beate Marie Ebor', ex una parte, et Robertum Sallay, armigerum, filium et heredem Willelmi Sallay, quondam civis Ebor', ex altera parte, pro quadam domo predicti Roberti in cornerio cujusdam gardini tenementi predicti Roberti in Bouthom, quod est in tenura Johannis Kirkeby, *litster,* ubi duo latera predicte domus edificantur et jacent ex utraque parte super quemdam murum terreum ibidem, quem predicti abbas et conventus clamant esse suum. Super quo venit Robertus Halton de Ebor', presbiter, deputatus et receptor reddituum et firmarum predicti Roberti in civitate Ebor' et suburbiis ejusdem, et clamavit predictum murum terreum esse jus predicti Roberti. Tandem tamen, sicut mos est predicte civitatis, partes predicte per certos deputatos suos venerunt coram Thoma Gare, maiore Ebor', quarto die Maii, 8 Henry v. (1420), et submiserunt se judicio et arbitrio scrutatorum cementariorum et carpentariorum civitatis predicte. Unde Johannes Ampilford et Johannes Thorp, cementarii, Johannes Hexham et Thomas Cunsburgh, carpentarii, scrutatores electi et jurati artificiorum predictorum de consensu predictorum deputatorum, super solum venerunt et predictos murum et domum suos visui apponentes, habita deliberacione diligenti in materia predicta inter eos, invenerunt quod predictus murus terreus fuit predictorum abbatis et conventus, et quod *lez gistes* et aliud meremium domus predicte super illum murum jacebant ad dampnum abbatis et conventus. Ideo scrutatores predicti considerabant et judicabant quod domus predicta, in quantum occupabat terram abbatis et conventus, esset amota et super terram propriam predicti Roberti ibidem adjacentem edificata; vel alias quod predictus Robertus pro predictis duobus lateribus domus predicte concordaret cum abbate et conventu memoratis. Considerabant insuper et judicabant iidem scrutatores quod, amota domo predicta ut prefertur, predicti abbas et conventus edificarent et perficerent murum suum lapideum, quem ibidem inceperunt ex interiori parte bundarum et metarum, per scrutatores predictos ibidem positarum, et quod de cetero predictus Robertus, nec per se nec per suos heredes vel tenentes, aliquas latrinas nec alia quecumque edificaret vel poneret, que predictum murum pejorarent seu predictis abbati et conventui dampnum facerent aliquale. Burton.

Memorandum quod Johannes Radclyff, civis et mercator, Ebor,' per scriptum suum obligatorium obligatus fuit Thome Farnlay, civi et *spuryer* Ebor', in duodecim libris sexdecim solidis et octo denariis solvendis ad terminum elapsum. Super hoc predictus Thomas assignavit et loco suo posuit Willelmum Nykson de (*fo.* 209, *b.*) Ebor', *mason*, attornatum suum ad petendum, recuperandum, et nomine suo recipiendum de Johanne Radclyff predicto predictas duodecim libras sexdecim solidos et octo denarios, prout in quadam litera attornacionis inde confecta plenius continebatur. Tamen ita contigit per infortunium quod predictum scriptum obligatorium fuit negligenter amissum inter Pavimentum et domum Johannis Rumby in Conyngstrete, et ea de causa solucio predicte summe tardata per Johannem Radclyff predictum. Unde demum quinto die Julii, 8 Henry v. (1420), predicti Thomas Farnlay et quamplures alii in magna copia venerunt coram Thoma Gare, maiore Ebor', et dixit se super solucione predicte summe ad tunc fore bene concordatum, et in presencia predicti maioris Johannis Waghen, *mercer*, Thome Roderham, Rogeri de Burton, clerici communis, Johannis Rumby, et aliorum, predictus Thomas Farnelay recognovit se literatorie constituisse predictum Willelmum Nykson, attornatum suum, modo ut prefertur. Et, ostensa litera attornacionis predicta, idem Thomas similiter recognovit ipsam literam esse factum suum. Et insuper in presencia maioris et aliorum predictorum sigillavit predicto Johanni Radclyff acquietanciam de solucione sibi facta summe predicte. Quam quidem acquietanciam predictus Thomas recognovit in presencia predicti maioris et aliorum predictorum esse factum suum. Et predicti Thomas Farnlay et Johannes Skyrmer pecierunt predictas literam attornacionis et acquietanciam inscribi et irrotulari hic in camera ad meliorem evidenciam in futurum, quarum tenores sequntur et sunt tales :—

Letter of attorney by Thomas Farnlay, citizen and spurrier of York, appointing William Nykson of York, *mason*, to receive from John Radclyff, citizen and merchant of York, payment of a bond of 12 *l*. 6 *s*. 8 *d*. 16 March, 7 Henry v. (1419-20).

Receipt by the said Thomas to the said John for the payment of the said bond. Seal. 18 June, 8 Henry v. (1420).

(*fo*. 210). Bond by John Bukkiller, citizen and merchant of Dansk, and John Dodyngton, citizen and merchant of York, to Robert Baurnburgh and John Dreng of Scardeburgh for 100 *l*. to be paid at Martinmas 1421. Seals. 5 August, 1420. Acknowledged before Thomas Gare, mayor, John Brounflete, chamberlain, and Roger de Burton, common clerk, 5 August, 1420, 8 Henry v.

Letter of defeasance by which the said bond for 100 *l*. is to be null and void, if the said John Bukkiller and John Dodyngton and Henry Helfeld shew letters under the seal of the city of Dansk, testifying that the ship called Marie Knyght of Dansk, of which Henry Strewyng of Dansk is owner and master, taken by the said Robert Baumburgh and John Dreng, with all its goods and merchandise valued at 100 *l*., belongs to the men and merchants of Dansk. Seals. Same date. Acknowledged as above by John Bukkiller and John Dodyngton and also by . . . . Crane of Scardeburgh attorney of Robert Baumburgh and John Dreng.

(*fo*. 210, *b*.) Two certificates of searchers of masons and wrights.[1]

(*fo*. 211). In crastino Sancti Laurencii Martiris, anno Domini millesimo cccxx^{mo} et 8 Henry v. (11 August, 1420), in camera consilii civitatis Ebor', venerunt in propriis personis suis Galfridus

---

1—Eng. Misc. *op. cit.*, pp. 16, 17.

Leventhorp de Bradforddale in comitatu Ebor', Alicia que fuit uxor Petri de Marton et Thomas Leventhorp, et predictus Galfridus recognovit se habere in manibus suis et custodia sua quasdam cartas et scripturas, tangentes jus et titulum heredum Petri de Marton in manerio de Askwyth in Wherfdale in comitatu predicto ; et juravit per bonam fidem suam corporis sui coram Thoma Gare, maiore Ebor', et Rogero de Burton, clerico communi civitatis Ebor', et aliis personis, quod ante mortem suam predictas cartas et scripturas sanas et integras deliberabit recto heredi predicti Petri de Marton et nulli alicui alteri, si ipsum Galfridum predictam Aliciam supervivere contingat. Qui quidem Galfridus et Alicia recognoverunt quod predicta Alicia nullas cartas aut scripturas penes se habuit manerium predictum tangentes. Et si predictam Aliciam ante predictum Galfridum mori contingat, tunc predictus Galfridus post mortem predicte Alicie omnes predictas cartas et scripturas deliberabit predicto Thome Leventhorp, qui pro presenti moratur in Heton in Bradforddale. Et hoc predictus Galfridus promisit, convenit et dixit se per fidem corporis sui bene et fideliter perimplendum et faciendum sine fictione quacumque. Qui quidem Thomas Leventhorp coram maiore et aliis personis predictis juravit super sancta Dei Evangelia per ipsum corporaliter tacta, quod predictas cartas et scripturas, cum ad manus suas devenerint, deliberabit rectis heredibus predicti Petri de Marton sine dolo vel fraude aut malo ingenio quocumque. Burton.

Bond by Andrew Newby, citizen and chandler of York, to Henry Markett, citizen and merchant, for a loan of 17 $li.$ 5 $s.$, to be repaid at the feast of the Invention of the Holy Cross next (3 May). Seal. 2 January, 8 Henry v. (1420–21).

Bond by the same to the same, for a loan of the same amount to be repaid on the feast of the Nativity of S. John the Baptist, next (24 June). Seal. Same date.

(*fo.* 211, *b*.) Bond by the same to the same for a loan of the same amount, to be repaid on the feast of S. Peter's chains next (1 August). Seal. Same date.

Inquisition held at York on Saturday before the feast of S. Bartholomew Apostle, 17 Richard ii. (23 August, 1393), before

Richard Basy, escheator, by virtue of his office; by oath of Robert Coke of Colliergate, Thomas Couper of the same, Richard del Howe of Conyngstret, John Housom of the same, Henry Snayth of the same, Roger de Pountfreit, skinner, Adam Hyde, William de Barton, tailor, John de Rasklelff, Adam de Horton, William de Morlay and Richard Wartre of Walmegate.

Maud de Kyrkby of York in the year 38 Edward iii. (1364-5), gave to Thomas de Folkerthorp, vicar of the church of S. Laurence in Walmegate in the suburb of the city of York, and to his successors, vicars, to provide a light of two torches in the said church, for her soul, two butts of land called Croftes in Walmegate lying between land of the nuns of S. Clement of York and land of William de Dalton, held of the king in chief in burgage, as parcel of the city, and of the yearly value of 3 s. 4 d. Licence to alienate in mortmain was obtained, and the vicar still holds the land.

Writ to the mayor and escheator of York, to hold the following inquisition, dated 12 March, 8 Henry v. (1420-21).

(fo. 212). Inquisition held at York on Wednesday after the feast of SS. Tiberius and Valerian martyrs, 9 Henry v. (14 April, 1421), before Richard Russell, mayor and escheator, by oath of John Thorpp, *mason*, John Pudsay, Thomas Forester, Richard Neuland, John Jakman, William Coklay, William Bulnays, Hugh Gyll, John Walker, Robert Hobshort, Henry Eslaby and Thomas Syke.

Richard le Scrop of Bolton, knight, deceased, held a tenement with a garden in Alde Conyngstrete of the clear yearly value of 16 s.; a tenement opposite the church of old St. Mary, of the clear yearly value of 10 s.; a chamber over the great gate, formerly of Richard Wateby, on Bysshophill, of the clear yearly value of 2 s.; two tenements by the said gate, of the clear yearly value together of 6 s.; a small house thereby, of the clear yearly value of 2 s.; a garden adjoining, of the clear yearly value of 4 d.; and a garden in Plughswayngate in a suburb of the said city of York, of the clear yearly value of 3 s., payable at Whitsuntide and Martinmas.

G

All the premises are held of the king in free burgage as the whole city is held. The said Richard died on the day of the beheading of S. John the Baptist, 8 Henry v. (29 August, 1420). Henry le Scrop, his son, is his heir, aged three years and more.

The writ to deliver the said tenements, houses, chamber and gardens to Margaret, late the wife of Richard le Scrope of Bolton, is written before, in this book folio lxvj^{to}.

(*fo.* 212, *b.*) Bond by Richard Bawtre of Scardeburgh, *merchant*, Ely Ward, John Besyngby the younger and Stephen Emeryk, citizens and merchants of York, to John Craven, citizen and *merchant*, for a loan of 79 *l.* 13 *s.* 4 *d.* To be repaid on the feast of Corpus Christi next. 15 June, 5 Henry v. (1404). Seals.

Littera testimonialis sub sigillo de Dansk.

Coram honorabilibus et magne sagacitatis viris, dominis maiore, ballivo et consulibus civitatis York in Anglia, amicis nostris presinceris, nos, proconsules et consules civitatis Danzik, cum tocius boni incremento, protestacione fide digna nostris in hiis scriptis publice profitemur quamdam navem, vulgariter apud nos Marienkneche nuncupatam, quam Robertus Baumburg et Johannes Dreng de Scardenburg, Henrico Strunyng, nostro comburgensi, gubernatori et magistro ejusdem navis, die Jovis ante festum Pentecostes proxime preterito, (8 May, 1421), in mari invadendo, cum bonis tunc temporis inibi onustatis, receperunt, pro quibus ex post Johannes Bokeler, mercator de Danzik, et Johannes Dodyngton, civis Ebor, se memoratis Roberto et Johanni Dreng in centum libris sterlingorum caucione fide jussoria, astrinxerunt, totaliter et nomine certis nostris civitatis Danzik inhabitatoribus et opidanis pertinere, et nulli alteri quovis modo. In cujus rei fidem et evidenciam pleniorem presentes nostras literas, quibus firmam et indubiam credulitatem adhiberi petimus, secreti nostri a tergo impressione fecimus communiri. Scriptum Danzig anno Domini mccccxxj^{mo} mensis Maii die decimoquinto.

Et sequitur de eodem. Ricardus Russell, maior civitatis Ebor, necnon vicecomites et aldermanni ejusdem, singularis

amicicie viris, ballivo et probis hominibus ville de Scardeburgh,
salutem in Illo, qui eterne dat dona salutis

. . . . on this day, the said John Bokeler came before
the mayor and shewed the above letter, fulfilling the conditions
for defeazaunce of the bond for 100 *l.* in which the said John
and John Dodington were bound to Robert Baumburgh and
John Dreng of Scardeburgh (see folio 210).

(*fo.* 213). Nos, igitur, racione intime dilectionis quam erga
vos gerimus, vobis consulimus necnon fervidis et sinceris rogamus
affectibus ut, visis predictis literis testimonialibus et presentibus
nostris literis, predictis Johanni et Johanni ut premittitur obligatis
scriptum suum obligatorium predictum liberari faciatis, sicut
decet, non solum nostris precibus et amore, sed pocius animad-
vertentes quanta dileccionis et favoris prosecucione voluntateque
placabili illi de civitate de Danzik predicta compatriotas nostras
in suis agendis negociis indies pertractare procurant. Vestram
amiciciam in perfecta et vera pacis caritate et unanime
dileccionis bono Deus augeat et custodiat nunc et semper.
Datum apud Ebor', sub sigillo officii maioratus predicte civitatis
Ebor', vicesimo septimo die mensis Maii, anno Domini millesimo
quadringentesimo vicesimo primo, regni vero regis Henrici
quinti post conquestum Anglie anno nono. Burton Roger. R.

(*fo.* 213, *b.*) Statutes of Parliament, 1 Henry v.[1]

(*fo.* 215, *b.*) Nota pro priore de Bolton in Craven Jhs.[2]

Coram Ricardo Russell, maiore civitatis Ebor', in curia sua
tenta ibidem primo die Marcii, 9 Henry v. (1421-22), venit quidam
Robertus de Bilburgh, capellanus perpetue promotus ad unam
cantariam in ecclesia Omnium Sanctorum in Northstrete in
civitate predicta, vocatam Bengechantre, attachiatus ad
respondendum priori et conventui de Bolton in Craven de placito,
quare ab eis injuste detinuit unum annuum redditum sex solidorum,
provenientem de omnibus mesuagiis dicte cantarie appropriatis
in Northstrete in eadem civitate, terminis Martini et Pentecostes
equis porcionibus eis solvendum ; et unde queruntur quod ab

1—**Statutes of Parliament II.**, pp. 170-174.
2—Jhs is doubtful.

eis (*fo.* 215, *b.*) detinuit annuum redditum predictum per sex annos ultimo elapsos etc. Et predictus capellanus peciit colloquium cum Nicholao de Blakburn et aliis nobilioribus advocatoribus cantarie predicte etc. Et super hoc, habito colloquio cum suis advocatoribus visisque evidenciis dictorum prioris et conventus, tam predictus Robertus, capellanus cantarie predicte, quam predictus Nicholaus, unus de nobilioribus advocatoribus cantarie predicte, cognoverunt predictum annuum redditum sex solidorum fuisse et esse jus ipsorum prioris et conventus et prioratus sui de Bolton imperpetuum, et de omnibus arreragiis satisfecerunt per manus predicti Nicholai priori predicto. In cujus rei testimonium sigillum officii maioratus predicte civitatis Ebor' huic presenti recordo est appensum. Datum apud Ebor' die, mense et anno predictis. Burton. R.

(*fo.* 216, *b.*) Certificatorium in cancellaria regis de nominibus vicecomitum (1421-2).

Certificate of searchers of masons and wrights.[1]

(*fo.* 217). Statutes of parliament; 2 Henry v.[2]

(*fo.* 218, *b.*) Statutes of parliament; 3 Henry v.[3]

(*fo.* 219). Memorandum quod die Veneris proximo ante festum Sancti Bartholomei Apostoli, anno Domini millesimo quadringentesimo vicesimo, 9 Henry v. (22 August, 1421), honesta mulier Maria Brathwayt, que fuit uxor Johannis Brathwayt, ex sua pura voluntate et devocione assignavit, concessit et dedit viginti marcas sterlingorum, ponendas et expendendas pro factura et edificacione cujusdam crucis nove lapidee in foro vocato Thursday market in civitate Ebor', pro bono statu suo, et pro salute anime predicti Johannis Brathwayt, et pro animabus omnium fidelium defunctorum. Et est penitus intencionis predicte Marie quod predicte viginti marce integraliter expendantur circa facturam crucis predicte, et quod ad nullos usus alios applicentur. Et predicte viginti marce sunt in manibus Johannis Sturtevaunt expendende modo premisso per surpervisum maioris, qui erit pro tempore civitatis Ebor'.

1—Eng. Misc. *op. cit.*, p. 17.
2—Statutes of the Realm, II., pp. 175-187.
3—Ibid., p. 191.

Sequitur clausula libertatis Fratrum Predicatorum Ebor' per quam clamant recipere fugientem ad locum suum tam pro debito quam aliis transgressionibus.

Quare volumus et firmiter precipimus quod predicti fratres et eorum successores habeant et teneant predictam capellam et partem predictam placie predicte cum omnibus libertatibus et liberis consuetudinibus ad eas pertinentibus per metas predictas, sicut predictum est. Hoc habetur ex concessione Henrici regis tercii. Alia clausula predictorum fratrum scribitur in folio clxxv^{to}.

(*fo.* 219, *b.*) Cronica de successionibus et gestis Archiepiscoporum Eboracensium, incipiendo ad Sanctum Paulinum usque ad mortem J. Thuresby, scripta per R. de B. clericum communem in anno Domini mccccxx et continet 88 capitula.

. . . .

(*fo.* 246, *b.*) Explicit cronica de successionibus et gestis notabilibus Archiepiscorum Eboracensium, incipiendo ad Paulinum et finiendo ad Johannem Thuresby, scripta propria manu Rogeri de Burton, clerici communis, tempore Ricardi Russell maioris. Burton, R.

Memorandum quod Johannes Ampilford et Willelmus Warter, scrutatores jurati arcium cementariorum et carpentariorum civitatis Ebor', ad requisicionem Cristofori Spenser, armigeri, et Roberti Belton de Ebor', *spicer*, tenentis Johannis Langton, chivaler, assignati fuerunt per Thomam Bracebryg, maiorem Ebor', ad scrutandum inter predictos Johannem Langton et Cristoforum de fundo cujusdam tenementi ipsius Johannis Langton in Conyngstrete in civitate predicta, in parte de novo edificandi et reparandi, jacentis inter tenementum Willelmi Seleby ex una parte, et tenementum predicti Cristofori ex altera parte, et inde fideliter judicandum secundum usum et consuetudinem civitatis predicte. Super hoc Johannes Ampilford et Willelmus, scrutatores predicti, super fundum tenementorum predictorum venientes, per avisamentum suum et aliorum artificum arcium predictarum inde captum die Dominica proxima ante festum nativitatis beate Marie virginis, anno Domini millesimo ccccxxiiij^to et 2 Henry vi. (3 September, 1424) ibidem, considerabant quod Johannes Langton predictus per Robertum, tenentem suum predictum, sicut indiguit edificaret et separaret tenementum suum predictum in visu positum in latitudine versus regiam stratam de Conyngstrete, sicut meremium suum hospitatum fuit ab antiquo linialiter a summo usque deorsum ad fundum, videlicet, per medium utriusque muri lapidei ex utraque parte, et a retro super ripam aque de Ouse, a statha tenementi Willelmi Seleby in tenura Walteri Luket, *skynner*, usque ad quemdam pilum ligneum, quem ipsi scrutatores tunc suis propriis manibus posuerunt versus fundum predicti Cristofori. Et tunc ibidem presentes fuerunt [1]predictus Robertus Belton pro parte Johannis Langton predicti, et pro parte Cristofori Spenser ex assignamento ejusdem dominus Willelmus, capellanus suus, Johannes Wyche, *taillour*, et Willelmus Housom, *wever*, tenens ipsius Cristoferi in tenemento suo predicto, et pro parte Willelmi Seleby, Walterus Luket predictus, astantibus Rogero de Burton, clerico communi et secretario civitatis predicte, Thoma Warde, *clerico*, Thoma Wederby et multis aliis.

Burton. R.

(*fo.* 247). Novit Ille, qui nichil ignorat et plebs conqueritur universa, quod ludus in die Corporis Christi in ista civitate, cujus institucio ob magnam devocionis causam et viciorum extirpacionem morumque reformacionem antiquitus facta fuit, heu plus solito impeditur pro multitudine paginarum, et nisi celerior et melior provideatur cautela, timendum est multo magis brevissime processu temporis impediri. Et artifices de *lez Payntours, Steynours, Pynners* et *Latoners* civitatis predicte, ad divisim ludendum duas paginas in ludo predicto antea assignati, unam, videlicet, de expansione et clavacione Christi ad crucem, alteram, vero, de levacione crucifixi super montem, intelligentes quod materie ambarum paginarum simul in una pagina possent inludi, abbreviacionem commodius ludencium oracul' audienti populo demonstrari, consenciebant pro se et aliis coartificibus suis in futurum quod una paginarum suarum amodo deleatur

---

1—A space is left here.

et altera sustentetur, secundum quod maior et consilium camere voluerint ordinare. Et super hoc scrutatores et artifices artificiorum predictorum venerunt coram Ricardo Russell, maiore Ebor', aldermannis et aliis probis hominibus, hic in camera consilii super pontem Use situata, ultimo die Januarii, 9 Henry v. (1421-22), et eis corum desiderium et intencionem monstrabant in premissis, videlicet, Willelmus Drax, Johannes Multon, Johannes Cave, Johannes Potell, Johannes Bryg, Thomas Midilton, Willelmus Couper, Johannes Scragge, Adam Mitton, Robertus Leche, Willelmus Crofte, Robertus Kyrkeby, Ricardus Lambert, Johannes Midylham, Thomas Steresacre de *pynnercrafte*, David Payntour, Willelmus Morlay, Johannes Gerard, et Willelmus Clyfton, de *payntourcrafte*, ac Thomas Cuke, Thomas Hirste, Thomas Hendechild, Johannes Wyman, Walterus Multon et Ricardus Marche de *steynourcrafte*. Unde predictus maior, aldermanni et probi homines hoc benigne acceptantes et predictos artifices pro eorum proposito laudabili commendantes, de suo et omnium artificum predictorum statuerunt et ordinarunt consilio quod ab hac die in antea pagina de *lez payntours* et *steynours* a ludo predicto penitus sit amota, et quod artifices de *lez pynners* et *latoners* super se assumant onus ludendi in pagina sua materiam loquelarum que per prius in pagina sua et in pagina de *les payntours* et *steynours* ludebatur, et quod *les payntours* et *steynours* singulis annis inter se de hominibus artificii sui colligant quinque solidos sterlingorum et illos annuatim solvant magistris pagine de *les pynners* et *latoners* pro tempore existentibus annuatim in vigilia Corporis Christi. Et si aliquo tempore in solucione hujusmodi defecerint, tunc volunt et concedunt se et universos successores suos distringi et stricte compelli in domibus et locis habitacionum suarum vel alibi, ubi melius et cicius distringi poterint, per maiorem et camerarios hujus civitatis pro tempore existentes, ad solvendum quadraginta solidos bone monete Anglie custodibus pagine de *les pynners* et *latoners*, qui pro tempore fuerint, die dominica dictum festum proximo sequenti, sine dilacione longiori, et districtiones in hac parte captas penes se retinere, quousque custodibus predictis de predictis quadraginta solidis unacum expensis et dampnis pro recuperacione eorum factis plenarie fuerit satisfactum.; ita semper quod maior, pro tempore existens, percipiat et habeat unam medietatem predictorum quadraginta solidorum ad usum communitatis, et custodes pagine de *pynner crafte* et *latoners*, qui pro tempore fuerint, alteram medietatem ad usum et sustentacionem dicte pagine sue. Ad quas quidem soluciones modo et forma prescriptis bene et fideliter faciendas ac presentem (*fo.* 247, *b.*) ordinacionem in omnibus tenendam et perimplendam, pro parte sua, David Payntour, Willelmus Morlay, Johannes Gerard, Willelmus Clyfton, Thomas Hirst, Thomas Hendechild, Johannes Wyman, Walterus Multon, et Ricardus Marche predicti se et successores suos arcium suarum obligant. Proviso omnino quod dicti artifices de *payntour crafte* et *steynours* de pagina de *pynner crafte* nec de eorum compoto imposterum se nullatenus intromittant. Burton, Roger.

[1]Ceste indenture, faite parentre nostre soveraine seigneur le roy, dune part, et Bartholemewe Seman autrement dit Goldebeter, maistre et overour de les moneys du Roy deinz la tour de Londres, dautre part, tesmoigne que le dit nostre soverain seignur ad ordenez et constitut le dit Bartholomewe gardein et changeour de sez eschangez dor et dargent en la citee Deverwyk, a tenir en lieus overtes et hautes rieus par lui et ses deputes sufficiantz, pur les queux il vorra respondre de le fiste de Seint Baptistre darrein passez tanque a le proschein parlement ensuant, et delors en avant tanque come il plerra a nostre dit soverain seignur le roy. Et serra le dit Bartholomewe tenuz de resceivre checun manere dor et dargent apportez as ditz eschanges, paiant a celui qui lapportera solonc le resonable value dicelle or ou argent, que serra apportez, rebatant ent solonc lafferant de cynk souldz pur lez seignurages et cunage, et quinsze deniers pur les change de la livre dor du poys de la tour de Londres sanz plus, lez quex cynk souldz et quinsze deniers se extendent solonc la ratte dune denier et maille a le noble du poys de mesme la tour. Les queux quinsze deniers pur la livre dor nostre dit soverain seignur, de lavis de son counseil, pur certeins causes voet et grante que le dit Bartholomewe eit et teigne devers lui mesmes et a son oeps propre sanz aucun accompt ent a rendre, le dit Baretholomewe supportant touz les charges, coustages, et expenses as ditz

---

1—R. Davies, Mints and Coinages of York, pp. 35, 36.

eschanges pur le temps partenantz et encumbentz. Et serra le dit Bartholomewe tenuz de paier a le poeple ce que a eux doit apparteiner pur tielle eschange bone et loiale monoye Dangleterre, et de tielle poys et alaye come serra et doit estre fait de droit en la toure de Londres, par poys ou par nombre al eleccion de celui qi le resceivra, de temps en temps sanz delaye ou difficulte queconque. Et si par cas en la dite monoye ensy appaier aucun defaute notable soit trovee en poys ou en alaye a leschanges susditz, que Dieu defende, que bien lerra a checun, qi tielle defaute trovera devaunt qil passera la place du dit eschange, de refuser, et que soit defective et refusable, et que sur ce le dit eschangeour soit tenuz de paier et delivrer sufficiante monoye pur icelle sanz daunger ou delaye. Et serra le dit eschangeour tenuz et obligez dapporter ou faire apporter tout lor et argent, qil resceivra en lez ditz eschanges, ou achatera par colour de son office en icelles, a la dite tour de Londres, pur y estre fonduz et fait en monoye par vieu et tesmoignance de lassaiour et contreroullour de nostre dit soverain seigneur illoeqes pur le temps esteant, en augmentacion et encrees de le monoye pur profit du roialme, et en ease de poeple, sanz estre venduz, alienez, ou mys a aucun autre oeps, sur pein au roy nostre dit seignur le double de ce qil avera ensy receux en les dites eschanges (fo. 248) ou achatera par colour de son dit office, et le navera mye apportez a la tour susdite. Et le dit eschangeour ad promys et est teuuz davoir et mettre en lez ditz eschanges sommes notables et competents dor et dargent pur lesploit et deliverance de le poeple as ditz eschanges repairantz, issint qils y ne soient tariez ne delaiez pur defaute de monoye. Et le dit Bartholomewe ad promys et se oblige a nostre soverain seignur le roy que pur profit ne singuler avantage qil purra prendre par cause des ditz eschanges en la dite citee, ne pur nulle autre cause voluntaire, il ne delivera nulle homme qapportera or ou argent a la dite tour de Londres, pur y estre cunez, ne qil artera ne compellera nulle persone par nulle manere colour de lesser davoir son or ou argent cunez en la dite toure de Londres pur aler a les ditz eschanges, mes qil les delivera aussitost et prestement a la dite toure, come il est tenuz par force des endentures parentre nostre dit soverain seigneur le roy et le dit Bartholomewe, come meistre et overour de les ditz monoys, sur ce faitz, sur peine de paier a la partie le double de ce dont mesme la partie serra grevee en ce cas. Et nostre dit seignur le roy ferra proclamer et defendre a touz ses liges et autres que nulle manere persone teigne nulle commun eschange en prive nappiert en la dite citee, ne riens preigne pur profit de tiel eschange forspris les eschangeours nostre dit seignur le roy, sur la peine et forfaiture contenuz en lestatut ent fait lan vynt et cynk de roy Edward tiez etc. De quele forfaiture le roy, de lavis de son counseil, voet que le dit Bartholomewe ait dousze deniers de la livre quaunt tiel cas cherra ; et a la suite du dit Bartholomewe ce soit proever et loialment adjugge. En tesmoignance de quele chose a la partie de ceste endenture, demurante devers le dit Bartholomewe, nostre dit soverain seignur le roy ad fait mettre son graunde seal. Donne a Westmostier, le xv jour de Juyll, lan du reigne de roy nostre dit soverain seignur primer.

Henricus, Dei gracia Rex Anglie et Francie et Dominus Hibernie, maiori et vicecomitibus civitatis Ebor', salutem. Precipimus vobis, firmiter injungentes quod, visa altera parte quarumdam indenturarum inter nos et Bartholomeum Seman, alias dictum Goldbeter, magistrum et operatorem monetarum nostrarum infra turrim London' ac custodem et campsorem cambiorum nostrorum auri et argenti in civitate nostra predicta tenendorum, de operacionibus et cambiis predictis debite faciendis confectarum, partem illam in singulas locis in civitate predicta, ubi melius expedire videritis, ex parte nostra publice proclamari et omnes articulos in eadem contentos, quantum in vobis est, in civitate predicta et suburbiis ejusdem firmiter et inviolabiliter observari faciatis juxta vim, formam, et effectum indenture predicte. Et hoc nullatenus omittatis. Teste me ipso apud Westmonasterium, xxiij die Julii, anno regni nostri primo.   Haselay.

(*fo.* 248, *b.*) In Magno Rotulo de anno viij° Regis Henrici quinti in civitate Ebor'.

Thomas Gare, nuper maior et escaetor Regis in civitate Ebor' ac suburbiis et procinctu ejusdem, reddit compotum de xiiij *s.* x *d.* de exitu ejusdem escaetrie, a tercio die Februarii, anno vij^{mo}, usque tercium diem Februarii tunc proximo sequentem ($14\frac{19}{20}$-$14\frac{20}{21}$), sicut continetur in compoto suo inde rotulo compotorum de escaetriis. In thesauro xxvj s. viij d. in ij talliis per dictum escaetorem de exitu ballive sue. Et habet superplusagium.

In Magno Rotulo de anno x^{mo} Regis Henrici quinti in civitate Ebor'.

Thomas Esyngwald, nuper maior et escaetor regis in civitate Ebor' ac suburbiis et procinctu ejusdem, reddit compotum de xiiij s. x d. de exitu ejusdem escaetrie in civitate et suburbiis predictis, videlicet, a tercio die Februarii, anno primo regis Henrici sexti, usque tercium diem Februarii, anno secundo (142⅔-142¾), scilicet, per unum annum integrum, sicut continetur in compoto suo. Rotulo compotorum de escaetriis. In thesauro xxvj s. viij d. in duabus talliis per dictum escaetorem de exitu ballive sue. Et habet superplusagium.

Memorandum quod ubi Johannes Bempton, civis et *barker* Ebor', ex capite suo proprio edificavit et de novo construxit quamdam domum retro et extra clausuram gardini sui, in vico de Northstrete, versus *le mote* civitatis super solum communitatis Ebor', extra cursum aliorum tenementorum vicinorum suorum ibidem adjacencium; super hoc Thomas Bracebryg, maior civitatis Ebor', vicecomitesque et aldermanni et plures alii concives ejusdem civitatis, accesserunt in propriis personis suis ad locum, ubi predicta domus stetit edificata, et ibidem viderunt diversas cartas et evidencias predicti Johannis, quas eis ostendit pro jure suo. Unde, ad peticionem predicti Johannis, predicti maior, vicecomites, et aldermanni assignarunt Johannem Ampilford, *mason*, Willelmum Ormsby et Willelmum Warter, carpentarios, scrutatores electos et juratos arcium suarum, ad scrutandum fideliter et vere judicandum secundum antiquam consuetudinem civitatis de domo predicta, utrum edificata fuit super solum proprium predicti Johannis vel non. Qui quidem scrutatores, habito inde avisamento diligenti inter eos, venerunt in propriis personis suis coram Thoma Bracebryg, maiore predicto, penultimo die Februarii, 2 Henry vi. (28 February, 1423-4), et per eorum sacramentum et discrecionem dixerunt quod invenerunt quod **domus predicta fuit edificata et posita super solum communitatis civitatis** predicte; ideo considerabant et judicabant quod **predictus** Johannes Bempton habeat solum suum sicut alii vicini sui ex utraque parte ibidem habuerunt et habent inclusum a tempore de quo non est memoria, per veteres sepes et muros suos et non ultra, et sic edificet et ponat domum suam et nullo alio modo.

Judicium scrutatorum predictorum, juratorum et assignatorum per maiorem supradictum de consensu parcium infrascriptarum, ad scrutandum quemdam fundum inter unum tenementum Roberti Burton, *barker*, in vico de Northstrete in civitate predicta, ex una parte, et quoddam tenementum in eisdem vico et civitate magistri, fratrum, et sororum gilde sive fraternitatis Sancti Christoferi, ex altera parte, secundum consuetudinem civitatis, videlicet, quod linea trahatur a tergo postis predicti Roberti versus regiam (*fo.* 249) stratam de Northstrete ante, linealiter et directe usque ad postem predictorum magistri, fratrum, et sororum versus gardinum retro, et quod ipsi magister, fratres, et sorores sumptibus et expensis suis amoveant postem suum intermedium inter postes predictos, ut predictus Robertus recte sursum possit ponere domum suam. Redditum fuit judicium predictum, coram maiore predicto, tercio die Marcii, 2 Henrr. vi. (1423-4).

[1]Judicium scrutatorum, proximo predictorum limitatorum et juratorum, coram Thoma Bracebryg, maiore predicto, ad scrutandum secundum consuetudinem hujus civitatis quoddam cornerium cujusdam domus decani et capituli ecclesie cathedralis Beate Petri Eboracensis, edificate de novo per Johannem Kyrkham, *plasterer*, tenentem suum, in cornerio boriali cimiterii ecclesie Sancte Margarete in Walmegate, Ebor'; et inde fideliter judicandum et certificandum utrum cornerium domus predicte fuit edificatum super solum proprium predictorum decani et capituli, vel super solum venelle regie ibidem adjacentis. Qui quidem scrutatores predicti, de voluntate et consensu maioris decanique et capituli predictorum, onus scrutinii et judicii hujusmodi licet cum difficultate quadam super se assumentes, scrutatis diligenter et nudatis antiquis bundis cimiterii et venelle predictorum et pavimenti antiqui ejusdem venelle, per eorum

1—In left margin is written "Venella juxta sementerii (*sic*) Sancte Margarete.

sacramentum in hac parte prestitum secundum suam discrecionem considerabant quod cornerium domus predicte fuit edificatum super solum venelle predicte. Et ideo judicabant quod cornerium domus predicte buttans super venellam predictam amoveatur ex utroque latere illius domus, per spacium unius ulne regie, et *la nayle* et dimidie *nayle* unius ulne regie ; et fiat illud cornerium quasi rotundum pro aisiamento cariagii ibidem transituri, sumptibus et expensis predictorum decani et capituli vel predicti tenentis sui, et quod linea trahatur directe a quodam lapide jacente subtus *le panne* ad aliud cornerium predicte domus versus orientem usque ad quamdam veterem arborem vocatam *Burtre,* versus le Kyrkestiyll, et secundum hoc tenens predictorum decani et capituli faciat clausuram gardini sui in latere boriali predicti cimiterii. Et redditum fuit judicium ibidem iiij^{to} die Marcii, 2 Henr. vi. (1423-4). Burton.

Memorandum quod ubi certi homines incluserunt et obstruxerunt quamdam venellam communem versus finem de Bouthum cum quadam porta, aperiente ultro in regiam stratam de Bouthum, sicut ipsa venella se extendit in longitudine a regia strata de Bouthum ante usque ad *les leys,* que quondam fuerunt Ranulphi del See, retro, et in latitudine inter grangiam et terram Ricardi Beverlay in tenura Willelmi Brame, *skynner,* ex una parte, et terram [1] in tenura Johannis Smyth de Bouthum, ex altera parte ; super hoc, ad clamorem et querelam multorum de communitate, Thomas Bracebryg, maior, et alii de aldermannis et viginti quatuor et communibus accesserunt ad venellam predictam, ut prefertur inclusam, et assignaverunt scrutatores supradictos cementariorum et carpentariorum ibidem presentes ad scrutandum et fideliter judicandum de quantitate latitudinis venelle predicte, et ipsam per metas bundandum. Unde scrutatores predicti limitabant venellam predictam esse apertam latitudinis unius ulne regie et dimidie ulne regie, et unius largi polliceti, a regia strata predicta directe usque ad *lez leys* predicta ; et ibidem palos pro metis posuerunt pro evidencia in futurum, et ostium (*fo.* 249, *b.*) et postes ad introitum ejusdem venelle versus stratam de Bouthum amoverant, et salices, ad

1—A space is left here.

alium finem ipsius venelle versus campum crescentes, absciderunt;
et foveam aquaticam ipsam venellam includentem versus *les
leys* predicta cum terra impleverunt pro communi passagio
hominum et jumentorum ibidem habendo. Burton. R.

Aldermanni, Thomas Bracebryg, maior, Robertus Howom,
Johannes Northeby, Henricus Preston, Thomas Esyngwald,
Willelmus Ormesheued, Petrus Buksy, Johannes Aldestanemor;
vicecomites, Willelmus Bedale, Willelmus Gatesheued; de
xxiiij^{or}, Thomas Doncastr', Johannes Pettyclerk, Thomas More,
Galfridus Savage, Robertus Yarom, Johannes Loftehouse,
Johannes Baynbryg, Johannes Somerby, Thomas Kyrkham;
camerarii, Nicholas Blakburn, junior, Thomas Roderham, congregati fuerunt hic in camera xiij^{mo} die Aprilo, 2 Henr. vi. (1424),
ubi venit coram eis Johannes Bempton, *barker*, et allocutus quare
ad preceptum et premunicionem maioris non amovit domum,
quam edificavit extra gardinum suum ad finem super solum
communitatis, secundum judicium scrutatorum inde redditum
in folio proximo precedenti scriptum. Et predictus Johannes
respondit quod domus illa non esset amota per eum nec pro eo
aliter quam pro tunc stetit, et dedit maiori et consilio camere
plura verba inobediencie et contradictionis, et propter hoc fuit
judicatus ad forisfacturam x *li*. secundum quandam antiquam
ordinacionem civitatis in hac parte editam, et missus in prisonam,
et exoneratus de libertate sua civitatis. Et super hoc idem
Johannes, capto avisamento meliori, certificavit maiorem quod
voluit humiliter in hac parte et cuncta facere que consilium camere
super eum judicare vellet. Unde maior convocari mandavit
aldermannos et consilium camere, videlicet, Robertum Howom,
Johannem Northeby, Henricum Preston, Johannem Moreton,
Thomam Esyngwald, Willelmum Ormesheued, J[ohannem]
Aldestanmor, Willelmum Bedale, Willelmum Gatesheued,
vicecomites, Johannem Hewyk, Thomam Doncastr', Thomam
More, Johannem Usburn, Galfridum Sauvage, Robertum Yarom,
Johannem Lofthouse, Thomam Aton, Johannem Bolton, Thomam
Davy et Thomam Snawdon de xxiiij^{or}, et alios, qui congregati
fuerunt hic in camera, xiiij^{mo} die Aprilis, anno predicto; et
coram eis venit Johannes Bempton predictus, et veniam peciit,
et se submisit gracie et judicio consilii camere, et promisit et

diem cepit quod predictum domum amoveret citra diem Martis proximo ex tunc sequentem, et ad solvendum in camera x *li.* predictas; et quod ista perficeret plegios invenit Robertum Burton et Thomam Snawdon sub pena xl *li.*, si defecerit. Et bene probatum erat quod predictus Johannes Bempton amovit domum predictam et eam posuit in ordine et cursu, secundum quod scrutatores judicabant. Et predictas x *li.*, solvit in camera et plegii sui exonerati fuerunt. Unde xix° die Aprilis, anno predicto, Thomas Bracebryg, maior predictus, et vicecomites predicti, necnon Robertus Howom, Johannes Northeby, Thomas Gare, Henricus Preston, Thomas Esyngwald, Johannes Aldestanemor, Galfridus Sauvage, Robertus Gare, Thomas More, Johannes Usburn, Johannes Bolton, Johannes Loftehouse, Thomas Snawdon, Robertus Burton, Johannes Baynbryg, Willelmus Craven, Nicholaus Blakburn, *junior*, et Johannes Raghton fuerunt hic presentes in camera, qui, considerantes humilitatem predicti Johannis Bempton, restituebant (*fo.* 250) eum ad libertatem civitatis, et forisfacturam x *li.* predictarum sub bono gestu suo in futurum sibi voce ipsorum omnium relaxabant.

Hoc est judicium Johannis Ampilford, *mason*, Willelmi Cunsby et Willelmi Warter, carpentariorum, scrutatorum juratorum artificiorum de *les masons* et *carpenters* in civitate Ebor', assignatorum per Thomam Bracebryg, maiorem ejusdem civitatis, ad scrutandum et fideliter judicandum inter parochianos ecclesie Sancti Michaelis ad pontem Use, in civitate predicta, et dominum Willelmum Kyddelam, capellanum cantarie Beate Marie Virginis in eadem ecclesia, secundum consuetudinem predicte civitatis, de quodam muro lapideo ipsius ecclesie, ex parte boriali ejusdem ecclesie, juxta tenementum predicte cantarie edificando per parochianos predictos, videlicet, quod parochiani predicti edificent murum suum lapideum predictum ex parte boriali predicte ecclesie, linealiter recte sursum a fundo cimiterii, sicut inceperunt contigue tenemento predicte cantarie ad finem australem ipsius tenementi, et quod predictus dominus Willelmus Kyddelam vacuet et deponat agestaciones suas pendentes ultra ad finem predictum ne impediant sursum edificacionem muri predicte. Et si contingat in futurum quod parochiani predicte ecclesie proponant edificare aliquas domos in cimiterio predicto ex parte occidentali tenementorum predictorum, quod tunc predictus dominus Willelmus et successores sui, capellani cantarie predicte, vacuent et deponant agestaciones suas tenementorum predictorum, ex parte occidentali eorundem, et dent parochianis predictis locum ut edificare possint ibidem linealiter recte sursum, secundum usum et consuetudinem civitatis predicte. Redditum fuit hoc judicium in festo Sancte Marie Magdalene, 2 Henr. vi. (22 July, 1424). Burton.

Grant by Robert Curtays the younger of all his goods to Sir Richard Denton, vicar choral of the cathedral church of S. Peter of York, John Waghen, mercer, and Edmund Barneburgh, sadler, citizens. Witnesses, Thomas Esyngwald, mayor, William Craven, Thomas Kyrkeham, sheriffs, William Barton, skinner, John Abywryk, citizens. York, 4 February, 1422, 1 Henry vi. Seal. Acknowledged before William Ormesheued, mayor, 8 October, 4 Henry vi. (1425). Burton R.

(*fo.* 250, *b.*) Johannes Ampilford, Thomas Best, et Johannes Hexham, scrutatores cementariorum et carpentariorum civitatis Ebor', quinto die Augusti, 3 Henr. vi. (1425), considerant quod quantum ad altam gutteram inter tenementum domini Henrici Broghton et tenementum Johannis Thorpe, in quo Johannes Lancastr' et Johannes Brystall inhabitant, in vico de Mykelgate, quod utraque pars sustentet et reparet illam gutteram ad aisiamentum utriusque partis, ita longe sicut servit utrique parti, quocienscumque indiguerit reparari seu emendari. Et quantum ad minorem gutteram, que jacet subtus altam gutteram extra murum tenementi predicti domini Henrici, super latus coquine predicti Johannis Thorpe, in tenura Johannis Bristall predicti, quod ipse Johannes tenens vel dominus suus sustentet et reparet illam per se sumptibus suis propriis. Et quod Johannes Lancastr' amoveat quemdam caminum, in quantum occupat super *le pan* predicti domini Henrici, nisi secum potuerit alias concordare. Et si contingat in futurum predictum caminum sic amotum iterum de novo fieri quod tunc ille caminus situetur integre per se super tenementum predicti Johannis Thorpe, modo in tenura predicti Johannis Lancastr', non frontatus ex aliqua parte super parietem vel super meremium tenementi domini Henrici de Broghton predicti.

Memorandum quod Willelmus Revytour, capellanus, qui obiit anno Domini millesimo ccccxlvj^{to}, tempore Willelmi Stokton, maioris civitatis Ebor', dedit et legavit usui capellanorum Sancti Willelmi super pontem Use unum librum vocatum **Legendum** pro toto anno, et unum alium librum vocatum **Gradale**, ac unum vestimentum integrum de albo serico, videlicet, unam casulam albam, ij tunicles, iij fanolles,[1] j stolam, et j novum autrecloth.

Adam Milorde natus infra civitatem de Parish infra regnum Francie virtute.[2]

(*fo*. 251). Memorandum quod secundo die mensis Junii, 9 Henr. v. (1421), Johannes Neuton de Ebor', *glover*, venit hic in camera coram Ricardo Russell, maiore, et ostendit quamdam literam patentem, cujus tenor talis erat.

A touz yceux que cestes presents lettres verront ou orront Robert Umfrevile, chivaler, lieutenant de Berewyk sur Twede, salutz en Dieu. Comme graunde merit soit et almoigne pur dire et tesmoigner a touz jours chose qest verraye, et tresgraunde petche ausi pur conceler la verite, et en case nomement ou estre purroit ou per de corps ou dez biens, pur ceo veulliez savoir de certein que plusours genz du cestez parties depar Johan de Neuton, demurant deins la dite citee Deverwyk, moy ount diligealment requises de certifier la natif estat del dit Johan et en quele partie il fuist nee de sa mier. Pur quoy vous plese a savoir que Henry del Strothir, esquier, frer et heir a monsire Thomas del Strothir, et diverses autres gentilles devaunt moy au Berewyk al faisaunce dicestes ount tout au plain jurez et recordez que le dit Johan fuist primerement nee de ventre sa miere en la ville de Neuton en Glendale, deins le counte de Northumbr', a la ligeance et foy nostre tres redoubte soverain seignur le roy; et que le pier dudit Henry fuist verraye pier a une Johan Grayden comme par bastardie, quel Johan Greyden fuist verraye pier a dit Johan Neuton, issint que le dit Henry del Strothir est uncle au dit Johan de Neuton. Entendantz bien de certein, treshonourez et tres entierment bien amez seignurs, que les ditz gentilles moy dient, si mestier soit, qils veullent venir en lours propres persones pur mesme ceo recorder,

---

1—Fanones but the MS. seems to have "fanolles."
2—This entry is unfinished in the MS.

tesmoigner et prover encountre ceux qi vuillent dire le contrarie. En tesmoignance de quelle chose a cestes lettres de recorde ay mys mon seal. Done a Berwyk suisdite le joefay prochein devant le fest de Pentecost, lan de grace mille quatre centintz vintisme, et de regne le Roy Henry quint puis le conquest septisme. (23 May, 1420). Burton.

John Loftehouse and Agnes Hugate.

Thys indenture bers wyttnes betwyx Johan Lofthous and Annas Hugayt that all hys obligacions ar payed that are in hyr hand, savand that John Lofthouse awe to the forsayde Annas in clere ix $li.$ xvij $s.$, all thynges rekynd betwyx tham. Wryten at York in the x yer of Kyng Herry, on the vj day of May, and hereto the partys settis thair seles to.

Release by Thomas Benson, citizen and draper of York, William Beverlay of Kyrkby in Kendale, and John Beverlay his son, to Robert Middilton, citizen and merchant of York, of all personal actions against the said Robert. Seals. 25 November, 1 Henry vi. (1422).

Thomas de Stragryfe, natus in Abirden in Scocia, juratus est homo Anglicus coram Thoma Esyngwald, maiore Ebor', xvij^{mo} die Januarii, 2 Henr. vi. (1423-4), et Thomas Harpour, *wever*, de Ebor', constituit se plegium pro es, etc.

Nicholaus del Furth, natus in Anguysh in Scocia, juratus est homo ligeus regis Anglie coram Willelmo Ormesheuyd, maiore Ebor', primo die Marcii. 3 Henr. (1424-5).

(*fo*. 251, *b*.) Nomina Scotorum juratorum coram Johanne de Bedale, maiore, de mandato Henrici Percy, comitis Northumbr', custodis de *lestmarchez* Anglie.

Stephanus Lyndesay, *baxter*, Scotus natus in Manymele in Scocia, virtute potestatis tradite per dominum Henricum Percy, comitem Northumbr', custodem de *lestmarchez* Anglie versus Scociam, juratus est primo die Septembris, 7 Henr. v. (1419), coram Johanne de Bedale, maiore Ebor', quod extunc erit fidelis ligeus regis Anglie et heredum suorum, et quod stabit legibus et consuetudinibus Anglie, et eas pro posse suo fideliter perimplebit ad totum terminum vite sue, per plegiagium Johannis Croxton, *baxter*, Ebor'.

Johannes Watson, *goldsmyth*, natus est in Scocia et potestate qua supra, juratus est coram Johanne de Bedale, maiore predicto, in forma predicta, ij^{do} die Septembris, anno predicto, per plegiagium Willelmi Herte, *spuryer*, de Ebor'.

Johannes Marsshall, *cocus*, natus in Louthian in Scocia, potestate qua supra, juratus est coram maiore predicto in forma predicta, secundo die Septembris, anno predicto, per plegiagium.[1]

Willelmus Jonson, natus in Lethcogh in Scocia, potestate qua supra, juratus est coram maiore predicto in forma predicta, iiij^{to} die Septembris, anno predicto, per plegiagium Johannis Boune et Roberti Hilton, *cordewaners*, Ebor'.

Johannes Martyn, Scotus, natus in villa Sancti Johannis in Scocia, potestate qua supra, juratus est coram maiore predicto in forma predicta, quinto die Septembris, anno predicto, per plegiagium Thome Appilton de Ebor', *goldsmyth*.

Johannes Andrewson, Scotus, natus in Anewe in Gualguidia Scocie, potestate qua supra, juratus est coram maiore predicto in forma predicta, v^{to} die Septembris, anno predicto, per plegiagium Johannis Rumby de Ebor', *salsermaker*.

Marjoria Forester, nata in Jeddeworth, quando erat de ligeancia regis Anglie, potestate qua supra, coram maiore predicto, jurata erat in forma predicta, ix° die Septembris, 7 Henry v. (1419).

Johannes Kede, *baxter*, Scotus, ostendit literam Johannis filii regis, custodis de *lestmarche*, de data xx° die Augusti, 6 Henr. v. (1418), quod juratus erat coram eo ligeus regis Anglie et heredum suorum.

Thomas Blount, Scotus, juratus erat ligeus regis Anglie et heredum suorum coram Henrico Percy, comite Northumbr', custode de *lestmarche*, prout litera ejusdem testabatur, quam dictus Thomas monstravit, de data apud Topclif, xx^{mo} die Augusti, 6 Henr. v. (1418).

Margoria Henrydoghter, Scota, in vigilia exaltacionis sancte Crucis, anno predicto (13 September, 1418), potestate qua supra, jurata erat coram Johanne de Bedale, maiore predicto, et plegios invenit Johannem Skelton et Ricardum Gednay, *taillours*, Ebor'.

1—No pledge is named.

Margareta Thornour, Escotte, jurata coram Henrico Percy, comite Northumbr', custode de *lestmarche* versus Scociam, xiiij die Septembris, 7 Henr. v. (1419), et super hoc ostendit literam dicti comitis de data in manerio suo de Topclif, die et anno predictis.

. . . . Wyseman . . . . natus in Scocia juratus . . . . viij die Marii, 10 Henr. v. (1422) et invenit pleg . . . .

Johanna Sandeland, nata in Edenburgh in Scocia, jurata est coram Thoma Esyngwald, maiore, xviij die Decembris, 2 Henr. vi. (1423), plegio Andrea Ferrour sub pena xx *li*.

(*fo*. 252). Willelmus Henryson, Scotus, venit coram Johanne de Bedale, maiore predicto, vij° die Septembris, 7 Henr. v. (1419), et ostendit literam dicti comitis, de data apud Howeden, ultimo die Septembris, anno sexto regis predicti (1418), quod tunc juratus erat coram eo ad ligeanciam regis Anglie.

Henricus Smyth, Scotus, venit coram maiore predicto et ostendit literam Johannis filii regis custodis de *lestemarchez*, quod juratus erat coram eo apud Leycestr', xij° die Maii, 2 Henr. v. (1414).

Johannes de Halywell, Escot, juratus erat coram Henrico Percy comite predicto, xxiij° die Septembris, anno regni regis predicti sexto (1418), prout litera ejusdem comitis, quam monstravit, testabatur de data apud Werkeworth, die et anno predictis.

Thomas Gyselay, *taillour*, capitur per suspicionem pro Scoto, venit coram Johanne de Bedale, maiore predicto, et probavit per sufficiens recordum quod natus erat in Rokesburgh sub ligeancia regis Anglie.

Jacobus de Erthe, natus in Halton in Louthyan, Scotus, potestate qua supra, juratus est coram maiore predicto in forma predicta, xvj^{mo} die Septembris, 7 Henr. v. (1419), et plegium invenit Johannem Thornour, *galegemaker* de Ebor.'

Katerina Dykson, nata in Lowthian in Scocia, potestate qua supra, jurata erat coram maiore predicto in forma predicta in vigilia Michaelis (28 September), anno predicto.

[1]Johannes de Neuton in Glendale venit coram Johanne de Bedale, maiore predicto, ix° die Septembris, 7 Henr. v. (1419), et ostendit literam Henrici de Percy, quondam comitis Northumbr', custodis de *lestmarche*, de data apud Bernardcastell, xij die Julii, 3 Henr. iv. (1402)[1] Vacat.

Johannes Wylby de Meneros, Scotus, juratus est esse ligeus et fidelis homo regis Anglie et heredum suorum, ut in forma consueta, coram Thoma Gare, maiore Ebor', xix° die Novembris, 8 Henr. v. (1420).

Vicesimo tercio die Novembris, 8 Henr. v. (1420), Robertus Johanson venit coram Thoma Gare, maiore Ebor', et quandam literam ostendit sub hiis verbis :—

Johan fitz du Roy, connestable Dengletere et gardein del Estmarche vers Escoce, a toutz ceulx qui cestes noz lettres verront ou orront salutz. Savoir vous faisons que le vynt et primer jour de Januer, lan du regne de nostre tresredoute seignur le roy Henri quint puis le conquest primer (1413-4), Robert Johanson Descoce a sa diligente supplicacion jura sur les saintz evangelies, par lui corporelment touchez, devant nous judicielment seiantz deins nostre manoir de Semere, pour estre foial Englois et liege a nostre dit seignur le roy et a ses heires et successours, roys, et au corone et roialme Dengleterre tout son vivant, et aussi dobeier de haut en bas a les loyes et custumes du dit roialme. En tesmoignance de quelle chose nous avons fait faire cestes noz lettres patentes, enseallees de la seal de nostre office. Donne a nostre dit manoir lan et jour avantditz.

Willelmus Andrewson, de Edenburgh, Scotus, juratus est ut in forma consueta coram Thoma Gare, maiore Ebor', in festo Sancti Antonii, 8 Henr. v. (17 January, 1420-1).

Laurencius Alanson, natus in Egerston in Foresta de Jeddeworth, juratus est in forma supradicta, coram Ricardo Russell, maiore Ebor', 8 Henr. v. (1420).

. . . . de . . rston in Scocia juratus est in forma . . . . xxiij . . . .

1—1—This entry is crossed through and in the margin is written, " Vide in prima parte folii proxime presidente," see p. 113.

Jacobus Thomson, Scotus, natus in Aberden, juratus coram Henrico Preston, maiore xxv° die Novembris, 1 Henr. vi. (1422).

Ordo paginarum ludi Corporis Christi tempore Willelmi Alne, maioris, anno regni regis Henrici quinti post conquestum Anglie tercio, compilata per Rogerum Burton, clericum communem, in anno Domini millesimo ccccxv.[1] R.B.

(ff. 252, b to 254, b.) . . . .

(fo. 254, b.)

Portours	... ... viij torch'	Chaloners	... iiij torch'
Coblers	... ... iiij torch'	Fullers ...	... iiij torch'
Cordwaners	... xiiij torch'	Girdellers	... torch'[2]
Cottellers ...	... ij torch'	Taillours	... torch'$\frac{2}{3}$
Wevere servauntz...	iiij torch'	Et lviij cives civitatis hab-	
Carpenters	... vj torch'	uerunt torcheas similiter die	
		Corporis Christi.	

Ordinatum est quod *portours coblers* eant antea primo. Et tunc a dextris *websterservauntz* et *cordwaners*. Et ex opposito, *fullers, cuttellers, girdellers, chaloners, carpenters, tailliours*. Et tunc boni cives, et postea xxiiij, xij., maior, et iiij^{or} torchee magistri Thome de Bukton.

Proclamacio ludi Corporis Christi facienda in vigilia Corporis Christi.[4]

(fo. 255.) Second list of plays.[5]

Potters	viij torch'
Glovers	iiij torch'
Smyths	iiij torch'
Wevers	viij torch'
Corpus Christi	x torch'
Willelmus Selby pro anima magistri	
Thome Bukton	iiij torch'
Fisshers	ij torch'

1—This list of plays is given by Miss Toulmin Smith, *York Mystery Plays*, pp. xix to xxvij.
2—The number of torches is not given.
3—Here is written:—Respice ulterius in folio sequenti.
4—See Drake, p. xxij.
5—See Davies, pp. 233-236. At the foot of the folio, in the middle of the line, is Ranell. If more was written, it is illegible.

Quod *goldsmyths, pewderers, cordewaners, girdellers* . . .
assise panis et servisie, vendentes candelarum de Pyris, juners
et . . . quod . . . plasteriorum et tegulariorum . .
karvers . . . de . . . .

(*fo.* 255, *b.*) Fait a remembrer que le xij jour de Juyn, lan xiij., Alisander Jonson de Lawatre de Scoce terre feust jure destre loial liege etc., per plegge Johan Rumby, Deverwyk, *saucer.*

Johannes Buteler, natus in Normannia, juratus est quod erit fidelis homo ligeus regis Anglic, ut in forma, xxvj die Septembris, 4 Henr. vi. (1425), coram Willelmo Ormesheued, maiore etc., per plegiagium Johannis Hobson et Johannis Spynk de Askham.

Memorandum quod Johannes Fynlawson de Cumbrenaunt, Scoticus, juratus est ad sancta Dei evaungelia, vj^{to} die Junie, 3 Henr. v. (1415), quod ipse amodo erit fidelis ligeus dicti domini regis et heredum suorum, et quod fideliter ad omnes leges et consuetudines regni Anglie pro posse suo stabit, et eas custodiet et perimplebit ad terminum vite sue, etc.

[1]Memorandum quod Johannes Martyn, natus in Crakevergus in Hibernia, moram trahens in Scocia per decem anuos, juratus est ut supra, xxviij die Augusti, 5 Henr. v. (1417), coram Willelmo Bowes, maiore Ebor', quod ipse amodo erit ligeus fidelis dicti domini nostri regis Anglie et heredum suorum, et quod fideliter ad omnes leges et consuetudines regni Anglic stabit, et eas custodiet et perimplebit ad terminum vite sue etc.[1]

Memorandum quod dominus Willelmus Robertson, presbiter, filius Roberti Smyth de Athington in Scocia, juratus est ad sancta Dei evaungelia, xiij° die Aprilis, anno Domini m° ccccxix°, 7 Henr. v., coram Johanne de Bedale, maiore Ebor', quod ipse amodo erit ligeus fidelis dicti domini regis et heredum suorum, et quod fideliter ad omnes leges et consuetudines regni Anglie stabit, et eas custodiet et perimplebit ad terminum vite sue etc.

Memorandum quod Archebaldus Jonson, natus in castro de Bostrevyn in Scocia, juratus est ad sancta Dei evaungelia, xxvij^{mo} die Maii, anno Domini et regis predicto, coram Johanne de Bedale, maiore Ebor', quod amodo erit ligeus fidelis domini

---

1—1—This entry is crossed through.

nostri regis Anglie et heredum suorum, et quod fideliter ad omnes leges et consuetudines regni Anglie stabit, et eas custodiet et perimplebit ad terminum vite sue.

Memorandum quod Stephanus Lyndesay, *baxter*, Scotus, natus in Manymele in Scocia, juratus est primo die Septembris, 7 Henr. v. (1419), coram Johanne de Bedale, maiore Ebor', virtute potestatis sibi tradite per Henricum Percy, comitem Northumbr', custodem de *lestmarche* versus Scociam, quod ipse amodo erit bonus et fidelis ligeus domini regis Anglie et heredum suorum, et fideliter ad omnes leges et consuetudines regni Anglie stabit, et eas perficiet et custodiet ad terminum vite sue, et Johannes Claxton, *baxter*, plegius.

Johannes Goatson, *goldsmyth*, natus in Scocia, juratus est ij^{do} die Septembris, anno regni regis predicto, coram Johanne de Bedale maiore predicto, de mandato predicti comitis, custodis de *lestmarche*, quod extunc erit fidelis ligeus domini regis et heredum suorum, et leges et omnes consuetudines regni Anglie custodiet, et eis stabit ad terminum vite sue, per plegiagium Willelmi Herte, *spuryer*.

Et eodem die juratus est, modo premisso, coram maiore predicto, Johannes Marsshall, *cocus*, natus in Lowthian in Scocia, et plegius.[1]

x^{mo} die Septembris, anno regni regis Henrici v^{to} x^{mo}[2] 12 (1422) Johannes Williamson, Scotus, natus in Clydesdale juratus est, coram Henrico Preston, maiore, modo et forma premissis.

(*fo.* 256). Juramentum custodis mercati bladorum super Pavimentum et Coppergate.

Memorandum quod Ricardus de Rykhall, *cordewaner*, x° die Februarii, 12 Ric. ii. (1388-9), admissus fuit ad custodiendum forum bladorum ex ista parte Use, et juratus est. Idem renovavit juramentum suum xv die Februraii, anno xvj (1392-3).

Memorandum quod quidam Johannes de Marton captus fuit per suspectum pro Scotico et exploratore, et die Lune, in vigilia Sancti Bartholomei, 13 Ric. ii. (23 August, 1389). Johannes de Berden, Johannes de Doncastr' et Willelmus de Marton,

---

1—The entry ends thus.
2—There was no month of September in 10 Henry V., the reign of Henry VI. began 1 September.

draper, manuceperunt et recordati fuerunt, quod predictus Johannes de Marton est fidelis Anglicus et ligeus domini regis Anglic, et sic ad requisicionem dictorum proborum liberatus est.

Memorandum quod iij die Septembris, 13 Ric. ii. (1389), Johannes de Selby, Gilbertus de Twys et Johannes de Draycotes, *taillour*, manuceperunt coram maiore in camera ad defendendum dictum maiorem M' S,[1] et ballivos indempnes, pro deliberacione corporis Hugonis Cooke, *taillour*, pro uno *chapelet* domine regine subtracto, pro quo dictus Hugo calumpniatus fuit, etc.

Memorandum quod Willelmus Inkelyng, armiger, recepit de Johanne Payntour unum . . . . ys, depictatum cum aquila argentea, in camera maioris die Lune proximo ante . . . festum Omnium Sanctorum, 13 Ric. ii. (25 October, 1389).

Memorandum quod iij° die Novembris, 13 Ric. ii. (1389), quidam Johannes de Chilton recognovit coram maiore et aliis probis hominibus in camera, quod ipse manucepit et acquietavit Willelmum de Petthow de Ebor', de redempcione sua centum marcarum versus dominum Jacobum de Sandylandes de Scocia, *chivaler*, qui cepit dictum Willelmum in prisonatum suum, et quod dictus Willelmus amodo non calumpnietur versus ipsum Jacobum seu dictum Johannem in hac parte.

Memorandum quod Henricus de Brynsall, vocatus Wolleman, admissus fuit ad officium curatoris debito modo et fideli excercendum inter mercatorem et mercatorem et ad hoc juratus est xxiiij die Januarii, 13 Ric. ii. (1389-90).

(*fo.* 256, *b*.) Memorandum quod Ricardus de Crosseland juratus est x° die Octobris, 8 Ric. ii. (1384), ad custodiendum fideliter forum bladorum de Mikelgate. Idem juratus est coram Johanne de Bracebryg, maiore, xiij° die Februarii, anno xvj (1392-3).

Memorandum quod dominus Johannes de Ryse cepit ix archas pro districtione redditus x *s*. de Willelmo Cristendom, deliberatas die Sabbati in prima septimana Quadragesime, 12 Ric. ii. (6 March, 1389).

1—MS. maiorem, scilicet ? M. would probably mean manucaptores, but this does not seem to suit the grammar.

Willelmus de Chyvyngton, Scotus, juratus est fidelis ligeus domini regis, xviij die Januarii, 14 Ric. ii. (1390-1).

Walterus Gare, juratus ad custodiendum fideliter forum piscium apud pontem de Ouse etc., xv die Februarii, anno xj^{mo} (1387-8), et fide et fideliter presentandum defectus etc.

Johannes Dorlyng, *sadler*, captus, in prisona detentus ut Scoticus per Willelmum Foughler, *draper*, unde litere testimoniales venerunt de Beverlaco etc. Et quia dictus Johannes juratus est ad libertatem etc., invenit manucaptores quod ipse sit residens et paratus ad respondendum ad standum recto, si quis loqui voluerit contra eum etc., Johannes de Cotyngham, Willelmus de Semere, Robertus Spine, et Thomas de Bedale.

Memorandum quod xvj die Januarii, 21 Ric. ii. (1397-8), in camera maioris super pontem Use in Ebor', Thomas de Staynlye, nuper maior civitatis Ebor', deliberavit Willelmo de Hugate de Ebor' quandam commissionem domini regis, tangentem liberacionem bonorum et catallorum dicti Willelmi, nuper forisfactorum pro quadam felonia etc. Qui quidem Willelmus in fide sua promisit coram Willelmo Frost, tunc maiore, Thoma Gra, Thoma de Holbek, Thoma de W . . . . tunc camerariis, Roberto del Gare, Willelmo de Chestre et aliis, ad restituendum dictam commissionem dicto Thome, vel eciam ad sessandum totaliter processum in hac parte, ita quod dictus Thomas sit inde quietus etc.

Johannes de Eddenham, de Scocia, venit in camera coram Willelmo Frost, tunc maiore, et probis hominibus, decimo septimo die Junii, 2 Henr. iv. (1401), et optulit se ibidem ad essendum fidelis ligeus domini regis, et ad hoc firmiter tenendum, tactis sacrosanctis Evangeliis, corporaliter prestitit juramentum.

Memorandum quod in crastino Sancti Hillarii (14 January, 1404-5) Willelmus Johanneson de . . . . . et Thomas Darrawell, de Brenskelf, optulerunt se coram Willelmo Frost, tunc maiore Ebor', ad essendum fideles ligei dicti domini regis, et ad hoc firmiter tenendum, tactis sacrosanctis Dei Evangeliis, corporale prestiterunt juramentum.

Stryngers.

(*fo.* 257). Inprimis, pro bona regula et meliori regimine habenda in arte quadam, que vocatur *stryngercrafte*, in civitate ista Ebor' inter homines artis illius, et ne populus domini nostri regis per malum opus per homines artis illius sit deceptus, de consensu Henrici Preston, maioris Ebor', et consilii camere hujus civitatis Ebor' ordinatum est quod homines artis predicte habeant scrutatores inter se et de se ipsis, ad scrutandum et videndum quod omne opus in arte sit bene et debite operatum ad commodum domini regis et populi sui, et quod *lez strynges* pro arcubus, qui inventi erunt defectivi, sint forisfacti et portentur huc in cameram et ibidem remaneant comburendi. Et super hoc Thomas Conysholm et Willelmus Pannall electi sunt et jurati scrutatores artis predicte.

Item, quod nec vir nec mulier artis predicte capiat aliquem in apprenticium ad docendum illum artem illam pro minori termino quam pro quatuor annis, sub pena quatuor solidorum, camere et arti predicte equaliter applicandorum, tociens quociens hujus constitucionis contrarium factum fuerit.

Item, quod nec vir nec mulier occupet ut magister in civitate ista priusquam receptus sit in libertatem hujus civitatis, et scrutatus si sit habilis ad operandum in arte predicta, sub pena xx *s.*, usibus predictis equaliter applicandorum.

Item, quod nullus artis predicte capiat nec ponat aliquem extraneum in opere in arte predicta, priusquam extraneus ille examinatus sit et scrutatus quod habilis sit ad operandum in arte predicta, sub pena xx *s.*, usibus predictis equaliter applicandorum.

Item, quod nec vir nec mulier artis predicte sit contrarius nec rebellis scrutatoribus ipsius artis, cum ad scrutandum venerint in ea, sub pena iij *s.* iiij *d.*, usibus predictis applicandorum, quociens aliquem vel aliquam contigerit contrarium hujus constitucionis facere.

Goldsmyth.

In nomine Domini, Amen. Non est pretermittendum sed pocius memorie commendandum quod aurifabri hujus civitatis Ebor' annis preteritis onus grave et expensas excessivas pro duabus paginis suis in ludo Corporis Christi portabant; jamque mundus alteratus est super ipsos, et ipsi plus solito in bonis pauperiores sunt effecti et viis et modis superpremissis. Sectam fecerunt frequentem maioribus et consilio camere pro subsidio habendo in hac parte in suorum importabilium onerum relavamen; vel alias, quod exonerarentur de una paginarum suarum cum causantibus expensis, que ea occasione indies excrescunt, onus utrarumque paginarum suarum non potuerunt sine nimio eorum incommodo diucius sustinere. Ex altera parte, vero, quia cementarii hujus civitatis murmurabant inter se de pagina sua in ludo Corporis Christi, ubi Fergus flagellatus erat, pro eo quod materia pagine illius in sacra non continetur scriptura, et magis risum et clamorem causabat quam devocionem, et quandoque lites, contenciones et pugne inde proveniebant in populo, ipsamque paginam suam raro vel nunquam potuerunt producere et ludere clara die, sicut faciunt pagine precedentes, ipsi igitur cementarii affectabant desiderio magno ab hujusmodi pagina sua exonerari, et alteri assignari, que conveniens est scripture sacre, et quam producere et ludere poterunt clara die. Et pro hujusmodi suis desideriis perimplendis ambe partes predicte instanciam fecerunt, et preces penes maiorem et consilium camere pro eorum bono consensu et voluntate gratuita in hac parte habendis. Unde Thomas Snaudon, maior, necnon aldermanni et consilium camere hujus civitatis voluntates et desideria hominum arcium predictarum benivole acceptantes, et ea honestati consona reputantes, considerabant quod aurifabri predicti in diminucione gravium onerum suorum exonerentur de una (fo. 257, b.) paginarum suarum, scilicet, Herodis. Et similiter quod cementarii predicti sint exonerati et quieti de pagina Fergus. Et quod ipsi cementarii habeant eis et arti sue predictam paginam Herodis, quam aurifabri per prius habebant, suis expensis in ludo Corporis Christi producendam et ludendam honestiori modo quo decet, in laudem civitatis, tociens quociens ludum predictum ludi contigerit in civitate predicta.

(fo. 257 b.) Recordum pro Johanne Robertson libertatum de Appilby. Omnibus et singulis ad quos [sic] noticiam presentes litere pervenerint vel auditum, nos maior et communitas burgi domini regis de Appelby, in comitatu Westmorel[1], salutem in Eo, qui est omnium vera salus, ac honoris prosperitatisque continnuum incrementum. Cum christianissimus et excellentissimus rex

1—*Sic.*

Henricus, pater [sic] domini Johannis, quondam regis Anglie, concesserit et per cartam suam racionabiliter confirmaverit burgensibus suis de Appilby omnes libertates et liberas consuetudines, quas cives et burgenses domini regis de Ebor', ex concessione dictorum Henrici et Johannis, quondam regum Anglie, habent et possident in presenti; et quod dicti burgenses de Appilby liberi sint et quieti de tolloneo, stallagio, pontagio, muragio, chiminagio, et lastagio per totam terram Anglie, quantum ad dominum regem pertinet atque spectat, prout in literis patentibus dictorum Henrici et Johannis, quondam regum Anglie, ac in diversis literis patentibus omnium regum Anglie post ipsos successive in Anglia regnancium, dictis burgensibus de Appelby confectis plenius declaratur. Et quia Johannes Robertson, unus burgensium dicti domini regis burgi de Appelby predicti, ad presens et per tres annos ultimos ante datam presencium inmediate elapsos, existens, ad partes mundi varias se divertens cum suis mercandisis et causa mercandisandi, a quibusdam dicti regni incolis et ministris, dictarum concessionum et libertatum nesciis et ignariis, extitit quam plurmum fatigatus, arestatus, prepeditus, molestatus, ut asserit, et vexatus, contra vim, formam et tenorem concessionum earumdem libertatum, in ipsius Johannis Robertson dampnum non modicum ac dicti domini regis contemptum manifestum. Quocirca vos omnes et singulos, quorum interest et intererit in hac parte, requirimus efficacius et rogamus quatinus eundem Johannem Robertson, burgensem predicti burgi, contra formam et tenorem dictarum concessionum et confirmacionum libertatum predictarum nullatenus molestetis in aliquo nec gravatis, sed cum penes vos pervenerit, ut unum burgensium dicti domini regis favorabilius admittatis. In cujus rei testimonium sigillum commune dicti burgi de Appelby presentibus est appensum. Datum in burgo predicto, sexto decimo die mensis Aprilis, 8 Edw. iv. (1468).

Plasterarii et Tegularii domorum.[1]

(*fo.* 258). Cum nuper quedam controversia mota fuisset inter magistros artificii tegulariorum domorum hujus civitatis,

1—In right margin is written " Plus inde super xlv folio in libro majoris registri."

ex una parte, et magistros artificii plasterariorum ejusdem civitatis, ex altera parte, tandem partes predicte submiserunt se stare et perimplere arbitrio et judicio Thome Esyngwald, nuper maioris istius civitatis predicte, et quatuor personarum indifferencium per ipsum eligendarum. Unde Thomas, maior predictus, de bono avisamento elegit Johannem Stayneburn, Johannem Huthwait, Willelmum Scoreburgh, et Ricardum Neuland, tanquam personas indifferentes, ad indifferenter tractandum inter partes predictas, et eas finaliter concordandum de et super omnibus litibus et querelis inter ipsas partes motis et pendentibus indecisis. Qui quidem quatuor arbitratores, de consensu et assensu maioris predicti, prece eciam et instancia parcium predictarum, inter easdem partes tractabant et eas concordabant et judicabant, quod universi homines arcium predictarum ammodo sint amici et unanimes, semper in vera caritate viventes, et quod ordinacionum articuli subscripti plane teneantur et plene perficiantur ex utraque parte, sine contradiccione persone cujuscumque.

Ad honorem Dei, et pro commodo tocius populi domini regis, et emendacione certorum defectuum et misprisionum usitatorum publice ante hec tempora in artibus predictis, per avisamentum quatuor arbitratorum supradictorum et communem assensum omnium magistrorum arcium predictarum, quedam ordinaciones statuuntur et sunt tales.

In primis, ordinatum est quod quilibet plasterarius exercens et operans plasteraturam et tegulaturam, sit contributorius in solvendo utrique pagine ipsarum arcium. Et e contra quod quilibet tegularius, operans tegulaturam et plasteraturam, sit contributorius in solucione utrique paginarum predictarum, sub pena iij *s.* iiij *d.* usui communitatis, et iij *s.* iiij *d.* paginis predictis applicandorum.

Item, quod quilibet tegularius, qui operatur tantum tegulaturam, solvat annuatim ambabus paginis predictis iij *d.*, et non ultra. Et quod quatuor magistri eligantur annuatim equaliter ad gubernandum ambas paginas arcium predictarum.

Item, quod duo scrutatores annuatim eligantur indifferenter, videlicet, unus de utraque arte, qui sint boni, honesti, et bene operari scientes, in festo translacionis sancti Thome Cantuariensis

THE ORDINANCES OF THE PLASTERERS (1422) 127

archiepiscopi (July 7), ad scrutandum, supervidendum, et presentandum fideliter maiori pro tempore existenti defectus et forisfacturas inventos in artibus predictis. Et quod uterque scrutatorum illorum sit alter alteri bonus, humilis et obediens sicut decet.

Item, quod nullus magister arcium predictarum capere presumat aliquem sibi in apprenticium pro minore termino quam pro termino septem annorum, sub pena vj *s*. viij *d*. modo quo premittitur solvendorum.

Item, quod si aliquod opus arcium predictarum scrutari contigerit per scrutatores earumdem arcium, et illud per eorum judicium et presentacionem inventum fuerit defectum, tunc factor illius operis perdet et solvet camere et artibus predictis iij *s*. iiij *d*. per equales porciones.

Item, quod nullus magister arcium predictarum ponat aliquem apprenticium vel servientem suum, qualiscumque fuerit, ad operandum in plasteratura vel tegulatura extra presenciam magistri sui, nisi ita sit quod hujusmodi apprenticius vel serviens prius scrutati fuerint per scrutatores predictos, et approbati per eos, et allocati quod artem suam sciunt, et quod boni operatores teneantur. Et si quis magister contrarium fecerit, incurret penam iij *s*. iiij *d*. usui camere et paginarum predictarum, tociens quociens culpabilis inventus fuerit.

Item, quod artifices arcium predictarum eant cum paginis suis predictis, et eas producant per civitatem omnes tanquam iidem homines.

(*fo*. 258, *b*.) Item, per quatuor arbitratores predictos, Johannes Symond, *plasterer*, et Ricardus Watson, *tyler*, electi sunt scrutatores, ad gubernandum et scrutandum artes predictas tanquam eosdem homines, ab hac die in antea usque ad predictum festum translacionis sancti Thome proximum futurum. Et quod tunc magistri ambarum arcium predictarum eligant duos scrutatores annuatim in dicto festo, ad scrutandum et gubernandum bene et honeste artes predictas, et omnes defectus in eisdem artibus inventos presentandum maiori in forma supradicta.

Item, ordinatum est per quatuor arbitratores predictos cum integro assensu et unanimi consensu ambarum arcium predictarum, quod si aliqua persona unius artis vel alterius ab hac die in antea reprobare presumat alium in verbo vel in facto, quod possit legitime probari per recordum vel testimonium vicinorum pro aliquo delicto vel aliqua re inter ipsos habito vel facto, a principio mundi usque in hunc diem, quod quilibet, qui inventus fuerit in defectu, solvat vice qualibet xij *d.* operi pontis Fosse sine dilacione vel pardonacione aliqua, tociens quociens aliquis talis inventus fuerit in defectu.

Facte fuerunt iste ordinaciones suprascripte ultimo die mensis Marcii, anno Domini millesimo quadringentesimo vicesimo quarto, 2 Henr. vi., tempore Thome Bracebrig, maioris.

Burton, R.

Parchemeners.

Per avisamentum et consensum omnium magistrorum artificum artificii de *lez parchemeners* hujus civitatis Ebor' consensum et ordinatum est in tempore Thome Esyngwald, maioris, quod scrutatores illius artificii pro tempore existentes libere scrutari possint in artificio illo quociens viderint oportunum ; et si quis artificii predicti rebellis fuerit contra eos, sui officii [1]debite[1] execucionem facientes, quod solvat tunc camere consilii ad opus communitatis et sustentacioni pagine et aliorum onerum artis predicte, xl *d.* per equales porciones dividendos.[2]

Item, quod nullus artificii predicti vendat nec vendicioni exponat aliquod pergamenum ovinum vel vitulinum in aliquo loco infra istam civitatem Ebor', suburbia, nec precinctum ejusdem, nisi in propria shoppa vel infra locum habitacionis sue, sub pena predicta modo quo premittitur persolvenda.

Item, quod nullus artificii predicti per se ipsum nec aliquem alium nomine suo, conducat, procuret, vel culiet aliquem servientem artis predicte a servicio magistri sui, cui servit, sub pena predicta predictis usibus applicanda.

Item, quod nullus artificii predicti capiat nec conducat aliquem servientem artis predicte ad sibi serviendum, nisi ipsum

---

1—1—Interlined.
2—Blank space possibly a clause erased, shewing through from the other side of the folio.

conducat et capiat ad sibi serviendum et occupandum in omni modis rebus et serviciis ad predictam artem pertinentibus, sicut usus fuerat ab antiquo, sub pena perdicionis summe predicte tociens quociens convictus fuerit in hac parte predictis usibus persolvende.

Item, quod nullus magister nec serviens artificii predicti aliquibus diebus sabbati, nec in vigiliis sanctorum, post horam prandii duodecimam, trahat nec radat, anglice, *nouther drawe na shafe*, aliquod genus pergameni, sub pena iij *s.* iiij *d.*, solvendorum modo quo prefertur.

(*fo*. 259). Item, si aliquis artificii predicti magister vel serviens operetur rem aliquam predicto artificio pertinentem cum aliquo homine alterius artificii infra civitatem istam, vel in patria ad extra, in prejudicium artis predicte, infra istam civitatem, si magister sit, quod tunc solvat viginti solidos, modo predicto solvendos; et si serviens sit, et convictus fuerit in hoc puncto, si quis magister artificii predicti civitatis predicte ponat ipsum decetero in opere aliquo artificii predicti, perdet et solvet predictam summam xx *s.*, modo quo premittitur applicandam.

Item, quod nullus magister artificii predicti capiat aliquem in apprenticium suum pro minori termino quam pro septem annis simul, et hoc unum ad semel, et hoc per indenturam et recognicionem inde factam scrutatoribus artificii predicti, sub pena vj *s.* viij *d.*, usibus predictis equaliter applicandorum.

Statutes of Parliament; 2 Henry vi.[1]

(*fo*. 263). Grant of a subsidy on wool, 3 Henry vi.[2]

(*fo*. 264). Inquisition held at York on Monday after the feast of S. Andrew Apostle, 4 Henry vi. (3 December, 1425), before William Ormesheued, mayor and escheator; by oath of Thomas Karre.[3]

Ralf late Earl of Westmorland held jointly with John Park, chaplain, and John de Morton, who are still living, by enfeoffment of Richard Kylkenny, a messuage in Walmegate in the city of

---

1—Statutes of the Realm, II., pp. 216-227.
2—Rolls of Parliament, IV., p. 275.
3—A space is left for the names of the other jurors.

York, called Fournour Inne, with all solars, cellars, shops and gardens thereto belonging; worth by the year, beyond reprises, five marks.

He held jointly with John de Morton, by enfeoffment of William Ledes and Christofor Malore a messuage in Skeldergate with a garden and dovecote, and with other tenements in Kyrkelane and Loumelith, together with the advowson of a moiety of Old S. Mary's church upon Bysshophill, of which Sir Richard Ilklay is rector; worth by the year, beyond reprises, 40 s.

He held jointly with John Alwent, chaplain, and John de Morton, who are still living, by enfeoffment of Henry Nessefeld, a messuage upon Castelhill, which William Heseham now inhabits, together with all shops, tenements, gardens and dovecotes between the said messuage and the bridge of York Castle; worth by the year, beyond reprises, 40 s.

He held jointly with John Morton, by enfeoffment of John Kenlay the younger, a messuage in Mekilgate late in the tenure of Thomas Howeden, *bower*, with two cellars, lying in breadth between the churchyard of S. John the Evangelist at the bridge of Use and land formerly of John de Sutton, together with the advowson of a chantry at the altar of S. John the Baptist in the said church; worth by the year, beyond reprises, 6 s. 8 d.

He held jointly with John Morton, by enfeoffment of Robert Coverham, various tenements in Petirgate and Grapelane; worth by the year, beyond reprises, five marks. All the premises are held of the King in burgage, as is the whole city of York. He died 21 October last (1425). Ralf Nevill, son of John Nevill knight, is his kinsman and heir, aged nineteen years, two months and more.

(*fo.* 264, *b.*) Grant of a subsidy on wool; 4 (Henry vi.)[1]

Girdlers; John Lyllyng.[2]

(*fo.* 267, *b.*) Grant by the parliament of 6 Henry vi. of a subsidy of 2 s. from every parish containing ten households, of which the church is of the yearly value of 20 s., and ascending

1—Rolls of Parliament, IV., p. 302.
2—Eng. Misc. *op. cit.*, pp 1-10

at the same rate, to be paid at Whitsuntide next. And of a subsidy of 6 s. 8 d. on the knight's fee from freeholders, descending at the same rate to the fourth part of a fee ; to be paid at the feast of the nativity of S. John the Baptist next.[1]

(fo. 268). Commission to Thome Leverton, Robert Fereby, Henry Rothewell, and Roger Othehaye to collect the said subsidies in the city and suburbs of York ; and to hold inquisition therefor in presence of the mayor, sheriffs and four or six of the good men of the city. Westminster, 6 April, 6 Henry vi. (1428).

Virtute cujus commissionis predicti commissionarii xxj die Maii, anno predicto (1428), apud Ebor', venire fecerunt coram eis Willelmum Bowes, maiorem civitatis predicte, Thomam Carre, et Nicholaum Blakburn, vicecomites ejusdem civitatis, ac alios sex de dignioribus et probioribus dicte civitatis, in quorum presencia dicti commissionarii secundum formam et effectum dicte commissionis diligentem inquisicionem fecerunt de quibuscumque articulis in hac commissione contentis ; per sacramentum Henrici Skyrmer, Willelmi Barton, Roberti Allerton, Reginaldi Bawtre, Ricardi Bukden, Willelmi Gyselay, Andree Ferrour, Johannis Preston, *buklermaker*, Johannis Catryk, Johannis Pudsay, *wever*, Ricardi Knyght, Willelmi Bostan, Johannis Bell, Thome Forester, Roberti Bolton, Ricardi Bryan, Willelmi Houeden, Willelmi Scoreburgh, Willelmi Brandesby, Henrici Hayrster, Ricardi Crokeham, Roberti Gray, Ricardi Clynt, Ricardi Newland, Roberti Belton[2] (fo. 269), Johannis Staynburn et Willelmi Masham, veram noticiam plenarie habencium de omnibus et singulis articulis supradictis. Qui quidem juratores dicunt super sacramentum suum quod in civitate predicta et in suburbiis ejusdem sunt triginta novem ecclesie parochiales et non plures. Et in qualibet parochia ecclesiarum predictarum existunt decem inhabitantes domicilia tenentes, et unde quilibet ecclesia est veri valoris annuatim prout patet in sequentibus, videlicet, ecclesia Beate Marie Veteris est veri valoris annui decem librarum. Et ecclesia Beate Marie Episcopi est veri valoris annui sex librarum. Et ecclesia Sancti Nicholai in Mikelgate est veri

1—Rolls of Parliament, IV., p. 318.
2—Cf. Drake, *op. cit.*, p. 234.

valoris annui sex librarum. Et ecclesia Omnium Sanctorum in Northstrete est veri valoris annui octo librarum. Et ecclesia Sancti Martini in Mikelgate est veri valoris annui sex librarum. Et ecclesia Sancti Gregorii est veri valoris annui quadraginta solidorum. Et ecclesia Sancti Johannis Evaungeliste, ad pontem Use, est veri valoris annui octo librarum. Et ecclesia Sancti Michaelis in Ousegate est veri valoris annui decem librarum. Et ecclesia Sancte Marie in Castelgate est veri valoris annui sex librarum Et ecclesia Sancti Petri Parvi est veri valoris annui septem librarum. Et ecclesia Sancti Sampsonis est veri valoris annui octo librarum. Et ecclesia Sancte Trinitatis in curia regis est veri valoris annui octo librarum. Et ecclesia Sancte Trinitatis in Guthrumgate est veri valoris annui quatuor librarum tresdecim solidorum et quatuor denariorum. Et ecclesia Sancti Michaelis de Berefrido est veri valoris annui duodecim librarum. Et ecclesie Sancte Elene in Stayngate est veri valoris annui sex librarum. Et ecclesia Sancti Wilfridi est veri valoris annui quinque librarum. Et ecclesia Sancte Crucis in Fossegate est veri valoris annui undecim librarum, Et ecclesia Sancti Salvatoris est veri valoris annui octo librarum. Et ecclesia Sancti Johannis in Hondegate est veri valoris annuatim viginti solidorum. Et ecclesia Sancti Dionisii est veri valoris annui septem librarum. Et ecclesia Sancte Margarete est veri valoris annui septem librarum. Et ecclesia Sancti Petri in lez Wylughes est veri valoris annui viginti solidorum. Et ecclesia Sancte Elene ad Muros est veri valoris annui quadraginta solidorum. Et ecclesia Sancti Cutberti est veri valoris annui trium librarum. Et ecclesia Sancte Marie in Layrthorp est veri valoris annui quadraginta solidorum. Et ecclesie Sancti Olavi est veri valoris annui viginti quatuor librarum. Et ecclesia Sancti Mauricii est veri valoris annui quadraginta solidorum. Et ecclesia Sancti Johannis del Pyke est veri valoris annui quatuor librarum. Et ecclesia Sancti Mauricii est veri valoris annui novem librarum. Et ecclesia Sancti Edwardi est veri valoris annui viginti sex solidorum et octo denariorum. Et ecclesia Sancti Nicholai est veri valoris annui quinque librarum. Et ecclesia Sancti Martini in Conyngstrete est veri valoris annui decem librarum. Et ecclesia Sancti Andree est veri valoris annui trium librarum sex solidorum et octo denariorum. Et ecclesia Omnium Sanctorum in Pavimento est veri valoris annui novem librarum. Et ecclesia Sancti Clementis est veri valoris annui viginti solidorum. Et ecclesia Omnium Sanctorum in Peseholme est veri valoris annui trium librarum. Et ecclesia Sancte Elene in Fysshergate est veri valoris annui viginti solidorum. Et ecclesia Omnium Sanctorum in Fysshergate est veri valoris annui viginti solidorum. Et ecclesia Sancti Georgii est veri valoris annui quatuor librarum. Item predicti juratores dicunt super sacramentum suum, quod Johannes Thwaytes est seisitus de terris et tenementis in dominico suo ut de libero tenemento, et ea tenet immediate per integrum feodum militis, et predictus Johannes, nec aliqua alia persona tenet aliqua alia terras sive tenementa in civitate predicta nec in suburbiis ejusdem, per feodum militis integrum nec per aliquam partem feodi militis. Pretextu quarum commissionis et inquisicionis dicti commissionarii levari fecerunt ad opus domini regis de parochianis (*fo.* 296, *b*.) predictis predicte ecclesie Sancte Marie Veteris viginti solidos. Et Sancte Marie Episcopi duodecim solidos. Et ecclesie Sancti Nicholai in Mikelgate duodecim solidos. Et ecclesie Omnium Sanctorum in Northstrete sexdecim solidos. Et ecclesie Sancti Martini in Mikelgate duodecim solidos. Et ecclesie Sancti Gregorii quatuor solidos. Et ecclesie Sancti Michaelis in Ousegate xx *s*. Et ecclesie Sancti Johannis Evangeliste sexdecim solidos. Et ecclesie Sancte Marie in Castelgate duodecim solidos. Et ecclesie Sancti Petri Parvi quatuordecim solidos. Et ecclesie Sancti Sampsonis sexdecim solidos. Et ecclesie Christi in curia regis sexdecim solidos. Et ecclesie Sancte Trinitatis in Guthrumgate novem solidos quatuor denarios. Et ecclesie Sancti Michaelis de Berefrido viginti quatuor solidos. Et ecclesie Sancte Elene in Stayngate duodecim solidos. Et ecclesie Sancti Wilfridi decem solidos. Et ecclesie Sancte Crucis in Fossegate viginti duos solidos. Et ecclesie Sancti Salvatoris sexdecim solidos. Et ecclesie Sancti Johannis in Hundegate duos solidos. Et ecclesie Sancti Dionisii quatuordecim solidos. Et ecclesie Sancte Margarete quatuordecim solidos. Et ecclesie Sancti Petri in lez Wylughs duos solidos. Et ecclesie Sancte Elene ad Muros quatuor solidos. Et ecclesie Sancti Cutberti sex solidos. Et ecclesie Sancte Marie in Layrthorp quatuor solidos. Et ecclesie Sancti Olavi quadraginta octo solidos. Et ecclesie Sancti Mauricii quatuor solidos. Et ecclesie Sancti Johannis del Pyke octo solidos. Et ecclesie Sancti Laurencii octodecim solidos. Et ecclesie Sancti Edwardi duos solidos octo denarios. Et ecclesie Sancti Nicholai in Walmegate decem solidos. Et ecclesie Sancti Martini in Conyngstrete viginti solidos. Et ecclesie Sancti Andree sex solidos octo denarios. Et ecclesie Omnium Sanctorum super Pavimentum octodecim solidos. Et ecclesie Sancti Clementis duos solidos. Et ecclesie Omnium Sanctorum in Peseholm sex solidos. Et ecclesie Sancte Elene ad Muros duos solidos. Et ecclesie Omnium Sanctorum in Fysshergate duos solidos. Et ecclesie Sancti Georgii octo solidos. Que quidem summe, de predictis parochianis per dictos commissionarios in forma predicta levate, in omnibus se extendit [sic] ad summam viginti trium librarum quatuor solidorum octo denariorum per dictos commissionarios domino regi solvendam, pro dictis parochianis ad festum Pentecostes proximo futurum post datam commissionis predicte. Insuper predicti commissionarii levari fecerunt de predicto Johanne Twhaytes pro terris et tenementis suis predictis summam vj s. viij d. solvendam domino regi ad festum nativitatis Sancti Johannis Baptiste tunc proximo futurum. In quorum omnium testimonium sigillum officii maioratus presentibus est appensum. Datum apud Ebor. etc.

(*fo.* 270). Noverint universi per presentes me Nicholaum Blakburn, seniorem, civem et mercatorem Ebor', dedisse, concessisse et intuitu caritatis presenti scripto meo confirmasse dilecto michi in Christo, domino Willelmo Revetour, capellano, cantariam perpetuam sex marcatarum annui redditus in capella Sancti Willelmi super Pontem Use, per Ricardum Toller, quondam civem Ebor', mediante licencia domini Regis, ab antiquo fundatam, et nunc per mortem domini Johannis Ry...e, ultimi capellani ejusdem, vacantem, de meo patronatu existentem ac ad meam donacionem spectantem, ex dono et concessione Willelmi May de Cottesmore in Roteland et Matildis, uxoris sue, consanguinee et heredis Roberti filii Willelmi de Bergh, consanguinei et heredis Ricardi Toller predicti, habendum et tenendum predictam cantariam, cum suis juribus et pertinenciis universis, predicto domino Willelmo Revetour unacum predicto annuo redditu sex marcarum per ipsum dominum Willelmum percipiendo, sicut hucusque percipi consueverit simul cum omnibus libris, vestimentis, et ceteris ornamentis et rebus aliis, ad dictam cantariam qualiter. cumque spectantibus, ad totam vitam ipsius domini Willelmi libere, integre, bene et in pace sine occasione, impedimento, perturbacione, aut expulsione mei predicti Nicholai, aut aliquorum heredum, assignatorum vel executorum meorum seu alterius cujuscumque. In cujus rei testimonium sigillum meum presentibus apposui. Hiis testibus Nicholao Blakburn, juniore, Thoma Carre, vicecomitibus dicte civitatis, Ricardo Russell, Willelmo Ormeshede, Johanne Aldestanemore, Johanne Bolton, aldermannis, Johanne Loftehouse et aliis. Et quia dicta cantaria, in capella Sancti Willelmi super pontem Use in civitate Ebor' fundata existit, ut prefertur, et in ea eidem cantarie serviri oportebit, sigillum igitur officii maioratus ipsius civitatis presentibus apponi procuravi. Et nos Willelmus Bowes, maior dicte civitatis, ad peticionem Nicholai Blakburn senioris predicti, sigillum nostri officii maioratus presentibus apponi fecimus in fidem et testimonium omnium premissorum. Datum apud Ebor' decimo die Augusti, anno Domini millesimo quadringentesimo vicesimo octavo. 6 Henr. vi. Burton, R.

Mercers.

Henricus, Dei gracia rex Anglie et Francie et dominus Hibernie, omnibus ad quos presentes litere pervenerint, salutem. Sciatis quod cum quamplures homines mistere mercerie civitatis nostre Ebor', abundantes pro tempore et multum locupletes tam in mercibus quam in aliis rebus secularibus, postmodum, per maris infortunium aliosque casus fortuitos, ad tantam devenerint miseriam et inopiam, quod parum aut nichil habuerunt, unde vivere aut se ipsos possent sustinere, nisi elemosina, ope et relevamine Christi fidelium et Deo devotorum. Unde diverse valide et potentes persone mistere predicte ejusdem civitatis, zelo caritatis fervide et accense, id pie intuentes, et ab egestate et miseria hominum predictorum sua viscera non claudentes, terras, tenementa, et redditus infra civitatem predictam et suburbia ejusdem seu alibi infra regnum Anglie, ad honorem Dei et in auxilium et relevamen pauperum et indigencium mistere predicte, necnon sustentacionem unius capellani divina singulis diebus celebraturi, licentia nostra mediante, adquirere proponant, ut accepimus. Nos laudabile propositum piamque intencionem personarum predictarum in hac parte merito commendantes, et ut tanti tamquam salubris et meritorii operis subsequentis, quod nedum in amorem Dei et proximi, verum eciam in divini cultus augmentum, liquido se extendit, immunes nos reddamur. Nos, de gracia nostra speciali ac de avisamento et assensu consilii nostri, et pro quadraginta et una libris et undecim solidis nobis solutis in hanaperio nostro, concessimus pro nobis (*fo.* 270, *b.*) et heredibus nostris, quantum in nobis est, gentibus mistere predicte, quod ipsi decetero sint una communitas et perpetua, et quod eadem communitas eligere possit die annunciacionis Beate Marie quolibet anno de se ipsis unum gubernatorem et duos custodes, ad supervidendum, regendum et gubernandum misteram et communitatem predictas; et quod ipsi sic electi gubernator et custodes communitatis mercatorum civitatis nostre Ebor' decetero nuncupentur; et quod iidem gubernator et custodes et successores sui sint persone habiles et capaces ad perquirendum terras, tenementa et redditus, ac alias possessiones quascumque, habendas et possidendas sibi et successoribus suis, gubernatori et custodibus mistere predicte, imperpetuum; et quod ipsi gubernator et custodes implacitare possint et ab aliis implacitari coram quibuscumque judicibus, tam secularibus quam ecclesiasticis, per nomina gubernatoris et custodum communitatis mercerorum civitatis nostre Ebor'; et quod habeant commune sigillum pro negotiis communitatis predicte deserviturum. Et ulterius, de uberiori gratia nostra, concessimus eisdem gubernatori et custodibus et successoribus suis, quod ipsi terras. tenementa et redditus infra civitatem nostram Ebor' et suburbia ejusdem, que de nobis seu de aliis in liberum burgagium tenentur, ad valorem decem librarum per annum adquirere possint, habenda et tenenda sibi et successoribus suis in auxilium et relevamen pauperum et indigencium communitatis predicte, ac sustentacionem unius capellani divina singulis djebus pro salubri statu nostro, dum agimus in humanis, et pro anima nostra, cum ab hac luce migraverimus, ac pro anima carissimi domini et patris nostri, necnon pro animabus omnium fidelium defunctorum, juxta ordinacionem ipsorum gubernatoris, custodum et communitatis et successorum suorum in hac parte faciendam celebraturi imperpetuum ; statuto de terris et tenementis ad manum mortuam [1]non[1] ponendis edito, seu eo quod terre, tenementa, et redditus sic adquirenda de nobis teneantur in liberum burgagium sicut tota civitas Ebor', non obstante. Dum tamen per inquisicionem inde capiendam et in cancellariam nostram vel heredum nostrorum rite retornandam compertum sit, quod dicta adquisicio terrarum, tenementorum et reddituum predictorum fieri poterit absque dampno et prejudicio nostri et heredum nostrorum aut aliorum quorumcumque. In cujus rei testimonium has literas nostras fieri fecimus patentes. Teste Humfrido Duce Gloucestr', custode Anglie, apud Westmonasterium, duodecimo die Julii, anno regni nostri octavo (1430).

(*fo.* 271). Bond by William, abbot, and the convent of Blessed Mary of Jervaulx, to the dean and chapter of York, for 100 *l.*, to be paid at Martimas next. Seal. In the chapter house of Jervaulx, 24 May, 1470. Acknowledged by Sir William Heslyngton, monk of Jervaulx, in the name of the abbot and convent, before William Holbek, mayor, and the chamberlains, 20 May, 12 Edward iv. (1472).

(*fo.* 271, *b.*) Hec indentura testatur quod nos maior et communitas civium civitatis Ebor' concessimus et ad firmam dimisimus Johanni Kyrkham, plasterario, concivi nostro, quoddam tenementum nostrum de novo edificatum in vico de Hertgate, in civitate predicta, prout jacet ibidem in fronte versus vicum predictum ante, usque ad terram Fratrum Minorum retro, habendum et tenendum tenementum predictum cum suis pertinenciis predicto Johanni et assignatis suis de nobis, maiore et communitate predictis, a festo Pentecostes anno Domini millesimo quadringentesimo tricesimo quarto, ad totum terminum vite ipsius Johannis, reddendo inde annuatim nobis et successoribus nostris, seu custodibus pontis Use civitatis predicte, qui pro tempore fuerint, nomine firme viginti sex solidos octo denarios sterlingorum ad duos annos terminos, ad festa Sancti Martini in

1—1—Interlined.

yeme et Pentecostes, per equales porciones. Et si predicta firma a retro fuerit, in parte vel in toto, ad aliquem terminum solucionis prenotatum in quo solvi debeat ultra unum mensem, tunc bene licebit nobis, maiori et communitati predictis, et successoribus nostris, seu custodibus pontis Use predictis, in toto tenemento predicto, et in qualibet parcella ejusdem, distringere et districciones captas fugare et asportare, ac penes se retinere, quousque de predicta firma et arreragiis ejusdem, si que fuerint, nobis plenarie fuerit satisfactum. Et nos, maior et communitas supradicti, et successores nostri predictum tenementum nostris sumptibus et expensis, quociens opus erit, infra terminum predictum competenter sustentari et reparari faciemus ; et illud idem tenementum cum suis pertinenciis predicto Johanni pro annua firma predicta, in forma premissa, ad terminum vite ipsius Johannis warantizabimus et defendemus. Et ulterius concessum et concordatum est per nos, maiorem et communitatem predictos, pro nobis et successoribus nostris, quod Johannes Kyrkham predictus durante vita sua habebit et occupabit per se ipsum duas parvas domos, predicto tenemento proximo contiguas et adjacentes, et in eis hospitabitur calcem et *plaster,* quandocumque voluerit, sumptibus et expensis propriis ipsius Johannis, et, cum premunitus fuerit per nos vel custodes poncium Use et Fosse dicte civitatis nostro nomine, nobis vel ipsis custodibus vendet, et inveniet in omnibus temporibus oportunis quamlibet melam calcis pro decem denariis et non ultra, et quemlibet bussellum plastri pro quatuor denariis et non ultra, ad reparacionem omnium antiquarum domorum rentalium conmunitatis predicte, que die confectionis presencium edificate existunt. Et ipse idem Johannes pre aliis hominibus, si voluerit, predicta calcem et plastrum, per se vel servientes suos ad hoc habiles et idoneos, bene et artificione[1] operabitur, capiendo de nobis, maiore et communitate, seu custodibus predictis salarium suum, sicut usus communis erit in civitate predicta. Et si nos maior et communitas predicti, vel successores nostri, aliquo tempore in futurum edificari fecerimus aliqua tenementa nostra de novo, quod tunc predictus Johannes, si voluerimus, nobis

---

1—*Sic.* Artificiose on p. 139.

providebit de calce (*fo.* 272) et plastro pro illis tenementis nostris necessariis meliori precio quo sciverit, vel alias, quod nos, ipsi maior et communitas, et successores nostri providebimus ubi melius poterimus de calce et plastro ad edificacionem illorum tenementorum nostrorum de novo faciendorum necessariis; et predictus Johannes illam calcem et plastrum operabitur bene et artificiose super nova tenementa predicta pre alio homine quocumque si voluerit, capiendo a nobis et successoribus nostris pro salario suo, sicut modus capiendi erit in civitate predicta, sicut predictum est. Predictus eciam Johannes, pro bona husbandria sua et supervisu tenementorum communitatis in hiis omnibus, que ad artes suas pertinent, habebit annuatim de nobis. maiore et communitate predictis, togam ejusdem secte, cum sementario et carpentario nostris capitalibus maioris et communitatis predictorum et successorum nostrorum; et regardum pecunie sicut maior et camerarii dicte civitatis, qui pro tempore erunt, secundum discretiones suas fieri viderint faciendum. In cujus rei testimonium sigillum officii maioratus civitatis predicte, et sigillum Johannis Kyrkham predicti, partibus hujus indenture sunt alternatim appensa. Datum apud Ebor' tercio die Maii, anno Domini supradicto, 12 Henry vi. (1434).

Willelmus Ormesheued, Nicholaus Blakburn, Johannes Bolton, Thomas Gare, Willelmus Bowes, junior, Nicholaus Usseflete, Nicholaus Wyspyngton, Thomas Riddelay, aldermanni, Johannes Warde, Willelmus Craven, Johannes Doddyngton, Willelmus Grillington, Johannis Roghton, Robertus Yarom, Johannes Thrysk, Ricardus Bukden, de xxiiij^{to}, Ricardus Shirwod et Willelmus Burton, vicecomites, omnes isti in vigilia Sancti Thome apostoli, 15 Henr. 6 (20 December, 1436), congregati fuerunt in camera consilii super pontem Use, coram Ricardo Warter, maiore, et de consensu et assensu omnium predictorum regardum in dicta indentura contentum, et dicto Johanni Kyrkham concessum erat taxatum ibidem ad xiij *s.* iiij *d.* solvendos annuatim prefato Johanni Kyrkham ad terminum vite sue etc.

Constituciones de lez patoners, botellers et bowgemakers **ordinate** et concesse, tam per assensum maioris et consilii camere, quam per consensum omnium artificum arcium predictarum, xxj^mo (1471) die mensis Octobris, anno regni regis Edwardi quarti undecimo, sequntur et sunt tales. (*fo.* 272, *b*.)

The daie and yere abovesaide, it was ordayned agreyde and establisshed, as wele by the assent of William Holbek, maior of the cite of York, John Gillyot, John Marshall, John Glassen, Christofer Marshall and William Lambe, aldremen, William Wright, Richard Claybroke, William Thorp, John Breerton, William Welles, John Lightlope, William Shirwod, Thomas Alan, of the nombre of the xxiiij^to, assembled in the counceil chamber upon Owsebrig, as also by the special instance, consent, and prayer of John Richardson and Richard Osgodby, serchiours within the same cite of the forsaide craftes, Robert Jakson, Nicholaus Garnett, Richard Berden, John Broun and John Myn, citisins and artificers of the same craftes, that from hensfurth ther shall no maister of the saide craftes take noo printes, but for the terme of vij yeres to geddre, and but one at ones, or the tyme of vj yeres of the said vij yeres be perfitely passed, uppon payn of iij *s.* iiij *d.*, to be payed evenly to the chamber of this cite and to the saide craftes, whan so ever that ony man of the same craftes dose the contrarie of this ordynance. But if so be that any of the saide apprintece eyther discesse or departe frome his service at ony tyme within the saide vj yeres, that than it shalbe levefull to every maister stonding in that case, to take ane other apprintece in the fourme aforewriten, this ordynance in ony wise notagaynstonding, etc.

Item, if that ony straunger of the saide craftes, or of any of thaime com to this cite, and woll set upp and occupye as a maister in the same craftes or in ony of thaime, he shall paye at his first settyngupp or occupyyng as a maister within the fraunchies of this cite vj *s.* viij *d.*, to the saide chamber and craft evenly to be devided, etc.

Item, that noo man of the saidez craftes shall set up and occupie as a maister within this cite, afore that he be examyned and approved able and sufficiently lerned and enfourmed in that behalf to occupye as a maister for the common profeit and wele of the kinges liege people, and also worship of the cite, opayn of lesyng of xiij *s.* iiij *d.*, to be payed evenly in fourme afore writen, etc.

Item, that no maister of the saidez craftes shall take, receyve, nor sett on wark ony man that hath ben servant or apprintece in the saide craftes, or in ony of the same craftes within this cite or withoute, but if the saide servand or apprintice have a generall acquitance or ane other laufull discharge of his maister, that he seruffed afore, upon payn of xiij *s.* iiij *d.*, to be payed in fourme aforewriten.

Item, that ther shall no man of thies craftes make ony boulgeys, boulgett, ne bowbages of sheepe leder, opayn of iij *s.* iiij *d.*, to be payed as is afore writen, as oftyn tymes as ony man of the same craftes offenden ayenst this ordynance in ony wise, etc.

(*fo.* 273). Item, if ony servant or apprintece of any of the saide craftes untruely withdrawe any maner of thinge from his maister, or from any othir man to the value of viij *d.*, and therapon be atteynte and convict, he shall therfore be punysshed by the advice of the mair for tyme beyng, and by the consent of the serchiours of the saide craftes for the tyme also beyng; and if he be foundon gilte at any other tyme therafter of untrouthe of les or of more, than he to forswere the saide cite and craftes for evermore, etc.

Item, if ony man of the saide craftes be rebell and disobeysaunt unto his serchiours of the same craftes for tyme beyng, in laufull doynge of thair office at ony tyme, he shall forfett and pay iij *s.* iiij *d.* in fourme afore writen, as oft tymes as he offendes in that part.

Item, what maister of the saide craftes or of any of thaime so ever comys not in his person to every assemble and congregacon duely warned therunto by his serchiours for the wele, honour, and profeit of this cite and of the saide craftes, shall forfett and pay at every tyme so fayling iiij *d.* to the saidz chamber and craftes, etc. Oles then he have a resonnable excuse to be proved of trouthe tofore the same serchiours.

Item, yt ys ordayned and establysshed that yif any maister, servant or apprentez of any of the s[aide]¹ craftes frome hensfurth take upon hym to make or shappe any maner of patens, belowx, bo[. .]¹ ledder-kannez, bowgez, bowgett, bowebage, quyver, cloothsak, trunkes or malez or any other m[aner]¹ of stuff aperteynyng to the saide craftes or to any of thayme, within the houses or chambres of [any]¹ tanner, shomaker, glover, whitetewer, couurour or girdiller within this cite, suburbes, or pres[inctes]¹ of the same, withoute licence of his serchiours of the saide craftes for tyme beynge, shall forfe[tt]¹ xx d. to the chambre of this cite and to the chargeys of the said craftes evenly, as often as eny abovesaide offenden contrarie to this present ordynance without any maner of pardone.

(*fo.* 273, *b.*) Aldermanni, Willelmus Ormesheued, Nicholaus Blakburn, Johannes Bolton, Thomas Snaudon, Thomas Gare, Willelmus Bedale, Willelmus Bowes, junior, Ricardus Louth, Nicholaus Usseflete, Nicholaus Wyspyngton; vicecomites, Johannes Thrisk, Ricardus Bukden; de xxiiij[or], Thomas del More, Robertus Jarom, Willelmus Craven, Johannes Ward, Willelmus Grillington, Johannes Ratcliff, Johannes Rukeby, Robertus Ebchester; all these were gadred afore Richard Warter, maire of the citie of York, in the counseil chambre upon Ousebrig of the said cite, the xxij day of September, 15 Henr. vi. (1436), and ther be thadvise and thassent of hem al Thomas . . . . alderman for thoffence and disobeisance doon bi hym to the said Richard Warter maire in the gildhall of the same cite the xxj day of the said moneth in the said yere was excluded of his f . . . . e fourme and theffecte of an ordinance made in such cases. And then upon Monday, the xxiij day of the same moneth in the said yere in the gildhal aforesaid the said Thomas . . . . in the presence of the same maire and all the said worshipful persones, and of the comonalte of the said cite, oppenly confessed the said offense and disobeidaunce, bicause of which he submitted hym meekely to the correccion of the said mair, and before the said worshipful persones and the comanalte . . . besech the said mair to forgeve hym and. . . hym to favour

---

1—The rest of the word is cut off at the edge of the folio.

and to grace ; which submission made, the maire goodly with warme wordes and tendre admitted the said submission, and touk hym to favour and grace and restited and restored hym to his f . . . . . and to the state of alderman in fourm as he stood in afore.

And the xxj day of Septembre, 15 Henr. vi. (1436), bi thadvise and thassent of the said maire, of al the said worshippul persones, and of al the communatte of the said cite, in the said gildhall, it was accorded and granted that Thomas Bracebryg should be discharged of al offices within the cite and of al other occupacions and labours to the parliamentz.

(*fo.* 274). A folio has been cut out here, but there is no break in the old numeration of the folios.

Adonqes serra agarde qe le defendant soit arrestu par son corps, et qile face fyn pur le contempt; et quant il est issint arrestu, il trovera sufficeantz plegge de venir adonqes al proschein court de respondre al partie, sur peine limite a devant la ou *cap(ias)* est agarde. Et si tiel defendant face plusours delaies, et tesmoigne soit par le sergeant qe le defendant est futif ou noun sufficeaunt, adonqes serra agard le *cap(ias)* de prendre son corps, ou darester et preiser les biens de mesme le defendant auxi come forrein attachement. Et si aucuns parties veignent et pledent al enquest ou en juggement, adonqes ils serront rewles solonc les usages de la citee, sanz aucun esson aver en tielx accions personeles, devaunt ou apres. Et coment qe un tiel defendant, qad plede al enquest, face defaut apres lenquest joynt, ne purquaunt sil veigne apres, quaunt lenquest serra charge, il avera sez chalangez a les jorrours, et dirra ses evidences, nient contresteant le defaut. Et apres ceo qe les parties soient a issue denqueste, mesmes les parties ne sont pas demandables, si noun qe lenquest soit somons. Et en plee de dette le defendant poet gager sa leye par usage de la citee qil doit riens al pleintif, cestassaver, qil soit homme enfranchise deinz la citee ou reseant deinz mesme la citee, ovesque sa septisme maine, ly mesmes nommez pur un ; et purront tielx defendantz faire lour leyes mayntenant en courtz sur la ley gage, sils oient gentz prestz, ou autrement averont jour de faire la leye al prochein court suant. Et si le defendant soit forein, estrange et ment resident en la citee, il purra gager et faire sa leye maintenant ove la tierce main, ly mesmez nommez pur un, qil doit riens al pleintif et issint estre quitz; et sil neit deux hommes prestz a faire le serement ovesqe luy, adonqes le defendant, al request de pleintif, doit aler en gard dun sergeant de la court a sis esglises pluis proscheins a la gihall, et deinz mesmes lesglises jurra qe serement qil fist en la gihall fuist bon, et adonqes serra le defendant demesme a la gihall et avera son juggement destre quitz, et le pleintif serra amercie. Et en mesme le manere serra fait en nulles accions personels la ou la leye est acceptable. Et la ou femmes en tielx cas sont compledez, et gagent lour leye, et les purront faire lour leye ovesqe hommes ou femmes a lour volunte. Et si homme enfranchise deinz la citee soit emplede par voie de trespas pur biens emportez ou pur baterie, la ou nul sank est espanduz ne coupe apparaunt, et pur autre trespas suppose estre faitz encontre le peas, tiel frank homme issint enplede poet gager et faire sa leye par usage de la citee, qil nest pur coupable, ove la septisme main, come devaunt est dit.

Item, accion de dette et de covenant sount maintenables devers executours et administrours sanz especialtee; et tieux executours et administrours, par usage de la citee, quaunt ils venount en respouns, poent aver lour leye par taunt des mains come la courte vouldra agarder sur tielx paroles, qils savoient riens del duyte, ne del contract, ne del covenant, et qils entendent par lour consience, par lour testatour a soun moriant riens devoit al pleintif, ne nulle covenant ly a neynt enfreint, et par tiel manere estre desous jugez. Et si homme soit emplede par pleint de dette pur vitailles dispenduz en la meson le pleintif pur ferme de mesons allowes appellez *houshire*, en tieux cas le defendant navera mye sa leye ne nulle protection en tielx cases ad estre allowe. Et la ou femme coverte de baron use aucune crafte deinz la dite citee a par luy soul, douut le baron se melle riens, tiel femme serra charge comme femme sole de tout ceo qe touche son dit crafte; et si le baroun et sa femme soient enpledez en tiel case, la femme pledera come femme sole en court de recorde, et avera sa leye (*fo*. 274, *b*.) et autres avantages par voie de plee come femme sole; et si ele soit condempne ele serra commys al prison tanqe ele soit fait gree, et le baroun ne ses biens ne serront mye en tiel case chargez nenpechez.

Item, si une femme, come femme sole, allowe aucun maison ou shoppe deinz la dite citee, ele serra charge de paier la ferme de dite meason ou shoppe, et serra enplede et pursuy come femme soule par voie de dette, si mestier soit, nient contresteant qele fuist coverte de baroun al temps de lessement, nient sachant le lessour.

Item, si pleint de trespas soit fait devers une homme et sa femme de trespas fait par la femme soulement, adonqes la femme respoundra soole sanz soun baroun, si le baroun ne viegne mye, et avera plee comme femme sole; et si ele soyt atteint de trespas, ele serra condempne et commys a la prisone tanqes ele eit fait gree.

Item, si pleint de trespas soit fait par le baroun et sa femme de baterie fait al femme, en tiel case la femme serra receu pur luy et pur son baron de pursuire et recoiler ses damages vers le defendant, coment qe le baron ne soit mye present.

Item, la ou pleint de dette est fait devers le baron, et le pleintif counte qe le baron fist le contract ovesqe le pleintif parmy le main la femme le defendant, adonqes mesme le defendant avera eide de sa femme et avera jour tanqe al prochein court de conseiler ovesqe sa femme, et *idem dies* serra done al pleintif; et quaunt aucune defendant en plee de dette ou autre accion personelle gage sa leye come frank homme de la citee, et le pleyntif demanda coment frank, y coment qe le defendant die, le qil nie soit frank par nestre ou par redempcion, et sil die qil frank par redempcion, le pleintif purra dire qe le defendant eit soun recorde a prochein court; et sile faile de son record, adonqes il serra atteint et convicte en la cause. Et si le defendant allegge qil est frank par nestre, le pleintif purra dire qil ne fuist nee deinz la citee, et ceo serra enquis par enquest pres deinz la dite citee de tiel lieu ou le defendant voudra allegger qil fuist nee, et cele issu est peremptorie.

Item, la ou deux ou plusours sount obligez deinz la citee par obligacion de dette, et chescun deux en lentier, adonqes si un des obligez paie lentiertee, ou cely a qi obligacion est fait pursuye deinz mesme la citee et recovere le dette vers un dez obligez soulement, adonqes cely qad paie le dette, ou issint est condempne, purra suyr devers autres obligez par pleint de dette, jointement

K

ou generalment, pur contribucion faire, issint qe chescun paiera pur lafferant solonk lusage de la citee.

Item, quaunt pleint de dette est fait devaunt aucun des ditz viscountz, et tesmoigne soit par le ministre que le defendant nest sufficiant deinz la citee, et soit allegge par le pleintif qe le defendant ad biens et chateux ou dettes en autre mains ou en autre garde deinz la dite citee, et prove soit par mesme le pleintif qe tielx biens et chateux soient arrestiez, et les dettes defenduz, adonqes al suyte et suggestion de tiel pleintif serront tielx biens et chateux, ou qils soient trovez deinz la citee, arrestuz, et les dettez defenduz en les mains de dettours, al peril de pleintif; et sur ceo le pleintif pursuera as quatre courts devant mesme lez viscountz devant qi la pleint fuist afferme, tanqe le defendant soit quatre fortz demande. Et si le defendant ne veigne al quarte court et eit fait quatre defautes, adonqes serront les biens et chateux issint arrestuz, preisez et liverez al pleintif. Et si les biens ne soient mye a la value del dette, adonqes les dettes defenduz es mains des dettours serront levez et liverez a mesme le pleintif tanqe al somme en demande, et tielx arrestez des biens et defenses de deniers sount appellez foreins attachementz, solonc la custume (*fo.* 275) de la citee; et sur ceo le pleintif trovera sufficiant seurtee al court par plegges avant ceo qe la leve luy soit fait, sur tiel condicion de faire restitucion al defendant de toutz les biens et chateux issint prises, ou de la price de ycelx, et de les deniers des queux il avoit execucion. Si issint soit qe le defendant veigne deinz lan et le jour prochein ensuant en la court, et ce purra descharger et justifier par la ley qil ne devoit riens al pleintif al temps de la pleint fait, et si mesme le defendant voudra venir deinz lan et le jour, comme devant est dit, de ly justifier et pleder ovesqe le pleintif, adonqes il avera *scire facias* hors de mesme le record devers la partie qe avoit tiel execucion, de lui garnier de venir al prochein court, sil sache rien dire pur qoy restitucion ne serra mye fait en manere avantdit; et si celui, vers qi le *scire facias* est suy, sort garny et face defaute, ou sil soit tesmoignee qil nad riens deinz la citee ou il poet estre garny, et ne veigne mye al prochein court, adonqes cely que suyst le *scire facias* avera restitucion de tieux cely biens et chateux issint preisez ou de la price, et de toutz les deniers dount la partie avoit la liveree par le forein attachement, et en mesme le manere avera restitucion, sil luy purra discharger par voie de plee; et en mesme le manere serra restitucion faite solonc lafferant, si le defendant se purra discharger de parcelle de le dette, coment qil ne se purra discharger de lentier. Et si la partie, qe avoit tiel execucion, ne soit mye sufficiant de faire restitucion en manere avantdit, adonqes ses ditz plegges serront en chargez. Et si cely, sur qi tiel forein attachement est fait, ne veigne mye deinz lan et le jour de ly justefier, come dit est, adonqes il serra forsclose en apres. Et fait assaver qe pendantz tielx foreins attachementz, si aucun autre veigne en court de record avant le quarte defaute recorde ou avant execucion sue, et soit prest de prover qe les biens arrestuz furent ses biens propres a temps del rest fait, et unqore sont, et nient a cely come qi biens ils feurent arrestuz, et qe mesme cely come qi biens ils furent arrestuz navoit nulle proprete en mesmes les biens, ne nulle autre forsque luy mesmes, a le value de iiij $d.$, adonqes il avera le prove et avera la livere de touz tielx biens issint arrestuz, ou de parcelle diceux solonc ceo qil ad fait la prove; et issint avera un servant la prove des biens son maistre, esteanz en sa garde, solonc discrecion de la court. Et auxint si le defendant en tiel forein attachement veigne en court al quarte defaute recorde ou devant, il serra receu de pleder ovesqe le pleintif, et en mesme le manere serra receu, sil veigne avant execucion sue, issint qe le pleintif soit present en court ou autrement garny; et en mesme le manere en tielx foreins attachementz ceux en qi mains aucuns biens sont issint arrestuz par suggestion de les pleintifs, et ceux en qi mains aucuns deniers sount defenduz, purront venir en court de recorde devant mesmes lez viscountez et estre excusez et dischargez par lour serement, qils navoient nul tielx biens en lour garde, et qils devoient nulle denir a ceux defendantz a temps qe les arrestez et defensez furent issint faitz en lour mains.

Item, la ou homme est enplede devant un des viscountz de Loundres par pleint de dette, et le pleintif mette avant obligacion portant date en Loundres en prove de la deutee, de qele qe la dite obligacion soit simple ou endosse ou par endentures de cest, en tiel case par usage de la citee le defendant ne serra mye receu de pleder nulle acquitance ne reles del pleintif portant date en forein countee, ne nulle paiement estre fait, ne condicion ou autre matere, si noun tiel matere qe purra estre enquis et trie deinz mesme la citee ; et si aucun defendant en tiel case plede aucune tiele acquitances ou reles, ou allege aucun paiement ou autre matere estre fait en forein countee hors de la dite citee pour ouster la court (*fo.* 275, *b.*) de jurisdiction, qe tiel defendant ne voille autre chose dire il serra conclus par defaut de respons ; mais si issint soit qe lendossement del obligacion ou les endentures ent faitz facent expresse mencion de faire ou perfourmir aucun condicion ou autre matere aillours hors de la citee, et tiel matere soit allegge par le defendant, adonqes la court surserra et serra dit al pleintif qil suy a la commune ley. Et en mesme la manere est usee en pleint de trespas et en autres accions personeles des bargainez et contractz faitz deinz la dite citee, lez defendantz ne serront mye receux de pleder nalegger matere hors de la dite citee, si noun tiele matere qe purra estre enquis et trie deinz mesme la citee.

Item, la ou obligacion est mys avaunt qe porte date en nulle certein lieu, et le pleintif en countant allegge qe la dite obligacion fuist faite en certein paroche deinz la citee de Loundres, et le defendant de sa partie allege qe mesme lobligacion fuist faite en certein lieu hors de la citee, et ceo soit prest daverrer, et ovesqe ceo plede forein matere illoqes en voidance du dite obligacion, et le pleintif tende daverrer par pais qe la dite obligacion fuist faite deinz la citee de Loundres en manere come il ad counte, en tiel case est usee de prendre lenquest en Loundres, de la paroche ou le pleintif ad countee qe lobligacion fuist faite, si le pleintif le prie, et si trove soit qe lobligacion fuist faite en Loundres, sicome le pleintif ad suppose par soun compte, adonqes serra le defendant condempne en le dette et en damages et taxer par mesme lenquest.

Item, la ou obligacion est fait en la double par endossement ou par endentures, et la partie oblige soit emple et commisse lobligacion, et le jour de paiement soit encoruz, come apparer poet par mesme lobligacion, nepurquant le pleintif doit recoverer fors tantsoulement le clere dette quest aderere, et ceo par le serement le pleintif, ou par loial enformacion de soun attourne, si le pleintif ne soit mye present, et nemy le double dette contenuz deinz la dite obligacion, et ses damages ly serront taxez par la

courte solonk le temps passe, par lour discrecion ou par enquest.
Et coment qe le defendant en tiel case encountre tiel obligacion
faite en le double plede qe nient est son fait ou qil ad parfourne
les jours de paiement contenuz en lendossement ou en lendentures
ent faites, ou autre matire semblable, et sur ceo se mette en enquest,
et trove soit encontre le defendant par voirdit denqueste, unqore
le pleintif recovera riens mes ceo qest trove due clerement par
enquest, cestassaver, le seingle deute et ses damages taxez par
mesme lenqueste, et le defendant en tiel case ferra fyn pur countre-
dite de son fait, et en les autres cases serra amercie.

Item, la ou obligacion est faite de certein somme sur diverses
condicions a perfournir par lendossement ou par endentures ent
faitz, et sur ceo pleint son fait, et les parties soient a travers et a
issue sur aucun condicion especialle enfreinte, et trove soit par
enqueste al myse des parties encountre le defendant, qest issint
oblige et qil ad enfreinte cele condition, unqore le pleintif ne
recovera mye lentier obligacion, mes il recovera les damages
queux il ad sustenuz par cause de cele condicion enfreinte, et
les damages ly serront taxez par mesme lenquest, et lobligacion
ly serra save pur server les autres condicions en apres, mais
aucuns sont aderere de ceste custume.

Item, si obligacion de dette soit mys avaunt, et le defendant
allegge qil ad acquitaunce ou endentures ou autre chose enseale
par le pleintif, les queux li purront vailler et discharger vers le
pleintif, si il avoit les prest en poigne, et die outre qe lez ditz
munimentz sount en forein countee et hors de la citee, et ceo soit
prest a jurer, adonqes mesme le defendant apres son serement
fait avera jour assigne par la court daver sez ditz munimentz
ensealez a certein court apres, solonc la distance del lieu, et sur
ceo trovera plegge a son peril ; issint qe sil veigne a dit jour done
et porte mesme le fait enseale, qil il alleggea, adonqes il serra
receu de pleder et de prendre ses avantagez par mesme le fait ;
et sil face defaut a cel jour ou (*fo.* 276) sille faille de ceo qil
alleggea, adonqes il serra condempne en la dite obligacion et
damagez serront taxez par la court, save qe le pleintif ou son
attourne serront examinez sur la duete.

Item, si pleint de dette soit fait sur un frank homme et
resident deinz la citee, la ou par la leye de la citee il averoit un

sommons par cause de sa franchise, si le pleintif veigne al viscount et face amesner ovesqe luy sis ou quatre frank hommes et creables de dite citee, qe voillent tesmoigner qe le defendant soit fugitif, et qe se voit retrere et absenter, adonqes le dit viscount par lour tesmoignance poet arester le defendant par son corps ou par ses biens auxi come dun forein.

Item, les viscountz poent tenir plees des prises de neymes en lieu de *replegiare*, et avowerie poet estre fait et retourne a garde en tielx plees auxi come en *husteng'*, si la cause ne touche mye frank tenement, et tiel suite est appelle *de placito convencionis et detencionis catallorum*, et pleggez serront trovez de faire retourne des biens ou de la value auxi come en *replegiare*.

Item, use est en tielx accions personeles devaunt les viscountz a primer jour quaunt les parties appergient et le pleintif ad counte devers le defendant, mesme le defendant respondra mesme le jour sanz aver aucun jour autre pur emparler; et en mesme le manere si le defendant plede aucun plee ou matire allegge encountre le pleintif, mesme le pleintif repliera maintenant sanz aver aucun jour autre pur enparler sanz assent des parties.

Item, si aucuns custumes ou usages soient pledes ou allegges en courtz des viscountz, dount les viscountz ne lour mynistres ne soient mye pleinement enfourmez, adonqes tieux custumes et usagez serront discuz par le mair et aldermans, et ceo avaunt juggement sur ceo rendu. Et fait assaver qe nulle ajournement est fait en court des viscountz, ne nulle jour done par prefixion, mes soulement qe les parties gardent jour al prochein court generalle, sil ne soit sur aucun cause especialle.

Item, accions de dette sont maintenables par usages des simples grantz et de assignementz et de plegiage et de covenant simplement sanz especialtee.

Item, une taille de dette enseale par usage de la citee est auxi fort come une obligacion, et la ou pleint de dette est fait par tiel taile enseale soit mys avant en prove del deute, le defendant navera mye sa leye qil doit riens naver matire, nient plus qe encontre une obligacion, einz il dirra bien qe le jour de paiement est autre qe le pleintif nad countee.

Item, lez viscountz de Londres usent, et chescun deux par soy, de prendre reconuzances de dette en lour courtz de qeconqe somme; et si le jour de paiement soit passe et les deniers nient paiez, adonqes il suyt cely a qi la reconisance fuist fait, sil soit deinz lan, touz les biens et chateux le reconissour trovez deinz la citee serront preisez et liverez al partie tanqe al value del dette contenuz deinz la dite reconisance, sanz extendre terre del reconissour, et si lan soit passe, adonqes *scire facias* serra suy devers le reconissour de venir, et sil sache rien dire pur quoy execucion ne serra mye fait de ses biens, come devant est dit.

Item, les ditz viscountz poent par usage tenir qeconqes prisoners, devant eux condempnez ou commys en lour garde, sibien a lour mesons ou ils sount demurrantz et a lour countours come en les communes gaoles, issint qils soient toutfoiz detenuz en garde et nient alantz a large hors des mesons ne des contours suisditz.

Item, les plegges et mainpernours[1] et attournes, prises et receux deinz les countours des viscountz et autre proces illoeqes duement faitz, sount tenuz de record sibien come a les courtz tenuz deinz la gyhalle.

Item, chescun alderman de Loundres poet par usage recorder attourne en plees pendantz en courtz des viscountz.

Item, quant une enquest parentre parties est jointe et jure devant les viscountz en plees personeles, si les parties voillent absentier, la courte par usages poet doner le . . enquest pur eux aviser de lour voirdoit tanqe a autre jour apres, en manere come les parties poent accorder, et ceo al peril del pleintif, si aucun juror devye ou autre case aveigne en le mesme (*fo.* 276, *b.*) temps.

Item, lez jurours qe sont sommons en enqueste ne sount mye amerciez coment qils facent defaute outre iij *d.*; mais sils traient longement et ne voillent mye venir, les viscountz par usage poent firmer lour *huys* de les constrendre de venir.

Item, les enquestes de office, qe sount prisez par lez viscountz denquerer des affraies et batteriez faitz encountre la pees, ne sount mye traversables par novelles enquestes par usage, mes

---

1—This word is not very legible.

al suyte de partie, chescun partie avera response nient contresteant celle enquest doffice.

Item, en pleintes de dette et accompte et autres personeles contractz faitz parentre merchant et merchant, si le pleintif counte qe le defendant, a aucune ville merchant ou a lieu merchandable deinz le roialme, bargaigna ou achata de mesme le pleintif aucuns merchandises ou resceust ses deniers pur luy paier, liverer, ou ent rendre accompt en aucun lieu deinz la citee de Loundres, en tiel case le defendant par usage serra mys a respoundre, nient contresteant qe le contract se fist hors de la cite. Et si les parties soient a travers et pledent a issue denqueste, adonqes serra lenqueste prise des gentz de la dite citee, cestassaver, des merchantz passantz parentre la dite citee et la ville merchant ou le contract est suppose, a celle entent qe tielx merchauntz passantz poent aver notice de dit contract.

Item, les viscountz de Loundres ount usez de tout temps de tenir pleez devant eux parentre quiconqes merchantz, la ou ambideux parties sount merchauntz, de touz bargainez et contractz personeles, qe touchent merchandises faites outre le meer a ville merchaunt ou a lieu merchandable, la ou les bargaines et contractz sount faitz par expresse parole sur paiementz ou liverez de merchandises, ou de rendre accompt deinz la dite citee de Loundres, et en tiel case si les parties descendent en issue denqueste, adonqes serra lenqueste pris des genz demurantz deinz mesme la citee, cestassaver, des merchauntz passantz qi usent de passer outre meer, qi poent mieux aver conisance de les bargaines et contractz susditz. Et si aucun estraunge merchaunt et alien soit partie al plee, et tiel enquest soit apprendre, adonqes le merchaunt alien avera la moite de lenquest de sa lang.

Item, si pleint de dette soit fait, et tesmoigne soit par le ministre qe le defendant nist my resident deinz la citee einz qil se ad retreate et esloignez ses biens, et tesmoigne soit qil ad terres ou tenementz deinz mesme la citee, adonqes al suyte de pleintif mesmes les terres et tenementz par usage de la citee serrount extenduz et liverez a mesme le pleintif, a tenir par mesme lextente, tanqe il eit ent leve les deniers a luy duez, trovant suerte de sustener les tenementz covenablement, et auxint de paier al defendant lez deniers ent receux en le mesme temps; si issint soit qe mesme le defendant veigne en court de record deinz un an et un jour apres la livere fait, et luy purra descharger qil doit riens al pleintif.

Item, les viscountz usent dexaminer les parties en touz accions personeles pendantz devant eux, si aucun des parties le prie et de proceder a jugement, solonc ceo qe trove est par examinacion.

Item, la ou aucun accion personele est pendant devant aucun des ditz viscountz, ou aucun matire soit allegge par le defendant en barre daccion ou chose materielle, pur delaier le pleintif, et le pleintif se mette sur le serement le defendant peremptorie qe le plee en lexcepcion, done par mesme le defendant, ne soit mye veritable, adonqes le dit defendant, sil soit en court ou il soit resident deinz la citee, qil purra bonement venir par discrecion de la court, adonqes il serra serementez sil voille qe son plee en lexcepcion, quele il ad done, est bone et veritable; et sil veigne et refuse de faire tiel serement, adonqes il serra tenuz auxi come (*fo.* 277) convict en la cause ; et sur ceo le pleintif recovera ceo qest en demande, solonc ceo qe purra estre trove par examinacion del pleintif, ou par enquest doffice si mestier soit; et sil face le serement le pleintif serra ouste de la suyte. Et en mesme le manere serra le pleintif ouste de sa suyte ou de sa accion, sil ne voudra jurer de sa part qe sa suyte ou autre matere allegge par luy ne soit bon et veritable; et si tiel serement soit mys sur la pleintif et le pleintiff face le serement, il recovera par mesme le serement, si lexcepcion soit material. Et issint sount tieles serementz peremptoires dune part et dautre, solonc la matere de les excepcions.

Item, si homme soit arestu par pleint de dette ou par autre accion personele, et trove meynprise de venir prest al prochein court devant les viscountz, de respoundre al partye a quele court, coment qe le defendant soit demande en covenable temps de venir et saver sa meynprise, et face defaut, et defaut soit recorde, unqore, si mesme le defendant veigne sciant mesme le court, il serra receu de de [*sic*] pleder, sauf en tiel case, il ad perdu lavantage de gager sa ley coment qil purroit aver ewe sa leye, sil eust venuz par temps.

Item, la ou les partyes apergent en court des viscountz use est qe les pleintifs poent amender lour pleynts et lour billes tout temps, avant ceo qe mesmes les parties soient a issu enpledez en jugement en court de record.

Item, en accion daccompt devant lez viscountz le pleintif, par usage de la citee, ne purra mye counter qe le defendant fuist son baillif en nulle case, mais receivour de ses deniers ou de ses biens.

Item, accion daccompt est maintenable par usages devers une femme sole et devers enfantz deinz age, sils soient . . [1] ou sils teignent communes shopes de mestier ou de merchandises, et accions de dette en mesme la manere de ceo qe touche lour mestier ou lour merchandises.

Item, la ou plus sont pendanz devant viscountz use est de tout temps, qe le mair de Loundres, qi soit pur le temps, poet mander les viscountz de faire venir la querelle et le proces devant luy et les aldermans, pur terminer et discusser mesme la querele devant eux, ou de . . ander ladite querelle devant mesme . . daler avant en le proces, solonc ceo qe le mair et aldermans . . . . . et de commander lez viscountz de surseer a lour voluntee.

Item, quant action est lye deinz la dite citee par obligacion en certein . . . et certein . . . . le quel dettour fuist tenuz sufficeant a temps qil fuist . . . . est devenuz futif ou noun sufficeant, adonqes si le creanceour veigne devant le mair ou viscountz du dite citee fesant tiele suggestion, et amesne ovesque luy vj ou iiij gentz creables de mesme la citee, qe voillent loialment tesmoigner qe le dettour se voet retreer et esloigner ses biens hors de la citee . . qil ne . . mye sufficeant de faire le paiement, adonqes le mair ou un des viscountz devant queux la suggestion est faite usent darester le dettour, coment qe le jour contenu deinz lobligacion ne soit mye venuz, et de tenir mesme le dettour en presone tanqe le jour de paiement soit venuz, et autrement qil trovera plegge de tenir mesme le jour; et en mesme le manere darester pur *housebire* devant le jour, si le tenant soit futif.

1—A word here is faded.

Item, si frank homme de la citee trove soi dettour sodeine‑ment . . . . mesme la citee, qel dettour se ad retreate a devant ou soit futif, et le quele dettour voilleit eschaper avant ceo qe le creanceour purra aver un ministre de faire . . . . use est, en tiel case, que le frank homme mesmes par eide de ses veisyns . . . . poet arrester son dit dettour, et ly amesner tanqe al office dun des viscountz, et illoeqes faire sa suyte come la ley demande.

Item, touchant . . . . (*fo.* 277, *b.*) a prendre de pleintz en courtz de viscountz, use est, si les demandes soient de xl *s.* ou de deins, de prendre iiij *d.* pur lamerciment, et sils passent xl *s.*, use est de prendre xij *d.* pur lamerciment.

Item, si une fermer deinz la citee soit futif ou retret, par qi ses biens deinz sa meson soient arestuz ou preises al suyte des partyes par pleint, unqore le lessour appelle *landlord* serra devant touz autres pur la ferme de sa measson aderere par un an, et pur taunt de somme serront biens deinz la dite meason lessez en mesmes les measons al oeps le dit *landlord*. Et coment qun tiel fermer deinz la dite citee face felonie ou autre contempt par qi ses biens et chateux soient arestablez ou forfitables, unqore le lessour, par usage de la citee, serra servey de sa ferme aderere par un an, come devant est dit, des biens trovez deinz mesme la meason.

Item, la ou tenantz deinz la citee tiegnent a volunte et voillent aler hors et surrendre lour measons, ils ferront garnisse‑mentz al lessour devant lour departyr, cestassaver, des mesons qe voisent ferme pur xl *s.* et dedeinz serra fait garnissement par un quarter devant, et si la ferme de la meson passe xl *s.* le serra fait par demy an devant le departyr al peril del tenant, et en mesme le manere serra fait garnissement al tenant, si lessour voet ouster le tenant.

Item, quant homme est condempne al suyte de partye en dette ou en damages devant les viscountz, la partie qad issint recoverer poet eslire daver le corps celuy qest condempne commys al prison, tanqe il eit fait gree, ou daver execucion de ses biens a son perille etc. Burton, R.

Litera papalis de admissione et recepcione Johannis Kempe nuper Londoniensis episcopi in archiepiscopum Eboracensem.[1]

(*fo.* 278). De festo Corporis Christi.[2]

In nomine Domini, Amen. Ex consuetudine quadam per nonnulla annorum et temporum curricula usitata universi artifices civitatis Ebor' suis sumptibus annis singulis ludi fecerunt quemdam ludum sumptuosum, in diversis paginis compilatum veteris et novi testamenti representacionum, per diversa loca predicte civitatis, in festo Corporis Christi, quamdam processionem solempnem ad tunc similiter facientes, ob reverenciam corporis sacramenti Corporis Christi. Incipiendo ad magnas portas, prioratus Sancte Trinitatis Ebor', et sic processionaliter eundo ad ecclesiam cathedralem Eboracensem; et deinde ad hospitale Sancti Leonardi Ebor', sacramento predicto ibidem relicto. Precedentibus numeroso lumine torchearum, et magna multitudine sacerdotum in superpeliciis indutorum, et subsequentibus maiore et civibus Ebor' cum alterius magna copia populi confluentis. Super hoc, quidam vir maxime religiosus, frater Willelmus Melton, ordinis Fratrum Minorum, sacre pagine professor, verbi Dei famosissimus predicator, ad istam veniens civitatem, in suis sermonibus diversis ludum predictum populo commendavit, affirmando quod bonus erat in se et laudabilis valde. Dicebat, tamen, quod cives predicte civitatis et alii forinseci in dicto festo confluentes ad eandem, non solum ipsi ludo in eodem festo, verum eciam comessacionibus, ebrietatibus, clamoribus, cantilenis, et aliis insolenciis, multum intendunt, servicio divino officii ipsius diei minime intendentes. Et quod dolendum est, ea de causa, amittunt indulgencias in ea parte felicis recordacionis per Urbanum papam quartum graciose concessas, illis, videlicet, Christi fidelibus, qui in matutinali officio festi ejusdem in ecclesia in qua idem festum celebratur interfuerint, centum dies; qui vero misse totidem; qui autem in primis ipsius festi vesperis interfuerint, similiter centum; qui vero in secundis totidem; illis,

---

1—Printed in Drake, App. lxvi.
2—Cf. Drake, *op. cit.*, App. p. xxix. Davies, *op. cit.*, 243. Toulmin Smith, *op. cit.*, xxxi.

vero, qui prime, tercie, sexte, et none ac completorii officiis interfuerint, pro qualibet horarum ipsarum quadraginta dies; illis, autem, qui per octabas illius festi matutinalibus, vespertinis, misse, ac predictarum horarum officiis interfuerint, centum dies singulis octavarum ipsarum diebus ; sicut in sanctis canonibus inde editis plenius continetur. Et ideo ipsi fratri Willelmo salubre videbatur, et ad hoc populum civitatis inducebat, ut ludus ille fiat in una die, et processio in die altera, sic quod populus convenire possit ad ecclesias in festo predicto et interesse servicio ecclesiastico pro indulgenciis consequendis. Unde Petrus (*fo*. 278, *b*.) Bukcy, maior hujus civitatis Ebor', Ricardus Russell, nuper maior stapule apud Calesiam, Johannes Northeby, Willelmus Bowes, senior, Johannes Moreton, Thomas Gare, senior, Henricus Preston, Thomas Esyngwald, Thomas Bracebryg, Willelmus Ormesheued, Johannes Aldestanemore, aldermanni ; Ricardus Louthe, Johannes Dodyngton, vicecomites ; Johannes Hewyk, Thomas Doncastre, Johannes Usburn, Thomas More, Robertus Yarom, Robertus Midelton, Galfridus Sauvage, Thomas Snawdon, Johannes Loftehouse, Johannes Bolton, Johannes Lyllyng, Johannes Gascoigne, Willelmus Craven, Thomas Aton, Thomas Davy, Johannes Baynbrig, Thomas Kyrkham, Willelmus Bedale, Willelmus Gaytesheued, Johannes Louthe, et Johannes Warde, de numero viginti quatuor, congregati fuerunt hic in camera consilii hujus civitatis, sexto die Junii, anno gracie millesimo quadringentesimo vicesimo sexto, regni vero regis Henrici sexti post conquestum Anglie anno quarto, et per dicta, exhortaciones et monita salubria predicti fratris Willelmi propensius excitati, et optime advertentes quod delictum non est, nec Deum offendit si bonum in melius commutetur. Habito igitur inter eos diligenti tractatu de materia prelibata, suum unanimum et expressum dederunt consensum quod casus iste primitus communitati in aula communi publicetur, et habito communitatis assensu, quod extunc premissa in melius reformentur. Super quo maiore predicto et communitate istius civitatis in aula communi ejusdem congregatis, x^{mo} die predicti mensis Junii, anno predicto, factaque ibidem publicacione solempni premissorum, ordinatum erat de communi assensu, qu^od ludus ille solempnis, qui ut prefertur ludi consuevit in ipso festo

Corporis Christi, amodo ludatur singulis annis die Mercurii, vigilia ejusdem festi, et quod processio fiat semper modo solempni in die ipsius festi ; sic quod universus populus, tunc in predicta civitate constitutus, vacare possit devote matutinis, misse, vesperis, et aliis horis ejusdem festi, et particeps fieri indulgenciarum, in ea parte, a predicto Romano pontifice Urbano papa quarto graciosius concessarum.¹ Burton, R.

Eisdem eciam die, loco et anno, exhortacione predicti fratris Willelmi causante, et primo ordinatum erat per maiorem et communitatem, quod nullus vitalarius nec artifices de cetero teneant shoppas seu fenestras apertas, nec stalla vel scabella ponant apud domos suas in loco vocato Thursdaymarket, nec alibi infra civitatem istam vel suburbia ejusdem, nisi tantum in tempore necessitatis in subito adventu dominorum vel dominarum vel extranearum personarum ad civitatem istam, ad emendum vel vendendum aliquod genus marcandisarum, vel ad emendum vel vendendum carnes, pisces, aut aliqua alia victualia, aliquibus diebus Dominicis, sed quod shoppe et fenestre universorum hominum in diebus Dominicis teneantur clause, a nocte cujuslibet diei Sabati usque ad auroram diei Lune proximo subsequentis, tabernariis et cocis communibus pro aisiamento hominum viatorum, piscenariis eciam pontium Use et Fosse a Carnipreviis usque ad festa Pasche tantum exceptis. Et quod emptores captoresque et provisores victualium faciant provisionem suam pro victualibus suis emendis et expendendis in diebus Dominicis in diebus Sabbatorum precedencium, sic quod expletis sex dierum negociis et laboribus universis, populus diem septimum, scilicet Dominicum, sanctificare possit in requie ad laudem Dei, qui in die septimo requievit ab omni opere quod patrarat, et curis mundi relictis ad ecclesias accedere et matutinis, missis et vesperis personaliter interesse, sub pena sex solidorum octo denariorum usui communitatis istius civitatis applicandorum et solvendorum per quoscumque marcandisantes artificesque alios et vitalarios quoscumque, qui in aliquo tempore hujus contrarium fecerint in futurum. Burton, R.

1—In the left margin :—" Vide melius infra vijum folium sequentem " is written.

¹Memoratus insuper frater Willelmus, volens peccatum destruere, et amator honestatis, predicando, ymmo exhortando, audientem populum inducebat, ut amoveri facerent universas publicas concubinas in fornicacione vel adulterio delinquentes et pronubas de corpore civitatis. Unde de consensu maioris et communitatis ordinatum erat quod antiqua constitucio civitatis de meretricibus edita execucioni mandetur, et quod non inhabitent civitatem, sed quod ipse et omnes pronube eam exeant infra octo dies proximo sequentes, sub pena imprisonamenti corporum suorum, nisi ita fuerit quod ipse pronube infra idem tempus venerint coram maiore, et sufficientem invenerint securitatem quod omnino dimittent usum et officium receptandi vel hospitandi aliquos in fornicacione vel adulterio delinquentes. Burton. R.¹

De Fullonibus et tonsoribus.

(*fo.* 279). In vigilia Epiphanie, 3 Henr. vi. (5 January, 1424-5), Thomas Bracebryg, maior hujus civitatis, Ricardus Russell, maior stapule lanarum apud Calesiam, Johannes Northeby, Willelmus Bowes, Johannes Moreton, Henricus Preston, Thomas Esyngwald, Willelmus Ormesheued, Petrus Bukcy, Johannes Aldestanemore, aldermanni; Johannes Warde, unus vicecomitum; Johannes Hewyk, Thomas More, Galfridus Sauvage, Robertus Yarom, Johannes Waghen, Thomas Snawdon, Robertus Yarom, Johannes Loftehouse, Johannes Bolton, Johannes Baynbrig, Thomas Davy, Johannes Gascoigne, Thomas Aton, Johannes Lyllyng, Willelmus Bedale et Willelmus Gaytesheued, de xxiiij^or, congregati fuerunt hic in camera consilii et consenserunt et ordinarunt inter alia quod fullones hujus civitatis Ebor' habeant scrutinium suum de panno fullito per fullones forinsecos, ita quod non ostendant eis odium nec maliciam in scrutando et quod fullones universi hujus civitatis libere possint tondere, si voluerint, universos pannos per ipsos fullitos, si scienciam tondendi habuerint, sine aliquo dando tonsoribus hujus civitatis. Sed si hujusmodi fullones super se ceperint per consuetudinem tondere aliquos pannos majores vel minores, qui non crunt de fullitura

1—Cf. Drake, *op. cit.*, App. xxxii.

sua propria, quod tunc sint contributorii cum tonsoribus ad paginam suam et alia onera sua. Et eciam consenserunt quod Robertus Pennok habeat ad firmam tenementum communitatis in Hertillane pro iiij^{or} marcis per annum ad terminum sex annorum, ita quod plegios inveniat pro firma.

(*fo.* 279). Bond by Cecily Ferrour, late the wife of William Ferrour formerly of Newcastle-upon-Tyne, daughter of William Steward formerly of York, painter, to William Skyrwyth, clerk, for 40 *s.* to be paid at Martinmas next. 19 November, 6 Henry vi., (1427). Seal. The said William has five other bonds, each for 40 *s.* to be paid at Martinmas in each of the next five years. If Cecily pay to him 8 *l.* at Martinmas next, she shall be quit of the remaining 4 *l.*, and the said bonds shall be void.

Constituciones cocorum.[1]

(*fo.* 279, *b.*) In primis, it ys ordand the xj day of Septembre in the yere of oure Lord mccccxxv, 4 Henry vi., be William Ormesheued, than mair of this cite of York, that fra than furth nullus forinsecus admittatur infra civitatem istam, nec toleretur parare prandia in generalibus festis vel nuptiis, sepulturis, nec in congregacionibus gildarum vel fraternitatum, nisi sit admissus et juratus ad libertatem hujus civitatis, et sustineat expensas et onera arti cocorum pertinencia, sicut artifices artis hujusmodi in civitate faciunt annuatim.

Item, quod uxores aliquorum alterius artificis neque pinsant, bulliant neque assent in shoppis publicis ad vendendum per retalliam, nisi sint habiles ut occupent, pro honore civitatis et hominum artis predicte.

Item, quod omnes illi qui occupant et tenent shoppas apertas vel focos in arte predicta, sint sub correccione scrutatorum ejusdem artis, si aliquam fecerint offensam vel defectum in arte predicta, et quod supportent onera et expensas illius artis annuatim sicut alii ejusdem artis faciunt infra civitatem predictam, et si quis recusaverit articulos predictos [2]seu aliquem eorum[2] perimplere,

---

1—In left hand margin, " Iste ordinaciones reformantur tempore Thome Harrison, maioris," is written.
2—2—Interlined.

THE ORDINANCES OF THE COOKS (1425)

quod sit expulsus de arte et solvat camere sex solidos octo denarios sterlingorum [et arti per equales porciones dividendos.[1]]

Item, quod nullus cocus communus asset aliquas carnes in diebus dominicis ad vendendum nisi adventus dominorum vel alique magne congregaciones populi peregrinorum et aliorum extraneorum contigerint esse in civitate, sub pena vj $s.$ viij $d.$, camere et arti predicte equaliter applicandorum; et quod bene liceat in adventu hujusmodi dominorum et congregacionibus hominibus artis predicte habere carnes et victualia in domibus suis et assare si voluerint absque solucione alicujus forisfacture.

Et pro eo quod in tempore antiquo quando coci communes hujus civitatis usi fuerunt emere pisces recentes maris, et ipsos per retalliam ad eorum libitum vendere, tunc contributorii fuerunt pagine piscenariorum, sed quod modo prohibiti sunt ne aliquos pisces maris recentes amodo vendant nisi quos coxerint, assaverint vel pistaverint, sicut ad eorum artificium pertinet; ideo ordinatum est quod ammodo non sint contributorii pagine piscenariorum, sed quod inde pro perpetuo sint quieti.

Et xviij die Octobris, 24 Henr. vi. (1445), de consensu omnium artificum cocorum hujus civitatis, videlicet, Willelmi Burgh, Roberti Popilton, Johannis Marsshall, Willelmi Bridehill, Roberti Hall, Johannis Chaumbre, Roberti Pothowe, Roberti Brereton, Radulphi Couk, Gilberti Couk, Johannis Gaunton, Thome Burgh, Ricardi Dygby, Thome Gerade, Walteri Couk et Thome Arden, ordinatum est quod quilibet, qui de cetero incipiet occupare ut magister in arte sua in civitate ista, et non fuit apprenticius in arte illa in civitate ista, quod in prima occupacione sua ut magister solvat vj $s.$ viij $d.$ camere consilii ad usum communitatis et artificii equis porcionibus dividendos.

Memorandum that the xvj day of Decembre, 24 Henry vii. (1508), the hole occupacion of the coukes personally afor John Dogheson, maire of the cite of York, William Neleson and Alan Staveley, aldermen, as weell by the assentt of the sayd occupacion, as by the commandment of the sayd maire for the weell of the sayd craft, shall of new every ij yere chose ij serchours. And

---

[1]—Written in a later hand.

also award which apperith more playnly of the bakke syde of thare ordinance, and in record of the same agrement they have gevyn xvj *d.* to the chambre.[1]

(*fo.* 280). A cancelled copy of the first six lines of the commission to collect the subsidies of Henry vi. given on fo. 268.

Tanners.

In nomine Domini, Amen. Cum magna et diutina varietas lisque et discordia mote et pendentes fuerint inter homines artificii tannatorum hujus civitatis Ebor', ex una parte, et homines artificii allutariorum hujus ejusdem civitatis, ex altera parte, pro scrutinio habendo cujuscumque corii tannati, tandem amicabili quarumdam personarum indifferencium mediante tractatu ambe partes predicte, pro se et universis hominibus arcium suarum predictarum presentibus et futuris, et maxime pro bona reformacione pacis inter ipsos habenda et tenenda inter eos in futurum, assecurabant se et plene consenserunt perficere et perimplere ordinacionem et judicium nostri Willelmi Bowes, maioris, aldermannorum et consilii camere hujus civitatis Ebor' in materia ista. Et super hoc nos predicti maior, vicecomites, aldermanni et consilium dicte civitatis, visis et intellectis peticionibus, evidenciis et allegacionibus utrarumque arcium predictarum, pro pace reformanda inter easdem, primitus et ante omnia ordinamus et judicamus quod universi homines arcium predictarum civitatis predicte sint ammodo boni amici simul, quilibet alteri, et non amplius discordes pro aliquo dicto vel facto hucusque in materia varietatis, litis, et discordie predictarum.

Item, ordinamus et judicamus quod omne corium tannatum portandum de partibus in et ad civitatem istam Ebor' vel suburbia ejusdem, sive corium ipsum sit alicujus tannatoris sive alicujus allutarii, seu alterius persone cujuscumque hujus civitatis vel extranei, integre portetur ad quemdam locum infra aulam communem, et quod corium illud ibidem totum expectet quoadusque fuerit scrutatum per scrutatores certarum arcium, ad hoc ut sequitur assignandos.

1—In a different and later hand.

Item, quod capiantur octo persone in scrutatores, videlicet, due persone de discrecioribus tannatorum, due de discrecioribus allutariorum, due de discrecioribus zonariorum, due de discrecioribus curiatorum hujus civitatis Ebor', ad scrutandum quodcumque corium tannatum, portandum de partibus ad civitatem istam ; et si in tempore scrutinii sint nisi sex hujusmodi scrutatorum presentes, tunc duo ex illis erunt tannatores, duo allutarii, unus curiator corii, et unus de arte zonariorum ; et si in tempore scrutinii sint nisi tantum quatuor presentes, tunc de qualibet predictarum quatuor arcium capietur unus ad scrutandum.

Item, quod predicti scrutatores in primo introitu suo ad officium suum scrutinii sint jurati ad scrutandum bene et fideliter omnimodum corium tannatum, portatum in locum predictum, et fideliter certificandum singulos defectus inveniendos in aliquo corio ibidem sine favore aliquo ; quod quidem corium veniens de partibus hospitabitur integre in loco predicto et in nullo alio quousque scrutatum (*fo.* 280, *b.*) fuerit, sub pena forisfacture ejusdem corii ad usum communitatis civitatis predicte, in quorumcumque manibus illud corium sit inventum alibi quam in predicto loco hospitatum.

Item, quod si aliquis allutarius vel aliquis alius emere voluerit aliquod corium, quod erit tannatum hic in civitate ista, de aliquo tannatore istius civitatis, ad operandum illud infra civitatem istam, quod tunc allutarius ille et omnes alii veniant ad domum tannatoris et videant ibidem corium, et dicant tannatori quale et quantum corium ab eo pro tunc emere voluerint, et statim cum concordati fuerint de precio, antequam allutarius vel aliquis alius habeat liberacionem illius corii, tannator cujus est cariari faciet sumptibus suis corium illud ad predictum locum, et ibi scrutatum erit per scrutatores predictos et signatum sigillo eorumdem scrutatorum.

Item, quod si predicti octo scrutatores seu sex, aut quatuor eorum ad minus, in forma predicta presentes, inveniant aliquod corium tannatum portatum ad locum predictum male tannatum seu defectivum, tunc presentabunt defectum illum domino maiori hujus civitatis, qui pro tempore fuerit, ut defectus ille judicetur et puniatur secundum quantitatem delicti.

Item, quod si predicti octo scrutatores, seu sex, aut quatuor eorum ad minus, in modo et forma predictis non fecerint scrutinium suum diligenter, debite, et fideliter, secundum quod ad id jurati erunt, et super hoc coram maiore, qui erit pro tempore, convicti fuerint, quod tunc teneantur perjuri, et eis ex tunc nulla fides adhibeatur, et quod ipsi nicholominus finem faciant juxta discrecionem maioris et consilii camere pro tempore existencium.

Item, si quis allutarius post hoc inveniat defectum notorium in aliquo corio tannato, cum pervenerit ad manus suas, quod tunc allutarius, quiscumque fuerit, presentet illum qualibet vice maiori hujus civitatis pro tempore existenti, ita quod audire poterit et terminare defectum tam ad sectam regis quam ad sectam cujuscumque alterius conqueri volentis, vel alias convincere culpabiles per debitam examinacionem eque bene ad sectam regis quam partis virtute cujusdam statuti regni Anglie inde editi et provisi.

Item, quod quilibet possessor alicujus corii tannati, ducti de patria ad civitatem, si sit domesticus et concivis hujus civitatis, solvat pro qualibet dacra corii obolum pro firma domus ad usum et commodum hujus civitatis, et si possessor alicujus corii tannati ad civitatem istam ducendi, si extraneus seu extra civitatem istam maneat, quod tunc solvat pro qualibet dacra corii sui denarium pro firma domus ad usum communitatis predicte ; et quod quilibet tannator hujus civitatis, qui ex nunc vendiderit aliquod corium suum alicui allutario hujus civitatis tannatum infra istam civitatem, quod tunc solvat pro qualibet dacra corii ad locum predictum ducenda obolum pro firma domus.

Tanners.

(*fo.* 281). Memorandum quod cum inter ceteras ordinaciones et constituciones factas in secundo tempore officii maioratus Willelmi Bowes, maioris istius civitatis Ebor', de modo et forma scrutinii corii tannati extunc habendi in civitate ista, ordinatum fuerit et stabilitum, quod si aliquis allutarius vel aliquis alius emere voluerit aliquod corium tannatum hic in civitate ista de aliquo tannatore istius civitatis ad operandum illud infra civitatem istam, quod tunc allutarius ille et omnes alii venirent ad domum tannatoris, et viderent ibidem corium, et dicerent tannatori quale et quantum corium ab eo pro tunc emere voluerint, et statim cum concordati fuerint de precio, antequam allutarius vel aliquis alius habeat liberacionem illius corii, tannator ille cujus erit cariari faceret sumptis suis corium illud integre ad quemdam locum infra aulam communem hujus civitatis ibidem expectandum quousque scrutatum foret per scrutatores certarum arcium ad hoc assignandarum, prout in ordinacionibus plenius continetur. Tamen quia per lapsum temporum nimis tediosum laboriosumque hominibus apparuit et dampnosum, quod cum tannatores hujus civitatis corium suum vendiderint allutariis vel aliquibus aliis apud domos suas, quod corium illud singulis vendicionum temporibus per tantam distanciam cariarent extra domos suas ad locum aliquem infra aulam predictam, ut ibidem corii sui scrutinium expectarent; igitur Ricardus Russell, maior dicte civitatis, necnon aldermanni et universi probi homines de jurato consilio dicte civitatis considerabant magna incommoda et dampna, que tannatoribus dicte civitatis presentibus et futuris de corio suo occasione et causa tanti cariagii huc et illuc possent verisimiliter pervenire, ipse ergo Ricardus Russell, maior, aldermanni et probi homines predicti, dictorum tannatorum tediosis laboribus parcere et eorum excessiva incommoda precavere volentes, ad rogatum magnum et peticionem humilem tannatorum predictorum, ipsos in omnibus ad regimen artis sue eorum ordinacioni in alto et basso submittencium, in vigilia purificacionis Beate Marie, 8 Henr. vi. (1 February, 1429-30), omnes et singulos tannatores civitatis predicte primitus et ante omnia libertati sue predicte civitatis, de qua propter eorum transgressiones erant exonerati, resitituebant, et super hoc considerabant et ordinabant quod tannatores predicte civitatis extunc in omnibus punctis modo fideli et debito gubernarent artem suam ad honorem hujus civitatis et commodum populi domini nostri regis, et quod inter se suum exercerent et haberent scrutinium corii de tannatura sua propria infra artem suam per scrutatores proprios artis sue juratos, et liberum passagium qua voluerint per terram et per aquam cum corio tannaturo proprio, sigillo suo consueto et antiquo sigillando, sine calumpnia vel impedimento aliquorum hominum aliarum arcium, ita plene et libere sicut habuere et usi fuere ante tempus confeccionis constitucionum et ordinacionum predictarum, que tempore predicti Willelmi Bowes provise et edite fuerint, ut prefertur, ita quod tannatores ipsi presentes et futuri cariari et portari facerent omne illud corium, quod de extraneis ement tannatoribus, ad locum scrutinii aulam communem predictam ibidem scrutandum in forma ordinacionis inde facte.

Tanners.

(*fo.* 281, *b.*) Ultimo die Decembris, 16 Edward iv. (1476), Thomas Wrangwish, maior hujus civitatis Ebor'; aldermanni, Thomas Nelson, Johannes Gilyot, Johannes Marshall, Willelmus Snaweshill, Christoferus Marshall, Johannes Glasen, Johannes Tonge, Robertus Amyas; xxiiij^{or}, Ricardus Cleybroke, Thomas Catour, Johannes Letheley, Thomas Aleyn, Thomas Maryot, Willelmus Chymney, Alanus Wilberfosse.

At whiche day in the counsaile chaumbre of this citie of York, by the instaunce and ful humble supplicacion of all the hole craft of the tanners of the saide cite, it was enacted, ordeined, and established by thassent of all the counseil of the chaumbre from hynsefurth perpetually to be observed and keped. First, if ther be any maner man that is not of the tanner craft, and shall hapen to wedde and take to wife a widowe of the same craft, then that man shall paie er he occupie, and by his sersours of the saide craft admitted therunto, xl *s.*, the oone half unto the chaumbre of the citie, and the other half to the supportacion of the pageaunt and charges of the saide craft.

Item, if ther be any tanner of the contre that hath not be apprentice within this citie, and will sett upp the craft and occupie as a maister within this citie, that then he shall paie at his upset xiij *s.* iiij *d.*, to the chaumbre and craft as is aforesaide.

Item, whosomever of the saide craft that is deuly warned by his sersours to appere afore theyme, for any matter concernyng the honour of the citie and the wele of his said craft, and willfully absent hym and com not, to lese and paie at every tyme ij *d.*, in manere and fourme abovesaide.

Item, if ther be any man of the saide craft that after the sersours have made dewe serche of his leder, and fynde it not sufficiantly barked, and warne hym to amend it, and then the saide man take upon hym to sell any of the saide leder not sufficiantly barked, to paie and lese iiij *s.* in like maner and fourme as is aforesaide.

(*fo.* 282). Item, if ther be any man, maister or servant, in the saide occupacion that takith vpon hym to teche any other personne that is not of the saide craft, in any poynte belonging to the saide craft, or to make lethir hungry within his owne howse, he to paie vj *s.* viij *d.*, to be devided in manere and fourme aforesaide.

Item, that the sersours of the saide craft shall yerely have and resceive of every foreine barker that commyth to this citie and accustumably sellith rede ledir or byeith rouch within this saide citie, that they paie unto the sustentacion of the pageaunt of the saide craft yerely, iiij *d.*

Cuuryours.[1]

(*fo.* 283). Reverendo domino suo, maiori hujus civitatis Ebor', omnes magistri *de la curyour craft* istius civitatis, eorum pauperem statum considerare et qualiter annuatim onerantur cum pagina in ludo Corporis Christi et aliis oneribus eis quasi importabilibus, et eis graciose concedere quod nullus artificii predicti capiat aliquem apprenticium in arte predicta pro minore termino quam sex annorum, sub pena vj *s.* viij *d.*, camere consilii civitatis et arti predicte ad sustentacionem pagine sue equis porcionibus solvendorum, per magistrum qui contrarium fecerit, et sub pena forisfacture apprenticii contra formam istius ordinacionis capiendi. Et quod quilibet magister artis predicte, statim cum aliquem apprenticium acceperit, solvat pro illo in primo introitu suo xij *d.* camere predicte et alios xij *d.* arti predicte.

Item, quod quilibet serviens, in arte predicta conducendus et mercedem vel salarium recipiens, solvat annuatim iiij *d.* magistris

---

1—In left margin, "Plus inde in alio libro super xxj folio." In right margin, "Iste ordinaciones de novo corriguntur, alie ordinaciones nove istis opponuntur tempore Edwardi Fawcet, maioris," is written.

pagine predicte, ¹si fuerit apprenticius ad artem illam in civitate predicta, et si non fuerit apprenticius, solvat annuatim ad paginam predictam viij $d.$¹

Item, quod quilibet serviens, qui bene et fideliter servivit magistro suo in arte predicta per sex anuos vel amplius secundum terminum inter eos concordatum, solvat in prima levacione shoppe sue iij $s.$ iiij $d.$, pro sustentacione pagine predicte. Et si aliquis extraneus venerit ad civitatem ad occupandum artem predictam, et non fuit apprenticius in arte predicta in civitate predicta, quod solvat vj $s.$ viij $d.$ camere consilii predicti, et vj $s.$ viij $d.$ ad sustentacionem pagine sue ad primam levacionem shoppe.

Item, quod nullus artificii predicti ponat aliquem in opere aliquo artis predicte, nisi prius inveniatur abilis per scrutatores artis predicte ad operandum, sub pena vj $s.$ viij $d.$, camere et arti predictis equis porcionibus applicandorum.

Item, quod nullus artis predicte ponat in opere aliquem, qui erit male fame aut vite inhoneste, sub pena iij $s.$ iiij $d.$, solvendorum arti predicte, si hoc inveniri et probari possit per scrutatores artis predicte.

Item, quod nullus magister artis predicte procuret nec conducat aliquem servientem alicujus hominis artis predicte infra terminum suum, sub pena vj $s.$ viij $d.$, camere et arti equaliter solvendorum; et quod nullus ²artis predicte² conducat aliquem talem servientem nisi pro uno anno integro, si aliquis alius artis predicte ipsum conducere voluerit et cui ipse servire voluerit sub eadem pena modo predicto solvenda per conducentem; ita semper quod serviens ille magistrum suum cui servit premuniat per quarterium anni an sibi voluerit servire vel non.

Item, si aliquis extraneus ad civitatem istam venerit ad operandum in arte predicta, quod sit conductus per aliquem magistrum ejusdem artis ad operandum cum eo per unam septimanam, et cum alio magistro ejusdem artis per aliam septimanam, et sic de septimana in septimanam quousque servierit omnibus magistris servicium suum habere volentibus, unicuique per septimanam suam, sine licencia scrutatorum artis predicte, nisi

1—1—Added in a later hand.
2—2—Interlined.

extraneus ille voluerit conductus esse in adventu suo cum aliquo magistro ipsius artis per unum annum integrum, sub pena vj *s.* viij *d.*, modo premisso solvendorum per magistrum, qui contrarium hujus ordinacionis fecerit in futurum.

Item, quod nullus *de le couureourcrafte*, utrum sit de libertate civitatis, vel non, excitet nec procuret per donum vel per empcionem aut vendicionem aliquem custumarium alterius hominis ejusdem artificii, sive custumarius ille fuerit *cordwaner*, *girdeler*, *cardemaker* vel *sadeler*, in dampnum seu prejudicium alicujus alterius artificii predicti, sub pena vj *s.* viij *d.*, solvendorum modo predicto.

Item, vij^{mo} die Februarii, 2 Henr. vi. (1423-4), concordatum est per omnes magistros artificii predicti quod die Dominica post festum purificacionis Beate Marie proximo futura (4 February, 1424-5) eligant novos scrutatores suos pro anno futuro, et quod die Dominica proxima post festum Corporis Christi eligant magistros pagine sue, et quod veteres magistri pagine sue tunc sursum reddant compotum de occupacione sua de anno preterito, et sursum liberabunt omnia instrumenta sua pagine et ludo suis pertinencia ad custodiam et manus scrutatorum, sub pena vj *s.* viij *d.*, predictis usibus applicandorum.

Item, quod nulla mulier serviens alicui artis predicte operatur seu laborat in dicta arte seu aliqua parcella ejusdem, nisi tantummodo uxor ejus, qui est vir[1] vel ut vir[1] habetur et reputatur in eadem arte, sub pena vj *s.* viij *d.*, forisfaciendorum arti et camere in forma predicta.

(*fo.* 283, *b.*) Item, ordinatum est quod si aliquis artificii predicti premunitus sit per aliquem, qui est vel erit ejusdem artificii, ad interessendum cum scrutatoribus et magistris ejusdem et communicandum de negociis et materiis artem predictam tangentibus, et non venerit et non habuerit justam causam se absentandi, perdet et solvet iiij *d.*, in custodia scrutatorum artis predicte expectaturos vice qualibet qua inventus fuerit culpabilis predictis usibus applicandos.

Item, si aliquis artificii predicti inventus fuerit rebellis vel contrarium fecerit alicujus ordinacionum predictarum in aliquo

---

1—The word 'vir' is doubtful, possibly jur, *i.e.*, juratus.

puncto, quod super eum probari poterit per scrutatores suos et duos magistros ejusdem artificii eis electos, quod perdat penam et penas superius limitatas. Et ad omnes istas ordinaciones fideliter tenendas omnes [1]magistri[1] artificii predicti sunt jurati in quantum lex regni permittit et consuetudo laudabilis civitatis.

(*fo.* 284). Item, quod curiatores hujus civitatis decetero non capiant corium tannatum alicujus allutarii curiandum, nisi allutarius ille liberet sibi sufficientem et necessariam stuffam pro curiacione corii sui vice qualibet, ita quod corium illud cum stuffa liberata debite et fideliter curiari et parari possit, sicut deberet pro bono usu et utilitate populi domini regis ; et ut hoc melius observetur consideratum est quod certe persone artis curiatorum hujus civitatis sint per maiorem, qui erit pro tempore, assignate et jurate ad supervidendum et scrutandum quod universi curiatores sufficientem et necessariam stuffam capiant pro coriacione cujuscumque corii eis liberandi ad coriandum, sicut natura et qualitas corii requirunt, ita quod corium illud sit forte et habile usui hominum et aquam expellat.

Item, quod si probari possit super aliquem curiatorem quod non recepit stuffam sufficientem ad curiacionem corii, seu quod non fecerit debitam diligenciam et scienciam suam ad coriandum bene et fideliter corium ductum ad manus suas, quod quociens hoc probari poterit super eum, quod perdat libertatem suam in civitate ista, et alio modo puniatur per discrecionem maioris et consilii camere secundum qualitatem delicti.

Item, quod nullus allutarius hujus civitatis quamdiu occupaverit artem allutarii, utatur vel exerceat artem curiatoris nec secum teneat in domo sua vel aliena aliquem de arte curiatorum de consensu suo ad curiandum aliquod corium alicujus allutarii, sub pena gravis punicionis per maiorem et consilium camere, et forisfacture corii, qualibet vice quod probari poterit super eorum aliquem.

Item, quod scrutatores predicti habeant sigillum eis limitatum pro signacione corii, quod invenerint defectivum, cum nota differencie a sigillo quod tannarii hujus civitatis ab antiquo

---

1—1—Interlined.

habuerunt inter eos, quod quidem sigillum semper expectabit sub certis clavibus clausum ab uno tempore scrutinii usque ad aliud.

Item, quod quodlibet corium coriatum veniens de partibus in civitatem istam, cujuscumque hominis fuerit, integre portetur ad locum predictum infra aulam communem, ut ibi inde scrutinium fiat per scrutatores juratos artis curiatorum hujus civitatis, sub periculo incumbenti, solvendo firmam domus, sicut superius est expressum.

Item, quod omnes articuli premissi stent in suo pleno robore et virtute a festo Sancti Andree apostoli, 7 Henr. vi. (30 November, 1428), et quod pixis ordinetur, omni hora expectans in loco predicto, ligata posti cum catena ferri cum [1]quatuor[1] clavibus diversis, ad imponendum sigillum predictum, a tempore unius scrutinii usque ad aliud, et quod unus cujuslibet arcium predictarum habeat unam de clavibus predictis in custodia sua, et scrutinium tentum erit singulis septimanis diebus Martis, Jovis et Sabbati, in loco predicto, et tempus scrutinii incipiet ad horam nonam usque ad horam decimam ante prandium; et predicti scrutatores semper erunt parati singulis septimanis et diebus ad horam predictam ad custodiendum scrutinium suum, et quod se non absentent sub pena perjurii et gravis punicionis per maiorem et consilium camere, vice qualibet qua inveniri poterunt in defectu.

(*fo.* 283, *b.*) In Nomine Domini, Amen. Cum nuper in tempore Henrici Preston, maioris, de avisamento consilii camere, pagina *de lez salsemakers*, ubi Judas se suspendebat et crepuit medius in ludo Corporis Christi; et pagina *de lez tilemakers*, ubi Pilatus condempnavit Jhesum morti; et pagina *de lez turnours, hayresters* et *bollers*, ubi Jhesus ligatus erat ad columpnam et flagellatus; et pagina molendinariorum, ubi Pilatus et alii milites ludebant ad talos pro vestimentis Jhesu, et pro eis sortes mittebant, et ea partiebantur inter se, fuerunt combinate simul in unam paginam, ceteris predictis paginis pro perpetuo exclusis; que quidem pagina decetero vocabitur pagina condempnacionis Jhesu Christi. Super hoc artifices arcium predictarum contendebant inter se de modo solucionis ad paginam

1—1—Interlined.

predictam.¹ Tandem tamen mediante bono tractatu Thome Bracebrig, maioris, universi artifices predicti posuerunt se in judicio Willelmi Scoreburgh, Johannis Stayndurn, *draper*, Roberti Bolton, *kambesmyth*, et Ricardi Neuland, tanquam indifferencium personarum; et ipsi, onus hujusmodi super se assumentes, ipsas artes, ut sequitur, concordabant, scilicet, quod *les salsemakers* et *tilemakers* decetero portent onus et expensas pagine predicte, et ipsam in bono et honesto modo annuatim ludendam producent, cum ad hoc premuniti fuerint, sicut inde coram maiore, pro tempore existente, voluerint respondere. Et quod molendinarii in vigilia Corporis Christi annis singulis imperpetuum solvent et liberabunt a *lez salsemakers* et *tilemakers*, in manus, scilicet, magistrorum pagine predicte, decem solidos sterlingorum in auxilium expensarum ipsius pagine, sub pena xiij *s.* iiij *d.*, camere hujus civitatis et reparacioni pagine predicte equaliter dividendorum; et quod unus vel duo molendinariorum eant cum pagina in die ludi ejusdem, et cum *lez salsemakers* et *tilemakers* in cibo potuque solacia percipiant. Et quod *lez hayresters*, et illi qui eis antea solverunt annuatim, liberabunt in vigilia Corporis Christi custodibus pagine predicte in auxilium expensarum ejusdem pagine quinque solidos, sub pena decem solidorum modo quo premittitur solvendorum, et quod unus eorum circumeat cum ludo et pagina predicta cum magistris ejusdem et cum eis solacia habeat si voluerit. Et si ipsa aliquibus temporibus reparacione indigeat, quod molendinarii sint contributorii ad tercium denarium expensarum, et *les hayresters* ad medietatem summe solvende per molendinarios supradictos, et quod unus molendinariorum et unus *de lez hayresters* supervideant expensas circa reparacionem pagine predicte cum magistris ejusdem pro tempore existentibus. Et quod nulla quatuor arcium predictarum ponat aliqua signa, arma, vel insignia super paginam predictam, nisi tantum arma hujus honorabilis civitatis. Et quod nullus quatuor arcium predictarum litiget, nec aliquam discordiam faciat cum aliquo earundem arcium pro aliquo puncto pagine predicte, sub pena iij *s.* iiij *d.*, usui operis pontis

1—R. Davis, *op. cit.*, p. 235. He quotes the first eleven lines, Miss Toulmin Smith requotes Davies' Extract and adds more lines, xxv.

de Fosse applicandorum, per quemlibet qui fecerit contrarium in hac parte, et hoc tociens quociens super hoc sufficienti recordo convictus fuerit in futurum. [1]Huic eciam concordie additum est et ordinatum, primo die Septembris, 11 Henr. vi. (1432) . . . . in tempore Thome Snaudon, maioris, per consideracionem et arbitrium Johannis Staynburn, Roberti Bolton, Ricardi Neuland predictorum, et Johannis Man, ut personarum indifferencium, per univeros artifices salsariorum et *tylemakers* predictorum electorum, quod salsarii annuatim imperpetuum in vigilia Corporis Christi liberent a *les tylemakers* pro parte sua ludi pagine predicte quinque solidos in moneta, sub pena x *s.*, solvendorum equaliter camere et commodo pagine predicte. Et quociens dicta pagina reparacione indiguerit, quod tunc salsarii solvant unum denarium, sicut *les tylemakers* solvent annuatim ; et quod reparacio illa supervideatur per duos homines unius artis et duos alterius, et quod duo vel tres salsariorum (qui) circumeant cum pagina predicta in die et ludo Corporis Christi simul habeant solacia sua, si voluerint. Burton, Rog.

Ordinacio pro tilers et wryghtis.

(*fo.* 284, *b.*) Memorie vero hominum commendandum est quod die Veneris in septimana Pentecostes, anno 3 Henr. vi. (1 June, 1425), Willelmus Ormesheued, maior, Johannes Northeby, Willelmus Bowes, Johannes Moreton, Thomas Gare, Thomas Bracebryg, Petrus Bukcy, aldermanni ; Johannes Louthe, unus vicecomitum ; Johannes Hewyk, Johannes Usburn, Robertus Gare, Thomas More, Johannes Lyllyng, Thomas Snawdon, Johannes Gascon, Johannes Baynbryg, Willelmus Craven, de numero viginti quatuor ; et Thomas Ward, homo legis, congregati fuerunt hic in camera, et coram eis veniunt Johannes Bobeon, Willelmus Kyrkeby, Johannes Hexham, Johannes Mosse et Willelmus Warter, carpentarii, pro se et universis hominibus artis sue hujus civitatis Ebor', et Johannes Ase, Willelmus Coupeland, Johannes Kyrkham, Johannes Symond et Ricardus Watson, tegularii domorum, pro se et omnibus hominibus artis

1—From "Huic" to the end is added, but in the same hand.

tegulariorum ejusdem civitatis, et submiserunt se judicio maioris
et consilii camere de et super factura novorum lodiorum que
vocantur *draghtlouers* venalium. Qui considerabant quod omnes
homines utrarumque arcium predictarum sint adinvicem
amici boni, et quod in signum amicitie inter eos firmande isti
artifices hic presentes simul oscularentur, et sic factum est; et
pro eo quod invenerunt quod capitalis factura lodiorum, que
vocantur *draghtlouers*, pertinuit et pertinet principaliter ad
carpentarios, ideo considerabant quod omnes tegularii, tam
presentes quam futuri hujus civitatis, facientes hujusmodi lodia
et ea vendentes, sint contributorii ad paginam carpentariorum
annuatim ad unum denarium tantum, primo termino solucionis
incipiente ad festum Corporis Christi anno isto; et quod tegula-
tores domorum decetero ponant lodia super domos universas
sive sint de factura sua propria vel de factura carpentariorum,
bene, debite, et fideliter, sine murmure vel contradiccione; ita
quod hujusmodi lodia priusquam ponantur super domos sint
scrutata per scrutatores carpentariorum, et quod optimum
lodium decetero vendatur pro x d., et non ultra; secundum
vero lodium minoris quantitatis pro viij d., et aliud lodium tocie
quantitatis pro vj d., sive sint de factura hominum unius artis
vel alterius. Et quod omnes districciones tegulariorum, ante hec
tempora capte et tente per carpentarios pro solucione ad paginam
carpentariorum, sint deliberate tegulariis sine aliquo inde solvendo
carpentariis, et si quis obedire noluerit, quod habeat imprisona-
mentum ad voluntatem maioris, pro tempore existentis, et
consilii camere, et solvat xl s. ad opus communitatis. Et quod
ammodo emendent et ponant vetera lodia super domos sicut
consueverunt, sub pena supradicta. Burton, Rog.

Ordinacio broggos [*sic*] *lanarum.*

(*fo.* 285). Memorandum quod ij^{do} de Julii, 6 Henr. vi. (1428),
Willelmus Bowes, maior hujus civitatis Ebor', Ricardus Russell,
Johannes Moreton, Thomas Gare, Thomas Bracebryg, Willelmus
Ormesheued, Johannes Aldestanemore, Thomas Snawdon, alder-
manni ejusdem; Nicholaus Blakburn, junior, Thomas Carre,
vicecomites; Thomas More, Johannes Gascoygne, Willelmus

Craven, Willelmus Bedale, et Willelmus Gyrlyngton, de numero xxiiij^{or}, congregati fuerunt hic in camera, et consencientibus illis ordinatum est pro utilitate communi quod omnes extranei, de quacumque parte venientes ad civitatem istam Ebor' cum lana venali, illam portet integre ad forum et mercatum Jovis in eadem civitate, et illam ibidem publice in aperto vendicioni exponat, et in nullo loco alio ; et vendat tribus diebus mercati in singulis septimanis contingentibus, et non ante horam nonam, nec in aliis domibus nec hospiciis, sub pena vj s. viij d. solvendorum camere et arti ; et quod forinsecus non vadat cum lana sua venali de domo ad domum infra libertatem hujus civitatis. Sed si forinseci aliqui dimittant lanam aliquam invenditam in mercato predicto in aliquibus diebus mercatorum, quod tunc hospitetur et custodiatur in domibus hospiciorum suorum per supervisum Thome Addyson ad hoc assignati, et cujuslibet alterius ad hoc postea assignandi, et reportetur in mercatum die proxima mercati, ut vendatur per supervisum eorumdem ; et quod nullus vendat lanam aliquam nisi in mercato predicto nisi sit de libertate hujus civitatis sub pena forisfacture illius lane ; et quod nullus hujus civitatis se intromittat de lana alicujus extranei, nisi tantummodo ille cujus lana est vel aliquis de suis, et quod nullus liber homo sit socius cum aliquo extraneo, nec cooperiat lanam suam in locis suis sub pena forisfacture libertatis sue ; et quod nullus de libertate hujus civitatis capiat aliquem extraneum ad vendendum lanam suam in mercato, ac si esset lana alicujus extranei, sub pena forisfacture libertatis sue ; et quod omnes venientes cum lana venali facient warantam universis emptoribus lanarum, quod lane sue venales erunt concordantes et ejusdem secte cum vellere superiori, et eque bene infra sicut extra in pannis in quibus lane involvuntur ; et si aliqua lana inveniatur non concordans deliberabitur venditori, et quod solucio sibi fiat pro lana illa que bona fuerit et concordans, sub pena vj s. viij d. ; et super hoc proclamacio facta fuit, et broggatores lanarum ordinati et jurati, Johannes Sylton, Johannes Marche, et Robertus Appilby, et quod capiant pro labore suo duos denarios de sacco de emptore, et quod universi tenentes domos in libertate civitatis pro lanis suis ibidem hospitandis sint contributorii ad paginam broggatorum singulis annis in ludo Corporis Christi. Burton. Rog.

Marsshals.[1]

(*fo.* 285, *b.*) Memorandum that thise are the ordenauncez underwryten that are made, grauntend and stabled be the assent and consent of all the hale crafte of the marsshals in the cite and the subbarbes of Yorke, and the ordenauncez trewly forto be haldyn and forto be keped for evermore be all the ahle crafte beforsayd, the whylk was made and grauntend be the persones underwryten apon the Sononday [*sic*] nexte befor the feste of the purificacion of oure Lady (26 January), in the yhere of oure Lorde mccccix, 11 Heur. iv.

Walterus Holme, Willelmus Huntyngton, Thomas Marsshall. Ricardus Wykeham, Willelmus Hoton, Willelmus Innocent, Johannes Burn, Johannes Travers, Johannes Shupton, Willelmus Newland, Thomas Grenewod, Johannes Warkeworth, Thomas Holton, Radulphus Marsshall, Johannes Cowesby, Willelmus Newsom, Johannes Neuton, junior, Johannes Heburn, Robertus Carylhyll, Ricardus Gillyot, Johannes Melsynby, Thomas Burton, Ricardus Bradschawe, Hugo Mannyng, Robertus Westefeld, Robertus Johnson, Johannes Knyght.

In primis, it is ordand be the assent of all the hale crafte beforsayd that ilkane of tham sal be obedient to thair sercheours of the same crafte, and com to tham when thai are warned, upon the payn of xij *d.*, for any thyng that touches the reule or the governaunce of the crafte, bot yf he haf resonable cause to be excused by, the to [*sic*] halve to the chambre and the tother halve to the crafte forto be payd, als ofte tyme als any of the sayd crafte is funden gylty in the said article.

Item, it is ordand that the padghand maistres of the said crafte sall warn all the crafte, als ofte tymes als thai sall be charged be the sayd sercheours, apon the payn of xx *d.*, forto be payd in the fourme beforsayd.

Item, it is ordand that no man of the sayd crafte sall putte nor sette no hors shoue apon no hors fete that are pared be any other man, bot if that same man haf gyffyn hym upp, apon the

---

1—" Iste ordinaciones reformantur tempore Roberti Maskue, maioris," is written in the margin.

THE ORDINANCES OF THE MARSHALS (1409)

payn of xl d., forto be payd als oftetymes als any person is fouden gylty in the same poynt.

Item, it is ordand that no man of the sayd crafte sall putt no cure to no hors that is or sall be under the cure of ane other man of the same crafte, bot that same other man haf clerely giffen up the same hors, apon payn of xl d., for to be payd als oftetymes als any of the same crafte is funden gylty in the fourm beforsayd.

Item, it is ordand that no man of the sayd crafte take no hors for to sho or hele of no man that is customer to any of the sayd crafte, and he haf knawlege that the said customer awe any monee to the tother man, apon the payn of xl d. for to be payd in the fourm beforsaid.

Item, it is ordand that if any of the said crafte undertake for to hele any hors, and he be noght of sufficiant cunyng, and than he send for ane other man of the same crafte, that same man sal com at the forsaid sande and sall do his cure to the sayd hors, so alway that he haf resonabyll salare for his travail; and what person of the said crafte that refuses for to com in the maner beforsayd sall pay xx d. in the fourm beforsayd.

(fo. 287). Item, it is ordand that no man of the sayd crafte sall putte nor sette no sho to no hors fote apon the Sonondays to no custumer, bot if it so be that the same custumer be putt to travell at the same day and nedelyng behoves for to travell, and also to husbands of the cuntre and to straungers that sodanly comes to hym, the whilk is nedefull, and what person that dose contrary he for to pay xl d. in the fourm beforsayd.

Item, it is ordand that no man of the sayd crafte sall go to innes, bot if he be sente after, upon the payn of xl d., forto be payd in the fourm beforsayd als ofte tymes als any person of the sayd crafte is funden gylty.

Item, it is ordand that no man of the sayd crafte sall procure nor cherys no custumer fra ane other man of the same crafte, nor serife hym unto the tyme that he haf full knawlege that thai be fully accorded and agreed of all rekenyng, upon the payn of xl d., to be payd in the fourm beforsayd als ofte tymes als any person of the sayd crafte is funden gilty in the same poynt.

Item, [1]it is ordand that no maistre sall sett no servant of the sayd crafte upon wark for les terme than for a hale yher aponles than he haf beyn apprentesse in the same cite; bot if any maistre sett hym apon warke for a wouke and ane other maistre for ane other wouke, and than the tane of the maistres forto occupy hym for a hale yhere, and what maistre that dose the contrary sal pay vj s. viij d. in the fourm beforsayd.

Item, is is ordand that no person of the same crafte sall sett upp no shopp nor occupy als maistre in the sayd crafte wythin the franchyse of this cite, before the tyme he be dewly and trewly serched, and funden, and approved for ane able werkman be the serchours of the sayd crafte to occupy als maistre to the avayle of the kyngys poeple, worship also for thys cite, and honeste for the crafte. And yf he take apon hym at any tyme to set uppe and occupy als maister in the sayd crafte, before he be serched and abled agayns the wyll of the sercheours and gude men of the crafte, he to forfet xx s. to the chambre and the sayd crafte be even porcions at ilka tyme he dose it.

Item, that ylk man of the sayd crafte come to Seynt Loy evensangs and hys messes at Seynt William chapell on Ousebryg, and to hys mete, opayn of vj d. to Seynt Loy lyght, bot if he be seke or els that he hafe a resonable lettyng to excuse hym by.

[2]Item, it is ordenyd by the assent of all the holl crafte that no man of the said craft shall wyrke no other men servantes, nor prentyses, nor jourman, unto suche tyme as he be clere of his said maister uppon payn of vj s. viij d., the one half to the chambre and the other to the crafte, as ofte tymes as any of the said crafte is found gyltie in the same.

[3]Item, that no maister of the said crafte shall take any apprentys for lesse terme then vij yeres, and the vij yere to be hyerd as his master and he can agree, uppon payn of vj s. viij d. to the chambre and crafte by evyn porcions. And that every person, as well forren as apprentys, to pay iiij d. to the crafte at the entryng of his name into there bookes.[2]

1—This clause is crossed through and vacat written by the side.
2—Printed by Miss Toulmin Smith, Antiquary, XI., pp. 106–107.
3—These two ordinances are written in a later hand. Against each ordinance a few words referring to the contents are written.

(*fo.* 286).[1] And all the hole craft of the smythes in the said citee on the morn after the feste of the Concepcion . . . .[2] xliij hafe agreed and boun thaim to offre at both the festes of Saint Loy and to kepe the firste feste halyday in the . . . .[2] aboun rehersed.

And after this bothe the said craftes afore William Bowes, the yonger, mayre of the said citee, on the morn after the Concepcion, ccccxliij [*sic*] hafe assented and frely boun thaim the . . . .[2] what man so evere settes up and occupies as maistre . . . .[2] settyng up xviij *d.* to the mayntenyng of the said torches and lyghtes, and who so evere . . . . . .[2] forfaite vj *s.* viij *d.*, to be payd to the chambre and the craft be even porciones.

(*fo.* 286, *b.*) Walt. Marshall, Rog. Marsshall, Ric. Bradeshaw, Rob. Watson, Rad. Loksmyth, Rob. Lutton, Rob. Leysmyth, Th. Bew.

Marsshals and smyths.

(*fo.* 287, *b.*) Memorandum, whare a lang stryfe and debate was moeved and hadde betwix the marsshals and smyths of the cite of York, in alsmykell that the smyths alleged and sayde that the marsshals occupyde thair craft and had tharof the maste part of thair lyvyng, and tharfo thay chalenged of tham to pay to thair pageand ; and the marsshals alleged agayn that certeyn smyths wroght and sald diverse thynges pertenant to thayr crafte, and tharfor thay asked of tham pagand sylver. And thus thay war many dayes and yerys in variance, and ayther crafte trubild other, and yerely tuke and held distresse of other so ferr furth that many yerys mairs and the chambre was hugely vexed wyth tham. Neverthelesse at the last thurgh the gude consell and mediacion of John Aldestanemore, mair, bathe the craftes beforesayde put tham in the jugement and awarde of William Barton, skynner, John Huthwayt, taillour, Robert Allerton, barker, and John Neuton, glover, and assured tham to stand and abyde fully thair award in hegh and in lawe; if thay

1—This folio is interleaved.
2—The ends of the lines are evidently missing.

myght accord tham of the demandes and maters abouensayd.
And if thay four varyed in any poynt and myght noght accord,
than thay four arbitruors suld hafe recource to the mair and
consell of the chambre, and the partyes abide thair jugement.
And her apon the sayd four arbitruros, at the request of the sayd
mair and prayer of the sayd partyes, tuke apon tham to trete in
this mater indifferently, and all as a man, and to make an nend,
if thay myght ; and so when thay had lang tyme tretyd in this
mater indifferentely, and herd and understand wele the allegeance
and evidence of bathe sydes, than at the last thay come before
William Bowes, mayr, all four arbitrours, the sevent day of
Apryll, 6 Henry vi. (1428), and thar, in presence of the mayr, thay
sayd that thay ware fully accorded of the poyntes and the
variance betwix the sayd craftes, and thair accordement was
this :—that the sayd craftes suld hafe thair serchours, and thair
serche, and thayre pageant maisters yerely, als thay hafe had in
tymes passed ; and that a man of the a crafte and a man of the
tother crafte suld walke to gyder yerely, and gedyr uppe thair
pageant sylver of men of bathe craftes, and of thair bather costages
bryng furthe thair bather playes, and uphald thair torches in
the procession of Corpus Christi day and all thair lyghtes in the
mynster and in other places ; and ayther crafte hafe trewe
rekkenyng of other, and yf any mone leve unspendyd at thair
rekkenyng, that it be spendyd to the oeps and the profyte of
bathe the sayd craftes. Burton.

Marshalles and smythez.

(*fo.* 288). Memorandum, that the xiiij day of December, the
yere of our Lorde mccccxliij, in the counseil chaumbre of the
citee of York, before William Bowes, maire of the same citee, by
the ful assent and consent of the craftes of marsshalles and
smythes of this citee of York and suburbes of the same, thies
ordenauncez undrewriten wer made and grauntted to be kept for
ever more ; that is to say, that al the lightes and torches that
langes to both the saide craftes, as wele in the mynster as in
other places, fro nowe furth be made at the costes and expenses
of both the said craftes, and spended to the use of eithere of

THE ORDINANCES OF THE MARSHALS (1443 ?)

thaym, as wele in the procession upon Corpus Christi day, as at beriall of every man and of thaire wifes that er or shalbe of the said craftes.

Item, it is ordaned that the pageant of both the saide craftes fro nowe furth in the play of Corpus Christi be joyntly broght furth at the costes of bothe the said craftes, and that every man of the said craftes shalbe prevy to the receytes and expenses of al money that shal be receyved to the said pageantes, as wele pageant silver as other; and that the pageant maisters of both the said craftes shal make thair rakenyng and gife accompt evere yere fro nowe furth upon Sononday next before Missomerday, upayn of iiij s., to be payed that oon half to the chaumbre and that other halfe to the said craftes.

Item, that every maister of the said craftes shal com to Seint William chapell upon Ouse brigg every yere, to thair devyne service of Seint Loy, upon the morn after Missomerday, that is to say, to the first evensang and to messe upon the morn, and kepe it dere [sic] haliday, and com to thair mete al togeder upayn of vj d. to be payde to the said craftes, bot if he have a resonable excusasion. And also that every man of the said craftes shal com to messe at the said chapell every yere upon the morn after Seint Andrewe day. ×

Item, that every man of the said craftes as oft tymes as thay shalbe warned by thair serchours forto mete and com to geder for eny gode rule to be made in the said craftes, or for eny thinges that er profitable and worship to this citee, shal com at thair warnyng o payn of forfatour of a liber wax to the lightes of the said craftes.

Item, that every man of the said craftes, that has bene pryntes within this citee, shal pay at his first settyng upp as a maister in the said craftes xviij d., to the lightes of the said craftes, except thaym that er fraunchestmen sonnes of the said craftes within this citee.

(fo. 288, b.) Item, if eny man of the saide craftes com to this citee, that has not bene pryntes within this citee, and wil occupy as maister, he shall pay at his first settyng upp ij s. to the lightes of the said craftes, etc.

Item, if eny aliene com to this citee and will occupy as maister, he shal pay at his first settyng upp vj *s.* viij *d.*, that one halve to the chaumbre and that other halve to the craftes.

Item, it is ordayned, by the ful assent and consent of both the saide craftes, that every man of the same craftes that shalbe founde rebell or disobeiant unto his serchours, shal lose xij *d.* to be payed in the forme aforewriten, as oft tymez as he be found gilty in that by halve.

Billa ista presentata fuit coram maiore supradicto die, anno et loco supradictis, per Walterum Marsshall, Radulphum Loksmyth, Ricardum Bradshawe, Robertum Lutton, Robertum Watson, Thomam Bewe, Rogerum Smyth, et Robertum Cotes, in nomine omnium artificiorum predictorum.

Pro Eustachio Hunter.

Henricus Percy, comes Northumbr' ac gardianus *Estmerc* Anglie versus Scociam, omnibus ad quos presentes litere nostre pervenerint, salutem. Sciatis quod die confectionis presencium Eustachius Hunter, Scotus, oriundus in Scocia, coram nobis super sancta Dei evaungelia per ipsum corporaliter tacta juravit quod de cetero erit verus et fidelis Anglicus ac fidem et ligenciam geret domino nostro Regi Edwardo Anglie, qui nunc est, heredibus et successoribus suis, ac omnes leges, custumas, et consuetudines dicti regni Anglie, a supremo usque ad inferiora, in omnibus obediet et confirmabit durante tota vita sua. In cujus rei testimonium has literas nostras fieri fecimus patentes. Datum apud castrum nostrum de Alnewyk, ultimo die mensis Octobris, 11 Edw. iv. (1471). Presens scriptum irrotulatum fuit tempore Johannis Tonge, nuper maioris civitatis Ebor', et sacramentum suum coram ipso super sancta Dei evaungelia prestitit quod perimplebit et custodiet omnia et singula premissa etc.

(*fo.* 289). De carnificibus quod possint vendere carnes usque ad octavam pulsacionem in mane singulis diebus Dominicis, non obstante alio priori statuto prohibente.[1]

1—In the margin, "Vide de ista materia in vij^{mo} folio precedenti," is written.

BUTCHERS' SHOPS TO BE OPEN ON SUNDAYS (1428)

Duodecimo die Aprilis, 6 Henr. vi. (1428), Willelmus Bowes, maior, Ricardus Russell, Johannes Northeby, Johannes Moreton, Henricus Preston, Thomas Esyngwald, Willelmus Ormesheued, Johannes Aldestanemore, Thomas Snaudon, aldermanni ; Nicholaus Blakburn, Thomas Carre, vicecomites ; Johannes Hewyk, Thomas More, Robertus Middelton, Willelmus Craven, Thomas Kyrkeham, Thomas Acton, Willelmus Bedale, Willelmus Gaytesheued, Johannes Warde, Johannes Brounflete, de numero xxiiij^{or}, congregati fuerunt hic in camera, et audita gravi querela multorum de communitate civium hujus civitatis quod carnifices ejusdem die Dominica proximo precedente in mane tenebant fenestras suas et shoppas clausas, nec vendere voluerunt carnes aliquas populo venienti ad emendum, ad gravem injuriam et scandalum civitatis nisi remedium apponatur. Super hoc igitur ordinatum erat, ad honorem civitatis et aisiamentum populi, quod decetero universi carnifices dicte civitatis teneant singulas shoppas et fenestras suas apertas, et carnes venales in eis habeant, et publice vendicioni exponant, ad serviendum populo emere volenti, singulis djebus Dominicis, in mane usque ad octavam pulsacionem campane orilogii communitatis super pontem Use, sic quod carnifices misse sue parochiali possint interesse. Et ab illa hora octava teneant shoppas suas clausas usque post vesperas hora consueta completas in ecclesiis parochialibus, et ipsis vesperis completis, quod extunc dicti carnifices teneant fenestras et shoppas suas apertas pro carnibus ad cenas hominum providendis. Et si quis carnificum ordinacionem istam non perimpleverit, quod solvat vj *s.* viij *d.*, usui communitatis, nomine pene, pro vice qualibet qua hujus ordinacionis contrarium fecerit, et super hoc per recordum sufficiens convincatur. Et subsequenter eodem die hec presens ordinacio fuit per maiorem et communitatem hujus civitatis in gilda aula ejusdem confirmata, et de consensu omnium approbata. Burton.

Universis Sancte Matris Ecclesie filiis, ad quos presentes litere pervenerint, officialis curie Ebor', salutem in Domino sempiternam. Noverit universitas vestra quod Robertus Ingylby, armiger, Robertus Selby, Ricardus Rameshede, cives Ebor', Johannes Dubber, Johannes Burneley, merceri, Johannes Pacok, Johannes Burneby, clerici, Robertus Feriby, *wefear*, et Robertus

Forster, *walker*, de Ebor', nuper coram nobis ad premunicionem
Isabelle, relicte Johannis Bowland, nuper civis et merceri civitatis
Ebor' defuncti, ac Johannis Ford, ejusdem civitatis merceri,
executorum testamenti ipsius defuncti, personaliter comparentes,
jurarunt et quilibet eorum juravit ad sancta Dei evaungelia per
ipsos corporaliter tacta super requirend(is) ab eisdem confessiones
publicas et verba, quasi in extremis per dictum defunctum prolata
concernentibus, plenam et meram dicere veritatem. Qui quidem
Robertus Ingylby, Ricardus Rameshede, Johannes Pacok,
Johannes Burneby et Johannes Dubber, sic jurati et per nos
diligencius requisiti, dixerunt, et quilibet eorum dixit, in suo
hujusmodi juramento, quod die Veneris proximo post festum
Omnium Sanctorum ultimo preterito (4 November, 1429), personaliter presentes fuerunt ipsi jurati infra domum habitacionis
predicti Johannis Bowland, qui tunc in vico vocato saynt Andrewgate civitatis predicte situata inhabitavit. Ubi et quando idem
(*fo.* 289, *b.*) Johannes Bowland, infirmitate pestilencie vexatus
graviter et detentus, sane tamen et bone memorie existens, ut
dixerunt, de qua infirmitate die Sabbati proximo tunc sequente
moriebatur, juravit et dixit palam publice et expresse per fidem
suam et juramentum suum, et sicut ipse salvaretur et foret unus
in extremo judicio salvandorum, quod domino Roberto Stavelay,
rectori sive preposito ecclesie de Kyrkbyorblawers, nichil debuit
racione alicujus scripti obligatorii seu quovis alio modo, sed ipse
dominus, ut ipse idem Johannes Bowland dixit in fide sua hujusmodi et juramento, sibi debuit octo vel novem libras pecunie.
Prefatique Johannes Burneby, Robertus Feriby et Robertus
Forster, jurati et per nos interrogati, dixerunt, et quilibet eorum
dixit in juramento suo coram nobis prestito, ut prefertur, quod
sepius anno presenti et modicum ante predictum diem Sabbati
audiverunt predictum Johannem dicere et jurare quod ipse
predicto domino Roberto Stavelay rectori sive preposito de
Kyrkbyorblawers, non debuit arum [*sic*] aliquod vel argentum;
et dixit idem Johannes temporibus hujusmodi quod, si posset
ipsum dominum Robertum capere in civitatem Ebor', ipsum pro
pecuniis sibi debitis, et pro finali compoto habendo inter ipsos
faceret arrestari. In quorum omnium testimonium atque fidem
has literas nostras fieri fecimus testimoniales, sigillo officii nostri

pendente signatas. Datum Ebor', xij die mensis Decembris, anno Domini millesimo cccc^{mo} viciesimo nono.

Henricus, Dei gracia rex Anglic et Francie et dominus Hibernie, omnibus ad quos presentes litere pervenerint, salutem.[1] Sciatis quod, de gracia nostra speciali et de avisamento et assensu dominorum spiritualium et temporalium ac communitatis regni nostri Anglie in ultimo parliamento nostro existencium, auctoritate ejusdem parliamenti, et pro quinque marcis nobis solutis in hanaperio nostro, concessimus Henrico Market infra partes Almannie oriundo, quod ipse et heredes sui de cetero sint indigene et taliter tractentur, teneantur, reputentur, et gubernentur, prout veri et fideles ligei nostri infra regnum nostrum Anglic oriundi. Et quod predictus Henricus et heredes sui predicti terras, tenementa, redditus, advocaciones, servicia, reversiones, et alias possessiones quascumque infra dictum regnum nostrum et alibi infra dominium et potestatem nostra perquirere, dare, concedere, alienare, et eisdem gaudere et heredari possint, adeo libere et pacifice sicut aliquis alius ligeorum nostrorum predictorum infra regnum predictum oriundorum ; habendum et tenendum predictas terras, tenementa, redditus, advocaciones, servicia, reversiones, et alias possessiones quascumque, sibi et eorum heredibus et assignatis, aut alio modo quocumque, absque aliqua impeticione vel gravamine imperpetuum. Et quod predictus Henricus et heredes sui predicti in omnibus curiis nostris et placeis, tam infra regnum nostrum predictum quam alibi, omnimodas actiones reales, personales et mixtas, habere et prosequi, ac in eisdem curiis et placeis implacitare et implacitari, respondere et responderi possint eisdem modo et (*fo.* 290) forma, et adeo libere et integre sicut aliquis ligeorum nostrorum infra regnum, dominia et potestatem nostra predicta oriundorum. Et ulterius concessimus quod predictus Henricus et heredes sui predicti omnimoda privilegia et consuetudines habere et eis uti et gaudere possint, prout ligei nostri predicti habent, utuntur et gaudent, eo quod predictus Henricus in partibus predictis oriundus fuit, ut premittitur, non obstante. Proviso semper quod predictus Henricus et heredes sui predicti nobis homagium ligeum faciat,

---

1—Pat. R., 8 Henry VI., pt. 2, m. 35.

ac lotto et scotto contributores existant, necnon taxas, tallagia, et alia denaria et onera quecumque solvant, prout alii infra regnum nostrum predictum oriundi facere consueverunt et tenentur. In cujus rei testimonium has literas nostras fieri fecimus patentes. Teste me ipso apud Westmonasterium, vicesimo sexto die Februarii anno regni nostri octavo (1429-30).

Per peticionem in parliamento.

[1]Honorabili et prepotenti domino et semper dilecto Henrico de Borssalia, domino de Campveer, de Sandenburch et de Vlyssyng, benivoli vestri vobisque et vestri omni tempore amici, maior, vicecomites, et aldermanni civitatis Ebor' in Anglia, reverencias et honores multiplices, sicut decet. Vera siquidem concordia, amor solitus continuataque amicia, quos inter vos et nos diebus antiquis effectualiter crevisse et nullatenus decrevisse cognovimus, nobis magnam prebent leticie causam, et non immerito occasionem gaudendi ministrant. Novitque Deus, qui nichil ignorat, et concors vulgi sentencia scit testari, quod nichil hucusque ex parte nostrorum concivium intercessit, nec dante Domino quidquam de velle nostro, verbo vel facto procedet, quod mutue nostre dileccionis nedum et plusquam triplicem pacis inviolate funiculum dissolvet. Animadvertimus enim unavobiscum quam fructuosa et utilis sit hominibus virtus unitatis, que nunquam divisionem capit, et quam bonum sit eciam et jocundum habitare fratres semper in unum. Ex altera, tamen, parte modo unum quod nobis multum displicet per vestras literas experimur, quod quidam Johannes Wacker, vester naucterus notabilis et subditus de Campveer, cum navi sua et attinenciis ejusdem et aliis bonis suis per quosdam ligeos domini nostri, regis Anglie, et precipue de Novo Castello, captus est, spoliatus, privatus, et dire ab eisdem modo hostili tractatus; super quibus reformandis a nobis opem et auxilium postulasti, ut ubi requiritur et oportunum fuerit, et precipue ad illos de Novo Castello et de Hull quos precipue presens tangit negocium ita solicitari velimus, ut idem Johannes de navi, bonisque, et rebus suis, ad ipsum et suos complices dumtaxat pertinentes liberacionem habeat, ut est juris. Super hoc preclara vestra dominacio scire dignetur, quod in

---

1—In the left margin, " Litera responsiva litere domini de Campveer."

hominibus villarum Novi Castelli et de Hull, in hiis que extra libertatem nobis concessam transgressi (*fo.* 290, *b.*) fuerint, nullam punicionem aut jurisdictionem habemus, quo causante ipsos ad nostrum examen vocare non possumus, ut veniant ad respondendum super transgressionibus supradictis. Unum tamen veraciter unanimes profitemur, quod si probabiliter quisquam de concivibus nostris culpabilis inventus fuerit in premissis, vel eciam si auctoritatem haberemus de delinquentibus hiis qui extra nos sunt, non dimitteremus multum quousque juxta totum posse nostrum dictus Johannes de dampnis, que occasione premissa passus est, debitam et celerem consequeretur emendam, et potissime vestrarum precum instancia et pro Deo. Unde vestram preclaram nobilitatem fervidis et sinceris interpellamus affectibus, ut in hiis que ad nos non pertinent punienda, nostram impotenciam habere dignemini excusatam, licet autem, ut scribitis, omnes de corona nobili Anglicana et in rebus publicis simul gaudere debent et tristari. Hoc non negamus. Veritas tamen est quod nos, sicut et singule civitates et burgi regni Anglie, ex concessionibus et beneplacitis regum ad certa franchesias, libertates, et priviligia, inter nos exercenda, separatim limitamur et terminos nostros in hiis preterire non debemus, nec audemus eis abuti, ne forsan priviligia nobis et eis concessa ea occasione amittantur, quod avertat bonus Jesus. Nos, nichilominus, considerantes tenerrime que petitis ac desideriis cordis vestri quantum in nobis est inclinare et favere volentes, pro remedio contra transgressores predictos in hac parte habendo indubitanter promittimus et concedimus una voce, quod nostras interponemus partes et curas viis et modis quibus juste poterimus, omni segnitie et mora postpositis, penes maiores et legis ministros Novi Castelli et de Hull, ut si eis inter se modo aliquo constare possit de nominibus delinquencium in premissis contra Johannem Wacker predictum, in pacis boneque dilectionis inter terram et terram hucusque nutrite perturbacionem, quod tunc ipsi in signum futuri amoris et justicie complementum per stricte punicionis rigorem compellant, aut compelli faciant in quantum possunt, hujusmodi delinquentes, ut jam dictus Johannes, navis, bonorumque et rerum suorum, quibus privatus et spoliatus erat, debitam et integram restitucionem habeat, sine diminucione aliqua vel concelamento quocumque, sic quod ipsis transgressionibus et aliis imposterum cedat in terroris exemplum. Reverende domine, o si stemus et perseveremus invicem in amicicia vera et non ficta, et concedente Altissimo, non deficiet ex parte nostra nec concivium nostrorum, et si, quod absit, hujus contrarium per aliquos sub potestate nostra et districtu constitutos contigerit evenire, Deum vocamus in testem, quod hoc probato noctes ducemus insompnes quousque id, quod injuriatum est, ad vestrum honorem et subditorum vestrorum justiciam fuerit reformatum. Et pax Dei, que exsuperat omnem sensum, statum vestrum in sublimitate gradus custodiat et longitudine dierum adimpleat, ad sui laudem in amplitudine caritatis. In cujus rei testimonium sigillum officii maioratus civitatis Ebor' predicte presentibus est appensum. Datum apud Ebor', vicesimo die Augusti, anno Domini millesimo quadringentesimo tricesimo tercio.

(*fo.* 291, *b.*)[1] In Dei nomine, amen. Anno Domini millesimo cccclxxvij° et 17 Edw. iv., per avisamentum Johannis Tonge, tunc maioris, et tocius consilii camere, quod pagina purificacionis beate Marie Virginis de cetero ludebit [*sic*] annuatim in festo Corporis Christi sicut alie pagine. Et super hoc concordatum est quod cementarii istius civitatis pro tempore existentes portant onera et expensas pagine predicte, et ipsam in bono et honesto modo annuatim ludendam producent in ordine, cum ad hoc premuniti fuerint, sicut inde coram maiore, pro tempore existente, voluerint respondere. Et quod laboratores istius civitatis, annuatim decetero, videlicet, *kidberers, garthyners, erthewallers, pavers, dykers, groundwallers with erthe*, qui nunc sunt et pro tempore existent, in vigilia Corporis Christi annis singulis imperpetuum solvent et liberabunt infra cameram consilii istius civitatis camerariis ejusdem pro tempore existentibus tresdecim solidos et quatuor denarios, in auxilium expense ipsius pagine, sub pena viginti sex solidorum et octo denariorum camere hujus civitatis et reparacioni pagine predicte equaliter dividendorum. Hoc facto, predicti laboratores decetero sint quieti de omnibus et singulis aliis paginis infra istam civitatem ludendis. Et insuper quod dicti

---

1—Folio 291 (cclxxxi) is blank. First 14 lines quoted by Miss Toulmin Smith, xxi.

cementarii habebunt annuatim in vigilia Corporis Christi tresdecim solidos et quatuor denarios de camerariis istius civitatis, pro tempore existentibus, et quod dicti cementarii annuatim producent dictam paginam ac portabunt omnes expensas et onera decetero dicte pagine pertinencia, sicut volunt annuatim respondere maiori, pro tempore existenti, penam forisfacture in aliis paginis inde edite et provise. Et quod magistri pagine dictorum cementariorum cant et circuant cum prefata pagina in locis ex antiqua consuetudine. Et quod dicti laboratores inter se singulis annis elegent [*sic*] quatuor homines in scrutatores, et ipsi colligent de omnibus et singulis laboratoribus, laborantibus infra istam civitatem, suburbia et libertatem ejusdem, predictam summam tresdecim solidorum et quatuor denariorum, et illam summam liberabunt infra cameram istam sicut predictum est, sub pena predicta. Et si contingat quod aliquis de laboratoribus predictis ad aliquod tempus sit rebellis et reneiet solvere, tunc predicti quatuor homines vel unus illorum habebunt unum servientem camere ad clavam, et ipse transibit cum eis in omnibus temporibus necessariis et oportunis ex precepto maioris pro tempore existentis etc. Et quod quilibet trium[1] occupacionum laboratororum predictorum, videlicet, *erthwallers*, *pavers*, et *groundwallers* solvant, et quilibet eorum per se solvat annuatim dicte pagine iiij *d*., et alii laboratores prescripti ij *d*., sub pena xij *d*. etc., camere et dicte pagine equaliter solvendorum etc.

Tapitours.[2]

(*fo*. 292). Voiez plusours et aulters ordynanucz de cest occupacion, faitz xiiij jour d'August, lanne notre seignour le roy E. vi. synke, come pleynement appiert en livre Thome Appleyard, adonsques mairour (1552).

In primis, ordinatum est et concordatum, tam pro communi utilitate tocius populi domini regis quam artificiorum artis predicte, quod nullus artifex artis supradicte operabitur in eodem artificio, nisi dum lux diei sibi ad operandum racionabiliter sufficere

---

1—MS. trior, (triorum).
2—Above these ordinances is written, ": Iste ordinaciones reformantur tempore Christoferi Herbert, maioris."

poterit, cum instrumento dicte artis vocato *Shotill*, sub pena decem solidorum, solvendorum tociens quociens aliquis eorum contra dictam ordinacionem deliquerit, duas partes communitati hujus civitatis, et terciam partem dicte arti ad sustentacionem pagine et ludi Corporis Christi, per dictos artifices sustentate.

Item, quod nullus magister dicte artis capiat aliquem apprenticium pro minore termino quam pro septem annis simul ; et quod nullus magister ejusdem artis procurabit nec desiderabit apprenticium alterius magistri dicte artis, utrum sit plene etatis vel infra etatem, nisi prius concordet cum magistro illius apprenticii sub pena xxx *s*., quorum due partes camere et tercia pars artificiis supradictis erunt applicande.

Item, quod nullus magister artis predicte, nec uxor ejus, neque aliquis serviens ejusdem, transiet vel laborabit publice vel occulte cum mercatoribus ementibus *coverletta* seu *tapita* infra civitatem predictam ; sed ut ipsi emptores cant et libere emere valeant pro libito voluntatis sue, ubicumque voluerint, sine impedimento aut procuracione alicujus artificii predicti, in prejudicium seu detrimentum alterius artificii ejusdem artis, sub pena vj *s*. viij *d*., duas partes communitati et artificio predicto terciam partem, ut supra, etc.

Item, quod de omnibus pannis tam *coverlettis* quam *tapettis* forisfacturis, seu indebite operatis per quod forisfaciendi sint, communitas civitatis predicte habeat duas partes dictorum pannorum forisfactorum, et artificiarii dicte artis terciam partem, ut supra.

Item, quod nullus magister artificii predicti assumat aliquem in apprenticium suum in arte predicta erudiendum, nisi ille apprenticius sit natus sub potestate et legiancia domini regis nostri Anglie, et liber homo, sub pena xl *s*., duas partes dicte communitati et arti predicte terciam partem, ut supra, etc.

(*fo*. 292, *b*.) Item, quod si aliquis alienigina natus extra terram, sub potestate et legiancia regis nostri Anglie existentem, occupare voluerit ut magister in artificio supradicto infra libertatem civitatis predicte, solvat in prima occupacione sua ut magister in arte predicta communitati dicte civitatis xxvj *s*. viij *d*., et predicte arti xiij *s*. iiij *d*.

THE ORDINANCES OF THE TAPITERS (UNDATED)

Item, quod nullus magister artificii supradicti ponat aliquem extraneum ejusdem artis, qui subito veniet ad hunc civitatem, in opus vel laborem dicte artis antequam per scrutatores artis supradicte, pro tempore existentes, examinetur quod sit abilis et sufficienter eruditus in arte supradicta, sub pena x s. solvendorum forma supradicta. Et ulterius ordinatum est quod ille magister ejusdem artis, cui aliquis hujusmodi extraneus prius venerit, postquam examinatus fuerit et per dictos scrutatores habilis probatus et inventus fuerit ad serviendum et occupandum in eadem arte, habebit dictum extraneum pro salario competenti pre aliquo alio magistro ejusdem artis etc. [1]Proviso quod nullus magister conducet talem extraneum sine cognicione scrutatorum aut maioris.[1]

Item, quod quilibet magister artificii supradicti in propria persona sua cum pagina dicte artis in festo Corporis Christi transiet, et laborabit pro gubernacione ejusdem, quousque ludus dicte artis in locis assignandis et ordinandis per civitatem juxta ordinacionem ejusdem civitatis debite fuerit perimpletus, nisi aliquis eorum senectute, debilitate, seu infirmitate, aut alia causa excusacionis legitime et probabilis fuerit impeditus, quo casu contingente alium deputatum sufficientem loco suo providebit et ordinabit; et si aliquis eorum defecerit in aliqua parte hujus ordinacionis, solvat communitati et arti xij *d.* equis porcionibus applicandos, etc.

Item, quod nullus occupabit ut magister dicte artis nec utensilium anglice vocatum *a lome* levabit infra libertatem dicte civitatis, nisi prius fuerit apprenticius in eadem arte infra libertatem predictam, seu alibi in eadem arte sufficienter eruditus fuerit, sub pena xl *s.*, duas partes communitati et terciam partem arti persolvendas, et forisfacture libertatis sue deinceps infra eandem civitatem ulterius occupande. Proviso semper quod si contingat infuturo aliquem hominem ducere in uxorem aliquam mulierem hujus civitatis, que prius fuisset uxor alicujus viri defuncti, magistri dicte artis in eadem civitate, et voluerit occupare artem predictam infra eandem civitatem post sponsalia inter eos celebrata, quod ipse solvat xl *s.* communitati et arti predictis

---

1—In margin, "Addita tempore Thome Appleyerd, maioris," is written.

equaliter dividendos, antequam occupaverit in arte predicta, et extunc bene licebit sibi occupare et exercere in artificio supradicto quamdiu voluerit; ita semper quod (*fo.* 293) habeat hominem sufficientem instructum et in arte predicta eruditum, ad supervidendum et gubernandum opera servientum suorum in artificio predicto facienda, insuper observando et perimplendo omnia alia onera, statuta, et ordinaciones dicte artis, ordinata et imposterum ordinanda pro utilitate et comodo civitatis predicte, etc.

Item, quod omnes illi, qui utuntur artificio sepedicto infra dictam civitatem cujuscumque condicionis fuerint, conveniant et compareant in locis necessariis et oportunis, quociens et quandocumque premuniti fuerint, pro bono statu, regimine, et gubernacione dicte artis. Et si quis eorum infuturo cum premunitus fuerit ex causis predictis comparere noluerit, nisi legitime impeditus fuerit per sufficientem probacionem secundum discrecionem maioris, pro tempore existentis, forisfaciet et persolvet communitati et arti predictis iij *s.* iiij *d.*, equis porcionibus applicandos, etc.

Item, quod nullus artificii predicti recipiat filum alterius alicujus ad operandum secundum formam artis sue, nisi imponat et operetur filum illud seu aliud filum ejusdem qualitatis et bonitatis seu melioris in hujusmodi opere, et illud opus operetur tempore competenti absque aliquo defectu in substancia et opere artis supradicte, sub pena x *s.* solvendorum communitati et arti predictis equis porcionibus. Et si quis artificii predicti fecerit aliquem defectum sive transgressionem in aliquo opere dicte artis pertinentem sive spectantem, et ille vel illi cui seu quibus hujusmodi transgressio facta fuerit causam transgressionis sue scrutatoribus dicte artis ostendere voluerit seu voluerint, tunc ipsi scrutatores ejusdem artis pro tempore existentes scrutinium sufficienter super hujusmodi delictum secundum effectum juramenti sui facient, et dampna ejusdem transgressionis juste et plene taxabunt secundum quantitatem delicti; que quidem dampna idem artifex, sic delinquens per judicium dictorum scrutatorum, parti sic lese satisfaciet infra quadraginta dies tunc proximo sequentes, sub pena vj *s.* viij *d.* solvendorum communitati et arti equis porcionibus. Et si aliquis dicte artis, qui transgressus fuerit in forma predicta et non fecerit parti lese debitam satisfactionem secundum judicium scrutatorum predictorum infra quadraginta dies post scrutinium et judicium inde reddita, quod ex tunc ipse artifex sic delinquens lapso quadraginta dierum spacio cessit de occupacione sua in arte illa, quousque plenariam satisfactionem transgressionis supradicte fecerit in forma predicta, sub pena forisfacture libertatis sue civitatis predicte, etc.[1]

Carpenters.

(*fo*. 293, *b*.) Ordinacio carpentariorum civitatis Ebor', facta et confirmata quarto die Junii, 2 Edw. iv. (1462), per Johannem Thrisk, maiorem civitatis Ebor', et totum consilium camere ejusdem civitatis, sequitur in subscriptis.

In primus, it is ordeigned that, if any straunge carpenter com within the fraunchies and liberties of this citee, and occupie as a maistre in any poynt pertenyng unto the saide craft, he shal pay yerely, as lange and whensome ever that any suche straunger comes to this citee, to the charges of thair pageant and light on Corpus day Christi, iiij *d*.; and if any suche straunger walde be obstenate or refuyse to pay the said iiij *d*. yerely, when he occupies within the fraunchies of the saide citee, that than the maire for the tyme beyng and the counseill of the chaumbre shal supporte the said craft to streyne the saide straungers as the lawe will.

Item, that every free man of this citee, that occupies as maister in the saide craft, not beyng of the fraternite of the same, shal pay yerely to the chargies aforewriten as other wrightes doo, that be of the same fraternite.

Item, if any man of the said crafte presume uppon hym self to occupie as a maister in the same craft within the libertie of this citee, and his wark be fon unable and unsufficiently wroght by the serchours for the tyme beyng, at the instance of thaym that the warke is wroght unto, than he shall pay to the chaumbre and the craft by even porcions vj *s*. viij *d*. as oft tymes as he shalbe founde defective in that byhalve.

1—At the end, " Plus inde in secundo folio sequente," is written.

Item, if any man of the saide craft that is freman of this citee be rebell unto his serchours or be obstenate and contrarious ayeinst in any maner of poynt concernyng the wele and worship of this citee and of the saide craft, or that wil not com to his serchours, when he shalbe warned to assemble and mete with thaim and his craft, to say and to shewe his advise in al materes demaundable at any tyme for the wele and profeite of the same, withouten that he have a reisonable excuyse, he shall pay iij $s.$ iiij $d.$ in the fourme aforwriten, etc.

($fo.$ 294). Grant to John Nevell, lord Mountague, for term of life, of the subsidy and ulnage of sale cloth, with the forfeitures of the same in the county of York, Kyngeston upon Hull, and the city of York and suburbs. (8 July, 1 Edward vi.)[1] (1461).

Sadlers.

($fo.$ 295). The $xxiij^{to}$ daye of Feberyere in the xij^{to} yere of King Edward the iv. (1472-3), it was ordayned and ennacted, as wele by the mair and counsaill of the chamber of this cite of York, as by the assente and consente of all the maisters of the crafte of sadlers within this cite of York, for tyme beyng, in and for the appeasyng of divers controversiez than moved emonges thayme of the same crafte within the same cite, in that from now farthe yerely withoutyn ende all the maisters of the saide crafte within the same cite and suburbez of the same, for tyme beyng, shall be warned by thair serchiours of the saide crafte, for tyme being, in the vigill of the conversion of Saynt Poull, to mete in a convenient place within the same cite in the daye of the conversion of Sainte Poull than next aftre felowyng, thar and than to chuse ande elect thre serchiours of newe to be and occupy for the yere felowyng, in the maner and fourme that ensuyth. Firste, the thre olde serchiours shall than and thare put in thre names of the moste discrete and moste able maisters of the saide crafte, such as hath nat ben serchiours within the same crafte by the space of two yerez next tofore that of . . eding. And if all othir maisters of the saide crafte, or the more numbre of thaym

---

1—The date is not given in the Patent Roll, 1 Edward IV., pt. 4, m. 2.

als are so assembled, woll able and admitte the same thre lites
so put in to be thair serchiours for the yer felowyng, that than
it be leefull to the same thre litez so put, abled, and admitted for
to occupy and be serchiours of the saide occupacion within the
saide cite for the yere than next ensuyng. And if all the maisters
of the saide occupacion, or the more numbre of thamme than
and thar assembled, wolle nat able, admitte, ne chuse the same
thre litez so than thar put yn, ne none of thayme, that than it
shall be leefull to all the maisters of the same occupacion, or to
the more numbre of thayme thar so being elected to chuse and
eslyt othir thre able maisters of the same occupacion to be . . .[1]
serchiours within the saide occupacion for the yere than felowyng,
if the numbre of the saide maisters of the same occupacion than
for tyme beyng within the same cite woll suffise therunto. Forseyne alway and except any maister of the same occupacion
hereafter to yiffe, have, or bere voice in or to his aune election
to be serchiour in that occupacion.

Tapiters.[2]

(*fo*. 295, *b*.) The xij^t daie of the moneth of Julye in the
xiijth yere of our liege lord the King Edward the iv^t., in the
counsaill chambre of this cite, it was ordained as wele by the [*sic*]
Christofer Marshall, maire of the cite of York, as also by the assent
and consente of the godemen of the crafte of tapiters within the
cite of York, whos names ben ensuyant, for perpetuelly to be
observed and kepped, as wele for wele and worship of the saide
cite, as also for the worship and honeste of thaime of the same
crafte.

Firste, that every coverlett, called worstede ware of the
moste assisse, shall halde and contente in lengthe thre yerdes and
ane halfe, and in brede ij yerdes ande ane halfe; and also every
coverlett, called worsett ware of the leste assisse, halde and contente
in lengthe iij yerdes and a halfe quarter, and in brede ij yerdes
and j quarter. And every tapett,[3] called quarter clothe, shalde

---

1—Illegible.
2—" Plus in tercio folio precedente," is written above.
3—Nota. There is a statute for assisses to be kept, " anno regni regis
Henrici VIII., 34, c. 10," is written in the left margin.

halde and contene in lengthe two yerdes ande ane halfe, ande in brede j yerde and iij quarters. And if ther be any fraunchised man of the crafte aforesaide, within this cite, suburbez, and fraunchez of the same, make or do make any coverlettes or tapittez of thaire owen or of othir mens, whilke er called sale ware, agayns this ordynance in fourme and maner abovesaide, that than he or thay, so foundon defectyfe, brekyng the saide ordynance of the saide lengthe and brede, by the serchiours of the saide craft for tyme beyng to be foundon, shall paye vj s. viij d. als often tymez as he or thay offendyn in that behalfe, to be employed evenly to the common wele of this cite and to the saide crafte.

Item, it is ordayned that every maister of the saide crafte may from nowefurth have two apprentessez at ones in that craft and no moo, and who of the same craft that dothe the contrarie shall forfaitt xl s. to the communalte of this cite and to the said crafte by even porcions, as oft tymez as he or they er offenden, etc.

Johannes Tesedale, Elyas Cure, Ricardus Kyd, Robertus Scathelok, Willelmus Rile, Johannes Bukler, Thomas Calas, Johannes Hovell, Thomas Pymerton, Robertus Fraunsez, Willelmus Symson, Johannes Scathelok, Willelmus Houke, Johannes Brokholes, Willelmus Palson, Ricardus Gurnard, Radulphus Dent, Thomas Kechynner, Robertus Bukler, Nicholaus Pymerton, Willelmus Gude, Willemus Harbard, Thomas Santon, Christian Erl, Androus Blithe, Ricardus Sharpels, Thomas Raa.

Item, it is ordeined and awarded by Thomas Wrangwishe, then maire of this saide citie, and the chaumbre of the same, with the hoole assent and concent of all the hoole craftes of the tapiters and lynenwevers, that whereby a decre, awarde and juggement by William Holbek, late (fo. 296) maire of this saide citie, made and yeven betwene the hole craftes of tapiters and lynenwevers of the saide citie, that the saide craft of lynenwevers shuld from thensefurthe yerely paie unto the saide craft of the tapiters vj s. for all manere dewtes, charges and accustumes, to the aide and supportacion of thaire pageant in the plaie of Corpus Christi, as more pleynely it apperith in the saide decre and awarde. The saide tapiters at the special desire and request of the saide Thomas Wrangwishe, maire, clerely, freely, and holey for evermore herafter have remised and released unto the saide craft of lynenwevers the saide vj s. And also it is ordeined that either of thaire craftes shalbe free from any serse, contribucion or dewtie from other form this day furth. And if it happen any of the saide tapiters hynsefurthward to have or sett upp any lynen lome or lomes, the whiche hath apperteyneith and belongith to thaire craft and occupacion of olde tyme, the saide lomes and warkemen therin to be examened and sersed by the sersours of the saide lynenwevers at all tymes, the saide tapiters payng unto thayme none pageant sylvere for the same had afore tym.

Also the saide tapiters shall have and yerely perceyve of the litsters, by the handes of the pageaunt maisters of the saide lytsters, in the feste of Corpus Christi, to the supportacion and sustentacion of the pageaunt of the tapiters iij s. iiij d. of lawful money of England. Also that the saide tapiters shall yerely have and percieve to the sustentacion of thaire pageaunt of every upholder and comon seller of coverlettes within this citie and libertie of the same, ij d.

Item, it is ordeyned that no man of the said craft of tapiters by the assent and concent of the hole craft frome nowe forth shall set up ne occupie no mo lomes moo then two, ne no mo standyng within his house within the liberte and franches of this cite, uppon payn of xl s., tociens quociens, the tone half to the chaumbre, the tother half to the craft[12]; and that it shall be leefull for any maister of the sayd occupacion to werk in the said ij lomes, coverlettes, or in thon coverletes, and thother to be a bedlome at their pleasure.[2]

Ista prescripta ordinacio inter *tapitours* et *dyers* adnullata est tempore Johannis Gylliot, maioris, per ejus assensum et tocius consilii camere, xxvij° die Novembris, 6 Henr. vii. (1490).

(*fo*. 296, *b*.) Item, it is ordeined and enacted by all the hole assent of the saide craft of the tapiteres that whosomevere from hynsfurth shall take upon hym to set upp of newe in the saide craft within this citie, and hath not be apprentice within the same citie at the saide craft, to paie at his upset xiij s. mj d.

1--In margin, " xix° die Augusti, 16 Edw. IV. (1476)," is written.
2--2--Addit. tempore, Tho. Appleyerd, maioris.

And if he hath be apprentice within this saide citie at the same craft, then he to paie at his upsett vj s. viij d. to the chaumbre of the saide citie and craft by even porciones.

Item, it is ordeigned ande enacted in the tyme of John Fereby, beyng maire of this wirshupful cite, the secund day of Septembre, the xviij yere of Kyng Edward the iv^t. (1468), as wele by the assent ande consent of the said maire and the hole counsell of the chaumbre, as by the godemen of the tapiters of this said cite, suburbes, and precinctes of the same, that from this day forward it shalbe lefull to the said tapitours and every iche of thayme that nowe is, or for tyme shalbe, to colour and litt thare awne garnez withoute lettyng or interupcion of eny dyer of this said cite, and also withoute payment of eny dewtie to the said dyers as have ben hertofore, bot they of eny such dewtie to the said dyers be clerelie discharged. Moreover it is agreid that non of the said tapiters colour ne lit non other mannes garn ne cloth bot is awn, and he that so doeth contrarie this ordinaunce that lawfully can be proved of right lese ande pay without pardon vj s. viij d., tociens quociens, unto the use of the commonaltie of this cite, to be resavyd by the hondes of the chaumberleyns for the tyme beyng. And more over the said tapiters bynde thayme and there successours yerelie to bere all the chargez of thare pageaunt ande torches as have ben accostomed by thame to do afore tyme ; and yerely to pay and content v s. of true Inglissh money within this chaumbre, to be resavyed by the hondes of the chaumberleyns for the tyme beyng, to the use of the commonaltie of the same cite, etc., solvendos infra mensem Junii quolibet anno.[1]

Ista prescripta ordinacio *de le tapitours* cancellata et adnullata est tempore Johannis Gylliot, maioris, per ejus assensum et tocius consilii camere, xxvij° die Novembris, 6 Heur. vii. (1490).

(*fo.* 297). De xij, Thomas Neleson, maior ; Ricardus Wartre, Johannes Thrisk, Johannes Carre, Willelmus Holbek, Thomas Barton, Thomas Danby, Johannes Catryk, Robertus Colynson ; vicecomites, Johannes Glasyn, Willelmus Wright ;

1—The whole of this ordinance was cancelled, but the cancelling lines were erased from the last part.

legisperiti, Guido Rouclyff, recordator, Johannes Thwaytes, Henricus Thwaytes, Nicholas Girlington, Johannes Thweynge; de xxiiij, William Aberford, Johannes Gudale, Willelmus Stanes, Thomas Scauceby, Ricardus Thornton, Nicholaus Holgate, Robertus Perte, Johannes Marton, Thomas Curtas, Thomas Beverlay, Willelmus Barlay, Johannes Strensall, Johannes Gyllyote, Johannes Voure, assembleez en la counseil chaumbre le x jour de Septembre, 34 Henr. vi. (1454), ounte ordine et estable que la somons de lez aldermanz et xxiiij du counseile de dite chaumbre de ceste jour en avaunt soit tenuz et observez en la manere et fourme quensuite; ceste assavoir, que au qile joure qascun dez ditz xij aldermanz et xxiiij du dite counseile ou de cez successoures soite summone destre devaunt le maire qore est, ou que pur le temps serra, et ne vient point al heoure assigne par le dite mair, paiera a chescun foithe iiij $d.$, sil ne poet estre excuse par son seremente faite devaunt le dite mair, qil ne fuist mie a lostel de cele heure quaunt il fue summone, issint qil ne fuist mie sachaunt de sa summons, ou qil fuiste distourbe par reisonable encheson, dount il ne poiet venir. Et que chescun mair pur le temps esteiant face levier les ditz amerciamentz issint perduz du temps en temps, saunce ascun delay ou pardone, sur peine de double somne en son fee par lez chaumbrelaynes de dite cite, que pur le temps serront, accompter; et que mesmez lez amerciamentez issint leviez soient dispenduz sur ledificacion de la Guihall de mesme la citee, et pur ledificacion dicelle, toucz les ditz amerciamentez tourneront al use et profette de la commonaltee de mesme la cite as toutz joures. Et sile aveigne que lez sergiantz de le mair ne ferroient lour summons en due et sufficiante fourme par consideracion du mair et cez counseillers, que adonques mesme le sergiante paiera le amerciamente de celluy que ferra defaute de son apperance al heure a luy assigne.

(*fo.* 297, *b.*) Recordum pro Andrea Lam, pistore, defamato pro Scotico, patet in subscriptis. Raufe Huthum, esquire, to al those that this present writyng shall se or here, gretyng. For as much as it hath pleasid my lord of Northumberland, warden of the Estmarch and Middelmarch of England towarde Scotland, to have yeven and committed unto me ful power to attach and arrest al maner Scottes and alyenees within his said wardanrye, by the auctoritie of our sovereigne lorde the Kynge to hym committed in that behalve, by which power so be my lorde of Northumberland to me yeven and committed, I, the forsaid Rauffe, have yeven and committed full power to my welbelovyd Richerd Stirton and Walkyn Coursour to attach and arest al maner Scottes and alyenees within the said wardanrye. By the which power, the forsaid Richard and Walkyn attachied and arest Andrewe Lam of Hesill for a Scottys man, the which Andrew Lam by thaym so attachied and arest, they broght afor me to Lekenfeld, the xx^t day of October, and thare he, be me examyned in that behalve, preved hym self a Englesh man born, wherfore I, the forsaid Raufe, by the auctoritie of my office strately charges and commaundes all maner of men, that they nether vex ne trobell the said Andrewe for the cause before rehersed, but hym peseable suffir to rest as trewe Englissheman. In wittenesse of this I, the forsaid Raufe, have putte the seall of my office, yeven at Lekenfeld the xx^t day of October, 11 Edw. iv. (1471).

(*fo.* 298). Robertus Colynson, maior; Johannes Thrisk, Willemus Stokton, Thomas Barton, Thomas Danby, Johannes Catryk, Nicholaus Holgate, *aldermanni*; Willelmus Aberford, Johannes Goodale, Willelmus Stanes, Ricardus Thornton, Robertus Perte, Johannes Marton, Thomas Curteis, Thomas Beverlay, Johannes Gyllyot, Willelmus Wryght, Johannes Ince, Willelmus Cleveland, de xxiiij^{or}, congregati fuerunt in camera consilii civitatis Ebor', viij° die Aprilis, 35 Henr. vi. (1457), et ibidem legi fecerunt coram eis eas literas domini regis sub ejus privato sigillo maiori, vicecomitibus, et aldermannis dicte civitatis, que sequntur in hiis verbis:—Trusty and wele beloved, now be it that all insurrections, riottes, assembles, unlawful conventicles, confederacees, and congregacions made by any persone or persones within this oure royalme, ben by oure lawes in all wise forbyden, yit that notwithstanding we have understond that divers gret riottes and assembles of oure peple have be made and committed within oure citee of York, by the which gret slaughters, murders of oure peple, and other mischeves were like to ensue that we ne wolde. Therfore we, in eschewyng and puttyng downe of all suche misruled persones, wol and streitly charge you that, inmediatly after the sight of thees oure lettres, ye do make open proclamacions on oure behalfe, as ofte and in such places within oure said citee as shalbe thought necessarie, that no persone, ne persones, of what condicion or degre thei be of, tak upon to make any insurrections, riottes, assemblees, conventicles, confederacions, within oure said citee, nor bere, ride, ne goo, with wapen defensively arraied within oure said citee ne fraunchises thereof, thorough the which oure pees might of lykelyhode be broken; except such officeres as ben assigned and deputed within oure saide citee for keping of oure said pees, upon payne of forfaitour of all their goodes and thar bodies at oure will; chargyng you more over that in case any such persone or persones of suche and like disposicion as is abovesaid be founde within oure saide citee or fraunchesis therof, that then without any delay ye arrest hem, and send hem in all goodly haste unto oure presence with the cause of their arrest; to the intent that we, by thadvis of our counseil, may provide and ordeyn such punysshment for hem as all othere shal nowe take therby example. And we wol that ye leve not this, as ye love and tendre the prosperite, welefare, and rigtful reule of this oure royaume, and as ye wol eschewe oure grevouse displesour, and also upon the faith and ligeance that ye and everich of you owe unto us. Yeven apon oure preve seal at Coventree, the xj^e day of March (1456-7).

Quibus hiis auditis et intellectis, ordinatum est et statutum quod ordinacio facta et provisa, die Lune proximo post festum Circumsisionis Domini, 24 Henr. vi. (3 January, 1445-6), tempore (fo. 298, b.) Thome Crathorn, maioris, in omnibus observetur, que est talis, videlicet, quod nullus concivis hujus civitatis, infra eandem civitatem commorans, decetero utetur vestura vel librata alicujus domini, militis seu generosi, nec alicujus alterius, contra formam statuti domini regis inde editi, sub pena foris- facture libertatis et franchesie sue civitatis predicte, et quod extunc non recipietur ad libertatem ejusdem civitatis, nisi persolvat ad usum dicte civitatis c s. ad minus, et ultra secundum discre- cionem et consideracionem maioris et consilii camere dicte civitatis, pro tempore existencium. Et quod maior dicte civitatis, pro tempore existens, faciat execucionem hujus ordinacionis in futurum sub pena xx li., ad usum et proficuum dicte civitatis persolvendarum, tociens quociens necligens fuerit in dicta execucione facienda. Et si quis de libertate dicte civitatis contra istam ordinacionem pro aliquo homine ejusdem civitatis laboraverit, seu aliquam instanciam seu deprecacionem fecerit, c s. usui communitatis antedicte de bonis suis forisfaciet et persolvet, per maiorem in forma predicta levandos. Addendo huic ordinacioni quod singulis annis sequentibus illa ordinacio legatur immediate post electionem servientum maioris ad clavas, die Lune proximo post festum Sancti Blasii (February 3), coram communitate ibidem tunc presentibus [sic], ad eam intencionem quod ipsi melius illam ordinacionem observare et custodire poterint.

Willelmus Holbek, maior ; aldermanni, Willelmus Stokton, Thomas Barton, Thomas Neleson, Nicholaus Holgate, Johannes Marton, Willelmus Barlay ; vicecomites, Johannes Coupland, Willelmus Bradley ; Willelmus Abirforde, Robertus Perte, Willelmus Stanes, Thomas Scausceby, Ricardus Thornton, Johannes Strensall, Willelmus Wright, Johannes Ince, Willelmus Cleveland, Johannes Marshall, congregati fuerunt in refectorio fratrum Augustinensium, in festo Sancti Blasii, 37 Henr. vi. (3 February, 1458-9), pro electione maioris, et per assensum ac unanimem consensum omnium et singulorum concivium dicte civitatis ibidem congregatorum ordinaverunt et stabiliverunt quod si quis concivis dicte civitatis, qui ab hac die in antea subtraxerit vel detinuerit a maiore et communitate dicte civitatis, sive eorum suecessoribus, aliquem redditum, exeuntem de terris seu tenementis suis, aut de terris seu tenementis alicujus alterius, de quo redditu dicti maior et communitas vel eorum predecessores legitime seisiti et possessionati fuerunt, vel si terram aut solum inclusum tenuerunt aliquo tempore anni, in quibus iidem maior et communitas et predecessores sui communam pro averiis suis de jure aut de consuetudine habuerunt seu habere debuerunt, quod ipse infra annum postquam subtraxerit vel detinuerit hujusmodi redditum, seu terram aut solum inclusum tenuerit, ubi dicti maior et communitas communam pro animalibus suis habuerunt, de libertate et franchesia, eisdem maiori et communitati per dominum nostrum regem Anglie et ejus progenitores concessis et confirmatis, penitus sit expulsus et exoneratus etc.

(*fo.* 299). Nicholaus Holgate, maior ; Willelmus Stokton, Thomas Barton, Thomas Neleson, Johannes Merton, Willelmus Barlay, Willelmus Abirford, Willelmus Stanes, Thomas Scauceby, Robertus Perte, Thomas Curtays, Johannes Gyllyote, Johannes Voure, Willelmus Wright, Johannes Ince, Willelmus Cleveland, congregati in camere consilii civitatis Ebor', xxvij die Aprilis, 37 Henr. vi. (1459), ex corum unanimi assensu et voluntate ordinatum et stabilitum fuit quod ab hac die in antea nulli alienigine, venientes de partibus extraneis ad civitatem predictam, hospitentur, nec eorum aliquis hospitetur, infra eandem civitatem, suburbia, et libertatem ejusdem, nisi solummodo in hospicio maioris et communitatis, ad signum Tauri in Conyngstrete, nisi aliter licensientur per maiorem, qui pro tempore fuerit, sub pena xl *s.*, usui communitatis ejusdem civitatis forisfaciendorum per ipsum seu ipsos, qui tenuerit seu tenuerint hospicium et contrarium huic ordinacioni fecerit seu fecerint in futurum. Et ulterius ordinaverunt et consenserunt quod Johannes Newhall, *girdiller*, deinceps non assumetur neque eligetur in maiorem, vicecomitem, custodem poncium, nec ad aliquod aliud officium seu statum electivum per maiorem et communitatem infra civitatem predictam ; sed ab omni hujusmodi officio et statu electivo penitus exoneretur. Et postea in festo Sancti Johannis Beverlaci, videlicet, vij die Maii, anno supradicto, in presencia plurimorum concivium dicte civitatis Ebor' in Guihalda congregatorum, ordinaciones predicte per predictum maiorem recitate et per clericum communem perlecte fuerunt, et de eorum communi assensu et voluntate affirmate fuerunt, prout superius conscribuntur.

Nicholaus Holgate, maior ; Johannes Thriske, Willelmus Holbek, Willelmus Stokton, Thomas Barton, Thomas Neleson, Ricardus Lematon, Thomas Beverlay, Willelmus Barlay, de xij ; Johannes Coupeland, vicecomes ; Willelmus Abirford, Ricardus Thornton, Robertus Perte, Thomas Curtas, Johannes Gylhote, Willelmus Wright, Johannes Ince, Willelmus Cleveland, congregati in camera consilii civitatis predicte, xxij die Marcii, 37 Henr. vi. (1458-9), consenserunt et ordinaverunt quod si aliqua secta seu querela tempore futuro incepta fuerit versus aliquem maiorem seu vicecomitem hujus civitatis, postquam exoneratus fuerit de officio suo predicto, pro aliqua re vel causa per ipsum seu per ejus mandatum facta, pro libertate, jure, jurisdictione, proficuo seu honore hujus civitatis, tempore quo stetit in officio suo supradicto, quod extunc vicecomites dicti civitatis, succedentes et imposterum existentes, nec eorum ministri seu officiarii, non capient aliquos fines nisi per consideracionem maioris et consilii ejusdem civitatis pro tempore existencium. Et ulterius concesserunt solvere per manus camerariorum dicte civitatis pro una pipa vinii rubii, medietatis unius dolii vini rubii.

Condicatum per dominum Henricum, comitem Northumbrie, solvere iij *li.* (?) Ricardo Percy fratri suo et Katerine uxori ejus, in plenam solucionem et satisfactionem pro certis offensis, transgressionibus, causis, et querelis, per Willelmum Shirwod nuper unum[1] vicecomitum ejusdem civitatis et illis in comitiva sua existentibus apud Walton factis, aut per ipsum Willelmum et Willelmum Bracebrig, alterum vicecomitem ejusdem civitatis, apud Coopemanthorp seu alibi aliqualiter factis sive perpetratis.

Lytsteres.

(*fo.* 299, *b.*) Thomas Beverlay, Johannes Thrisk, Willelmus Stokton, Thomas Barton, Thomas Neleson, Ricardus Lematon, Nicholaus Holgate, Johannes Marton, Willelmus Barlay, Johannes Ince, de xij ; Christoforus Both, Johannes Marshall, vicecomites ; Willelmus Abirford, Willelmus Stanes, Thomas Scauceby, Ricardus Thornton, Thomas Curtays, Johannes Gyllyote, Johannes Voure, Johannes Glasyn, Willelmus Wright, Willelmus Cleveland, Johannes Coupeland, de xxiiij, were assembled in the counseill chaumbre of the citee of York, the xxij day of Maii, 38 Henr. vi. (1460), considering the grete decay of this citee, that dayly decresces by the withdraght of toll and murage due to the maire and communaltie of this citee, not only by colour of merchauntez, concitisyns of this same citee, in bryngyng in and sendyng forth of diversez goodes and merchaundisez of other mennes undre colour of thaire awne propre goodez and merchaundisez, and of other concitisynes of the same citee in propreyng and affermyng diverse manere of graynes to be boght

1—MS., unius.

by thaym in utwarde parties of this realme of Englond, and to com to this at thaire aventour ; but aswele by bryngyng in and havyng out of this citee of woll, clothe, and garnes of many diverse mennes of the contre by dyers of this citee, without payng of toll and murage ; and also by makyng of colorable covenauntez with foraynes to bryng diverse goods and merchaundisez to a certayne place nere the fraunches of this citee, and than thay of this citee to bere almanere of charges fro thence to this said citee, to thentent forto defraude payment of toll and murage of this same citee, contrarye to the grauntz and confirmacions of our sovereigne the kyng and his progenitours, and also contrarye to the ordenauncez and thaccustomes of this same citee. Therefore, it is ordaned and establisshed for the reformacion of the premissez in the manere and fourme that felowes by the hole advise and ful consent of all the commons of the said citee.

First, that if any merchaunt fraunchest of this citee send forth into any parties within this realme to be solde, or bryng in from any parties within the said realme by water or by lande, iren, oyle, tarre, wyne, wax, sope, wadde, mader, alom, tynne, lede, or any other manere of merchaundisez, of what condicion as evere it bee, shalbe sworn uppon a bouke that it is his awne propre goodez and merchandisez, commyng in or goyng forth at his awne propre aventour, so that if it happyn to be perisshed or lost in any manere of wise by lande or by water, it to rest soill uppon hym selfe and on noon other person ; and that it is not boght ne soulde to thentent to deferre or defraude the ministres óf this citee of the toll and murage or any thing due unto this citee by any manere of colour.

Item, that if any fraunchestman of this citee by any manere of corne in the contree uppon condicioun that it shal com to this citee at his cost and aventour, that as wele he that selles it, if he resorte or com to this citee, as he that byes it, shal swere uppon a bouke that the bargan and covenaunt was so treuly made without fraude and colorable ymaginacion in the manere and fourme aforsaide.

Item, if it happyn at any tyme here after that any fraunchest⁻ man of this citee bye or sell any manere of goodes or merchandisez upon condicioun to resceyve at a place nere adioynyng to ye boundes of the fraunches of this citee, to thentent to defraude or dissayve the ministres of this citee of thaire toll or murage by covenaunt made bitwix hem and his merchauntz, or make any untrue (*fo.* 300) othe for any goodes or merchandisez to be boght or soulde, and that proved uppon him, he shal pay double toll and murage for the same goode or merchaundisez, and overe that be discharged of his fraunches within this citee, and not to be admitte there to agayne, withoute assent of the hole counseill of the chaumbre or the more partie of thayme.

Item, that almanere of dyers, concitisynes of this citee, that brynges in any manere of wolles, clothe, or garnes to be litted within this citee fro nowe forth, pay toll and murage after the forme and effecte of the grauntes and confirmacions therof graunted by oure sovereigne lorde the kyng and his progenitours, and also after the custome and ordenauncez of this citee at the commyng in, in like forme as the awners foreyns shulde doo if thai broght it thaym selfe, and no thing at the hafeyng forth. Forsene alway that if any persone or persones bryng or sende any woll, clothe, or garn to litt to this citee for thaire awne propre clothing or thair familier servantz by ane othe to be made by the awner or by the brynger, be it dyer or other persone, pay no toll ne murage.

Walkers.

Johannes Gillyot, maior; Willelmus Stokton, Nicholaus Holgate, Thomas Beverlay, Thomas Scauceby, Johannes Marshall, Johannes Kent, aldermen; Willelmus Crossely, Johannes Cotes, vicecomites; Willelmus Abirford, Johannes Strensall, Ricardus Thornton, Johannes Glasyn, Willelmus Wright, Willelmus Shirwood, Christoforus Bothe, Ricardus Claybruke, Willelmus Thorp, de xxiiij^{or}.

The vth day of Marche, in the fourt yere of the reigne of King Edward the fourt (1463–4), at the suyte and request of the walkers, inhabitauntz within this citee, by the discrecion of the maire, aldremen and counseill of the chaumbre, with'assent of the commons in the guyldhall, it is considred and undrestoude howe that in tyme passed men of the said craft of walkers, inhabitauntes within the saide citee, wer wont to full and wirke all manere of clothe made within this citee, and also grete parte of clothe made in the contree aboute the saide citee, at whiche tyme were many honest and thrifty men of the said craft inhabitaunt in the same citee, and nowe thay be fewer and porer for lak of wark, that gothe at thies dayes into the contree. And therefore, it is this day ordeyned, establisshed and by common assent agreed, that no man of this citee delyvere any clothe within the fraunchesse therof to any foreyn walker to full or to wirk, nor noo clothe fulled or wroght by any foreyne walker of any mannes of this citee risseyue within the fraunchesse o payne of ij s., to be forfaite als oft tymez as any suche persone doo the contrarie, two parties therof unto common availe and proffeite of this citie and chaumbre of the same, and the other haulf to the crafte of the walkers, soo that the said walkers and theire successours wirke and full the clothe of every mannez, als wele and at as reisonnable price as other foreyn walkers dose at this day. Forseyne alway that if it can be thoght to (fo. 300, b.) the maire, aldremen and counseill of the chaumbre and comons at eny tyme after this to be eny hurt, prejudice, or inconvenient in this ordenaunce or any parte ther of to the comon wele, worship, [1]or proffite of this citee, that than it shalbe lefull to thayme to adnull, adde, correcte, refourme, and amende this ordenaunce, and every parte ther of, after thaire wisdomes and discrecions, to the honour of the citie and wele of the craft.

Also, that every forcine walker commyng to this citie and hathe not be apprentise therin at the saide crafte, and wil sett up as a maister, and therto be founden able and worthy bothe in connyng and honour by the sersours of the saide crafte, that then he shall paie at his upsett xiij s. iiij d., the oone haulf to the chaumbre and use of the citie, and the other haulf to the craft of the walkers.[2]

1—" Plus inde folio cclxx precedente," is written in the left margin.

2—In the margin, Ista ordinacio iterum reformatur et confirmatur sub communi s(igillo)? ultimo die Ma**, 16 Edw. IV. (1476), tempore Thome Wrangwishe, maioris, civitatis Ebor'.

Glasyers.

Johannes Gillyot, maior; Johannes Thrisk, maior stapule; Willelmus Holbek, Willelmus Stokton, Nicholaus Holgate, Thomas Beverlay, Thomas Scauceby, Johannes Marsshal, *merchant*, Johannes Kent, Johannes Marsshal, *drapour*, Johannes Voure, aldermanni; Willelmus Abirford, Ricardus Thornton, Johannes Strensall, Willelmus Wright, Willelmus Shirwood, Christoforus Bothe, Ricardus Claybruke, Willelmus Skynner, Christoferus Marsshal, Willelmus Thorp, Willelmus Crosseby, de xxiiij^{or}, were gadred in the counseill chambre of the city of York, the second day of October, the fourth yere of the reigne of King Edward the fourth, where it was ordeyned, agreed, and establisshed by all the hole craft of glasyers of this citee of York, that is to say, Mathewe Pety, Thomas Mylet, William Inglissh, Robert Shirlay, John Colke, Rauff Shuttilworth, Robert Hudson, and Thomas Coverham, that is to say, that they shall emonges hem selfe every yere in the fest of Seint Luke chese hem two serchours to have reule and thoursight of almanere of thynges, that shall be made in the saide craft, and to see that it be wele, truely, and substancially wroght, and that therin be noo disceyt unto the kynges peple, upon [1]payne of forfetur of vj *s.* viij *d.* to the chaumbre and craft by even porcions.[1]

Item, if any man of the said craft [1]be rebell and[1] disobey, distourbe or lett the said serchours to have or to use their deue[2] serche in all thynges pertenyng unto the same craft, [3]or els that he come not at all suche tyme and place as he shalbe warned[3] [4]to appere afore his said sersours[4] [5]and craft, he shall lese and pay[5] vj *s.* viij *d.* to the chaumbre and to the saide craft by even porcions as oft tymez as [6]he is founden culpable in the same.[6]

1—1—Interlined.
2—Interlined.
3—3—Interlined.
4—4—Written upon an erasure.
5—5—Interlined.
6—6—Written upon an erasure. In the margin is written, 'Thes ordinances are reformed and newly agreed upon and corrected, *tempore maioratus Edwardi Fawcett, maioris, ut patet* in the black boke in paper, 1598.'

Item, that ther shall noo man of the saide craft take any apprentece in the same for lesse terme than for vij yere to gedder, and bott oon at once unto the tyme that iiij yere of the said vij yeres be fully complete, opeyne of lesyng of vj s. viij d. to be payed in the manere and fourme aforewriten, as oft tymez as any man dose the contrarye of this ordenaunce. Forseyne alway that if any arrour, inconvenyent, or prejudice appere to the maire and counseill of the chaumbre in any partie of this ordenaunce at any tyme here after, that than it shalbe lefull to the maire (*fo.* 301) and counseill for the tyme beyng to amend the saide ordenaunce by thare discrecions for the wele, honour, and common proffett of this citee and craft.

Item, that no maister of the said craft supporte any maner of foreyner within this citee or without ayeinst any other maister in any poynt concernyng the wele, worship and proffecte of the same craft, opayne of leisyng of xiij s. iiij d. to be payed as is aforewriten, [1]and that noo foreyne sett up a shop as a master in the said crafte unto suche tyme he aggre with the serchours of the said craft for a certain some.[1]

Item, if any man of the said craft that dwelles within this citee, outher fraunchest or unfraunchest, drawe hym to any lordship or maistership other than to the maire of this citee for the tyme beyng, for any manere of mayntenaunce of any querrell ayeinst any other man of the same craft, he shall lese and pay xl s. in the manere and fourme aforewriten, as oft tymes as he dose ayeinst this ordenaunce.

[2]Item, whosomevere of the saide craft discovereith and reveles the counsailes and privetees of his saide craft to any personne not being of his saide craft, and also inhabiting and abideing within this citie, that as oftens tymes as he shalbe founden defautie in the same, to paie xiij s. iiijd. in manere and fourme aforesaide.[2]

[3]Item, whosomevere of the saide craft shall doo from hynse furth any untrewthe vnto the valeu of xij d. or be founden untrewe of his tonge, that then he shall paie and forfet x s. in manere and

---

1—1—Interlined.
2—2—Added in a different hand.
3—3—Added in a different hand at the bottom of fo. 300, b.

o

fourme aforesaide, and overe that he to be avoided from the saide craft vuto the tyme that he fynde sufficiant suretie of his trewthe and goode bereing to the saide craft frome thynse furthe, and then to be readmitted and accepted by the sersours and all the hole craft.³

Lytsters.

Att the speciall instance, request, ande prayer of alle the godemen of the craft of littesters of the cite of York, thees ordynaunces undrewriten ben ordayned and establisshed to be kepped within the same cite by all the maisters of the said craft from nowe furth duryng for evermore by the advise, counsaill, and consent of Christofre Marsshall, maire of the same cite, and the counsaylours of the same cite, thanne for tyme beynge, for the worship of the saide cite, profect of the kinges liege people, and honeste of the same craft.

In primis, it is ordayned that if any maister of the same craft within this cite discese, havyng a prentez or apprentessez in that occupacion, which have nat fullfilled the full termes and yeres of thaire couvenance in that behalf, that it shall nat be lefull to any maister of that craft within the same cite to take any such apprentes into his service in that occupacion, eyther as hyerdman or yit journayman, unto such tyme as the same apprentez hafe fulfilled and seruffed oute the residue of his forsaide yeres and termes with some other maister of that same craft within the same cite, uppon payn of forfayting of vj s. viij d. as oft tymes as any maister of the same craft doth the contrarie, evenly to be devyded betuyx the chambre of the same cite and the saide occupacion.

(*fo*. 301, *b*.) Item, it is ordayned that no maister of that crafte within the same cite shall sett no straunger of the same crafte, commyng to this cite, frome noweforth on warke in that occupacion, or tyme be that the sercheours of the same craft for tyme beyng have examyned, approved, and abled the same straunger, under payn of forfayting of vj s. viij d., to be payde in fourme abovesaide.

Item, that ther shall noo maner of man, deynisin, ne straunger, take apon him to sett upp for himsilf as a maister litster in that craft within the same cite, afore the tyme that he be suffisauntly examyned serched, approved, and admitted by the serchiours of the said crafte, for tyme beyng, and iiij maisters of the moste able and discrete of the same craft, uppon payne of lesyng of vj s. viij d. to be payed in fourme aforewriten.[1]

Item, it is ordayned, ennact, and establisshed that what maister of the same occupacion within this cite that fro nowefurth takes any othir mans servant, of that occupacion, into his service withoute licence of his maister, for tyme beyng, shall forfaite vj s. viij d. to be employed as is aforesaide.[2]

Item, it ys fermely ordaned that none of the maisters of that occupacion within this cite shall fro nowefurth drawe, ne wyrke to any other man of that occupacion within the saide cite, which is vnfraunchised, and that all tho that ben fraunchised within the forsaide cite of the same occupacion shall at all dayes wirke whare thayme pleas, [3]ande thay to have als gode a pennyworth for a penny as thay of the same occupacion may holde thaire owen, and who dothe the contrary shall forfait iij s. iiij d. in fourme abovesaid.

Item, it is ordayned that what maister of that occupacion that hereafter holdeth in his service any maner of servante in that occupacion, that is proved fals suffisauntly to the valuer of xij d. or ovir, shall lese and forfaite vj s. viij d. in maner and fourme aforesaide.

Item, it is ordaned that in case be that any variaunce hereafter behappen to fall betuyx any tweyn maisters of that occupacion within the same cite for any mater or cause, that touchez ther crafte in any poynte, that than it shall nat be levefull to neyther of thayme to suye other in any forreyn courtes in that behalfe, but firste he or thay that so feyl him or thayme greved shall com unto the serchiours of the same craft for tyme there being, and ther shewe his or thaire grevaunce to thentente that the same serchiours by the advice of iiij of the moste able and

---

1—Upset in margin.
2—Drawyng in margin.
3—'Wher he best lyke or that no man doo vy to tak his work uppon,' interlined.

moste discrete (*fo.* 302) personnes of the same crafte may here thaire grevaunces betuyx the same parties by gode deliberacion, and therapon the same serchiours and iiij men to put gode rule betuyx the same partiez in that behalf, and the same partiez to obbey and fulfill the same rull in alle thinges, under payn of lesyng of xiij *s.* iiij *d.* to be payde be him disobeying in fourme aforesaid.

Item, it is ordaned that if any man or woman so occupyyng that occupacion within this cite fro nowfurth be foundon rebell, or disobeysant unto the serchiours of that occupacion for tyme beynge, in the tyme of thaire due serch making in that behalfe, that than he or she, that so is foundon rebell or disobeysaunt and thairof convyct, shall pay and forfayt iij *s.* and iiij *d.* in maner and fourme aforewriten.

Item, that all maner of men and women, within this liberte littyng any maner of colours as grene, rede, dorrey, yalowe, or any othir colour in woll, clothe, or yarne, to be put to sale in any maner of behalfe, shall be nowe from this tyme furth yerely serched duely by the serchiours of the saide crafte for tyme being in that behalfe, and if the saide colours or any of thaime be foundou deceyvably dyed by any personne within this cite and liberte of the same, that thanne he or she, that so disceyvably littes and colours, shall forfett a certayne broke or payne after the quantite of the defalte by the advice, jugement, and discrecion of the maire of the saide cite, for the tyme beyng, vnto the chambre of this cite and to the saide crafte, evenly to be devyded, as often tymez as any offenden in that behalf; every man ande woman within this saide cite ande liberte of the same, littyng wolle, clothe, yarne, or any othir thing to thaire owen were, and to the were of thaire owen householdes in every thinge except.

[1]Tempore Johannis Gylliot maioris civitatis Ebor'.

Tempore Johannis Person et Cuthberti Brounlee, scrutatorum *de le dyers*.

1—The whole of this entry is written on half a sheet of parchment cut off from fo. 302, it is interleaved between ffs. 301, 302, and is not numbered.

THE ORDINANCES OF THE TAPITERS (1490)

Johannes Gylliot, maior; Ricardus Yorke, miles, Johannes Fereby, Johannes Newton, Nicholaus Lancastr', Willelmus Chymney, Willelmus Todd, miles, Robertus Hancok, Johannes Harper, Willelmus White, Willelmus Fairefax, *recordator*; Willelmus Barker, Alexander Dauson, *vicecomites*; Thomas Allen[1] . . . . wer assembled in the counsail chaumbre apon Ousebrig, the xxvij day of September, the vj yere of the reign of our soveren lige lord king Henry the vijth (1490), and ther and then determyned, assented, and fully concludet contynualie herafter to be observed and kept that the tapitours of this cite and libertie of the same that erre or for tyme shalbe dying eny maner yarnes, cloth, or woll, as in dorry, reid, yalowe, or eny other colour, to be contributory to the dyers of this cite, that erre or for tyme shalbe, in paing of pagent silver, as thay have doon in tymes past, that is to say, every tapitour so dying to pay yerelie to the[2] . . . .

(*fo.* 302). [3]Item the xxvij day of Septembre, 6 Heur. vii. (1490), wer assembled in the counsall chambre apon Ousebrig the right worshipful sir John Gillyot, maire of this worshipful cite; Richerd Yorke, knyght, John Fereby, John Neweton, Nicholas Lancastr', William Chymney, William Todd, knyght, Robert Hancok, John Harper, William White, William Fairefax, recorder, aldermen; William Barker, Alexander Dauson shereffes; Thomas Allan, William Spence, William Tayt, Richerd Clerk, Miles Grenebank, John Hag, George Kirke, Robert Johnson, Thomas Folneby, and Thomas G . . . and ther and then determyned and fully concludet contynualie herafter to be observed and kept that the tapitours of this cite and fraunches of the same, dying eny maner yarnes als reid, dorray, yalowe, or eny other colour in woll or cloth, be contributory to the dyers of the same cite, that erre or for tyme shalbe, in paing of pagent silver as they have done in tymez past, that is to say every tapitour so dying to pay yerelie to the pagent . . . . ere of the said dyers x *d.* per annum . . . rebell . . . . the same payment to

---

1—The parchment is cut off and the top of the letters of the next name can be seen.
2—The parchment is cut off here.
3—This entry comes after the litsters' ordinances. It is pasted on to the top half of fo. 302.

forfet and pay without pardon iij *s.* iiij *d.* . . . . . camere¹
. . . . in the tyme of Thomas Wrangwish, late maire, or eny other to the . . . . notwithstonding.²

(*fo.* 302, *b.*) Release by Richard Roos, esquire, to Isabel Roos of Laxton, co. Nottingham, widow, Robert Roos of the same, esquire, and sir William Roos, rector of the parish church of Laxton, of all actions against them had by reason of a recovery by writ of *Quare impedit,* of the parish church of Laxton, 4 July, 14 Edw. iv. (1474). Seal. Acknowledged in the mayoralty of John Gillyott, mayor, same date.

Release by John Byrdsall, citizen and merchant of York, to John Stokesley, citizen, and Mary his wife, and Hugh Lincoln of York, tailor, and Ellen his wife, of two mesuages and a garden in the street of S. Saviour in York, formerly of Henry Scoreby, formerly of York, merchant. Witnesses, Thomas Wrangwys, mayor, Alan Wilberfosse, Thomas Scotton, sheriffs, John Tonge, John Feriby, John Tuse of York, merchants, George Souleby, gentleman, York, 7 August, 16 Edw. iv. (1476). Seal. Acknowledged in the mayoralty of Thomas Wrangwishe, 26 August, 16 Edw. iv.

(*fo.* 303). ³Writ of *supersedeas* to the mayor and sheriffs of the city of York not to carry out the outlawry, pronounced in the court of husting of the city of London against Richard Blakburn, late of London, grocer, otherwise called Richard Blakburn, late of the city York, yeoman, in a plea of debt brought at the suit of Thomas Sergaunt, citizen and grocer of London; the king's court having revoked the said outlawry, which was pronounced by error. Westminster, 8 July, 17 Edw. iv. (1477) Trinity, xvij, Rot. xxxj.

(*fo.* 303, *b.*) Release by Isabel Langthorn, one of the daughters and heirs of William Langethorn, late citizen and merchant of York, to Nicholas Pereson of York, dyer, of a messuage in Mikelgate, formerly of the said William Langthorn. Witnesses, John Tonge, mayor, Robert Ancok, William Spence,

1—This word is interlined.
2—These ordinances are faintly crossed through, the interlined parchment is not.
3—This entry is crossed through.

sheriffs, John Hagg, William Dekyn, Thomas Davison, John Speller. York, 25 [sic] October, 17 Edward iv. (1477). Acknowledged before John Tong, mayor, 24 [sic] October, 17 Edw. iv.

(fo. 304). Memorandum quod sexto die Februarii, anno Domini millesimo cccc^{mo} decimo octavo, Willelmus Wright, maior civitatis Ebor', presentavit dominum Willelmum Metcalf, capellanum, ad cantariam ad altare Sancti Nicholai confessoris, in ecclesia Sancte Trinitatis in Gotheromgate, pro anima Elie Wandesford, clerici, et omnium fidelium defunctorum.

Memorandum quod Henricus Dyconson, capellanus, presentatus erat ad cantariam Willelmi Selby ad altare Beate Marie Virginis, in ecclesia Sancti Michaelis de Belfray, xiiij° die Februarii, anno Domini millesimo cccc^{mo} xviij°, post mortem domini Petri Danyell, ultimi capellani ejusdem, cum omnibus terris, tenementis, redditibus, firmis, et proficuis etc. Data fuit ista presentacio, tempore venerabilis viri Willelmi Wright, maioris civitatis Ebor' etc.

Shipmen ordinances.

(fo. 304, b.) Vicesimo septimo die Martii, 18 Edw. iv. (1478), Johannes Fereby, maior, Johannes Marshall, Willelmus Snawsell, Ricardus Yorke, Willelmus Lambe, Thomas Wrangwish, Johannes Tonge, Johannes Glasyn, Robertus Amyas ; Robertus Hancok, Willelmus Spence, vicecomites ; Thomas Catour, Johannes Lightlop, Willelmus Chymney, Nicholaus Pereson, Thomas Alleyn, xxiiij, wer assembled the same day in the counsell chambre of [sic] Ousebrig, and ther and then be a hole assent and consent it was enacted and establisshed that the shipmen of this cite, that nowe er or for tyme shalbe, have certan ordynances under writen. Firste, that every man occupiyng eny shipping at the stahe [sic] of this worshupful cite and is fraunchest, whether he be denisen or forant dwellyng, be contributori to the said shipmen, that is to say, every man salyng as maister with a freman pay yerely ij *d.* ; and he that salys as a felowe, pay j *d.*, to the sustentacion and upholdyng as well of the pageant of Noe as of the bringing furth and beryng ef certan torches before the shryne of Corpus Christi yerely. And he that is rebell and wilnot pay his duety, as it is above rehersed, to rynne in the contempt of xx *d*., that to be paid without pardon, the on halfe to the profect of the chaumbre and the comons of this cite, and the other half to the sustentacion of the chargez of the said shipmen. And also that the said shipmen yerelie from this yere forward elect and chuse thame seircheours and pageant maisters in the secund Sonday of Clene Lentyn, uppon [payn] of forfatour of iij *s*. iiij *d*. to the chaumbre of this cite. And that the olde pageant maisters yerelie yelde and yif accompt to the olde seirchours and all the said feliship of shipmen. And in like case the olde seirchours to yif accompt to the newe sercheours of all ther resaytes and paymentes don and takyn be thame durant ther hole yere. And also it is enacted that if eny man be warned by the said seircheours for tyme beyng to mete at convenient place, for eny thing concernyng the wele and profect as wele of this said cite as of the sciens and craft of the said shipmen, and is rebell and wilnot com as he is warned, to forfait and pay xl *d*., the on halfe to the chaumbre and the other half to our said chargez by even porcions without pardon. And, also, it is enacted that salte, granes, fuell, and all other thinges lying in ship at the said staith, and lieth not in his course as hym aght forto doo, and is warned by the said seircheours for tyme beyng to vire his said ship, and is rebell and wilnot, he to ryn in the contempt of xl *d*., that to be paid without pardon in maner as it is bove [*sic*] rehersed, by evyn porcion.

(*fo*. 305). In Dei nomine, Amen. Nonodecimo die Februarii, anno ab incarnacione Domini millesimo cccclxxvij°, Johannes Brigham, molendinarius molendinum aquaticum [*sic*] castri, Anglice vocat(orum)[1] *Castelmylnes,* adeundo in communi vico, inter cornerium capelle Sancti Georgii et dictum molendinum aquaticum, per Galfridum Studert et Thomam Hancok, servientes Radulfi Hastynges, armigeri, adtunc escaetoris comitatus Ebor', ut utlagatus extiterat, captus et ad dictum castrum adductus, inibi detrusus erat. Postea vero, Ricardo Nele, justiciario domini regis, adveniente ad assisas et deliberacionem gaole castri predicti unacum vicecomite ac aliis militibus armigeris

---

1—MS. molendinu aquaticu—vocitat.

aliisque pluribus, nobilis vir, Johannes Fereby, tunc maior istius civitatis, Milonem[1] Metcalf, tunc hujusce civitatis recordatorem, Thomam Wandesford, armigerum ad clavam, et Thomam Davyson subclericum ad dictum Ricardum Nele, domini regis justiciarium tunc in judicio infra castrum predictum, pro tribunali sedente, eum, humiliter supplicando, ut ille justicia suadente limites dictorum civitatis et castri inspiceret prefatum Johannem Brigham, aut vere et infra limites preasserti castri per dictos servientes escaetoris captum decernendo aut infra limites *ast* et bundas ante dicte civitatis dictum Johannem Brigham captum declarando determinaret. Qui, vero, dictus Ricardus Nele justiciarius, die Jovis in quarta septimana Quadragesime, dictum vicum communem, quo dictus Johannes Brigham captus extiterat, convocatis secum domino Ryther, milite, vicecomite predicto, Hugone Hastynges, milite, Jacobo Danby, armigero [pronunciavit].

(*fo.* 305, *b.*) Recordum pro Rolando Brice allocatur coram Johanne Fereby, maiore, iij die Augusti, 18 Edw. iv. (1478), sequitur. To all men to whom this present writing shall com, gretyng. Ande for asmuch as it is meretorys and medefull to bere witnes and recorde in materes of trouth, we therfore Humfre, lorde of Dacre, lieutenaunt of Carlell, Thomas, prior of Carleill, John, prior of Lanercroste, Richerd Salkeld, Richerd Denton, esquires, Henry Denton, maire of the cite of Carleill, John Appilby, Robert Skelton, Thomas Coldell, Richard Coldell, Alane Blenerhasset, and Thomas Denton, citezyns of the same, John Soureby, John Wardropp, and William Richardson, recordes and certifies for trouth be this our writinge that Rollande Brice, dwellyng in Yorke, is ane Inglishman borne, and was cristined in the kirke of Brampton in Gillesland, in the countie of Cumbrelande, and hade to his godfadres William Richardson and Rollande Bires, and to his godmodre, Marion Robynson, the wiffe of William Robynson, and in ratifying and affirmyng of this our letter testimoniall we have put to our sealles. Yeven at Carleill the xix[th] day of the moneth of July, 18 Edw. iv. (1478).

(*fo.* 306). Grant by Thomas, prior, and the convent of the Holy Trinity of York, by advice of John Sothill, esquire, their

1—The MS. has no verb in this sentence.

founder, to Richard Blakburn, in recompense for service, of a dwelling-house in Mikelgate now in the tenure of Nicholas Haliday, between tenements of the said priory on either side, and extending from the high street of Mikelgate in York before, to a garden of the priory in the tenure of Maud Belamy behind; to hold for term of life, at a yearly rent of 6 *s.* 8 *d.* Seal. In the chapter-house, 24 September, 1477. Acknowledged in the mayoralty of John Tong, 20 November, 17 Edw. iv. (1476).

(*fo.* 306, *b.*) Grant by Thomas Saxton of the city of York, corveser, of all his goods, to sir Thomas Darnton, prior of the priory of the Holy Trinity of York, and Richard Blakborn, gentleman, servant of the said prior. Seal. Witnesses, Henry Hudson, chaplain, Richard Russell, spicer, William Spencer, 19 September, 16 Edw. iv. (1476). Acknowledged before John Tonge, mayor, 17 February, 16 Edw. iv. (1476-7).

(*fo.* 307). Release by John Bernardcastell to Ralph Bygod, knight, etc., of lands in the city and suburbs of York. York, 3 January, 33 Henry vi. (1454-5).

(*fo.* 307, *b.*) Grant by Henry Gascoigne, esquire, to Thomas Hemylsay of York, Guy Fayefax, John Evenwod, clerk, and John Thwenge, and the heirs of Thomas, of a yearly rent of six marks, payable at Christmas and the feast of S. John the Baptist from Henry's lands in Mekelfeld by Abirford in the West Riding and Naburn in the East Riding; the grant is not to take effect as long as the grantees hold without ejection or lawful recovery a tenement, late of the said Henry, in Kyngeston upon Hull, which John de Lutton and John Grymesby, chaplains, formerly held by enfeoffment of Henry Wyman, late citizen and merchant of York, lying in length between Hulstrete east and a street called Marketgate west, and in breadth between a tenement formerly of Roger le Taverner, Hugh le Taverner and Walter le Taverner south, and a tenement of the archbishop of York, north. Seal. York, 31 October, 1455, 34 Henry vi. Acknowledged before Richard Lematon, mayor, 25 October, 34 Henry vi.

(*fo.* 308, *b.*) Grant by William Northerby, son and heir of John Northerby late of York, merchant, being of the full age of twenty-one years, to Robert Mauleverer, Richard Wyman, esquires, and John Popelay, gentleman, of a tenement in Skeldergate in York. Witnesses, William Gascoyng, knight, William Skargill, esquire, William Abirford of York, merchant, John Selby of the same, tapiter, and Alexander Metham of the same, gentleman. Seal. 8 June, 35 Henry vi. (1457). Acknowledged before Robert Colynson, mayor, 9 June, 35 Henry vi. Letter of attorney by the same, citizen and merchant of York, appointing Thomas Thornton and Thomas Pille to deliver seisin of the said tenement. Seal. Same date. Acknowledged as above.

(fo. 309). Cum quedam controversia mota fuisset inter Robertum Colynson, civem et mercatorem Ebor', ex una parte, et Thomam Burnell de Calisia, mercatorem, ex altera parte, propter incidicionem aque pluvialis de tenemento dicti Thome in gardinum predicti Roberti in Northstrete in Ebor', contra consuetudinem civitatis predicte, tandem tamen, mediante [ali-] quorum amicorum tractatu, tam predictus Robertus quam prefatus Thomas per Thomam Curteis, deputatum et attornatum ac receptorem reddituum et firmarum ejusdem Thome Burnell in civitate predicta, submiserunt se, sicut mos est in eadem civitate, judicio et arbitrio scrutatorum cementariorum et carpentariorum ejusdem civitatis. Unde Johannes Porter, magister lathamus ecclesie Cathedralis beati Petri Eboracensis, Robertus Couper, magister lathamus civitatis Ebor', Johannes Foulford et Robertus Jakson, carpentarii, scrutatores artificiorum predictorum, ad hoc specialiter electi et jurati de consensu predictorum Roberti Colynson et Thome Curteis, et prehabita deliberacione matura et diligenti, iidem scrutatores considerabant et judicabant, videlicet, quod tam predictus Robertus Colynson quam prefatus Thomas Burnell, heredes et assignati sui, evacuabunt et conducent omnimodam aquam pluvialem super domos suas predictas cadentem super solum suum proprium absque pejoracione seu dampno aliquali alterius partis in futurum.

(fo. 309, b.) Grant by John Blakburn of York, goldsmith, and Elizabeth his wife, to Richard Atkynson of Newark, mercer, for term of life of Elizabeth, of the messuages without Mekillythbarr in the suburb of the city of York, which she had for term of life. Witnesses, John Thwenge, William Crofte, Thomas Clerke, Adam Gunby of York. 13 October, 37 Henry vi. (1458).

(*fo.* 310). Placita assisarum apud civitatem Ebor' coram Johanne Nedeham et Ricardo Knyght, eidem Johanni ac Radulfo Pole, justiciariis domini regis ad assisas in civitate predicta capiendas, hac vice associato, presencia predicti Radulfi non exspectata, virtute brevis domini Regis, si non omnes, die Jovis proximo post festum Sancti Petri ad Vincula, 6 Henr. vi. (3 August, 1458).

Civitas Ebor'. Assisa venit recognitura si Willelmus Bradley de Ebor', mercator, injuste et sine judicio disseisivit priorem ecclesie sive prioratus Sancte Trinitatis de Kirkham de libero tenemento suo in civitate Ebor' post primam etc. Et unde idem prior, per Willelmum Stillyngton, attornatum suum, queritur quod disseisivit eum de decem et septem solidatis redditus cum pertinenciis etc. Et predictus Willelmus Bradley non venit, set quidam Thomas Cotes respondet pro eo tanquam ejus ballivus, et nichil pro eo dicit quare assisa predicta remanere debeat etc. Ideo capiatur inde inter eos assisa etc. Et super hoc predictus prior pro titulo liberi tenementi et assisa de redditu predicto habendis dicit, quod redditus ille est redditus oneris exiens de quatuor mesuagiis cum pertinenciis in parochia ecclesie Sancte Crucis in Conyngarth in civitate predicta, ex opposito finis occidentalis ejusdem ecclesie, unde solum super quo mesuagia illa edificantur quondam fuit Ade Carpentarii, et postea prioris et conventus ecclesie sive prioratus predicti. Et dicit, quod idem nunc prior et omnes predecessores sui, priores ecclesie sive prioratus Sancte Trinitatis predicti, successive fuerunt seisiti in jure ejusdem ecclesie sive prioratus de redditu predicto exeunte de mesuagiis predictis, in dominico suo ut de feodo, singulis annis ad festa Pentecostes et Sancti Martini in yeme per equales porciones solvendo, a tempore cujus contrarii memoria non existit. Et petit assisam etc. Recognitores videlicet Willelmus Crathorn, Johannes Brereton, Ricardus Claybruke, [Johanne]s Wardrop, Thomas Tutbag, Ricardus Croull, Thomas Atkynson, Johannes Bedale, Johannes Kirke, Ricardus Crokelyn, Johannes Lynton, et Johannes Whyr[yg] exacti veniunt, qui ad veritatem de premissis dicendam electi, triati et jurati, dicunt super (*fo.* 310, *b.*) sacramentum suum, quod idem nunc prior seisitus fuit de redditu predicto cum pertinenciis in dominico suo ut de feodo et jure ecclesie sive prioratus sui Sancte Trinitatis predicti, quousque predictus Willelmus ipsum inde injuste et sine judicio, set non vi neque armis, disseisivit. Recognitores predicti, quesiti qualis redditus predictus redditus existit et quale jus predictus nunc prior habet in eodem redditu, et quis predecessorum suorum fuit inde seisitus ut in jure ecclesie sive prioratus sui predicti, tempore domini Henrici nuper regis Anglie tercii post conquestum, et qualiter disseisina ejusdem redditus facta fuit, et que dampna idem prior sustinuit occasione desseisine predicte, et si habeatur aliqua fraus sive collusio inde inter predictum priorem et prefatum Willelmum Bradley contra formam statuti quo cavetur ne terre sive tenementa ad manum mortuam deveniant quoquo modo prelocuta, dicunt super sacramentum suum, quod redditus predictus est redditus oneris exiens de predictis quatuor mesuagiis in titulo predicto specificatis cum pertinenciis. Et quod predictus nunc prior seisitus fuit de redditu illo, per manus predicti Willelmi Bradley, nunc tenentis mesuagiorum predictorum cum pertinenciis, ipseque prior et omnes predecessores sui, priores prioratus predicti successive per manus omnium aliorum tenencium mesuagiorum illorum, pro tempore existencium, seisiti fuerunt de redditu predicto cum pertinenciis exeunte de eisdem mesuagiis, in dominico suo ut de feodo et jure ecclesie sive prioratus illius, singulis annis ad festa predicta equis porcionibus solvendo, a tempore quo non extat memoria. Et quod quidam Ricardus Memthorp, quondam prior ecclesie sive prioratus predicti, predecessor predicti nunc prioris, fuit seisitus de redditu predicto cum pertinenciis exeunte de mesuagiis predictis ad festa predicta equis porcionibus, in dominico suo ut de feodo et jure ejusdem ecclesie sive prioratus, tempore dicti domini Henrici nuper regis Anglie tercii post conquestum, per manus Ade Neirum et Ranulfi de Floyter, tunc tenencium mesuagiorum illorum, et quod predictus redditus per unum annum proximo precedentem festum Sancti Martini in yeme proximum ante diem impetracionis brevis originalis assise predicte, scilicet, primum diem Januarii ultimo preteritum, eidem nunc priori aretro fuit non solutus, per quod ipse in eodem festo ad mesuagia predicta venit, et ibidem decem et septem solidos de redditu illo per annum illum eidem nunc priori sic aretro existenti et non soluto de prefato Willelmo Bradley, tunc tenente mesuagiorum illorum cum pertinenciis, peciit. Et idem Willelmus redditum illum eidem nunc priori reddere tunc ibidem penitus recusavit et objurgavit. Et sic dicunt quod idem Willelmus ipsum nunc priorem inde injuste et sine judicio in forma predicta disseisivit ad dampnum ipsius nunc prioris, tam occasione assise predicte quam pro redditu predicto sic aretro existenti, ultra misas et custagia sua per ipsum circa sectam suam in hac parte apposita, quadraginta solidorum, et pro misis et custagiis illis quinque marcarum. Et dicunt quod non habetur aliqua fraus sive collusio inde inter ipsum nunc priorem et prefatum Willelmum Bradley contra formam statuti predicti prelocuta. Ideo consideratum est quod predictus nunc prior recuperet seisinam suam de redditu predicto cum pertinenciis per visum recognitorum assise predicte et dampna sua predicta per recognitores predictos ad octo marcas in forma predicta assisa. Et dictus Willelmus Bradley in misericordia etc.

(*fo*. 311). Grant by Robert Thorp, of Holme in Spaldyngmore, gentleman, and Alice his wife, to John Thweng of York, gentleman, John Cawton and William Myrthefeld of York, chaplains, of a tenement with a garden in Fysshergate in York, lately held by John Rolston, of Margaret Catour, formerly the wife of Thomas Catour, late of York, salsemaker. York, 2 April, 37 Henr. vi. (1459). Acknowledged before Nicholas Holgate, mayor, 3 April, 37 Henry vi.

(*fo*. 311, *b*.) Grant by Thomas Rodirham, citizen of York, to William Couper of York, pinner, of two selions of land in the parish of S. John in Hundegate in York. York, 3 March, 1427, 6 Henry vi.

Bond by the master and hospital of S. Leonard of York, to the mayor and commonalty of the city, in 40 *s*. that whereas Alice, late the wife of Thomas Esyngwald, late mayor, has given 20 *l*., to the hospital, they will celebrate the obit of the said Thomas on 10 September yearly during the life of Alice, and after her death, her own obit also, on the same day, with *Placebo* and *Dirige*, mass of the dead and ringing of the great bells ; in the daily Mass of Requiem they shall be bound to pray for Thomas and Alice in the prayer *Inclina Domine*. The following sums shall be distributed

EUFEMIA LANGTON'S BEQUEST TO THE FRIAR PREACHERS 223

yearly; to the brothers saying Mass 10 s. 10 d., to be divided equally immediately after the offertory of the Mass, as is the custom; to the chaplain of the infirmary 3 d.; to the clerk of the church 2 d.; to the clerks and choristers for ringing the great bells 8 d.; to the town crier for proclaiming the obit 4 d.; in the chapter house of the hospital 8. 1436. Deed tripartite. Seal.

(fo. 312, b.) Grant by Robert Davyson, of York Castle, to Ralph, baron Graystok, knight, Thomas Wytham, esquire, and John Shirwood of York, gentleman, of a yearly rent of six marks. 1 July, 3 Edward iv. (1463). Acknowledged in the mayoralty of Thomas Scauceby, 3 July, 3 Edw. iv.

(fo. 313). Grant by Thomas Howren, John Evenwod of York, clerks, and Christofer Dobley, chaplains to Thomas Neleson, citizen and merchant of York, of the lands in the city and suburbs, which they had by enfeoffment of William Stokton, citizen and merchant. York, 18 August, 3 Edw. iv. (1463). Acknowledged before Thomas Scauceby, mayor, 8 September, 3 Edw. iv. (1463).

Universis et singulis Christi fidelibus has literas tripartitas indentatas inspecturis vel audituris, frater Johannes Multou, prior ordinis fratrum predicatorum civitatis Ebor', et ejusdem loci conventus, salutem in Domino nostro Jhesu Christo. Veraciter agnoscimus, ad memoriam reducentes grata et acceptabilia beneficia et dona, que honorabilis et discreta domina ˙Eufemia Langton nobis ante hec tempora contulit, successoribus nostris et domui nostre predicte multipliciter valitura, et precipue pro quadam summa pecunie, quam eadem domina Eufemia jam tarde nobis tribuit intuitu caritatis ex affectione speciali, quam nobis et ordini nostro gerit; que summa pecunie pro redempcione quorundam jocalium, librorum, et vestimentorum, ac aliorum diversorum ornamentorum, pro debitis nostri conventus antedicti diversis personis impignoratorum plenius persolvit et convertitur. Que bona, ornamenta (fo. 313, b.) et jocalia, nisi manus pietatis prefate Eufemie nobis cicius occurrissent, conventus noster predictus bonis et ornamentis illis pro perpetuo caruisset. Et quia benefactoribus ad antitoda [sic] naturaliter obligamus, ne gratis acceptorum contra naturam immemores videamur, nos, igitur, prior et conventus predicti, de nostro unanimi consensu et voluntate, que spontanea ac de licencia et assensu venerabilis in Christo patris, fratris Johannis Kyng, sacre sciencie professoris, nostri provincialis in Anglia, pro nobis et successoribus nostris imperpetuum promittimus, et bona fide concedimus, ac, juramento corporali super sancta Dei evaungelia prestito, nos et successores nostros predictos stringimus et obligamus, quod pro bono statu et laudabili prosperitate ejusdem domine Eufemie, Johannis, Roberti, Henrici, Willelmi, Thome, et Margarete, liberorum ejusdem Eufemie, et pro animabus domini Johannis Langton, militis, parentum ipsius, et omnium progenitorum et amicorum suorum, ac pro animabus predicte domine Eufemie cum ab hac luce migraverit, et omnium amicorum et progenitorum suorum, et omnium fidelium defunctorum specialiter quibus supradicti Johannes et Eufemia obligantur, vel a quibus aliquid immerito habuerunt vel eorum alter habuit, quod singulis diebus imperpetuum, exceptis djebus ab ecclesia approbatis, scilicet, triduo ante Pascha, faciemus unam missam de beate Maria Virgine celebrari ad altare sancte Trinitatis in ecclesia conventuali antedicta, inter horam octavam et horam novenam, per unum fratrem nostri ordinis et conventus cum oracionibus in eadem :—"Deus, qui caritatis dona sancti spiritus tuorum cordibus fidelium infudisti, da famule tue Eufemie, famulis et famulabus tuis, Johanni, Roberto, Henrico, Willelmo, Thome, et Margarete, filiis et filiabus eorundem, et omnium parentum, amicorum, consanguineorum [sic] et benefactorum suorum, pro quibus tuam deprecamur clemenciam" etc. et oracione :—"Inclina, Domine, aurem tuam ad preces nostras, quibus misericordeam tuam supplices deprecamur ut animam famuli tui Johannis Langton, militis, et animas omnium parentum, progenitorum et amicorum predictorum Johannis et Eufemie, quas de hoc seculo migrare jussisti" etc. usque ad finem, publice in eisdem oracionibus et missis recitand(o) nomina ut superius scribuntur, pro maiori noticia et devocione amicorum et Christi fidelium hujusmodi audiencium. Ad quam quidem missam pulsetur tribus pulsacionibus cum parva campana, et vocetur imperpetuum Langton messe. Et frater, qui missam celebrabit, jurabit super sancta Dei Evaungelia quater in anno, scilicet, omni quarterio anni semel, quod sine fictione, fraude, seu dolo, celebrabit missam illam pro bono statu dicte domine Eufemie, filiorum et filiarum ejusdem, et pro animabus domini Johannis Langton, militis, omniumque parentum, progenitorum, consanguineorum et amicorum predictorum Johannis Langton et Eufemie defunctorum, et omnium aliorum quibus ipsi obligantur. Et idem frater servabit et fideliter custodiet cotidie horam superius assignatam, nisi fuerit racionabiliter premunitus ad expectandum super adventum predicte domine Eufemie, aut aliquorum heredum vel liberorum aut executorum ejusdem Eufemie. Et concedimus, (*fo.* 314) quod nomina et cognomina predicte domine Eufemie, filiorum et filiarum ejusdem vivencium, cum nominibus Johannis Langton, militis, parentum, progenitorum, amicorum et benefactorum suorum, quibus ipsi obligantur, scribantur in una cedula, et ponatur super altare antedictum ante oculos dicti sacerdotis imperpetuum missam predictam celebrantis; et eciam eadem nomina et cognomina in martilogio nostro scribantur, et in cotidiano nostro capitulo singillatim recitabuntur, pro quibus dicemus in eodem capitulo devociones et suffragia, sicut pro aliquibus aliis benefactoribus ibidem dicitur vel dicere teneamur. Insuper nos, predicti prior et conventus, de licencia superius recitata, obligamus nos et successores imperpetuum, quod hora nona dicta in choro dicte ecclesie nostre inmediate dicetur a conventu nostro ibidem omni die Psalmus *De profundis* cum oracione fidelium ut supra, et quod omnino in die parassaphe dicentur septem psalmi penitenciales cum letania ab omnibus et singulis fratribus ejusdem conventus pro bono et salubri statu prenominatorum vivencium ac defunctorum. Similiter, de eadem licencia superius recitata, obligamus nos et successores imperpetuum ad unum annualem obitum pro anima venerabilis predicti Johannis Langton, militis, animabus parentum omniumque progenitorum ac amicorum ejusdem, quem quidem obitum celebrari faciemus in choro nostro predicto solempniter et devote, cum nota et aliis ornamentis convenientibus, prout moris est, cujus exequie celebrentur in vigilia Sancti Mathie Apostoli et missa in crastino, ad cujus exequias pulsetur tribus pulsacionibus distincte, et ad missam similiter, cum magna campana nostra, et dicentur in eisdem exequiis et missis annuatim oraciones speciales videlicet "Deus indulgenc(ie)" et "Inclina Domine" etc. in forma superius expressa, cum aliis oracionibus convenientibus pro defunctis imperpetuum. Insuper volumus et concedimus, quod postquam dicta Eufemia ab hac luce migraverit, in vigilia sive [die?] migracionis ab hoc seculo unum alium obitum cum *Placebo* et *Dirige*, ac missa in crastino, cum nota in capis ceterisque ornamentis convenientibus in choro nostro predicto devote et solempniter annuatim imperpetuum celebrari faciemus a toto conventu domus nostre antedicte, cum oracionibus :—" Deus indulgenc(ie), Domine, da famule tue Eufemie, animabus liberorum suorum nominatim et decedencium, parentum, fratrum suorum, omniumque progenitorum, consanguineorum et amicorum suorum, quorum anniversaria " etc. et " Quamvis, Domine, pro tua pie(ta)te misere(re) famule tue Eufemie " etc., cum aliis oracionibus et suffragiis consuetis, ad cujus exequias et missam annuales pulsetur distincte tribus pulsacionibus magne campane nostre. Et ulterius nos, predicti Prior et conventus, ex nostris unanimi consensu et assensu, de licencia prefati nostri reverendi patris provincialis, pro nobis et successoribus nostris volumus, et per presentes concedimus, recipimus, et admittimus, prefatos Eufemiam, Johannem, Henricum, Robertum, Willelmum, Thomam, et Margaretam, liberos ejusdem Eufemie, ac omnes heredes et pueros de eorum seu de eorum alicujus corpore vel corporibus legitime exeuntes, plenarie fore fratres et sorores in dicto nostro capitulo, et quod imperpetuum sint, et quilibet eorum (*fo.* 314, *b.*) sit, participes et particeps de cetero omnium et singulorum missarum, predicacionum, jejuniorum, peregrinacionum, abstinenciarum, vigiliarum, oracionum ceterorumque bonorum operum et suffragiorum spiritualium, que per nos et successores nostros predictos fient ad laudem et honorem Dei. Et quandocumque Deo placuerit prefatam Eufemiam, seu aliquem vel aliquos liberorum suorum predictorum, vel aliquem seu aliquos pueros eorundem liberorum ab hac luce migrare, tam cito sicut vera noticia[1] ad nostras aures ve noticiam devenit, obligamus nos et successores nostros ad mittendum nomina eorum singulorum sic decedencium, tociens quociens ita eveniet in futurum, omnibus et singulis locis ordinis nostri per totam Angliam per ordinacionem capituli provincialis, ut fiant pro eis omnino in quolibet loco *Placebo* et *Dirige* cum aliis oracionibus et suffragiis ecclesie, prout

---

[1]—Repeated in MS.

tenemur facere pro aliquo fratre nostre professionis. Et pro majori noticia et memoria omnium premissorum, nos, predicti prior et conventus, obligamus nos et successores nostros, quod presentes litere tripartite publice legantur coram omnibus fratribus dicte domus annuatim imperpetuum bis, videlicet, in die Cene Domini et xv° die Septembris. Ad quas quidem convenciones superius expressas et omnibus et singulis ex parte nostra bene et fideliter absque fraude, seu dolo, seu malo ingenio, tenendas, observandas et perimplendas, nos, iidem prior et conventus, de licencia antedicta, obligamus nos et successores nostros ac omnia bona nostra consecrata et non consecrata, ubicumque fuerint inventa, prefate Eufemie, heredibus et liberis suis antedictis, ita quod tociens quociens ita evenerit in futurum, quod absit, quod nos, prior et conventus, vel successores nostri imposterum dictas devociones et observaciones vel aliquam earundem partem aliquo die contra formam superius recitatam subtraxerimus vel necligenter dimiserimus, concedimus nos et successores nostros predictos teneri et firmiter per presentes obligari maiori civitatis Ebor', qui nunc est, et successorebus suis maioribus, qui pro tempore crunt, ac dictis liberis prefate Eufemie, heredibus et executoribus eorundem, conjunctim et divisim, in centum solidis sterlingorum nomine pene solvendis et forisfaciendis indilate tociens quociens hujusmodi casus evenerit in futurum; de qua summa centum solidorum quadraginta solidi remaneant ad usum camere civitatis antedicte, et sexaginta solidi residui dictorum centum solidorum distribuantur inter pauperes et egenos per dictum maiorem seu liberos dicte Eufemie die anniversarii sui imperpetuum, quandocumque et quocienscumque hujusmodi casus evenerit in futurum. Volumus eciam et concedimus nos, prior et conventus antedicti, pro nobis et successoribus nostris in futurum, quod pro necligencia seu omissione aliquarum ordinacionum prescriptarum bene licebit prefate Eufemie, dum vixerit, heredibus et executoribus suis, et post ejus decessum, prefato maiori et communitati et successoribus suis maioribus, vel heredibus et liberis eorundem Johannis et Eufemie, dictam ecclesiam (*fo.* 315) conventualem cum omnibus domibus, terris et tenementis nostris eidem pertinentibus, quibuscumque privilegiis sive libertatibus non obstantibus, libere ad eorum

placitum intrare et ibidem distringere, districtionesque sic captas
libere abducere, effugere et asportare, sive fuerint consecrata
sive non consecrata, et ea penes se retinere quousque sibi de
predictis centum solidis una cum misis et expensis ea occasione
habitis plenarie fuerit satisfactum et persolutum, tociens quociens
hujusmodi casus evenerit, refutando et recusando omnimoda
privilegia et libertates, tam papales quam regales, nobis seu loco
nostro predicto concessa aut imposterum concedenda in hoc casu
tantum. Obligamus enim nos et successores nostros per presentes,
quod non licebit nobis nec alicui nostrum nec aliquo alio quocumque in futurum aliquem rescussum facere aliquibus temporibus
pro vel in districtionis hujusmodi capcione, nec aliquas literas
monicionis sive sentencias excommunicacionis in isto casu
prosequi vel denunciare, nec aliquod replevium capere, nec
placitum per breve nec aliquo alio modo prosequi nec manu-
tenere coram aliquibus judicibus spiritualibus vel temporalibus.
Ad quas quidem convenciones bene et fideliter tenendas et in
omnibus et singulis ut supra scribuntur ex parte nostrorum,
prioris et conventus, et successorum nostrorum pro perpetuis
futuris temporibus duratur(as), absque fraude, dolo, seu malo
ingenio, bene et fideliter perimplendas et observandas, nos, prior
et conventus supradicti, obligamus nos et successores nostros
ac omnia bona nostra consecrata et non consecrata prefate
domine Eufemie, heredibus et liberis suis antedictis et eorum
cuilibet conjunctim et divisim imperpetuum, licencia plena et
consensu nostri predicti venerabilis patris provincialis ad omnia
et singula premissa optenta. Et ad hec tenor ejusdem sequitur
in hec verba :—Universis pateat per presentes quod ego frater
Johannes Kyng, sacre sciencie professor, provincialis fratrum
ordinis predicatorum in provincia Anglia, in capitulo meo provinciali, xv die mensis Augusti celebrato, anno Domini infrascripto,
quasdam literas pro et ex parte fratris Johannis Multon, prioris
fratrum predicatorum Ebor', et ejusdem loci conventus, super
quibusdam composicionibus, pactis et convencionibus inter
eosdam priorem et conventum ex una parte, et prepotentem
dominam Eufemiam Langton, nuper uxorem Johannis Langton,
militis, ex altera parte, factis nuper et habitis pro nonnullis
devocionibus, oracionibus, missarum celebracionibus, obitibus et

aliis divinis obsequiis et suffragiis, ab eisdem priore et conventu et successoribus suis et singulis fratribus ejusdem conventus pro quibusdam animabus defunctorum, et pro bono et salubri statu predicte Eufemie et aliarum diversarum personarum superstitum imperpetuum faciendis; et debite supportandis, prout in dictis literis plenius continetur, michi presentatas, visas, inspectas, et cum matura deliberacione intellectas, et ad instanciam et specialem requisicionem predicti fratris (*fo*. 315, *b*.) Johannis Multon, prioris, et conventus sui, postquam vidi et intellexi dictas composiciones et convenciones fore verisimiliter Deo gratas, dictis priori et conventui ac successoribus suis utiles et multipliciter profituras, ac cciam tam vivis quam defunctis salutiferas et imperpetuum valituras; ipsas composiciones et convenciones omnes et singulas, quantum in me est, pro me et successoribus meis admisi et approbavi et ratificavi, necnon admitto, approbo, et per presentes confirmo et ratifico, necnon de consensu et assensu omnium et singulorum fratrum ordinis antedicti in capitulo nostro provinciali supradicto congregatorum, concessi dicto fratri Johanni, priori, et conventui licenciam pro se et successoribus suis dictas convenciones et composiciones cum suis emergentibus, incedentibus, dependentibus et connexis, ad finem debitum plenarie et omnibus perficere et perimplere. Et ego predictus frater Johannes Kyng, prior provincialis provincie Anglie, recipio et admitto predictam dominam Eufemiam, liberos suos antedictos, necnon parentes, fratres et sorores, necnon eorundem omnium et singulorum liberos et heredes, et de eorum heredibus in heredes in futurum provenientes fore participes per divinam clemenciam omnium suffragiorum spiritualium fratrum nostri ordinis tam presencium quam futurorum, videlicet, omnium missarum, oracionum, jejuniorum, vigiliarum, predicacionum, abstinenciarum, peregrinacionum, laborum ceterorumque bonorum spiritualium, que per fratres nostri ordinis predicti et eorum successores imperpetuum fient, ad laudem et honorem Dei in futurum. Et quandocumque contigerit, quod aliquis vel aliqua predictorum liberorum ejusdem Eufemie aut heredum suorum imposterum ab hac luce migrare(t) volumus quod eorum nomina sic decedencium in nostro provinciali capitulo recitentur, et pro eis injungantur exequie et misse solempnes cum aliis suffragiis et oracionibus ecclesiasticis in singulis ecclesiis nostri ordinis per totam provinciam, sicut pro fratribus nostri ordinis defunctis fieri consuevit. In quorum omnium et singulorum prout suprascribuntur testimonium presentibus literis nostris tripartitis indentatis sigilla conventui pertinencia, scilicet, sigillum officiale mei, prioris, et sigillum nostrum commune conventus nostri predicti, cuilibet parti dictarum literarum tripartitarum ut predicitur apposuimus ; et pro majori securitate omnium premissorum sigillum predicti venerabilis patris nostri provincialis cuilibet parti earundem literarum tripartitarum apponi procuravimus et apponi fecimus, quarum unam partem penes nos et conventum nostrum predictum, alteramque vero partem penes heredes et executores dicte Eufemie, et terciam partem penes maiorem et communitatem civitatis Ebor' antedicte, volumus imperpetuum remanere. Et ego frater Johannes Kyng, provincialis, cuilibet parti dictarum literarum tripartitarum, ad instanciam et specialem requisicionem dictorum prioris et conventus, in plenam confirmacionem et affirmacionem et ratificacionem omnium (*fo*. 316) prescriptorum, sigillum meum provincialis[1] [*sic*] antedicte apponi feci. Datum in meo provinciali capitulo Glocester', celebrato in festo Assumpcionis beate Marie Virginis, anno Domini millesimo quadringentesimo sexagesimo tercio.

Inquisition held at York, 6 July, 4 Edward iv. (1464), before John Gillyot, mayor and escheator, by oath of William Bouland, John[1], William Knolles, John Croull, Walter Graystok, John Thomlynson, William Graunge, John Treman, Thomas Elyson, John Hill, Thomas Makblythe, William Speller and Robert Leper.

Brian [Davell][1] held no lands at the time of his death ; but held previously the manor of Bilton and four messuages, seven and a half bovates of land, twenty acres of pasture and twenty acres of wood in the vill of Bylton ; the manor is held of Thomas, Lord Lescrop of Upsall, by fealty and rent of 9 *l*. 12 *s*., and is of the clear yearly value of 10 *s*., and the messuages, land, pasture and wood are held of the prior and convent of S. John the

---

1—The MS. has no surname here.

Evangelist of Helaghpark by fealty and rent of one red rose at the feast of S. John the Baptist, and are of the clear yearly value of 10 s.

He held the manor of Tokwyth of Robert Roos of Ingmanthorp by fealty and rent of 1 d.; of the clear yearly value of six marks.

He held the manors of Busterdthorp and Middilethorp of the abbot and convent of Whitby by fealty and rent of 10 s.; of the clear yearly value of six marks. He held a yearly rent of 6 s. from ten tenements of Brian Stapilton, knight, in the city of York. He held a toft and croft in the vill of Marston of the abbot and convent of S. Mary of Fountains by fealty only; of the clear yearly value of 20 d. He held seven messuages, seven and a half bovates of land in the vill of Bishopthorp, otherwise called Thorp Anderowe, of the king by fealty and rent of two marks; of the clear yearly value of 40 s.

By charter shewn to the jurors dated 11 Oct., 1 Edw. iv. (1461) he granted all the premisses to Guy Fairfax, Thomas Davell and Henry Davell, his brothers. He died 6 March last (1463-4).

Elizabeth Davell is his kinswoman and heir, daughter and heir of William Davell, eldest son of the said Brian, and is aged six years and more.

(*fo.* 317). Bond by the wardens and convent of Friars Minors of the city of York, to the mayor and communalty in 40 s., that whereas William Butler of Selby and Cecily and Constance deceased, late his wives, have been benefactors to the convent, and William has given to them a certain sum of money, they will celebrate their obit as follows :—Daily in the Mass of Blessed Mary during the life of William the collect *Omnipotens Sempiterne Deus* shall be said and after his death, *Inclina*; their obit shall be said solemnly with note on 21 July yearly with *Placebo* and *Derige*, and mass of requiem at the high altar. Deed tripartite. Seal. In the chapter-house 12 January, 1464, 4 Edw. iv. (1464-5).

(*fo.* 317, *b*.) Grant by William Vescy, citizen and merchant of York, to William Burges, chaplain, and Robert Boteler of York, yeoman, of the lands and tenements in Conyngstrete which he inherited after the death of Joan Burton, his mother. Five witnesses. York, 24 April, 5 Edw. iv. (1465). Acknowledged before Thomas Neleson, mayor, 9 May, 5 Edw. iv.

(*fo.* 318). Grant by the said William and Robert to the said William Vescy of the said lands and tenements, which they had by his grant; to hold for term of life, with remainder for term of life to Alice Holegate, wife of Nicholas Holegate, citizen and merchant, daughter of master Roger Burton, formerly of York, clerk, and of Joan his wife, sister of the said William Vescy, with successive remainders to William Holegate, son of Nicholas and Alice, in tail, and to the right heirs of Alice, and then of William Vescy. Witnesses, Thomas Neleson, mayor, John Brereton, William Snawfell, sheriffs, William Wright, *draper*, John Sherwod, William Spence, citizens of York. Seal. York, 26 April, 5 Edw. iv. (1465). Acknowledged as last deed.

(*fo.* 318, *b.*) Grant by John Warthill, son of Nicholas Warthill, clerk of the city of York, to Maud, wife of John Radclyff, gentleman, and John Radeclyff otherwise called John Warthill, their son, of the lands in Heslyngton, Gatefulford and Waterfulford, which he had by enfeoffment of the said Nicholas Warthill his father. Seal. Witnesses John Thweng, gentleman, Thomas Staynton, Ralf Makblyth, Henry Burdclever, John Stalon. 15 November, 5 Edw. iv. (1465).

Letter of attorney by the same, appointing William Watson of York, chaplain, to deliver seisin of the said lands. Same date. Seal.

Will of John Warthill of the city of York, clerk; dated 12 Sept., 1465. Proved, 14 February, 1465.

(*fo.* 319. *b.*) Grant by Richard Busshebury, citizen and grocer of London, to John Scargill esquire, and John Knapton, clerk, of a tenement called le Graunge in Westharford. Names of witnesses. 25 September, 6 Edw. iv. (1466). Acknowledged before John Kent, mayor, 6 Oct., 6 Edw. iv. Release (*fo.* 320) by the same of the same to the same, same witnesses. Westharford 30 Sept., 6 Edw. iv. (1466). Acknowledged as last deed.

(*fo.* 321). Grant by Henry Willesthorp, rector of the church of Braffynton, to Roger, son of Thomas Willesthorp, of the lands which Henry had together with John Elton and others

GRANT TO A CHANTRY IN THE CATHEDRAL (146⅞) 233

now deceased, by enfeoffment of the said Thomas, in the vill of Knapton by Acom, to hold from Whitsuntide 1443 for term of seven years, with successive remainders in tail male at the end of the said term, to George, Christopher, and Thomas Willisthorp, brothers of Roger, and to the said Roger; in tail to Katharine Tanfeld and Joan Sparowe, their sisters; successively in tail male to Miles, son of Richard Willesthorp, son of Robert Willesthorp, their uncle; to Peter Willesthorp, son of William Willesthorp, their uncle; and to James Willesthorp; and to the right heirs of the said Thomas Willesthorp, father of the said George. Seal. Witnesses, Roger Warde, Robert Roos, knights, Richard Aldeburgh, Richard Banke, Brian Dayvell. 20 January, 21 Henry vi. (1442–3). Acknowledged in the time of John Marsshal, mayor.

(*fo.* 321, *b.*) Confirmation by William Sharpils of York, fletcher, of the following deed of his brother.

Grant by Robert Sharpils of Kyngeston-upon-Hull to William Snawesell of York, goldsmith, John Thurynge of York, gentleman, John Saxton, clerk, and Thomas Eston, chaplain, of his lands in Huntyngton and Clifton by York. Seal. Witnesses, John Cotes of York, Christopher Mowbray, Stephen Talbot, John Shirwod, gentleman, William Heynde, goldsmith, William Hardy. 7 June, 4 Edw. iv. (1464). Confirmation dated 13 May, Edw. iv. (1467). Seal.

(*fo.* 322). Release by the said William of the same to the same. Seal. Witnesses, Robert Holme, gentleman, master William Huet, clerk, William Welles, vintner, all of York, 20 May, 1 Edw. iv. (1461).

(*fo.* 322, *b.*) Grant by William Wright, citizen and weaver of York, and Marion his wife, to John Cawod, vicar choral in the cathedral church of S. Peter of York, and chaplain at the altar of S. Stephen, and his successours, chaplains at the said chantry, of a yearly rent of 13 *s.* 4 *d.*, which he and the chaplains his predecessors have received, time out of mind, at Martinmas and Whitsuntide, from a tenement in Colyergate, which William and Marion now inhabit in her right, lying in breadth between a tenement late of Simon de Waghen and a tenement belonging to a chantry in the church of S. Saviour of York; to pray for the souls of William and Marion, and of Adam Helmesley and Sir George Helmesley, chaplain, brother of Marion. Seals. York, 3 March, 1467 ; 7 Edw. iv. (1467-8). Acknowledged before William Snawsill. mayor, 4 March, 8 Edw. iv. (1467-8).

(*fo.* 323). Grant by Eufamia, lady (domina) of Heslarton, and Robert Bukton, rector of the church of Louthorp, to Denise, formerly wife of Thomas Stodehagh of Pokelyngton, for term of life, of the lands which they have of her grant in the vill of Hasthorp, with remainder to William Hungate of Brunby, for term of life, and successively in tail male to Thomas and William his sons, and then to the right heirs of the said William the father. Seal. Witnesses, Thomas Ughtred, knight, John Aske, Walter Rudstane, Robert de Fenton, Richard Curtays of Pokelyngton. Sutton-upon-Derwent. 5 Jan., 10 Rich. ii. (1386-7).

(*fo.* 323, *b.*) Omnibus et singulis ad quorum noticiam presentes litere pervenerint vel auditum, nos, maior et communitas burgi domini Regis de Appelby in comitatu Westmorl'. salutem in Eo, qui est omnium vera salus ac honoris prosperitatisque continuum incrementum. Cum christianissimus excellentissimus rex, Henricus, pater domini Johannis, quondam regis Anglie, concesserit et per cartam suam confirmaverit burgensibus suis de Appelby predicta omnes libertates et liberas consuetudines, quas cives et burgenses domini regis de Ebor' ex concessione dictorum Henrici et Johannis, quondam Regum Anglie, habent et possident in presenti, et quod dicti burgenses de Appelby liberi sint et quieti de tolneo, stallagio, pontagio, muragio, chiminagio et lastagio per totam terram Anglie, quantum ad dominum Regem pertinet atque spectat, prout in literis patentibus omnium regum Anglie, post ipsos successive in Anglia regnancium, dictis burgensibus de Appelby confectis, plenius declaratur. Et quia Willelmus Bower, alias dictus Willelmus Wilson, unus burgensium domini regis dicti burgi de Appelby, ad presens et per unum annum ultimum elapsum ante datam presencium existens et extiterit ad partes mundi varias se divertens et laborans cum suis mercandisis et causa mercandisandi, a quibusdam dicti regni incolis et ministris, dictarum concessionum et libertatum nesciis et ignaris, extitit quamplurimum fatigatus, arestatus, prepeditus, (fo. 324) molestatus graviter, ut asserit, et vexatus contra vim, formam et tenorem concessionum dictarum libertatum, in ipsius Willelmi Bower, alias dicti Willelmi Wilson, dampnum non modicum ac dicti domini regis contemptum manifestum. Quocirca vos omnes et singulos, quorum interest vel intererit in hac parte, requirimus efficacius et rogamus quatinus eundem Willelmum, burgensem dicti burgi, contra formam et tenorem dictarum concessionum et confirmacionum libertatum predictarum nullatenus molestatis in aliquo nec gravetis, set, cum penes vos pervenerit, ut unum burgensium dicti domini regis favorabilius admittatis et recipiatis. In cujus rei testimonium sigillum commune dicti burgi de Appelby presentibus est appensum. Datum in burgo predicto, vicesimo die Maii, 17 Edw. iv. (1477).

Release by Elizabeth, late the wife of Brian Davell, late of Bilton, esquire, deceased, sister and heir of William Garton, monk, likewise deceased, to Thomas Davell the younger, her son, of eight messuages, five hundred and eighty acres of land, thirty acres of meadow, and a yearly rent of 40 s., in Menthorp, Osgodby, Dugelby, Northduffeld, Swynton and Malton, granted by fine by Guy Fairfax, serjeant at law, Thomas Davell, the elder, and Henry Davell, brothers of the said Brian, to Brian and Elizabeth for term of life with remainder to the said Thomas Davell, the younger, their son. Seal. 10 September, 8 Edw. iv. 1468. Acknowledged before William Snawefill, mayor, 27 September, 8 Edw. iv.

(fo. 325). Grant by John Hertyng of York and Ellen his wife, late the wife of John Bedale, citizen and mercer of York, to John Bedale, son and heir of the said John Bedale and Ellen, of the lands in the city and suburbs of York, which his said father and mother jointly had by enfeoffment of John Lekkys of York, chaplain, and John Calton, citizen and mercer of York. Seals. Witnesses, William Snawsill, mayor, William Welles, John Lethelay, sheriffs, William Wright, Robert Butler, William Spence, John Crounour, citizens of York. York, 26 Sept., 8 Edw. iv. (1468). Acknowledged before William Snawsill, mayor, 3 Oct., 8 Edw. iv. (1468).

Release by the same of the same to the same. York, 1 Oct., 8 Edw. iv., 1468. Acknowledged as the last deed.

(*fo.* 326). Grant by Thomas Dayvell, son of Brian Dayvell, late of Bylton, esquire, deceased, to Elizabeth Dayvell, his mother, for term of life, of a yearly rent of twelve marks payable at Whitsuntide and Martinmas from a messuage, five hundred and eighty acres of land and thirty acres of meadow in Menthorp, Osgodby, Dugilby, Northduffeld, Swynton and Malton. Seal. 16 Sept., 8 Edw. iv. (1468). Acknowledged in the mayoralty of William Snawsill, 30 Sept., 8 Edw. iv.

Release by Elizabeth Dayvell, late the wife of Brian Dayvell late of Bilton, esquire, deceased, sister and heir of William Garton, monk professed, to Thomas Dayvell her son, of the manor of Sallay by Ripon, and of sixteen messuages, six hundred acres of land, fifty acres of meadow and 40 *s.* of rent in Sallay by Ripon, Menthorp, Osgodby, Dugilby, Northduffeld, Swynton and Malton, which Guy Fairfax, sergeant at law, Thomas Dayvell and Henry Dayvell, brothers of Brian had by fine by grant of the said Brian and Elizabeth ; also of all her lands in the said places ; also of the lands in the vill of Sallay, which the said Guy, Thomas and Henry had by grant of the said Brian, dated 11 Oct., 1 Edw. iv. (1461). 6 Oct., 8 Edw. iv. (1468). Acknowledged in the mayoralty of William Snawsill, 7 Oct., 8 Edw. iv.

(*fo.* 326, *b.*) Release by the said Elizabeth, to Guy Fairfax, serjeant-at-law, and Henry Davell, brother of Brian, her late husband, of the manors of Bilton and Tokwyth, and of twenty messuages, one hundred and twenty acres of land, forty acres of meadow, thirty acres of pasture, twenty acres of wood, and 20 *s.* of rent in Bilton, Tokwith, Middilthorp, Marston, and York in the county of the city of York, which the said Guy and Henry together with Thomas Dayvell, brother of Brian, had by fine, by gift of Brian and Elizabeth ; also of the manor of Bustardthorp, in the county of the city of York, which Guy, Thomas and Henry had by gift of Brian ; also of the lands in Bilton, Tokwith, Middilthorp, Marston and York, which they had by grant of Brian, dated 11 Oct., 1 Edw. iv. (1461). 6 Oct., 8 Edw. iv. (1468). Acknowledged as the last deed.

(*fo.* 327). Release by Thomas Dayell, brother of Brian Dayvell late of Bilton, esquire, deceased, to Thomas Dayvell the younger, son of the said Brian, of the lands released to the said Thomas the younger, by Elizabeth Dayvell, by deed dated 6 Oct., 8 Edw. iv. (1468). Seal. 30 Sept., 8 Edw. iv. (1468). Acknowledged in the mayoralty of William Snawsill, 8 Oct., iv.

(*fo.* 312, *b.*) Release by the same to Guy Fairfax, serjeant-at-law, and Henry Dayvell, brother of the said Thomas, of the lands released to Guy and Henry by Elizabeth Dayvell, by deed dated 6 Oct., 8 Edw. iv. Seal. 20 May, 4 Edw. iv. (1464). Acknowledged as above.

(*fo.* 328). Release by William Wakefeld, esquire, to Robert Ughtred, knight, James Ughtred, and George Ughtred, clerk, sons of the said Robert, of the manor of Wasshand in Holdernesse; with clause of warranty against the abbot of Westminster. 21 Sept., 9 Edw. iv. (1469). Seal. Acknowledged before Richard York, mayor, 29 Sept., 9 Edw. iv.

(*fo.* 328, *b.*) Release by Thomas Scauceby, citizen and merchant of York, and William and Thomas Scauceby his sons, to Margaret, formerly the wife of John Legh, daughter and heir of Thomas Duffeld, of all actions against her. 15 Oct., 1470. Seal. Gunby. Acknowledged before William Holbek, mayor, 24 April, 1471. Similar release by the said Margaret to the said Thomas, William and Thomas. Seal. Same date. Gunby. Acknowledged as the last deed.

(*fo.* 329). Grant by Thomas Gibson, chaplain, to John Scargill, son of Roger Scargill, esquire, and to Alice his wife, and the heirs of John, of the lands, which he had by enfeoffment of the said John, in a hamlet called Bulerode, within the township of Dewsbery, and in a hamlet called Byrtby within the township of Schadiwell. Seal. Witnesses, Robert Nevile, esquire, Sir Thomas Clarell, vicar of the parish church of Ledes, Peter Symson, Thomas Man. 7 March, 4 Edw. iv. (1463-4). Acknowledged before John Gillyott, mayor, 16 March, 14 Edw. iv.

Parchemeners.

(*fo.* 329, *b.*) Facta fuit ista ordinacio subscripta iiij^{to} die mensis Junii, 14 Edw. iv. (1474), tempore Johannis Gillyott,

maioris hujus civitatis. Johannes Gillyott, maior; Willelmus
Holbek, Thomas Neleson, Johannes Marshall, Willelmus Snawsell,
Christoforus Marsshall, Johannes Glasslyn, Johannes Tonge,
Willelmus Lambbe, de xij^{ti}; Thomas Maryott, vicecomes;
Willelmus Wright, Ricardus Claybruke, Willelmus Thorp,
Johannes Touthorp, Johannes Lightlop, Robertus Amyas,
Johannes Fereby, Henricus Stokton, Thomas Kaytour, at the
instance and reasonable supliment and prayer minystred by
John Woddall of the cite of York, parchemenmaker, by bill unto
alle above writen, within the counsayll chambre of the same
city, the day yere above saide. It was ordaned, ennacted and
stablisshed by alle above writen, that frome nowefurth it shall be
levefull to all the maisters of the forsaide crafte of parchemen-
makers, within the cite of York, subburbes, and precinctes of the
same, and to every maister of the same crafte there occupyyng
now, and that hereafter shall occupy as maisters or maister within
the same cite, subburbes, and precinctes of the same in the same
crafte, to take into thaire services, and into every of thaire services
in that craft, iij, ij, or j apprentesses or apprentes tageders attones
by indenture to be made betwyx theyme in that behalfe for such
yeres and termes as the maisters or maister on that one partie,
and the same apprentes can agre emonges theymsiffe, any acte,
ordynaunce or constitucion made in the dayes and tyme of
Thomas Esyngwald, standing maire of the forsaid cite of Yorke,
to contrarie of this present ordynaunce not agaynstynge.

(*fo.* 330). Memorandum quod vicesimo die Januarii,
18 Edw. iv. (1478-9), personaliter in camera consilii coram Johanne
Fereby, tunc maiore civitatis, pro tribunali sedente, Johanne
Harper, Ricardo Clerke et Ricardo Hardesang, tunc camerariis
ejusdem, et aliis probis hominibus tunc et ibidem existentibus
dompnus Thomas Wenslagh, monachus ac prior prioratus domus
beate Marie de Wardell, in comitatu Cumbr', Nicholaus Warwyk,
filius Johannis Warwyk, domini de Warwyk in eodem comitatu,
Robertus Iveson, Alexander Iveson, *taillour*, Johannes Maclyney,
taillour, Thomas Blakelok, litteratus, Ricardus Ormesby, *taillour*,
Christoforus Barrey, *wever*, Thomas Richerdson, *wever*, et
Willelmus Hetherington, filius Johannis Hetheryngton de
Coreburgh in comitatu Kariol', nati in partibus borialibus et in

LEASE OF THE PLAY OF CORPUS CHRISTI (1468)   239

comitatibus Cumbr' et Kariol', jurati super sancti Dei evaungelia per eos corporaliter tacta, quod [*sic*] cum Johannes Richerdson, *milner*, scandilizatus est per inimicos suos ac ministros diaboli tanquam natum Scotum et domini nostri regis inimicum, dixerunt, et quilibet corum per se dixit, super sacramenta sua predicta, quod dictus Johannes Richerdson est ligeus homo domini nostri regis Anglic, qui fuit filius Georgii Rycherdson, natus in villa de Crosby juxta Karliell', ubi tota ejus parentela nata fuit; et hoc sunt et erunt parati ad omne tempus probare, prout etc.

(*fo.* 330, *b.*) Memorandum that on 15 Nov., 15 Edw. iv., 1475, before Thomas Wrangwisshe, mayor, William Tayte, Richard Marston and John Tyrell, chamberlains, John Claybruke, son of Richard Claybruke, citizen and baker of York, acknowledged two charters.[1]

Grant by Thomas Roos, knight, lord Roos of Hamelak, Trussebut and Belvere, to his servant John Hemylsey, of his lands upon Bisshophill, otherwise called Bychehill Lomelyth, or elsewhere in the parish of old S. Mary, within the liberty of the city of York; and also in Yolton. He appoints John Evenwod and Nicholas Botman, chaplains, his attorneys to deliver seisin Witnesses, Thomas Chaworth, John Souche, Henry Perpoynt, knights, Ralf Leek, Robert Wesyngham. Seal. 12 Sept., 21 Henry vi. (1442). Acknowledged by John Hemylsey of York, gentleman, before Thomas Wrangwisshe, mayor, William Tayte, Richard Marston and John Tyrell, chamberlains, 15 Nov., 16 Edw. iv. (1476). Grant by John Hemylsey of York to John Claybruke, of the same lands, 14 Nov., 16 Edw. iv. (1476). Acknowledged as above.

(*fo.* 331, *b.*) Omnibus hoc scriptum visuris vel audituris maior et communitas civium civitatis Ebor', salutem in Domino sempiternam. Noveritis nos concessisse et ad firmam dimisisse Henrico Watson et Thome Diconson, *pikemongers*, ludum sive lusum Corporis Christi annuatim ludendum in alta strata de Ousegate, inter tenementa modo in tenura prefatorum Henrici et Thome, scilicet, apud finem pontis Use, ex parte orientali, habendum et tenendum dictum ludum sive lusum a festo Corporis

---

1—This entry is unfinished and crossed through.

Christi, anno Domini millesimo cccclxxviij°, usque ad finem duodecim annorum proximo sequentum plenarie, reddendo inde annuatim nobis, prefato maiori et successoribus nostris, videlicet, ad manus camerariorum, qui pro tempore fuerint, undecim solidos legalis monete Anglie ad opus communitatis civitatis predicte annuatim durante termino predicto, scilicet, infra sex dies proximo sequentes festi [sic] Corporis Christi predictum, sub pena amissionis ludi predicti presenti dimissione in aliquo non obstante ; ita, scilicet, quod dictus ludus sive lusus ad stallagium minime ludatur. Et nos, predicti maior et communitas, et successores nostri dictum ludum sive lusum pro firma xj s. predicta usque ad finem xij^{cim} annorum predictorum, ut predictum est, contra omnes gentes warantizabimus et defendemus. In cujus rei testimonium etc.

(fo. 332). In Dei Nomine Amen. Anno ab incarnacione immortalis Dei millesimo ccccxxviij°, mense vero Septembris, die vicesimo, [sic] illustrissimus ac uti fama omnium fert metuendissimus ast christianissimus Edwardus, Dei gracia rex Anglie et Francie, et dominus Hibernie, magna ducum, marchionum, comitum, baronum caterva, aliorumque regni procerum eum comitante certis ob causas[1] e borea vero omnibus ferme majoribus natu undique ad eum catervatim confluentibus Pontefractum versus adventaret, Johannes Fereby, nobilis hujusce alme urbis ea vice maior, unacum plerisque hujus civitatis nobilioribus preasserto domino regi paulo minus duobus miliaribus ultra Wentbrig obviam fecerunt, dictumque dominum regem usque Pontefractum concomitabantur; ibique a prefato metuendissimo domino regi [sic] aliisque regni proceribus, per dictum maiorem ejus complices valecapto, preassertus maior cum complicibus suis aliisque dictam civitatem Ebor' domumque venerat; dehinc unius septime curriculo vix effluxo, idem dominus rex cum quampluribus regni magnatibus hanc civitatem Ebor' advenit, cui a prefato prenobili viro Johanne Fereby, maiore, aldermannis, singulisque aliis de camera equitare valentibus, ceteris hujusce urbis majus honestis civibus, quid equo, quid pedibus, obviam itum est, condonataque fuerant preasserto exemio principi et regi in

1—Certis ob cas in MS.

exenniis secundum quod in illius anni libro clare conscriptum liquet; vicesimoque octavo ejusdem mensis luce hac alma civitate London' versus abierat.[1]

Judicium Scrutatorum.

(*fo.* 332, *b.*) Judicium Johannis Bell et Willelmi Madder, scrutatorum cementariorum civitatis Ebor', Jacobi Whynfell et Johannis Burgh, scrutatorum carpentariorum ejusdem civitatis, juratorum et assignatorum per Christoforum Marshall, maiorem civitatis predicte, secundum consuetudinem ejusdem civitatis de consensu parcium infrascriptarum ad supervidendum, scrutandum et judicandum reparacionem sive clausuram cujusdam gardini, in contraversia [*sic*] pendentis inter Johannam Gylliot, viduam, de Ebor', ex una parte, et Reginaldum Grenehode de Ebor', ex altera parte; quod quidem gardinum jacet in Havergate in civitate predicta, inter terram ejusdem Reginaldi, ex parte australi, et terram Thome Barton de Rydale, ex parte boriali; redditum in camera consilii civitatis predicte coram maiore supradicto, decimo die mensis Octobris, 13 Edw. iv. (1473). We the seircheours aforewriten fynde and awarde that the reparacion and closyng of the said garthyn belongeth and apperteneth unto the same Johannet, to be made at all tymes on the south side of the same garthyn, contenyng in length lxxiiij yerdes, etc.

Recordum pro Johanne Loksmyth.

Memorandum that the xxvij[ti] day of Aprile, 21 Edw. iv. (1481), cam personalie into the counsell chaimbre of Ousebrigg on Johannet Loksmyth, the wiffe of John Loksmyth of Burghbrig, in the countie of Yorke, smyth, and thare and then from the right worshipfull Sir William Tankerd, the steurd of Burghbrigg, a letter broght and shewid unto Robert Amyas, than beyng maire of the cite of Yorke, the which letter shewid that the said John Loksmyth and Johannet, his wiffe, was burges of the said town of Burghbrigg, and aght for to have and resave the privelige there-unto belonging and to the ducherie of the forest of Knaresburgh.

1—Cf. Drake, *op. cit.*, p. 114.

The which letter so redd and understond, the said maire admit the said John and Johanna his wiffe as a fre burges, and from this present day forward as long as it can be laufully proved, thai soo stondyng to be fre and discharged in paying of tolles, murages, and all other thinges to the same belonging, within the cite of Yorke, suburbes, and procinctt of the same etc.

(fo. 333). Grant by Robert Shepherd of Selby and Agnes, his wife, to John Dyvelyn, citizen and tailor of the city of London, of land in Selby, which Robert and Agnes had by grant of Henry Hodilstone of Gygleswyk and Christine, his wife, and late of Richard Vescy, late of Selby; viz., three acres of land in an assart called Madenakes, between the common way leading to Thorp, and abutting upon le Damryddyng; four acres and a half in a field called Langmorez; two acres between an assart called Smythland and a place called " Bitwene the Waters " on one side, and a lane leading to the bridge of Wystowe on the other side, and abutting at one end upon land of the monastery of S. German of Selby, and at the other end upon land late of William Hathilsey; and three selions in an assart called Crosseriddyng toward Wistowe. Seals. Witnesses, Robert Derkyn, gentleman, William Pavstron. chapman, William Baker of Selby. 4 May, 10 Edw. iv. (1470).

Acknowledged before William Holbek mayor, 5 May, 10 Edw. iv.

(fo. 333, b.) Release by the same to the same, of two parts of the said lands, and to John Hakynsey, son and heir of Thomas Hakynsey and of Alice, his wife, daughter and one of the heirs of Richard Vescy, formerly of Selby, of the third part, which he claims to have inherited after the death of the said Alice. Seal, same witnesses, 5 May, 10 Edw. iv. (1470). Acknowledged as above.

Tapiters and lynnen wevers.[1]

(fo. 334). Tenor cujusdam arbitrii, judicii et decreti, facti per Willelmum Holbek, maiorem civitatis Ebor', inter artifices de lez tapiters, ex una parte, et artifices artis de lynnenwevers in civitate predicta, sequitur et est talis.

1—The whole of these ordinances is crossed through.

THE ORDINANCES OF THE TAPITERS (147½)

To all christen people be it knawen that, where afore this it was used within the cite of York and suburbez of the same of auncien tyme that ech lynnenwever, holding and occuppyng lynnen loymes or lynnen loyme, payyed yerely into the craft and occupacion of tapiters, within the saide cite for everiche lynnen loyme that he helde and occupyed, within the saide cite and suburbez of the same, ij $d.$ to the sustentacion of the charges of the saide crafte of tapiters within the same cite for the tyme beyng; and also that all thoo of the same crafte of lynnenwevers, within the saide cite and suburbez of the same, were used at all dayes and tymez to be serched by the serchiours of the said craft of tapiters for tyme beyng withoute interrupcion unto nowe late, that is to saye the xx^{ti} day of Januarie in the xj^{th} yere of the reigne of King Edward the $iiij^{th}$ (1471-2), that a grugge of variance was moeved in that behalf emonges the saidez tweyne craftes within the same cite ; wherapon alswell Elias Cure and William Calcrofte, serchiours of the saide craft of tapiters, then for tyme beyng within the said cite, by thassent and agremente of all tho othir of the same craft of tapiters, whose names ensuye for thaime and ther successours, on that one partie, and Patrik Haull and William Sandy, serchiours of the said craft of lynnenwevers within the said cite for tyme beyng, and by thassent of all tho othir of the said craft of lynnenwevers within the saide cite, whose names ben under writen, for thaime and ther successours, on that othir partie, at York, in the counseill chambre of the said cite, by mediacion of ther bother freyndes, the daie and yere abovesaid, submitted and compromytted thayme to stande and obbey to th'awarde, ordynance, decre, and jugement of William Holbek, maier of the said cite, in and apon the premissez and gruge aforforsaid. And therapon the saide maire, than and ther takyng apon (*fo.* 334, *b.*) hym the charge of th' awarde, ordynance, decre, and juygement in that behalf betwyx the saidez partiez, hering also the articlez, compleyntes, grugge and replicacions of the bothe saide partiez, the daie and yere above-saide, awarded, ordeyned, decreed and adjugeide in fourme felowing.

Firste, that from hensfurth withouten ende ther be named, had and taken yerely tweyne able personnes of thoccupacion and craft of lynnenwevers within the saide cite by thaime of the same craft of lynnenwevers to be serchiours of the saide craft of lynnenwevers, and to serche within the same craft duely at all tymez hereafter, and that the saide craft of tapiters within the saide cite shull be discharged clerely of all maner of serche and intromytting of theyme and of every of thaime of the saide craft of lynnenwevers of the same cite and suburbez of the same. And forthermore the saide maier awarded and adjugeyde that the serchiours of the saide craft of lynnenwevers within the saide cite for tyme beyng yerely withoute ende pay, or make to be payed, within viij dayes next felowyng the feste of Corporis Christi, into the handes of the serchiours of the said craft of tapiters of the same cite for tyme beyng, laufull money of England to the sustentacion of the yerly chargez of the said craft of tapiters of the said cite; and ovir all abovesaid the said maier awarded and adjugeyde that Richard Kydde, Thomas Pennythorne, and William Palson, tapiters, shulde have and occupye at ther pleasier, ech of thaime, one lynnen loyme during ther lyves naturell, withoutyn thing yelding to the saide serchiours of the forsaide craft of lynnenwevers for the saide thre lynnen loymes. Forseyn alway that every tapiter of the saide cite and suburbez hensfurth havyng and occupyyng herafter eny lynnen loyme or loymes lynnen within the same cite and suburbez, othir than the thre tapiters above named for ther thre lynnen loymes, shull paye yerly unto the saidez serchiours of the saide craft of the lynnenwevers for tyme beyng, and to ther successours serchiours of the same, for every lynnen loyme ij d. And also the saide maier awarded and adjugeyde that from nowe furth every tapiter and lynnenwever occupyyng and holding (fo. 335) eny lynnen loymes or lynnen loyme within the saides cite and suburbes be serched and under the serche of the serchiours of the saide craft of lynnen wevers of the saide cite for tyme beyng, as in that behalf. Forseyn and except alwaye that when soever hereafter that the serchiours of the saide craft of lynnen wevers for tyme beyng and ther successours, serchiours of the same make defalt in payyng of the . . . .[1] in fourme abovesaid, and

---

1—n (nichel) is written in the erasure.

that duely proved tofore the mair for tyme beyng, that than it shalbe levefull from thensfurth unto the saide serchiours of the saide craft of tapiters and ther successours, serchiours of the same, to take and perceyve yerly of every lynnen wever of the saide cite and suburbes for every lynnen loyme, that thaie halde and occupye, and to have the serche apon the sayde lynnenwevers, as was used within the same cite afor the tyme of this awarde, ordynance, decre, and jugyement yeven, this awarde, ordynance decre, and jugement nat agaynstonding.

Nomina tapitariorum :[1]—Johannes Tesedale, Robertus Scathelok, Nicholaus Pymerton, Willelmus Holme, Ricardus Sharpyls, Johannes Howell, Thomas Calis, Willelmus Rybe, Johannes Bukler, Ricardus Kydde, Robertus Fraunceys, Johannes Sharp, Willelmus Bukler, Thomas Raye, Radulphus Dent, Andreas Blithe, Thomas Pennythorn, Ricardus Gurnerd, Johannes Brokholez, Christianus Erle, Thomas Santon, Willelmus Sharp, Willelmus Palson, Thomas Pymerton. Nomina de *lez lynnenwevers* :—Johannes Tailliour, Willelmus Kilburn, Nicholaus Frieston, Johannes Thweyng, Willelmus Sesay, Jacobus Dam, Robertus Barre, Johannes Moore, Willelmus Clerk, Willelmus Dale, Thomas Morland, Johannes Gillyn, Nicholaus Monkegate, Thomas Thomson, Johannes Perte, Thomas Asarlay, Johannes Audley, Johannes Candall, Willelmus Westwyk, Thomas Geffray, James Handelay, Willelmus Bracebrig, Willelmus Colson, Willelmus Waldby.

(*fo*. 335, *b*.) In festo Sancti Blasii Episcopi 14 Edw. iv. (3 February, 1474-5) xij^{cim}, Johannes Gillyott, maior, Willelmus Lambe, Willelmus Holbek, Willelmus Snawsell, Christofus Marsshal, Johannes Glassyn, Johannes Tonge, Willelmus Wellez; xxiiij^{or}, Johannes Newton, vicecomes, Johannes Howthorp, Johannes Lethelay, Thomas Alan, Henricus Stokton, Henricus Willyamson, Thomas Maryott.

[1]—In margin (fo. 334), "Cassatur et adnullatur istud arbitrium, ordinacio, decretum et judicium, quia textores linei sequentes assumpserunt super se onus cujusdem pagine vocate Fergus annuatim per ipsos lu^{d}en^{d}e etc. ex assensu tapitariorum, et habent novas constituciones et ordinaciones, ut in libro papiro de tempore Thome Wrangwishe, maioris," is written.

Omnes prescripti necnon tota communitas civitatis Ebor' fuerunt congregati in Guyhald ejusdem civitatis, die et anno supradictis, where and thanne it was fully aggreyde, ordayned, and establisshed of one assente and consente the effect, intente and purpose of a bill to the mair and counsaill abovesaide, the day yere and place abovesaide, by the hole commonalte of the said cite be frome nowefurth within the same cite fermely holden, observed and kepped for evermore, as enenste the yerely eleccion of chambrelayns to be had frome yere to yere, within the forsaide cite, the fourme of whiche bill felowith ande ys suche.

To thair worshipfull lord the mayre, and thair worshipfull masters, his brederen, the aldremen, and counsaylours of the chambre of the saide citee.

To whome mekely besekes the pore commonalte of the forsaide cite to remembre the grete povertie of this cite ande the downe gate of our common rente, the whilke was wonte to be upphald to the chambre and to kepe the cite oute of dette; and nowe it is so as youre lordship ande maisterships understandes that every man, that have lyvelod within the cite, abates of his ferme to gett tenandes to his lyvelod, so that the common rente ys greatly abated of thare fermez, so that it ys nott ahill to kepe the chambre oute of dett, and so yt lyes in dekey ande the chambre rynnes in dett, and men kan not gett tenaundes therto withoute more sufficient reparacion, than we understand may be had, withoute the supportacion of you. And thus, we thynke with goode supportacion ande avise of your lordship and maistership for alsmuch as we ben all one bodye corporate, we thynke that we be all inlike prevaliged of the commonalte, which has borne none office in the cite. Wherefore we desyer ande besekes your forsaide lordship ande maistershipps, that frome hencefurth that ye elect ne chuse any chambrelaynes, but suche as hafe ben brigmaisters afore, and borne thair charge worshipfully; ande that ye chuse non odir what degre that ever thay be off, but if thay pay to the reparacion of the common rente at the leste xl *s.* and that to be delivered to the handes of the brigmaisters, that shall be chosen to occupy for the common rente the yere next ensuyng, or els the saide brigmaisters so chosen for that yere stande dischargeyd to that be payde to ther handes to the reparayhyng of the common rent. And also we beseke youe, that ye from hensfurth chece no brigmaisters but of the moste able men in goodes and discrecion to occupy the forsaid officez, for none envy of no persone ne persouns.

(*fo.* 336). In festo Sancti Blasii episcopi 14 Edw. iv. (3 Feb., 1474–5).

For washyng above the Piddynghole.

The day yere and place aforesaide, it was ordayned forthermore by thassent of all above writen, that frome nowefurth that there be no tanner of this cite, ner none othere man ne woman of this cite, so hardye to lye, caste, or wesshe, any maner of lymed skynnez or ledir or any inmetys or corrupcion of bestes abouen the Puddyng Hole for corrupcion of the water of Ouse, upon the payn of xij $d.$ to be forfayte and payde by hym, that offendith, als oftyn tymes as enny maner of man so traispasseth to the common availe of this cite.

(*fo.* 336, *b.*) Letters testifying that Thomas Bakhus and Robert Elwald were not Scotsmen.[1]

(*fo.* 337). [2]Memorandum that the xth of Juyu, 22 Edw. iv. (1482), cam to fore Richerd Yorke, in the secound tyme of his marialtie, into the Counsell Chaimbre, aswele the craftes of the cutlers and bladesmythez as loksmythez and blaksmythez, and ther and then of a variaunce and debate bond depending betwix the said craftes maid a ful acorde and grement herafter to be kept, that is say, that the said craftes of cutlers and bladesmythez be as on togydders in all maner of charges to ther said craftes belonging, and to be discharged from the blaksmythez for all maner of things to thame belonging, that is to say, from lightes, offerandes, and all other things, except the said bladesmyth to yif yerelie every man of the same iiij $d.$ to the blacksmythez and in case like. And if eny man of the craft of blaksmythez or other take uppon thame within this cite to wirke eny thing belonging to the bladesmythez to be contributory to thame, and also yerelie every of the said craftes to chese uppon thame self seircheours, to thentent that dewe serche may be maid for the wele of the

1—Eng. Misc., *op. cit.*, pp. 37–38.
2—Vacat written in left margin.

kynges people; and every craft yiff warnyng to other, whan they shall go of seirch, and what person that shall offend to eny of the seircheours in ther seirch laufully don, or to be rebell to thame, to forfet and pay withoute pardon xij d., the on halfe to the chaimbre, and the other half to the craft, that awe to make the seirch, by even porcions, and that the bladsmythez shall alway serche all and every manere of egelome or egetole, where so evere thay may be founden in the handes of the maker or makerz of the same.

(*fo*. 337, *b*.) Letters concerning the nationality of Andrew Lambe.[1]

(*fo*. 339, *b*.) Award of John Sutton, Walter Johnson, masons, John Couper and Michael White, wrightes, concerning land in dispute between Sir William Cokkay, priest, and Thomas More.

We, Michael Clerc and John Braidley of the craft of wrightes, John Patrik of the craft of tilers, serchours, sworne upon the holy evangelistes indifferently to serch and examyn the reparacion of a house in Bowthom, within the suburbs of the citie of York, hanging in travaux betwix the right worshipfull Thomas Darell, squire, of that oone partie, and Thomas Wandesforth, gent, of that other partie, personally appering bifore Sir William Todde, knight, maier of the citie of York, the eght day of the moneth of January, 3 Henr. vii (1487–8), after due serch maid by us of the said house, and all circumstance of the same, awardeth and jugeth betwix the said Thomas and Thomas in fourme folowing. That is to say that the said Thomas Wandesforth of his proper costez and expensez (*fo*. 340) shall cause and make to be thekid suffisauntly the house of the said Thomas Darell, as far as the rynnyng rofe of a house of the said Thomas Wandisforth, lait standing ther, was joynyng of the house of the said Thomas Darell.

Blaksmyth and Blaydsmitties.

Memorandum that the xxv[th] day of Jun, 8 Henr. vii (1493), came tofore Nicholaz Lancastr', in the secund tyme of his mairaltie, in the counecil chamber, as well the crafte of blaksmythez as loksmythes and bladsmythez, and ther be their concentes and

---

[1]—Eng. Misc., *op. cit.*, pp. 43–44.

agrementes desired of the said maire for appeasing of diverse matiers of variencez and oftentymez moved betwix the said craftes of blaksmythez and bladsmythez, for serch makyng of diverse instrumentes in their occupacions, and paing pajaunt silver ather to other craft etc. That frome hensforth the same blaksmythez may be separate and discharged clerly from the bladsmythez, as well of serche makyng in eny thing pertenyng to tham as of paying tham pajaunt silver or ony other dewties. And in like case, the said bladsmythez to be discharged in all maner thynges forsaid enenst the said blaksmythez, acordyng to whose desire it was ordenid and enacted by the said maire and the hole counceil, the said xxvth day of Jun, the viijth yer of the reign of Kyng Henry the vijth, as it apperith in the pauper buke of the said maire the secund tyme etc. That frome hensforth ather of the said occupacions be clerly discharged from other, not payng pajant silver, ne none serch makyng of ony axez or other egelome, or any other instrumentes in other of the said occupacions, but the serchourz of ather occupacion to make serch within thame selff, and that all blaksmythz wurkyng ony axes or egetoile pay yerly amongst tham to ther pageunt silver xvj $d.$ for that cause, besydes his other pajant silver that thai pay otherwies to ther craft. Also that ony other ordinaunce betwix the said occupacions otherwiez tofor maid notwithstondyng, and the same soo tofore maid, to be void and cancelled etc.

(*fo.* 340, *b.*) Memorandum that William Erews and Robert Davisone, seircheours of the masons, John Haxby and Michael Clerke, seircheours of the wrightes within the cite of Yorke, have bene and takyn the seirche of a grounde that stude in variaunce betwix William Mowbray and John Arthington, without the barr of Walmegate, buttyng uppon the Kynges streit forward, and a common lane called Horselane bakwerd, according to the custom of the cite, the xxx^{ti} day of August, 17 Edw. iv., 1477, by the comaundment of John Tonge, than beyng mare of the said cite. And efter the examinacion, gode advise and great deliberacion by us had, as wele by substanciall writyng undre sealles, as by the instruccion ande recorde of honest personez thare beyng present, having perfite notice and knawlege of the said grounde, we have founde that the tenaunt of the saide John Arthington

have wrongfully holden and occupied certen grounde of the saide
William Mowbrey, by the space of viij yere last passed, afore this
present day; which grounde after oure consciens and wisdomez
we have departed frome the grounde of the saide John Arthington.
Ande we deme and awarde that the saide William Mowbray shal
have the said grounde delyverd and laid to his grounde thare beyng
ayane to hym and to his heires for ever, that is to say, the saime
breid bakwerd as the frounte of his house to the kynges streit
forwerd.

(*fo.* 341). Memorandum that we, Thomas Gaytclyffes, John
Cayrok, serchours of masounes, within this citee of York, John
Forster and John Merdlay, alias Williamson, serchours of
wryghtes within the saide citee, have bene and takyn of a grounde
that stode in variaunce betwix thabbot and convent of Rivaux,
on the oon partie, and the dene and chapiter of the Cathedral
Kyrke of Saint Peter in York, on that other partie; lying
buttyng opon the water in Laierthorp, in subarbes of the saide
citee, buttyng opon the water of Fosse at the west ende, and on
a commone lane that leedes frome the hie strete of Laierthorp
unto ij closez belangyng som tyme to the parsonage of Seint
Marye Kyrke in Layrethorp. And accordyng to the custume of
the same citee, the ix day of Marce, 8 Edw. iv. (1467-8), by the
comaundement of William Snawesill, than beyng maire of the
same citie, and after the examinacion, good advise, and grete
deliberacion by us hadde, as wele by substanciall wrytyng undre
sealez, as by the instruccion and recorde of honest personnes
havyng perfite notice and knawlynge of the saide grounde, we
have founde that the tenauntes of the saide abbotes and convent
have wrangwisly halden and occupied xviij poules feet of the
grounde of the saide deanez and chapiter, the whiche xviij fote
of ground we have demed and awarded shalbe departed from the
grounde of the saide abbot and convent, and delivered and laide
unto the grounde of the saide deane and chapiter, to have and to
holde to thayme and to thaire successours for evermore etc.

Memorandum that this is the awarde and juygement of
William Hyndeley, John Sutton, John Haxby, and Richard
Bisshop, serchiours of the masons and wrightes, in the cite of
Yorke, assigned and lymytt by William Lambe, maire of the cite

of Yorke, with the full assente ande consente of William Snawsell, aldreman of the saide cite, for his partye, ande sir William Watson, vicare of Saynte Georg churche in Fysshergate, ruler and gouvernour of a chaunterie belongyng to the saide churche, on that othir partie, to serche ande deme a guttur apon a tenement in Walmegate in Yorke perteynyng to the saide chaunterie, and a pales perteynyng to a tenement of the saide William Snawsell, nowe in the halding of one Robert Yereslay, at the este ende of Fossebrigge in Walmegate. Firste the saide iiij serchiours awardes and demes betwyx the saide partiez for thair bother ease, that the forsaide William Snawsell shall abide with the voydance of the waterfall of the forsaide guttur, ande in like fourme the saide vicare, as by right ande duete belongyng to the saide chaunterie, shall bere the charge of the uphaldinge and makyng of the forsaide pales at alle dayez, at his owen propre costes and expensez. Snawsell. Judicium scrutatorum redditum fuit vj die Marcii, 15 Edw. iv. (1474-5).

(*fo.* 341, *b.*) Deed of delivery to Agnes Manwel, widow, of her portion of the goods of her late husband Richard; viz., 31 *l.* 18 *s.* 2½ *d.*; to hold to her use and pleasure by Edward Bygod. 18 June, 17 Edw. iv. (1477). Acknowledged before John Tonge mayor, same date.

(*fo.* 343).[1] De curia maioris civitatis Ebor', et custumis civitatis ejusdem in diversis casibus terminabilibus in eadem curia.

La Courte du mair este tenu per custume de la cite devaunt lez mair et aldermans, que sont pur le temps in le chaumbre de Guyhall ou en le Guyhall; et ceo de jour en jour a lour volonte. Et la sount treetes, termines et discusses lez plees et materes touchauntz apprenticialtees, et autres busaignes de mesme la cite; et illouques sont redresses et correctez les defautes et mesprisons de ceux que font encontre les custumes et ordenauncez de la cite, sibien al suyte dez parties come per enqueste de office, et en autre manere, per suggestion, solonc ceo que lez cases demandant; et la usent de justifier lez pestures, braisioures, vitaillers et gentz de toutz mistieres; et de treiter et ordiner

1—Folio 342 is blank.

pur le governall de la cite et pur le sustienaunce de la peis nostre seigneur le roy, et autres poyntes necessaries de la dite cite, et pur profette de ceux, que repairent a mesne la cite, per lour discrecions solonque ceo que le temps demande.

Item, lez officers et ministres de la cite troves in defaute sont justiciables devaunt mesnes lez mair et aldermans, sibien al suyte dez parties pro processes faite come en autre manere solonque discrecion dez ditz mair et aldermans.

Item, lez ditz mair et aldermans et seut longs tener et determiner plees de dette et autre accions personelx parentre merchaunt et merchaunt par ley de merchundyes, que cy pleindre voilont, et processe serra fait divers lez partiez. Item, lez mair et aldermans ou lez mair et (*fo.* 343, *a.*) chaumbreleyns del dit cite pernont devaunt eux en la dite chaumbre recoinersance de dette de toutz ceux que entrent le fraunchiese de le dite cite, queste appelle fraunchessilvere, et autres duetes parteignauntz as ditz mair et commonalte; et si le jour de paiement soit encurrue, adonques les mair et chaumbrelayns pur le temps esteiantz hors de ceste recorde avera execucion de toutz lez biens de le dettour, et pur defaute dez biens vers le corps du dite dettour.

Item, lez assisez de noisancez sont rennuables par bill devaunt lez mair et aldermans, le quele bill serra servie par lez bailiffes, et lez parties serront sommones quatre joures devaunt encountre le lundie adonques prochien ensuant, et adonques lez mair et aldermans devoient procedre en le plee come assise le commune ley.

Item, lez mair et aldermans ount tout temps use de fair ordenauncez (*fo.* 343, *b.*) penalx sur vitailers et pur aver governall de la cite et de la peis solonque lour discrecion et advicez, et mesmes les ordenaunces proclaymer deins le dite cite overtement pur estre tenuz et gardees en nome de nostre seigneur le roy et les mair et aldermans, sur le payne ente ordeine, es mesmes lez peines levire de teutz ceux que font encountre lez ordenaunce suisdite.

Item, lez mair et aldermans aunt tout temps use de faire venir devaunt eux lez mailefeisours, que ount este pris et arrestuz deins le dite cite pur messangees et fauce novelles, ymagenes en disturbance de la peis, feisours et countrefeitours de faux seials et faux charties, et pur autre defautes notaries ; et ceux que sount trovez culpables de teux mailefeites par conisance des parties, ou par enquestes ent pris, sount punys par iowes de pilorie, au autrement chasties par enprisonement, solonque lour desert et solonque reisonable discreccion des ditz mair et aldermans.

Item, fait assavoir que toute la cite Deverwik est teuuz de nostre seigneur le roy en fraunk burgage et sance mesne, et toutz lez terres et tenementz, rentz et servicez deins la dite cite et lez suburbes dicelle, sibien en reversion come en demeasne, sont devisables par usage de la dite cite, issint que homes et femmes par usage de la dite cite preint deviser lour tenementz, rentz, et reversions deins la dite cite et suburbes dicell, a qi qils voueront, et de quele estate qils voudront, et poient auxi deviser novell rent a prendre de mesme lour tenemente en manere come meux lour semblera par lour testament de lour darreine volonte.

Item, celly qui tenierent tenemente joyntement avesque autres poiet·deviser ceo que a luy affert sance autre severance fair, mais enfaunte deins age ne pet my faire devyise. Et toutz les testamentez par queux ascuns tenementez sont devises poient estre enrolles en[1] (*fo.* 344) le Guyhall de recorde, al pursuyte de chescomque poiet prendre avauntage par mesmes lez testmentez, et les testamentez, que devoient issut[2] estre enrolles, serront enportes ou fait venir devaunt lez ditz Mair et aldermans en pleine courte du mair, et la serra le dite testament proclayme par le sergeaunt, et illouques prove par deux prodhomes bien cunez, les quex serront serrementes et examines severalment de teutz lez circumstances de le dit testement, et de lestate le testatour, et de son seiall, et si les proves soient troves bones et loialx et accordantz, adonques serra la dit testament enrolle in mesne la Guyhall de recorde, serra paie le fee pur le enrollement. Et null testament monpatife [*sic*] nautre testament poiet estre de recorde, si nome que le seall le testatour soit mys a mesme le testament ; mais lez testamentz que poient estre troves bones et loyals sont effectuels, nient contrestant qils ne soient my enrolles de recorde.

1—This word is repeated.
2—*Sic*, issint ?

Item, par auncien custume de la citee Deverwik, les citizeins ne ministres de mesme la citee ne devoient my estre entendantz a nully maundement, ne nully seal, sinouue a lez maundementz et seal nostre seigneur le roy inmediate; ne null ministre nostre seigneur le roy nautre devoit faire session, ne null execucion, deins le dite cite ne deins le fraunchise dicelle, par terre ne par eawe, si nouns soulement lez ministres de la citte suisdite.

Item, par auncien custume de la cite toutz lez libertes, privileges et autres custumes partenauntz a mesme la citee soiloient estre recorde et declares per bouche, sance estre mys ou maundez ailliours en escriptz.

(fo. 344, b.) Item, leawe de Ouse si avaunt, come lez boundes de la fraunchise de la citte purportent, est parcell de la citee, et mesme leawe et quauntque appent al dite eawe deins la dite fraunchise tout temps ad este en governalle de mesme la citee, come parcelle de la citee suisdite, sibien lune partie de leawe come lautre; et lez maire et baillifes du dite citee, qont este pur le temps, ount use de tout temps de faire arrestes et execucions al suyte dez parties en la dite eawe de Ouse, ceste assavoir del weste partie de dite eawe de Ouse, comenchaint a une fontaine appele Bampton Welle, tanque a le Bisshopflete; et del Est partie de mesme leawe de la bounde, assigne de la fraunchise du dite cite vers le south, en lez prees de Fulford de South, une fountaine appelle le Haukeswell, tanque a une seuwer in le Fetesenge en lez prees de Clyfton versus le North.

Item, per auncien custome de la citte, nulle home demuraunt deins mesme la citee soiloite estre prise ne amesne hors du dite citee, par colour ne clayme de villinage, avaunt ceo que le matere fuiste discusse per course de ley.

Item, lez constablez, sergiantez et autres gentez et officers de la dite citee de aunciom temps ount use de amesner a la Kidcote, et illouques enprisoner, lez trespassours alantz nutaundre encountre le peese, et autres homes et femmez, chapelleinz et homes et femes de religion, troves nutandrez en lieu suspectez ovesqes ascun feme, et eux amesner devaunt le ordenarie destre punye solonque le ley de Saynt Eglys.

Item, les prisoners que sont condempnes ou arrestuz deins la dite citee, et sount comys a prison au suyte de partie, et puis sount maundez par briefe (*fo.* 345) al Eschekre ou en autre place de roy ovesque lour causes, mesmes les prisoners, apres ceo qils soient deliveres en court le roy, devoient estre remandes al dit cite pur respondre a lez parties et attendre lur deliverance la.

Item, sy ascun meason deins la dite citee soit ardante, issint que le flamne de la fue soit veu horse de la meason, celly qeste demurante en la dit meason, paiera a lez bailifs de la cite xl $d.$, pur ceo qil ne garde son fuie, par quell le pople nostre seigneur le roy sount affraiez.

Item, lez mair, aldermans et bailifes, et toutz autres officers et ministres dudit citee sount electifes en la manere et fourme qensoite, ceste assavoir en la feste de Saynt Blayse, quaunt le mair serra eslue, lez comunes de la dit citte serrount par usage ensembles en la Guyhall, et le mair que fuiste en lane passe nemera deux ou trois ditz des ditz aldermans, et mesmes les comons ferront eleccion dune dez aldermans du dite citee destre lour mair pur lan prochien ensuant, le quelle alderman issint esluz destre lour maire, sil soite presente en la ditee cite, serra jurez apartement, devaunt toutz lez comunes en la fourme qensuyte cy apries . . . . . Et sil ne soit presente en la dite citee, il preindra son serrement en la maner et fourme avaunt dite, devaunt lez ditz comunes en la Guyhall le lendymayne prochien ensuant, apres sa primer venu a la dite citee. Et avera le dit mair governal de mesme la citee desouth nostre seigneur le roy pur lan ensuant, et prendre le dit mair 1 $li.$ pur lan a cez costagez et expensez pour sey et cez officers selonc lez usagez de mesme la citee.

(*fo.* 345, *b.*) Et adonques toutz les aldermans et xxiiij[or] de comune counseill, que sont presentez, ferront une serrement en manere qensuyte etc. Et adonques le comune clerk liesra le serrement de lez comunes suisditez, en manere et fourme qensuyte que faite, toutz lez comunes teundront suise lour mains de perfourner le dite serrement. Et le mair, qest pur le temps, par custume de la dite cite, pur mayntenaunce de la peies et tranquillite deins mesme la citee, ad poier darrester et enprisoner lez distourbers de la peies, et autres mesfeisours pur rebellitez, malevoise, paroiles et autres defautez, solonc sa discrecion, sance estre de cea enpechez ou enpleddz en apres, et sil serra enpeche ou enpledde pur ascun tile fait, il serra defendu a lez costz de la comunalte.

Le sermont du mayeur.

Ce oyes, bone gens, que je serray foial et loyal a nostre seigneur le roy, et la ditte cite salveray et garderay a nostre seigneur le roy et a ses heirs, et les fraunchises, droites, loyes, usaiges et custumes dicelle, en tous points maintendray et avanceray, et comune droit as riches et as poures feray, et ce pour riens ne lerray sy Dieu meide et lez saints.

Le serment de trent et six personns du counseil.

Vous jures que vous serres prestes a la commandement du maieur, autant de fois que vous serres summones et commandes, a luy consellier, assister, supportier et maintenir en tous poins, pour lamour et prouffite du dit maieur et mesme la cite.

Le serment de les communes fait au mayeur.

Et la communalte du dite citie leverount leurs mains sus, et jurount a dit maieur pour maintenir et perfournir le serment devantdit, en tous poins a lour povoir.

Chamberlaynes.

(*fo.* 346). Item, en la mesme feste de Saint Blaise, apries la election du dit maieur en la maniere et fourme avaunt ditz, tous les aldermans et vingt quatre adoncques estiauns presents en la Guyldehall departerount de la dite Guyldhall a la chambre du counseil. Et illosques eslirount trois preut homes et de mieulx vaillants et plus descreites du dit cite pour estre chambrelains pour lan ensievant; les quelz chambrelains ainsy esleuz prenderount leurs sermentz devant le maieur en la chambre du consiel susdite en la maniere quel sensieut.

Le serment des trois chambirlains.

Vous jures que serres prestes en tout ce que pourrez, que vous loyaulment recepueres et leveres les debtes et lez arrerages des tallaiges, et aultre debtes deuez a la dite comunalte. Et les testes de ceux, des quelx vous recepueres, acquiteres, et les proffites et avauntages de la communealte ferres, et largent que vous recepueres en les besoignes de la cite, bien et loyaulment emploires et despenderes. Et loyaul accompte de la recepte renderes, quant vous serres requis et demandes a vostre povoir et scient, sy Dieu vous eide et tous lez Saintz.

Item, mesmes le maieur et aldermans et vingt quatre de la comune counsiell illousques eslier ount deux gardiens pour la pount de Ouse et deux aultres gardiens pour la pount de Fosse, lesquels brigmaisters serront jurees devant le maieur et chambirlains en la dite chambre en la maniere que seusieut; les quelx gardeurs arrount la charge et gouvernance desditz pountz et de lez tenementes appartenantes as lesditz pountes, par le surveu dudit maieur et ses chambirlains pur lan estiantes.

Le serment des quatre brigmaisters.

Vous jures que vous surverres la chapele sur la pount de Ouse, et de [sic] les chapilleins et clercs de icelle chapelle, et des maisons, rentes, et toutes aultres choises audit pount, ou aucunes aultres rentes a vostre dite office appartenantes. Et les despences de la dite chapelle bien et duement en loyaulte ferres, et tous les fermes, rentes et issues accompt renderes, sy Dieu vous eit et lez saints. Et mesmes lez gardiains renderont leur accomptes chescun an en la dite feste de Saint Blaise, devant lez dites communes en la guyhall, la quelle accompt serra preuve et examine en la fourme come les accomptez des chambirlains susditz, jusques quilz soyent examines et deliveres par la mayeur et les aldermans et la counsiel de la chambre.

Chambre.

(*fo*. 346, *b*.) Item, le lundi prochain apries la ditte feste de saint Blayse serrount les comune clerc et tous les sargiants du maieur esluz par les dits maieur, aldermans, et par les comuns susdits en la Guyldhalle pour lan ensievant. Et en cas que ascun deux trapasse de vie en mort dedens la dit an, ou soit descharge par aucune causse ou dessiert ressounable, adoncques la mayeur pour la temps estiant prendera ung aultere officier en lieu dicell que ainsy trepasse ou meursse, pour occupier jusques a la dite feste de saint Blaisse, et en mesme le lundi serrount tous les dits officiers jurees devant les comunes en la maniere que sensieut.

Le sarment de les sargiantz du maieurs.

Vous jures que serrez loialx a nostre seigneur le roy et a ceste citee Deverwyk, et que bien et loyaulment ferres les commandementes du dit maieur, et de tous vostre somons et attachementes ferres droittement sans aucune couleur, deceyt ou faintisme, quaunt vous serres requis, et tous aultre pointes appartenants a vostre office loyaulment vous ferres comme Dieu vous eit et les sains.

Aldermanni.

Item, les aldermans serrount esluz par les maieur et aldermans pour le temps estieantz, dedens quarante jours prochian ensieuantz apries le trepasse de vie en mort, ou descharge par aucune cause ressounable, par le dit maieur et aldermans confederee, affin que la nombre soit des aldermans fournis deudens le dessus escript quarante jours. Et lesdits aldermans ainsy esluz ferrount serments en la mesme fourme et maniere comme les trente six counssilliers susditz. Et mesme les ditz aldermans ount povoir par les ussaiges de la dite cite les contectours et aultres malfacteurs et les commettre en garde de les viscountes de la dite citee, et lors demorount jusques quilz soyent ressounablement punys.

Item, apres que aucun persoun soit esleu ung alderman, et quil soit jure, et le office dung alderman occupie, ordonne et establie est, que jamais apries per lusaige du ditte cite ne serra enpanellez ne nommes pour estre mis sur aucune enqueste deudens la ditte cite, ne en les franchisses de mesme la citee.

(*fo.* 347). Item, les mayeur, aldermans et vingt quatre de comune conselle de la dite citee ount use de eslier trois prudomes de mesme la citee pour occupier et minestrer loffice de coronniers.

Cest assavoir ung des trois serra demourant entre lieau de Ouse et de Fosse, et ung aultre demoura de par de la dite yeau de Ouse, et ung aultre demoura depar de la Fosse. Et les ditz trois persouns serront souffissauntes descris persouns et ables et de bonn renomee. Et apries quilz soient esleuz a le dite office de coronniers, ilz serrount jurees pour loyaulment faire lour dit office devant les dit maieur, consiell et comunalte, plainement en la countee en la maniere que sensieut.

Vicountes ou baillyffs.

Item, la ussiage est dedens la ditte citee que en la feste de saint Matheu principallement serrount esluz trois bonns et loyaulx proudhomes en la Guyldhall du ditte citee, pour occupier et faire loffice de bailliefes, tous ceulx que pardevant ont occupie et fait la dite office resarvees et exceptes, et lours charges deuement avoyent porte de la dite office, lesquelx balliefes ainsy esleux serrount pressentes a la communalte. Et sy ilz soyent convenables aus ditz comunes par la dit comunalte acceptez serrount. Et les ditz bailliefes serrount jurees devant la maieur en la court ou en aultre lieu dedens la dite citee, ou la maieur plaira. Et lesditz bailliefes paient et sount accomptables anuellement a leschequer nostre seigneur le roy pour la ferme dudit citee, et pour le baillewike de Ansty seloncque la coustume de la ditte citee, pour laquelle cause lez ditz balliefes doivent avoir tous les profitz et commodites a la ditte (*fo.* 347, *b.*) office de ancien temps appartenantes. Et lesditz bailiefes arront frank eleccion de tous leurs officiers et sarviteurs et bailliefes, ausy bien dedens la ditte citee come en la baillywik de Aynsty, et de les gaoliers de lours gaoles appartenants a lour ditte office, a lour voulente et plaissir, nient estiant encontre les ordenances faites sur les memes sarviteurs par la conseile dudit citee, sy comme la loy vuelt. Et les ditz bailiefs receveront lour office par endentoures faitz entre eulx et lour predicessours le jour de Saint Michiell, au premier coup de vespres sonnant a leglise de Saint Michiell pres de le pount de Use. Et pour lesdites choise fare et accomplir en la fourme et maniere devant dit, chescun deulx trouvera et mettre deux souffisauntes homes pour lour plegges. Et puis le dixhuit jour de May, lan nostre siegneur le roy Richard le secounde la dixnoefeme de mesme nostre signour, le roy Richard ottroya et garanta povoir as ditz citezins, leurs hoirs et successours, de eslier deux prodhomes de mesme la citee en viscountes en lieu et place desditz trois bailifes, lesqueulx viscountz serrount eslieus chescun an en la feste de saint Matthieu lapostre, et apries lour elieccion ilz trouveront chescun deux plegges, et serrount jurees en la mesme maniere et fourme, comme lesditz bailifes souloient estre. Et les noms desditz viscountz, ainsy eslieuz, serrount anuelement presentes en la chauncerie nostre seigneur le roy soulz la comune seal dudit citee.

Lordenance pour les gardeurs de les messeures et poisses de la Citee.

Item, lez ditz maieur, aldermans et vingt quatre de la counsiel du chambre de la dite citee ount accoustume et usee de eslier deux prodhomes pour avoir et occupier desoubz la maieur la garde de lestanderd dedens la fraunchisse dudit citee. Cest assavoir des boussels, demi boussels, galon, demi gallon, et de toutes aultres manieres de messures et de poisses, et pour occupier et loyaulment faire la dite office, ilz serrount jures devant le maieur. Et les ditz deux homes ainsy jures sellerount toutes messeures convenables, affin que nulles aultres messures ne serount occupies dedens le mesme citee ne franchisse. Et ilz prenderount pour lour seall launcien fee et salaire a celle office accustumes.

Serchours.

(*fo.* 348.) Item, ilz ount use et accoustumee que les maisters de chescun mestier du dit cetee eslierount deux prudhomes ou pluseurs, sy mester soit, lesquelx serrount nomes serchours pour garder, sourveier et examiner le dit mestier, seloncque les ordonnances et statutez en mesme le mestier sont faitz et ordonnes. Et sy aucune defaulte troverount au maieur pour le temps estieant presenterount. Et a ce loyaulment faire ilz serrount jures devant le maieur.

Constablez.

Item, ait este use et accustumee de esher en chescune paroche ung, deux ou trois connestables pour garder et mayntenir le paix, lez queulx serrount esluz parmy toute la citee chescun an le secounde lundy prochain apries la feste de Saint Blase, devant les aldermans et gardains de la warde, et presentez au maieur, ou a son lieutenant, et lours nomes enrolles. Et lesditz serrount jures quilz serrount a tous heures prestes pour apaissier toutes debattes, haynes, et executer et justifier toutes fellonies, ou deroberies, ou burgaries faites dedens la dicte citee, et les maulxfacteurs amerrount a la loy, affin quilx pourrount estre justifies par justice. Et lesditz connestables serrount prestes pour poursuir touts fellouns et aultre malfacterure, affin quilz ne eschaperount sans permission. Et les ditz connestables serrount attendantes aux ditz maieur, bailiefs, et aldermans, quant de besoing serra.

Gardeyns dez chieffs dez Portes.

Item, ait este use et accoustume de eslire ung ou deux prudhomes, lesquelx jures et lours noms enrolles, pour la garde des chieffs de chescune porte de la citee, lesquelx doyvent tous jours estre prestez de faire ce que lour serra commande de par la maieur et la comunalte.

Forfettours del Fraunchese.

Item, ordonne est et assentus de tamps que nulluy retient memoire, que sy aucune parsonne, que soit fraunchisse dedens la dicte citee, pregne en maintenance auscune cause ou querelle encountre la fraunchisse et libertes de mesme la citee, ou faissaunt suyte, par la quelle suyte les franchisses et libertees dudite citee soit endomages ou enblessies, celluy que ainsy forfait, et son trespas prouve devant lez maieur et bailiefs du dite citee, ou devant aucun aultre juge en court de recorde ou autrement, soit outrement forjuge de son franchisse et de tous autres bienficez parteignauntz as fraunchisses et libertees de la dite citee.

De comunibus placitis Ebor' in Guyhald.

(*fo.* 348, *b.*) En comunes plees plediables briefs, appelles *Ex gravi querela*, pour avoir execucion des tenementz hors de testamentz, que sont enrolles de recorde ou autrement en la Guyhale, brief de dowere, *unde nichill habet*, brief de coustumes, et de serevices en lieu de *cessavit*, briefs darrour de jugementz donnees devant les bailiefs, briefs de waste, briefes *de particione facienda* entre parteneres, brief de *Quid juris clam* . . . . , *per que servicia* et autres, les queux briefes sont closes et directez as maieur et bailiefes, et auxsi *replegiare* des neymes et distresse a torte prises sont pledables devant maieur et baliefes en mesme le Guyhall de comune plees par plaint sance brief. Et fait assavoir que mesmes lez bailiefes sont ministres de faire loffice et service et servir tous lesditz briefes et *replegiare* par precepte de maieur directe as ditz bailliefs, et la prochesse est tiell. En primes, en brief de *Ex gravi querela* premunicion serra fait a lez tenantz, cest assavoir, par trois jours devant le lundie, come de plee de terre, et ainsy serra fait de tous autres somons touchaunt mesme la court, et sy la premunicion soit faite et tesmoigne par les bailiefs ou sez ministres, lez tenantz pourront estre essonnie une fois. Et sy lez tenantz faice default a le dit premunicion, tesmoigne adoncques serra agarde le grande cap. . . Et silz apperrent, ilz povent estre essonnie apries la veue, et sur ce toute autre proces serra fait plainement. comme dit est en brief de droit patent en la Guyhall de plee de terre.

Dower.

Item, en brieff de dowere *unde nichil habet* les tenauntz averont a le commencement trois somons et une essone apries le trois somons, et puis arrout la veue, et apries la veue une essone, et les tenantz ou tielle brief de dowere arront le veue comment ils entreront par mesme le baron, que murrust seisse, et auxi les tenantz pourront vouchier a garrant et estre essone apries chescun apparance, et toute autre processe serra fait comme en brief de droit en Guyhall de plee de terre. Et sy le mandant recoure dowers vers le tenant par defaulte, ou par juggement en loy, en tiel brief de dowere, et mesme la fame demandant allegie en court de recorde, que son baron morust seisse, adoncques la maieur maundera as bailifes par precepte quilz fachent somondre enqueste de les voissins ou lez tenementez sont encountre la prochain courte de comune plees, denquerer si le baroun morust seisse et de la value de les tenementez et de lez damagez. Et si elle recovere par enqueste lez damagez serrount enquis par mesme lenqueste.

Rent and Services.

(*fo.* 349). Item, en brief dez custumes et servicez les tenauntez averont trois somons et trois essones, et averont auxi la veue, et pourront voucher a garrant deniszein et forcine, et serront essonnies et arront excepcions, et tout autre processe serra fait sy come declaire est devant en brief de droit en la court de plee de terre. Saufe sy le tenaunt fache defaulte apries defaulte, adoncques le demandant arra jugement de recoverer et tenir par ung an et ung jour, sur tiel condecion que le tenaunt pourra venir dedens mesmes lan et jour prochain ensuiant, et faire gree de lez arrerages, et trover seurte, come la courte agarde, de paier la rente ou le services loyaulement en apries, et ravoier ses tenauntz. Et dedens queux an et jour le tenaunt poet venir et faire le demandant venir en court per *scire facias*, et reavera ses tenantz, feissant come devant est dit, adoncques apries lan et jour le demandant avera *scire facias* deviers le tenaunt. Et sy lez bailifes retourneront que le tenaunt soit garny de venir et respondre, sil sache rien dire adonques, le jugement serra que le demandant ne doyt my recoverer lez tenementz quitement a luy et a ses heires a tous jours, seloncq la custume de la citee susditte.

Wast.

Item, en brief de waste processe serra fait devers lez tenauntz par somons, attachement et distresse, accordant a le statute ens faite; et sy le tenaunt viegne et pledee, adoncques avera ung esson, et ainsy apries chescun apparance; et sil fache defaulte a la graunde distresse, adoncques serra maunde as bailiefes par precept de maieur que les ditz bailifs voisent a le lieu vastee et enquerront de la waste et des damaiges seloncq lestatute, et quilz retourneront lenqueste a la prochain courte des comunes plees, et la playntife recovera le lieu wastee et lez damages en tribill par le statute.

Replegiare.

Item, en *replegiare* la processe est tiel, sy ascun home preugne distresse en autre soile dedens mesme le citee, celluy a quy mesmes lez biens sont, pourra venir a ung dez bailliefs, et avera ung ministre par comandement de court dalier a la partie que prent lez biens, et sil puet avoir la veue de ceux biens, il ferra prissier mesmes les biens par deux prodomes, et adoncques serra ung pleint fait et entre en la paupier des bailliefs en tiel maniere, *Talis queritur versus talem de maniis* [sic] *suis injuste captis in domo sua vel in libero tenemento suo in tali parochia.* Et mesme la partye trouvera illosques deux plegges souffissauntes de poursuyr et faire (*fo.* 349, *b*) retorne de lez biens, ou le pris, en cas que retorne soit agarde, et ainsy avera la deliverance, et les parties arrout jour pour prefixion a le prochain court des comunes plees. Lez bailiefes ferra une cedulle contenant tout le matiere et le plaint, et portera mesme la cedulle a mesme le court, et la serra mise en filace. Et les parties serront demandez a quel jour lun et lautre pourront estre esson de comune essone, et a quelle jour que le plaintif fauche default, retournee serra agarde a lavowant. Et retourne en tiel cas est agardeable trois foiz par la coustume, et a la tierch fois nient replevisable; et a quelle heure que lavowant face defaulte, adoncques serra agarde que lez neimes demourent a la plaintife, *videlicet, morentur nemia,* sans aucun domage recoverer. Et sy ainsy soit que lez bailliefes ne povent avoir veue de le destresse prisse, adoncques ilz certeferont en la dit court, et la serra agarde la withernam, et sur ce proces serra fait. Et si les parties veignent, et avower soit fait, et pleddent a juggement ou a issue denqueste, adoncques serra juggement donne ou proces fait de faire venir lenqueste, seloncque ceo que le cas demande, et lez parties pourront estre esson apries chescun apparance. Et si la partie clayme proprete en la destresse, adoncques ce certifie en la court, et proces serra fait par precepte as bailliefes, de trier la properte etc. Et coment que la partie soit essonnie de sarvice le roy, ou *replegiare,* et al jour quil ait par lession face defaute, ou ne porte mye son garrant, il emportera nulle pennance.

De particione facienda.

Item, en brief *de participacione facienda,* pour faire departicion entre partiniers des tenementez en Everwyk, brief close serra directe as maieur et bailiefes contenant le matiere seloncque la fourme de tiel brief. Et lez parties serront garnis par precept de la maieur directe as baliefes, et lez tenantz pourront estre essoygnez, et sils veignent ilz pourront plaidier lours matieres, et silz fachent default la departicion serra agarde par defaulte. Et tous juggements, que sont donnes en plee de terre en la dit court, serront donnes devant le maieur et aldermans par bouche de lour recordeur.

Exigences et utlariez.

Et lez exigencez de tous utlariez et wayveries agardes devant lez ditz bailieffes, par brief de exigence a deux directe par le maieur, serront enrolles devant lez bailiefes et mandes en la chambre de la Guyhall suisdittes.

(*fo.* 350). Et sait assavoir que tous lez amerciamentes incidentez des ditz plees de terre serront levez par lez ministres dez bailifes, et egallement devises a le ussaige de ditz bailiefes et comunalte de mesme la citee.

Item, les aldermans Deverwyk serront somones de venir a le dite courte de plee de terre par le sergiant du maieur, que portera son mase.

De assisa mortis antecessoris en Everwyk.

Item, les assises de mort dauncestre sont tenus et terminables devant lez maieur et bailiefs d'Everwyk chescun lundy a la Guyhall, comme avaunt est dit, dont le proces est tiel, cest assavoir :—Celluy que vuelt avoir tiel assis, vendra devant le maieur et bailifs en la chambre du Guyhall a aucun lundi, sy comme dit est en assise de fresshforce, et ferront une bille contenant la forme *dassise de mort dauncestre* seloncque le cas, et la quelle bille serra enrolle, et apries le comune clerk ferra une aultre bille, contenant toute la matiere de la primier bille, faissant mencion de le title et de le congregation des maieur et aldermans. Et tiel bille serra mande as bailiefes pour servir seloncque la custume, la quelle brief serra sarvie par aucun sargant de bailiefes ; cest assavoir, le dit sergant le mersquedi prochain apries le liverie de la dit bille as ditz bailiefes ferront somons a lez tenantes de lez tenementez demandez par tesmoignaunce de deux frank homes de la citee, quilz soyent a la Guyhall le lundi prochain ensuiant pour oyr la recongnissance, silz vuellent encontrer ; quele lundi le demandant pourra suyr la samadi prochain devant darraier et somonder les jurrours, et ainsy en apries encountre lez lundis de viij jours en viij jours de sa volunte. Et ainsy pourront lez tenantz suyr, silz veullent, pour leur deliverance, et lez arraymentz des panelles dez tielz assises serront faitez par les maieur et bailiefes, et lours ministres, ou par le maieur et aldermans, si aucun des parties le voudera demander, sur reissounable cause, en maniere com usse est en assise de fressheforce; et en tiel assisses de mort dauncestre lez parties pourront estre esson comme a le comune loy, et lez tenantz pourront vouchier a garrant dedens la citee et auxi en forein counte sole.

(*fo.* 350, *b.*) Nationality of Bertram Dawson.[1]

(*fo.* 352, *b.*)[2] Clausula testamenti Willelmi Fereby, filii Roberti Feriby, civis Ebor', inpressa, qui obiit anno Domini millesimo cccc^{mo}, terciodecimo quarto die mensis Augusti.

Item, lego Roberto filio Johannis de Rilleston, totum illud tenementum meum, cum omnibus edificiis et pertinenciis suis, in vico de Mikilgat Ebor', quod habui ex dono et feoffamento Roberti Fewlar, civis Ebor', prout jacet in latitudine inter terram quondam Johannis de Sadyngton, ex parte una, et terram quondam Willelmi Ripon ex altera, et extendit se a strata regia de Mikylgate ante usque ad vicum dictum Northstrete retro,[2] tenendum et habendum prefatum mesuagium cum omnibus edificiis et pertinenciis suis, prefato Roberto Rilleston et heredibus de corpore suo legitime procreatis per servicia inde debita et consueta, libere, bene et pacifice inperpetuum. Et si prefatus Robertus decesserit sine herede de corpore suo legitime procreato, tunc volo quod dictum tenementum, quam primo de ipsius morte constiterit, per maiorem et vicecomites civitatis Ebor', qui pro tunc fuerint, vendatur, et quod una medietas precii pro eo recepti sustentacioni pontis de Fosse applicetur, et altera medietas per manus officialis curie Ebor' inter pauperes parochianos de Appilton, Whistan, et Foxholez distribuatur pro animabus omnium fidelium defunctorum. Et volo quod dictus officialis habeat pro labore suo xiij *s.* iiij *d.*

1—Eng. Misc., *op. cit.*, pp. 51–52.
2—Folios 351–352 are blank.

Datum quoad consignacionem nono die mensis Marcii, anno Domini mcccc^{mo} quarto decimo.

Memorandum that on 3 November, 20 Edw. iv. (1480), before John Marshall, mayor, Robert Williamson of York, founder, shewed the following writ of *de non molestando*.

Writ to the keepers of the peace and justices of the county of the city of York not to proceed against the said Robert for any offences, committed before 4 November, 1 Edw. iv. (1461), in accordance with the pardon granted to him by letters patent dated 6 March last. York, 26 Sept., 5 Edw. iv. (1465).

(*fo.* 353). Nationality of John Richardson.[1]

Johannes Nevill, comes Northumbr' et dominus de Monte Acuto, ac gardianus Estmarchie Anglie versus Scociam, universis et singulis ad quos presentes litere pervenerint, salutem. Noveritis nos, die confeccionis presencium, recepisse fidem et sacramentum Johannis Birkched de ·Ebor', milner, oriundi de Scocia, super sacrosanctum evangelium corporaliter jurati, quod erit fidelis Anglicus, fidem et ligienciam geret supremo domino nostro regi Edwardo, qui nunc est, heredibus et successoribus suis, Anglie regibus, ac omnes leges, custumas, et consuetudines regni Anglic, a superiori usque ad inferiorem, in omnibus obediet et conservet durante tota vita sua. In cujus rei testimonium presentibus sigillum nostrum apponi fecimus. Datum apud castrum nostrum de Alnewyk, quinto die Novembris, 4 Edw. iv. (1464).

Pro hominibus ville de Hamiburg.

(*fo.* 353, *b.*) Edwardus, Dei gracia rex Anglic et France, et dominus Hibernie, universis et singulis vicecomitibus, maioribus, ballivis, ministris, et aliis fidelibus suis, ad quos presentes litere pervenerint, salutem. Cum secundem consuetudinem in regno nostro Anglie hactenus optentam et approbatam homines de antiquo dominico corone Anglic quieti sint et esse debeant de theoloneo, pavagio, muragio, et passagio, per totum regnum nostrum Anglie; vobis mandamus quod homines ville de

1—Eng. Misc., *op. cit.*, p. 35.

Hamiburg in comitatu Ebor', que est de antiquo dominico corone Anglie, sicut per certificacionem thesaurarii et camerarii Henrici Sexti, nuper de facto et non de jure regis Anglie, eidem nuper regi in cancellariam suam de mandato suo missam plene liquet, ad hujusmodi theoloneum, pavagium, muragium, seu passagium de bonis et rebus suis prestandum non distringatis contra consuetudinem supradictam; et districtionem, si quam eis ea occasione feceritis, sine dilacione relaxetis eisdem. Teste me ipso apud Westmonasterium, xxx die Octobris, anno regni nostri sexto decimo (1476). Morton.

Omnibus Christi fidelibus ad quos presentes litere pervenerint, Johannes Tonge, maior civitatis Ebor', vicecomites, et aldermanni ejusdem civitatis, salutem in domino sempiternam. Cum nobis intimatum et conquestum existat per homines ville de Hamiburgh in comitatu Ebor', que est de dominico corone Anglie, quod ipsi per collectores theolonii civitatis predicte multipliciter vexati et perturbati existunt, contra tenorem literarum patentium de diversis concessionibus et confirmacionibus per nonnullos reges, progenitores domini regis nunc, concessis, ac per ipsum dominum nunc regem eisdem hominibus de novo confirmatis, quas quidem literas patentes prefati homines nobis, prefatis maiori, vicecomitibus et aldermannis, in camera consilii dicte civitatis super pontem Use die confeccionis presencium monstraverunt, ac publice lege fecerunt; in quibus inter alia sic contineter, quod predicti homines ville de Hamiburg in comitatu Ebor', qui nunc sunt et qui pro tempore erunt, soluti et quieti sint in civitatibus, burgis, foris et nundinis (*fo.* 354) quibuscumque, in transitu pontium et pontium maris, et in omnibus locis per totam terram nostram, de teoloneo, pontagio, passagio, pedagio, lastagio et de omnibus aliis tallagiis occasionibus inde quibuscumque prout in literis predictis continetur. Nos vero, predicti maior, vicecomites et aldermanni, premissa considerantes, mandamus et quacum [*sic*] in nobis est precipimus, firmiter injungentes omnibus et singulis collectoribus theolonii, pontagii, passagii, pedagii, lastagii et tallagii in civitate predicta, suburbiis et libertate ejusdem, qui nunc sunt et qui pro tempore erunt, quod nec ipsi collectores nec eorum aliquis de cetero exigant seu capiant, aut exigat seu capiat, de prefatis hominibus ville de Hamiburg, nec eorum aliquo, aliquod hujusmodi theoloneum, pontagium, passagium, pedagium, lastagium sive tallagium pro aliquibus bonis, catallis, mercandisis, rebus seu averiis suis quibuscumque infra civitatem predictam, suburbia et libertatem ejusdem, quovismodo aliquo tempore in futurum existentibus sive venientibus etc. In quorum omnium testimonium sigillum officii maioratus civitatis apponi fecimus. Datum apud Ebor', vii die Februarii, anno regni regis Edwardi quarti post conquestum Anglic decimo septimo (A.D. 147$\frac{7}{8}$). Lancastria.

(*fo.* 354, *b.*) Letter of attorney by Robert Kelam, citizen of London, and Isabel his wife, late the wife of John Bedale, gentleman, appointing George Lovell of Skelton, esquire, to receive the rents now owing for their lands and tenements in the city of York, late of the said John Bedale, and to survey, repair, and lease the said lands and tenements, according to his discretion, and if necessary to sell the same. Seal; also seal of Thomas Hill, grocer, citizen, and alderman of London. London, 26 March, 14 Edw. iv. (1473-4).

(*fo.* 355). Universis sancte matris ecclesie filiis, ad quos presens scriptum pervenerit, Johannes Tong, maior civitatis Ebor', patronus cantarie in honore sancti Petri in ecclesia parochiali sancti Martini in Conyngstrete dicte civitatis, pro animabus Johannis Braithwate, quondam mercatoris et maioris dicte civitatis Ebor', et Marie uxoris sue, benefactorum suorum ac omnium fidelium defunctorum fundate, erecte et stabilite, salutem. Sciatis quod cum cantaria antedicta certis tenementis et redditibus, pro nunc in tenura Johannis Otteley, Thome Thorp, Margarete Clerkson, Alicie Taite, Margarete Yarwit, Johannis Gill, Agnetis Tanner, et Agnetis Thorp in Conyngstret dicte civitatis Ebor', parcellatim existentibus et situatis dotata, ad tantam hiis diebus provenit exilitatem et ruinositatem, quod capellanus eidem deserviturus ex provenientibus ipsius cantarie honeste vivere ac onera eidem incumbencia supportare nequaquam potest; adeo quod eadem cantaria a quocumque capellano diu viduata fuerat, in animarum fundatorum ejusdem grave dispendium. Hinc est quod ego, Johannes Tong, maior et patronus antedictus, pio affectu salutem animarum predictarum merito cupiens, ac unione, annexione et combinacione ejusdem cantarie et cantarie Sancti Michaelis in ecclesia parochiali Sancte Elene in Stanegate dicte civitatis, pro animabus Radulfi Horneby et Johanne uxoris sue, antecessorum, benefactorum omniumque heredum ac omnium fidelium defunctorum erecte et fundate, auctoritate ordinaria canonice facta, assensu et consensu prestant', ex assensu et consensu expressis heredum fundatorum dicte cantarie Sancti Petri, ipsam jamdictam cantariam Sancti Petri, ex causis premissis et aliis me et conscienciam meam in hac parte canonice moventibus, ad altare Sancti Michaelis in dicta ecclesia parochiali Sancte Elene per capellanum cantarie in honore ejusdem ibidem fundate deserviturum, et pro animabus fundatorum predictorum imperpetuum celebraturum, harum serie transfero in quantum de jure potero, proviso quod ego, predictus Johannes Tong, et successores mei, maiores dicte civitatis Ebor' pro tempore existentes, ad dictas cantarias unitas et combinatas secunda vice ex nunc qualitercumque, et extunc qualibet vice quomodolibet vacaturas imperpetuum, loci ordinario capellanum ydoneum valeant presentare. In cujus rei testimonium sigillum officii maioratus dicte civitatis Ebor' presentibus est appensum. Datum apud Ebor' decimo die Februarii, 17 Edw. iv. (1477-8).

(*fo.* 355, *b.*) Memorandum, that where a contraversie and a debate was hangyng betwix Thomas Neleson, alderman and merchant, of the cite of Yorke, and William Neleson, son of the same Thomas Neleson, of the on partie, and William Scauseby, son and heire of Thomas Scauseby, alderman and merchant of the same deseised, of the other partie, of and apon a bargan maid betwix the said parties of certan tenementes lying in Thuresday market in the cite of Yorke; the which contraversie and debate was understondet by the right wirshupfull Sir John Tong, than beyng maire of the cite of Yorke, (who) tuke the said contraversie and debate to rest uppon hym, and the right wirshupfull Sirs Richerd York, alderman, Miles Metcalf, recorder, of the same cite, William Todd, merchaunt, and Nicholas Pereson, late shireffes of the same, and by gude deliberacion called tofore thame the said parties; they, understonding the said contraversie and debate, maid a full end in all thinges dependyng betwix the said parties:—that is to say, that the said Thomas Neleson and William, his son, shold have and joy peseable for ever to thare heirs and assignes all thocs landes and tenementes, rentes and servis, the which the said William Scauseby had in the Thuresday market by dissent, as son and heire of the said Thomas Scauseby. And in acomplishement of the same the said Thomas Neleson and William his son, by jugement and awarde of the said maire and all other above writen, yaff the said William Scauseby a certan sowme of money. That done and fulfilled, the said William Scauseby, of his own fre will ancoart, not constrenyd, afore us, the said William Scauseby, swore uppon the holy Evaungelist corporalie touched that the said Thomas Scauseby, his fader, died not seised of the said landes, tenementes, rentes, and servis, in Thuresday market above writen, ne of no parcell of thame.

(*fo.* 356). Release by John Fox, clerk, John Gurnard, chaplain, and William Scauseby, citizen and merchant, all of York, to Thomas Neleson, citizen and merchant, and William Neleson his son, of the lands in Thuresday market, which they had among other lands in the city and suburbs of York, and in Kirkebymoresyde, by enfeoffment of William Scauseby, citizen and merchant of York. Seals. Witnesses, John Tonge, mayor, Robert Hancock, William Spense, sheriffs, Thomas Wrangways, Robert Wrangways, Robert Amyas of York, merchants. 12 Feb., 17 Edw. iv. (1477–8). Acknowledged before John Tong, mayor, 24 January, 17 Edw. iv. (1477–8). Release by the said William Scauseby, to the said Thomas Neleson and William Neleson of the said lands in Thuresdaymarket. Seal. Witnesses, John Tonge, mayor, Robert Hancok, William Spense, sheriffs, Thomas Asper of York, gentleman, Adam Gunby of York. 10 Feb., 17 Edw. iv. (1477–8). Acknowledged as the last deed.

(*fo.* 356, *b.*) Omnibus Christi fidelibus, presentes literas visuris seu inspecturis, nos Johannes Carlell, maior, et Willelmus Scott, vicecomes ville Novi Castri super Tynam, Johannes Cok, Robertus Chaimbre, Johannes Sample, Willelmus Rodum, Johannes Essyngton, et Johannes Fissher, aldermanni ejusdem ville, Ricardus Stevynson, nuper maior dicte ville, Willelmus Haysand, mercator, et Robertus Batson, scissor, de eadem villa, salutem in omnium Salvatore et in dubiis firmam adhibere fidem. Cum enim inter cetera pietatis officia id maxime arbitramur necessarium, et ut veritati testimonium perhibeamus, hinc est quod lamentabilis querela ad nos dilata est per discretam mulierem de civitate Ebor' Elizabeth Troghton.[1]

(fo. 357). An unfinished entry about the castle mills given in full on fo. 305.

(fo. 357, b.) An indenture made between the master of the hospital of Saint Thomas of Canterbury etc. and the master of the gild of Corpus Christi.[2]

In Dei Nomine, Amen. Anno ab Incarnacione millesimo ccccxxviij° cumque illustrissimus metuendissimus ast Christianissimus princeps Edwardus Dei gracia Anglie et Francie rex.[3]

(fo. 359). Grant by Thomas Howme of York, gentleman, to George Soulby and John Rawdon gentleman, William Shaffton, wawker, and Symon Bedale, berker, all of York, of his lands and tenements in Monkgayte in the suburb of the city; viz., ten tenements lying together before the churchyard of S. Maurice and the walls of the city. Seal. Witnesses William Holbek, mayor, John Stokton, and Robert Harwod, sheriffs, Sir Edmund Pawner, parochial chaplain of S. Maurice, Robert Atkynson. Seal. York, 14 January, 12 Edw. iv. (1472-3).

Grant by Thomas Home of York, gentleman, to Thomas Tubbac of York, merchant, of three acres, three roods of meadow in the fields of Bisshoppthorpp, by the bank of the Use, in the county of the city of York. Seal. Witnesses, John Sharppe, Nicholas Halyday, Robert Walton, Robert Egill, John Walker, Robert Lassell, John Browne, William Atkynson, William More, and others of the vill of Bisshoppthorpp. Bisshoppthorpp, 26 June, 14 Edw. iv. (1474).

(fo. 359, b.) Grant by Thomas Tubbac of York, merchant, to Thomas Home of York, gentleman, and Joan his wife, and the heirs of Thomas Home, of three acres, three roods of meadow in the fields of Bisshoppthorp, by the bank of the Use. Witnesses as above. Bisshoppthorpp, 28 June, 14 Edw. iv. (1474).

Resignacio et presentacio cantarie in capella Sancti Willelmi super pontem Use.

1—This word is crossed through.
2—R. H. Skaife, op. cit., pp. 270-273, gives this in full.
3—This entry is unfinished in the MS.

A CHANTRY IN ALL SAINTS' (150⅞)

Memorandum quod decimo die mensis Julii, anno Domini millesimo quingentesimo septimo, Cuthbertus Cotes, capellanus, resignavit cantariam in capella Sancti Willelmi super pontem Use, cujus quidem presentacio spectat Willelmo Bulmer, militi. Que quidem resignacio facta fuit in presencia Johannis Birkhed, maioris civitatis Ebor', et aliorum etc., die et anno predictis.

Et postea terciodecimo die Julii, anno predicto, Johannes Palyser, capellanus, presentatus fuit ad cantariam predictam per predictum Willelmum Bulmer, et per predictum maiorem admissus fuit ad eandem cantariam, tercio die Augusti, anno Domini millesimo quingentesimo septimo et 22 Henry vii.

(*fo.* 360). Beginning of a writ of *non molestando* to the mayor and escheator of the city of York, concerning the custody of the temporalities of the archbishopric, vacant by the death of Laurence [Booth], which the king granted to Thomas Rotherham, lord chancellor, by letters patent dated 24 March last, Edward iv.

Presentacio cantarie in ecclesia Omnium Sanctorum in Northstret pro animabus Johannis Catton etc.

Memorandum quod sexto decimo die Marcii, 23 Heur. vii. (1507–8), Robertus Lelograve, capellanus, presentatus erat ad cantariam ad altare beate Marie Virginis in ecclesia Omnium Sanctorum in Northstrete per resignacionem Johannis Chatburn, ultimi capellani ejusdem, cum omnibus proficuis, ac sex marcarum et duorum solidorum annuatim, solvendorum per manus camerariorum hujus civitatis pro tempore existentum ad festa Pentecostes et Sancti Martini in yeme per equales porciones etc.

Memorandum quod sexto die Januarii, anno Domini millesimo quingentesimo nono, Laurencius Brownflete, capellanus, presentatus erat ad cantariam ad altare Sancte Katerine in ecclesia Sancti Johannis Evaungeliste in Mekilgate . . . .[1] ultimi capellani ejusdem, cum omnibus proficuis. Data fuit ista presentacio tempore Georgii Esser, maioris civitatis Ebor', ut in elaps[1] . . . . agentis pro animabus Ricardi Watby et omnium fidelium defunctorum.

1—A space is left here.

Memorandum quod xxi° die Marcii, 8 Henr. viii. (1516-17), Willelmus Lowson, capellanus, presentatus erat ad cantariam Rogeri Marre, quondam . . . . y de Qhyx [ley], capella Sancti Willelmi super pontem Use, per resignacionem Henrici Burton, capellani ejusdem, cum omnibus proficuis etc.

Memorandum quod primo die Junii, 9 Henr. vii. (1517), Johannes Smyk, capellanus, presentatus erat ad cantariam perpetuam in capella sancti Willelmi super pontem Use, fundatam pro animabus Roberti Wistowe et Eluesie, uxoris sue, ac Roberti Wistowe et omnium fidelium defunctorum, per resignacionem Willelmi Gurnell, ultimi capellani ejusdem, cum omnibus proficuis etc. una cum quadraginta solidis sterlingorum pro celebracione misse . . . . etc. Data fuit ista presentacio tempore Johannis Dogeson, maioris civitatis Ebor' etc.

(*fo.* 360, *b.*) Bond by John Hopton of Waterhay in the parish of Rothwell, gentleman, Thomas Shipton, Richard Shipton, John Cusson, William Saule of Tollerton, husbandmen, and Robert Robynson of Alne, husbandman, to Thomas Neleson the elder, citizen and merchant of York, in 60 *l.* to be paid at the feast of S. Peter's Chains next. Seals. 9 April, 21 Edw. iv. (1481). The condition of this bond is that it shall be void upon payment by the sum of 40 *l.*; viz., 40 *s.* at the feast of S. Peter's Chains (1 August) next, 40 *s.* at the feast of the Purification (2 February) then next; and thus 40 *s.* half yearly until the said 40 *l.* be paid. Acknowledged in the time of Robert Amyas, mayor.

Henricus, comes Northumbr', dominus honorum de Cockermouth et Peteworth, ac gardianus Est et Middel marchiarum Anglie versus Scociam, omnibus ad quos presentes litere pervenerint, salutem. Sciatis quod Adam Roosse in Scocia natus, super sacrosancta Dei evaungelia per ipsum corporaliter tacta, prestitit juramentum quod vita sua durante erit legius et fidelis subditus domino regi nostro, qui nunc est, et successoribus suis, regni Anglie regibus, et quod ejusdem regni legibus et statutis, tam provisis quam providendis, fideliter obediet et inviolabiliter observabit. In cujus rei testimonium presentibus sigillum mei officii gardianitatis feci apponi. Data in castro meo de Aylenewyk, xxviii° die Junii, 20 Edw. iv. (1480).

(*fo.* 361). Nationality of John Hans.¹

(*fo.* 361, *b.*) Grant by Robert Langton, esquire, to Alexander Aunger, gentleman, and Robert Ledes, of the lands in the city of York, which he had together with Henry Langton esquire his brother, deceased, by release of lady Eufemia Langton, their mother. Seal. Witnesses, Robert Amyas, mayor, John Newton, alderman, Miles Willesthorp, esquire. 8 July, 21 Edw. iv. (1481).

(*fo.* 362, 362, *b.*) Nationality of Alexander Ambler, John Meldroun, John Malson.²

Ordinacio vinteriorum.

(*fo.* 363). Ordinacio vynteriorum civitatis Ebor', facta et confirmata . . . . 22 Edw. iv. (1482-3), per Ricardum Yorke, majorem civitatis Ebor', et totum consilium camere ejusdem, ac cum assensu et consensu omnium magistrorum artis predicte, sequitur in subscriptis.

In primis, that it be not leful to eny maner of man within this cite to set upp and to occupie as a maister vynter retaling wynes, that is to say reid clarett or white, afore the tyme that he be examyned and seirched by the seircheours of the same occupacion for tyme beyng, whether he be able and sufficiant in conyng and knowlige of and in that feit and occupacion or noo, uppon the payn of forfatour of vj *s.* viij *d.*, evenlie to be employed unto the common wele of this said cite and the craft abovesaid, withoute pardon.

Item, it is ordeigned that from this day forwerd, it be not leful to eny maner merchaunt estraunger, infraunchest, to sell or retaill eny wynes, that is to say reid claret, white or rynnesshe, or eny other wynes by retaill within this said cite afore the tyme that the said estraunger be fraunchesed and admitted for a freman of this same cite, and that that wyne or wynes be sufficiantly serched and founden gude and able merchaunt and trewe stuff by the seirchours of the said occupacion for tyme

---

1—Eng. Misc., *op. cit.*, p. 39.
2—Eng. Misc., *op. cit.*, p. 39-40.

beyng, uppon payn of forfatour of xiij *s*. iiij *d*., to be paid in maner and forme above writen withoute pardon.

Item, it is ordeigned fermelie from this day forwerd to be kept that every man retaling eny maner wynes, that is to say, reid claret, white, or eny other maner swete wynes, ether growing or confect within this cite, from noweforth be contributorie unto the yerlie chargies and expenses of the said craft and occupacion, as in and unto the bringyngfurth yerelie of ther pageant in the fest of Corpus Christi and other ther charges yerelie; forsene alwey that no man retaling wynes within this cite, suburbes and precinctes of the same, be not overcharged in paing of pageant silver, bot at they pay after ther othes ton and ton like, etc.

Item, it is enact and ordeigned that from hensforth, it be leful unto the seirchours of the said occupacion for tyme beyng within this said cite to seirch dewlie and understond, from tyme unto tyme and als oft tymes as theym shall seme necessarie for the wele of the kynges lige people, almaner wynes such as shalbe (*fo.* 363, *b.*) putto sale by retaill, to thentent that therbe no maner of corrupt wynez unholesum for manys body put unto sale within this same cite; and if the said seircheours for tyme beyng, opon ther said seirch makyng at eny tyme herafter, fynde and take eny maner man retaling or utteryng eny maner of corrupt and unholesum wynes within this said cite, that than not onelie the said seirchours shall charge the man, havyng the said unholesum and corrupt wynes, to surseisse of eny forther utteraunse or retaling therof, bot also the same seirchours incontynent adcerteyn and enfourme the maiour of this said cite for tyme beyng, or his lieutenaunt, of the said offence, as often tymes as eny man shalbe founden delinquent in that behalf, to thentent that dewe punycion may be in that partie; and if eny maner man herafter within this said cite be founden disobeaunt unto the said seircheours in ther dewe seirch makyng in that behalfe that than he so disobeyng pay for every [tyme][1] that he so disobeith vj *s*. viij *d*., to be enploed evenlie, as is abovesaid, withoute eny remission.

Item, it is ordeigned and enact aswele for the wirshop of the said cite and honestie of the same occupacion, as also for the

---

1—Omitted in the MS.

common wele of the kynges people, that it be not leful to eny maner man, retaling wynez hcrafter within this said cite, to hold or have eny servant, man, childe, or woman to retaill his wyne, which is corrupt and unclen nature, uppon the payn of forfatour of xx *s.*, to be enployd as is abovesaid.

Item, it is ordeigned and constitued that wo so ever occupies or herefter shall occupie, as a maister vyntener retaling wyne within this cite, that and he be dewlie warned by his seircheours of the said occupacion for tyme beyng forto be and appere in his propre persone at eny assemble generall or eny other leful congregacions, eyther concernyng for the common wele of this cite or for the convenient wele, honestie, and profect of the said occupacion, and comys not, shall forfet and pay vj *d.* for every tyme that he so offendeth, to be converted (*fo.* 364) unto the uses beforsaid, oules than he have a resonable cause for his excuse in that behalfe.

Item, it is ordeigned and constitued that wo so ever of the said occupacion of vynters resavyth eny maner pottes of eny other mannes of the same crafte, of eny other mannes marke, and thame kepys or raisseth the marke of, that can be laufully proved, shall forfet and pay withoute pardon iij *s.* iiij *d.* to the chambre and craft by even porcions.

(*fo.* 364, *b.*) Nationality of Alexander Ambler.[1]

Carpenters.

(*fo.* 365). In the honour of God, and for the weile of this full honourabill cite of York, [2]and of the carpenters inhabit in the same,[2] at the speciall instaunce and praier of James Whynsell, Michell Clerk, John Haukysby, John Hyrst, Robert Ostyrby, Richard Bysshop, Christofur Mure, Thomas Denton, William Johnson, John Bell, Ricardus Tod, John Burgh, Thomas Freman, John Bradley, William Stanowse, the elder, William Stanowse, yonger, Thomas Hall, William Dykson, John Silwyrtop, Thomas Hunt, John Sande, Robert Williamson, William Portjoye, John Meidley and Richard Wylys, carpenters of this full nobill cite,

---

1—Eng. Misc., *op. cit.*, pp. 41, 42, 43.
2—2—Interlined.

ar ordenyd the xxij^{ti} day of Novembyr in the xxij^{ti} yere of the reing of king Edward the iv. (1482), in the secund tym of the mairalte of the ryght honorabill Richard York, mair of the said cite, by the autorite of the holl counsell of the said full honourable cite, for ewyr to be kept thez ordinaunces filluyg.

Furst, for asmoch as here afore thar hath beyn of old tym a broderhode had and usyd emong the occupacion and craft above said, the wich of long continuance have usid, and as yit yerly usis to fynd of thar propir costes a lyght of diwyrs torchis in the fest of Corpus Christi day, or of the morn aftir, in the honour and worship of God and all saintes, and to go in prossession with the same torchis with the blessid sacrament from the abbey foundyd of the Holy Trenite in Mykylgate in the said cite on to the cathedrall chyrch of Saint Petir in the same cite ; and also have done and usyd diwyrs odir right full good and honourabill deidis, as her aftir it shall more playnly apeir. It is ordenyd and establyshid be the said mair, aldermen (fo. 365, b.) and all the holl counsell of the said full nobill cite, be the consent and assent of all tham of the said occupacion in the said cite, that the said fraternite and bredirhode shalbe here aftir for ewyr kept and continend, as it has beyn in tymis passid, and that every brodir thar of shall pay yerly for the sustentacion thar of vj d., that is to say, at every halff yer iij d., providyng allway that every man of the said occupacion within the said cite shalnot be compellid ne boundyn to be of the said fraternite ne brodirhod, ne noyn to be thar of bot soch as will of thar free will.

Also, it is ordenyd and stablishid be the auctorite abovesaid for ewyr to be kept by consent and assent of the said bredir, that all the said bredir of the said fraternite shalbe togiddir ij tymys in the yere, that is to say, the furst tym the Sunday next aftir Saint Elyn day, and the secund tyme the Sunday next afore or next aftir the fest of all Halows, at adyr of the wich days ichone of the said bredir shall pay j d. to the behove of the said bredirhode, and also the said bredirhode shall cause, at adyr of the said days, a trentall of messis to be said and done in the Freir Austens of this cite, in the worship of God and of all Sayntes, for the saulles of all the bredir and systyrs passid her afore of the said fraternite and brodirhode, and that every brodir, that than is absent and not thar, shall pay a pound of wax to the behove of the said fraternite, and vj d. to the behove of the chambir of thys full nobill cite, withowt he have a resonabill excuse.

(fo. 366). Also, it is ordyend that thar shalbe iiij kepers of the said fraternite, the wich shall make thar reknyng every yer odyr of Saint Petir day or of Saint Mathie day in wyntyr, apon the payn of forfatour what keper fayls so to doo, withowt he have a resonabill excuse, iij s. iiij d. to the behove of the chambyr of thys cite and of the said fraternite, betwyx tham evynly to be devydyd.

Also, it is ordeynd that yf ony of the said fraternite dy, the said bredirhode shall gyfe for a trentall of messis to be dooyn for hys sawll in the said Freir Austens, v s.

Also, it is ordeynd, that if ony of the said bredir dy or ony of thar wiffes, that the said torchys shalbe born with tham to thar beryall, withowt ony thyng gyffyng thar for, bot onely of devocion; and when ony of the said bredir is deid, tha that has the torchys in kepyng shall warn all thar bredir, when that ony is so deid, to cum to the beriall of thar brodir apon the payn of forfatour of iiij d., to be forfaite be the kepers tharin defective, to the behove of the comunalte of thys cite and of the said fraternite, betwyx tham evynly to be devydid, and the said kepers of torchys shall gar beer the said torchis to the beriall of the deth person, and bryng tham home agane of the bredir cost, and not of the cost of the deid person, yf he be beryd within the fraunchez of thys cite.

(fo. 366, b.) Also, it is ordenyd that if ony of the said bredir dy, that what broder of hys, that is not at hys beriall, shall pay halff a pound of wax to the behove of the said lyght, and the valeu of halff a pound of wax to the behove of the communalte of this cite, bot yf he have a resonabill excuse, that is to say, that he was not warnyd or odyr resonabill cause have.

Also, it is ordenyd that yf ony of the said fraternite fall to povert, so that tha may not wyrk, or happyn to be blynd, or to leis thar gudes by unhapp of the world, then the forsaid bredyrhode to gyffe tham iiij d. every weke, as long as tha liff, by way of almusse, so that he that is so fortunyd have trewly fullfillid the ordinauncez above wryttyn.

Also, it is ordenyd that what brodir shall so be admittyd to take almous, shalbe sworn a pon a buke that he shall trewly lyffe apon hys allmous and hys awn gude, without wast or gyffyng away of tham, and what so ewyr he levys at hys dying that longys to hym selff, hys dettes payd and hys beriall resonably done, shall remayn to the said fraternite as thar own propre gudes.

Also, it is ordenyd that yf ony of the said bredir have nede to a warkman at ony tym, and a nodir of hys bredir is owt of wark and has no wark to doo, that the said brodir, that has neid of a warkman, shall rather take in to wark hys brodir of the said fraternite then ony odyr that is not brodyr, yf he will wyrk as he may deserif, apon the payn of forfatour of xx d., to be payd by hym that (fo. 367) doos the contrary, the sum xx d. to be devydid as is above said.

Also, it is ordenyd that thar shalbe every yer a brodir chosyn and assigned of the said fraternite, to whom every brodir that is owt of wark shall make knawlege that he is owt of wark, so that he that wold have a warkman may have knawlege of hym that is owt of wark.

Also, it is ordenyd, that as oft as the said kepers or ony of the said kepers willes the bredir of the same for the wele of thys cite and of the said fraternite to cum to gyddyr, to gyfe thar advisez and counsell in soch thynges as tha shalbe demandid of, and ony brodir faill and cum nott without a resonabill cause of excuse, he shall leys xl d. as oft tymys as he so offendes, in the furm above said to be devydid and paid.

Also, it is ordenyd that it shalbe lefull to ony of the offisours, that is to say, ony of the serjantz of the mair for the tym beyng, be the commaundment of the mair, with the said kepers or sersourz or ony one of tham, as wele to distreyn for the dewte dewe to the said bredirhode, as wele for the said subsedy of vj d. yerly, as for all odir thynges dewe to the said fraternite, as for the dewty dewe to the comunalte of thys cite, be the gudes and catell of tham that so aws the said dewte; and yf tha be lett of thar distres, or rescous thar of be to tham made, he that tham so lettes or rescous to tham so makys shall forfait vj s. viij d., in the form abovesaid to be devydyd and paid.

THE ORDINANCES OF THE CARPENTERS (1482)

Also, it is ordenyd that yf ony be boundyn prentyse in the said occupacion [1]or cny to the same belonging[1] within thys cite, that the maister that so taykes hym preutes shall pay within the furst (*fo.* 367, *b.*) halff yer that the said prentis is so boundyn prentys vj *s.* viij *d.*, in the furm abovesaid to be devydyd.

Also, it is ordenyd yf a yongman, that is not cunyng in wark of the said occupacion, cum in to thys cite to lern the said occupacion bettyr, yf he be hyryd in the said occupacion for mete, drynk, and xx *s.* be yere or above, than hys said maister, that so hyrys hym, within a quarter of a yer than next aftir shall pay xx *d.*, in the furm above said to be devydid; and yf he hyr hym ondyr the some of xx *s.*, the said maister, that so hyrys hym, shall pay xl *d.*, in the furm above said to be devydid and paid. Also the said maister shall not thake more a pon hym of whos werk, he that is not cunyng wyrkes, then he that is not cunyng in that occupacion can deseryff, a pon the payn of xl *d.*, in the furm abovesaid to be devydid and paid.

Also, it is ordenyd that none of the said occupacion shall sett ony of wark within the said cite owr xiiij days, except that he be boundyn servant for the holl yere or boundyn apprentys, a pon the payn of xl *d.*, in the furm aforsaid to be devydid and paid.

Also, it is ordenyd that yf ony that has beyn prentys in the said occupacion within thys cite, will at the end of hys prentishode sett upp and wyrk as a maister in the said occupacion within thys cite, he shall pay for hys upsett xx *d.*, in the furm abovesaid to be paid and devydid; and yf he take apon hym to wyrk as a maister within thys cite, and was newyr prentys thar in, he shall pay for hys upsett vj *s.* viij *d.*, in lyk form to be paid and devydyd.

Also, it is ordenyd that all wryghtys, sawers, carvers, (*fo.* 368) jyoners, and cartwryghtes, and all odyr that occupiis as maistyrs, or that her aftir shall occupy as maisterz in ony of the said mystyrs, craftes, or occupacions within thys said cite and every of tham, shalbe equale and lyke of charge every yere from hens forward to the charge and cost of bryngyng furth and playng of the pagent of the wryghtes of Corpus Christi day, and of the charge of the fyndyng of the said lyght the morn aftir Corpus Christi day,

1—1—Interlined.

so that no maister of the said occupacions ne craftes pay to the said chargis of the said play or to the said lyght more one than a nodyr.[1]

Also, it is ordenyd that yf ony maister of the said occupacions of wryghtes, sawers, carvers, yonours or cartwryghtes hyr ony yorney man servant, or take aprentys to wyrk within thys cite, that the maister that so hym hyrys or settes hym on wark shall pay to the sustentacion of the said pagent and lyght every yere iiij $d.$ for every person that he so settes on wark or hyrys.[2]

Also, is it ordenyd that yf ony of the said fraternite or ony of the said occupacions and craftes of wryghtes and other above rehersed be rebill to hys sersour, or lee a nodyr of hys bredir or ony of the same occupacions in males, or call hym fals, or stryk hym, or profir hym ony stroke, at eny assemble for the wele of the said craftes, he thar in defective shall forfate vj $s.$ viij. $d.$, in the maner and furm abovesaid to be devydid and paid.

(fo. 368, b.) Also, it is ordenyd by the actorite abovesaid that yf ony of the said fraternite, or eny of the said craftes, discowyr or disclose the counsell or ony thyng that the said bredir or ony of said occupacions or eny of tham says at the day or days of thar assemblys, that tha meit for the weill of thys cite and of the said occupacions, that he or tha that so disclosys the said counsell shall forfate as oft tymys as tha ar thar in foundyn defective xl $d.$, in the furm abovesaid to be devydid and paid.

Also, it is ordenyd that yf ony wyrk ony wark within this cite, libertes and precintes of the same, ony thyng pertenyng to the said occupacion of wryghtes, that is unsufficiently, unabill, and unwarkmanly wroght, that the sersours of the said occupacion at the desyr of the awner of the same wark shall serch it, and yf it be foundyn unsufficiently wroght be the syght of the said sersowrs, he or tha that heryn be foundyn defective shall as oft tyms as tha be foundyn defective forfate vj $s.$ viij $d.$, in the form abovesaid to be payd and devydyd; and our this, he that is so defective shall make sufficient amendes to the pairte tharby grevyd or hurt.

1—"In the play of Corpus Christi day the lyghts of the morn," is written in the right margin.
2—"Which servandes and apprentes shall pay to the play and light."

Also, it is ordenyd that yf the sersowrs of the said occupacion fynd a defaute in the said occupacion and present it not to the mair and the chamberlayns for the tym beyng, that the sersour shall for hys consillment as oft tyms as eh thar in is foundyn defective forfate to the wele of the communalte of thys cite xl d.

Wrights.

(*fo.* 369). iiij^{to} die Junii, anno regni regis Henrici octavi secundo (1510), Johannes Shawe, maior; Brianus Palmes, recordator; Michael Whyte, Georgius Kirk, Thomas Gray, Willelmus Neleson, Alanus Staveley, Johannes Dogheson, Bartramus Dawson, Willelmus Wilson, Johannes Hall, aldermanni; Johannes Langton, Johannes Gegges, vicecomites; Robertus Petty, Thomas Bankhous, Johannes Elles, Thomas Braxe, Johannes Beysby, Willelmus Huby, Johannes Thornton, xxiiij^{or}, assembled in the councell chalmer uppon Ouse brighe, it was agreed by all the sade presence that, consyderyng a bill of supplicacion which was putt in to the sade councell by the craft of wrightes of this cite of and for certeyn poyntes, which was expedyent to be had unto the sade ordinance, which premysses consydered, it was fully determyned that this addicion folowyng shuld be kept for evermore.

Furst, that yf eny straunge carpenter com to this cite and occupy the sade craft with eny man in the sade cite, what so ever he be, by the space of a weyk, that then he to pay iiij d., and so as many as ther his to pay iiij d. a pece. And yff they wirk by the space of a monthe that then thay to pay ij s. a pece, and so to wirk the hole yere yff it be of on mans wark; and yff he or they remove fro on mans wark to a nother, to pay other ij s., [in] maner and forme above sade, to chalmer and craft by evyn porcions; and so as ofte as they chaunge to pay in lyke maner ij s.

Cappers.[1]

(*fo.* 369, *b.*) In the honour of God, at the speciall request of all the hole craft of cappers, the xx day of the moneth of

---

1—In the left margin, "This company is joyned to the hatters, haberdashers and feltmakers, tempore Roberti Watter, maioris, 1591," is written.

Decembyr, in the xxij^{ti} yere of the reing of king Edward the iv. (1482), in the secund tym of the mairalte of Richard York, mair of this full nobill cite of York, thez ordinaunces filluyng be the said mair and the hole counsell of the said cite wer enact and ordenyd to be annexid and ayonyd, as a nordinaunce adyonyd to odir ordinauncez of the said occupacion, comprisid in this registir, the xxiiij^{ti} lefe, and as wele the said ordinaunce in the said lefe as thez ordinaunces filluyng for ewyr to be kept and holdyn.

Furst, it is ordenyd that no maner of person shall take apon tham to occupy as a maister in the said occupacion to the tym that he be foundyn abill by the sersors of the same craft; and he that dose contrary to thys ordinaunce to forfait and pay xiij *s.* iiij *d.*, the too halff tharof to be paid to the comunalte of thys cite, and the todir halff to the supportacion of the charges of the said occupacion; providyng all way that the mair for the tym beyng have the examinacion and coreccion her of.

Also, it is ordenyd what person that cumys in by redempcion to the libertes of thys cite, that is foundyn abill to occupy as a maister in the said occupacion, shall pay at hys furst uppset vj *s.* viij *d.*, in the furm aforsaid to be payd and devyded (*fo.* 370); and that every person fraunchesid as aprentis shalbe admitit as a maister to occupy in the said craft, withowt ony thyng giffyng or payng for hys uppsett.

Also, it is ordenyd that yf ony maister of the said occupacion take ony apprentis, the maister shall shews the indenturs of the said apprentis to the sersors of the said occupacion within xiiij days that he cumys to hym, and than to pay ij *d.* in the form abovesaid.

Also, it is ordenyd yf thar be ony of the said occupacion be attayntid with ony falshode or theft to the valew of xij *d.*, that than he, that so is foundyn fals, shalbe dischargid of the said occupacion and newyr aftir to wyrk in thys cite.

Also, it is ordenyd that no maner of stranger shall wyrk with any maister of the said occupacion to he be abyld by the sersours, and who so dothe contrari to these ordinance that takys ony soch to wyrk with hym at every tym to pay vj *s.* viij *d.*

in the form abovesaid, and the mair for the tym beyng, with the said sersours to examyn the same.

Also, it is ordenyd yf ony of the said occupacion croche or mak to be crochid ony maner of wark in the said occupacion, wych crochyng is a dissavabill color for the kynges peepill, at every tym to pay iij *s.* iiij *d.*, in the form abovesaid.

Also, that no maistre of the said occupacion gyff no werk to wyrk to no maner of person dwellyng in Seynt Mary gate, ne in Seint Leonardes, ne odyr placez ne santuaries within this cite, wher we have no power to correk tham, and that no meistre of the said craft uttyr their werk, which can lawfully be provyd at ony tym, he sall pay iij *s.* iiij *d.*, in the fourm abovesaid.

(*fo.* 370, *b.*) Also, that the serchourz and pajaunt maistrez, beyng for the yere, gyff yerly ther accompt on the Sunday next eftyr the fest of the nativite of Seynt John Baptist of all their receites and paymentes, and who so dois the contrarie to this ordinaunce shall pay at every tym vj *s.* viij *d.*, in the fourm abovesaid withowt pardone.

Also, that if the serchourz of the said occupacion, for the tym beyng, be neglygent and wilnot dewly serch and present the defawtes of them that ar foundyn defectyff, for luff or faivor or malice of ony person that belongith to tham to serch, that als oftymez that may be approbayt of tham or ony of thame by the holl occupacion lawfully, then the serchourz or serchour to pay at every tym vj *s.* viij *d.*, in maner and fourm above writtyn.

Also, it is ordeynyd that no man ne woman, that is abild, or he or she shalbe abyld, to be of the said occupacion within this cite and subberbys of the sam, shallnot from hens forward wyrk ony wark pertenyng to the said occupacion within thys cite and suburbs of the sam to no person, man, ne woman, bot to soch as beyn abyld, and heraftir shalbe abyld to wyrk in thys cite in the said occupacion of capmakers, uppon the payn of vj *s.* viij *d.* to be forfaite by tham doyng the contrary to this ordynans, the said vj *s.* viij *d.* to be devydyd in the form abovesaid.

(*fo.* 371). Release by William Hodlow, son and executor of John Hodlow late of York, merchant, to John Gilyot, merchant of York, of all actions against him. 3 June, 1489, 4 Henry vii. Acknowledged in the church of All Saints in the city of York, before John Harper, mayor, 4 June, 4 Henry vii.

Hatmakers.[1]

(fo. 371, b.) Thordinaunce of the craft of hatmakers, incorporate and made in the tyme of Michaell White, maire, in the neynth yere of the reigne of King Henry the vijth (1493-4), and past be acte in the councell chambre, xiiijth day of February, etc., as in buke of actes, the same yere, it appereth.

First, that noo maner of man from hensfurth occupie as a master or servant in the said occupacion unto suche tyme that the serchours for the tyme being find hyme able and sufficient to wirk in the said occupacion, and if he be foundou able and apprentise in the said occupacion, than he admitted able to be a master in the said occupacion, pay at his entre iij s. iiij d., that is to say, the oone half to the chambre of the citie and the other half to the supportacion of ther craft and padgeant. And if he be a stranger and not franchest, come in by redempcion and never was apprentice, than to pay xx s. by evene porcions, to be devided as is above said.

Also, that no maner of maner [sic] of man within this citie presume on hyme to sett any man in the said occupacion to occupie, bot if he be fondon an able man of his owne handes to wirk in the said occupacion, and so to be admitted by the serchours of the same; and he that doth contrary ther in, for evere tyme fondon so giltie, pay xx s., by evene porcions to be devided in fourme abovesaid.

Also, that noo man of the said occupacion take a prentise to the said occupacion for lesse termes then vij yeres; and also that his master within xiiij days that he takes hyme to apprentise shew his indentures[2] to the seirchours for tyme being; and he that doeth the contrarie and therof convict, to pay withoute parden vj s. viij d., by even porcions to be devided in fourme abovesaid.

1--In the right margin, " This and cappers are joyned together into one company, Roberti Watter, maioris, 1591," is written.
2—About two words erased here.

THE ORDINANCES OF THE HATMAKERS (149¾)

Also, that no man of the same craft procour ne desire the apprentice of a other maister, whethre he be within age or at ful age, withoute so be that he first agre with the maister of the same apprentice, apon the payn of forfatour of vj s. viij d., by even porcions to be devided in fourme abovesaid.

Also, that every yere the seircheours of the said craft be chosen by the maisters of the same of the Monday in the secound weke of Lentyn, and what maister that is werned to be at a convenient place for the same entent, or for eny other thing toching the wirshup of this cite or the common wele of the said craft, and is absent withoute a resonable excuse, to forfet for every tyme xij d., to be devided in maner and fourme abovesaid.

(fo. 372). Also, that if eny herafter of the same craft woll set upp as maister in the same and hath tofore ben apprentice within this said cite, and fully and truelie hath served his apprentishode, and abled by his said seircheours that he be connyng in the same for the common wele and wirshup of this cite, shall pay at his first setting upp as master vj s. viij d., in maner and fourme above writen. And if he be a forant and woll com to this cite to set upp as maister in the same, and never was apprentice within the same cite, shall pay at his first setting upp xx s., to be devided in maner and fourme abovesaid.[1]

Also, by vertu of the same ordynaunce, forasmuch asmuch stuffe at diverse tymes commeth to this cite and sold within the same to the kinges people, which stuffe is dissavable to the byers, that it be leful to the seircheours of the same craft to serch all such stuffe to ther craft belonging being owte of the merchauntes hondes; and what man, that is disobeaunt to the said seircheours in ther seirch laufully doon, forfet and pay withoute parden vj s. viij d., tociens quociens, which defaltes so found by thame withoute eny conseilment to present thame to the maiour, chamberlens, or the common clerk for tyme being, and the same sowme of forfet to be devided in maner and forme abovesaid. And also it is ordeigned by vertu of this same ordynaunce, what forant commyng to this cite or herafter shal com with eny such stuffe to sell, to be contributorie yerelie to the sustentacion of

1—"Vac" is written after this.

bringing forth of thare pageant, that is to say, every such person iiij *d*.; and he that is disobeaunt and wilnot pay the same, when by the pageant maisters he is required, to forfet xij *d*. tociens quociens, to be devided in maner and fourme abovesaid withoute pardon.

Also, if it so happen eny forent man of the craft abovesaid to com to this cite and offer hym self to be set apon warke in that occupacion, that it benot lefull to eny maister of the same craft to set eny such man of warke unto the tyme the seircheours of the craft have seirched the same man, and that man so seirched and abled by the seircheours to be set apon warke by the seircheours to such a man of the same that hath most nede of such a warkman; and what man, that settes eny such man of warke withoute the advise of his seircheours for tyme being, to forfet withoute pardon vj *s*. viij *d*., to be devidet in maner and fourme abovesaid; providet alwey that it benot leful to noon such alien ne forent commyng to this cite to wirke with eny man within this cite and libertie of the same, efter this present day, bot with a maister of the same craft.

Item, that it be lefull to the serchourz of the said craft for the tyme being to serch all maner stuff, belonging to the said craft maid within this citie, or the suburbes of the same and the contrey, which is broght to this citie to be sold, and being oute of merchaundes handes and fun unhable be the said serchours, it to be forfeyt, and the person in whos handes the said unhable stuff is foun to forfeyt and pay iij *s*. iiij *d*., to be devyded in maner and fourm to forsaid.

(*fo.* 372, *b*.) Memorandum that where certain maters of variaunces, dettez, debatez, and demaundez was hanging indecided betwix the right honourable and worshipfull Sir William Todde,[1] knight, maier of the cite of York, of that oone partie, and Richard Polyngton of the same, fisshmonger, of that other partie, in the which grete expensez hath be maid hertofore, the said parties, at last wolling to have an end in and upon the said maters, aswell for the good as otherwise, now of lat the x day of Septembre, 3 Henr. vii. (1487), hath compromitte themself to

---

1—R. H. Skaife, *op. cit.*, p. 65.

stand and obbey thaward, laude and jugement in and upon the same of Richard Burgh, squir, and Thomas Foulnalby, gentilman, merchaunt of the citie of York, arbitours indifferent betwix the said parties, soo that ther award, laude, and jugement had be yevene by theme of this halve the fest of Saint Michael last past. And in caas the said arbitours culd not aggre, nor bring the said parties to rest in and upon the premisses by the said fest, that then they to stand and obbey the word, laude, and jugement in the same upon the moost reverend fader in God the Archbishop of York, impare indifferent in that partie; which arbitours not atteynyng to bring the said parties to any perfite end in the said maters of this halve the said fest, the said moost reverend fader in God, impare in that partie, wolling quietnesse and rest to be had betwix the said parties, after mature examinacion in and upon all variaunces, dettes, debates, and demaundes, depending betwix tham by reason of any mater or cause from the begynnyng of the world unto the xxj^{ti} day of the moneth of Octobre, the yere of our Lord mccclxxxvij and the yere of the reigne abovesaid, awarded and jugged that the said Richard Polyngton, after humble submission to be maide by hyme unto the said Sir William Todde and knowlegeing of his misreportes and unfitting langage had ayenst hyme before his brethern aldermen and other of the counsaill of the citie of York, shall content and pay unto hyme xxiiij li of laufull Inglissh money at iij payments; that is to say, in the fest of Saint Thomas thappostill next comyng viij $li.$, and in the said fest of Saint Thomas, which shalbe in the yere of our Lord mccclxxxviij, viij $li.$, and in the said fest of Saint Thomas, which shalbe in the yere of our Lord a mccclxxxix, viij $li.$; and from hensfurth the said Richard to be of (*fo.* 373) good bering as well in wordez as dedes ayenst the said Sir William Todde. And that either partie to other shall yeve other generall acquitance for all maner of maters past bifore the said xxj^{ti} day of Octobre. Which award laude and jugement both the parties above writyn have emologate. R.

Writ to the mayor and escheator of the city of York to assign dower to Elizabeth, late the wife of Richard Fitz Hugh, knight, deceased, whose lands are in the king's hands by reason of the minority of George Fitz Hugh, his son and heir; the escheator in the counties of Nottingham and Derby has been directed to take her oath not to marry without the king's licence. Westminster, 8 May, 3 Henry viii. (1511).

(*fo.* 373, *b.*) Release by Alice Gascoigne of Burnby, late the relict of Ralph Gascoigne deceased, to dame Agnes Ratclyff, late the relict of Richard Ratclyff, knight deceased, of the manor of Bolton, formerly of Robert Lokton, esquire, deceased. Seal. 18 March, 4 Henry vii. (1488-9).

(*fo.* 374). Lease by Christofor Nuport, esquire, to Edward Forster of York, tailor, of a messuage in York (one cellar now in the tenure of John Harper, merchant, and another celler in the tenure of Katharine Lain excepted), lying in breadth between land of Richard Yorke, knight, and land of the chantry of S. Katharine, virgin, in the church of All Saints on the Pavement, and in length from the Pavement before to land of William Yngilby, knight, behind; to hold from Whitsuntide next for term of twenty years at the yearly rent of 20 *s*. Seals. Witnesses John Gylliot, mayor, John Elwald and John Norman, sheriffs, John Harper of York, merchant, Humfrey Maners, gentleman, Richard Symson of York, wiredrawer. 3 December, 6 Henry vii. (1490). Acknowledged in the mayoralty of John Gylliot, 9 December, 6 Henry vii.

(*fo.* 374, *b.*) Memorandum quod Johannes Birkehede, natus in Tybers in Scocia, juratus est ad sancta Dei evaungelia, vij^{mo} die mensis Februarii, anno Domini millesimo cccclxxvij^o et 17 Edw. iv., coram Johanne Tong, tunc maiore civitatis Ebor', quod ipse amodo erit ligeus fidelis dicti domini regis et heredum suorum, et quod fideliter ad omnes leges et consuetudines regni Anglie stabit, et eas custodiet et perimplebit ad terminum vite sue etc.

Memorandum quod David Robynson, natus in Coupir in Fiffe in Scocia, juratus est ad sancta Dei evaungelia, iij die[1] Augusti, anno Domini millesimo ccccxxviij^o et 18 Edw. iv., coram Johanne Fereby, tunc maiore civitatis Ebor', quod ipse amodo erit ligeus fidelis dicti domini regis et heredum suorum, et quod

1—The MS. has "anno Augusti anno."

fideliter ad omnes leges et consuetudines regni Anglie stabit, et eas custodiet et perimplebit ad terminum vite sue etc.

Memorandum quod Stephanus Watson, milner, natus in Caudestreme in Scocia, juratus est ad sancta Dei Evaungelia, xiiij° die Septembris, anno Domini millesimo cccclxxviij° et 18 Edw. iv., coram Johanne Fereby, tunc maiore civitatis Ebor', quod ipse amodo erit ligeus fidelis dicti domini regis et heredum suorum, et quod fideliter ad omnes leges et consuetudines regni Anglie stabit et perimplebit, ac eas custodiet et perimplebit ad terminum vite sue etc.

Memorandum quod Adam Marshall, *tyler*, natus in castro de Rokesburgh in Scocia, juratus est ad sancta Dei evaungelia, ultimo die Septembris, anno Domini millesimo cccclxxviij°, 18 Edw. iv., coram Johanne Fereby, maiore civitatis, quod ipse amodo erit ligeus fidelis dicti domini regis et heredum suorum, et quod fideliter ad omnes leges et consuetudines regni Anglie stabit et perimplebit, ac eas custodiet et perimplebit ad terminum vite sue.

Johannes Gilliot, maior.

For the almus women of Ousebrig.

(*fo.* 375). Memorandum that in the tyme of the right worshipful Sir John Gylliot, maier of this worshupful cite, that where a rerage was behynd unpaid unto the almus women of the Masyndewe apon Ousbrig, of a fee farm rynnyng oute of a tenement withoute Skeldergate posteron, the which was wont to pay of tyme that mynde is ij *s.* vj *d.*; the whilke fee ferm hath ben unpaid unto the said almus women by the space of xviij yeres past; and nowe the said tenement is sold by William Hungate, gentilman, yonger, and takyn down by John Gaunt and John Martyndale for the nown payment of the said fee ferm, the said maire caused his servantes to the maise to arrest all the lymmer, plaister, and all other stuffe so takyn doun, unto the tyme the arrerage of the said fee ferme werr unto the said almus women fully content and paid; wher apon the said William Hungate labored unto the said maire for agrement of the said fe ferm. The said maier by gude deliberacion and advise of his counsaill agreid with the said William Hungate, he to content and pay in

✗ full contentacion of the said fee ferm to the said almus women xx s. for the arrerage past, the which xx s. the said William content and paid to the almus women abovesaid, and so he and the ground where the said tenement stude of the arrerage past of the same, from the begynnyng of the world unto the day of writing of this presentes, which was the xxiiij^{ti} day of Novembre, 6 Hen. vii. (1490). And over this, the said William Hungate to the said maire hath promysed, and by this writing bound hym and his heires for ever to the said maier and his successours, maires, to content and pay yerelie for ever to the almus women abovesaid, that is or for tyme shalbe, for the said ground xij d. of lawful money of England, and in defalt of noun payment of the said xij d. yerelie to be paid in maner and fourme aforesaid, it to be lefull to the said almus women, by the supportacion of the maier for tyme being, to enter the said ground and the same to enjoy to thame and ther successoures for ever, and the said William Hungate and his heires clerlie therof to be excludet etc.

(fo. 375, b.) Johannes Gilliot, maior, xx die Januarii, 6 Heur. vii. (1490-1), Johannes Harper, maior, Ricardus York, miles, Johannes Newton, Nicholas Lancastr', Willelmus Chymney, Willelmus Todd, miles, Robertus Hancok, Johannes Gylliot, assembled in the counsail chaimbre of Ousebrig, and ther and then of oon assent and consent elect and chuse the right wirshupful Thomas Scotton, merchaunt, to be of the noumbre of the wirshupful aldermen and in dede so chosyn alderman in the roume and place of Thomas Wrangwish, late alderman, in the tyme of the right wirshupful John Gylliot, maier, the xj day of May, next felowing the date above writen, he being in the church of All Hallowe apon the Payment, tofore hym, Sir Rycherd Tunstall, knyght, John Fereby, Nicholas Lancastr', William Chymney, Robert Hancok, John Harper, and William White, aldermen, the said Thomas was sent fore. He personalie appering ther and then to fore tham presentlie tok his oth, and so sworn occupieth the roume of a alderman. xvij. die Novembris, 6 Henr. vii. (1490), John Gylliot, maior, Ricardus Tunstall, miles, Willelmus Snawsell, Johannes Fereby, Johannes Newton, Nicholaus Lancastre, Willelmus Chymney, Willelmus Todd, miles, Willelmus White,

Thomas Scotton, assembled in the counsail chaumbre and ther and then, for so much as the right wirshupful John Tong, alderman and late maire of this wirshupful cite, is gretlie disesid and broken by greit sekenyesse, by reason wher of the roume of aldermanship by hym is not kept ne occupied, he willing to surseisse and of the same to be discharged, in his oun propre person in the church of Saynt Leonard, desired the said maier in the presence of Robert Hancok, alderman, that he might be discharged.

(fo. 376). Johannes Gilliot, maior; William Snawsell, John Fereby, John Newton, Nicholas Lancastr', Willelmus Chymney, Robertus Hancoke, Johannes Harper; Willelmus Barker, Alexander Danson, vicecomites; Thomas Catoure, Willelmus Spence, Willelmus Tayte, Ricardus Clerk, Johannes Hagge, Michael Whyte, Milo Grenbank, Ricardus Hardsang, Thomas Fynche, Willelmus Barker, baker, Roger Appylby, George Kyrk, Robert Johnson, Thomas Fulnaby, Thomas Grey, at the whiche day assembled in the counsaill chaumbre of Ousbridge. For so myche as the ryght wurshipfull Sir John Vavasour, late recorder of this wurshipfull cite, nowe beyng oon of the kygnges juges and the place of recordership void, it is by the said presence fully determyned and concluded, that the right wurshipfull Sir William Fairefaxe, for certane consideracions, is most able and beneficiall for that rowme. And so by the hole assent and consent of the seid presence, the said William Fairfaxe is elect and chosen to be recorder of this cite, and then and ther sworne and admitted in the said office, then beyng present Sir Guy Fairefaxe, knyght.

xvij die Novembris, 6 Henr. vii. (1490) within writen. Forsomych as the right wurshipfull Sir John Tonge, alderman, and late maire of this cite is grety diseased and broken by gret sekens, by reason wherof the rowme of aldermanshyp by hym is not kept ne occupied, he, willyng to surssece of the same, hath disired diverse tymes to be discharged, and this same day shewed by Humfrey Maners, gentilman, that he willed and dysired hym for to desire the maire and aldermen, for Godes sake, he might be discharged, for that he was in that case, he might not yife his attendaunce (fo. 376, b.) upon the counseill accordyng to his othe and dewte. The said mair and alderman and Sir Richard Tunstall beyng in the counsaill chambre and in counsaill with thaym, the

premyssez considered, hath of on assent and consent elect and
chosen in the rowme and place of the said right wurshipfull sir
John Tong to be and occupied as an alderman Mychaell Whyte,
dyer, and thereto sworne afore the seid presence.

xx^{mo} die Decembris, 6 Henr. vii. (1490). John Gilliot,
maior, Ricardus York, miles, Willelmus Snawsell, Johannes
Newton, Willelmus Chynney [sic], Willelmus Todde, miles,
Robertus Hancoke, Johannes Harpour, Willelmus Whyte, Michael
Whyte, Willelmus Fayrfax, recordator, Thomas Catour, Thomas
Aleyn, Willelmus Tayte, Willelmus Spence, Ricardus Clerk,
Johannes Hagge, Milo Grenbank, Willelmus Barker, *baker*,
Thomas Fynch, Johannes Shawe, Georgius Kyrk, Robertus
Johnson, Alexander Dauson, at the which day the presence
abovesaid assembled in the councell chambre of Ousebryge.
For as much as the right wurshipfull maistyr John Harryngton,
baculer in the law and late comon clerk of this citie of York,
haith surrendyd and yevyn up into the handes of the mayr and
the councell of the same the office of comon clerkship abovesaid,
by reson of which surrender the said offyce stondes void; it is
be the said presence fully determyned, concludyd, and ennactyd,
that Robert Plumpton for certein consideracions is most able
and beneficyale for that rowm and offyce. And so be the holl
assent and concent of the said presens the said Robert Plumpton
is elect and chosyn to be common clerk, and afore the said presens
sworn acordyng to the auncyen custom of the said citie.

(*fo.* 377). Grant by Ralf Clyfton, son and heir of Thomas
Clifton, late of Bisshopthorp, in the county of the city of York,
gentleman, to Miles Willesthorp, esquire, of the manor of
Bustardhorp in the county of the said city, and all the lands in
the vill, hamlet, or territory of Bustardthorp, extending in length
from the highway of the vill of Drynghouse west to the Ouse
east, and the moor of Bustardthorp, extending in length from a
place called Spittillflatt west in Bustardthorp to a close of pasture
called Bustardhall, and in breadth from a common pasture
called Knasemyer north to the common pasture of Middelthorp
south. He appoints Cristofor Bentlay, attorney to deliver
seisin. Seal. Witnesses Thomas Wrangwish, mayor, John
Gilyot, Thomas Fynch, sheriffs, Richard Yorke, John Tong,

alderman. 12 Dec., 2 Rich. iii. (1484). Acknowledged before Thomas Wrangwish, mayor, 24 Dec., 2 Rich. iii. (*fo.* 377, *b.*) Release by the same of the same to the same. Witnesses, Henry Banke, Cristofer Bentley, Thomas Tutbag. Seal. 20 Dec., 2 Rich. iii. (1484). Acknowledged as the last deed.

(*fo.* 380).[1] Torchys ordinaunc how they shall goo in ordyr.

In primiz for the coblers ...	iij^{or} Thorchys.
Item for the porters ...	viij Torchys.
Item for the ropers and heirsters ...	ij Torchys.
Item for the glovers per se ...	iiij Torchys.
Item for the buchers by tham self ...	iiij Torchys.
Item for the bakers of the left hand ...	vj Torchys.
Item for the fullourz of the right hand ...	vj Torchys.
Item for the carpenters goyng by tham self	vj T.
Item for the smythis goyng of the right hand ...	iiij T.
Item for the coverlet wevers goyng on the left hand ...	iiij T.
Item for the fysshmongers fysshers and maryners goyng to geder by tham self	xiiij T.
Item for the wevers goyng of the right hand ...	xvj T.
Item for the cordwaners goyng of the left hand ...	T.
Item for the taillourz goyng by tham self	viij^t T.
Item for the mercers ...	T.
Item ilkon of the xxiiij^{ti} and of the aldermen ilkman a torche ...	T.
Item for Corpus Christi Gild ...	T.

Testamentum Thome Drawswerd[2] anno M°D° xxix.

Item I wyll after my wyfe death to Saynt Crystefor Gyld ij tenementes being in Bergate and Feysgate for evermore. The mayster for the tyme beyng every yere in Saynt Martyn Kyrke evermore uppon Monday next after the translacion of Saynt Thomas, and Messe upon Tewysday after, in this maner followyng. First to the curate for messe and dyrayge vj *d.*, to the clarke for

---

1—Folio 378, *b* is blank, 379 follows.
2—R. H. Skaife, *op. cit.*, pp. 151.

messe and dyryge and ryngyng x *d*., to every prest in the parishe iiij *d*., to the under clarke ij *d*., to scollers j *d*., ¹to the parson for wax viij *d*., and a hedemes penny. To every power boddy in the massyndewe j *d*., and every yere iiij loode of wodd. And if the mayster for the tyme being wyll not make yt, then I wyll that the maister of Corpus Christi have the land to the use of Corpus Christi Gyld and performe the obbott, as is afforesayd.¹

(*fo*. 380, *b*.) Thaward yevene betwix John Tong, alderman of the citie of York, and Richard Thorneton, spicer and citizin of the same.

In the name of God, Amen. We, Henry Williamson, John Harpour, Richard Laton, notary, and John Beseby, citizins of the citie of York, arbitours indifferently chosen betwix the right worshipfull John Tong, alderman of the said citie, of that oone partie, and Richard Thorneton, spicer and citizin of the same, of that othre partie, in and upon all and almaner maters, controversies, demaundes, and debates depending betwix them, awardith, demeth and ordynneth as ensuyth. First, we award, deme and ordan that the said Richard Thorneton shall discharge and clerely acquite the said John Tong of the kinges writte of *sub pena*, purchesid ayenst hyme by the said Richard Thorneton, contrarie to the ordinaunce of the said citie. Also we ordan, award and deme that the said John Tong, his heyres, or his executours, ne any in his or there name, during the lif of the said Richard Thorneton, and his heyres of his bodie laufully begoten, shall make any title or clame in or upon a tenement with thappurtenaunce without Walmegate barre, as it lieth there betwix the livelode of the monasterie of Kirkham, of the suth partie, and the livelode of Sir James Danby, knight, of the north partie, and the kinges strete before, and a close belonging to James Charleton, gentilman, of the bakeside. Also that the said John Tong shall putt hyme in his utmast devour to make a due serche for the evidence of the said tenement, and them foundon to be put into indifferent man or mens bandes for the sure and sauffe keping of the same, as well for the right and title

---

1—Testamenta Eboracensia, Surtees Soc., 79, pp. 267–269. Here the scholars are given iiij *d*., possibly the municipal scribe copied wrongly.

THE ORDINANCES OF THE PINNERS (1478) 297

of the said John Tong as the said Richard Thorneton. And if it fortune the said Richard Thorneton to dye without heyres of his bodie lawfully begoten, then the same tenement with thappurtenaunce, as it is tofore bounded, with the evidence therof, remayne unto the said John Tong and his like heyres for ever, according to the last will of Richard Thorneton.

Pynners and Wyerdrawers.

(*fo.* 379).¹ In the tyme of the right wirshipful Sir William Wellys, beyng maiour of this wirshipful cite, it is ordeigned that where the pageant of the craft of pynners is chargeable and in compareson noon to bring furth the pageant of the same, that from this day forwerd, it be leful yerelie to take and perseve of every forant comyng to this cite and wirkynge in eny poynt belonging to the tincler craft, or that makes hekilles of wire, or candelstikkes of white or blak plate, ij *d.* to the bringyng furth of the sayd pageaunt. And he that is rebell and wilnot pay the said ij *d.* yerelie, when he is required by the said seircheours or pageaunt maisters, shall forfet and pay withoute pardon xij *d.*, the on half to the chaumbre and the other half to the craft by evyn porcions.

Item, in the secund tyme of the marialtie of right wirshupful Sir Richerd Yorke, beyng maior of this wirshipful cite, by the assent and consent of the same maiour and the hole counsell of the chaumbre, it is graunted vnto the said craft vnto the said craft [*sic*] of pynners, that the same craft of pynners and wyredrawers from thes present day forwerd be on craft, that is to say, that all those, that makes pynnes or draweth wyre, or makes fisshe hukes or shobokilles, yerelie to be contributorie of and to the upholdyng of ther pageaunt and other charges to the said craft belongyng, accordyng to the auncheaunt ordynaunce above writen.

Item, that yerelie the pagiaunt maisters of the said craft make accompt to the said hole craft of pynners and $_{wi}{}^{re}d_.^{r}aw^{er}{}_{s}$ of all ther receytes and charges of ther pageaunt within xviij days next ensuyng the fest of Corpus Christi. And they that is rebell

1—Interleaved between folios 380–381, no old numeration.

and doeth the contrarie this ordynaunce, to forfet at every tyme vj s. viij d., that is to say, the on halfe to the chaumbre of this cite, and the other halfe to the charges of the said pageaunt and craft withoute eny pardon.

(fo. 380). Johannes Dobson, natus in Brigeam in Scocia, juratus est ad sancta Dei evangelia, sexto die Novembris, anno Domini millesimo cccclxxviij° et 18 Edw. iv., coram Johanne Fereby, maiore civitatis Ebor', quod ipse amodo erit ligeus fidelis dicti domini regis et heredum suorem, et quod fideliter ad omnes leges et consuetudines regni Anglie stabit et perimplebit, ac eas custodiet et perimplebit ad terminum vite sue etc.

(fo. 381). Memorandum it is the xvth day of May, the fifth yere of the reign of our sovereyn lige lorde Kyng Henry the sevent (1490) ordeigned and establisshed by thassent and agrement of the right wirshipful Sir John Gylliot, merchaunt, then being maiour of this wirshipful cite, at the special instance and prayer of Thomas Rooke, thelder, Robert Gybbon, William Gybbon, Nicholas Kechyn, Thomas Rooke, yonger, Thomas Penpugh, William Johnson and Roger Emson, citesyns and coblers of this said cite, according unto a ordynance maid and registerd in the thik pauper boke, in the myddes of the same, the xj day of May, the iiij^{t} yere of the reign of King Edward the fourth, as in the same more planelie doeth appere, that every man from hens forth occupying the said occupacion of coblers, within this cite and fraunches of the same, yerelie content and pay to the sustentacion of the torches by the said coblers yerelie born to the honour of Corpus Christi, that is to say iiij d., except all the personez in the said ordynaunce ben except, as in the same more planelie doth appere; and who that is rebell contrarie this ordynaunce shall forfet and pay withoute pardon vj s. viij d. to the chaumbre and craft without parden.

(fo. 381, b.)[1] Memorandum that Thomas Wandesforth, esquier, to the maire the xxiiij day of Novembre, 18 Edw. iv. (1478) delyverd into the comon hall of this cite vij fire pannys, that is to say on of thayme for my lorde the maire, ande for every warde

---

1—Headed "Folio ultimo." The following folios are of paper and have no old numeration.

CITY ORDNANCE (1478)

on, to the hondez of John Sponer, yoman sergaunt in the warde of the said comon hall.

This parcell of ordynancez was put in the keping of John Pattan, teller. First iiij gonne chaimbres, xiij gonstones, ij bottes of iren of halfe a yarde long and more, ij slottes of iren, with two cheynez, ij pynnes of iren with two cheynes, a pynne of iren for a whele, and v capones of wodd.

Memorandum, that this parcell was delivered to William Jacson, keper of the craen, by the chamberleins in the time of William Channey, maier of this citie, that is to say John Elwald, William Barker, John . . . ton, and W. Paintour. First sex brasse weghtes of iij qu. and vj $li.$ a p[ece]. Item delivered C qu. of brasse and vij $li.$ Item vj C and viij $li.$ lede. Item a cabyll, ij pare slynges. Item a bale of wodd, j pare skales. Item j pare of yrne lynkes and the capill.

GLOSSARY.

AHLE, 176, hale, whole.

ALLUTARIUS, 164, shoemaker; Ducange has, qui pelles et coria parat.

ALS, 62, an intermediate form between the fuller al swa, also, and the modern as, chiefly northern, though also in Wyclif. N.E.D.

ANEWE, 114. Mr. Hannay, of the General Register House, who has given me generous help in identifying these place names, suggests Anworth.

ANGUYSH, 114, Angus.

ARBITRUROS, 180, O.F. arbitreor, earlier equivalent of arbitrator, 1382, Wyclif, 1 Esdr., viii., 23; Ordeine domesmen and arbitrouris. N.E.D.

ASTELWOD, 54, O.F. astelle, splinter, split wood; logs of wood for burning, cf. Norwich Records II., p. 59. Treasurers' Roll, 1412–3, " venegar, 2d., candell, 1½d., fagets and astel, 5d."

ATHINGTON, probably Haddington.

AUTRECLOTH, 113, altar cloth, cf. York Fabric Rolls, Surtees Soc., 35, p. 267, " the begh auter, Item, the litile awterse is so ragged and torne that it were grete shame to se suche in any uplandishe towne."

AVAYLE, 178, see Mem. Bk., I., p. 255.

AVENTOUR, 205, chance, risk. O.F. aventure, L. adventura.

BAILWICK, 38, originally a district or place under the jurisdiction of a bailiff, but used in English history as a general term including sheriffdom, c. 1460. N.E.D.

BARKER, 179, a tanner, 1402. Test. Ebor', I., 289. Lego uxori Ricardi Skyrtynbek, barkar, j togam. N.E.D.

BAROUN, coverte de, 144, protected by a husband, an old legal term for a married woman. Early M.E. barun, baroun, anciently applied to the freemen of London, York and some other places, who were homagers of the King, bound to suit and service, also until the 18th c. to the freemen of the Cinque Ports and till the Reform Bill of 1832, to the burgesses returned by these ports to Parliament.

BATHER, 180, bother, 243, both see N.E.D.

BOLLER, 171. The N.E.D. gives this as bowlmaker, with a query, neither this nor hayrester as horsehair worker seems quite satisfactory.

BOSTREVYN, 119, possibly Botruvyn (Botriphine) in Banff.

BOTELLERS, 139, leather bottle makers.

BOULGEYS, 141, M.E. bulge, O.F. boulge, adapted from Latin bulga, leather knapsack, earliest example, 1230. N.E.D.

BOULGETTE, 141, O.F. boulgette, a pouch, the earliest example given by the N.E.D. is 1550, this is 1471.

BOWGEMAKERS, 139, bougemakers, wallet or bag makers.

BRANDRETH, 78, a gridiron.

BREDIR, 278, plural form of brother, still used in northern England and Scotland.

BREWLED, 54, a brew-lead, " a leaden vessel used in brewing, cf. culyngledes. The lead for boiling was fixed like a modern copper, over a grate, and, so long as there was plenty of water in it, it would not melt; see Skeat's Notes to Chaucer, p. 24." Durham Account Rolls, Surtees Soc. III., p. 897.

BRODERHODE, 2-8' not found in O.E., whereas childhood, maidenhood, wifehood and other genuine derivatives in hood go back to an O.E.— Hád. Earliest examples 1388, Wyclif 1, Macc. xii., 10. To renuee britherhod [in 1382 bretherhed] and frenschip.

BROGGOS, 174, broggers, an unexplained corruption of broker ; Anglo-French has broggour, beside brocour ; in this extract the word obviously means the men who collect the wool from the farmers and probably the spinners in the district, and act as middlemen between the merchants and the producers. In the great woollen trials of the seventeenth century several witnesses assert that if the Yorkshire clothiers would sort their wool as carefully as the clothiers in Wiltshire do, then Yorkshire cloth would be as good as Wiltshire. Possibly the relaxation of these fifteenth century rules for broggers, tyrannical as they seem, led to depreciation in the quality of the cloth.

BURGAGE, 66, " in free burgage as is the whole city " an old tenure : from early times there had been in the older boroughs men, who paid rent and no service, this tenure became distinctive of the boroughs ; thus the abolition of labour service, and the introduction of burgage tenure, is of the utmost importance.

BUSOIGNE, 57, see Mem. Bk. I., p. 256.

BUTTANS, 109, for abbutare, abbotare, adjoining, Ducange.

BUTT, 97, a measure of land, cf. selion, of uncertain derivation, Anglo-Latin butta, buttis ; Ducange identifies butta terrae, with French, bout de terre. N.E.D.

CASULA, 113, a chasuble, med. L. Casubula dim. of casa cottage. Du Cange. N.E.D.

CARLELAXAES, 79, possibly adaptation of F. Carrelet, dim. of carrel, carreau, file : axes with sharp points ; carle meaning rough, clumsy seems also admissable.

CERTIORARI, writ of, 85. A writ issued by a superior court, which demands at the request of a party, whose case has been unfairly tried in a lower court, that the record of the inferior court should be sent to the superior court.

CHALMER, 283, chamber, L. camera.

CHALONER, 118, a maker of chalons ; chalon, woollen stuff apparently, as stated by Du Cange, it takes its name from the place where it is manufactured, Chalons-sur-Marne, in France. Not given in Godefroy nor in Cotgrave, cf. Shalloon, cf. Chullour iii.

CIPHI, 13, cups.

CLERICUS COMMUNIS, 76, clerk of the mayoralty and commonalty, common clerk, town clerk.

CLOTH, 195, a definite quantity of woven fabric, according to 1 Rich. III., c. 8, " Every hole wolen cloth called brode cloth . . . shal . . . hold and conteyn in leenght xxiiij. yerdes . . Every half cloth of the seid hole cloth . . . holde and conteyne xij. yerdis in leynght."

COMMUNITAS, 137, the community, the body of citizens that is of men who had been enrolled as freemen. " Communitas civium civitatis Ebor'."

CORDWANER, 118, see Mem. Bk. I., p. 256, shoemaker. Coventry Leet Book has cordener, 581, 705 ; corviser, 203, 249 ; Norwich Records has cordwan, shoeleather, p. 200.

CROCHE, 285, croceam, from Latin croceus, saffron coloured.

CROFT, 97, O.E., craft enclosed field.

CUMBRENAUNT, 119, Cumbernauld in Dumbartonshire.

CUNNING, 177, skill (O.E. cunnan, M.E. cunnen) in its earliest sense to know, c. 1374 Chaucer Troylus, v., 866. Crysede . . . Als ferforthe as she konnynge hadde or myght answerde hym. N.E.D.

DEFEASANCE, letter of, 95, O.F. defesance, from desfaire undo. N.E.D.

DENIZEN, 210, O.F. deinzein, L. de-intus, within + — ein L. aneus.

DISCUS, 13, a dish, a local and obsolete measure by which ale and wine were sold. Durham Acct Rolls, vol. III., p. 910.

DISSAVABILL, 285, possibly disavailable, disadvantageous.

DORRY, 212, F. doré pa. pple of dorer :—L. denaurare to gild ; bright yellow.

DRAGHTLOVER, 174, louver, O.F. lover, med. L. lodarium, lodium, a domed turret-like erection on the roof of the hall or other apartment in a mediæval building, with lateral openings for the passage of smoke.

EGELOME, 249, edgeloom, edged tool, loom an implement of any kind, obsolete except in Scotland and the north.

EGERSTON, 117, Edgerston, near Jedburgh.

EGETOILE, 249, edged tool, sharp-cutting tool. C. 1350 Will. Palerne 3755 and if any eggetol wol entre in-to his bodi.

ESCAETOR, 90, escheator, the official who collected the King's dues or forfeits which frequently fell to him. Cf. Norwich Records, I., p. lxi.

EXCUSASION, 181, Fr. excusation, L. excusation-em, c. 1380 Wyclif Sel. Wks., III., 440. Worldliche excusacioun shal not thenne assoyne, defence, apology.

FANOLLES (?), 113, fanones, fanonellus, idem quod faniculus, dimin. a fano, manipulus sacerdotalis, Ducange. Eucharistic vestment, strip about three feet long hanging from the left arm. N.E.D. Durham Account Rolls, II., 509.

FOREIGN, 207, not necessarily alien, strange, from another town or county.

FULLER, 159, see Mem. Bk., Vol. I., p. 257.

GARE, 84, chiefly Scottish and northern dialect, to do, to make, to cause, to perform. 1460 Towneley Mystery, E.E.T.S. IV., 104. Thi lufly chere makes my hert glad, and many a time so has it gart. N.E.D.

GARN, 198, Yarn, see Mem. Bk. I., p. 258.

GEAUGE, 90, gauge, O.N.F. guage, of unknown origin, wanting in the other Rom. languages ; the O.Fr. word is found along with the related verb, gauger in the thirteenth century. 1357 Act 30, Ed. III., stat. 1, c. 5. Les tonelx de vin duissent contenir certain nombre des galons solonc launciene gauge.

GILD OF THE HOLY TRINITY, 70. The history of this gild and its connexion with the gild of the fraternity of S. Antony I have reserved for the volume dealing with the mystery of mercers and gild of the blessed Mary and the Holy Trinity.

GIRDELERS, 119, according to the ordinances of 1417 their principal work was " castyng sadiller nayle, broches, or chapes," that is nails used in the ornamentation of saddles, and coverings for the points of scabbards or sheaths, see Mem. Bk., p. 183. In Coventry there were two distinct crafts, the girdlers and the girdlemakers, the former corresponding to the York girdlers, the latter " girdulmen," having no counterpart there, see Coventry Leet Book, pp. 181, 183, 705–6. The girdlemen took over the wire after it had been annealed and probably drew it through " a gurdel," or used " a gurdel " in handling the wire, see the extremely interesting note by Miss Dormer-Smith, p. 849, cf. Victoria History of Yorkshire, Vol. II., p. 333. According to the regulations of the cardmakers' mystery, any York man, who brought cardleves, *i.e.*, sheets of leather into which the teeth of a woolcard were inserted, from Coventry to sell in York was fined 40s.

GISTES, 93, the right of pasture for cattle, the usual meaning does not seem applicable here.

GRADALE, 113, gradalia, graduals, grails, the books containing the music sung at the mass, obsolete : med. L. gradale, late Latin gradalis, what is gradually sung after the epistle.

HALTON, 116, a very common name : probably it is Hatton, parish of Ratho, W. of Edinburgh.
HAYRESTER, 171, from Hairster, a worker in horsehair. N.E.D.
HOPIR, 90, a basket, a. 1300, E.E. psalter lxxx. 7.   His hend in hoper served thai. N.E.D.

JEDDEWORTH, 115, Jedburgh.
JAPIECA, japicea. 88, se decompose en ja pièç à = il y a déjà une pièce de temps, un bout de temps, un certain temps. I am indebted to Monsieur G. Clédat, doyen de la Faculté des Lettres de l' Université de Lyon, professeur de langue et littérature du moyen-âge for this explanation.

KAMBESMITH, 172, comb-maker, a common Teutonic substantive O.E. comb, camb.
KIRKE, 217, 250 ; the northern English and Scotch form of the word church, cf. O.E. circe, O.N. Kirkja, Danish Kirke, Swedish Kyrka.

LATONER, 102, a worker in latten, *i.e.*, a mixed metal resembling brass, O.F laton ; 1392-3 Earl Derby's Exped. (Camden) 157. Et ij latoners per ij dies ij *s*. N.E.D.
LERRAY, 256, 1st person future of an O.F. verb laier, to leave, omit, neglect.
LETHCOGH, 115, Linlithgow.
LEWDE, 83, the lewde frer of Munk grace, a lay brother, in Anglia . . . viii., 116-30, wee made hym a conuers, that is to saye a lewde frere.
LINTHEAMINA, 78, a sheet, cf. Norwich Records, I., p. 205. " Et unum chalonem de reyns (a blanket of Rheims) . . . et una lintheamina (sic) precii xviii. similiter."
LITEZ, 195, elite, elect, c. Scotland and north, c. 1450 S. Cuthbert (Surtees) 6519 and cuthbert to hexham lyte.
LIVELOD, 246, O.E., liflad, from lif, life, lad subsistence, a. 1300, Fall and Passion, 37, in E.E.P. 13. In the vale of aboir his livelod he [Adam] must swink sore.
LOME, 197, loom, see Mem. Bk., I., 260.
LYTTESTER, 46, dyer, see Mem. Bk., I., p. 260.
LYSTER, 210, see littester, Mem. Bk., I., p. 260.

MANYMELE, 114, Monymele in Fife, the seat of the prelates of S. Andrews.
MENEROS, 117, possibly Montrose.
MERCER, adapted from F. mercier, L. merciarius from L. merci, merx, merchandise. The earliest example given is c. 1123. Stephanus mercer. Mercator L. mercator, merchant, O.F. marchand, earlier marcheant popular Latin mercatantem pr. pple of mercatare freq. of mercari to trade. All three forms occur in Memorandum Book and Freemen's list, apparently there was little distinction made between the three classes, cf. H. Pirenne, Belgian Democracy, p. 15.
MOTLEMAKER, iii., mottle a kind of woollen yarn of variegated colour. N.E.D., the earliest example given is from the " Daily News " of 20th June, 1887.

GLOSSARY

MORTMAIN, license in, 97, By the statute De Viris Religiosis no religious persons were to acquire land. Pollock and Maitland, op. cit., pp. 333, 334.

MURAGE, 206, tax levied for building or repairing walls of towns, O.F. med. L. muragium.

MYKYLL, 62, mickle, much. Hampole Psalter Prol., in the translation i follow the lettre als mykyll as i may. N.E.D.

NEDELYNG, 171, necessarily ; need and ling ; néad lunga, nydlinga, a common Teutonic word ; M.E. nedlingis, needlings, of necessity.

PAGEANT, 181, 281, 297, a medieval mystery play. At York the whole series of plays seem to have been called the pageant, " omnes pagine ludi, vocati. Corpus Christi play," p. 63 ; the word is also used adjectivally, the padghand maistres, p. 176, pagand sylver, p. 179 ; the word is also used for the stage or platform on which the scene was acted, p. 32, " domus ad hospitandum paginas suas " ; " circa reparacionem pagine," p. 172. The word in the preceding sense is known only in English, and in the Anglo-Latin pagina. The two main early senses were " scene displayed on a stage," and stage on which a scene is exhibited, see N.E.D. Pageant.

PAN, 112, in timber-framed house, the beam which rests upon and is fixed to the posts, and which supports the rafters, 1420, searchers verdicts in Surtees Misc. (1888) 15. In hys tenement in Coppergate in York walles even uppe thurgh fra the grunde uppe to the panne. N.E.D. There is another use of the word which might possibly apply—a square or compartment of timber framework filled in with bricks or plaster. N.E.D. gives no early example of the use of this word in the last sense.

PARCHEMENER, 128, a maker or seller of parchment, O.F. parcheminier (13th c. in Hatz-Darm.) in med. L. pergamenarius. N.E.D.

PARASSAPHE, p. 225, probably parasceve, a name for Good Friday, the day on which the seven penitential psalms are appointed to be said. Late Lat. parasceve day of preparation, cf. F. parascève.

PAUTENER, 61, a small bag, earliest example given by N.E.D. 1325, O.F. pautonniere (1419 in Godefroi).

PERAPCIDES, 13, parapsides, paropsis, vas escarium, plat, dishes or platters, properly square in form. Promp. Parvul.

PRENTES, 181, prentice, apprentice. The N.E.D. gives an example as early as 1300. Cursor M. 12233. O.F. aprentis from aprendre to learn.

PYNNER, 103, makers of pins and other articles of wire ; in Norwich in 1581 there was a project for providing a place at the Great Hospital where the pinner Dutchman might teach his science to children. Norwich Records, *op. cit.*, p. lxxxvii.

ROUCH, 167, hairy, shaggy, of hides undressed, untanned, c. 1375 ; Sc. Leg. Saints, xxxvi., 279. S. John Baptist with a belte of reuch skin made. Reg. Privy Council Scot., N., 356, Rouch Hydis and barkit leddir.

SAGGERS, iii., possibly makers of rough pottery. N.E.D. gives saggar a protecting case of baked fire-proof clay in which ceramic wares are enclosed ; or a maker of sagum. " In these Rolls denotes the textile called say, Serge : . . . sometimes it seems to be the same as worsted. Dur. Accts. R. Surtees Soc., Vol. 103, p. 957.

U

SCAPHE, 13, bowl, hec scapha Anglice bolle : Wright-Wülcker, Vocabularies, 660.
SEARCHERS, scrutatores, 74, 82, see Mem. Bk., I., p. 263.
SELION, 75, Ducange, a land measure of about twenty perches. A ridge of ground rising between two furrows, of no certain quantity, Durham Account Rolls, op. cit., p. 965. Anglo-Lat. Selion-em, mod. Fr. sillon. N.E.D.
SPICER, 61. M.E. spicer, O.F. espicier, a grocer.

TAPITER, 195, M.E. tapiser, a maker of carpets or tapestry. The York tapiter, however, undertook to make coverlets, to weave linen and to dye his own yarn and cloth. By a later statute the tapiters of York obtained the monopoly of coverlet making, 34 and 35 Henry VIII., cap. 10. The act cost the city more than 200£, York Munic, Rec., xvii., fol. 11 (May 1542), and on account of it the tapiters refused to pay either subsidy or auluage, S.P. Dom. Eliz., cclii., 2.

VILLA SANCTI JOHANNIS, 115, Dalry in the Stewartry—unless Perth is intended which, however, was a burgh.
VIRE, 216, an obsolete spelling of veer, M.L. virare vertere deorsum sursum. Ducange.
VIVARIUM, 80, a fish pond, cf. vijver, a sheet of water kept in motion by artificial means, in the Hague.

WADDE, 205, woad ; wad, or wode, for lystaris, gaudo : Promptorium, Parvulorum, Catholicon Anglicum, 405, note 4. Woad is the produce of Isatis tinctoria, and is still used as a blue dye, though largely superseded by indigo. Durham Account Rolls, p. 983.
WALKER, 206, fuller, see Mem. Bk., vol. I., p. 257.
WORTLED, 54, " a leaden vessel for wort, the infusion of malt previous to fermentation," Durham Account Rolls, op. cit, p. 988.

WORDS AWAITING EXPLANATION.

CAPONES OF WOOD, 299.
CAPILL, 299, the Durham Account Rolls, III., 900, has capillrapez, cable ropes, and caplin is a skull cap of iron. N.E.D.

HUNGRY, to make leather hungry, 167. " Ledderhungry, pro j pelle de ledir hungry, iiij s. ; Priory of Finchale, ccccxxxiv., perhaps leather from Hungray. We find in these Rolls a hide of ledder hungry, with dyghtyng, tewing, and factura of oxhides into the same. Dur. Acc. R., III., 930, 931. Grimm, Wörterbuch, sub hungern, "In der sprache der gerber heisst es, ' die leder haben in der grube gehungert,' ibid, sub Hungrig, hungrig in der gewerblichen sprache tuchwacher." " Kein fieming sal sin tuch czu hungrig machen by der gesaczten busze." Orloff, Rechtsquellen I., 291. Possibly a technical expression, it might mean to soak preparatory for the application of the tannic acid.

INDEX OF NAMES AND PLACES.

Abirden, 114
Abirford, Will., 199, 200, 203, 204, 206, 208, 219
Abirford, 218
Abywryk, Joh., 112
Acclom, Hen., 50
Acton, Tho., 183
Addyson, Tho., 175
Alan, Tho., 140, 245,
Alanson, Laur., 117
Aldeburgh, Ric., 233
Aldestanmore, Agnes, 68 ; Joh., 67, 68, 110, 111, 157, 159, 174, 179, 183
Aleyn, Tho., 166, 215, 294
Alkebarewe, Joh., 86
Allen, Joh., 213
Allerton, Rob., 131, 179
Alman, Joh., 60, 61, 90
Alne, 274
Alne, Ric. de, 20 ; Ric., 12 ; Will., 37, 42, 43, 44, 47, 51, 54, 69, 74, 76, 118,
Alnewyk, 267
Alwent, Joh., 130
Ambler, Alex., 275, 277
Ampilford, Joh. de, 23 ; Joh., 80, 82, 92, 106, 107, 101, 111 ; Rob. de, 17
Amyas, Rob., 166, 215, 238, 241, 271, 275
Anable, Joh., 33
Ancock, Rob., 214
Anderby, Ric., of S. Michael le Belfry, 23
Andrewgate, 184
Andrewson, Joh., 115, Will., 117
Anewe, 115, see glossary
Anguysh, Angus, 114
Antony, S. 70
Appelby, Appilby, 124, 125, 234
Appilby, Appylby, Joh., 217 ; Hen., 61 ; Nich., 35 ; Rob., 175 ; Rog., 293 ; Will. de, 21
Appilton, 266
Appilton, Tho., 115
Appleyard, Tho., 189, 191
Appylby, Phil, 75
Apylgarth, Rob., 18
Archibald, Rog., 25 ; Will., 25
Arden, 161
Arnald, Ric., 36
Artays, Joh., 78
Arthington, Joh., 249, 250
Asarlay, Tho., 245

Ascham, Joh. de, 18 ; Rob. de, 21
Ase, Joh., 173
Aske, Joh., 234
Askham, 37
Askham, Joh. de, 14, 69
Askwyth, 96
Asper, Tho., 271
Aspey, Joh., 56
Aspez, Joh., 60, 61
Atkynson, Ric., 219 ; Tho., 220 ; Will., 272
Aton, Tho., 56, 60, 61, 110
Athedill, Hen., 84
Athington, 119, probably Haddington
Audley, Joh., 245
Aukebarowe, Will., 56, 73
Aunger, Alex., 275
Austenmore, Joh., 56
Axiholme, Joh., 48

Bacoun, Ad., 69
Baker, Will., 242
Bakhus, Tho., 247
Bampton Welle, 254
Bank, Ad., del 12
Banke, Hen., 295 ; Ric., 233
Barbour, Tho., 48
Barker, Will., 213, 293, 299
Barlay, Will., 199, 202, 204
Barneby, Edw., 50, 112 ; Sym de, 21 ; Tho., 14, 32 ; Will. de, 15 ; Will., 34
Barnet, Will., 54
Baron, Joh., of S. Crux
Barr, Rob., 245
Barrey, Chris., 238 ; Rob., 30, 80
Barton, Joh., 23 ; Rob., 91 ; Rog., 9 ; Tho., 198, 200, 202, 203, 204, 241 ; Will., 44, 54, 77, 78, 97, 112, 114, 131, 179
Bassenheim, Sif. de, 2
Basy, Joan, 10 ; Rog., 10 ; Ric., 97
Batson, Rob., 271
Baumburg, Rob., 95, 98, 99
Bawtre, Reg., 131 ; Ric., 98
Baynbryg, Joh., 75, 79, 85, 86, 110, 157, 159, 173
Beaumont, Joh. de, 24
Bedale, Joh. de, 11 ; Joh., 62, 64, 78, 79, 82, 84, 85, 86, 87, 89, 90, 92, 114, 115, 116, 119, 120, 220, 269 ; Sym., 272 ; Tho. de, 122 ; Will., 110, 142, 157, 159, 183
Bedern, 42

INDEX OF NAMES AND PLACES.

Bedford, Duke of, Count of Richmond, and of Kendale, 57, 58
Belamy, Maud, 218
Beleby, Alicia de, 25 ; Joh. de, 25
Bell, Joh., 11, 57, 58, 59, 60, 61, 62, 131, 241, 277 ; Will., 11
Belton, Rob., 56, 101, 131
Belvere, 239
Bemeslay, Tho., 67
Bempton, Joh., 107, 110, 111 ; Will., 69
Benetplace, 35
Bengechantre, 99
Benson, Tho., 114
Bentley, Chris., 295
Berden, Joh de, 15, 16, 17, 28, 32 ; Joh., 120 ; Ric., 140
Bergate, 295
Bergh, Joh. de, 21 ; Will. de, 134
Bernardcastell, Joh. de, 28 ; Joh., 218
Berwick, 113, 114
Besyngby, Joh., 67, 85, 98
Beseby, Joh., 296
Best, Tho., 112
Beysby, Joh., 283
Beverley, 122
Beverlay, Hen., 25 ; Joh. de, 26 ; Joh., 47, 114 ; Ric., 109 ; Tho., 199, 200, 203, 204, 206, 208 ; Will., 114
Bew, Tho., 179, 182
Bilburgh, Rob., 99
Bilton, 230, 235, 236
Birkched, Joh., 267
Birkhed, Joh., 273, 290 ; Will. de, 30 ; Will., 91
Bisshopflete, 254
Bishophill, 66, 67, 84, 97, 239
Bishopthorp, Bisshopthorp, Bisshoppthorp, 231 294 272
Bitwene-the-waters, 242
Blakburn, Eliz., 219 ; Joh., 38, 46, 62, 64, 86, 91, 219 ; Nic., 38, 39, 41, 43, 74, 84, 86, 90, 111, 131, 134, 142, 174 ; Nic., the younger, 46, 55, 110, 135 ; Ric., 214, 218
Blakelok, Tho., 238
Blenerhasset, Al., 217
Blenkowe, Will. de, 38 ; Tho., 38
Blenkensope, Ric., 51
Blithe, And., 196, 245
Blount, Tho., 115
Bolron, Joh., 173
Boltby, Ric. de, of S. Clement's, 23
Bolton, 98, 99 ; prior of, 99, 100
Bolton, Joh. de, 14, 30, 35, 38, 39, 43, 44 ; Joh., 87, 91, 110, 111, 135, 139, 142, 157, 159 ; Hen. de, 11 ; Rob., 131, 172, 173 ; Will. de., 25, 34

Booth, Both, Bouthe, Cris., 204, 206, 208 ; Joh., 15, 52, 84, 86, 91 ; Laur., 273 ; Will. del, 14, 34, 38, 47, 68
Bootham, Bouthom, Bowthom, 60, 72, 93, 109, 248
Borssalia, Hen. de, lord of Camhour, 186
Bostan, Will., 131
Bostrevyn, 119, see glossary
Boteler, Rob., 231
Botman, Nic., 239
Botoner, Hugo, 22
Bouche, Joh., 62, 64, 74, 78 ; Mary, 78
Bouland, Will, 230
Boune, Joh., 115
Bower, Will., 234
Bowes, Will., 35, 39, 51, 52, 53, 54, 55, 58, 62, 64, 65, 68, 74, 75, 76, 79, 84, 86, 89, 90, 119, 131, 135, 139, 142, 157, 159, 164, 166, 173, 174, 179, 180, 183 : Hen., 66
Bowet, Hen., 43
Boydon, Joh., 48 ; Kat., 48, 49
Boynton, Kath. de, 44, 45
Bracebrig, Bracebryg, Bracebrygg, Ric., 119, 182 ; Tho., 35, 38, 52, 54, 55, 59, 60, 61, 62, 64, 74, 75, 84, 89, 91, 101, 107, 108, 109, 110, 111, 128, 157, 159, 172, 173, 174 ; Will., 204, 245
Brandesby, Will., 131
Bradeshagh, Ric., 48
Bradforddale, 96
Bradley, Joh., 277 ; Will., 220, 221, 222
Bradschawe, Ric., 176
Braffynton, 232
Braidley, Joh., 248
Brame, Will., 109
Brampton in Gilsland, 217
Brandesby, Will., 44
Brathwayt, Joh. de, 14, 16, 25, 38, 45 ; Joh., 52, 62, 64, 100, 269 ; Mar., 100
Braweby, Will., 85
Braxe, Tho., 283
Brayton, Will. de., 18
Brereton, Joh., 23 ; Tho., 90, 140, 161, 220, 232
Brice, Rol., 217
Bridehill, Will., 161
Bridlington, prior of, 55
Bridsall, Will. de, 23
Brigg, Ad. del, 7
Brigham, Joh., 216, 217
Brignall, Will. de, 7
Brisegreve, Will. de, 16

INDEX OF NAMES AND PLACES. 309

Brodok, Ric., 92
Broghton, Will., 18; Hen., 110, 112; Ric., 85
Broghtonlith, 46
Brokholes, Joh., 196, 245
Brome, Joh., 37
Broune, Joh., 21, 22, 140
Brounflete, Joh., 56, 85, 90, 95, 183; Laur., 273
Brounlee, Cuth., 212
Browne, Joh., 272
Bruges, 57, 87, 88
Brukeshagh, Will., 48
Brunby, Will., 234
Bryan, Ric., 85, 131
Brydlyngton, Joh., 44
Bryg, Ad. del, 63; Joh., 103
Bryghenhall, Joh., 54
Brynsall, Hen., 121
Brystall, Joh., 112
Bukden, Ric., 131, 139, 142
Bukey, Pet., 157, 159, 173
Bukkiller, Bokeler, Joh., 95, 98, 99
Bukland, Joh., 25
Bukler, Joh., 25, 196, 245; Rob., 196; Will., 245
Buksy, Pet., 38, 39, 52, 55, 74, 84, 89, 91, 110
Bukton, Tho. de, 32, 118; Rob., 234
Bulerode, 237
Bull, the, in Coney Street, 203
Bullyng, Rob., 69
Bulmer, Will., 273; Kath. de, 43; Will. de, 43
Bulnays, Will., 97
Burbryg, Tho., 23
Burbrigge, Adam de, 22
Burdclever, Hen., 232
Burdon, Joh., 27
Burgbrig, 241
Burgh, Joh., 241, 277; Ric., 28; Will., 161
Burn, Joh., 176
Burnell, Tho., 219
Burneley, Joh., 183, 184
Burton, Joan, 232; Hen., 274; Joh. de, 22; Joh. de, 23; Ric. de, 23; Rog. de, 47, 48, 49, 51, 53, 54, 62, 64, 65, 68, 69, 76, 94, 95, 96, 102, 118, 173, 174, 175, 232; Rob., 52, 54, 59, 60, 61, 79, 108, 111; Tho., 176; Will. de, 17, 22, 48; Will., 44, 139
Busshebury, Ric., 232
Bustardthorp, 231, 236, 294
Buston, Joh. de., 22
Buteler, Joh., 119; Tho., 50
Butler, Cec., 231; Con., 231; Rob., 235; Will., 231

Bychehill Lomelyth, 239
Bygod, Ed., 251
Bylton, Rob., 18
Byrdesall, Joh., 38, 214
Byrtby, 237
Bysshop, Ric., 250, 277
Bysshophill, 130

Cady, Maud, 92
Caen, 66
Calas, Tho., 196
Calcrofte, Will., 243
Caldecotes, Joh., 55
Calisia, 219
Calis, Tho., 245
Calthorn, Joh. de, 29
Calton, Joh. de, 31; Sim., 79
Campveer, Veere, 186
Candall, Joh., 245
Candestreme, 291
Candeler, Joh., 12, 51
Carleton, Carlton, Joh. de, 39; Rob. de, 22, 23; Tho., 48, 49
Carlell, Joh., 271
Carlisle, 217
Carnaby, Tho., 42
Carpentarius, Ade, 220
Carre, Tho.. 131, 135, 174, 183
Carum, Joh., 28
Carylhyll, Rob., 176
Carre, Joh., 198
Cartmell, Alicia de, 17; Joh. de, 17
Casawas, Perot de, 29
Castlegate, 63
Catclogh, Joh., 25
Cathedral, 108, 156, 219, 233, 278
Cathedral, Kirk, 250
Catlewe, Alic, 17; Joh., 17
Catour, Mar., 222; Tho., 7, 166, 215, 222, 293, 294
Catryk, Joh., 131, 198, 200
Catton, Joh., 273
Cauton, Ric., 33
Cave, Joh., 103
Cawod, Cawode, Joh., 233; Will. de, 12
Cawton, Joh., 222
Cayrok, Joh., 250
Ceszay, Joh. de, 14, 17
Chaimbre, Rob., 271
Channey, Will., 299
Charleton, Jas., 296
Chartres, Joh., 41, 75
Chatburn, Joh., 273
Chaumbre, Joh., 161
Chaundeler, Rob., 85
Chaworth, Tho., 239
Chester, Will., de, 17, 122

Chilton, Joh., 121
Chircheleghes, Rob., 92
Churches, see subject index
Chymney, Will., 166, 213, 215, 292, 293, 294
Chyvyngton, Will., 122
Clarell, Tho., 237
Claybroke, Cleybroke, Cris., 206, 208; Joh., 239; Ric., 140, 166, 220, 238, 239
Clegg, Joh., 48
Clementhorp, 40, 70
Clerk, Clerc, Clerke, Mic., 248, 249, 277; Ric., 213, 238; Tho., 219; Will., 245
Clerkson, Mar., 269
Cleseby, Ric., 51
Cleveland, Will., 200, 202, 203, 204
Clifford, Joh. de, 15
Clifton, Clyfton, 29, 233, 254
Clyfton, Will., 103, 104; Ralf., 294; Tho., 294
Clynt, Ric., 131
Clyveland, Will. de, 33
Cockermouth, Cokermouth, 274, 54
Cok, Joh., 271; Rob., 97
Cokkay, Will., 248
Coklay, Will., 97
Coldell, Tho., 217
Colke, Joh., 208
Colliergate, 97, 233
Colson, Will., 245
Colton, Abra. de, 7; Hen. de, 45
Colvell, Rob., 22
Colyer, Ad., 35
Colyngwyth, Alex. de, 22
Colynson, Rob., 198, 219, 200
Conyers, Rob., 66, 67
Conyngarth, 220
Conyngstrete, 18, 19, 24, 29, 35, 36, 63, 83, 92, 94, 97, 101, 102, 203, 231, 269
Conyshom, Tho., 123
Cook, Joh., 57, 58, 59, 60, 61, 62; Hugo, 121; Rob., 9; Rog., 31; Tho., 31
Coopemanthorp, 204
Coppergate, 31, 120
Corbrygge, Alan de, 21
Coreburgh, 238
Cotes, Cuth., 273; Joh., 206, 233; Tho., 220
Cotom, Rob. de, 25
Cottesmore in Roteland, 134
Cotum, Phil. de, 220
Cotyngham, Joh., 122
Coucher, Joh., 85
Couk, Gilb., 161; Rad., 161; Walt., 161
Coupeland, Joh., 204; Will., 54, 58, 173

Couper, Joh., 7; Rob., 219; Tho., 97; Will., 103, 222
Coupir, 290
Coursour, Wal., 200
Coventre, Will., 18
Coventry, 201
Coverham, Rob., 130; Tho., 208
Cowesby, Joh., 176
Crakynthorp, Joh. de, 23
Crathorn, 200
Crathorn, Will., 220
Craven, Joh. de, 28, 43, 44, 52; Joh., 62, 64, 98; Rob. de, 22; Will., 111, 112, 139, 142, 157, 178, 183
Crayk, Crayke, Joh. de, 23, 28, 33
Cristendome, Rob. de, 31; Will., 121
Croftes, 97
Croftes, Crofte, Will. de, 22; Will., 103, 219
Crokeham, Ric., 131
Crokelyn, Ric., 220
Crome, Rog., 67
Crosby, 239
Crosseland, Ric., 121
Crosseby, Will., 206, 208
Crosseriddyng, 242
Croull, Joh., 230; Ric., 220
Crounour, Joh., 235
Croxton, Agnes de, 54; Joh. de, 54; Joh., 114
Cuke, Rob., 21; Tho., 103
Cumbrenaunt, 119, see glossary
Cunsburgh, Cunnysburgh, Tho., 19, 93
Cunsby, Will, 79, 82, 111
Cure, El., 196, 243
Curtays, Curteis, Curtas, Ric., 234; Rob., 111; Tho., 119, 200, 204, 219
Cusson, Joh., 274
Cutberd, Joh., 56

Dalby, Rob., 48
Dale, Will., 245
Dalton, 46
Dalton, Joan de, 43; Will. de, 43
Dam, Jac., 245
Damryddyng, 242
Danby, Jac., 217; Jas., 296; Joh., 67; Tho., 198, 200
Danson, Alex., 293, 294
Dany, Tho., 91
Danyell, Pet., 215
Danzic, Dansk, 3, 10, 95, 98, 99
Danzic, 95, 98, 99
Darell, Tho., 248
Darnton, Tho., 218
Darrawell, Tho., 122
Darrell, Marm., 69

INDEX OF NAMES AND PLACES. 311

Danson, Alex., 213
Davell, Bri., 230, 235 ; Eliz., 231 ; Hen., 231 ; Tho., 231 ; Will., 231
Davy, Joh., 89 ; Tho., 47, 49, 51, 87, 110, 157, 159
Davyson, Davison, Rob., 223, 249 ; Tho., 215, 217
Dawson, Bert., 200, 283
Dekyn, Will., 215
Dene, Tho., 80
Dent, Rad., 196, 245
Denton, Ric., 112, 217 ; Tho., 217, 277
Derby, Will., 65
Derfeld, Joh., 20
Derkyn, 242
Devyas, Will., 10
Dewsbury, 237
Dey, Joh., 92 ; Tho., 92
Diconson, Dyconson, Hen., 215 ; Tho., 239
Disford, Will., 23
Dobley, Chris., 223
Dobson, Joh., 298
Dodmor, Rob., 56
Dodyngton, Doddyngton, Joh., 68, 73, 95, 98, 99, 139, 157
Dogheson, Joh., 161, 214, 283
Dolfyne, Rob., 22
Doncastre, Joh. de, 28, 30, 120 ; Hen., 40 ; Tho., 38, 52, 62, 64, 74, 75, 84, 86, 91, 157
Donyngton, Will. de, 22
Dorlyng, Joh., 122
Douglas, Count of, 33
Drawswerd, Tho., 295
Drax, Will., 103
Draycotes, Joh. de, 121
Dreng, Joh., 95, 98
Driffield, Ric. de, 21 ; Step. de, 22 ; Tho. de, 23 ; Will. de, 21
Drynghouse, 294
Dubber, Hen., 85 ; Joh., 183, 184
Duffield, Joh., 731, 73 ; Marg., 89, 237 ; Tho., 89, 237
Dugelby, 235, 236
Dunbar, 27
Dunnyng, Rob., 48, 82
Durem, Duresme, Joh., 46, 47 ; Sim. de, 32 ; Tho., 79 ; Will. de, 12
Dygby, Ric., 161
Dyghton, Joh. de, 25
Dykes, Will. del, 54
Dykryng, 55
Dykson, Kat., 116 ; Will., 277
Dyvelyn, Joh., 242

Ebchester, Rob., 142
Eddenham, Joh. de, 122
Ede, Rob., 19
Edenale, 38
Edenburgh, 116
Egerston, 117, see glossary
Egill, Rob., 272
Elbing, 2, 3, 6
Ellerbek, Rob. de, 30, 31
Elles, Joh., 283
Elton, Joh., 232
Elyson, Tho., 230
Elvyngton, Sim. de, 15 ; Joh., 66
Elwald, Joh., 290 ; Rob., 247
Emlay, Tho., 40, 51, 85
Emson, Rog., 298
Enghebert, Hen., 82
Erews, Will., 249
Erl, Chris., 196, 245
Erthe, Jac. de, 116
Eryome, Joh., 22
Escrik, Tho. de, 22
Eseby, Will., 54, 56, 87
Eshwra, Ric. de, 22
Eslaby, Hen., 97
Esser, Geo., 273
Essheton, Joh. de, 29
Essyngton. Joh., 271
Esyngwald, Al., 222 ; Tho., 62, 64, 69, 74, 75, 84, 86, 91, 106, 110, 111, 112, 116, 126, 128, 157, 159, 222, 238
Eston, Tho., 233
Eton, Ric., 87, 88, 89
Etwald, Joh., 299
Eure, Rob. de, 30
Even, Joh., 239
Evenwod, Joh., 223

Fairfax, Fairefax, Farefax, Guy, 218, 231, 235, 236, 237, 293 ; Will., 213, 293, 294
Farleham, Joh., 28
Farlyngton, Rob. de., 23
Farnham, 76
Farnlay, Tho., 94, 95
Fawcett, Ed., 167
Fencotes, Will., 46
Fendard, Ric., 56
Fenkel Street, 35
Fenton, Rob. de., 234
Fenwyk, Will., 56
Fergus, 124
Feriby, Joh., 198, 213, 214, 215, 217, 238, 290–293 ; Rob., 44, 183 ; Will., 18, 260
Ferrour, Ferur, And., 61, 116, 131 ; Cec., 160 ; Ric., 79 ; Will., 160
Ferrybridge, 16

Fetesenge, 254
Fewlar, Rob., 266
Feysgate, 295
Fissher, Joh., 271
Fitz Hugh, Eliz., 289; Geo., 290; Ric., 289
Fysshlendyng, 53
Fysshergate, 222
Flasby, Joh. de, 21; Rob. de, 23
Flaynburg, Rob. de, 22
Floyter, Ran., 221
Folkerthorp, Thom. de, 97
Folneby, Tho., 213
Forester, Al., 46; Geof., 48; Mar., 115; Tho., 97, 131
Forster, Ed., 290; Joh., 250; Tho., 75
Foss, 16, 44, 48
Fossbridge, 7, 33, 68, 72, 128, 138, 158, 173
Fossgate, 7, 19, 48
Foulford, Joh., 219
Foughler, Will., 122
Foulnabey, Tho., 289
Fountains, 231
Fournour Inn, 130
Fowton, Rob. de, 18
Fox, Joh., 271
Foxholez, 266
Fraunsez, Rob., 196
Freman, Tho., 277
Freres, Will. del, 12
Frieston, Nich., 245
Frost, Will., 6, 9, 14, 53, 122
Fryston, Agn. de, 45; Tho. de, 9; Will. de, 45
Fulford, 70
Fulnaby, Tho., 293
Fulthorp, Will., Sir, 39
Furth, Nic. del, 114
Fuyster, Dav., 47
Fynche, Tho., 293, 294
Fynlawson, Joh., 119

Gammyl, Rob., 48
Gardener, Hugh, 17, 51; Joh., 33; Ric., 29
Gare, Rob. del, 12, 30, 37, 122; Rob., 30, 46, 49, 62, 64, 79, 84, 111, 173; Tho., 52, 53, 62, 64, 79, 80, 86, 87, 90, 91, 93, 94, 95, 96, 106, 111, 117, 139, 142, 157, 173, 174; Walt., 122
Gargrave, Joh., 77
Garleker, Tho., 54
Garnett, Nic., 140
Garth, Tho. del, 17; Tho., 18, 20, 30, 69; Will., 235

Gascoigne, Alice, 290; Hen., 218; Joh., 55, 68, 157, 159; Ral., 290; Ric. de, 6; Will., 6
Gatefulford, 232
Gatesheued, Will., 51, 110
Gaunton, Joh., 161, 291; Rob., 34
Gayteclyffes, Tho., 250
Gayteford, Joh., 21
Gaytesheued, Wm., 157, 159
Gednay, Ric., 115
Geffray, Tho., 245
Gegges, Joh., 283
Gerard, Joh., 103, 104; Tho., 161
Gerardus, 42
German, S. of Selby, 242
Gervas, Joh., 44, 45
Gibson, Tho., 237
Gilbert, 34
Gildhall, Guehald, Guyhall. Guyhale, 142, 143, 203, 206, 246, 251, 253, 255, 256, 258, 259, 261, 262, 265, 298
Gill, Gyll, Hug. de, 66, 89, 90; Joh., 269
Girdelergate, 37, 44
Girlington, Gyrlyngton, Nic., 199; Will., 175
Gisburn, Gyseburn, Joh. de, 33; Step., 63
Gillyot, Gyllyot, Gilyot, Gylliot, Joh., 140, 166, 197, 198, 199, 200, 203, 204, 206, 208, 212, 213, 214, 230, 238, 240, 241, 245, 285, 290, 291, 293, 294, 298; Ric., 176
Girdlergate, 37, 44, 45, 63
Giry, Will., 12
Glasen, Joh., Glasson, Glasyn, Joh., 140, 166, 198, 204, 206, 213, 238, 245
Glover, Ed., 33
Gloverlane, 45
Goatson, Joh., 120
Goddesbroke, Tho., 73
Goldebeter, 104, 106
Gothland, Joh., 21
Gothrumgate, 27, 37
Gotteshalve, Joh. de, 33
Gower, Alice, 67; Adam, 67
Gra, Graa, Grey, Gray, Geo., 293; Rob., 131; Tho., 1, 5, 6, 8, 14, 16, 28, 45, 85, 122, 283
Gradale, 113
Gradon, Joh. de, 28
Grape Lane, 130
Graunge, Will., 230
Graystok, Ralph, baron, 223; Walt., 230
Grene, Ric., 69
Grenebank, Miles, 213, 293, 294
Grenehode, Reg., 241
Grenewod, Tho., 176

INDEX OF NAMES AND PLACES.

Greteham, 48
Grice, Rob., 66
Grillington, Will., 139, 142
Grimston, Grymston, Rob. de, 22; Sim., 89
Grissop, Will., 89
Grymesby, Joh. de, 218
Gudale, Joh., 199, 200; Will., 54
Gude, Will., 196
Guienne, 65
Gunby, Ad., 219
Ganby, 237
Gundall, Gundeale, Jord., 22; Tho., 22
Gurnell, Will., 274
Gurnard, Joh., 271; Ric., 196
Gurnerd, Ric., 245
Gybbon, Rob., 298; Will., 298
Gygleswyk, 242
Gyllyng, Will. de, 21
Gyselay, Tho., 116; Will., 131

Hackenberger, Alric., 6
Hag, Hagge, Hagg, Joh., 213, 215, 293, 294
Hakynsey, Alice, 242; Joh., 242; Tho., 242
Halgarthdyke, 76
Halghton, Joh. de, 26
Haliday, Nic., 218
Hall, Joh., 67, 283; Rob. del, 27; Rob., 161; Tho., 277
Hallowe All, 292
Halton, probably Hatton, par. of Ratho, west of Edinburgh
Halton, Rob., 93
Halygaste, 10
Halywell, Joh., 116
Halyday, Nic., 272
Hamelak, 239
Hamerton, Joh, 39, 40
Hamiburg, 267
Hancock, Tho., 216; Rob., 213, 215, 271, 292, 293, 294
Handelay, Jam., 245
Hans, Joh., 275
Harbard, Will., 196
Hardwyk, 10
Hardy, Will., 233
Hardesang, Ric., 238, 293
Harfleur, 65
Harington, Will. de, 37
Harper, Harpour, Joh., 213, 238, 290, 292, 293, 294, 286, 292, 296; Tho., 214
Harpham, Rob., 15, 63
Harryngton, Joh., 294; Will., 37
Harwod, Rob., 272

Haselay, 106
Hasthorp, 234
Hastynges, Rad., 216, 217
Hatterbergh, 67
Hatlessay, Hathelsay, Joh., senior, 25; Joh., junior, 25; Tho. de, 22
Haukeswell, Ric., 75, 76
Haukeswell, 254
Haukysby, Joh., 277
Haule, Pat., 243
Havergate, 241
Haxby, Joh., 79, 249, 250; Tho. de, 23
Haxholme, Walt. de, 22
Hay, Rog. del, 54, 77
Hayne, Rob., 9
Hayrster, Hen., 131
Haysand, Will., 271
Heburn, Joh., 176
Hebbe, Joh., 48
Heceham, Edm., 48
Hedon, Will. de, 22
Helagh park, 231
Helfeld, Hen., 95
Helithwayte, 46
Hellowe, Phil. de, 23
Helmeslay, Ad., 234; Alice, 37; Geo., 37, 234; Will. de, 32, 35, 37, 38
Helperby, Joh. de, 23
Helysbech, Tho. de, 22
Hemmyngbrough, Tho. de, 34
Hemylsey, Joh., 239; Tho., 218
Hendechild, Tho., 103, 104
Henrydoghter, Mar., 115
Henryson, Will., 116
Herbert, Chris., 189
Herod, 124
Herte, Will., 115, 120
Hertillane, 160
Heryse, Joh. de, 23
Heseham, Ad., 82, 85; Joh., 82
Hesill, Tho. de, 24
Heslarton, 234
Heslyngton, 232
Heslyngton, Will., 137
Hessay, Ham. de, 35
Hesyll, Tho., 36
Hetherington, Will., 238
Heton, 96
Hewik, 46, 47
Hewester, Law., 92
Heworth, Phil. de, 22
Hewyk, Joh. de, 8, 45; Joh., 9, 35, 38, 39, 52, 55, 62, 64, 74, 75, 84, 85, 86, 91, 157, 159, 163, 183; Tho., 79
Hexham, Joh., 93, 112, 173
Heynde, Will., 233
Hichenberg, Alric, 2
Hill, Joh., 230; Tho., 269

Hillom, Joh. de, 7
Hilton, Rob., 115
Hirste, Tho., 103, 104
Hobshort, Hobschort, Joh., 66 ; Rob., 54, 97
Hobson, Joh., 119
Hodilstone, Chris., 242 ; Hen., 242
Hodlow, Joh., 285 ; Will., 285
Hogin, Joh., 28
Holbek, Tho., 51, 66, 122 ; Will., 44, 137, 140, 196, 198, 202, 237, 238, 243, 245, 272
Holderness, 237
Holgate, Alice, 232 ; Nic., 199, 200, 203, 204, 206, 222, 232 ; Will., 232
Holm, Holme, Nic., 42 ; Joh., 67 ; Rob., 33, 43, 44, 233 ; Walt., 176 ; Will., 245
Hohme, 222
Holmes lez, 33, 70
Holton, Tho., 176
Home, Joan, 272 ; Tho., 272
Honorius III., 68
Hopton, Joh., 274
Hoperton, Rob. de, 12, 28
Horle, Tho., 34
Horneby, Rad., 270 ; Rob. de, 23 ; Tho. de, 15, 85 ; Will., 37
Horselane, 249
Horton, Ad. de, 97 ; Joh. de, 21
Hoser, Joh., 35
Hosyergate, 47
Hoton-on-Derwent, 53
Hoton, Hen. de, 22 ; Will., 176
Houke, Will., 196
Housom, Will., 49
Houson, Joh., 97
Hovell, Joh., 196
Hovyngham, Joh. de, 21 ; Rob., 67 ; Will. de, 9 ; Will., 49, 51
Howe, Ric. del, 97
Howeden, Houeden, Howdon, Joh., de, 14, 25, 30, 32, 45 ; Tho. de, 6 ; Tho., 130 ; Will., 131
Howell, Joh., 245
Howeram, Tho., 53
Howham, Rob. de, 32
Howme, Tho., 272
Howom, Howome, Rob., 17, 52, 62, 64, 74, 79, 84, 110, 111 ; Tho. de, 247
Howran, Howren, Tho., 51 ; Tho., 223
Howrom, Tho., 14
Howthorp, Joh., 245
Huby, Will., 283
Hudson, Hen., 218 ; Rob., 208
Huet, Will., 233
Hugate, Agnes, Annas, 114 ; Will. de, 122

Hugate, Will. de, 9
Hugon, Rob., 89
Hulke of Selykey, 56
Hunt, Tho., 277
Hulstrete, 218
Humfre, lord of Dacre, 217
Humphrey, Duke of Gloucester, 137
Hundegate, 222
Hungate, Will., 234, 291, 292
Hunter, Eus., 182
Huntyngton, 233
Huntyngton, Will., 176
Huse, 68
Hutham, Rauf., 199
Huthwayt, Joh., 85, 126, 179
Huton, Joh. de, 22
Hyde, Ad., 97
Hyndeley, Will., 250
Hynelay, Hen. de, 10
Hyngbryg, 65, 81
Hyrst, Joh., 277

Ilklay, Ric., 130
Ince, Joh., 200, 202, 203, 204
Inglissh, Will., 208
Ingmanthorp, 231
Ingylby, Rob., 183, 184 ; Will., 76, 290
Inkelyng, Will., 121
Innocent, Will., 176
Irland, 65
Ithen, Joh., 65
Iveson, Rob., 238

Jacson, Jakson, Rob., 140, 219 ; Will., 299
Jakman, Joh., 97
Jeddeworth, 115, see glossary
Jerusalem, Jerosolamitane, 5, 76
Jesus Christ, 48
Joan, 38
Johannensson, Gilb., 27
Johannes, S., 115, see glossary
Johanson, Rob., 117
John, Duke of Bedford, 117
Johnson, Rob., 178, 213, 293, 294 ; Walt., 248 ; Will., 277, 298
Jonby, 38
Jonson, Alisand, 119 ; Arch., 119 ; Will., 298
Jubritgate, 63
Judas, 171

Karre, Tho., 129
Kaytour, Tho., 238

INDEX OF NAMES AND PLACES. 315

Kechyn, Nic., 298
Kechynner, Tho., 196
Kede, Joh., 115
Kelam, Isa., 269 ; Rob., 269
Keldsyk, Marg., 54 ; Will. de, 54
Kelfeld, Tho. de, 14
Kempe, Joh., 156
Kendall, Will., 54
Kenlay, Joh. de, 34 ; Joh., 130 ; Kath., 34, 35
Kent, Joh., 206, 208, 232
Kepewyk, Will. de, 33
Ketyll, Rob., 85
Kidcote, 254
Kiddelay, Tho., 139
Kilburn, Will., 245
Kingston, Kyngeston-super-Hull, 10, 56, 218
Kirk, Kirke, Kyrk, Geo., 213, 283, 293, 294 ; Joh., 220
Kirkeby, Kereby, Kyrkeby, Joh., 47, 69, 82, 84, 93 ; Maud de, 97 ; Rob. de, 38 ; Rob., 103 ; Will., 173
Kirkebymoresyde, 271
Kirkham, 220, 296
Knapton-by-Acom, 233
Knapton, Joh., 232
Knaresburgh, 46, 241
Knasemyer, 294
Knolles, Will., 230
Kuyght, Joh., 176 ; Ric., 131, 220
Kyd, Ric., 196
Kydde, Ric., 244
Kyddelam, Will., 111
Kyghlay, Tho. de, 21, 23
Kylburn, Tho. de, 7
Kylkenny, Ric., 129
Kyllynghall, 46
Kyng, Joh., 228, 229, 230 ; Ric., 27
Kyrkby-in-Kendale, 114
Kyrkbyorblawers, 184
Kyrkelane, 130
Kyrkestiyll, 109
Kyrkham, Joh., 82, 108, 137, 138, 139, 173 ; Tho., 110, 112, 158
Kyrkla, 56
Kyrkton, Will. de, 22
Kyrspyn, Joh., 77
Kyrtlyngton, Joh. de, 21

Lacer, Rob., 18
Laierthorp, 250
Lain, Kat., 290
Lam, And., 199, 200
Lambbe, Will., 238
Lambe, Will., 140, 215, 245, 250
Lamberd, Will., 46, 79
Lambert, Ric., 103 ; Will., 46, 84, 91

Lancaster, Joh., 112 ; Nic., 213, 248, 292, 293
Lanercoste, prior of, 217
Langlaythorp, Will. de, 45
Langthorn, Isa., 214 ; Will., 214
Langtoft-super-le-Wald, 40
Langtoft, Tho., 22
Langtofte, 75
Langton, Cris., 101 ; Euf., 223–230 ; Hen., 224, 226 ; Joh. de, 44, 45, 101, 102, 223–230, 283 ; Marg., 224, 226 ; Rob., 224, 226, 275 ; Tho., 224, 226 ; Will. de, 224, 226
Lassell, Rob., 272
Lasynby, W., 44
Latham, Hug., 92
Lathes, Rob. de, 54
Laton, Rei., 296
Laxton, Joh., 69, 85
Layrthorp, 6
Laysyngby, Will., 39
Leche, Rob., 103
Ledes, 237
Ledes, Ledys, Ag. de, 41, 47 ; Joh. de, 15, 22 ; Rad., 23 ; Rob., 33, 38, 46, 275 ; Tho. de, 40, 46 ; Will. de, 6, 21, 46, 130
Lee, Will. del, 82
Leck, Ralf, 239
Legh, Joh., 237
Leicester, 50
Lekenfeld, Will., 41, 200
Lelograve, Rob., 273
Lematon, Ric., 204, 218
Leper, Rob., 230
Lescrop, Hen., 29, 51, 98 ; Joh., 27 ; Marg., 98 ; Ric., 97 ; Tho., 230
Lethcogh, 115, see glossary
Letheley, Joh., 166, 235, 245
Letteby, 69
Leuesham, Joh. de, 39 ; Will. de, 15
Leventhorp, Gal., 96 ; Tho., 96
Leverton, Laur. de, 7 ; Tho., 131
Levyngton, Joh., 34
Leycestr, 116
Leysmyth, Rob., 179
Lightlope, Joh., 140, 215, 238
Limesey, R. de, 42
Lincoln, Ellen, 214 ; Hugh, 214
Littester, Step., 1
Lofthouse, Loftehouse, Joh., 55, 68, 74, 75, 91, 110, 111, 114, 135, 157, 159
Loksmyth, Johannet, 241 ; Rad., 179, 182
Lokton, Rob., 46, 52, 62, 64, 74, 75, 84, 86, 290
Lokwood, Rob., 91
London, 1, 3, 5, 7, 73, 242
London, Ric., 34

Longmorez, 242
Longespy, Bert., 29
Lonsdale, Rob. de, 66
Lough, Joh., 57, 58, 60
Loumelith, 130
Lound, Alex. del, Sir, 39
Louthe, Joh., 56, 58, 157, 173 ; Rob. de, 14, 38 ; Rob., 35 ; Ric., 142, 157 ; Will., 90
Louthian, 115
Louthorp, 234
Lovell, Geo., 269; Rob., 53 ; Will., 53
Lowson, Will., 273
Lygeard, Ric., 44
Lyland, Robt. de, of S. Crux, 22
Lyllyng, Joh., 68, 130, 157, 159, 173
Lyndesay, Joh., 27 ; Step., 114 ; naturalization repeated, 120
Lynton, Joh., 220
Lyons, Will., 7, 44
Lyvelandes, Joh., Tho., 6
Lyverton, Tho., 48, 49
Lukes, Joh., 22
Lund, Joh., 41
Lutton, Joh. de, 18, 218 ; Rob., 179, 182

Maclyney, Joh., 238
Madder, Will., 241
Madenakes, 242
Makblyth, Ralf., 232 ; Tho.,
Malehys, Tho., 69
Malore, Chris., 130
Malson, Joh., 275
Malton, 235, 236
Malton, convent of, 37
Malton, Rob., 32
Man, Joh. de, 17, 51 ; del, 66 ; Joh., 76 ; Tho., 237
Maners, Hum., 290, 293
Mannyng, Hugo, 176
Manymele, 114, 120, see glossary
Manwel, Ag., 251 ; Ric., 251
Marche, Joh., 175 ; Ric., 103, 104
Marie Knyght, the, 95, 98
Mariemburg, 2, 5
Market, Markett, Hen., 185, 96
Marketgate, 218
Marketsted, le, 76
Marre, Rog., 273
Marshall, Marsshal, Maresshall, Ad., 291 ; Chris., 140, 166, 198, 208, 210, 238, 241, 245 ; Joh., 22, 77, 115, 120, 140, 202, 204, 206, 208, 233, 238, 261 ; Rad., 176 ; Ric., 50 ; Rob., 233 ; Rog., 179 ; Tho., 176 ; Walt., 66, 179
Marston, Ric., 239
Marston, 231, 236

Marton, Alice de, 96 ; Joh. de, 120, 121 ; Joh., 199, 200, 202, 204 ; Pet. de, 96 ; Will. de, 120
Martyn, Joh., 115, 119
Martyndale, Joh., 291
Mary of York, 65, 66
Marygate, S., 285
Maryot, Tho., 166, 238, 245
Masham, Will., 131
Maskue, Rob., 176
Mason, Rob., 68
Massam, Will. de, 23
Masyndew, Mesendu, Massyndewe, 233, 291, 296
Mauldson, Rob., 67
Mauleverer, Hanl., 6 ; Rob., 218
May, Mat., 134 ; Will., 134
Meidley, Joh., 277
Mekelfeld, 218
Mekillythbarr, 219
Meldroun, Joh., 275
Melsynby, Joh., 176
Melton, Will., 156, 157, 159
Meneros, S., 117, see glossary
Menithorp, Ric., 220
Menthorp, 235, 236
Mergrave, Joh., 47
Merdlay, Joh., 250
Merston, Rob. de, 21, Laur. de, 22
Merton, Joh., 203
Metcalf, Mil., 217, 270 ; Will., 215
Micklegate, Mykelgate, Mikelgate, Mikilgate, 21, 63, 68, 112, 214, 218, 266
Micklegate Bar, 89
Middilthorp, Middilethorp, 231, 236, 294
Middilton, Midelton, Midilton, Midylton, Middleton, Joh., 13 ; Ric. de, 22 ; Rob. de, 33, 34, 37 ; Rob., 39, 53, 75, 84, 85, 86, 114, 157, 183 ; Tho. de., 22 ; Tho., 103
Midylham, Joh., 103
Mikellyth, 37
Miles, Adam, 24
Miller, Will., 66
Milnestrete, 92
Milorde, Ad., 113
Mitton, Adam, 103
Molcroft, Joh. de, 18
Molendinis, Tho. de, 22
Monastery of S. Peter, 63, 75
Monkegate, Nic., 245
Monkgate, 24, 272
Monymaker, And., 35
More, Joh. att, 33 ; Joh., 245 ; Tho. del, 52, 55, 62, 64, 142 ; Tho., 79, 86, 91, 110, 111, 157, 159, 173, 174, 183, 248 ; Will., 272

INDEX OF NAMES AND PLACES. 317

Moreton, Morton, Joh. de, 53, 68, 71, 73, 77, 83, 84, 90, 129, 130 ; Joh., 34, 46, 52, 54, 62, 64, 67, 74, 75, 76, 79, 86, 157, 159, 173, 174, 183 ; Rog. de, 92
Morlay, Will. de, 97 ; Will., 103. 104
Morland, Tho., 245
Mosse, Joh., 79, 82, 173
Mowbray, Chris., 233 ; Will., 249, 250
Moys, Joh., 21
Multon, Joh., 103, 223, 229 ; Walt., 103, 104
Munckgate, Munkegate, Ad. de, 21 ; Joh. de, 42 ; Joh., 48 ; Will. de, 23
Munkgate, 24
Mure, Chris., 277
Mureton, Joh., 47
Muston, Will. de, 7, 52
Mykellyth, 28, 37, 63, 84
Myn, Joh., 140
Mylet, Tho., 208
Myrthefeld, Will., 222

Naburn, 218
Nassington, Tho., 21
Nedeham, Joh., 220
Neirum, Ad., 221
Nele, Ric., 216
Nelson, Tho., 166, 198, 202, 204, 223, 232, 238, 270, 271, 274, 283 ; Will., 161, 270, 271
Nesefield, Nessfield, Hen., 40, 46, 47
Neusom, 46
Neuton-in-Glendale, Northumberland, 113
Neuton, 50
Neutour, 33
Nevil, Neville, Nevile, Nevell, Joh., 267, 194 ; Ralf., 130 ; Rob., 237
Newark, 219
Newby, And., 96
Newburgh, convent of, 37
Newcastle, 186, 187, 271
Newland, Neuland, Joh. de, 9 ; Ric., 35, 44, 85, 97, 126, 131, 172, 173 ; Will., 35, 50, 67, 85, 176
Newton, Neuton, Joh. de, 43, 116 ; Joh., 113, 179, 213, 245, 275, 292, 293, 294 ; Joh., junior, 176 ; Rob. de, 79 ; Tho. de, 30 ; Tho., 44, 56
Newsom, Will., 176
Noah, 215
Norman, Joh., 290
Normandy, 78, 119
Normanton, Rob. de, 16
Northby, Northeby, Joh., 35, 46, 47, 48, 49, 51, 52, 53, 54, 58, 62, 79, 87, 111, 157, 159, 173, 183, 218 ; Will., 218

Northduffield, 235
Northstrete, 21, 28, 46, 63, 99, 107, 108, 109, 219, 266, 273
North Street End, 63
Norton, Will., 34, 69 ; Ric., 67, 78
Norwich, 33
Nuport, Chris., 290
Nykson, Will., 94, 95

Odo, 42
Ormesby, Ric., 238 ; Will., 108
Ormesheued, Ormeshed, Will. de, 42, 43, 55, 62, 64, 74, 75, 79, 86, 91, 110, 112, 114, 119, 129, 135, 137, 139, 142, 157, 159, 160, 173, 174, 183
Orwell, Rob., 61
Osebaldwyk, Joh. de, 9
Osgodby, 235, 236
Osgodby, Ric., 140 ; Tho., 23
Ostyrby, Rob., 277
Otherhaye, Rog., 131
Ottelay, Joh., 269 ; Rob. de, 21, 24, 35 ; Will. de, 21
Overfulford, 39
Ouse, 254
Ousebridge, 46, 51, 53, 122, 138, 158, 257
Ousegate, 72, 239
Orre, Will., 21

Pacok, Joh., 183, 184
Palmer, Will., 25
Palmes, Brian, 283
Palmour, Will. de, 33
Palson, Will., 196, 244, 245
Paltan, Joh., 299
Palyser, Joh., 273
Pannall, Will., 123
Paris, Joh., 70 ; Step. de, 14, 15
Park, Joh., 129
Paston, Joh., 7
Patricius, 21
Patrik, Joh., 248
Patrik, Brunton, 23
Patrikpole, 35, 37
Pavement, 63, 94, 120
Pavstron, Will., 242
Pawner, Ed., 272
Payne, Tho., 23
Payntour, Dav., 103, 104 ; Joh.. 121 ; Will., 299
Pelleson, Will., 36
Pennok, Rob., 160
Pennythorne, Tho., 244, 245
Penpugh, Tho., 298
Penrith, Joh. de, 28 ; Joh., 79, 84, 86, 89, 91

INDEX OF NAMES AND PLACES.

Percy, Hen., 77, 84, 114, 115, 116, 117, 120, 182, 204; Kat., 204; Ric., 204; Rob., 76; Tho., 76
Pereson, Person, Joh., 212; Nic., 214, 215
Perpoynt, Hen., 239
Perte, Joh., 240; Rob., 199, 200, 202
Petergate, 63, 130
Peteworth, 274
Petthow, Will., 121
Petty, Rob., 283
Petyclerk, Peticlerk, Joh., 52, 55, 68, 74, 79, 84, 110
Piddynghole, 247
Pilate, 171
Pille, Tho., 219
Poiler, Will., 54, 77
Plughewayngate, 97
Plumpton, Rob., 294
Pogethorpe, Joh., 69
Pokelyngton, 234
Pole, Joh., 220; Rad., 220
Polyngton, Ric., 288
Pomfrayt, Ric. de, 23
Pontefract, 240
Popelay, Joh., 219
Popilton, Joh. de, 14, 15; Rob. de, 9; Rob., 161
Porter, Joh., 219
Portjoye, Will., 277
Potell, Joh., 103
Pothowe, Rob., 161
Pountfreyt, Rog., 51, 97
Preston, Hen. de, 9; Hen., 51, 52, 62, 64, 74, 79, 80, 84, 86, 90, 91, 110, 111, 118, 120, 123, 157, 159, 171, 183; Joh., 77, 131; Will. de, 72, 73, 74
Proktour, Rob., 41
Prussia, 1, 2, 3, 4
Pygot, Joh., 46
Pykering, Pikering, Joh. de, 21, 22, 23; Joh., 18; Will. de, 22
Pymerton, Nic., 196, 245; Tho., 196, 245
Pudsay, Joh., 97, 131

Queldryk, Joh. de, 21
Quixlay, Joh. de, 31; Sim. de, 6, 14, 17, 31, 33, 70

Raa, Tho., 196
Radclyff, Radclif, Radeclyff, Joh., 94, 95, 142, 232; Maud, 232
Raghton, Joh., 10, 111
Ralf, Earl of Westmorland, 129
Ramshede, Ric., 183, 184

Randolf, Walt., 13
Rasklelff, Joh., 97
Ratclyff, Ag., 290; Ric., 290
Rathbon, Dav., 47
Rawdon, Joh., 272
Raye, Tho., 245
Revetour, Revytour, Will., 113, 134
Ricall, Joh. de, 23
Richardson, Richerdson, Rycherdson, Geo., 238, 239; Joh., 140, 239, 267; Tho., 238; Will., 217
Richemond, Ric., 76
Richmond, 46
Riddelay, Tho., 139
Rile, Will., 196
Rilleston, Joh., 266
Ripon, 46, 47, 76
Ripon, Rypon, Joh. de, 17, 28, 30, 85; Nich. de, 21; Rob. de, 10, 23; Will., 266
Rivaux, 250
Robertson, Joh., 124, 125; Will., 119
Robton, Tho. de, 25
Robynson, Dav., 290; Mar., 217; Rob., 274; Will., 217
Roderham, Rotherham, Tho., 35, 44, 50, 110, 222, 273
Rodes, Will., 46
Rodum, Will., 271
Roghton, Joh., 139
Rokesburgh, Roxburgh, 116
Rolston, Joh., 222
Rooke, Tho., 298
Roosse, Roos, Ad., 274; Isa., 214; Ric., 214; Rob., 231, 233, 239; Will., 214
Rose, Hugh, 13
Roseton, Rog. de, 15
Rotenstein, Con. de, 1, 5
Rothwell, 274; Hen., 56, 131
Rouclyff, Gui., 199
Roundell, Will., 9
Rowlay, Will., 54, 77
Roxburg, 291
Ruddestan, Rudstane, Joh. de, 32; Walt., 234
Rukeby, Joh., 142
Rumby, Joh., 94, 115, 119; Will. de, 30
Russell, Ric., 35, 46, 52, 54, 74, 75, 79, 80, 84, 97, 98, 99, 103, 113, 135, 157, 159, 164, 174, 183, 218; Rob., 41
Rust, God., 82
Rybe, Will., 245
Rydale, 241
Rykhall, Ric., 120
Ryllyngton, Will., 67
Rymyngeton, Beat. de, 40

INDEX OF NAMES AND PLACES.

Ryse, Joh. de, 121
Ryther, 217
Ryver, Tho., de la, 19

Sadyngton, Joh., 266
Salkeld, Ric., 217
Sallay, Sallaye, Rob., 93 ; Will. de, 8, 28, 32 ; Will., 85
Sallay-by-Ripon, 236
Salton, Joh. de 22 ; Will. de, 22
Salvayn, Ger., 39 ; Tho., 73, 74
Sample, Joh., 271
Sande, Joh., 277
Sandeburgh, 98
Sandenbuch, 186
Sandes, Will. del, 54
Sandy, Will., 243
Sandylandes, Jac. de, 121 ; Joh., 116
Santon, Tho. de, 43, 44 ; Tho., 46, 51, 52, 62, 64, 74, 75, 84, 86, 89, 196, 245 ; Will., 35
Saule, Will., 274
Sauvage, Gal., 52, 74, 86, 91, 110, 157, 159 ; Geoff., 54 ; Rob., 15, 17, 28, 29, 30, 33, 35 ; Tho., 110 ; Will., 69
Saxton, Joh., 233 ; Hugo de, 21 ; Tho., 218
Scarburgh, Will. de, 22
Scardeburgh, Scardebrough, 67, 95, 98, 99
Scargill, Alice, 237 ; Joh., 232, 237 ; Rog., 237
Scathelok, Joh., 196 ; Rob., 196, 245
Scauceby, Tho., 199, 203, 204, 223, 237 ; Will. de, 24, 25, 237, 270, 271
Schadiwell, 237
Schale, Joh., 23
Scharrowe, Joh., 69
Schirbron, Shirrun, Joh de, 21 ; Will. de, 21
Scorburg, Will., 66
Scoreburgh, Wlll., 76, 126, 131, 172, 173
Scoreby, Hen., 214
Scott, Will., 271
Scotton, 76
Scotton, Joh., 76 ; Tho., 214, 292, 293
Scragge, Joh., 103
Screkyngton, Will. de, 21
See, Joh. del, 44 ; Ran. del, 30, 109 ; Ric. del, 30, 31
Selby, 242
Selby, Seleby, Joh. de, 121 ; Joh., 219 ; Hugh, 33, 51 ; Rob., 183 ; Will. de, 6, 14, 17, 18, 30, 32, 38 ; Will., 36, 51, 52, 53, 62, 64, 85, 101, 102, 118

Selwyrtop, Joh., 277
Seman, Bart., 104, 105, 106
Semer, Will., 85, 122
Seland, 56, 58
Sergaunt, Tho., 214
Sesay, Will., 245
Setrington, Setryngton, Alan de, 22 ; Joh. de, 22
Shaffton, Will., 272
Shalford, 83
Shalford, Rog., 85
Sharowe, Joh., 9
Sharp, Joh., 245, 272 ; Will., 245
Sharpels, Sharpils, Ric., 196, 245 ; Will., 233
Sharrowe, Joh., 77 ; Tho., 44
Shawe, Joh., 283, 294
Sheffeld, Will., 66, 67
Shelton, Joh., 47
Shepherd, Agnes, 242 ; Rob., 242
Sherman, Will., 27
Sherwood, Shirwood, Joh., 54, 223, 232, 233 ; Ric., 139 ; Will., 140, 206, 208
Shipton, Tho., 274
Shirlay, Rob., 208
Shrewsbury, 47, 48
Shupton, Joh., 176
Shuttilworth, Rauf., 208
Sibille, Walt., 1, 3
Skathelok, Joh., 79
Skeldergate, 10, 130, 291
Skeldergate end, 63
Skelton, 89
Skelton, Joh. de, 16 ; Joh., 115 ; Rob., 217
Skynner, Will., 208
Skyres, Will., 51
Skyrmer, Hen., 131 ; Joh., 94
Skyrwyth, Will., 160
Smyth, Hen., 116 ; Rob., 119 ; Rog., 182 ; Tho., 14, 16, 25, 109
Smythland, 242
Snasell, Snawesell, Snawsill, Will., 215, 232, 233, 234, 236, 238, 245, 250, 251, 292, 293, 294
Snaudon, Snawdon, Joh., 84 ; Tho., 52, 53, 55, 58, 62, 64, 68, 74, 81, 91, 110, 111, 124, 142, 157. 159, 173, 174, 183 ; Joh., 76
Snayth, Joh. de, 9 ; Hen., 97
Somerby, Joh., 10, 54, 62, 64, 110
Sonyngton, Joh., 217
Sothill, Joh., 217
Souche, Joh., 239
Souleby, Geo., 214, 272
Sourby, Soureby, Ric., 35, 49, 51, 56, 217
Spaldyng, Joh., 54

320   INDEX OF NAMES AND PLACES.

Spaldyngmore, 222
Sparowe, Joan, 233
Speller, Joh., 213 ; Will., 230
Spense, Will., 213, 214, 215, 235, 271, 293, 294
Spenser, Spencer, Chris., 75, 101, 102 ; Ric., 35, 42, 43, 52, 62, 64, 74 ; Tho., 85 ; Will., 218, 232
Spine, Rob., 122
Spittillflatt., 294
Sprottesburgh, Rob., 50
Sprotton, Joh. de, 22
Spynk, Joh., 119
Stafford, John, 51, 85
Stalon, Joh., 232
Staneby, Rad. de, 23
Stanes, Will., 199, 220, 203, 204
Stanowse, Will. the elder, 277 ; the younger, 277
Stapilton, Bri. de, 66 ; Bri., 231 ; Joh. de, 66 ; Miles de, 66 ; Miles, 84 ; Will. de, 38
Staple, 27
Staveley, Alan, 161, 283 ; Rob., 184
Staynburn, Joh., 126, 131, 172, 173
Staynelay, Staynlay, Stanlay, Joh. de, 45 ; Tho. de, 10, 14, 33, 122 ; Tho., 36
Staynton, Tho., 232
Stele, Joh., 51
Steresacre, Tho., 103
Stertevaunt, Stertevant, Stirtavant, Sturtevant, Joh., 47, 67, 84, 100
Stevynson, Ric., 271
Steward, Will., 160
Stillyngton, 220
Stillyngton, Styllyngton, Joh. de, 17, 25, 28 ; Rob., 54
Stirton, Ric., 200
Stodehagh, Den., 234 ; Tho., 234
Stok, Ad. del, 10
Stokesley, Joh., 214 ; Mary, 214
Stoket, Nich., 3
Stokton, Hen., 238, 245 ; Joh., 43 44 ; Joh., 45, 238, 272 ; Tho., 45 ; Will., 113, 200, 202, 203, 204, 206, 208, 223
Stonegate, Stayngate, 18, 22, 63, 82, 85
Stowe, Will., 46
Stragryfe, Tho. de, 114
Straunge, Hugo, 30
Strensall, Joh., 199, 202, 206, 208 ; Tho. de, 54 ; Will. de, 42, 54
Strewyng, Hen., 95
Strothir, Hen. del, 113 ; Tho. del, 113
Strunyng, Hen., 98
Stryghtlay, Ric., 77
Strykell, Rog., 39 ; Will., 39
Stubbes, Tho., 41

Suthewell, Joh., the younger, 40 ; Joh., 18
Sutton-upon-Derwent, 234
Sutton, Joh. de, 130 ; Joh., 82, 248, 250 ; Tho., 66 ; Walt. de, 21
Swaynland, Will., 23
Swyne, Joh. de, 23
Swynton, 235, 236
Syker, Tho., 30
Symond, Joh., 44, 45, 127, 173
Symondson, Joh., 77
Symson, Pet., 237 ; Will., 196, 290
Sylton, Joh., 175

Tailboys, Walt., 39
Taillour, Joh., 245
Taite, Tayte, Alice, 269 ; Will., 293, 294
Talbot, Step., 233
Talkan, Rob. de, 14 ; Rob., 63
Talke, Rob., 17
Tanfeld, Tanfield, Kat., 233 ; Will., 46, 76
Tankerd, Will., 241
Tanner, Ag., 269
Taverner, Hugh, 218 ; Rog. le, 218 ; Walter le, 218
Tayt, Will., 213, 239
Tesedale, Joh., 196, 245
Thomas, Count of Dorset, 65
Thomlynson, Joh., 230
Thomson, Jac., 118 ; Tho., 245
Thornhill, Rog. de, 10
Thornour, Joh., 116 ; Mar., 115
Thornton, Joh., 283 ; Ric. de, 21 ; Ric., 18, 199, 200, 202, 204, 206, 208, 296, 297 ; Rob., 89 ; Tho., 219 ; Will. de, 18
Thorp, 242
Thorp Anderowe, 231
Thorp, Thorpe, Thorpp, Alice, 212 ; Joh. de, 21 ; Joh., 80, 93, 97, 112 ; Rob., 222 ; Tho. de, 21, 24 ; Tho., 269 ; Will., 140, 206, 208, 238
Thouthorp, 89
Thresk, 58-61
Thresk, Thrisk, Thyrsk, Thirsk, Joh. de, 20, 21 ; Joh., 139, 142, 193, 198, 200, 204, 208 ; Will. de, 22
Thruslane, 72
Thuresby, Ric., 68 ; Will., 68
Thursday Market, 270, 271
Thurverton, Rob. de, 22
Thurynge, Joh., 233
Thwaytes, Thwayt, Hen., 199 ; Joh., 133, 199 ; Tho., 26
Thweynge, Thweng, Joh., 199, 218, 222, 232, 245

INDEX OF NAMES AND PLACES. 321

Tirwhit, Rob., 39
Tod, Todde, Ric., 277 ; Will., 213, 248, 270, 277, 288, 292, 294
Toftes les, 32, 53
Tokwyth, 231, 236
Toller, Ric., 134
Tollerton, 274
Tong, Tonge, Joh., 166, 182, 188, 214, 215, 218, 238, 245, 249, 251, 268, 269, 271, 290, 293, 296, 297
Topclif, 115, 116
Topcliff, Topclyff, Joh. de, 14, 21, 30 ; Walt. de, 10 ; Will. de, 23
Toucotes, Jac., 82
Touthorp, Joh., 238 ; Will. de, 10
Tower of London, 104, 105, 106
Travers, Joh., 25, 176
Tremen, Joh., 230
Trepland, Joh., 35, 54
Trogton, Eliz., 272
Trussebut, 239
Tubbac, Tho., 272
Tundue, Will., 13, 85
Tunstale, Ric., 292, 293
Tup, Rob., 89
Tuse, Joh., 214
Tutbag, Tho., 220, 295
Twenge, Joh., 219
Twys, Gilb., 33 ; Gilb. de, 121
Twyslyngton, Ad. de, 23
Tykyl, Joh. de, 21
Tylehouse, 42
Tyrell, Joh., 239

Ughtred, Geo., 237 ; Jam., 237 ; Rob., 237 ; Tho., 234
Ulron, Joh., 23
Ulskelf, El. de, 30
Umfrevile, Rob., 113
Unkthorp, Alice, 46 ; Joh., 46
Uppestall, Pet., 49, 50
Upsall, 230
Urban Pope, 156
Usseburn, Usburn, Joh., 38, 52, 62, 64, 74, 86, 91, 157, 163
Ussflete, Nic., 139, 142

Vavasour, Joh., 293
Vasour, Sim., 33
Verdnell, Rob., 23
Vescy, Ric., 242 ; Will., 231, 232
Vlyssyng, 186
Voure, Joh., 199, 203, 204, 208

Wacker, Joh., 186, 187
Wadman, Will., 82

Waghen, Joh., 52, 53, 55, 58, 62, 64, 68, 74, 76, 77, 81, 84, 85, 86, 91, 94, 112, 159 ; Sim., 233 ; Rob. de, 15, 31, 32
Wakefield, Ric., 51, 237
Wakeman, Joh., 56
Waldby, Will., 245
Wales, Edw., prince of, 31
Walker, Joh., 97, 272 ; Nic., 55 ; Ric., 66
Walmegate barre, 75, 296
Walmgate, 43, 44, 48, 97, 108, 129, 130, 249, 251
Walleworth, 50
Walpod, Sidfrid, 2
Walrode, Con. de, 2, 6
Walter, Joh., 78
Waltham, Joh., de, 20
Walthewe, Will., 76
Walton, Rob., 272
Wandesford, Wandesforth, Ag. de, 40 ; El., 215 ; Tho., 217, 248, 298 ; Will., 62, 64
Warcope, Rob., 51
Ward, Warde, Ely., 98 ; Joh., 139, 142, 157, 159, 183 ; Rob., 14, 30 ; Rog., 233 ; Tho., 102, 173 ; Will., 54, 56
Wardale, Tho., 48, 92
Warkeworth, Joh., 176
Warterton, Rob., 77
Warthill, Joh., 232 ; Nic. de, 10 ; Nic., 20 ; Will. de, 21
Wartre, Ric., 97, 142, 198 ; Will., 101, 107, 111, 173
Warwyk, Joh., 238 ; Nic., 238
Waryn, Tho., 18
Wasshand, 237
Watby, Ric., 97, 273
Waterfulford, 232
Waterhay, 274
Wath, Joh., 69
Watson, Joh., 115 ; Hen., 239 ; Ric., 127, 173 ; Rob., 179, 182 ; Step., 291 ; Will., 232, 250
Wederby, Tho., 102
Well, Joan de, 42 ; Rog., de, 42
Welles, Will., 140, 233, 235, 245, 297
Wenceley, Rob., 77, 78
Wenslagh, Tho., 238
Wentbridge, 240
Werkeworth, 116
Wersworth, Joh., 69
Westerdale, Dion, 85
Westerfeld, Rob., 176
Westharford, 232
Westminster, 78
Westwik, Westwyk, 40, 46
Westwyk, Will., 245

v

Westyby, Nic., de, 9
Wesyngham, Rob., 237
Wetherby, Tho., 76
Weton, 46
Weyts, Jaq., 87, 88
Whallesgrave, 67
Whallesgrave, Will., 67
Wheldale, Joh., 10 ; Tho. de, 27
Wherfdale, 96
Whetall, Tho., 75
Whistan, 266
White, Mic., 248, 283, 286 ; Will., 213
Whittik, Tho., 77, 85
Whixley, Sim. de, 14
Whynfell, Jac., 241, 277
Whyryg, Joh., 220
Whyte, White, Mic., 248, 283, 286, 292, 293 ; Will., 292, 294
Wighton, Joh. de, 28
Wilberfosse, Alan., 166, 214
Willesthrop, Chris., 233 ; Geo., 233 ; Hen., 233 ; Jam., 233 ; Miles, 233, 275, 294 ; Pet., 233 ; Ric., 233 ; Rob., 233 ; Tho., 233 ; Will. de, 33
Williamson, Bea., 79 ; Hen., 245, 296 ; Joh., 67, 120 ; Rob., 277
Wilson, Will., 234, 283
Wirkesworth, Tho., 19 ; Will. de, 10
Wistowe, Elue., 274 ; Rob., 274
Woddall, Joh., 238
Wode, Joh., del, 11
Woderof, Joh., 6
Wortelay, Will., 38, 85
Wrangways, Rob., 271 ; Tho., 271
Wrangwishe, Tho., 166, 196, 207, 214, 215, 239, 245, 292, 294, 295
Wrench, Rob., 17, 30
Wright, Pet., 66 ; Will., 140, 198, 200, 203, 204, 206, 208, 215, 233, 235, 238

Wyche, Joh., 102
Wyclyf, Rob., 22
Wyghton, Will. de, 18
Wykeham, Ric., 176
Wylby, Joh., possibly Wylly, Wylie, though the MS. has a letter more like " b " than " l," 116
Wyllardeby, Tho., 76
Wylys, Ric., 277
Wyman, Hen., 34, 35, 38, 63, 218 ; Joh., 103, 104
Wymmer, Marg., 69
Wynkburn, Will, 38, 52, 54, 79
Wyseman, no Christian name, 116
Wyspyngton, Nic., 139, 142
Wystowe, 242
Wytham, Tho., 223
Wytton, Will. de, 25

Yarom, Yarum, Yharom, Jarom, Hen. de, 17 ; Rob., 9, 39, 40, 55, 56, 57, 58, 74, 75, 79, 84, 86, 91, 110, 139, 142, 157, 159
Yarwit, Mar., 269
Yereslay, 251
Yermuth, 56
Yhedyngham, Will. de, 23
Yhedyngton, Rob., 21, 22
Yhucflete, Will. de, 22
Yolton, 239
Yolton, Step. de, 32
Yore, 29
York, Yorke, Ric., 213, 215, 237, 247, 270, 277, 278, 290, 292, 294
York Castle, 130

INDEX OF SUBJECTS.

Abbot, of Fountains, statute merchant and the, 30 ; Brian Davell, tenant of the, 231 ; of Jervaulx, bond to dean and chapter, 137 ; of S. Mary's, dispute between Robert Sallay and, 93 ; of Meaux, dispute between Prior of Carmelites and, 80 ; of Whitby, Brian Davell, tenant of the, 231

Advowson of S. Mary the Elder, 130

Agreement between surgeon and patient, 17, 25, 26 ; about pageant house in Toft Green, 42, xlii.

Aldermen, 9, 55, 81, 91, 109, 142, 159, 166, 199, 200, 202, 206, 208, 246, 252, 265, 286 ; election of, 258, 292, 293, 294, ix., x. ; of weavers, 30

Aliens, Johannes Artays, 78, 79 ; Johannes Walter, 78, 79 ; Johan Cook, 57–62 ; Perot de Casawas, 29 ; naturalization of, 49, 50, 113–122, 185, 186, 217, 267, 298, xiii., xxiii., xxvii., xxviii.

Almswomen, in Maison Dieu, 33

Antony, gild of S., 70

Appleby, burgesses of, charter of, 124, 125, 234, 235

Apprentices, 14, 29 ; cappers', 284 ; cooks', 161 ; curriers', 167 ; glasiers', 209 ; listers', 210 ; marshals', 178 ; patoners', 139 ; parchmentmakers', 128 ; tapiters', 197 ; number of, 196, 238 ; to be tried in mayor's court, 251, lv., lvi.

Apprenticeship, seven years', 127, 129, 140, 178, 190, 209, 286 ; 4 years', 123, lv., lvi.

Archbishop of York, 43 ; as arbiter, 289 ; tenement of, 218 ; treasury of, 37 ; le Halgarthdyke of the, 76 ; mint of the, 42, 43 ; chronicle of, 101 ; printed in The Historians of the Church of York, Rolls Series, vol. ii., pp. xxvii., 312–387

Arms, men and, requisitioned, 84

Assembly of the city, in S. William's Chapel, 17 ; in the council chamber on Ousebridge, 30 ; in the common hall, 52, 53, 63, 81, 91, 107, 109, 157, 202, 257

Assize, fresh force, 11, 12, 85 ; mort d' ancestor, 265 ; novel disseisine, 39 ; of cloth, 195, 196

Attachment, defence in foreign, 147

Attempt to avoid payment of bequest to Maison Dieu, 291, 292

Attornment for tenement in Skeldergate, 10

Award, house in Bootham, 248 ; in Horselane, 250 ; in Walmgate, 296 ; of xiii*s*. 4*d*. for unjust verdict, 17 ; fishmonger to pay 24£ for insulting mayor, 289 ; to settle dispute between John Tong and Richard Thornton, 296

Bailiffs, 11, 12, 255, 259 ; replaced by sheriffs, 259, v., vi ; court of, 11, 12 ; of Shrewsbury, 47

Bedern, le, 42

Black Death, ii.

Boatbuilders, 70

Bollers, 171

Bond, with double penalty, 149 ; between merchants of Danzic and Scarborough, 95, xxv., xxvi. ; bond by master of S. Leonards to mayor, 222 ; by wardens of Friars Minors, 231

Botellers and bowgemakers, ordinances of, 139–142

Bolton, Prior of, defrauded by chaplain, 99, 100

Boroughbridge, Sir William Tankerd, steward of, 241

Breach of sequestration, 143

Broggers, dealing with non citizens, 175 ; ordinances of, 175, 176

Building on common land, 107, xvii.

Bull, the, in Coney Street, hostel for aliens, 203

Cappers, ordinances of, 283–286

Carpenters, ordinances of, 193, 194, 277–283

Case in sheriff's court, 61, 62, x., xi.

Castle mills, 216

Chamber, sergeant of the, 33, 257, 258

Chamberlains, 277 ; oath of, 257

324

INDEX OF SUBJECTS.

Chantry in All Saints', North Street, 99, 100, 273, 274; in the cathedral, 233; in S. George's, Fishergate, 251; in S. Helen's, Stonegate, 18, 270; in S. John's, Micklegate, 273; in S. Martin's, Coney Street, 18, 269, 270; in S. Mary's the Elder, 18; in S. Mary's, Castlegate, 18; in S. Michael's-le-Belfry, 215; in S. Sampson's, 18, 137; in S. Saviour's, 18, 233; in Holy Trinity, Fossgate, 19; in Holy Trinity, Goodramgate, 215; in S. William's Chapel, Ousebridge, 18, 39, 40, 51, 53, 134, 272, 273, lxiii.-lxvii.

Churches, All Saints', Fishergate, 133, 134; All Saints', Peaseholm, 133, 134; All Saints', North Street, 18, 21, 99, 100, 132, 133; All Saints', Pavement, 133, 134, 286, 290, 292; S. Andrew's, 23, 132, 134; S. Anne's, Fossbridge, 68; S. Clement's, 23, 133; S. Crux, 21, 132, 133; S. Cuthbert's, 132, 133, 134; S. Dionisius, 22, 48, 49, 132, 133; S. Denis, 44; S. Edward's, 132, 134; Friars preachers, church of, 27, 28; S. George's, 133, 134, 251; S. Gregory's, 21, 132, 133; S. Helen's, Fishergate, 133; S. Helen's-on-the-Walls, 132, 133, 134; S. Helen's, Stonegate, 18, 22, 132, 133; S. John's-del-Pyke, 23, 132, 133; S. John's, Hundgate, 132, 133; S. John's, Ousebridge, 21, 130, 132; S. Lawrence's, 134; S. Leonard's, church of, 293; S. Margaret's, London, 50; S. Margaret's, Walmgate, 108, 132, 133; S. Martin's, Coney Street, 18, 21, 24, 132, 134; S. Martin's, Micklegate, 21, 132, 133; S. Maurice's, 132, 133; S. Mary's, Castlegate, 18, 23; S. Mary's Episcopi, 131, 133; S. Mary's the Elder, 18, 21, 131, 133; S. Mary's, Layerthorp, 132, 133, 250; S. Michael's-le-Belfry, 20, 23, 132, 133; S. Michael's, Ousebridge, 111, 132; S. Nicholas', Micklegate, 21, 23, 131, 132, 133; S. Nicholas', Walmgate, 134; S. Olave's, 22, 132, 134; S. S. Peter's the less, 21, 132, 133; S. Peter's cathedral church, 42, 63, 75, 93, 108, 219, 233, 250;

Churches (con.)—
S. Peter's-in-lez-Wylughes, 132, 133; S. Sampson's, 18, 21, 132, 133; S. Saviour's, 132, 133; S. Stephen's, Caen, 66; Holy Trinity, 18, 63, 217, 218, 278; Holy Trinity in curia regis, 132; Holy Trinity, Goodramgate, 132, 133, 215; S. Wilfrid's, 18, 132, 133; S. William's Chapel, 18, 40, 51, 53, 68, 72, 113, 178, 181, 272, 273, 274

City, freedom of, 217, 165, 261
Clause of will of Henricus Lescrop, 29
Cobblers and Corpus Christi
Common clerk, 96, 99, 101, 102, 104, 174, 175, 183, 294
Communitas, 52, 81, 183, 246
Cooks, ordinances of, 160, 161
Cordwainers not to be curriers, 170
Corpus Christi, see pageant
Council chamber, on Ousebridge, 68, 74, 75, 76, 78, 79, 84, 87, 95, 103, 110, 139, 166, 173, 175, 180, 195, 199, 200, 203, 204, 208, 213, 215, 238, 241, 247, 248, 283, 293, 294; in common hall, 52, vii.
Counsaylours of the chamber, 246
Crane, the new, 81, 82
Cross, on highway to Fulford, 39; in Thursday market, 100
Court of Chivalry, 57; of Husting (London), 214; of mayor and bailiffs, 259, 260, 12, 13,; of mayor and sheriffs, 259, 260; of mayor and aldermen, 251-253, vii., viii.; sheriff's court of personal action, 57-62, xi.; sheriff's court of London, 143-155, x.

Dean and chapter, 108, 250
Dearth of pinners, 297, xlvii.
Debt, 77; Duke of Exeter and payment of, 83, 84; incurred in Bruges, 87, 88; action for, 56, 144-150
Debtor, in sanctuary, 27, 28, 101
Decay, of the city, 246, 247; of weaving, 207; of country towns, ii.
Deeds, lost, 94; enrolled in council chamber, 95
Defeasance, 44; indenture of, 45, 95

INDEX OF SUBJECTS.

Disputes, between, two aldermen, 270, 271 ; blacksmiths and cutlers, 247-249 ; carpenters and skinners, 79 ; gild of S. Antony and Holy Trinity, 70-73 ; mayor and tanners, 165 : mayor and fishmonger, 288 ; plasterers and tilers, 125, 126, 128 ; tapiters and linen weavers, 243, 244 ; about, boundary, 80 ; building on common land, 107 ; goods lost in wreck, 56, 165 ; gutter, 112 ; payment of porters, 41 ; serf, 6
Ditches, 89
Domesday book, v., vi.
Dordrecht, bond to merchant of, 82, xxvii.
Dower, 262 ; assignment of, 289, 299
Dyers, to pay toll unless wool dyed be for their own use, 206 ; ordinances of, 210-212 : not to sue in foreign courts, 211

East marches, 84, 113-122, 199, 274
Edward IV. at Pontefract and Wentbridge, 240
Edward, Black Prince, death of, 31
Election of, bailiffs, 259 ; bridgemasters, 257 ; chamberlains, 256 ; common clerk, 257, 294 ; mayor, 255 ; recorder, 293 ; sargeants, 257, 258 ; searchers, 260 ; the sheriffs, 75, 260, 292, 293 ; members of parliament, 87
Enclosure, 110
Escheator, mayor as, 51, 66, 83, 85, 97, 106, 107, 129, 289
Exchequer, false statement in, 44
Exeter, duke of, 83
Ex-mayors, suits and complaints against, 203, 204
Ex-sheriffs, the twenty-four to be, 75

Fairfax, Sir William, recorder, 293 ; Sir Guy, 218, 236, 293
Felon, property of, 54, 62 ; from Bruges, 57-62
Fergus, mistery play of, 124, xlix., l.
Fifteenth, collectors of, 76
Fine, of vis. viijd. for calling a man an usurer, 67 ; of 10£, for disobedience to mayor, 110 ; of friars preachers if chantry duties not done, 227 ; levied and collected by sheriffs, 52

Firepans, 298, 299
Firewood for poor, 296
Fishermen, feud with country fishermen, 72
Foreign trade, 10, 14, 29, 56, 65, 66, 82, 87-89, 95, 98, 99, 205, xix.-xxvii.
Forgiveness for homicide of a father, 30, 31, xviii., xix.
Forfaiture of liberties of the city, 38 ; of franchise, 111, 165, 175, 201, 261
Fossbridge, money left to rebuild, 266
Foundation of a gild without royal license, 71
Franchise, parliamentary to citizens in assembly, 87, xiv. ; bounds of city's, 254 ; penalty for wearing livery, loss of, 200, 201
Fraternity, of carpenters, 193, 277-280 ; name of, xxxix. ; poor and blind and, 279 ; not compulsory on mistery, 278 ; women members of, 279 ; members of, to employ other members, 280, xxxiii.-xl. ; of S. Christopher, 108
Freemen of the city, not to be partners with men from the country, 175
Freemen, sons of, not to pay fee when beginning as masters, 181
Freshforce, assize of, 85, 265
Friar of Munk Grace, 83, 84
Friar, Willelmus Melton, and feast of Corpus Christi, 156-159
Friars minors, 231
Friars preachers, and right of sanctuary, 101 ; and Euphemia Langton, 223-230 ; and riots of 1381, 69 ; prior of, in York, 229 ; in England, 229
Fullers of York, to search country fullers, 159, see walkers

Garden in Havergate, 241
Gaol, Kidcote, 254
Gate keepers, 261
Gate, of Friars Preachers' Convent, 69
Gild or common hall, meetings in, 52, 63, 85, 86, 90, 157, 183, 203, 206 ; building of, 199, ii. ; elections in, 251-261
Gild of Corpus Christi, 295-296 ; Holy Trinity and S. Antony, 71, 72 ; of S. Christopher, 108, 295
Gilds, craft, see misteries

INDEX OF SUBJECTS.

Glasiers, ordinances of, 208–210; mayor and council and, 209; attempt to evade mayor's court by, 209
Glover's, stall at the great gate of the cathedral, 93
Goldsmiths, 123, 124
Gonstones, 299
Governing Body, v.–xii., see mayor, twelve or aldermen, twenty-four or councillors.
Grants, to a chantry in cathedral, 233; of Davell family, 235–237; of goods to mercers, 34; of house in Micklegate, 218; of land in Cokermouth, 54; of land in Hosiergate, 47; of manor of Lettby, with service, 69; of manor of Wasshand, 237; of property to Willelmus de Nessefield, 46; of property in Fishergate and Hundgate, 222; of a rent under condition, 218; of a tenement in Skeldergate to Robert Mauleverer, 218; of a tenement in Monkgate, 272
Guardian of England, John duke of Bedford, 46
Halygaste, ship named, 10
Hamiburg, Hemingborough, royal borough of, 267–269
Hatmakers, ordinances of, 268–288; foreigners and, 287
Hawkers of wool, 175
Helaughpark, prior and convent of, 230
Helmeslay chantry, 37
Henry I., charter of, vi.
Henry II., charter of, earliest charter in possession of the city, vi.
Henry III., 221
Henry IV., Joan, wife of, 38
Henry VI., proclamation against wearing liveries, 200, 201; grant of subsidy from every parish to, 130–135
Herbage, 89
Holland, 186
Hospital, of Jesus Christ and the Blessed Virgin, 48; of S. Leonards, 222; of S. Nicholas, without Walmgate bar. 75; of S. Thomas of Canterbury, 272
Hulke of Selykey, ship named, 56
Hull, piracy by men of, 186–188; tenement in, 218; voyages to, 10, 56

Indenture, Johannes Kirkham to supply council with lime and plaster at fixed price in return for house and warehouses, 138, 139
Inquisition, about two messuages, three shops and a solar in Walmgate and Girdlergate, 43, 44; about a messuage and garden held in free burgage, 66; about goods and chattels of a felon, 53, 54; about cargo lost at sea, 56
Insolence of porter to alderman, 55, 76; to mayor and council, 110, 111
Inventory of goods of an outlaw, 77, 78

John, charter of, 125
Judas, mistery play of suicide of, 171
Jurisdiction, see courts
Jury, in assize of freshforce, 85; and mercer's disobedience to searchers of mistery, 9; and property of Richard Lescrope, 97; and property of Holy Trinity, Kirkham, 220–222; and shipwreck, verdict sealed, 56
Justice, to be done alike to rich and poor, 256
Justices of assize and gaol delivery, 216, 217, 220; of the peace, 73, 74

Kambesmyth, 172
Kidbearers, 188
Kidcote, 254
King, Johannes, prior of the friars preachers of Engand and gift of Euphemia Langton, 229
Kings, John, duke of Bedford, constable of England, son and brother of, 57, 58
Kirkham, prior of, and four messuages in Coyngarth, 220–222
Kissing, as seal of peaceful settlement of disputes, parson of Patrickbrunton and Nicholaus de Skelton, 15; tilers and wrights, 174
Knaresborough, duchy of the forest of, 241
Knights, 213, 223, 237, 239, 241, 288, 289, 291, 292, 294, 296, 298
Kyrke, S. Mary's, 250
Kyrke, cathedral, of S. Peter's, 250

INDEX OF SUBJECTS.

Land, two butts given to provide a light of two torches in S. Lawrence's, 17

Langton, Euphemia, chantry, obit, gifts, 223–230, see friars preachers

Latoners and their pageant, 102, 103

Lead, 205

Leases, of herbage called moat, 89; of land, in Hoton-on-Derwent, 53; in Pavement, 290; in Walmgate, 15; of messuage in Gloverlane, 45; by Mayor and community to Johannes Kyrkham, 137; of station in Ousegate for acting of mistery plays, 239

Leather, to be searched in common hall, 162; rescinded 166; red, 167; to make hungry (?), 167

Leonards, S., 222, 285

Lescrop, will of Hen., 29; property of Richard, 97

Letters, from mayor of Appleby, 125, 234, 235; from magistrates of Bruges, 88; of Danzic, 98; from King of Jerusalem, 76; from mayor of Newcastle, 271, 272; from bailiffs of Shrewsbury, 47; from lord of Veere, 186–188; from York to bailiffs of Scarborough, 99

Liberty, of city, 123; of castle and city, 217; of S. Leonards, 285; of S. Mary's, 285, iv., v.

Licence in mortmain, 42, 97

Lights, in minster and other places, 180; in procession of Corpus Christi, 118, 295, see mistery and procession

Linen weavers, 243, 244

Listers, ordinance of, 204–206, 210–212; mayor's court and, 211

Liveries, proclamation against, 200–202

Looms, 243, 244

Lord mayor, dominus maior, 163, lii.; reverendus dominus, 167.

Loss of deeds, 94

Loy, S., evensong, masses and lights, 178, 181

Maison Dieu, 33, 34, 291, 292, 296

Market Thursday, customs in, 13; cross in, 100; Sunday trading in, 158, 159

Market, cattle in Toft Green, 53

Marshalls, ordinances of, 176–179; smiths and, 180–182

Master mason of cathedral, 219

Mayor, first vi., election of, 255; alteration of election of, viii.; bailiffs and, 11, 12, 31; oath of, 256; powers and duties, vi.-ix.; letters to and from, 47, 88, 98, 99, 125, 234, 235, see assemblies, courts, escheator, insolence; mayors, see Joh. Aldestanmore, Rob. Am. Jas. Will. Alne, Joh. de Bedale, Nic. Blackburn, Joh. Bolton, Will. Bowes, Tho. Bracebrigg, Pet. Buckey, Rob. Colynson, Joh. Couper, Joh. de Craven, Joh. Feriby, Will. Froste, Joh. Gare, Tho. Gilliot, Joh. Gisburn, Will. de Helmeslay, Will. Holbec, Nic. Holgate, Joh. de Howden, Rob. Howom, Ric. Lematon, Joh. de Morton, Tho. Neleson, Joh. Northby, Will. Ormsheued, Hen. Preston, Joh. Quixlay, Ric. Russell, Tho. de Santon, Rob. Sauvage, Tho. Scawsby, Will. de Selby, Tho. Smith, Tho. Snawden, Will. Snawesell, Joh. Stokton, Will. Stokton, Rob. Talken, Joh. Thirsk, Joh. Tonge, Will. Welles, Tho. Wrangwish, Hen. Wyman, Ric. Yorke

Mayor of staple, 27; at Calais, 159, lxvii., lxviii.

Meaux, abbot of, 80

Mercers, charter of, 135–137, xxix.-xxxi.

Merchants, foreign, see aliens

Merchant statute, 45, 46, 252, lxvii., lxviii.

Mills, castle, 216

Mint and moneyers, archbishop's, 42–46, 104–106

Misteries, broggers, 175; cappers, 283–286; carpenters, 193, 194, 277–283; cooks, 160, 161; curriers, 167–171; fullers and shearers, 159; goldsmiths, 123, 124; hatters, 286, 288; labourers, i.e., kidbearers, garthyners, erthewallers, pavers, dykers, groundwallers with erthe, 188; listers, 204–206, 210–212; marshals, 176–179; parchment makers, 128, 129, 237, 238; patoners, botellers and bagmakers, 139–142; plasterers and tilers, 126–128; payntours, stainers, pynners and latoners, 102, 103; pinners and wiredrawers, 297, 298; sadlers, 194, 195; saucemakers, 171, 172; shipmen, 215, 216; stringers, 122,

Misteries (con.;—
123; tanners, 162-167; tilers and wrights, 173, 174; wrights, 283; wrights, sawers, carvers, jyoners, and cartwrights, 281; vintners, 275; walkers, 206, 207, li., lxii.

Mistery plays, stations for acting, 63, 64; new station in Ousegate, 239, 240; shortening and combination of, 102-104; goldsmiths and, 123, 124; friar Melton and, 156-159; procession and, 157; titles of; the Condemnation of Jesus Christ, 171; the Elevation of the Cross, 102; Fergus, 123, 124; Herod, 123, 124; Noah. 215; the Nailing of Christ to the Cross, 103, 104; Pilate and the soldiers cast lots for the vestments of Jesus, 171; the Purification of the blessed Virgin, 188; the Hanging of Judas, 171; the Scourging of Jesus, 171, xli.-li.

Monastery of S. Peter's, 75

Municipal officers, election of, 256-261; oaths of, 257, 258

Names of marshals, 176; of tapiters, 196; of tenants in Coney Street, 269

Naturalization of Hen. Market, 185; of Scots, 33, 34, 113-123, 182, 199, 200, 217, 266, 267, 298; of Pet. van Upstall, 49, 50

New crane, 81

Newcastle, mayor, sheriffs and aldermen of, 271, 272; pirates from, 186-188

Norwich, iii., vii.-ix.

Novel disseisin, 39

Oaths, of bridgemasters, 257; of chamberlains, 257; of the commons, 257; of councillors, 256; of mayor, 256; of sargeants, 258

Obit, of William and Alice Helmeslay, 37, 38; of Constance, Cecily and William Butler, 231; of William Drawsword, 296

Ordinance against liveries to be read annually, 201, 202

Ordinances, craft, see misteries

Ordnance in common hall, 298, 299

Outlaw, inventory of goods of, 77, 78

Outlawry, 265

Pageant master, 179, 180, 297, 298

Pageant silver, 180

Pageant house, 32

Pageants, see mistery plays

Painters and stainers, 103-104

Parchment makers, 128, 129, 237, 238

Parishes in York, 131-135

Patoners, 139-142

Pinners, 102, 103, 297, 298, xlvii.

Pipe rolls, 55, 73, 83, 90, 92, 106, 107

Plasterers, 126-128

Poor, 33, 34, 246, 279, 280, 291, 292, 296

Porters, strike of, 76

Precautions against defective work, 123

Priests, and mortuaries, 17-24, see chantry.

Procession of Corpus Christi, lights for, 32, 118, 295; riot during, 70, 79; plays and, on different days, 157, 158; friar Wilellmus and, 157-159

Receiver of archbishop of York, 36

Record, attested by Humphrey, lord Dacre, Thomas, prior of Carlisle, prior of Lanercost, and mayor of Carlisle, 217

Recorder, 84, 199, 213, 293, 294, viii., ix.

Rector of Kyrkbyorblawers, 184

Rector of Laxton, 214

Rectors and vicars of York, 18, 21-24

Registers, Northern, 76

Releases, of action of debt, 34, 54; of land in Menthorp, Osgodby, Dugelby, Northduffield, Swynton and Malton, 235; of manor of Jonby, 38; of manor in Bilton and Tokwyth, 236; of messuage in Walmgate, 68

Remyngton, Beat. de, prioress of Clementhorp, 40

Rent, 263; red rose as, 231; of six marks from Rob. Davyson of York castle to Ralph, baron Graystok and Thomas Wytham, 223

Repairing, pageant, 172; pageant house, 32

Replevin, replegiare, 263

Restitution of liberties of York, 38

Retail, no sale by, at the crane, 81

Riots in York, 69

INDEX OF SUBJECTS.

River, jurisdiction over, 254; cleansing, 70; Foss, 44, 80; bridge of, 128, 138; Ouse, 41, 53, 70, 102, 130, 247, 272; bridge of, 46, 51, 53, 138, 178, 181, 239

S., Antony, gild of, 71–73; Christopher, gild of, 108, 295; Leonards, hospital of, 222; Loy, lights of, 78, 181; Nicholas, hospital of, 75; Thomas, hospital of, 28, 272
Sadlers, 194
Sanctuary, rights of, 27, 28, 101, 285, lxix.
Saucemakers, pageant of, 171–173
Scales, 90, 299; of staple, 82
Scotsmen, forbidden office or entrance of common hall, 84, 86, see aliens.
Searchers, 241, 260, see misteries.
Seed onions, 13
Selby, monastery of S. German of, 242
Seman, Bar., master of the royal mint, 104–107
Service of daughter, 29
Shearers and fullers, 159
Sheriffs, 24, 39, 45, 52, 54, 55, 60, 61, 62, 68, 74, 75, 84, 86, 87, 91, 110, 139, 142, 159, 173, 174, 183, 202, 213, 238, 245, 283, 293; custumal, account of, 259, 260, x., xi.
Ships, Halygaste, 10; the Hulke, 56; Mary of York, 56, 65; Marie Knyght of Danzic, 95, 98; from Campveer, 186–188, xxiv., xxv.
Shipmen, ordinances of, 215; pageant of, 215
Shipping, rules for, iron, oil, tar, wine, 205
Shipwreck, 56, 135, 205, xxvii.
Shoemakers and tanners, 162–167
Shotill, 190
Shrewsbury, David Fuyster of, buyer of bows, 47
Skinner, Simon de Durrne, and obligatory skilled foreman, 32
Smiths and marshals, 179–182
Soap, 205
Solars and shops, of Johannes de Stokton, 43
Stainers and painters, 102
Staith, cargoes at the, 216
Stall, glover's at cathedral gates, 93
Staple, mayor and constables of, 27; mayor of, 159, 208; exemption from law of, 65, 66; scales of, 82

Statute merchant, 45, lxviii.
Strike, of porters, 41
Stringers, ordinances of, 122, 123
Submission of an alderman, 143, viii.
Subsidy on wool, 130
Sunday, work on, 129, 158, 161, 177, 182, 183
System of hiring servants, 168

Tanners, ordinances of, 162–167
Tapiters, ordinances of, 189–193, 195–198; linen weavers and, 242; names of, 145, 196
Taxes, manner of collection, 90, 91; in Bootham, 73; tenths and fifteenths, 76; on parishes, 130–134; names of commissioners of, 131, see pipe rolls
Tenants, and the court, 263; and briefs of *ex gravi querela*, and *particione facienda*, 262; lower rents and, 246
Testaments, see wills
Theft of taxes, 62
Thirty-six, council of, in custumal, 256
Thursday market, cross in, 100; custodian of, 25; customs of, 13; land in, 271; prohibition of Sunday trading in, 158
Todde, William, mayor, abuse of, Richard Polyngton, aldermen, 288, 289
Tofts, cattle market in lez, 53; pageant house in, 32; gates of friars preachers in, 69
Tolls, John and Johannes Loksmyth of Boroughbridge exempt from York, 241, 242
Torches in Corpus Christi procession, 32, 295, 298; in S. Lawrence's, 97; of Thomas de Bukton, 32, 118
Town crier, 38
Treaty with Teutonic Knights, 1–6
Trinity, Holy, abbey of, *i.e.*, priory of, 278
Twelve, the, later aldermen, 52, 79, 84, 91, 198, 238, ix., x.
Twenty-four, the, or councillors, 52, 62, 74, 75, 79, 84, 91, 110, 173, 198, 215, 283, x., xi.

Ulnage of cloth, grant of, to Joh. Nevell, lord Montague, in county of York, Kyngeston-upon-Hull and city and suburbs of York, 194

INDEX OF SUBJECTS.

Ultra, tam citra mare quam, on both sides of the sea, 14, xxiv.
Union, of the chantry of S. Michel in S. Helen's and S. Peter in S. Martin's, Coney Street, 269, 270
Uppestall, Petrus van, a native of Brabant, 49, 50, xxvii.
Upsall, Thomas, lord Lescrop of, lord of the manor of Bilton, 230

Value of parishes of York, 131–134
Veere, lord of, and pirates of Hull and Newcastle, 186, 187, xxvi., xxvii.
Verdict of master masons of cathedral and searchers of carpenters, 219
Vicar, choral, grant to, 112, 233; habitation of, 42; 17-25
Vintners, ordinances of, 275–277; servants of, to be clean and healthy, 277
Vivarium of Foss, 80

Walkers, ordinances of, 206, 207; complaint of lack of work of, 207
War, prisoners in, bond invalid in case Johannes de Kenlay, 35; prisoners of, from Normandy, 78, 79; with France, 65, 66, 78, 79; with Scotland, 84, 86
Waste, 263
Weights and measures, 10, 13, 90, 260

Wills of, Thomas Drawswerd, bequests to poor, 295, 296; Ric. Revytour, bequest of books and vestments to S. William's chapel, 113; of Henry Lescrope, 29; Ric. de Wardeby, bequest to poor in Maison Dieu, 33
Wine, red, white and Rheinish, 275–277; measures of wine, 10, 13, 90, 260
Women, in misteries, 122, 123, 160, 161, 166, 191, 192, 276, 277; in Maison Dieu, 33, 291, lx., lxi., lxxi.–lxxiv., see Mar. Brathwayt, Euphemia Langton
Wrights, dispute between tilers and, 173, 174; ordinances of, 283; cart, 281; bond of 100£ by ten, 79, 248
Writ of, dower, *unde nichil habet*, 262, to deliver tenements to Margaret Lescrope, 98; Eliz. Fitzhugh and oath not to marry without King's licence, 290; *non molestando*, 267, 273; *quare impedit*, 214; subpena, 296; supersedeas, 24, 38, 214
Wynton, Winchester, bishop of, 43

Yarmouth, 56
Yolton Step, and Corpus Christi torches, 32
York, Mary of, ship called, in return for service in French war, right to sail anywhere at pleasure of master, 65, 66

SURTEES SOCIETY.

BALANCE SHEET, 1913-14.

JOHN GEORGE GRADON, TREASURER

Dr. *From 1st January*

	£	s.	d.
To Balance from 1912	601	11	0
,, Subscriptions received from 1st January, 1913, to 31st December, 1914	624	15	6
,, Bank Interest	31	5	0
,, Amounts received for Sale of Books by Treasurer	5	7	6
	£1262	18	6

OUNT WITH THE SURTEES SOCIETY.

st December, 1914. **Cr.**

	£ s. d.	£ s. d.

VOL. 122. VISITATIONS OF THE NORTH IN 1552 AND 1557:—
    By paid A. Reid and Co., on account for printing..   60 0 0

VOL. 123. REGISTER OF JOHN LE ROMEYN:—
    By paid Knight and Forster, for printing 75 16 9
    ,, ,, Leighton and Co., for binding 11 13 0
                                                                 87 9 9

THIRTEENTH CENTURY ASSIZE ROLL:—
    By paid Mitchell Hughes and Clarke, on account for printing 34 12 0

VOL. 125. CITY BOOK OF YORK:—
    By paid B. Johnson, on account for printing ..   60 0 0

MISCELLANEOUS:—
    By paid W. Brown, Secretary, for two years' allowance to June, 1914 .. .. .. 60 0 0
    ,, ,, J. G. Gradon, Treasurer, the like 30 0 0
    ,, ,, Andrews and Co., on account for rent of warehouse, insurance and postage of Vols. to Members 40 0 0
    ,, ,, Veitch and Sons, for stationery 1 18 6
    ,, ,, Veitch and Sons, for cheque book .. 0 2 6
    ,, ,, Treasurer, for postage and expenses (two years) 8 17 0
                                                                 140 18 0

    Balance in hands of Treasurer 879 18 9

                                                                 £1262 18 6

Audited and found correct,
                        STANLEY C. DAVIS.

25th March, 1915.